SOCIAL STRATIFICATION
IN THE UNITED STATES

SOCIAL STRATIFICATION IN THE UNITED STATES

Jack L. Roach
University of Connecticut

Llewellyn Gross
State University of New York at Buffalo

Orville R. Gursslin
Ohio University

PRENTICE-HALL, INC.

Englewood Cliffs, New Jersey

Prentice-Hall Sociology Series

Herbert Blumer, *editor*

Prentice-Hall International, Inc., *London*
Prentice-Hall of Australia, Pty. Ltd., *Sydney*
Prentice-Hall of Canada, Ltd., *Toronto*
Prentice-Hall of India Private Ltd., *New Delhi*
Prentice-Hall of Japan, Inc., *Tokyo*

13-818641-3

Library of Congress Catalog Card Number: 69-13586

Printed in the United States of America

Current Printing (last digit) : 10 9 8 7 6 5 4 3 2 1

PREFACE

Plato said that all men are equal in respect to their origin from the same earth and the same Creator; he was neither the first nor the last to enunciate a principle of equality. This fundamental equality of men has been attributed to their rational endowment and natural humanity, to their status in social customs, and, perhaps most significantly, to beliefs in justice inherited from the past. However, the ideal that all men should be treated as either numerically or proportionally equal by society and the law is less a reality than a prophetic hope. The discrepancy between the two, so vividly apparent today, has been one of the principal sources of sociological interest in stratification.

Following a century or more of intermittent studies social research has now accelerated to the point where specialized scholars have difficulty keeping abreast of relevant monographs and journals. The amount of stratification literature is more than sufficient to justify a text on the United States alone. Moreover, outstanding contributions from European and non-Western countries are available. To include such materials would have meant either a prohibitively large volume or a reduction in the initial outline of the book. Focusing on American society seemed especially desirable in view of the appearance of a new edition of *Class, Status, and Power* by Reinhard Bendix and Seymour Lipset. This volume and *European Social Class*, by Bernard and Elinor Barber, are substantial treatments of stratification in European and other countries.

Briefly, then, the present text is a survey and critique of sociological writing on stratification in the United States with emphasis on the past two decades. Although it gives substantial attention to substantive studies, the core of the book is devoted to salient theoretical and methodological issues. In most instances these issues revolve around current explanations of stratification: functionalism, social conflict, and synthetic theories. The special relationships of stratification to social pathology, to social mobility, and to power are assessed in the same terms.

Considering the heightened interest in problems of poverty and ethnic relations, our chapters on the lower class and Negro class structure could be doubled without doing justice to the flood of research. It appeared preferable to limit the treatment of poverty and the Negro group to brief surveys and to refer the reader to the expanding literature on these topics.

While this text is intended for the first course in social stratification, much of its contents should be useful to the advanced student. The extended treatment of theory and methodology is designed both to give the beginning student a basic comprehension of the literature and to be a resource for seminar instruction.

Is class, status, or power the prime element in systems of inequality? What are the relationships among these elements? Authors start from different premises (explicitly or implicitly) and develop divergent explanations. Some view strata largely as the outcome of subjective dispositions (e.g., values and attitudes); others turn to objective grounds (e.g., income and wealth) as keys to class differentiation. These are but a few of the many theoretical diversities discussed in the text. Students who seek certainty in a single authoritative view of stratification should look elsewhere. But for those who wish to understand the intricacies of a complex subject, the present volume should be helpful.

Herbert Blumer and Leonard Reissman reviewed an early draft of the manuscript. Their thoughtful comments and encouragement are acknowledged with deep appreciation. Thanks are due Genevieve Gross and Janet Roach for cheerfully relieving us of some of the more unpleasant editorial tasks. We wish also to express our gratitude to Pamela Fischer for her excellent editorial counsel.

JACK L. ROACH
LLEWELLYN GROSS
ORVILLE R. GURSSLIN

CONTENTS

SOCIAL STRATIFICATION
IN THE UNITED STATES

PART ONE

THEORY AND METHODS

CHAPTER ONE

Introduction

To what extent do members of a society have the same or different beliefs, values, and patterns of conduct? What accounts for the similarities and dissimilarities? Such questions as these are among the central concerns of sociology. If we assume that social stratification is a significant source of variability in social behavior, the study of stratification gains paramount importance in sociology.

A widely acknowledged universal disposition of humans is their capacity to notice things, to discern likenesses and differences, and to set apart one characteristic from another. This capacity leads them to separate sex and age groupings, to distinguish occupational and educational roles, and to accept differentiation generally in social life. The tendency to divide wholes into parts, to discriminate and differentiate, is opposed to the tendency to combine parts, to recognize similarity and commonality. Another acknowledged universal disposition is the readiness to appraise the utility or significance of any object or experience which influences survival and enhancement of life. Men judge and evaluate their surroundings.

Social stratification therefore has its roots in these two universal dispositions: the persistent search for differences and the equally persistent tendency to evaluate the differences in society. A person structures everything in his world of people, places, and events along these lines. Since time immemorial men have differentiated and evaluated, often in the most rudimentary and incomplete way.

Awareness of the ubiquitous inclination to find likenesses and differences in

3

social life and to evaluate such findings is no more than a first step, however, toward understanding the genesis, characteristics, and consequences of the complex phenomenon of stratification in modern industrial societies. Throughout history no line of social distinctions and no hierarchically established social pattern have received support from more than a minority of people. Although men generally rank and stratify, in doing so their disagreements outnumber their agreements.[1] No doubt this characteristic accounts, at least in part, for the dissension among scholars as to the nature of stratification in modern life. They couch explanations of the variant details of particular patterns of stratification in vocabularies ranging from the broadly discursive to the descriptive and statistical. They interlace ordinary usage with technical usage and link historical perspectives to psychological interpretations.

Some sociologists view differentially ranked positions as the outcome of accommodation, social cooperation, and normative consensus. Others believe such positions follow from conflict, conquest, domination, and economic power. Some hold that stratification is conducive to human survival, social achievement, and societal order. Others hold that it contributes to personal frustration, group deprivation, and social waste. In some cases, sociologists assume that ruling elites meet social needs by virtue of physical, moral, and intellectual endowments. In other cases, they direct their attention to the power of small groups in social organizations and to the influence of arbitrary or artificial social arrangements. Some sociologists contend that stratification is influenced in varying degrees by restless, aggressive, or ambitious people or by technology, by the division of labor, by population size and mobility, or by the growth of mass society.

The role of "values" deserves special mention. Values enter social stratification as elements of social integration and control or as incentives for competition, conflict, and group interest.[2] When values are expressed through the medium of politico-economic beliefs, they profoundly affect views about the proper study of stratification, the validity of findings, and the implications of conclusions. Because sociologists are not detached from the values of their societies, the patterns of

---

[1] For example, no sizable majority over a long period of time has accepted the ranking of specific values with reference to one another. Which is better—wealth, power, health, honor, or affection? What might be the most equitable or most "effective" distribution of these values? Abstractly and without reference to particular people or specific circumstances each is worth having. But within the contexts of everyday life, judgments on such matters vary over the widest possible spectrum.

[2] Studies in stratification not only describe social values but also may, in turn, contribute to their support. The *Yankee City Series* (W. Lloyd Warner *et al., Yankee City Series*, Vols. I–IV [New Haven, Conn.: Yale University Press, 1941, 1942, 1945, 1947]), for instance, was said to aid "understanding of the factors in the inefficient productivity of the industrial worker in the modern factory.... In the more recent *Social Class in America* [W. Lloyd Warner *et al., Social Class in America* (Chicago: Research Associates, Inc., 1949)] the utilitarianism of knowledge about social classes is more explicit for Warner and his colleagues specifically set forth the advantages of such information for teachers, school administrators, personnel directors, market analysts, and advertising executives." See R. C. Hinkle, Jr., and A. Boskoff, "Social Stratification in Perspective" in *Modern Sociological Theory*, eds. H. Becker and A. Boskoff (New York: The Dryden Press, 1957), pp. 384–85.

stratification to which they have become accustomed significantly influence their interpretations of them. Were such patterns entirely without influence, analyses of the ideological [3] characteristics of scholarly writings would not have repeatedly received critical attention during the last half century.[4]

Several writers have examined the relationships among social conditions, ideology, and class conceptions in American sociology. Probably the most thorough study is Charles Page's analysis of the contributions of Ward, Sumner, Giddings, Small, Cooley, and Ross—the fathers of American sociology.[5] Page shows how their economic and social orientations influenced the views of class these scholars held and how these orientations in turn related to the existing conditions of American society. Page puts it this way:

> Men's thoughts should be understood with reference to the cultures in which they take shape. This is true of the views expressed by the fathers of American sociology: Their theories, prophecies, and prejudices cannot be separated from their own world scene.[6]

While most of these early figures were influenced by European scholars—for example, Ward and Small by Ratzenhofer and Gumplowicz, and Sumner and Giddings by Darwin and Spencer—their thinking on class was "rooted mainly in the soil of American conditions."[7]

---

3 Ideologies are "systems of distorted and misleading ideas based on illusion. . . . The most frequent sense of ideology has come to be 'both the distortion of thought by interest—public or private, consciously or unconsciously known—and the study of such distortions. . . .' " J. Gould, "Ideology," in *Dictionary of the Social Sciences*, eds. J. Gould and W. Kolb (New York: The Free Press of Glencoe, Inc., 1964), p. 316.

4 One of the most noticeable characteristics of the stratification literature is the intensity of feeling that pervades so much of the writing. To be sure, arguments *ad hominem*, the erection of straw men, accusations of hidden biases, and other signs of subjectivism enter discussions on virtually any subject in sociology. But few specialties exhibit the heated exchanges and the acrimonious challenges to and defense of ideas so commonly found in this area. One might anticipate such a state of affairs in view of the many sensitive issues dealt with, directly or implicitly, by students of stratification—e.g., the functions of inequality, the distribution of rewards, the caste system in a democratic society, and the results of social mobility. Highly charged issues such as these tend to exacerbate divergent values and beliefs about the political and economic organization of society.

Note, for example, the tone of exchanges among those who have been contesting the merits of functional explanations since the early 1950s. Charges of ideological bias are especially in evidence in a set of papers which appeared in 1963. See Wilbert E. Moore, "But Some Are More Equal Than Others," pp. 13–18; Melvin Tumin, "On Inequality," pp. 19–26; and Moore, "Rejoinder," pp. 26–28; all in *American Sociological Review*, 28 (February 1963). Also, Walter Buckley, "On Equitable Inequality," *American Sociological Review*, 28 (October 1963), 799–801.

Contemporary American scholars also do not find it easy to write dispassionately about the subject of power. See, for example, the charges directed to each other by Robert A. Dahl and Thomas J. Anton, "Letters to the Editor," *Administrative Science Quarterly*, 8 (September 1963), 251–68.

5 *Class and American Sociology: From Ward to Ross* (New York: Octagon Books, Inc., 1964). (Published originally by The Dial Press, Inc., 1940.)

6 *Ibid.*, p. 3.

7 *Ibid.*, p. 250.

Page depicts the dilemma of several of the founding fathers who were acutely aware of the impoverished state of the laboring class but wanted to believe and basically did believe in the "American dream." While several of these eminent sociologists were known as the "left wing of the new economists," their social philosophy was essentially a middle-class American version of "left wing."[8] Most of them, for instance, advocated social reforms but firmly believed that the needed reforms should be and could be carried out within the general framework of the American society they knew. Cognizant of the extremes of wealth and poverty which effectively separated the great mass of the "have nots" from the "haves," they, nevertheless, viewed class divisions as rapidly diminishing. America, they felt, was steadily becoming a middle-class society. This goal, to them, was the hope of the future, for attainment of a middle-class society would eliminate the harmful aspects of the class system. As Page suggests, most of the fathers of sociology "gave voice to class theories which were, in the final analysis, highly colored by the 'classlessness' of the American scene."[9] Not only were they impressed with the anticlass characteristics of American democracy, but they also shared with the common man a readiness to conclude from slim evidence that America was in fact essentially classless.

Leonard Reissman[10] concisely summarizes the beliefs and conditions which led most Americans of that time ot oppose the notion that class was an important reality in their everyday lives. He refers to ingrained American values and rapid social and economic expansion as the major determinants:

> The antiaristocratic heritage, an antiradical philosophy, a frontier psychology, and a secularized Protestant ethic all were so deeply ingrained in the American value system that the realities of a class system could never come through to public awareness. Added to these beliefs were the facts of a rapidly expanding industrial system, the growth of cities, massive immigration, all of which hid some of the more obvious class differences and at the same time heightened the opportunities for social advancement.[11]

When the era of the founding fathers ended, scholarly attention to class diminished. In the late 1920s Robert S. and Helen Merrell Lynds' *Middletown*[12] and Pitirim A. Sorokin's *Social Mobility*[13] appeared, but these were exceptions to a general lack of interest in class by sociologists of that decade.[14] Milton Gordon[15] discusses reasons for this lull in attention. Along with the economic

---

8 *Ibid.*, p. 20.
9 *Ibid.*, p. 250.
10 *Class in American Society* (Glencoe, Ill.: The Free Press, 1959).
11 *Ibid.*, p. 30.
12 *Middletown* (New York: Harcourt, Brace and Co., 1929).
13 *Social Mobility* (New York: Harper and Brothers, 1927).
14Much of the work of the Chicago School during this period contributed to the class literature, but it subordinated class concepts to the relationship between ecology and social pathology.
15 *Social Class in American Sociology* (New York: McGraw-Hill Book Company, 1963).

prosperity of the period, which resulted in an appreciable rise in the living standard of the common man, probably the most significant factor was the heightened sensitivity to the Marxist connotations of class.[16]

The 1930s saw a marked resurgence of interest in class, precipitated largely by the catastrophe of the Great Depression. As Gordon indicates, economic determinism and concern over the maldistribution of income and wealth characterized this period.[17] In contrast to the case in the preceding decades, sociologists undertook a large quantity of field research on class. Most of this research centered on the measurement of socioeconomic status and the establishment of a variety of behavioral correlates of stratification. The result was a "raw empiricism" which had only a minimal connection with theoretical issues.

Contributions to the stratification literature continued to accelerate during the 1940s. While much was empirical research of a relatively low order, many elaborate studies used sophisticated designs and gave increasing attention to conceptual and theoretical problems. A series of community studies based on class concepts appeared in this decade. The most influential of these were W. Lloyd Warner's Yankee City series,[18] August B. Hollingshead's *Elmtown's Youth*,[19] and James West's *Plainville, U.S.A.*[20]

The contributions by Warner, in particular, have set the pace for much of the research since the 1940s. Not only did Warner's work stimulate a proliferation of empirical studies and support for more rigorous methodology, but it also was instrumental in emphasizing status and prestige as primary dimensions of stratification. In effect, the mounting preoccupation with status and prestige meant that the economic factor—a prime consideration in the Thirties—was relegated to secondary importance. The ending of the Depression, hastened by the war economy, contributed to the same trend. Moreover, as Reissman reminds us, from the beginning of American sociology the concept of status had more appeal than the concept of class with its economic overtones. Partly on observational grounds but also because of ideological influences, American sociologists have been especially attracted to status as a descriptive social category.[21] In Reissman's view:

> Warner's ideas were acceptable to social scientists and public alike in large measure because of the semantic shift he gave to class. "Status" can be translated into American symbols: into personal achievement, into social position in the social com-

---

16 *Ibid.*, p. 8.

17 *Ibid.*, p. 9.

18 The five volumes of the Yankee City studies by Warner and his associates are incorporated in a single edition. W. Lloyd Warner, ed., *Yankee City* (New Haven, Conn.: Yale University Press, 1963). Volume I, *The Social Life a Modern Community* (New Haven, Conn.: Yale University Press, 1941) is generally regarded as the basic work in the series.

19 *Elmtown's Youth* (New York: John Wiley & Sons, Inc., 1949).

20James West (pseud.), *Plainville, U.S.A.* (New York: Columbia University Press, 1945).

21 Reissman, *op. cit.*, p. 8. For a similar observation see Seymour M. Lipset, *Political Man* (Garden City, N.Y.: Doubleday & Company, Inc., 1959), pp. 408–9.

munity, and into a style of life. A "status" orientation and vocabulary can easily avoid the unwanted innuendoes of revolution, class struggle, and historical destinies that Marx attached so firmly to the idea of "class." "Status" stays within the grasp of individual control, where "class" is far outside, controlled only by superindividual forces in the social universe.[22]

Reissman thus contends that in large degree the reasons behind the concern of American sociologists for status are similar to those that motivate the concern of the ordinary man for the same concept.

The volume of stratification literature in recent years has reached such proportions that it is almost impossible to keep abreast of major works. A bibliography for the period 1946 through 1964 lists close to 1,500 items on the United States alone, and this is not an exhaustive compilation.[23] The concern with status, particularly occupational prestige, has remained in the forefront along with a continuing emphasis on methodological refinements. The current literature is characterized by a variety of developments, of which the most significant are the growing body of research on power, the trend toward comparative studies of mobility, the greater attention to the lower class, and the renewed interest in class consciousness. In addition to these substantive areas, an increasing number of contributions concern theoretical and conceptual issues, centering in large part on the functionalist interpretation of stratification.

Several decades ago, Page was able to sketch succinctly the founding fathers' conceptions of stratification, how their approach to the study of stratification related to their basic sociological thinking and to their economic and social orientations, and how these orientations originated in the conditions of American society at that time. For many reasons a comparable undertaking today would be far more difficult than it was for Page, who dealt with a period when American sociology was in its infancy. Not only were the half dozen figures he focused on the leading contributors to the literature on class, but they also represented a sizable part of the leadership in sociology. Page did not have to read between the lines or otherwise engage in speculation as to what their ideological positions might have been. In much of their writing, nonsociological as well as sociological, they directly expounded their political and economic views and their thinking about man's nature and his relationship to the state. Most of them were in the vanguard of social-reform movements or were active in political circles or, as with Sumner and Giddings, were champions of Social Darwinism. Furthermore, Page described events of the generation or two before him, thus having the advantage gained by looking backward.

Needless to emphasize, contemporary sociology is a vastly larger and more

---

[22] Reissman, *op. cit.*, p. 8.

[23] Orville R. Gursslin, Jack L. Roach, and Llewellyn Gross, *Social Stratification in the United States: A Classified Bibliography, 1946–1964* (Buffalo: State University of New York, 1965).

complex enterprise than it was during the time of which Page wrote.[24] Whereas Page could focus on those who were both the key figures in sociology and the primary contributors to the class literature, now social stratification itself is a major field in sociology, with numerous specialties within it. Who are the leading authorities on social stratification? How does one ascertain and account for their ideologies? What are the basic characteristics and trends of American society today? How are these societal conditions related to the values and belief systems of stratification students? While an adequate treatment of questions such as these would be a major undertaking, the contributions in this volume provide some of the substance required for a serious examination of the relationship between conditions of the sociohistorical situation and contemporary conceptions of stratification.

The present writers are not functionalists. Their preference is for theories of stratification which emphasize the role of family lineage and class history in the transmission of wealth, power, and position. (Cf. Walter Buckley's definition in Chapter Two.) Such theories are, however, of limited scope; they cannot claim to have universal application.

For any theory of stratification to be universal, its principal concepts would have to fulfill a number of scientific requirements. The same kinds of collectivities or subgroups would have to be ranked and evaluated in the same way by trained observers over an indefinite period of time. A constant relationship would have to exist between specifiable subgroups and the specifiable characteristics (status, power, possessions, etc.) of the strata to which they belonged. The facts that class categories and class membership are not fixed in any society, that successive generations of the same family often have different statuses, that property and power are acquired and lost, and that no group is assured stability in respect to occupational or educational rank testify to the mixture of constancy and inconstancy in patterns of stratification. Buckley's definition may be adequate for the short-run period of several generations, but it cannot be a statement of universal association so long as material gain, prestige, and power vary in the regularity with which they occur together.

In the above terms, stratification is not a known universal feature of all societies. Its varied appearance requires the combination of several conditions, some of which are more general or universal than stratification itself. These more general conditions, together with others of the same and lesser generality, are necessary to explain the special view of stratification which arises in any particular society.[25]

---

24 Some would also maintain that American society is far more complex than it was around the turn of the century; thus an analysis of the relationship between the sociologist of today and his milieu is a much more difficult task.

25 Much of Gerhard Lenski's theory is an attempt to unravel the variable conditions which give rise to different patterns of stratification. See, in particular, his discussion of the dynamics of distribution systems in *Power & Privilege: A Theory of Social Stratification* (New York: McGraw-Hill Book Company, 1966), pp. 43–72.

The chapters which follow will be best understood if these considerations are firmly held in mind.

SELECTED BIBLIOGRAPHY

BUCKLEY, WALTER, "On Equitable Equality," *American Sociological Review*, 28 (October 1963), 799–801.

CONNOLLY, WILLIAM E., *Political Science and Ideology*. New York: Atherton Press, 1967.

DAHL, ROBERT A., and THOMAS J. ANTON, "Letters to the Editor," *Administrative Science Quarterly*, 8 (September 1963), 251–68.

DAHRENDORF, RALF, *Class and Class Conflict in Industrial Society*. Stanford, Calif.: Stanford University Press, 1959. Chap. 1.

FARIS, ROBERT E. L., *Chicago Sociology, 1920–1932*. Chicago: Chandler Publishing Co., 1967.

GORDON, MILTON M., *Social Class in American Sociology*. New York: McGraw-Hill Book Company, 1963. Chaps. 1 and 2.

HEBERLE, RUDOLF, "Recovery of Class Theory," *Pacific Sociological Review*, 2 (Spring 1959), 18–28.

HINKLE, ROSCOE C., and ALVIN BOSKOFF, "Social Stratification in Perspective," in *Modern Sociological Theory*, eds. Howard Becker and Alvin Boskoff. New York: The Dryden Press, 1957.

LENSKI, GERHARD, "Social Stratification," in *Contemporary Sociology*, ed. Joseph S. Roucek. New York: Philosophical Library, 1958.

MURPHY, RAYMOND J., "Some Recent Trends in Stratification Theory and Research," *The Annals of the American Academy of Political and Social Science*, 356 (November 1964), 142–67.

NISBET, ROBERT A., "The Decline and Fall of Social Class," *Pacific Sociological Review*, 2 (Spring 1959), 11–17.

PAGE, CHARLES H., *Class and American Sociology: From Ward to Ross*. New York: Octagon Books, Inc., 1964. (Published originally by The Dial Press, Inc., 1940.)

REISSMAN, LEONARD, *Class in American Society*. Glencoe, Ill.: The Free Press, 1959. Chap. 1.

ROSE, ARNOLD M., "Concept of Class and American Sociology," *Social Research*, 25 (Spring 1958), 53–69.

CHAPTER TWO

Stratification Theory

Sociologists generally concur that social stratification in some form and degree is a feature of all societies. Opinions diverge however on how this claim is to be interpreted. The employment of idiosyncratic terms and the different procedures through which similar ideas are put to use obscure descriptions of social stratification. Bernard Barber, for example, defines it as "a structure of regularized inequality in which men are ranked higher and lower according to the value accorded their various social roles and activities."[1] A significant phrase in this definition is *regularized inequality*. Most definitions of social stratification contain this theme—expressed variously as a hierarchical structure, a system of inequality, or a systematic hierarchy. A related theme in many definitions is that of relative permanence of intergenerational continuity. As we shall see, this theme is widely debated in the professional literature.

Conceptions of social stratification vary in other ways. While some writers hold that stratification refers primarily to statuses, positions, or roles, others insist that it concerns persons or groups. Some definitions give explicit criteria for stratification, while others make reference only to some abstract scale of superiority-inferiority.

---

[1] *Social Stratification: A Comparative Analysis of Structure and Process* (New York: Harcourt, Brace & World, Inc., 1957), p. 7.

SOCIAL DIFFERENTIATION AND SOCIAL STRATIFICATION

Much of the variation in conceptions of social stratification occurs because writers define social differentiation and conceive of its relationship to social stratification in different ways.[2] Since social differentiation is the more general phenomenon, it is useful to examine its nature and also its connections to social stratification before proceeding further with the concept of stratification itself.

For most sociologists social differentiation refers to differences among roles, positions, or functions. Viewed in this way it is equivalent to division of labor. A representative of this view is Dennis Wrong, who describes social differentiation as "the existence of role differentiation or division of labor itself."[3] Other writers have an omnibus conception of social differentiation, applying it to "any difference between individuals, social positions, or groups."[4] However, Wrong's emphasis on positional differentiation is more typical.

Of greater significance are the differing conceptions of the relationships between social differentiation and social stratification. Sociologists generally agree that social stratification is a *type* of social differentiation wherein ranking is based on some criteria. But opinion varies concerning the degree of similarity between the two. Opinion also varies on the processes leading to the emergence of social stratification from the basic phenomenon of social differentiation. For example, some students see stratification as a rather simple extension, or elaboration, of differentiation. From their perspective, stratification is a natural, inevitable development from social differentiation. Man inherently evaluates, and stratification emerges from social differences being differentially evaluated. This orientation tends to minimize the distinctions between the two processes.

Other sociologists believe that important differences exist between social differentiation and stratification. The key distinction, they hold, is that stratification refers to a relatively enduring hierarchical system extending over several generations.[5] Although social differentiation may be represented by vertical distinctions, it does not necessarily imply a structure of inequality based upon superiority-inferiority. In this view, the process whereby social differentiation gives rise to stratification is a complex issue not adequately handled by resorting to a thesis of natural evolvement.

---

[2] As suggested in Chapter One, much more is admittedly at hand in the structuring of basic conceptions of social stratification. The fundamental roots probably originate in differing philosophical and ideological presuppositions concerning man's nature, the nature of society, and the relationship between the two. Additional comments along these lines are in this and the concluding chapter.

[3] "The Functional Theory of Stratification: Some Neglected Considerations," *American Sociological Review*, 24 (December 1959), 773.

[4] Barber, *op. cit.*, Chap. 1. Barber's views follow Parsons' interpretation of stratification, discussed subsequently in this chapter.

[5] See, for example, Walter Buckley, "Social Stratification and the Functional Theory of Social Differentiation," *American Sociological Review*, 23 (August 1958), 369–75. (Reproduced in this chapter.)

In brief, treating social stratification as a variation of social differentiation or as a relatively distinct phenomenon influences any inquiry into its basic nature and origins. If we see social differentiation and social stratification as virtually the same phenomena, then we can treat both as emerging from the same set of conditions. And we can argue that social stratification is as universal and necessary as social differentiation. If, on the other hand, we see social stratification as significantly different from social differentiation, then we cannot encompass both with the same explanatory scheme.

Regardless of the differences in usage of the two terms, certain distinctions are essential. Differentiation may occur in social systems without hierarchical organization,[6] but hierarchical organization cannot occur without differentiation. Thus, social differentiation is necessary but not sufficient for the emergence of hierarchical systems. Consequently, an explanation of hierarchical systems requires the postulation of additional conditions.

The ensuing discussion, and especially the papers on the functional interpretation of stratification, gives further attention to the problem of the relationship between social differentiation and social stratification, including the issue of the additional conditions necessary for the emergence of stratification.

FUNCTIONAL THEORY AND THE EXPLANATION OF STRATIFICATION

As in all of sociology, in social stratification the most widely accepted theoretical framework is that commonly known as *functionalism*. The significance of functional analysis in social stratification is most fully appreciated against the background of functionalism in sociology.

The principal objective of functional analysis in sociology is to explain a state of affairs in society by reference to the *consequences* of that state for the system as a whole. For example, proponents of this view say that the function (or consequence) of religion is group solidarity and the function (or consequence) of the family is the socialization of the child. In most cases they hold that the functions of such structures as religion or the family are *necessary* for the survival of society. Thus, the family serves the function of socializing the child, which is a *necessary condition* for the maintenance of group adaptation. Presumably, group adaptation or solidarity influences and is, in turn, influenced by other social structures. Implicitly, if not explicitly, functionalism assumes that under constant environmental and cultural conditions (values, norms, activities, roles, etc.) religion and the family function in the manner described. It is apparent, then, that functionalism seeks to explain a social pattern or structure

---

[6] The reference here is to the relatively enduring type of hierarchical system previously mentioned.

(e.g., the family) occurring in a system (the society in question) of relatively stable conditions (values, norms, and activities) so that the pattern or structure satisfies some need or requirement (e.g., the socialization of the child) necessary to the continued existence of the system.

In the light of this explanatory scheme, it should come as no surprise that functionalists regard stratification as a necessary structure in all societies. They hold that it is universally necessary because it fulfills fundamental needs vital to the functioning of the entire society. But, although stratification is a key structure in the maintenance of society, other societal structures also significantly influence it. The reciprocal relationships between stratification and other structures account for the variability manifested by systems of stratification in different societies.

Most theorists who write within a functional framework agree with W. Lloyd Warner's interpretation of the need for some form of stratification in any society:

> When there are large numbers of individuals pursuing diverse and complex activities and functioning in a multiplicity of ways, individuals' positions and behaviors are evaluated and ranked. This happens primarily because, to maintain itself, the society must coordinate the efforts of all its members into common enterprises necessary for the preservation of the group, and it must solidify and integrate all these enterprises into a working whole. In other words, as the division of labor increases and the social units become more numerous and diverse, the need for coordination and integration also increases and, when satisfied, enables the larger group to survive and develop.[7]

Briefly put, Warner claims that a stratification system is a necessary response to the societal imperatives of coordination and integration.[8] Without a system of stratification these basic functions could not be carried out and the society could not continue to exist. Beyond this broad assertion, however, Warner does not have much to say about how the phenomena of stratification arise and persist. Moreover, he provides little information on how stratification effectively serves the exigencies of integration and coordination. A small group of functional writers have undertaken these tasks. Particularly influential have been the contributions of Talcott Parsons[9] and a set of essays by Kingsley Davis and Wilbert Moore.[10]

---

7 *Social Class in America* (New York: Harper & Row, Publishers, 1960), p. 8. (Harper Torchbooks edition.)

8 As Cuber and Kenkel state, "The functional view holds that the existing differential distribution of privilege derives from the efforts of a society to fulfill its necessary goals." John F. Cuber and William F. Kenkel, *Social Stratification in the United States* (New York: Appleton-Century-Crofts, 1954), p. 28.

9 "A Revised Analytical Approach to the Theory of Social Stratification," in *Class, Status and Power*, eds. Reinhard Bendix and Seymour M. Lipset (Glencoe, Ill.: The Free Press, 1953), pp. 92–128.

10 "Some Principles of Stratification," *American Sociological Review*, 10 (April 1945),

Parsons' work and the views of Davis and Moore are complementary. Their arguments vary in level and scope of application, but they generally agree on basic assumptions. While not developed explicitly as an extension of Parsons' ideas, the Davis and Moore contribution supplements his framework by conveying some notion of the kinds of empirical content which can be subsumed under his highly abstract scheme. Together, their writings provide the essentials of functional thinking on social stratification.

Parsons derives his theory of stratification from his social-action framework. For this reason his basic conceptions of stratification do not correspond closely with either traditional or many contemporary views on the subject. To Parsons, stratification is an inevitable consequence of the elementary processes of human interaction. By subsuming stratification under interaction, Parsons attempts to encompass the stratification of any type of social system, large or small. Stratification can occur in any system, ranging from that of two individuals (alter and ego) to a total society, from a primitive tribe to a complex, industrial civilization.

Much of Parsons' treatment of stratification is a specialized version of his general sociological theory. It is not our intent to summarize his thoughts on the subject. Rather, we shall indicate the general nature of two fundamental aspects of his argument: the concept of evaluation and the premise of a common value system.[11]

Parsons maintains that an integral feature of human action is evaluation. Man, by his very nature, is an evaluator; he is continually evaluating entities in terms of their qualities and performances. Inherent in this process is a hierarchical characteristic or, in Parsons' words, "a differentiation of entities in a rank order of some kind."[12] The standards which determine the rank of the objects in an evaluation arise from the key premise in his interpretation of stratification. In Parsons' view, "it is a condition of the stability of social systems that there should be an integration of the value standards of the component units to constitute a common value system."[13] The stratification system, which expresses common values, performs this task of integration. Indeed, Parsons defines stratification as the "ranking of units in a social system in accordance with the standards of the common value system."[14]

Although sociologists commonly regard Parsons as the leading functional writer in sociology and although his contributions to a functional interpretation of stratification have been very influential, two of his students, Davis and Moore, have set forth the strongest case for the functional position. Attention in the Davis and

---

242–49. This essay is the one most commonly referred to in discussions of the Davis-Moore position.

[11] A fuller interpretation of Parsons' approach to stratification is given in Leonard Reissman, *Class in American Society* (Glencoe, Ill.: The Free Press, 1959), pp. 69–83.

[12] *Op. cit.*, p. 93.

[13] *Ibid.* Barber, a student of Parsons, states that, "when we say the stratification system is integrative, we mean, integrative to the extent that it expresses a common and shared set of values." *Op. cit.*, p. 9.

[14] *Op. cit.*, p. 93.

Moore formulation centers on the functional concept of basic societal requisites and the relationship of stratification systems to the satisfaction of these requisites. Like Parsons, they believe stratification meets the functional requisites of coordination and integration. Similar to Parsons', theirs is an equilibrium-integration model of society with emphasis upon the existence and role of common values in maintaining social order. In Reissman's words, the Davis-Moore theory of stratification is a "plausible extension of certain basic assumptions inherent in a functional view of society."[15]

The degree of attention given to this viewpoint over the past two decades occurs mainly for two reasons. First, as a model of the functional framework it uses widely accepted functional terms, concepts, and assumptions. Second, it is an explicitly reasoned scheme in which the authors attempt to state in detail the principles upon which their analysis rests.

Davis and Moore seek to "explain, in functional terms, the universal necessity which calls forth stratification in any social system."[16] They claim that the functioning of a society depends upon the adequate performance of different positions within it. Some of these positions are more important than others for the preservation or survival of the society. Moreover, some positions require different amounts of talent and training for their performance than do others. Since talent and training are scarce, the problem arises of finding the best means for inducing a sufficient number of qualified persons to assume the responsibilities of the more important positions. A system of attaching higher rewards to positions of greater importance solves this problem. Such rewards consist of those rights and perquisites which contribute to (1) sustenance and comfort, (2) humor and diversion, and (3) self-respect and ego expansion. In general, the more vital the position for the functioning of society the higher the rewards to persons occupying these positions.

> The rewards and their distribution become a part of the social order and thus give rise to stratification. . . . Social inequality is thus an unconsciously evolved device by which societies insure that the most important positions are conscientiously filled by the most qualified persons.[17]

The selection below is a shorter version by Davis of the formulation set forth by himself and Moore in 1945. We present this revised version rather than the more widely cited original essay since, as Davis rightfully claims, most critics of their thesis have overlooked the later statement, which contains important modifications.

---

[15] *Op. cit.*, p. 83.
[16] *Op. cit.*, p. 242.
[17] *Ibid.*, p. 243.

THE EXPLANATION OF STRATIFICATION*[1]

Kingsley Davis

University of California, Berkeley

Looking at the cultures of the world one finds that no society is "classless," that is, unstratified. There are some primitive communities so small that no class strata appear, the social organization resting almost entirely on age, sex, and kinship; but even here chieftainship, individual prowess, and clan or family property introduce an incipient stratification. As soon as greater size and complexity are attained, stratification unmistakably appears.

At the same time, although the principle of stratification is universal, its concrete manifestation varies remarkably from one society to another. Consequently, the explanatory task requires two different lines of analysis—one to understand the universal features of stratification, the other to understand the variable features. Naturally the two lines of inquiry are indispensable, but in what follows, because of space limitations, the emphasis will be on the universals.

THE FUNCTIONAL NECESSITY OF STRATIFICATION

Men have always dreamed of a world in which distinctions of rank did not occur. Yet this dream has had to face a hard reality. Any society must distribute its individuals in the positions of its social structure and induce them to perform the duties of these positions. It must therefore solve the problem of motivation at two levels: to instill in the proper individuals the desire to occupy certain positions and, once in these positions, the desire to perform the duties attached to them.

If the duties associated with the various positions were all equally pleasant to the human organism, all equally important to social survival, and all equally dependent on the same ability or talent, it would make no difference who got into which positions, and the problem of social placement would be greatly reduced. But actually it does make a great deal of difference who gets into which positions not only because some positions are inherently more agreeable than others but also because some require special talents or training and some have more importance than others. Also, it is essential that the duties of the positions be performed with the diligence that their importance requires. Inevitably, then, a society must have some kind of rewards that it can use as inducements and some way of distributing these rewards differently according to positions. The rewards and their distribution, as attached to social positions, thus become a part of the social order; they are the stratification.

One may ask what kind of rewards a society has at its disposal in distribut-

* Reprinted by permission of The Macmillan Company from *Human Society* by Kingsley Davis. Copyright 1948, 1949 by The Macmillan Company.

[1] This general theory of stratification is taken largely from Kingsley Davis and Wilbert E. Moore, "Some Principles of Stratification," *American Sociological Review*, 10 (April 1945), 242–47.

17

ing its personnel and securing essential services. It has, first of all, the things that contribute to sustenance and comfort—the economic incentives. It has, second, the things that contribute to humor and diversion—the esthetic incentives. And it has, finally, the things that contribute to self-respect and ego expansion—the symbolic incentives. In any social system all three kinds of rewards, as well as others, must be dispensed unequally as between different positions.

In a sense the rewards are "built into" the position. They consist in the "rights" associated with the position, plus what may be called its accompaniments or perquisites. Often the rights and sometimes the accompaniments are functionally related to the duties of the position. However, there may be a host of subsidiary rights and perquisites that are not essential to the function of the position and have only an indirect and symbolic connection with its duties, but which still may be of considerable importance in inducing people to seek the positions and fulfill the essential duties.

If the rights and perquisites of different positions in a society must be unequal, then the society must be stratified because that is precisely what stratification means. Social inequality is thus an unconsciously evolved device by which societies insure that the most important positions are conscientiously filled by the most qualified persons. Hence every society, no matter how simple or complex, must differentiate persons in terms of both prestige and esteem and must therefore possess a certain amount of institutionalized inequality.

It does not follow that the amount or type of inequality need be the same in all societies. We are simply trying to explain the universal fact of stratification, regardless of its particular form. The varying kinds of stratification are a function of other factors in addition to the broad functional necessity under discussion.

THE TWO DETERMINANTS OF POSITIONAL RANK

Granting the general function that inequality subserves, one can specify the two factors that determine the relative rank of different positions. In general those positions convey the best reward and hence have the highest rank which (a) have the greatest importance for the society and (b) require the greatest training or talent. The first factor concerns the relative functional contribution of the position as compared to others; the second concerns the relative scarcity of personnel for filling the position.

DIFFERENTIAL FUNCTIONAL IMPORTANCE

Actually a society does not need to reward positions in proportion to their functional importance. It merely needs to give sufficient reward to insure that they will be filled competently. In other words, it must see that less essential positions do not compete successfully with more essential ones. If a position is easily filled, it need not be heavily rewarded even though important. On the other hand, if it is important but hard to fill, the reward must be high enough to get it filled anyway. If it is unimportant and hard to fill, it will possibly be dropped altogether. Functional importance is therefore a necessary but not a sufficient cause of high rank being assigned to a position.

DIFFERENTIAL SCARCITY OF PERSONNEL

Practically all positions, no matter how acquired, require some skill or capacity for performance. This is implicit in the very notion of position, which implies that the incumbent must by virtue of his incumbency accomplish certain things.

There are ultimately only two ways in which a person's qualifications come about: through inherent capacity or through training. Obviously, in concrete activities both are always necessary; some capacity is necessary if training is to be effective, and some training is required if capacity is to express itself. But from a practical standpoint the scarcity may lie primarily in one or the other, as well as in both. Some positions require innate talents of such high degree that the persons who fill them are bound to be rare. In many cases, however, talent is fairly abundant in the population, but the training process is so long, costly, and elaborate that relatively few can qualify. Modern medicine, for example, is within the mental capacity of most individuals, but a medical education is so burdensome and expensive that virtually none would undertake it if the position of the M.D. did not carry a reward commensurate with the sacrifice.

If the talents required for a position are abundant and the training easy, the method of acquiring the position may have little to do with its duties. There may in fact be a virtually accidental relationship. But if the skills required are scarce by reason of the rarity of talent or the costliness of training, the position, if functionally important, must have an attractive power that will draw the necessary skills in competition with other positions. This means, in effect, that the position must be high in the social scale—must command great prestige, high salary, ample leisure, and the like.

AN APPARENT CRITICISM

One may object to the foregoing explanation of stratification on the ground that it fits a competitive order but does not fit a noncompetitive one. For instance, in a caste system it seems that people do not get their positions because of talent or training but rather because of birth. This criticism raises a crucial problem and forces an addition to the theory. It does not, however, upset the theory.

In the first place it should be apparent that our analysis concerns the system of positions not the individuals occupying those positions. It is one thing to ask why different positions carry different degrees of prestige and quite another to ask how certain individuals get into those positions. Most of the literature on stratification has tried to answer the second question (particularly with regard to the ease or difficulty of mobility between strata) without tackling the first. The first question, however, is logically prior and, in the case of any particular individual or group, factually prior.

In the second place, the functional necessities responsible for stratification do not operate to the exclusion of all other functions. There are certain additional functions, equally necessary, which have the effect of limiting and guiding stratification. For example, the necessity of having a social organization —the family—for the reproduction and socialization of children requires that stratification be somehow accommodated to this organization. Such accommodation takes the form of status ascription. The child, as mentioned before, receives initially the class status of his parents. Even in a highly competitive system this helps or hinders him throughout the rest of his life in the acquisition of adult statuses. In a less competitive system, such as is possible in stable agricultural societies, the influence of the parental position may tend to last through life. Although this seems to exclude functional importance, training, and talent, it is nevertheless true . . . that there is always some competition required, and for most positions some capacity and some training. Consequently it is still possible to explain on the basis of functional importance and scarcity of personnel the general hierarchy of positions. Even though a highcaste person occupies his high rank because of his parents, the reason for the high evaluation of the functions that his caste performs in the community cannot be found in this fact. The low estate of the sweeper castes in India, as compared with the priestly castes, cannot be explained by saying that the sons of sweepers become sweepers and the sons of Brahmins become Brahmins. There is a tendency for sweepers to have a low status and for priests to have a high status in every society. Thus the functional necessity behind stratification seems to be operative at all times, despite the concurrent operation of other functions.

CRITIQUES OF THE FUNCTIONAL EXPLANATION

The adequacy of the functional explanation of stratification rests, first, upon the adequacy of the functional argument generally. The following brief assessment concerns the logical structure and methodological consequences of functionalism not its empirical validity. Most critics of the functional interpretation of stratification are concerned with the latter.

Ernest Nagel and Harry Bredemeier, among others,[1] suggest that functional analysis rests on an untenable conception of the explanatory process. Functionalists not only explain social forms by their effects, which typically occur at some later period of time, but also give insufficient attention to the respects in which the activities of each part of the system causally determine the activities of every other part.

With reference to the explanation of a social form by its effect, Nagel indicates that the facts described by the functionalist can be rendered in nonfunctional language by stating the conditions under which the effect is obtained. If we grant this, then we can restate the functionalist argument as generally understood in the following manner. "In societies of a certain type, a necessary condition for the socialization of the child is the presence of the family"; or "children continue to be socialized only if the family behaves in a specified manner."[2] In

---

[1] Not discussed here, but of particular importance, is the incisive critique of functionalism by Hempel. See Carl G. Hempel, "The Logic of Functional Analysis," in *Symposium on Sociological Theory*, ed. Llewellyn Gross (New York: Harper & Row, Publishers, 1959), pp. 271–307.

[2] Ernest Nagel, "A Formalization of Functionalism," in *Logic Without Metaphysics* (Glencoe, Ill.: The Free Press, 1956), pp. 250–51.

Nagel's words, "the difference between a functional and a nonfunctional formulation is thus one of selective emphasis; it is quite comparable to the difference between saying that *B* is the effect of *A* and saying that *A* is the condition (or cause) of *B*."[3] Bredemeier's interpretation of causal determination is not unlike Nagel's. We may say that "a contributing cause of social adaptation is the family because it socializes the child" or that "the function of the family for social adaptation is the socialization of the child."[4] In the first statement the family is a contributing cause; in the second statement socialization of the child is the causal factor explaining the relationship between the family and social adaptation.

These authors suggest that functionalism typically neglects questions concerning the causal relevance of both environmental and intrasystem variables. All systems, functional or not, must assume some range of environmental variations beyond which the stability of relations among the system parts can no longer be maintained. On this assumption, we can take any system part as a causal determinant of any other part. Perhaps, then, such concepts as social adaptation are divisible into causal variables, with unknown portions accounting for the occurrence of the family, the socialization of the child, religion, and other structural characteristics of society.

The discussion of functional theory in general sociology has been paralleled by an extensive dialogue on its application to social stratification. Critics have written a number of papers since the original statement by Davis and Moore. Some of these represent extensions or enlargements of their framework; others clearly reject the formulation. The selections below cover a variety of methodological, empirical, and ideological issues. Since most of these papers use as a point of departure the initial controversy prompted by Melvin Tumin's critique of 1953, we present a review of his analysis first.[5]

Tumin questioned most of the basic premises either expressly set forth or implicit in the Davis-Moore thesis. In particular, he challenged the assumption that stratification is an inevitable and necessary feature of society. Even if stratification were a universal phenomenon, this universality by itself would not be proof of its necessity for societal functioning. And also the ubiquity of stratification in space and time does not constitute adequate evidence of its inevitability.

Tumin also questioned the functional importance or indispensability of certain positions for the survival of society. In his estimation, Davis and Moore's criteria of differential importance are a product of tautological reasoning and implicit value preferences. Further, he disputes the claim that a limited number of individuals have the talent or skill required for the functionally important positions.

---

[3] *Ibid.*, p. 251.

[4] Harry C. Bredemeier, "The Methodology of Functionalism," *American Sociological Review*, 20 (April 1955), 173.

[5] "Some Principles of Stratification: A Critical Analysis," *American Sociological Review*, 18 (August 1953), 387–93. We have not reprinted this essay here since subsequent selections recapitulate much of his argument.

The more rigidly stratified a society the less chance it has of discovering new facts about the talents of its members. "It is only when there is genuinely equal access to recruitment and training for all potentially talented persons that differential rewards can conceivably be justified as functional. And stratification systems are apparently inherently antagonistic to the development of such full equality of opportunity."[6]

With respect to the claim by Davis and Moore that a system of unequal rewards has the function of motivating persons to undergo the training required to fill the important positions, Tumin raises the possibility of alternative motivational schemes. He emphasizes the absence of any known reason why motivation should be contingent upon unequal rewards; hypothetically, alternative motivational schemes may be effectively induced by equal rewards. Man is and can be motivated by rewards other than the types of material and prestige rewards specified by Davis and Moore.[7] In brief, he suggests that a model of society can be outlined in which all indispensable functions are performed but without inequality as motive and reward.

In addition to challenging these basic assumptions of the Davis-Moore thesis Tumin directs much of his critique to refuting the empirical foundation upon which the thesis is presumed to rest. He presents a list of dysfunctions following from the consequences of social stratification. He treats these dysfunctions as alternative hypotheses regarding "the consequences of unequal distribution of rewards in a society in accordance with some notion of the functional importance of various positions."[8] Experts regard them as exemplary of the kinds of consequences which are often not taken into account in dealing with the problem.[9] Taken *in toto* they reduce the chances of a society for survival.

(1) Social stratification limits the discovery of the full range of talent in a society, hence limiting the possibility of expanding the productive resources of the society.

(2) Social stratification functions essentially as a conservative influence by providing the elite with the political power necessary to secure acceptance of a status quo ideology.

(3) Social stratification distributes favorable self-images unequally in a population, hence inhibiting the development of the creative potential inherent in men.

(4) Social stratification encourages hostility, suspicion, and distrust among the various segments of a society, hence limiting social integration.

(5) Social stratification distributes unequally the sense of significant membership in the society; hence it distributes the motivation to participate unequally in a population.

The controversy initiated by Tumin in 1953 has continued over the past decade

---

6 *Ibid.*, p. 389.

7 *Ibid.*, p. 391.

8 *Ibid.*, p. 393.

9 Tumin lists eight dysfunctions. We have combined some of these and generally paraphrased the material from his essay.

in the form of a series of essays and exchanges by Davis and Moore and their critics. Among the most significant of the latter are Walter Buckley, Dennis Wrong, George Huaco, and Arthur Stinchcombe.

Buckley raises a variety of issues. His key contentions are that Davis and Moore confuse social differentiation and social stratification (a conceptual problem we have already noted) and ignore the role of inheritance in the persistence of social inequality. Next to Tumin's analysis Buckley's paper is the most trenchant critique of the Davis-Moore framework.

SOCIAL STRATIFICATION AND THE FUNCTIONAL THEORY OF SOCIAL DIFFERENTIATION*†

Walter Buckley

University of California, Santa Barbara

There has been no dearth of criticism of the Davis-Moore theory of social stratification since its publication over a decade ago.[1] Particularly disturbing is the fact that what this theory views as virtues (or eufunctions) are the very factors that others overwhelmingly see as vices (or dysfunctions). The former characterizes stratification in terms of competitive achievement of position; a close correlation between superior capacities, importance of position, and high rewards; and its functional necessity to maintenance of the social system. The critics associate it with role-ascription and restriction of opportunity; absence of correlation between superior capacities, rewards, and positional importance; and disruption or discontinuity of the society. This gross difference of views has led several sociologists to seek out and find deficiencies in the functional theory. Among other shortcomings, its critics[2] have pointed out that the Davis-Moore theory is inadequate in its treatment of the concept of "functional importance"; it ignores possible dysfunctions

---

* From Walter Buckley, "Social Stratification and the Functional Theory of Social Differentiation," *The American Sociological Review*, 23 (August 1958), 369–75. Reprinted by permission of the American Sociological Association.

† Condensed version of a chapter of the writer's unpublished doctoral dissertation, "Sociological Theory and Social Stratification," University of Wisconsin, 1958.

[1] Kingsley Davis and Wilbert E. Moore, "Some Principles of Stratification," *American Sociological Review*, 10 (April 1945), 242–49.

[2] Cf. especially the critique of Melvin Tumin, "Some Principles of Stratification: A Critical Analysis," *American Sociological Review*, 18 (August 1953), 387–94. See also Melvin Tumin, "Rewards and Task-Orientations," *American Sociological Review*, 20 (August 1955), 419–23; Richard D. Schwartz, "Functional Alternatives to Inequality," *American Sociological Review*, 20 (August 1955), 424–30; Richard L. Simpson, "A Modification of the Functional Theory of Social Stratification," *Social Forces*, 35 (December 1956), especially p. 137.

and functional alternatives of stratification; it reifies "society" as "inducing" its members to assume positions and play roles; and in general it accepts outmoded concepts and assumptions of classical economics, such as "inherent scarcity" of social ends and the inviolability of competition, all of which result in a picture of theoretical necessity that reproduces with remarkable faithfulness a culturally circumscribed ideology. The view expressed by Lester F. Ward over half a century ago would seem to be still relevant:

> Here we encounter the great sullen, stubborn error, so universal and ingrained as to constitute a world view, that the difference between the upper and lower classes of society is due to a difference in their intellectual capacity, something existing in the nature of things, something preordained and inherently inevitable. Every form of sophistry is employed to uphold this view. We are told that there must be social classes, that they are a necessary part of the social order.[3]

The widespread acceptance of this theory in introductory sociology texts,[4] along with the recent appearance of Bernard Barber's detailed presentation of essentially the Davis-Moore functional view, demands further thought on the question of why the many cogent criticisms remain unanswered and especially why so much of current American sociological theory in this area remains isolated from and incompatible with the voluminous European and earlier American literature.

The present paper is concerned, not to review or revive earlier criticisms, but to point out what we believe to be a heretofore neglected basic conceptual flaw in the current functional theory of stratification and a problem focus that has still to be faced by an adequate theory. Whereas the excellent critique of Tumin and others was aimed mainly at the substantive content of this theory, the present analysis is aimed primarily at its methodological deficiencies.

To put the issue simply, and as the title of this paper suggests, the current functional theory of stratification is not a theory of stratification at all but something that more closely resembles a theory of certain aspects of social differentiation and hierarchical organization—a distinction, our argument insists, that is not merely one of arbitrary terminology.[5]

To begin with, it will be recalled that the Davis-Moore theory specifies the central defining criterion of the concept of stratification as follows: "If the rights and perquisites of different posi-

---

[3] *Applied Sociology* (Boston: Ginn and Company, 1906), p. 96.

[4] For example, see Arnold W. Green, *Sociology* (New York: McGraw-Hill Book Company, 1952). He states, on page 217: "Stratification is universal because it is necessary." It is of interest to note, however, that in the second edition, 1956, of this text the above statement is changed to read merely: "Stratification is universal."

[5] The distinction between stratification and differentiation has been made in some detail by, among others, Leopold von Wiese and Howard Becker, *Systematic Sociology* (New York: John Wiley & Sons, Inc., 1932, and Cecil C. North, *Social Differentiation* (Chapel Hill, N.C.: The University of North Carolina Press, 1926). The latter uses "social differentiation" as the generic term, subsuming under it the four main types: differences of function, of rank, of culture, and of interests.

And at least one other student of stratification has noted this basic flaw in Davis' theory: "Davis attempts a functional explanation of social stratification but, in fact, explains only social differentiation." Harold Pfautz, "Social Stratification and Sociology," *Transactions of the Second World Congress of Sociology*, Vol. II (London: International Sociological Association, 1954), p. 320, footnote 18.

tions in a society must be unequal, then the society must be stratified because that is precisely what stratification means."[6] We shall argue, however, that this is not precisely what stratification has meant to most students. It is (or was) rather firmly embedded in usage that stratification involves the existence of *strata,* generally agreed to refer to specifiable collectivities or subgroups that *continue through several generations* to occupy the same relative positions and to receive the same relative amounts of material ends, prestige, and power. The statement quoted above, on the other hand, refers only to the fact of the differentiation of social positions as seen at any one point of time and implies nothing about the existence of strata, which, to extend our above definition, implies groupings of individuals with biological and social continuity whose movements into the differentiated positions can be predicted to some degree (if only statistically).

Past stratification studies of importance have usually viewed strata, whether implicitly or explicitly, as historical developments. Without going back further, we recall the Marxian framework:

> From the serfs of the Middle Ages sprang the chartered burghers of the earliest towns. From these burgesses the first elements of the bourgeoisie were developed....
>
> We see, therefore, how the modern bourgeoisie is itself the product of a long course of development, of a series of revolutions in the modes of production and exchange....
>
> In proportion as the bourgeoisie, i.e., capital, is developed, in the same proportion is the proletariat, the modern working class, developed....[7]

And certainly Pareto's "circulation of the elites," Veblen's "leisure class," and Weber's "life-chances" and "life-style" lose much of their meaning outside of a developmental framework.

Turning to the early American sociological pioneers, we note that Ward and Cooley stressed continuity and inheritance of position as basic to class. Thus, for example, Cooley—who preferred the term "caste" or "caste principle" to refer to what we mean by strata or stratification—wrote:

> When a class is somewhat strictly hereditary, we may call it a caste—a name originally applied to the hereditary classes of India, but to which it is common, and certainly convenient, to give a wider meaning....
>
> On every side we may see that differences arise and that these tend to be perpetuated through inherited associations, opportunities, and culture.... Unlikeness in the constituents, a settled system, and a low state of communication and enlightenment favor the growth of caste, and vice versa. The first provides natural lines of cleavage and so makes it easier to split into hereditary groups; the second gives inheritance time to consolidate its power; while the third means the absence of those conscious and rational forces which are its chief rivals.[8]

Charles Page's study of the treatment of class by the American "Fathers" shows a similar general conception underlying the views of Small, Ross, and even Sumner.[9]

---

6 Davis and Moore, *op. cit.,* p. 243.

7 Karl Marx and Friedrich Engels, "The Communist Manifesto," in *The Making of Society,* ed. V. F. Calverton (New York: Random House, Inc., 1937), pp. 340, 341, 346.

8 Charles H. Cooley, *Social Organization* (Glencoe, Ill.: The Free Press, 1956), pp. 211, 217.

9 *Class and American Sociology* (New York: The Dial Press, Inc., 1940).

Of the contemporary students of stratification, we may mention R. H. Tawney, C. C. North, Wiese and Becker, Sorokin, Gerth and Mills, R. M. Williams, Jr., MacIver and Page, Harold Pfautz, and Kurt Mayer as a few of those (some, like Williams, with a functional orientation) who describe stratification as implying stratum permanence and hereditary inequality and not merely "achieved inequality."[10] Thus, North has argued:

It is frequently urged that this emergence of the class of those who control modern economic processes through the ownership of capital is not a case of privilege but of a natural evolution, whereby those whose abilities are adapted to the creation of capital and to the occupation of management and control naturally find their places in this position of power. In order to substantiate such a view it would have to be shown that the creation of capital was the work of such individuals and that they entered their vocations through a process of competitive adaptation. As a matter of fact all historical evidence points in exactly the opposite direction. . . .

Private property and the family, conservative government, legalization of class, occupational and religious differences, primogeniture, peonage, an aristocratic educational system, these are some of the socially created factors that tend to fasten upon the coming generations distinctions that have once become prevalent. Insofar as these factors

operate there are given to the members of the newer generations their respective places in the social system without reference to their own inherent qualities. But there is always the pretense that the inherent worth of the individual is the determining factor.[11]

For MacIver and Page,

A *system* or *structure* of social classes involves, first, a hierarchy of status groups; second, the recognition of the superior-inferior stratification; and, finally, some degree of permanency of the structure.[12]

And Mayer has recently stated:

Permanence is an important characteristic of social stratification. Rank hierarchies, like everything human, are changeable, but they tend to be relatively stable and enduring. Only those positions, therefore, which permit the exercise of power based on durable criteria, such as the possession of valuable material goods or the control of nonmaterial values like magic formulas or religious symbols, can become the bases of permanent social strata.[13]

In our judgment Davis and Moore have in effect disclaimed any interest in the problem of stratification per se by claiming to concern themselves only with the system of positions of a society. As if attempting to justify their avoidance of what has been the central conception of stratification, they state emphatically:

Throughout, it will be necessary to keep in mind one thing—namely, that the

10 R. H. Tawney, *Equality* (4th ed.) (London: George Allen & Unwin, Ltd., 1952); Wiese and Becker, *op. cit.*; Pitirim A. Sorokin, *Social Mobility* (New York: Harper and Bros., 1927); Hans Gerth and C. Wright Mills, *Character and Social Structure* (New York: Harcourt, Brace and Company, 1953); Robin M. Williams, Jr., *American Society* (New York: Alfred A. Knopf, Inc., 1955), p. 89; Pfautz, *op. cit.*, p. 314.

11 North, *op. cit.*, pp. 222, 265.
12 R. M. MacIver and Charles H. Page, *Society: An Introductory Analysis* (New York: Rinehart and Company, Inc., 1949), pp. 348–49.
13 *Class and Society* (Garden City, N.Y.: Doubleday & Company, Inc., 1955), p. 5.

discussion relates to the system of positions not to the individuals occupying those positions. It is one thing to ask why different positions carry different degrees of prestige and quite another to ask how certain individuals get into those positions. Although ... both questions are related, it is essential to keep them separate in our thinking. ... The first question ... is logically prior and, in the case of any particular individual or group, factually prior.[14]

Leaving aside the debatable assertion of priority, it should be noted that concern for the system of positions alone would have to stop with an analysis of their possible relations to and consequences for the system as a whole. When Davis and Moore go on, however, to speculate about processes motivating actors to fill these positions and the relation between the superior capacities or the training of actors and the highly rewarded positions they must fill, then Davis and Moore must relinquish their claim since they are clearly concerning themselves with characteristics of individuals and how these aid such persons in attaining certain positons. Whereas we concur in the view that differentiation of position on the one hand and the problem of individual attainment of those positions on the other are analytically distinct concerns, we are arguing that, not only must the distinction be consistently maintained, but, even more important, we cannot entertain a theory of stratification unless it focuses directly on the latter concern.

If we can agree that the term "social strata" refers to social groups or collectivities and not positions, and that stratification refers to the existence of strata in a society, then perhaps we should, logically, insist that stratification be defined in terms of groups or collec-

tivities, not positions. It might help to avoid confusion if we resist the current tendency to say, "Social stratification refers to the existence of a graded hierarchy of social positions" and to declare, instead, "Social stratification refers to the existence of a graded hierarchy of continuous social groups or collectivities." The difference of emphasis here can be crucial since the distinction between hierarchy of positions and hierarchy of groups opens up important questions. For example: To what extent, and how, does the former determine the latter, and vice versa? Would the range and particular structure of differential rewards and perquisites attaching to positions be what they are if it were not for the differential distribution of wealth, prestige, and power attaching to groups?

Failure to make and maintain the distinction between differentiation and stratification is brought out even more clearly in the recent volume by Bernard Barber, who builds the former concept into his definition of the latter. For Barber, stratification is "the product of the interaction of social differentiation and social evaluation."[15] It is "the result of the evaluations made of functionally important and differentiated social roles."[16] Thus, "a system of stratification can be seen as a system of facilities, rewards, and punishments allocated to the members of a society for the ways in which they perform its functionally essential and valued roles."[17] It follows then that "position in the system of stratification is determined on the whole by performance in functionally essential roles. ..."[18] And further, Bar-

---

[14] Davis and Moore, *op. cit.*, p. 242.

[15] *Social Stratification* (New York: Harcourt, Brace and Company, 1957), p. 2.
[16] *Ibid.*, p. 54.
[17] *Ibid.*, p. 20.
[18] *Ibid.*, p. 60.

ber concludes that stratification is inevitable because, first, some differentiation is essential in any society—it would be too wasteful to train all men for every specialized role, even if all were capable; and, second, differential evaluation of roles cannot be eliminated—not all roles are equally important. In sum, since Barber has defined stratification in terms of differentiation and since we can all generally agree that some social differentiation is essential, if not inevitable, then it logically follows that "some system of stratification is a functional requirement of societies."[19]

But Barber fails to include the central notion of strata in his definition of stratification and thus, like Davis and Moore, ignores the distinction between stratification and differentiation. This distinction may perhaps be brought out more clearly by the consideration that a nonstratified society (if the functionalist can, for the moment, grant such a possibility) containing no intergenerationally continuous strata: (1) would nevertheless be differentiated in terms of duties, rights, and perquisites, (2) might, without being inconsistent, recognize differential evaluation of roles (though not necessarily of persons), and (3) would still have the problem of training and selecting the new members for the various roles. The classlessness of the society would have nothing directly to do with its differentiation but would be manifested in the fact that a person's initial social position or milieu at birth would not be correlated with his adult social position, except perhaps to the very small extent that current fact and theory allow us to correlate validly the individual's biologically based capacities or

talents with his biological background. Stratified societies, on the other hand, have been viewed historically (as we have noted above) in terms of just such a correlation between individuals' initial social positions at birth and their adult social positions, giving rise to castes, estates, or classes. This is why the several recent empirical studies of *intergenerational* mobility, as distinct from career patterns per se, are crucial in establishing the fact and the extent of stratification.

The manner in which the functionalists present the stratification system as actually operating is rather the way in which many persons desire and believe that it would work in contemporary society if only the class structure did not exist to hinder it! As Mayer states,

> According to democratic ideology a person's social position should depend solely upon his own qualities and achievements and he should be free to rise above or fall below his parents' class and status groups in accordance with his personal capacities. Correspondingly, social classes should consist merely of temporary aggregates of individuals who happen to have achieved similar social positions at any particular time.[20]

Thus, it is precisely the issue of equality or inequality of initial opportunity to acquire the qualifications socially defined as necessary for achievement of functionally important positions that is conspicuously absent from the functionalists' theory.

The fact that differentiation and stratification are analytically distinct does not imply that they are not closely interrelated. Social differentiation accompanied by great inequalities in the

---

19 *Ibid.*, p. 19.

20 Mayer, *op. cit.*, p. 27.

distribution of wealth, power, and prestige can be seen to promote the development of more or less permanent strata; these, in turn, seem to promote the maintenance of large inequalities. Put otherwise, a classless society that nevertheless maintained great inequalities would seem to be as sociologically improbable as a stratified society maintaining no significant inequalities. Anthropological studies suggest, however, at the preliterate level at least, that such types of societies have existed. An important case in point is the Kwakiutl society of rank without class. Here is a society, according to a recent analysis,[21] with a proliferation of differentiated ranks and titles, but with each passed on from individual to individual, such that during his lifetime a person may be anything from a chief to a commoner. The result is that no classes can develop since no subgroup maintains a stable status over a long enough period for material, psychological, or subcultural distinctions to develop and persist.

Support for our basic argument is provided by the difficulties faced by the functionalist in attempting to square his theoretical formulation with research evidence. Thus, Barber, in discussing ethnic, racial, and religious criteria of stratification, drops his theoretical guard by suggesting that "there is *no necessary* reason why a member of a society born into any given ethnic, racial, or religious group in that society cannot learn to perform adequately in any social role that society includes, whether high-ranking or low-ranking."[22] If we extend this formulation to include any economic or social group in general, and no reason is given why we

may not, we arrive at the proposition that stratification is not necessary, or inevitable, after all. For an explanation of its ubiquity, then, we must turn, not to any functional necessity but to the sociocultural dynamics of particular times and places.

A second difficulty is involved in Barber's claim that "position in the system of stratification is determined on the whole by performance in functionally essential roles. . . ." Although Barber dedicates his book to Robert Merton, he apparently overlooks a telling point made by his mentor. After pointing out the great difficulties involved in trying to establish a "clear minimum inventory of 'functional needs' of social systems," Merton writes:

> Much the same can be said of the formally described need for motivating people to perform "the essential social roles" in a society. The criteria of the "essential" are of course heavily dependent on the social system as it exists at a given time. In actual practice, functional sociologists devote little attention to alternative roles "essential" to the modification of a social system in determinate directions.[23]

Furthermore, the empirical data Barber gathers together in later chapters show overwhelmingly that, even in modern democratic societies, the social positions of the majority of adults are at the same or very similar levels in the hierarchy as those of their parents. In other words, positions are determined on the whole by social inheritance, and only secondarily, *within this pattern*, by "performance." Although "performance" by itself may be important, it is the *chance to perform* that is at stake here.

---

21 Cf. Helen Codere, "Kwakiutl Society: Rank Without Class," *American Anthropologist*, 59 (June 1957), 473–86.

22 Barber, *op. cit.*, p. 60 (emphasis in original).

23 "Discussion," *American Sociological Review*, 13 (April 1948), 168.

Barber himself reaches this conclusion, although he fails to make explicit its implications for his functional theory: "It happens that every child is born into the social class of his parents, is socialized accordingly, and derives greater or fewer advantages or disadvantages from his initial class position. ... The family restricts equality of opportunity."[24] Barber seems to be trying to have and eat his cake. On the one hand, he states that position in a system of stratification is determined primarily by performance in functionally important roles. On the other hand, he declares that in no society can this be the case because it is inevitable that the family plays a central (according to his own interpretation, *the* central) role in determining position in the system; any other arrangement, he claims, would destroy the family (another confused but widely held hypothesis that we cannot discuss here).[25]

We note further that Barber's theory holds that social stratification is integrative for society "to the extent that it expresses a common and shared set of values."[26] But the empirical materials he uses show, in his own words, how

> family solidarity will cause the members of different classes to have different interests in social mobility ... different political interests ... different attitudes toward income- and inheritance-tax laws ... obviously, have different economic interests ... different educational interests. ... And so it will be with every other kind of social interest—recreational, "cultural," and even religious.[27]

Barber's conclusion from all this, however, is: "Thus the upper and the lower classes will have opposed interests *because* they share a fundamental value consensus."[28] Unless we have missed a subtle point here, we believe that a more warranted conclusion is that stratification, in principle as well as in practice, is incompatible with value consensus on any level.[29]

Finally, Barber's theoretical orientation and conceptual commitment lead him to see a direct correlation between functional differentiation and inequality:

> When we examine the evidence from many different societies, we discover a positive correlation between the amount of role differentiation and the development of a system of stratification. ...

---

24 Barber, *op. cit.*, p. 74.

25 Cf. Codere, *op. cit.*, for evidence that wide differences of rank could and did typically exist within the Kwakiutl family with no particular stress noted.

26 Barber, *op. cit.*, p. 9.

27 *Ibid.*, pp. 256–57.

28 *Ibid.*, p. 257 (emphasis in original).

29 Most students of society with a strong historical sense should find little difficulty in supporting the view that stratification has been, on balance, an actual or potential disruptive force. The fact that highly stratified societies like India have survived for many centuries proves, not that stratification is integrative as some claim, but only that a high degree of stratification can persist and the society "survive" at a certain level under such conditions as autocracy, little functional differentiation, and a low state of communication and enlightenment.

The question of whether functional differentiation per se is also, on balance, disintegrative is complicated by the difficulty of separating out the effects of stratification that, in practice, are closely intermingled with differentiation. Thus, it would seem that functional specialization, while leading to differences in *some* spheres of activity and outlook, need not lead to gross cleavages of a subcultural character such as stratification promotes. We might well subscribe to the perspective of C. C. North, who, accepting Durkheim's argument that increasing division of labor leads to organic solidarity of cohesive interdependence, notes also the disruptive potential of overspecialization and of individualistically oriented interest groups. North, *op. cit.*, Part IV.

Modern industrial societies, of course, are so highly differentiated that they all have elaborate systems of stratification. . . .[30]

But, we must ask, in what sense do modern societies have more highly developed and elaborated systems of stratification than, for example, India, Classical China, or feudal Europe? Do we not hold up such societies to students as models of highly elaborate stratified systems? Thus R. H. Tawney writes:

A community which is marked by a low degree of economic differentiation may yet possess a class system of which the lines are sharply drawn and rigidly defined, as was the case, for example, in many parts of the agricultural Europe of the eighteenth century. It may be marked by a high degree of economic differentiation and yet appear, when judged by English standards, to be comparatively classless, as is the case, for example, with some British Dominions.[31]

In sum, it would not seem unjust to say that the functionalists'[32] unique definition of stratification jetisons much of the previous work done in this area and promotes an insuperable discontinuity in sociological research.[33]

Press, 1949], Chap. 1.) Yet the frequent stress of functionalism on the "survival of society" easily leads one to look very hard for, or find very easily, some existing structural arrangement which, under the guise of explaining the survival of "society" (a very difficult concept to specify apart from the status quo), succeeds only in justifying the persistence of some existing *structure*, e.g., a class system. When we work in the other direction, however, starting with existing structures and seek their *consequences for or determinate relationships* to the total system in the present or future (a nonfunctionalist orientation), we are more easily humbled before the enormity of the task.

In any case, the student of sociology of knowledge might well argue that when we add to the logical structure of functionalism the factors of "human nature" and ethnocentrism, the probability is very great that some misuse will occur. Past experience would lend this some support. Cf. the writer's "Structural-Functional Analysis in Modern Sociology," in *Modern Sociological Theory in Continuity and Change*, eds. Howard Becker and Alvin Boskoff (New York: The Dryden Press, 1957), Chap. 8.

[33] A similar conclusion is reached by Jean Floud in her trenchant criticism of Theodore Geiger's functional orientation and concomitant confusion of social differentiation with social stratification. See "Social Stratification in Denmark," Review Article, *British Journal of Sociology*, 3 (June 1952), especially pp. 176–77.

[30] Barber, *op. cit.*, pp. 14–15.
[31] Tawney, *op. cit.*, pp. 52–53.
[32] Merton's view that the functional approach does not *logically* entail the difficulties discussed above is without doubt sound. (See R. K. Merton, *Social Theory and Social Structure* [Glencoe, Ill.: The Free

---

The paper by Wrong reassesses the Davis-Moore thesis in the light of the challenges put forth by its critics. In Wrong's opinion Buckley is overinvolved in definitional side issues and himself confuses social differentiation with social stratification. In general, he concludes, critics have not "dented the central argument that unequal rewards are functionally necessary in any and all societies."[1] Wrong, however, agrees with Buckley and Tumin that Davis and Moore do not deal sufficiently with the part played by inheritance in the perpetuation of in-

[1] *Op. cit.*, p. 772.

equality. Wrong believes this deficiency follows from their lack of historical perspective and their failure to take account of the role of social power in stratification.

THE FUNCTIONAL THEORY OF
STRATIFICATION*

Dennis H. Wrong

New York University

Nearly 15 years after its original publication, the issues raised by Kingsley Davis and Wilbert E. Moore in their article "Some Principles of Stratification"[1] are still being debated by sociologists. Critics of the authors' thesis have succeeded in showing that there are a great many things about stratification that Davis and Moore have failed to explain, but they have not succeeded in seriously denting the central argument that unequal rewards are functionally necessary in any and all societies with a division of labor extending much beyond differences in age and sex. On the other hand, the extreme abstractness and limited relevance of the Davis-Moore theory to the concrete historical world have been only partially recognized by its authors and their critics alike. Moreover, several of the theory's assumptions have yet to be made explicit, and a number of additional implications have been ignored by participants in the debate.

THE DEFINITION OF
STRATIFICATION

Walter Buckley's criticism of the Davis-Moore theory largely centers on the question of how stratification should be defined.[2] He accuses Davis and Moore of confusing *social differentiation*, the existence of specialized roles or of a division of labor, with *social stratification*, which he defines as a system of unequally privileged groups, membership in which is determined by the intergenerational transmission of roles, or of opportunities to attain them, through kinship affiliation. Davis has replied that what is or is not to be called stratification is purely a terminological question provided that a distinction is clearly made between the hierarchy of unequally rewarded roles and the way in which particular indivi-

---

* From Dennis H. Wrong, "The Functional Theory of Stratification: Some Neglected Considerations," *American Sociological Review*, 24 (December 1959), 772–82. Reprinted by permission of the American Sociological Association.

1 *American Sociological Review*, 10 (April 1945), 242–49. An extended and revised version of the theory which, as Davis has complained, the critics have largely ignored appears in Kingsley Davis, *Human Society* (New York: The Macmillan Company, 1949), pp. 366–78.

---

2 "Social Stratification and the Functional Theory of Social Differentiation," *American Sociological Review*, 23 (August 1958), 369–75.

duals are recruited in each generation to fill them.[3] Three relevant types of social organization, however, should be distinguished:

First, there is the existence of role differentiation, or division of labor itself, irrespective of whether or how the roles are ranked and their incumbents unequally rewarded. This is what is usually called *social differentiation*. Its causes and consequences, as Durkheim's famous study illustrates, can be discussed independently of the logically separable questions of how and why "horizontal" or "lateral" differences in position are transformed into "vertical" differences in rank.

Second, there are the unequal rewards distributed among the various roles making up the division of labor. The Davis-Moore theory tries to explain the ubiquity and inevitability of unequal rewards wherever role differentiation is highly developed.

Third, there is the tendency, a result of kinship loyalties, for roles and opportunities to attain them to be passed on from one generation to the next, giving rise to enduring classes or strata monopolizing certain roles and exhibiting a greater or lesser degree of solidarity and a common style of life.

Buckley accuses Davis and Moore of confusing the second and third types of social organization, but he himself confuses the first and second. The Davis-Moore theory, if it achieves nothing else, surely provides sound arguments for regarding the existence of a hierarchy of roles as a problem in its own right. Consider that Buckley's terminology would require him to describe an army which recruited all of its officers from the lower ranks as a differentiated

but nonstratified organization. And the same description would apply to the Catholic Church, where celibacy rules prevent the intergenerational transmission of roles. Admittedly, these types of hierarchy differ in important respects from hereditary class systems; if the term "stratification" is to be confined to the latter, however, another term is needed to distinguish armies, celibate priestly orders, and other bureaucracies from precivilized tribal societies, collegial bodies, parliaments, and similar nonhierarchical social structures.[4] But Davis and Moore are concerned with hierarchy or inequality per se: Such a distinction is only tangentially relevant to their argument.

THE FUNCTIONAL NECESSITY OF STRATIFICATION

What the critics of the Davis-Moore theory fundamentally object to is that in their view "the theory implies an assumption that any scheme of stratification is somehow the best that could be had, that the prevailing distribution of rewards comes into being somehow because it is 'functionally necessary.' "[5] The charge, repeated in some form by all of the critics, that Davis and Moore are "defending" or "justifying" the status quo, any status quo, rests on finding this implication in the theory. Yet it is not a logically correct implication, although it has never been explicitly disavowed by the authors.

All that the Davis-Moore theory actually asserts is that *if* the more impor-

[3] "The Abominable Heresy: A Reply to Dr. Buckley," *American Sociological Review*, 24 (February 1959), 82–83.

[4] They might usefully be called *ladder hierarchies* to distinguish them from *class* hierarchies.

[5] Richard L. Simpson, "A Modification of the Functional Theory of Social Stratification," *Social Forces*, 35 (December 1956), 132.

tant, highly skilled, and physically and psychologically demanding positions in a complex division of labor are to be adequately filled both from the standpoint of numbers and of minimally efficient performance, *then* there must be *some* unequal rewards favoring these positions over others. This proposition rests on certain assumptions about human nature. The important thing to note, however, is that it in no way denies that a particular distribution of rewards prevailing in a given historical society may vastly exceed the minimum inequalities necessary to maintain a complex division of labor.[6] Nor does it deny that some roles that are unimportant, unskilled, and pleasurable may be highly rewarded, provided only that they do not compete so successfully with roles possessing the opposite attributes that they reduce the quantity or the quality of candidates for the latter below some minimum level.[7] Nothing in their theory requires Davis and Moore to disagree with Tumin's claim that the "sacrifices" made by those who undergo professional training are overrewarded[8] nor with Simpson's contention that such roles as personal servant or kept woman may be highly rewarded although they make little contribution to society. Davis and Moore are committed solely to the view that there must be unequal rewards; *how* unequal these need to be or how strictly they must be apportioned according to functional importance and skill are separate questions the answers to which are not deducible from the theory.

The particular scale of unequal rewards prevailing in a society is likely so to shape people's expectations and sense of distributive justice that they will oppose efforts to alter it, even though no general sociological principle rules out the feasibility of a viable society in which the range of inequality might be far narrower. Notions of "fair price," "deserved recognition," and "proper return for services" may be invoked to protest increased taxation of large incomes, the imposition of wage cuts on manual workers, or even changes in wage and salary differentials between occupations differing in skill, responsibility, and traditional prestige.

Belief in the *legitimacy* of the existing scale of rewards, however, should be distinguished from the *power* possessed by threatened groups to resist any reduction in the size of their shares. The incumbents of the more functionally important and skilled roles are able to fight back by threatening withdrawal of their services if faced with a proposed distribution of rewards. This follows directly from the Davis-Moore principle viewed from a somewhat different perspective from that of its authors. Significantly, Davis and Moore have not formulated their theory in a way that focuses attention on the power element in stratification: They argue that unequal rewards are necessary to

---

6 Davis and Moore recognize the independent variability of the *scale of rewards*, or what they call "the magnitude of invidious differences," in listing it as a distinct "mode of variation" of stratified systems. *Op. cit.*, pp. 248–49. See also the very lucid discussion by Ralph Ross and Ernest van den Haag in *The Fabric of Society* (New York: Harcourt, Brace, 1957), pp. 121–22.

7 "Actually a society does not need to reward positions in proportion to their functional importance. It merely needs to give sufficient reward to insure that they will be filled competently." And, it should be added, in sufficient numbers. Davis, *Human Society*, p. 368.

8 Melvin M. Tumin, "Some Principles of Stratification: A Critical Analysis," *American Sociological Review*, 18 (August 1953), 390. Davis replies that Tumin ignores the "onerous necessity of studying," but no such defense is required to uphold his theory. Davis, "Reply," *ibid.*, p. 396.

attract individuals into the more important and skilled positions yet neglect to observe that once these positions have been filled their very importance and dependence on scarce skills gives their incumbents the power not only to insist on payment of expected rewards but even to demand larger ones. This power is inherent in the positions. The unequal rewards in wealth and prestige "attached to" the positions also give their incumbents greater opportunities to influence the general distribution of rewards in society and to protect or augment their own privileges. A further consideration is that the incumbents of the most highly rewarded roles are relatively few in number, which, as Michels and Mosca have taught us, facilitates collective organization and solidarity, preconditions for the effective exercise of social power.

Yet the history of left-wing parties and of labor movements in modern times demonstrates that the more numerous but individually less powerful occupants of the less-rewarded positions may organize to offset the initial power advantage of the privileged. By doing so they have succeeded often enough in effecting a redistribution of rewards in their favor. But the difficulties in organizing and maintaining solidarity among relatively poor, uneducated, apolitical, and geographically scattered majorities are formidable. That is why, as G. L. Arnold writes of the industrial worker, " 'Solidarity' is for him what 'honor' was to the feudal order and 'honesty' for the bourgeois: a claim which is felt as absolute because the existence of the individual depends on it."[9]

Reformist and revolutionary governments striving to alter the existing scale of rewards have often been forced to modify their egalitarian programs when confronted with the resistance of privileged groups. The threat or reality of a flight of capital has sometimes been employed to compel moderation of the policies of governments committed to greater economic equalization. The British Labour Party was forced to make concessions to the medical profession when socializing health services in England. Even unorganized lower strata may by passive resistance and what Veblen called "calculated withdrawal of efficiency" succeed at least in slowing up the pace of drastic changes imposed on them by centralized authorities: The Soviet regime from its earliest days repeatedly has made concessions to the peasants in the interests of higher agricultural productivity and has also found it expedient to restore "capitalist" incentives and wage differentials in industry.

These examples illustrate the eternal difficulties faced by reformers and Utopians in "making the leap from history into freedom." The progressive departure from egalitarian practices in the Soviet Union since the Revolution may indicate the "functional necessity" of maintaining a certain scale of unequal rewards in societies in the early stages of capital accumulation.[10] But neither the resistance aroused by efforts to modify existing inequalities in any society nor the possible need for wide inequalities in societies experiencing rapid industrialization justifies the conclusion that a more equal distribution of rewards is in principle incompatible with the maintenance of a complex division of labor.

Freud, in observing the social pathology of everyday life, spoke of a "narcissism with respect to minor dif-

---

[9] "Collectivism Reconsidered," *British Journal of Sociology*, 6 (March 1955), 9.

[10] Barrington Moore, Jr., *Political Power and Social Theory* (Cambridge: Harvard University Press, 1958), p. 137.

ferences," and students of bureaucratic organization confirm its reality when they report the immense significance people often attach to the door which is used to enter the place of work, the size and location of desks, the exact shade of cordiality of the boss's salutation, and so on. But can *all* differences, even those that are trivial in comparison with the inequalities we usually have in mind when discussing historical class systems, be abolished? Davis and Moore answer in the negative; a simple negative answer is all that their theory implies and all that any sociologist is entitled to mean in characterizing a "classless society" as a "sociological monstrosity" or a "contradiction in terms."[11]

It is worth noting that most egalitarian reformers in Western history have been concerned with narrowing the range of inequality and creating wider equality of *opportunity* rather than with the establishment of total equality of *condition:* the abolition of any system of unequal rewards altogether. And those who have favored the latter, notably sectarian Christian communists and Israeli *Kibbutznikim,* have been willing to pay the price set by Davis and Moore: foregoing the advantages of an elaborate division of labor and permanent commitment to an agrarian way of life. Marx relegated the achievement of his ideal society based on the principle "from each according to his quality, to each according to his need" to the "higher phase" of communism, when the state will have withered away, an economy of abundance will have been realized, and a division of labor will no longer be

necessary.[12] However difficult it may be to imagine technological innovations radical enough to make possible such a society,[13] there is nothing in its conception that violates the Davis-Moore principle. Moreover, the Marxist slogan refers only to *material* rewards. By recognizing different kinds of rewards, Davis and Moore do not rule out the possibility of a differentiated society in which complete income equality exists provided only that inequality of "psychological income" remains.[14]

The Davis-Moore theory, then, is formulated at so high a level of generality that it fails to rule out the "functional" viability of the major Utopian models of egalitarian societies which have been advanced by visionary thinkers since medieval times and even earlier. Although this may be regarded as evidence of the theory's undeniable validity, one may be disposed to conclude that, like other generalizations about the "universal functional prere-

---

11 E. Digby Baltzell, *Philadelphia Gentlemen: The Making of a National Upper Class* (Glencoe, Ill.: Free Press, 1958), pp. 1, 396.

12 Marx's view is stated most succinctly in *The Critique of the Gotha Programme,* Part I, Point 3, any edition.

13 And, barring the Malthusian problem which Marxists have notoriously slighted, it is not so difficult to imagine as it once was in view of the prospects of automation. As Meyer remarks: "Marx and Engels . . . had an idealized and quite premature conception of modern industrial society as a push-button shop, without realizing the complex technical demands such a society would make." Alfred G. Meyer, *Marxism: The Unity of Theory and Practice* (Cambridge: Harvard University Press, 1954), p. 81. See also Barrington Moore, *op. cit.*

14 Thus Walter Buckley is in error in suggesting that the Davis-Moore theory asserts that "some persons' incomes must always be greater or less than others." "A Rejoinder to Functionalists Dr. Davis and Dr. Levy," *American Sociological Review,* 24 (February 1959), 84–85. Tumin (*op. cit.,* p. 392) has noted the possibility of emphasizing one type of reward "to the virtual neglect of others."

quisites" of societies, it explains so little about concrete class structures, social inequalities, and the ways in which they arise and change that the theory's value is limited.

Yet by recognizing, if only implicitly, the separability of types of reward, the Davis-Moore theory is superior to other functionalist theories of stratification which tend to subsume all rewards under prestige or "differential evaluation."[15] Such theories require the questionable assumption that there is a single value-consensus in society. But there are always roles which *must* carry high material rewards to attract people to them in compensation for their abysmally low prestige—for example, hangmen, prostitutes, professional criminals. The independent variability of types of reward also helps to account for social change: That wealth or power can be gained in certain roles, even though their very existence may be deplored by prevailing mores and the resulting prestige judgments, encourages the spread of new activities, the rise of "new men" to foster them, and ultimately the development of new values, ideologies, and prestige rankings imposed by ascendant classes.

To avoid the "fallacy of misplaced concreteness," the Davis-Moore theory must be challenged on the ground of its psychological assumptions. Tumin is the only critic who has done so.[16] He suggests that motives other than desire for the prestige and material rewards attached to important and skilled roles might be institutionalized and might ensure competent role performance at less cost to society than unequal rewards. He mentions "joy in work" and "social duty" as possibilities. However, as Davis has pointed out in his rejoinder, Tumin blurs the distinction between prestige and esteem, between incentives for striving to attain positions and incentives for conscientiously fulfilling their duties once they have been attained. The motives Tumin mentions conceivably might induce people to carry out properly the duties of their positions, but, even if men were angels, the need for some selective system to allocate them to these positions in the first place would still exist. That exactly the right number of would-be doctors needed by society would feel an inner call to cure the ill at exactly the right time or that individuals, however beneficent their intentions, would spontaneously distribute themselves among positions in exactly the right proportions, to put it mildly, is an improbable supposition.

Tumin's point that sociology should not "shut the door on inquiry into alternative possible social arrangements"[17] is well taken, but the fails to propose any alternative to the Davis-Moore positional reward mechanism for recruiting individuals to their roles.[18] If we overlook the probability that the tendency to make invidious comparisons

---

[15] See, e.g., Talcott Parsons, "A Revised Analytical Approach to the Theory of Social Stratification," in *Class, Status, and Power*, eds. R. Bendix and S. M. Lipset (Glencoe, Ill.: Free Press, 1953), pp. 92–128; Bernard Barber, *Social Stratification* (New York: Harcourt, Brace, 1957), pp. 1–16.

[16] *Op. cit.*, p. 391.

---

[17] "Reply to Kingsley Davis," *American Sociological Review*, 18 (December 1953), 672.

[18] Earlier in his original article Tumin suggests that "a system of norms could be institutionalized in which the idea of threatened withdrawal of services . . . would be considered as absolute moral anathema." This observation, in common with his proposed motives for conscientiousness, indicates his exclusive concern with behavior *after* the various roles in a division of labor have been

both of unlike tasks ("prestige") and of performances of like tasks ("esteem") is rooted in the very nature of the self, we may concede that intrinsic job satisfaction and social duty might ensure high levels of performance in a static society where roles are ascribed at birth. But this does not appear to be what Tumin has in mind.

THE PROBLEM OF EQUALITY OF OPPORTUNITY

Davis and Moore see stratification as a sorting mechanism allocating the more talented and ambitious individuals to the more socially important and demanding roles by means of differential rewards which serve as incentives. Their model, as several critics have noted, is a special case of the market mechanism or price system of classical economic theory. And, just as the conditions for the "perfect" functioning of the market mechanism are never met by actual economies, so the stratification system never fully performs its imputed social function in actual societies.

In *Human Society* Davis has attempted to modify the theory to take into account the evident fact that differential rewards do not function as a selective mechanism for talent and industry when roles are ascribed to individuals at birth.[19] His arguments, which have been largely ignored by his critics, are worth examining in some detail. He begins by observing that the institution of the family limits the operation of the stratification system by giving to the children of the incumbents of roles in one generation relatively or absolutely greater opportunities to attain the same roles in the next generation. He shows in an analysis of the Indian caste system, however, that, despite its overwhelming emphasis on inherited status, the system cannot entirely preclude individual mobility because of caste fertility and mortality differentials, eventual changes in the physical environment giving rise to new roles and destroying old ones, and a number of other considerations.[20] He reiterates the distinction between the hierarchy of positions and the way in which individuals are recruited to them, pointing out that "the low estate of the sweeper castes in India, as compared with the priestly castes, cannot be explained by saying that sons of sweepers become sweepers and the sons of Brahmins become Brahmins." Since "there is a tendency for sweepers to have a low status in every society," Davis concludes that "the functional necessity behind stratification seems to be operative at all times, despite the concurrent operation of other functions."[21]

Now this argument actually does no more than assert that *over time but not necessarily "at all times"* differential

---

filled. But Davis and Moore are concerned with explaining how they come to be filled in the first place. As I have previously argued, they neglect the power to secure and enhance their rewards which accrues to role-incumbents once they have been recruited and trained. Tumin, however, makes the reverse error.

In a later article, "Rewards and Task-Orientations," *American Sociological Review*, 20 (August 1955), 419–23, Tumin also overlooks this crucial distinction, contending that parents perform their child-rearing tasks with dedication in the absence of expectations of unequal rewards; but, even if this be the case, motives for having children and for caring for them once they are born may be of a different order. And there is no assurance, of course, that people will reproduce at the rate which is optimal for society.

19 *Op. cit.*, pp. 369–70.
20 *Ibid.*, pp. 382–85.
21 *Ibid.*, p. 370. See also Davis, "Reply," *op. cit.*, p. 395.

rewards will operate as a selective mechanism. It lacks, but requires, a distinction analogous to that between the short run and the long run in economic analysis. By neglecting to make this distinction explicit the degree to which highly rewarded roles may be filled almost exclusively by ascription "in the short run" or "at any given time" is understated. Where inheritance of positions generally prevails, the existence of a system of unequal positional rewards favoring the important and skilled roles, far from reflecting a "functional necessity" that is currently "operative," can be understood only with reference to the past, to the events which shaped the system at the time when the society was developing a differentiated social structure.

Thus we arrive at the paradoxical conclusion that the Davis-Moore theory, especially when it is applied to rigid caste societies, is often a better theory of social origins than of contemporary functioning—an odd conclusion indeed in view of the antihistorical bias of functional explanations. The high estate of Brahmins can, in terms of the theory, be explained only if we assume that the promise of unequal rewards was once necessary to attract men to the priesthood before the hierarchy of positions had hardened into a hierarchy of hereditary strata. The truth of Schumpeter's assertion, alien to the spirit of functional analysis, is thus confirmed: "Any theory of class structure, in dealing with a given historical period, must include prior class structure among its data; and . . . any general theory of classes and class formation must explain the fact that classes coexisting at any given time bear the marks of different centuries on their brow. . . ."[22]

Schumpeter, like Davis, insists on the

ubiquity of mobility, even in relatively stagnant societies where legal and customary barriers between classes appear to be impassable. However, as in all of his writings, including his technical economic works, Schumpeter's approach is fundamentally historical: He clearly differentiates between a cross-sectional or short-run view of economies and social structures and a long-run view that takes into account changes in the position of families and firms within stable structures and, ultimately, changes in the structures themselves. Schumpeter sees the lineal family rather than the individual as the "true unit" of class and of mobility within and between classes; it may take generations for the representatives of a family line to inch their way upward in the class hierarchy to the point where an apparently secure hereditary class position is achieved. By looking at mobility in terms of family lines and generations, Schumpeter avoids the rival errors of viewing class position as entirely hereditary and immobile, on the one hand, and, on the other, of regarding existing inequalities as reflections of the actual distribution of ability and effort in the population. Lacking a truly historical perspective, the Davis-Moore theory, even in Davis' revised version of it, leaves itself open to the charge of committing the latter error, although Davis' later qualifications implicitly take into account time and change as crucial variables.

American sociologists often stress the

---

22 Joseph A. Schumpeter, *Imperialism*

and Social Classes (New York: Meridian Books, 1955), p. 111. Schumpeter's brilliant essay on social classes, first published in German in 1926, encompasses nearly all of the issues raised by the participants in the debate over the functionalist theory of stratification, including those raised by the present writer.

"dysfunctions" of the inequalities of opportunity that result from the inheritance of positions. When able and energetic individuals are prevented from competing for the most important and highly rewarded positions, the "efficiency" or "productivity" of society is alleged to suffer. This argument is a major one used by the critics of the Davis-Moore theory. Davis and Moore, however, themselves accept the argument when they insist that the function of unequal rewards is to allocate talent to the positions where it is most needed and answer their critics by claiming that this function can never be entirely suppressed. Yet for some important roles requiring subtle skills and character traits hereditary ascription may actually be a more efficient way of recruiting candidates. Some administrative and leadership roles are perhaps best filled by those who are "to the manner born," who have been subjected to a process of character-molding beginning in infancy and preparing them for later assumption of their roles. Obviously this does not apply to activities requiring genuinely scarce genetic aptitudes, for example mathematics and music. But such roles are largely technical and are usually, as Davis and Moore point out, less highly rewarded than administrative positions—religious, economic, or political—requiring "skill in handling people" or "capacity to make decisions," qualities which probably do not depend on rare genetic talents falling outside the range of endowment of the average man.

It is strange how insistence on the alleged "inefficiency" of unequal opportunities often leads sociologists to stress genetic endowment, the importance of which they are disposed to minimize in other connections. I suspect that this argument is another instance of the dangerous proclivity of contemporary social scientists to find "factual" or "instrumental" reasons for supporting views they ultimately favor on ethical grounds.[23] Nevertheless it is true, in a society with a growing population and an expanding economy, that barriers to full equality of opportunity may lead to shortages in the *supply* of candidates for important positions.[24] But this situation, clearly applicable to engineers, physical scientists, doctors, and other professionals in the United States today, does not necessarily imply deficiencies in the role performance of those who

---

23 Paul Kecskemeti, "The Psychological Theory of Prejudice," *Commentary*, 18 (October 1954), 359–66; also Bruno Bettelheim, "Discrimination and Science," *Commentary*, 21 (April 1956), 384–86; and Dennis H. Wrong, "Political Bias and the Social Sciences," *Columbia University Forum*, 2 (Fall 1959), 28–32.

24 Actually, societies face three distinct problems in "allocating" and motivating their members: The number of candidates for important roles must be sufficient; their talents and aptitudes, innate or previously acquired, must not fall below a certain level; and, once they have been trained and have assumed their roles, they must be induced to do their best. A solution to one of these problems is not necessarily a solution to the others.

If we wished to raise the intellectual level of the American academic profession, for example, two exactly opposite policies might prove effective. We might stop paying professors anything at all with the result that only men with a genuine love of learning and a profound dedication to the pursuit of truth would be willing to become mendicant scholars. Or we might raise professorial salaries so that the academy could compete with business and the highly paid professions in attracting able and ambitious men. Both of these policies might lead to greatly improved academic performance, but only the second would ensure an adequate supply of would-be professors to staff American colleges and universities. I am indebted for this (I hope) fanciful example to Russell Kirk, *Academic Freedom: An Essay in Definition* (Chicago: Henry Regnery Co., 1955), pp. 170–71.

are the beneficiaries of unequal opportunities. Nor should it be generalized to apply to all social orders where inequality of opportunity prevails, notably to static agrarian societies with caste-like stratification systems. The proponents of the view that inequality of opportunity is "dysfunctional" fail to distinguish between its effects when the *shape* or *profile* of the stratified occupational system is changing and under conditions where *pure mobility* alone is at issue.[25]

In hereditary class societies the desire for esteem rather than for prestige must suffice to motivate individuals to perform their roles competently.[26] Monopolizing the positions carrying high rewards, a ruling stratum is always subject to the temptation to become absentee owners embracing the values of Veblen's leisure class, which make a virtue of "functionless" activity and elevate what have previously been viewed as rewards for performance into criteria of worth in their own right. One of the patterns of conspicuous leisure described by Veblen is precisely the phenomenon noted by Richard Simpson: the creation by the privileged of new positions—servants, footmen, courtesans, and the like, whose function is to serve as lackeys catering to the most trivial wants of their masters. Davis and Moore note the existence of reward for "pure ownership" but add in a phrase with curious evolutionist overtones that it "becomes more subject to criticism as social development proceeds toward industrialization."[27]

It cannot be assumed, however, that a hereditary ruling class always degenerates into a "decadent" leisure class in the Veblenian sense. Clearly, there have been hereditary aristocracies deeply imbued with an ethos of honor, responsibility, and *noblesse oblige* serving to motivate conscientious role performance. Hereditary upper classes may even exhibit a stronger sense of duty and accountability to society than *arriviste* elites precisely because of their awareness that they are the recipients of "unearned" privileges which can only be justified by continuous effort.[28] Which model—Veblenian leisure class or responsible aristocracy—characterizes a hereditary class is a matter of the particular historical context.

Although American social scientists have stressed the "dysfunctions" for so-

---

25 For the concept of *shape* or *profile* of stratification, see Pitirim A. Sorokin, *Social Mobility* (New York: Harper, 1927), pp. 36ff. For the concept of *pure mobility*, see Natalie Rogoff, *Recent Trends in Occupational Mobility* (Glencoe, Ill.: Free Press, 1953), pp. 30–31; also Ross and van den Haag, *op. cit.*, Chap. 10, which contains an excellent general theoretical discussion of the different factors affecting mobility.

26 This is not, of course, strictly true: Important political, bureaucratic, and military roles may be filled only from the ranks of a hereditary upper class, but not all members of the class fill such roles. Thus prestige incentives may be effective in inducing feudal princes to strive to become and to remain the king's first minister, Junker landlords to seek to be generals, etc. This situation necessitates the familiar distinction between the "elite," those necessarily few men who possess actual decision-making powers, and the "ruling class," the larger stratum from which the elite is recruited.

27 *Op. cit.*, p. 247.
28 Baltzell, *op. cit.*, pp. 4–5. C. Wright Mills has suggested that the way of life of Veblen's leisure class is probably more characteristic of the *nouveau riche*, specifically of the self-made millionaires whose antics loomed so large on the American scene when Veblen was writing, than of established hereditary aristocracies. See Thorstein Veblen, "Introduction to the Mentor Edition," in *The Theory of the Leisure Class* (New York: Mentor, 1953), p. xiv.

ciety of inequality of opportunity, they have also been highly sensitive to the negative consequences for the *individual* of vertical mobility, upward or downward. But they have been extraordinarily remiss in exploring systematically the disintegrative effects for *society* of high rates of mobility, as well as the dangers posed by full equality of opportunity to other cherished values. Scores of books and articles have been written attributing neurosis, criminality, and demoralization to the competitiveness allegedly inspired by intense mobility strivings in a society which holds out the promise of high rewards to those who rise to the top.[29] But one can cite few writings by Americans which deal directly with the negative consequences for the social

structure of rapid mobility[30]—apart from Davis' argument, echoed by other functionalists, that the requirements for family solidarity set limits to complete equality of opportunity. However, a number of nonsociologists, many of them English, have recently become concerned with the question of just how much mobility and equality of opportunity a modern society can stand.[31] Will the trend toward the

---

[29] This was, in fact, a major theme, if not *the* major theme, of the most widely read works of American social science and social criticism in the 1930s and early 1940s. Representative are Karen Horney, *The Neurotic Personality of Our Time* (New York: W. W. Norton & Company, Inc., Publishers, 1937); Robert S. Lynd, *Knowledge for What?* (Princeton, N.J.: Princeton University Press, 1939), especially Chap. 3; Robert K. Merton, "Social Structure and Anomie," *American Sociological Review*, 3 (October 1938), 672–82. Treatments of American society in the books of Margaret Mead, Ruth Benedict, Lawrence Frank, Abram Kardiner, Elton Mayo, and others also stress this theme. Most of these writers fail to distinguish between the effects of competition per se and of competition under conditions where full equality of opportunity is manifestly absent. Merton, however, explicitly attributes the "strain toward anomie" he finds in American life to the "contradiction between cultural emphasis on pecuniary ambition and the social bars to full opportunity," but it is far from certain that the deviant and anomic responses he describes would disappear in an industrial society which successfully removed all major barriers to opportunity. In fact the cultural emphasis on success might very well be enhanced under such circumstances.

[30] The only examples I have found of American sociologists who have made the general point that rapid mobility may be "dysfunctional," as distinct from noting particular unpleasant consequences of recent mobility in analyses of ethnic prejudice or of "McCarthyism," are Baltzell, *op. cit.*, and Seymour Martin Lipset and Reinhard Bendix, *Social Mobility in Industrial Society* (Berkeley: University of California Press, 1959), pp. 260–65, 285–87. Lipset and Bendix mention the neglect of this topic by American sociologists and refer to an article by Melvin M. Tumin, "Some Unapplauded Consequences of Social Mobility in a Mass Society," *Social Forces*, 36 (October 1957), 32–37. This article, however, is chiefly concerned with the "unapplauded" consequences of status discrepancies between high occupational position and low ethnic or kinship status, and of mobility defined in terms of consumption gains alone.

[31] See Paul Kecskemeti, *Meaning, Value and Communication* (Chicago: University of Chicago Press, 1952), pp. 268–74; David Potter, *People of Plenty* (Chicago: University of Chicago Press, 1954), pp. 103–10; Peregrine Worsthorne, "The New Inequality," *Encounter*, 7 (November 1956), 24–34; C. A. R. Crosland, *The Future of Socialism* (New York: The Macmillan Company, 1957), Chap. 10; Ross and van den Haag, *op. cit.*, pp. 126–27, 132–34; Michael Young, *The Rise of the Meritocracy* (London: Thames and Hudson, 1958), *passim*; Raymond Williams, *Culture and Society, 1780–1950* (London: Chatto & Windus, Ltd., 1958), pp. 331–32. Of these writers only Young is a professional sociologist by background, and his entire book argues the undesirability of a society in which full equality of opportunity is institutionalized; see the review of his volume by Charles Curran in *Encounter*, 12 (February 1959),

replacement of class hierarchies by ladder hierarchies[32] in industrial societies eliminate the evils (or, if preferred, the "dysfunctions") which have been so widely attributed to inherited class privileges? Considering the charges of ideological bias which have been bandied about by both sides in the debate over the Davis-Moore theory, it is worth noting that in England staunch conservatives and confirmed socialists alike have raised this question. The following doubts have been expressed by at least two or more of the writers cited in notes 30 and 31:

1. Might not a self-made elite owing its position to demonstrated merit alone be even more intolerant and self-righteous in its attitude toward the lower strata than an elite owing its position largely to birth?[33]

2. Would not those who failed to achieve high positions feel even more guilt-ridden, demoralized, and alienated than at present if their failure were truly owing to proven lack of objective ability rather than to "accidents of birth" or "not knowing the right people," excuses which can now be employed as rationalizations for failure?

3. Is it really desirable that the lower strata should consist only of those who are genuinely inferior, thus depriving their ranks of a leaven of able and aggressive individuals to lead and represent them in conflicts of interest with the more highly placed groups and to contribute variety and liveliness to their social experience?

Let us ignore the extreme case of a brutal centralized totalitarianism which, as George Orwell has suggested, may actually be more compatible with a social structure resembling a ladder hierarchy than with a regime of hereditary social classes. Whether rapid mobility and full equality of opportunity in a democratic industrial society have the effects described above depends on a number of conditions, of which the major ones probably are the cultural value placed on upward mobility, the range of inequality or what I have called "the scale of unequal rewards," and the rate of economic expansion and technical progress. These

---

68–72, which makes precisely the Davis-Moore point that such a society is impossible because of man's "philoprogenitive" impulses.

[32] See note 4, above.

[33] "The Party is not a class in the old sense of the word. It does not aim at transmitting power to its own children, as such; and, if there were no other way of keeping the ablest people at the top, it would be perfectly prepared to recruit an entire new generation from the ranks of the proletariat. In the crucial years, the fact that the Party was not a hereditary body did a great deal to neutralize opposition. The older kind of Socialist, who had been trained to fight against something called 'class privilege,' assumed that what is not hereditary cannot be permanent. He did not see that the continuity of an oligarchy need not be physical, nor did he pause to reflect that hereditary aristocracies have always been short-lived, whereas adoptive organizations such as the Catholic Church have sometimes lasted for hundreds or thousands of years. The essence of oligarchical rule is not father-to-son inheritance, but the persistence of a certain world view and a certain way of life, imposed by the dead upon the living. A ruling group is a ruling group so long as it can nominate its suc-

cessors. The Party is not concerned with perpetuating its blood but with perpetuating itself. Who wields power is not important, provided that the hierarchical structure remains always the same." George Orwell, *1984* (New York: Harcourt, Brace, 1949), pp. 210–11. Too many American sociologists resemble Orwell's "the older kind of Socialist" in their views on stratification. Confusion of biological continuity with permanency of structure is particularly marked in Buckley's article, *op. cit.*, pp. 370–71.

factors of course are only partially independent of one another.

If the price of failure to rise socially —or even of downward mobility—is not too great, if a definite floor and ceiling are institutionalized to confine inequalities within tolerable limits, and if the general standard of living is high, then upward mobility, as David Potter has suggested, may come to be viewed as "optional rather than obligatory," and equality of opportunity need not produce a monolithic elite ruling over an inert mass. A diversified value system which recognizes and honors human qualities other than functional intelligence and single-minded ambition will be more likely to flourish.

Potter, David Riesman, W. H. Whyte, and others have noted the decline of the Protestant Ethic, the relaxation of the success drive, and the new importance of leisure as opposed to work in American life. There are also signs, however, that the decline of strong aspirations to occupational mobility has coincided with an increase of status-seeking in leisure pursuits and consumption behavior.[34] Davis and Moore and others who have theorized about the limits to equality in human societies have been chiefly concerned with the relationship of unequal rewards and mobility to the functional

division of labor; the newer forms of "status panic" raise questions of a cultural and psychological nature which fall outside the scope of theories that focus primarily on social structure.

Finally, if economic expansion and technical progress continue to change the shape of occupational stratification, producing "automatic" upward mobility by reducing the number of workers needed in low-status positions, the combination of hierarchy and equality of opportunity will be less likely to generate social tensions.[35]

All of the dimensions of hierarchy— the range of inequality, the shape of the hierarchical structure, the amount of mobility, and the ways in which each of these is changing—are empirically interdependent and jointly produce particular social consequences, although they can and must be analytically distinguished. American sociologists, reflecting the values of their own society, have been preoccupied with the amount of mobility to the neglect of the other dimensions.

CONCLUSION

If the inducement of unequal rewards is required to encourage men to convert their talents into skills, exercise their skills conscientiously, and undertake difficult tasks, it is also the case that, having won their rewards, they will use their superior power, wealth, and prestige to widen still further existing inequalities in their favor.

---

[34] See Tumin, "Some Unapplauded Consequences of Social Mobility in a Mass Society," *op. cit.* I have ignored in this paper the different types of mobility: occupational, status, consumption, etc. For a discussion of these, see Lipset and Bendix, *op. cit.*, pp. 269–77; also Lipset and Hans L. Zetterberg, "A Comparative Study of Social Mobility, Its Causes and Consequences," *Prod*, 2 (September 1958), 7–11. The fact that England has traditionally possessed a steeper status hierarchy than the United States and one in which status distinctions are much more sharply drawn probably accounts for the greater misgivings of English social analysts about the advantages of equality of opportunity per se.

[35] Inequalities of power are probably increasing as modern society becomes more bureaucratized at the same time that "consumer equality" is becoming more marked. For perceptive discussions of this trend, see Worsthorne, *op. cit.*, and Arnold, *op. cit.*; also G. L. Arnold, *The Pattern of World Conflict* (New York: The Dial Press, Inc., 1955), pp. 130–31.

And they are likely to do so even when their chances of passing on differential advantages to their children are strictly limited. Thus there may *never* be a correspondence between the existing scale of unequal rewards and the minimum scale required to maintain the social order—although democratic government and the organization of the lower strata to countervail the initial power superiority of the elite may stabilize or even narrow the existing scale. But conflicts between unequally rewarded groups and a sense of injustice on the part of the less privileged may be just as endemic in society as the necessity for unequal rewards itself. This of course is the central insight of the Marxist tradition. Sociologists pay lip service to the theoretical obligation to stress both the integrative and the divisive effects of social arrangements. The obligation applies with special force to discussions of stratification. Power, justice, and social necessity are perhaps ultimately incommensurable.

While a substantial body of literature has been devoted to assessing the merits of the Davis-Moore explanation of social stratification, the theory has generated few empirical studies.[1] The major obstacles to the conduct of relevant research are the highly abstract level of the Davis-Moore argument and the ambiguity of its basic propositions. The papers by Huaco and Stinchcombe clarify some of its logical implications, including its intervening conceptual operations, and suggest possible ways of testing its empirical consequences.

---

[1] Among the empirical investigations which have been guided in varying degrees by the Davis-Moore theory are Eva Rosenfeld, "Social Stratification in a Classless Society," *American Sociological Review*, 16 (December 1951), 766–74; Richard D. Schwartz, "Functional Alternatives to Inequality," *American Sociological Review*, 20 (August 1955), 424–30; Lionel S. Lewis and Joseph Lopreato, "Functional Importance and Prestige of Occupations," *Pacific Sociological Review*, 6 (Fall 1963), 55–59; Joseph Lopreato and Lionel S. Lewis, "An Analysis of Variables in the Functional Theory of Stratification," *Sociological Quarterly*, 4 (Autumn 1963), 301–10.

A LOGICAL ANALYSIS OF
THE DAVIS-MOORE THEORY*

George A. Huaco

Yale University

The recent exchange between Moore and Tumin suggests that a thorough logical analysis of the Davis-Moore theory of stratification is yet to be made. In these notes I attempt to contribute to such an analysis.

What are Davis and Moore trying to explain? Presumably their theory is

---

* From George A. Huaco, "A Logical Analysis of the Davis-Moore Theory of Stratification," *American Sociological Review*, 28 (October 1963), 801–4. Reprinted by permission of the American Sociological Association.

an attempt to provide a causal,[1] scientific explanation for what they mean by "stratification." Davis writes:

> The Davis-Moore article applies the term "stratification" to the system of unequal rewards attached to different positions in a society. It is the existence of such unequal reward systems that the theory tries to explain.[2]

And again:

> In so far as there is a difference between one system of stratification and another, it is attributable to whatever factors affect the two determinants of differential reward—namely, functional importance and scarcity of personnel.[3]

These two quotations present a simple or minimal assumption version of the theory. The steps of the argument run as follows:

(A) All societies have unequal rewards attached to different positions. (This empirical generalization is the dependent variable.)

(B) The state of affairs described in (A) is determined by two factors (which constitute the independent variables):

    (1) Different positions have unequal importance for the preservation or survival of the society.

    (2) Adequate performance in different positions requires incumbents equipped with different (and socially scarce) amounts of talent or training.

(C) The independent variables determine the dependent variable in the following manner: Incumbents with greater talent or training are induced to occupy the functionally more important positions by attaching greater rewards to these positions.

(D) It follows from (A), (B), and (C) that in all societies those positions which receive the greater rewards will be the ones which are functionally most important and will be the ones occupied by the most talented or qualified incumbents.

This is the causal, unqualified, and minimal assumption version of the theory. Before we examine it, we must contrast it briefly with three other versions of the theory: (1) the "consequential," (2) the qualified, and (3) the maximal assumption versions.

(1) The "consequential," or properly "functionalist," version of the theory examines consequences instead of causes:

> Social inequality is thus an unconsciously evolved device by which societies insure that the most important positions are conscientiously filled by the most qualified persons.[4]

Here "social inequality" (the system of unequal rewards attached to different positions) is said to have certain consequences; it is a determinant which insures "that the most important positions are conscientiously filled by the most qualified persons." Here the theorists have reversed the direction of causality. In the first version of the theory, unequal rewards are the *effect* of the operation of the mechanism surrounding unequal functional importance; in the second version of the theory, unequal rewards are the *cause* of the operation of the mechanism sur-

---

1 Kingsley Davis, "Reply," *American Sociological Review*, 18 (1953), 394.

2 K. Davis, "The Abominable Heresy: A Reply to Dr. Buckley," *American Sociological Review*, 24 (1959), 82.

3 K. Davis and Wilbert Moore, "Some Principles of Stratification," *American Sociological Review*, 10 (April 1945), 244.

4 K. Davis, *Human Society* (New York: The Macmillan Company, 1948), p. 367.

rounding unequal functional importance.

(2) The qualified version of the Davis-Moore theory introduces qualifications stemming from the differential impact of the family system.

> Since this is not the only functional necessity characterizing social systems, it is in actuality limited by certain other structures and requirements. Among the latter is the family, which limits vertical mobility by the mechanism of inheritance and succession. The family's limiting role, however, is never complete for there is some vertical mobility in any society. Thus the selective effect of the prestige system exists in its pure form only abstractly, not concretely; and the same is true of the inheritance of status.[5]

When this new qualifying factor is examined in conjunction with the earlier "consequential" version, some peculiar problems seem to be generated. The argument now runs as follows:

(a) In every society, inequality of rewards *insures* that the most important positions are filled by the most qualified persons.

(b) But you will not observe condition (a) in any existing society because in every society the presence of the family introduces status ascription, partially or almost completely (as in the Hindu caste system).

Now, if condition (a) exists and yet does not exist in any observable society, *where* does it exist? The answer, of course, is that the introduction of the family into the "consequential" version of the theory shows that the system of unequal rewards does *not*, in effect, *insure* what it is said to insure. What

---

[5] K. Davis, "Reply," *American Sociological Review*, 18 (1953), 395.

Davis and Moore seem to be trying to say is that if the family did not exist, then presumably the system of unequal rewards would insure, etc., but this is a counterfactual conditional and quite a different matter.

(3) The maximal assumption version makes stronger claims than those set forth in the minimal assumption version. At various times Davis and Moore have suggested that *only* unequal rewards can insure that the most qualified persons will occupy the functionally most important roles. This stronger claim is open to the charge (made by Tumin, Buckley, Schwartz, and Simpson) that Davis and Moore have ignored possible alternatives, or so-called "functional equivalents," to unequal rewards.

Let us now return to the causal, unqualified, and minimal assumption version of the theory. That all known societies exhibit systems of unequal rewards and that talent and training are scare resources are empirical generalizations about which no more need be said. The problematic core of the theory lies in the postulate that different positions have unequal functional importance for the preservation or survival of the society. The rest of these notes will attempt to elucidate this notion.

The postulate of unequal functional importance means that for any given society, the performance of some roles contributes more to the preservation or survival of that society than the performance of other roles. For this statement we need an independent definition of survival. We also need criteria to measure how much a given role contributes to survival vis-á-vis any other role. Davis mentions the following examples of such criteria.

Rough measures of functional importance are in fact applied in practice. In wartime, for example, decisions are made as to which industries and occupations will have priority in capital equipment, labor recruitment, raw materials, etc. In totalitarian countries the same is done in peacetime, as also in underdeveloped areas attempting to maximize their social and economic modernization. Individual firms must constantly decide which positions are essential and which are not.[6]

The difficulties with these examples are twofold:

(a) Each of them provides a dichotomous (essential/nonessential) criterion which seems to be tautologically derived from an overall system goal. But what we need is criteria that permit us to measure the *degree* of contribution to societal survival of any role vis-à-vis any other role; in short, we need ranking criteria.

(b) Each of these examples is drawn from a partially or totally planned economic system and, as such, useless for drawing inferences applicable to unplanned systems (and most societies throughout history have been unplanned).

Let us examine another attempt:

Unfortunately, functional importance is difficult to establish. To use the position's prestige to establish it, as is often unconsciously done, constitutes circular reasoning from our point of view. There are, however, two independent clues: (a) the degree to which a position is functionally unique, there being no other positions that can perform the same function satisfactorily; (b) the degree to which other positions are dependent on the one in question.[7]

The village idiot and the court jester were unique positions in medieval society. All positions in a modern army regiment are, in some sense, dependent on the position of supply sergeant. Even if we could develop a single, unified scale of positional dependency, we would still have to show that it had some empirical relevance to unequal functional importance (i.e., degree of contribution to the preservation or survival of a society).

As used by Davis and Moore, the notion of "unequal functional importance" shifts meaning. This shift occurs through the translation of "unequal functional importance" into "unequal functional necessity." Here the term "necessity" does double duty. In some formulations "unequal functional importance or necessity" means unequal contributions to societal survival; in other formulations "necessity" means analytical or logical necessity, and here the notion of "unequal functional importance or necessity" is removed from the empirical realm. In his recent "Rejoinder" to Tumin, Moore writes:

As I read the evidence, the evaluation of functionally differentiated positions is by no means as randomly variable as his discussion asserts or implies. I suggest that behavior relevant to the maintenance of order, the provision of economic support, the protection of the society, and the exemplifications of religious and esthetic values *always* involves differential position as well as merely personal valuation.[8]

This claim was previously made by Davis:

Owing to the universal necessity of

---

6 *Loc. cit.*

7 Davis and Moore, *op. cit.*, p. 244.

8 W. Moore, "Rejoinder," *American Sociological Review*, 28 (February 1963), 27.

certain functions in society, which require social organization for their performance, there is an underlying similarity in the kind of positions put at the top, the kind put at the middle, and the kind put at the bottom of the scale. . . . For this purpose we shall select religion, government, economic activity, and technology.[9]

This selection of four "necessary" societal "functions" is not only familiar, but it is also in the right order. As described by Davis,[10] the selected "functions" roughly correspond to the four analytical levels of a well-known model of society:

DAVIS	MARX
Religion	*Upper layer of superstructure*
Government	*Lower layer of superstructure*
Economic activity	*Relations of production*
Technology	*Forces of production*

The sole purpose of this comparison is to suggest that Davis and Moore's "universal" and "necessary" societal "functions" are really the various analytical parts of their implicit model of society or are derived by a series of hidden tautologies from such an implicit model. The "necessity" involved is clearly analytical or logical necessity. It follows from this that Davis' claim that what he has selected are four "universal" and "necessary" societal "functions" is simply a tautology.

There seem to be two possibilities for obtaining adequate criteria by which to determine the functional importance (or degree of contribution to

societal survival) of a given role vis-à-vis any other role:

(1) We can take the value and norm system of each culture as the criteria for that culture. (But this is the "extreme relativism" of Tumin, which Moore has rejected in the recent exchange,[11] and this possibility would also produce the circular reasoning which Davis has rightly rejected in one of the above quotations.)

(2) We can assert that, on the basis of experimental or quasiexperimental empirical evidence (and quite independently of the value and norm system of each culture), the sociologist is able to determine which roles make the greater contribution to the survival of a given society. (But in the present state of the social sciences, we have no such empirical evidence.)

In summary, "unequal functional importance" is a complete unknown; and, as it stands, it cannot serve as a legitimate explanation for "unequal rewards." Here it might perhaps be argued that the ingenuity of some future sociologist will eventually find empirical indicators for "unequal functional importance." This is possible, but we must remember that no "common sense" set of alleged indicators will do. If the notion of "unequal functional importance" means "unequal contributions of different roles to the preservation or survival of the society," then it follows from this that nothing short of a real empirical test—calling for painstaking and comprehensive comparative and historical analyses—will even begin to provide criteria for accepting or rejecting this notion.

---

9 Davis, *Human Society*, p. 371.
10 K. Davis and Wilbert Moore, "Some Principles of Stratification," *American Sociological Review*, 10 (1945), 244–46.

---

11 W. Moore, *op. cit.*, p. 27.

SOME EMPIRICAL CONSEQUENCES OF THE DAVIS-MOORE THEORY OF STRATIFICATION*†

Arthur L. Stinchcombe

The Johns Hopkins University

Davis and Moore's theory of stratification,[1] though frequently discussed, has stimulated remarkably few studies. Perhaps this is due to the lack of derivations of empirical propositions in the original article. I would like in this note to outline some empirical implications of the theory.

Davis and Moore's basic argument is that unequal regards tend to accrue to positions of great importance to society, provided that the talents needed for such positions are scarce. "Society" (i.e., people strongly identified with the collective fate) insures that these functions are properly performed by rewarding the talented people for undertaking these tasks. This implies that the greater the importance of positions, the less likely they are to be filled by ascriptive recruitment.[2]

It is quite difficult to rank tasks or roles according to their relative importance. But certain tasks are unquestionably more important at one time than at another, or more important in one group than another. For instance, generals are more important in wartime than in peacetime. Changes in importance or different importance in different groups have clear consequences according to the theory. If the importance of a role increases, its rewards should become relatively greater and recruitment should be more open.

The following empirical consequences of the theory are "derivations" in a restricted sense. We identify supposed changes in the importance of roles or identify groups in which certain roles are more important. Then we propose measures of the degree of inequality of reward and openness of recruitment which are consequences of

* From Arthur L. Stinchcombe, "Some Empirical Consequences of the Davis-Moore Theory of Stratification," *American Sociological Review*, 28 (October 1963), 805–8. Reprinted by permission of the American Sociological Association.

† This note was stimulated by a seminar presentation by Renate Mayntz, who focused attention on the problem of empirical investigation of functional theories.

[1] Kingsley Davis and Wilbert E. Moore, "Some Principles of Stratification," *American Sociological Review*, 10 (April 1945), 242–49.

[2] The theory holds that the most important positions, if they require unusual talents, will recruit people who otherwise would not take them, by offering high rewards to talent. This result would take place if one assumed a perfectly achievement-based stratification system. Some have asserted that Davis and Moore's argument "assumes" such a perfectly open system and hence is obviously inadequate to the facts. Since the relevant results will be obtained if a system recruits more talented people to its "important" positions but ascribes all others, and since this postulate is not obviously false as is the free market assumption, we will assume the weaker postulate here. It seems unlikely that Davis and Moore ever assumed the stronger, obviously false, postulate.

such changes. If changes in importance are correctly identified and if the measures of inequality of reward are accurate, then the consequences are logical derivations from the theory. If it turns out that generals are not more recruited according to talent in wartime, then it may be because the theory is untrue. But it may also be that generals are not in fact more important in wartime or that our measures of recruitment do not work.

Consequence 1. In time of war the abilities of generals become more important than in time of peace. According to the theory, this should result in the following types of restructuring of the stratification system during wartime (and the reverse with the onset of peace):

(a) The rewards of the military, especially of the elite whose talents are scarce, should rise relative to the rewards of other elites, especially those which have nothing to do with victory (e.g., the medical and social service elite charged with care of incurables, the aged, etc.).[3]

(b) Within the military, the degree of inequality of rewards should become greater, favoring generals for their talents are particularly scarce.

(c) Even standardizing for the increase in sheer numbers of high military officials (which of itself implies that more formerly obscure men will rise rapidly) there should be pressure to open the military elite to talent, and, consequently, there should be a higher proportion of Ulysses S. Grant type careers and fewer time-servers.

(d) Medals, a reward based on performances rather than on the authority

hierarchy, should behave the same way. They should be more unequally distributed in wartime within any given rank; new medals, particularly of very high honor, should be created in wartime rather than peacetime, etc.

Consequence 2. The kingship in West European democratic monarchies has consistently declined in political importance as the powers of parliament have increased (this does not apply, for instance, to Japan, where apparently the Emperorship was largely a ritual office even in medieval times). Modern kings in rich countries now perhaps have other functions than political leadership. Certainly the role requirements have changed—for instance, a modern king's sex life is much more restricted than formerly. Their rewards have also changed, emphasizing more ceremonial deference and expressions of sentiment, less wealth and power. It is not clear whether the ceremonial element has actually increased or whether the rewards of wealth and power have declined. Investitures in the Presidency in the United States and Mexico seem to have nearly as much pomp as, and more substance than, coronations in Scandinavia and the Low Countries. Changes in the nature of the role requirements and of the rewards indicate a shift of functions. At the least these changes indicate that some ceremonial functions of the kingship have declined much less in importance than the political functions. But to have a nonpolitical function in a political structure is probably to be less important in the eyes of the people. Consequently, historical studies of the kingship in England, Scandinavia, and the Low Countries should show:

(a) The decline of the rewards of kingship relative to other elites.

(b) Progressively more ascriptive recruitment to the kingship. This would

---

[3] This very interesting case is treated in Willard Waller, "War and Social Institutions," in *War in the Twentieth Century*, ed. W. Waller (New York: Dryden, 1940), pp. 478–532, especially pp. 500–511.

be indicated by (I) fewer debates over succession rules, less changing of these rules in order to justify getting appropriate kings, and fewer successions contested by pretenders; (II) fewer "palace revolutions" or other devices for deposing incompetent or otherwise inappropriate kings; and (III) less mythology about good and bad kings, concerning performance of the role, and more bland human interest mythology focused on what it is like to occupy an ascribed position.

Consequence 3. In some industries individual talent is clearly a *complementary* factor of production, in the sense that it makes other factors much more productive; in others, it is more nearly *additive.* To take an extreme case of complementarity, when Alec Guiness is "mixed" with a stupid plot, routine supporting actors, ordinary production costs, plus perhaps a thousand dollars for extra makeup, the result is a commercially very successful movie; perhaps Guiness increases the value of the movie to twice as much by being three times as good as the alternative actor. But, if an equally talented housepainter (three times as good as the alternative) is "mixed" with a crew of 100 average men, the value of the total production goes to approximately 103 per cent. Relatively speaking, then, individual role performance is much more "important" in the first kind of enterprise. Let us list a few types of enterprises in which talent is a complementary rather than additive factor, as compared with others which are more nearly additive, and make the appropriate predictions for the whole group of comparisons:

Talent Complementary Factor

Research
Universities

Entertainment
Management
Teams in athletics and other "winner take all" structures
Violin concertos

Talent Nearly Additive

Teaching
Undergraduate colleges
High schools
Manufacturing
Manual work
Groups involved in ordinary competition in which the rewards are divided among the meritorious
Symphonies

For each of these comparisons we may derive the following predictions:

(a) The distribution of rewards (e.g., income distributions) should be more skewed for organizations and industries [in the first group], whereas the top salaries or honors should be nearer the mean [in the second group]. In organizations with ranks, there should be either more ranks or greater inequality of rewards within ranks [in the first group].

(b) Since the main alternative to pure achievement stratification in modern society is not ascription by social origin but rather ascription by age and time-in-grade, seniority should determine rewards less in the systems [in the first group than in those in the second]. There are of course many ways to measure it. For instance, men at the top of the income distribution in [the first group] should have reached the top at an earlier age than those [in the second]. There should also be a higher proportion of people whose relative income has declined as time passes in the talent-complementary industries and groups.

Other easily accessible empirical consequences of the theory are suggested by the increased importance of the goal of industrialization in many countries since World War II, the rise in the importance of international officials during this century, and the increased importance of treatment goals in mental hospitals. Since these consequences are easy to derive, we may omit their explication here.

Another set of derivations can be made if we add a postulate that a bad fit between functional requirements and the stratification system makes people within the group (and particularly those strongly identified with the group) perceive the system as unfair. For example, this postulate together with the others would imply that, where talent is a complementary factor, those organizations with seniority stratification systems should create more sense of injustice than those in which the young shoot to the top. In addition, the alienation should be greatest among those *more* committed to group goals in seniority-dominated talent-complementary groups, whereas it should be greatest among those *less* committed to the group where there is an achievement system. All these consequences ought to be reversed, or at least greatly weakened, for groups where talent is an additive factor.

It may be useful to present briefly a research design which would test this consequence of the theory. Suppose we draw a sample of colleges and universities and classify (or rank) them on the importance of research within them. Perhaps a good index of this would be the number of classroom contact hours divided by the number of people of faculty rank on the payroll, which would be lower, the greater the importance of research relative to teaching.

Within each of the institutions we compute a correlation coefficient between age and income of faculty members. (Since the relation between age and income strikes me in this case as being curvilinear, some transformation of the variables will be appropriate.) The higher the correlation coefficient, the more seniority-dominated the stratification system of the institution.[4] The first hypothesis that we can immediately test is that this correlation coefficient should be generally smaller in research-dominated institutions. This is a direct consequence of the functional theory as originally stated.

Then we could divide institutions into four groups, according to whether they are research or teaching institutions and whether they are seniority-dominated or not. We could ask the faculty within a sample of such institutions a series of questions which would sort out those highly devoted to their work and to staying in the system, and those not highly devoted. At the same time we could ask them to agree or disagree with some such statement as: "Most faculty promotions in this school go to the people who deserve them most." According to the functional theory with the added postulate on the sense of justice, we could predict results approximately according to the pattern in Table 1.

But adding postulates goes beyond

---

[4] An elimination system, in which young people are either fired or given raises, depending on their performance, will also produce a high correlation between age and income within an institution and yet may produce (if the institutions with such elimination systems have markedly higher salary scales), in the higher educational system as a whole, a lower correlation. I doubt if the appropriate adjustments for this would substantially affect the analysis except for a very few institutions, but this is of course an empirical question. The adjustments could be made, theoretically, by including the people who have been fired, with their current incomes, in the institutions which fired them.

TABLE 1. HYPOTHETICAL PROPORTION THINKING "MOST FACULTY
PROMOTIONS GO TO THE PEOPLE WHO DESERVE THEM MOST"

	Institutions with			
	Substantial Research Functions and		Mostly Teaching Functions and	
	Achievement Systems	Seniority Systems	Achievement Systems	Seniority Systems
	Proportion Thinking the System Is Fair			
Faculty with				
Strong commitments	High	Low	Low	High
Weak commitments	Low	High	High	Low

the original theory into the mechanisms by which the functional requirements get met, which is an undeveloped aspect of functional theory generally.

I do not intend to investigate the truth of any of these empirical consequences of the theory here. The only purpose of this note is to point out that functional theories are like other scientific theories: They have empirical consequences which are either true or false. Deciding whether they are true or false is not a theoretical or ideological matter, but an empirical one.

ALTERNATIVE EXPLANATIONS: CONFLICT THEORY AND SYNTHETIC APPROACHES

In setting forth objections, critics of functionalism convey their own conceptions of the sources and their own reasons for the persistence of social stratification. Usually, however, their proposals tend to be allusive or prefatory in character. Although the Davis-Moore account may leave much to be desired as a bona fide theory, only in the past decade have competing formulations appeared comparable to, or extending beyond, their level of explanation. Several of these schemes are discussed below.

Conflict Theory

A major alternative framework for the explanation of social stratification comes from the conflict school in sociology. This body of theory, as it relates to stratification, has its immediate origins in Marxian conceptions of class dynamics. Although not so fully developed as functionalism, this school provides a significant competing frame of reference for understanding stratification.

The fundamental difference between functional and conflict interpretations of stratification lies in the emphasis of the former on integration and consensus in society, and, of the latter, on difference, discord, and coercion, which proponents see as pervasive in all forms of social organization. We compare these and other characteristics of the functionalist and conflict views in the following list:

Two Views of Social Stratification

THE FUNCTIONAL VIEW	THE CONFLICT VIEW
1. Stratification is universal, necessary, and inevitable.	*1. Stratification may be universal without being necessary or inevitable.*
2. Social organization (the social system) shapes the stratification system.	*2. The stratification system shapes social organization (the social system).*
3. Stratification arises from the societal need for integration, coordination, and cohesion.	*3. Stratification arises from group conquest, competition, and conflict.*
4. Stratification facilitates the optimal functioning of society and the individual.	*4. Stratification impedes the optimal functioning of society and the individual.*
5. Stratification is an expression of commonly shared social values.	*5. Stratification is an expression of the values of powerful groups.*
6. Power is usually legitimately distributed in society.	*6. Power is usually illegitimately distributed in society.*
7. Tasks and rewards are equitably allocated.	*7. Tasks and rewards are inequitably allocated.*
8. The economic dimension is subordinate to other dimensions of society.	*8. The economic dimension is paramount in society.*
9. Stratification systems generally change through evolutionary processes.	*9. Stratification systems often change through revolutionary processes.*

While this dual list of perspectives on social stratification is drawn from the writings of advocates of the two positions, not all would agree on the phrasing and the differentiation of characteristics. (Compare, for example, Ralf Dahrendorf's views given below and Gerhard Lenski's contrasting set of propositions discussed later in this chapter.) No doubt, more thorough analysis would lead to finer distinctions, best represented by separate and overlapping positions on several continua.

Dahrendorf, a leading conflict theorist, sees the origins of the controversy between functionalist and conflict writers in "utopian" and "rationalist" philosophies. These views, he suggests, are represented in modern sociology, respectively, by the integration theory of society (functionalism) and the coercion theory of society (the conflict school). He discusses some of the central tenets of each position in this selection from *Class and Class Conflict in Industrial Society.*

INTEGRATION AND VALUES VERSUS
COERCION AND INTERESTS*

Ralf Dahrendorf

University of Konstanz

Generally speaking, it seems to me that two (meta-) theories can and must be distinguished in contemporary sociology. One of these, the *integration theory of society*, conceives of social structure in terms of a functionally integrated system held in equilibrium by certain patterned and recurrent processes. The other one, the *coercion theory of society*, views social structure as a form of organization held together by force and constraint and reaching continuously beyond itself in the sense of producing within itself the forces that maintain it in an unending process of change. Like their philosophical counterparts, these theories are mutually exclusive. But—if I may be permitted a paradoxical formulation that will be explained presently—in sociology (as opposed to philosophy) a decision which accepts one of these theories and rejects the other is neither necessary nor desirable. There are sociological problems for the explanation of which the integration theory of society provides adequate assumptions; there are other problems which can be· explained only in terms of the coercion theory of society; there are, finally, problems for which both theories appear adequate. For sociological analy-sis, society is Janus-headed, and its two faces are equivalent aspects of the same reality.

In recent years, the integration theory of society has clearly dominated sociological thinking. In my opinion, this prevalence of one partial view has had many unfortunate consequences. However, it has also had at least one agreeable consequence, in that the very one-sidedness of this theory gave rise to critical objections which enable us to-day to put this theory in its proper place. Such objections have been stimulated with increasing frequency by the works of the most eminent sociological theorist of integration, Talcott Parsons. It is not necessary here to attempt a comprehensive exposition of Parsons' position; nor do we have to survey the sizable literature concerned with a critical appraisal of this position. To be sure, much of this criticism is inferior in subtlety and insight to Parsons' work, so that it is hardly surprising that the sociological climate of opinion has remained almost unaffected by Parsons' critics. There is one objection to Parsons' position, however, which we have to examine if we are to make a systematic presentation of a theory of group conflict. In a remarkable essay, D. Lockwood claims "that Parsons' array of concepts is heavily weighted by assumptions and categories which relate to the role of *normative* elements in social action and especially to the processes whereby motives are structured normatively to en-

---

* Reprinted from *Class and Class Conflict in Industrial Society* by Ralf Dahrendorf with the permission of the publishers, Stanford University Press. © 1959 by the Board of Trustees of the Leland Stanford Junior University.

sure social stability. On the other hand, what may be called the *substratum* of social action, especially as it conditions interests which are productive of social conflict and instability, tends to be ignored as a general determinant of the dynamics of social systems."[1] Lockwood's claim touches on the core of our problem of the two faces of society— although his formulation does not, perhaps, succeed in exposing the problem with sufficient clarity.

It is certainly true that the work of Parsons displays a conspicuous bias in favor of analysis in terms of values and norms. It is equally true that many of those who have been concerned with problems of conflict rather than of stability have tended to emphasize not the normative but the institutional aspects of social structure. The work of Marx is a case in point. Probably this difference in emphasis is no accident. It is nevertheless as such irrelevant to an understanding of or adoption of the alternative images of society which pervade political thought and sociological theory. The alternative between "normative elements in social action" and a factual "substratum of social action," which Lockwood takes over from the work of Renner, in fact indicates two levels of the analysis of social structure which are in no way contradictory. There is no theoretical reason why Talcott Parsons should not have supplemented (as indeed he occasionally does) his analysis of normative integration by an analysis of the integration of social systems in terms of their institutional substratum. However we look at social structure, it always presents itself as composed of a moral and a factual, a normative and

an institutional, level or, in the doubtful terms of Marx, a superstructure and a substratum. The investigator is free to choose which of these levels he wants to emphasize more strongly—although he may be well-advised, in the interest of clarity as well as of comprehensiveness of his analysis, not to stress one of these levels to the exclusion of the other.

At the same time, there is an important element of genuine critique in Lockwood's objection to Parsons. When Lockwood contrasts stability and instability, integration and conflict, equilibrium and disequilibrium, values and interests, he puts his finger on a real alternative of thought and one of which Parsons has apparently not been sufficiently aware. For, of two equivalent models of society, Parsons has throughout his work recognized only one, the Utopian or integration theory of society. His "array of concepts" is therefore incapable of coping with those problems with which Lockwood is concerned in his critical essay and which constitute the subject matter of the present study.

For purposes of exposition it seems useful to reduce each of the two faces of society to a small number of basic tenets, even if this involves some degree of oversimplification as well as overstatement. The integration theory of society, as displayed by the work of Parsons and other structural-functionalists, is founded on a number of assumptions of the following type:

(1) Every society is a relatively persistent, stable structure of elements.

(2) Every society is a well-integrated structure of elements.

(3) Every element in a society has a function, i.e., renders a contribution to its maintenance as a system.

(4) Every functioning social structure is based on a consensus of values among its members.

---

[1] David Lockwood, "Some Remarks on 'The Social System,'" *British Journal of Sociology*, 7 (June 1956), 136.

In varying forms, these elements of (1) stability, (2) integration, (3) functional coordination, and (4) consensus recur in all structural-functional approaches to the study of social structure. They are, to be sure, usually accompanied by protestations to the effect that stability, integration, functional coordination, and consensus are only "relatively" generalized. Moreover, these assumptions are not metaphysical propositions about the essence of society; they are merely assumptions for purposes of scientific analysis. As such, however, they constitute a coherent view of the social process[2] which enables us to comprehend many problems of social reality.

However, it is abundantly clear that the integration approach to social analysis does not enable us to comprehend all problems of social reality. Let us look at two undeniably sociological problems of the contemporary world which demand explanation. (1) In recent years, an increasing number of industrial and commercial enterprises have introduced the position of personnel manager to cope with matters of hiring and firing, advice to employees, etc. Why? And, what are the consequences of the introduction of this new position? (2) On the 17th of June, 1953, the building workers of East Berlin put down their tools and went on a strike that soon led to a generalized revolt against the Communist regime of East Germany. Why? And, what are the consequences of this uprising? From the point of view of the integration model of society, the first of these problems is susceptible of a satisfactory solution. A special position to cope with personnel questions is functionally required by large enterprises in an age of rationalization and "social ethic"; the introduction of this position adapts the enterprise to the values of the surrounding society; its consequence is therefore of an integrative and stabilizing nature. But what about the second problem? Evidently, the uprising of the 17th of June is neither due to nor productive of integration in East German society. It documents and produces not stability but instability. It contributes to the disruption, not the maintenance, of the existing system. It testifies to dissensus rather than consensus. The integration model tells us little more than that there are certain "strains" in the "system." In fact, in order to cope with problems of this kind we have to replace the integration theory of society by a different and, in many ways, contradictory model.

What I have called the coercion theory of society can also be reduced to a small number of basic tenets, although here again these assumptions oversimplify and overstate the case:

(1) Every society is at every point subject to processes of change; social change is ubiquitous.

(2) Every society displays at every point dissensus and conflict; social conflict is ubiquitous.

(3) Every element in a society renders a contribution to its disintegration and change.

(4) Every society is based on the coercion of some of its members by others.

If we return to the problem of the German workers' strike, it will become

---

2 It is important to emphasize that "stability" as a tenet of the integration theory of society does not mean that societies are "static." It means, rather, that such processes as do occur (and the structural-functional approach is essentially concerned with processes) serve to maintain the patterns of the system as a whole. Whatever criticism I have of this approach, I do not want to be misunderstood as attributing to it a "static bias" (which has often been held against this approach without full consideration of its merits).

clear that this latter model enables us to deal rather more satisfactorily with its causes and consequences. The revolt of the building workers and their fellows in other industries can be explained in terms of coercion.[3] The revolting groups are engaged in a conflict which "functions" as an agent of change by disintegration. A ubiquitous phenomenon is expressed, in this case, in an exceptionally intense and violent way, and further explanation will have to account for this violence on the basis of the acceptance of conflict and change as universal features of social life. I need hardly add that, like the integration model, the coercion theory of society constitutes but a set of assumptions for purposes of scientific analysis and implies no claim for philosophical validity—although, like its counterpart, this model also provides a coherent image of social organization.

Now, I would claim that, in a sociological context, neither of these models can be conceived as exclusively valid or applicable. They constitute complementary, rather than alternative, aspects of the structure of total societies as well as of every element of this structure. We have to choose between them only for the explanation of specific problems; but in the conceptual arsenal of sociological analysis they exist side by side. Whatever criticism one may have of the advocates of one or the other of these models can therefore be directed only against claims for the exclusive validity of either.[4] Strictly speaking, both models are "valid" or, rather, useful and necessary for sociological analysis. We cannot conceive of

society unless we realize the dialectics of stability and change, integration and conflict, function and motive force, consensus and coercion. In the context of this study, I regard this point as demonstrated by the analysis of the exemplary problems sketched above.

It is perhaps worth emphasizing that the thesis of the two faces of social structure does not require a complete, or even partial, revision of the conceptual apparatus that by now has become more or less generally accepted by sociologists in all countries. Categories like role, institution, norm, structure, even function are as useful in terms of the coercion model as they are for the analysis of social integration. In fact, the dichotomy of aspects can be carried through all levels of sociological analysis; that is, it can be shown that, like social structure itself, the notions of role and institution, integration and function, norm and substratum have two faces which may be expressed by two terms, but which may also in many cases be indicated by an extension of concepts already in use. "Interest and value," Radcliffe-Brown once remarked, "are correlative terms, which refer to the two sides of an asymmetrical relation."[5] The notions of interest and value indeed seem to describe very well the two faces of the normative superstructure of society: What appears as a consensus of values on the

---

[3] For purposes of clarity, I have deliberately chosen an example from a totalitarian state. But coercion is meant here in a very general sense, and the coercion model is applicable to all societies independent of their specific political structure.

[4] This, it seems to me, is the only—if

fundamental—legitimate criticism that can be raised against Parsons' work on this general level. In *The Social System*, Parsons repeatedly advances, for the integration theory of society, a claim that it is the nucleus of "the general" sociological theory —a claim which I regard as utterly unjustified. It is Lockwood's main concern also, in the essay quoted above, to reject this claim to universal validity.

[5] A. R. Radcliffe-Brown, *Structure and Function in Primitive Society* (Glencoe, Ill.: The Free Press, 1952), p. 199.

basis of the integration theory can be regarded as a conflict of interests in terms of the coercion theory. Similarly, what appears on the level of the factual substratum as integration from the point of view of the former model presents itself as coercion or constraint from the point of view of the latter. We shall presently have occasion to explore these two faces of societies and their elements rather more thoroughly with reference to the two categories of power and of role.

While logically feasible,[6] the solution of the dilemma of political thought which we have offered here for the more restricted field of sociological analysis nevertheless raises a number of serious problems. It is evidently virtually impossible to think of society in terms of either model without positing its opposite number at the same time. There can be no conflict, unless this conflict occurs within a context of meaning, i.e., some kind of coherent "system." No conflict is con-

ceivable between French housewives and Chilean chess players because these groups are not united by, or perhaps "integrated into," a common frame of reference. Analogously, the notion of integration makes little sense unless it presupposes the existence of different elements that are integrated. Even Rousseau derived his *volonté générale* from a modified *bellum omnium contra omnes*. Using one or the other model is therefore a matter of emphasis rather than of fundamental difference; and there are, as we shall see, many points at which a theory of group conflict has to have recourse to the integration theory of social structure.

Inevitably, the question will be raised, also, whether a unified theory of society that includes the tenets of both the integration and the coercion models of society is not at least conceivable—for as to its desirability there can be little doubt. Is there, or can there be, a general point of view that synthesizes the unsolved dialectics of integration and coercion? So far as I can see, there is no such general model; as to its possibility, I have to reserve judgment. It seems at least conceivable that unification of theory is not feasible at a point which has puzzled thinkers ever since the beginning of Western philosophy.

---

[6] As is demonstrated most clearly by the fact that a similar situation can be encountered in physics with respect to the theory of light. Here, too, there are two seemingly incompatible theories which nevertheless exist side by side and each of which has its proper realm of empirical phenomena: the wave theory and the quantum theory of light.

Synthetic Explanations

Dahrendorf's remarks on a synthesis of "the unsolved dialectics of integration and coercion" anticipate a recent work, *Power and Privilege*, by Lenski.[1] In Lenski's words, "a basic aim of this book is to speed the process [synthesis] by calling attention to the dialectical pattern in the development of thought in the field and by outlining the basic nature of the synthesis toward which we seem to be moving."[2]

---

[1] Gerhard Lenski, *Power and Privilege: A Theory of Social Stratification* (New York: McGraw-Hill Book Company, 1966). This account of Lenski's work attempts to consider only some of the central features of *Power and Privilege*. Thus, it does not include several secondary variables incorporated in his explanatory scheme. Only a reading of the original source can provide a complete understanding of this complex theoretical system.

[2] *Ibid.*, p. 19.

Like Dahrendorf, Lenski believes that functionalism and the conflict school in modern stratification theory developed out of long philosophical traditions. He discusses these traditions, labeled conservative and radical, with reference to their views on the distributive system. In summarizing this age-old controversy, Lenski concludes, "The only belief common to all conservatives has been their belief that the existing system of distribution was basically just; the only belief common to all radicals has been their belief that it was basically unjust."[3] He feels, however, that despite disagreement, the beliefs of each tradition reduce to a contrasting set of propositions about man and society.[4] These propositions deal with such issues as the degree to which inequality is maintained by coercion, the degree to which inequality in society generates conflict, the means by which rights and privileges are acquired, the role of the state and of law, and the basic problem of man's nature (e.g., the degree to which man requires external restraint and coercion).

Lenski's "synthesis" consists of a theory of the distributive system based on one or the other of these contrasting traditions or some mixture of the two as they relate to eight issues. In his final accounting Lenski concludes, "The synthesis can be said to resemble both of the older traditions—and neither. On three of the eight issues, it leans heavily in the conservative direction; on two, in the radical. On the remaining three it involves a complex mixture of elements of both traditions. . . ."[5]

Applicable to societies in which there is a continual threat to survival, Lenski's first law of distribution is based on the following propositions about the nature of man: (1) Cooperative activity is essential for attainment of man's needs and desired goals; and, (2) when man must make a choice, he is basically selfish— he will choose his or his group's interest over others. From (1) and (2), Lenski's first law follows: *"Men will share the product of their labors to the extent required to insure the survival and continued productivity of those members whose actions are necessary or beneficial to themselves."*[6] From Lenski's first law, in subsistence-level societies, the sharing of goods and services is necessary for individual and societal survival. Thus, in such societies we can expect substantial equality since goods and services are distributed on the basis of survival requirements.

Lenski's second law of distribution applies to societies with goods and services above those required for survival. The second law is initially derived from proposition (2) above and proposition (3), the scarcity principle: Goods and services are never sufficient for human needs. If (2) and (3) are valid, then it follows that (4) conflict occurs among men for control of the surplus and results in (5) growth of power,[7] the principal factor affecting the outcome of the conflict and the

---

3 *Ibid.*, p. 22.
4 *Ibid.*, p. 22–23.
5 *Ibid.*, p. 443.
6 *Ibid.*, p. 44.
7 Lenski uses the traditional Weberian conception of power—"the chance of a man or a number of men to realize their own will in a communal action even against the

disposal of the surplus. From (2), (3), (4), and (5), Lenski's second law follows: *"Power will determine the distribution of nearly all of the surplus possessed by a society."*[8] Thus, in societies having excess goods and services, the allocation of privilege is associated with the distribution of power. If power is unequally apportioned, so also is privilege. Since privilege thus depends upon the dynamics of power, Lenski gives considerable attention to the bases of power in his work, much of which documents the relationship between privilege and power in societies with varying degrees of surplus.

Just as "privilege is largely a function of power," Lenski further suggests "that prestige is largely, though not solely, a function of power and privilege, at least in those societies where there is a substantial surplus."[9] Lenski, then, addresses himself to a central problem discussed earlier—the relationships among the principal dimensions of stratification. His answer to this problem is that power is the primary source of variance in prestige and privilege.

We have seen that the importance of power hinges upon the presence of a surplus. What factor, then, influences the level of goods and services? Lenski's handling of this question highlights the other major tenet of his thesis: *Technology is the major determinant of societal surplus.* "Even though we cannot say that the surplus available to a society increases proportionately with advances in level of technology, such advances increase the probability that there will be a surplus and also that there will be a sizable surplus."[10] On the basis of this postulated relationship and in conjunction with the laws of distribution, Lenski derives the following hypotheses: (1) "In the simplest societies, or those which are technologically most primitive, the goods and services available will be distributed wholly, or largely, on the basis of need." (2) "With technological advance, an increasing proportion of the goods and services available to a society will be distributed on the basis of power."[11] If the distribution of power, privilege, and prestige varies with the size of the surplus and if this surplus, in turn, varies with the level of technology, then it follows that "the nature of distributive systems will vary greatly depending on the degree of technological advance in the societies involved."[12]

This last proposition provides the basis for Lenski's separate analysis of societies at different levels of technology. Using this approach, he hopes to (1) control for variables closely associated with technology, (2) determine the validity of the postulated associations, and (3) take into account second-order variations at

---

resistance of others who are participating in the action." Hans H. Gerth and C. Wright Mills, eds., *From Max Weber: Essays in Sociology* (New York: Oxford University Press, Inc., 1946), p. 180.

[8] Lenski, *op. cit.*, p. 44.

[9] *Ibid.*, p. 45. In postulating an association among prestige, power, and privilege, Lenski departs from the deductive approach. He supports the validity of this relationship by citing several empirical studies showing a high correlation among these factors.

[10] *Ibid.*, p. 46.

[11] *Ibid.*

[12] *Ibid.*, p. 47.

different levels of technology which may influence the relationships being tested.

Lenski applies his basic postulates to hunting and gathering, simple horticultural, advanced horticultural, agrarian, and industrial societies. In hunting and gathering societies, characterized by a rudimentary technology and a subsistence standard of living, he finds a considerable sharing of resources and a substantial degree of equality of privilege. At the level of simple horticultural societies a surplus begins to appear. The size and proportion of total goods and services increases at an accelerating rate up to and including those in industrial societies. According to Lenski's thesis we may expect that, with each increase in level of technology and consequent increase in surplus, an increasingly larger proportion of the goods and services is allocated on the basis of power, and inequality becomes more pronounced. Hence, inequality of privilege should be least marked in simple horticultural societies and most marked in advanced industrial societies.

Lenski impressively documents this relationship. He finds that, as technology advances, the system of stratification becomes more rigid and harsh and is based increasingly on fixed status with greater inequality of privilege—the exception being the situation in advanced industrial societies. "The appearance of mature industrial societies marks the first significant reversal in the age-old evolutionary trend toward ever increasing inequality."[13] Lenski advances a number of *ad hoc* hypotheses to explain this reversal. For example, "after a certain level of wealth has been attained, elites may prefer to sacrifice a portion of the economic surplus in order to reduce hostility and the dangers of revolution and to win for themselves a greater measure of respect and affection."[14] The institutionalization of democracy suggests another possibility: "Now the many can combine against the few, and, even though individually the many are weaker, in combination they may be as strong or stronger."[15]

Lenski presents these and other explanations to account for the greater equality in industrial societies. But perhaps the most significant reason he advances and that most consistent with his thesis is the influence of the growth of human knowledge on the increase in surplus. "Because of the great functional utility of so much of the new knowledge, a host of occupational specialists have appeared who are not interchangeable to any great degree. This introduces into the labor market certain rigidities which favor the sellers of labor, especially in an era in which demand for technical skills is rapidly rising." [16] In short, knowledge becomes, in industrial societies, an increasingly important source of power.[17]

---

[13] *Ibid.*, p. 308.

[14] *Ibid.*, p. 315. As Dahrendorf puts it in a review symposium on Lenski's work, "Yet as one reads on through hunting and gathering societies, simple horticultural societies, agrarian societies of various types and through stratification systems that are progressively involved, more differentiated, and increasingly various, one begins to wonder how Lenski is going to cope with industrial societies." Ralf Dahrendorf, "Review Symposium: Power and Privilege," *American Sociological Review*, 31 (October 1966), 716.

[15] Lenski, *op. cit.*, p. 318.

[16] *Ibid.*, p. 316.

[17] For a major presentation of this thesis, see Victor Thompson, *Modern Organization* (New York: Alfred A. Knopf, Inc., 1961).

We initially looked at Lenski's formulation in terms of his intent to advance a synthesis of functional and conflict theory. Whether he has, in fact, accomplished this goal is open to question. Although he has joined propositions from both schools, his emphasis on conflict and power places his argument more clearly within the conflict tradition. Privilege and prestige in his theory are distributed essentially on the basis of power, not on the basis of functional contribution.

Lenski's work is important in the study of American stratification because it contrasts advanced industrial societies, such as our own, with markedly different ones. It provides a theoretical perspective for viewing the structure and dynamics of strata in American society. Of perhaps greater importance, Lenski's work represents a considered attempt to develop a systematic theory of stratification, using, in part, a deductive scheme of reasoning. As Kurt Mayer concludes, "Lenski has set an important bench mark for the study of social stratification and every sociologist in his debt."[18]

Virtually all attempts to explain stratification by other than functional concepts emphasize processes of social conflict. The two efforts toward a synthesis discussed above—Dahrendorf's and Lenski's—try to utilize perspectives from these competing schools of thought. Perhaps such efforts augur well for the progress of stratification theory,[19] but a note of caution is in order. A synthetic theory of stratification should not be and need not be restricted to an integration of functional and conflict models. Illustrative of yet another possibility is Werner Cohn's ambivalence hypothesis, which is a modest synthesis of "traditional" conceptions of stratification and a perspective that is ordinarily overlooked. Unlike the functionalists he rejects assumptions of a well-integrated social system and of the differential functional importance of occupational roles. But he does not resort to conflict as an alternative explanation.

Cohn suggests that the high status of many positions in American society rests upon an interaction between two contradictory sets of standards—one stemming from invidious ranking, the other from charisma. The physician, for example, seems to combine charismatic attraction and high rank on the stratification scale. In brief, Cohn calls attention to the role of *nonrationality* in human behavior and in the operation of society as it relates to stratification. This, we feel, is the main value of his contribution, for the arguments of both conflict and functional theorists rest largely on premises of *rationality*. A more adequate synthesis, it would seem, should take account of the theme of nonrationality in explaining stratification.

---

18 "Review of Power and Privilege," *Social Forces*, 45 (December 1966), 284.

19 Compare, however, Dahrendorf's comment that there is no *a priori* reason "to assume that theories in which both equilibrium and coercion figure somewhat are bound to be superior to those that are apparently more one-sided." *op. cit.*, p. 717.

SOCIAL STATUS AND AMBIVALENCE*

Werner Cohn

University of British Columbia

We tend to think more highly of doctors than of doormen. That is to say, our society seems to accord more social status to some occupations than to others. In this paper we address ourselves to the problem of why that should be so. This question is related to but separate from the wider problem of why every human society seems to have a system of invidious ranking (social stratification), a matter which we plan to deal with in a subsequent paper.

Most of the discussion here centers around the social status of the physician since we believe him to be typical of high status occupations. Until this typicality has been further demonstrated, however, we restrict any claim for the validity of the present argument to the special case. Moreover, while it is hoped that this discussion of *high* social status will prove relevant for the whole range of statuses—low and middle, as well as high—such relevance, too, must await further verification.

In the 1947 study of occupational statuses by the National Opinion Research Center, physicians were rated second highest of ninety occupations by a cross section of Americans who were asked to give their "own personal opinion of the general standing" of these jobs.[1] Only the position of Supreme Court Justice was ranked above that of physician. The physician was followed, in order, by state governor, cabinet member in the federal government, diplomat in the foreign service, mayor of a large city, and college professor.

FUNCTIONAL VIEWS

The functional approach, as represented by Davis and Moore,[2] would hold that the high status of the physician arises from his great importance to the social system. It would be argued, presumably, that our society as now constituted is in great need of physicians and that by according them high status it assures itself at least some supply of this social commodity.

Tumin has noted some immediate objections to this view.[3] Professions that enjoy high status are not necessarily more important to society than those

---

* From Werner Cohn, "Social Status and the Ambivalence Hypothesis: Some Critical Notes and a Suggestion," *American Sociological Review*, 25 (August 1960), 508–13. Reprinted by permission of the American Sociological Association.

[1] "Jobs and Occupation: A Popular Evaluation," *Opinion News*, 9 (September 1, 1947), 3–13. Reprinted in R. Bendix and S. M. Lipset, eds., *Class, Status and Power* (Glencoe, Ill.: Free Press, 1953).

[2] Kingsley Davis and Wilbert E. Moore, "Some Principles of Stratification," *American Sociological Review*, 10 (April 1945), 242–49.

[3] Melvin M. Tumin, "Some Principles of Stratification: A Critical Analysis," *American Sociological Review*, 18 (August 1953), 387–94. The same issue of the *Review* includes replies by Davis and by Moore (pp. 394–97). For Tumin's rebuttal, see the *Review*, 18 (December 1953), 672–73.

that do not. Moreover, the status system cannot be shown actually to accomplish its presumed function of assuring a ready supply of valued people. The system may very well work to restrict unduly the number of physicians.[4] There are, however, even more far-reaching difficulties in the functional view. In what sense can it be said that society as a whole needs physicians more than it needs, let us say, artists?

The difficulty of determining societal needs may be illustrated by considering automobile accidents. For the victims, the accidents of course are undesirable. But not necessarily so for automobile dealers. Society has both automobile dealers and victims, and only special pleading can hold accidents to be good or bad for society as a whole. Unlike the organism, society cannot use the simple criterion of preservation of life. Society does not live in a biological sense and hence cannot die in that sense. If the preservation of individual life were used as the determining standard, most self-sacrifice and heroism would have to be condemned as harmful to the system.

When the functionalists speak of some positions as holding greater functional importance for the social system than others, they imply that the social system is more tightly integrated than probably is the case. Consequently, they are apt to neglect a whole range of contradictory values which constituent parts of society may esteem highly. Several writers recently have noted the undue emphasis in functionalism on social integration and social system, with an attendant neglect of social conflict, tension, and the relative autonomy of parts within a social system.[5]

In recognition of these difficulties in the functional view, Barber presents what appears to be a simpler "argument from usefulness":[6]

Doctors and street cleaners may be equally functionally necessary for the health of "society as a whole," but to the component members of society the skills of doctors are likely to be more valuable. The goal of "health for the society as a whole" is only comprehensible in terms of the health of the individual members of society. It is not hard to judge the differential value that doctors and street cleaners have for this goal.[7]

cussions of functionalism: Robert K. Merton, *Social Theory and Social Structure* (Glencoe, Ill.: Free Press, 1949), Chap. 1; Walter Buckley, "Structural-Functional Analysis in Modern Sociology," in *Modern Sociological Theory in Continuity and Change*, eds. Howard Becker and Alvin Boskoff (New York: Dryden, 1957), Chap. 8; Walter Buckley, "Social Stratification and the Functional Theory of Social Differentiation," *American Sociological Review*, 23 (August 1958), 369–75. See also "Stratification and Functionalism: An Exchange," with contributions by Kingsley Davis, Marion J. Levy, Jr., and Walter Buckley, *American Sociological Review*, 24 (February 1959), 82–86; and Philip Selznick and Gertrude Jaeger Selznick, "The Idea of a Social System" (paper read at the annual meeting of the American Sociological Association, September 1959).

The following valuable contributions to the discussion appear in Llewellyn Gross, ed., *Symposium on Sociological Theory* (Evanston, Ill.: Row, Peterson, 1959): Alvin W. Gouldner, "Reciprocity and Autonomy in Functional Theory," pp. 241–70; and Carl G. Hempel, "The Logic of Functional Analysis," pp. 271–307.

6 This phrase is taken from Hans Speier, "Social Stratification," in *Sociological Theory*, eds. L. A. Coser and B. Rosenberg (New York: The Macmillan Company, 1957), pp. 398–405. This is a condensation of an article that originally appeared in the *American Sociological Review* (April 1936).

7 Bernard Barber, *Social Stratification* (New York: Harcourt, Brace, 1957), p. 16.

---

4 Tumin, "Some Principles of Stratification . . . ," *op. cit.*, pp. 388–89.

5 I am indebted to the following dis-

By substituting the *individual* for *society* in his analysis, Barber seeks to escape the difficulties of demonstrating differential social usefulness of various occupations. But what evidence does he give for the physician's greater utility beyond the assertion that "it is not hard to judge"? Are doctors also more valuable than farmers, who produce most of our food? Barber's formulation seems to involve a value judgment which by its very nature seems unprovable. (We assume, of course, that Barber uses "health" as a symbol for general human needs. If he refers only to physical health, it may be granted that physicians are more immediately useful than street cleaners or farmers. But it remains to be demonstrated that medical treatment is generally more useful to an individual than clean streets or food.)

Should it be objected that Barber refers not to usefulness per se but rather to a relative scarcity of a given skill, Tumin's discussion (cited above), which indicates that scarcity of a skill may be interpreted as more the result than the cause of social status, would apply here as it does to the functionalist view. If wheat farmers, as a result of some status-derived power, were able to restrict their occupation to a select few, their skill would also become highly valuable in this sense. But in this case we should not use the scarcity value of their skill as a causal explanation for the high status of wheat farmers.

In their analysis of the hospital situation, Hughes, Hughes, and Deutscher also seem to have been influenced by the argument based upon usefulness: "To the doctors . . . who assume the greatest responsibility for the healing of the sick, most of the honor and glory are given—on the whole, willingly—and if other levels are accorded

smaller portions of deference, it is approximately *in the measure of their contribution*."[8] The argument from usefulness, as it appears on a popular level, is illustrated once more by the following quotation from a supervisor of nurses' training:

> After class, one of these students came up to me and said, "Miss . . . , I can see why I should stop to let someone like you go through a door ahead of me, but I can't understand why doctors should go first. I was taught that gentlemen should wait for ladies." So I had to explain to her that . . . not only are the doctors older than she and entitled to respect on that account, but that they *contribute more to the community* than she will. . . .[9]

In these views, the doctor's comparatively highly degree of usefulness is taken as self-evident without being subjected to further analysis. But many patients have learned that the nurse is the person frequently more concerned with his emotional well-being and may be more important and more useful to *him* in the hospital than is the doctor. Of course, the physician has specialized knowledge which the nurse lacks, but the nurse often has greater ability to contribute to the patient's overall well-being.[10]

It may be argued that it is a technologist's view of human comfort that holds the doctor to be necessarily more

---

8 Everett C. Hughes, Helen MacGill Hughes, and Irwin Deutscher, *Twenty Thousand Nurses Tell Their Story* (Philadelphia: J. B. Lippincott Co., 1958), p. 63 (my italics—W. C.).

9 Quoted by Albert F. Wessen, "Hospital Ideology and Communication Between Ward Personnel," in *Patients, Physicians, and Illness*, ed. E. Gartley Jaco (Glencoe, Ill.: Free Press, 1958), pp. 454–55 (italics in original).

10 *Ibid.*, pp. 462–64.

useful or important than the nurse. But in other occupational fields—the military, manufacturing, business—the man with highly specialized knowledge is usually subordinated to the more general manager or director.

Speier has pointed out that the argument from usefulness involves ultrascientific, moral evaluation.[11] In the case of the functionalists, this charge cannot be made directly since they speak in terms not of a general usefulness but a presumably morally neutral usefulness to a given system. However, since usefulness to society probably can never be shown objectively—society always involves a variety of disparate interests—we would hold that functionalism itself, like the argument from usefulness, embodies evaluative implications. In brief, we must reject both views because it cannot be shown that high status positions are in fact more useful to either society or individual than those of low status.

OTHER SOCIOLOGICAL EXPLANATIONS OF STATUS

There are sociological explanations of social status that do not suffer from these particular shortcomings. Simpson, for example, recognizes components of social status which cannot easily be viewed as rational either from the point of view of the social system or from that of the individuals involved, noting in particular "(1) effect from symbolic aspects of the work situation, (2) historical features of positions and their incumbents, and (3) custom evolved through historical accident."[12] Simpson's discussion shows that status is not necessarily based upon any objective usefulness to either society or individual, but rather upon an *imputed* usefulness, or a value attached to the position by a greater or lesser social consensus. We agree with this view but find it insufficiently developed: It fails to explain why such differential values are assigned to the various occupations.

A suggestion by Caplow to the effect that "behavior control" can account for a great deal of the mystery of social status does not seem convincing. "What this element represents is the status of the individual in the typical situations elicited by his occupational role, vis-à-vis his clients, customers, subordinates, pupils, passengers. . . ."[13] Caplow finds that this element of behavior control is highest in the cases of bankers, physicians, civil engineers, and so on, and lowest for hod carriers, street cleaners, ditch diggers, and the like. This interpretation, it seems, is marked by serious shortcomings. First, it is not at all clear whether the degree of "behavior control" can be determined objectively for any given occupation. (Caplow himself used the judgments of five raters, inviting the reader, however, to "substitute his own rating.") Secondly, a superintendent of schools, say, or an army captain, or a dean of men would appear to possess more behavior control than a physician, yet all of these occupations enjoy less status than the doctor's according to the NORC findings. Most importantly there is no convincing evidence that status is necessarily a result of behavior control (although it may be correlated with it) since relevant data could as well be

---

11 Speier, *op. cit.*, p. 404.

12 Richard L. Simpson, "A Modification of the Functional Theory of Social Stratification," *Social Forces*, 35 (December 1956), 132–37; quoted p. 137.

13 Theodore Caplow, *The Sociology of Work* (Minneapolis: University of Minnesota Press, 1954), pp. 53–56; quoted p. 55.

interpreted to indicate that behavior control is the *result* of status.

Another approach, and one frequently used, which analyzes occupational criteria of status in terms of other stratification criteria, is exemplified by Broom and Selznick, who write:

> Occupation serves as a clue to a number of important characteristics used in social ranking. It is normally used as a fairly good indicator of income, education, association with others, authority over others, contribution to the community or society, morality and responsibility, intelligence and ability. The occupation of physician, for example, is characterized by a very high degree of *all* of these features, and it has a consistently high rating."[14]

We agree that the occupational status of the physician correlates well with other stratification criteria. However, this kind of analysis fails to go very far. As in the case of Caplow's "behavior control," the factors cited by Broom and Selznick are as likely to be the result as the source of high status. This possibility holds particularly for the category "contribution to the community or society," which, as we have noted, depends upon social evaluation of usefulness. Such evaluation is the same as that by which status is determined, and the analysis, if it is intended as an *explanation* of high status, is largely circular. The same objection applies in substantially similar form to the other factors mentioned by these authors; even the social evaluation of "intelligence" is largely dependent upon social standards of useful personal characteristics.

14 Leonard Broom and Philip Selznick, *Sociology* (Evanston, Ill.: Row, Peterson, 1958), pp. 186–88 (italics in original).

THE AMBIVALENCE HYPOTHESIS

In an effort to overcome the objections to the theories discussed above and as a tentative formulation, we postulate an explanation for high status in terms of human irrationality. At the center of this hypothesis is the notion that social judgments are self-contradictory, or ambivalent.

It is suggested that social judgments are of two kinds. First, there are the criteria of invidious ranking (the stratification criteria), which in American society are primarily related to money, occupation, and formal education. Secondly, there are the "charismatic" standards, which are person-centered and are opposed to social stratification on the ground that it is external and (in the terminology of the Christian tradition) "worldly." Charismatic judgments are manifested by resistance to social stratification in religion, the arts, sexual practices, and so on.[15]

Considerations of social stratification interact with those of the charismatic in an ambivalent state of tension in probably all aspects of our culture. It appears, however, that this ambivalent interaction is sharper in some areas than in others and seems to be particularly poignant in the social role of the physician. The unusual degree of social affect imbedded in this role is a causal condition, it is argued, of the high status of the physician.

This rather contracted statement of the hypothesis may be amplified by

15 Cf. Werner Cohn, "Social Stratification and the Charismatic," *Midwest Sociologist*, 21 (December 1958), 12–18, in which the general notion of interaction between stratification and charisma is presented.

noting the dual role of the physician as healer (charismatic) and business man (social stratification). His charismatic role is symbolized by the ideal of the medical profession of treating the ill without regard to property, worldly position, and the like. The fact that this ideal meets head-on with the business requirements of our culture underlines the ambivalence inherent in the profession.

The standards of social stratification concern the outward, the show, impressing others through exhibition. In American culture, money is perhaps the most important symbol used for this external way of judging. This side of social life tends to ignore the nature of the individual, substituting for him an abstract measure of worth. For various historical reasons, the doctor has taken his place in the market place of the society, has been able to command a good price for his services, and has become endowed with external and formal qualifications of many kinds. He has gained a successful position in the system of social stratification.

But his total status cannot be explained merely in these terms since external success is probably also widely resented, at the same time that it is respected. The viability of the prophetic Judaeo-Christian religion, which teaches that it is better to be poor than to be rich and warns against the sham of worldly success, gives evidence of an important cultural strain which rejects the criteria of social stratification. Again, the doctor can qualify as outstandingly successful. He continues the tradition of Jesus as the healer; the services he renders are personal and do not seem to depend for their evaluation on money standards.

Thus the doctor, while occasionally the target of the negative side of this cultural ambivalence, on the whole seems to combine the positive aspects of both of these strategic ways in which roles are judged by our society. The priest, whose tradition deprives him (or so it seems) of the possibility of a worldly career, is suspected for his unworldliness and enjoys only a marginal prestige; the banker, suspected of being too worldly, enjoys a strictly limited status; but the doctor combines the functions of priest and banker and thus stands close to the pinnacle of the social order. In honoring him, we seem to be able both to eat and have our cake. (The Supreme Court Justice, the only position to have achieved a higher score than that of the physician in the NORC study, would appear to lend itself to a similar analysis: Here perhaps is the combination of clever politician and Biblical judge—the original judges were priests who pronounced oracles.)

A suggestion recently made by Brotz seems to be of relevance to our hypothesis. Brotz contends that in the United States political power is generally held by the middle, not the upper, class.[16] Politicians with upper-class backgrounds, like Nelson Rockefeller, find it necessary to affect middle-class or even lower-class manners of speech and custom. Why should this be so? The ambivalence hypothesis may suggest an answer. Our culture demands worldly success and distinction on the one hand, the value of equality and supremacy of the individual on the other. These conflicting aims seem to coexist in a dynamic tension in the middle class, the principal social background of American politicians.

From the analysis of high status as

---

[16] Howard M. Brotz, "Social Stratification and the Political Order," *American Journal of Sociology*, 64 (May 1959), 571–78.

proceeding from ambivalence, it follows that the status of the physician should not be altogether stable.[17] Let the doctor veer too far toward his role as business man or too far toward his role as priest, and his prestige is seriously endangered. At any rate, this would be the consequence of the hypothesis here posited and should be capable of empirical verification.

CONCLUSION

This paper attempts to put forward in a tentative way some consequences of a view of social stratification which we call the "ambivalence hypothesis." The hypothesis seems to promise more adequate explanations of status differences than functionalist and related positions. Unlike most functionalist interpretations, the hypothesis does not stipulate a well-integrated social system to which stratification phenomena are related.

We suggest that there are two fundamentally opposed, though dynamically related, value complexes in American culture—one labeled "social stratification," the other "charismatic."[18] This formulation, we believe, may permit more realistic analysis of the cultural grounds for social judgments.

---

[17] The NORC study, while it shows 67 per cent of the respondents designating the physician's standing as "excellent," also shows 30 per cent who viewed it as "good," and 3 per cent, as "average." Moreover, there is considerable popular resentment of the status and authority of the physician. One suggestive piece of evidence is the resistance to the medically endorsed fluoridation measure whenever it is brought to popular referendum. Cf. Donald R. McNeil, *The Fight for Fluoridation* (New York: Oxford University Press, Inc., 1957). Several professions prosper at least in part because of the mistrust of physicians, e.g., chiropractic, osteopathy, perhaps also optometry. Not all critics of the high status of the physician are unintelligent or uninformed. A voluminous literature attacks the practices of organized medicine, frequently taking the view that organized medicine in general, and by inference the individual practitioner as well, are socially harmful; see, e.g., Michael A. Shadid, *A Doctor for the People* (New York: The Vanguard Press, Inc., 1939); Alfred McClung Lee, "The Social Dynamics of the Physician's Status," *Psychiatry*, 7 (November 1944), 372–77; and various publications of the American Labor Health Association, the Physicians' Forum, and the Cooperative League of the USA.

[18] This usage is an example of the kind of "paired concepts" discussed by Reinhard Bendix and Bennett Berger in "Images of Society and Problems of Concept Formation in Sociology," in Gross, *op. cit.*, pp. 92–118. This article is a valuable discussion of some of the implications of the method used in the present paper.

We end this review of theories of stratification on a speculative note. If the diverse strains and conflicts engendered by patterns of stratification can be attributed partly to the nonrational origins of social institutions, could new social structures founded on the rational deliberation of interest groups alleviate these problems? Could common standards of value arise, with every group subordinating private interests to collective purposes? If all persons, groups, and social classes had the facilities necessary to achieve shared social norms, applicable to everyone as equals, each would be committed to the values upon which all were judged. On this assumption the achievement of shared norms would occur only through recognition of conflicting values and interests and through processes designed to adjudicate such conflicts. Acknowledging every claim for and against the social order would reduce conflict.

If stratification is based largely on nonrational values, why should sociologists view it as functional? If functional theories of stratification reflect socially privileged viewpoints, should not sociologists search for new theories—theories that appeal to values which are rational in import and universal in application? Can they speak meaningfully of common values without speaking to all men's conceptions of what is reasonable and just? And is not the response of those unfavorably situated in the hierarchies of society a necessary though insufficient test of whether any claim is indeed reasonable and just? Can common social values be validated without a rational integration of interests, each fully presented by its ablest exponents? How else can people of diverse interests acknowledge one another as persons and strive for consensus on common standards? Without this process, social integration, where it occurs, will rest largely on nonrational customs or illegitimate power.

SELECTED BIBLIOGRAPHY

ABERNATHY, GEORGE L., ed., *The Idea of Equality*. Richmond, Virginia: John Knox Press, 1959.

ANDERSON, C. ARNOLD, "The Need for a Functional Theory of Social Class," *Rural Sociology*, 19 (June 1954), 152–60.

BARBER, BERNARD, *Social Stratification: A Comparative Analysis of Structure and Process*. New York: Harcourt, Brace and Co., 1957. Chap. 1.

CHINOY, ELY, "Social Stratification: Theory and Synthesis," *British Journal of Sociology*, 8 (December 1957), 370–77.

CUBER, JOHN, and WILLIAM F. KENKEL, *Social Stratification in the United States*. New York: Appleton-Century-Crofts, 1954. Chaps. 3 and 13.

DAHRENDORF, RALF, *Class and Class Conflict in Industrial Society*. Stanford, Calif.: Stanford University Press, 1959. Part 5.

———, "On the Origin of Social Inequality," in *Philosophy, Politics and Society*, eds. Peter Laslett and W. G. Runciman. New York: Barnes & Noble, Inc., 1962.

DAVIS, KINGSLEY, "The Abominable Heresy: A Reply to Dr. Buckley," *American Sociological Review*, 24 (February 1959), 82–83.

———, "Reply to Tumin," *American Sociological Review*, 18 (August 1953), 394–97.

HARRIS, EDWARD E., "Prestige, Reward, Skill and Functional Importance: A Reconsideration," *Sociological Quarterly*, 5 (Summer 1964), 261–64.

HEMPEL, CARL G., "The Logic of Functional Analysis," in *Symposium on Sociological Theory*, ed. Llewellyn Gross. New York: Harper & Row, Publishers, 1959.

HUACO, GEORGE A., "The Functionalist Theory of Stratification: Two Decades of Controversy," *Inquiry*, 9 (Autumn 1966), 215–40.

LANDTMAN, GUNNAR, *The Origin of the Inequality of the Social Classes*. London: Routledge & Kegan Paul, Ltd., 1938.

LENSKI, GERHARD, *Power and Privilege: A Theory of Social Stratification*. New York: McGraw-Hill Book Company, 1967. Chap. 1.

LEVY, MARION J., JR., *The Structure of Society*. Princeton, N.J.: Princeton University Press, 1952. Chap. 7.

LEWIS, LIONEL S., and JOSEPH LOPREATO, "Functional Importance and Prestige of

Occupations," *Pacific Sociological Review*, 6 (Fall 1963), 55–59.

LOPREATO, JOSEPH, and LIONEL S. LEWIS, "An Analysis of Variables in the Functional Theory of Stratification," *Sociological Quarterly*, 4 (Autumn 1963), 301–10.

MOORE, WILBERT E., "But Some Are More Equal Than Others," *American Sociological Review*, 28 (February 1963), 13–18.

NORTH, C. C., *Social Differentiation*. Chapel Hill, N. C.: University of North Carolina Press, 1926.

OSSOWSKI, STANISLAW, *Class Structure in the Social Consciousness*. New York: The Free Press of Glencoe, Inc., 1963. Chap. 1.

PARSONS, TALCOTT, "A Revised Analytical Approach to the Theory of Social Stratification," in *Class, Status and Power*, eds. Reinhard Bendix and Seymour M. Lipset. Glencoe, Ill.: The Free Press, 1953.

QUEEN, STUART A., "Function of Social Stratification: A Critique," *Sociology and Social Research*, 46 (July 1962), 412–15.

SIMPSON, RICHARD L., "Modification of the Functional Theory of Social Stratification," *Social Forces*, 35 (December 1956), 132–37.

SJOBERG, GIDEON, "Contradictory Functional Requirements and Social Systems," *Journal of Conflict Resolution*, 4 (June 1960), 198–208.

SVALASTOGA, KAARE, *Social Differentiation*. New York: David McKay Co., Inc., 1965. Chap. 1.

TAUSKY, CURT, "Parsons on Stratification: An Analysis and Critique," *Sociological Quarterly*, 6 (Spring 1965), 128–32.

TAWNEY, R. H., Equality. London: George Allen & Unwin, Ltd., 1964. Chaps. 1–3.

TUMIN, MELVIN M., "On Equality," *American Sociological Review*, 28 (February 1963), 19–26.

———, *Social Stratification: The Forms and Functions of Inequality*. Englewood Cliffs, N.J.: Prentice-Hall, Inc., 1967. Chap. 12.

———, "Some Principles of Stratification: A Critical Analysis," *American Sociological Review*, 18 (August 1953), 387–94.

TURNER, ROY, "Functional Analysis and the Problem of Rationality," *Inquiry*, 9 (Autumn 1966), 262–73.

VAN DEN BERGHE, PIERRE, "Dialectic and Functionalism: Toward a Theoretical Synthesis," *American Sociological Review*, 28 (October 1963), 695–705.

WESOLOWSKI, WLODZIMIERZ, "Some Notes on the Functional Theory of Stratification," in *Class, Status, and Power: Social Stratification in Comparative Perspective* (2nd ed.), eds. Reinhard Bendix and Seymour M. Lipset. New York: The Free Press of Glencoe, Inc., 1966.

CHAPTER THREE

Social Class: Concepts and Research Methods

Systems of social stratification vary greatly from society to society, with wide differences in such characteristics as criteria for ranking, degree of inequality, number of strata, and distinctiveness of strata.[1] Yet some classification of stratification systems is possible and, for analytical purposes, is necessary. The most common subdivisions include *caste, estate,*[2] and *class* as major categories. Since the United States is usually understood to have a class

---

[1] Different writers have enumerated a variety of characteristics as criteria for "defining" degrees of distinctiveness among strata. These characteristics are of four general kinds: social-interactional (degree of residential or physical propinquity, rate of intermarriage among strata, frequency and intensity of interaction); cultural (correspondence of value systems among strata, degree of formal institutional support of distinctions among strata, degree of informal normative support of distinctions among strata); social-psychological (type and degree of class consciousness, class-linked psychological attributes); social mobility and change (ascription-achievement, change in criteria for placement).

[2] In an estate system the existence of unequal strata and placement in these strata are closely connected with land tenure. Since land is the basis of wealth, power, and prestige, one's position in the system generally corresponds to the amount of land one owns. While there can be considerable variation in the number of strata and in hierarchies within major divisions, an estate society generally consists of three distinct levels: nobility, clergy, and peasantry. The system is supported by law—distinctions of rank and respective rights and duties are institutionalized in the legal code. An estate system of stratification is essentially a hereditary system. One inherits status, based upon one's relationship to the land, and passes it on to descendants. Changes in status are infrequent and rest upon "royal grace" or formal acts by a superior.

For an extended account of an estate system, see Egon Bergel, *Social Stratification* (New York: McGraw-Hill Book Company, 1962) pp. 68–150.

system, we shall give primary attention to this type. The paragraph below describes the characteristics of a class system in its "purest" form—that is, as it would appear in a competitively open society. For purposes of comparison and to promote understanding, we follow this description with one of a caste system.

A class system is the prevalent type of social stratification in modern industrial society. This system of inequality, unlike castes or estates, requires no legal or other formally institutionalized support. Since opportunities for social mobility are held out to all members of the society, changes in ascribed status through personal accomplishments frequently occur. The society has no formal restrictions on social relations or on marriage among members of different strata. Thus, social organization along class lines is minimal and class boundaries are blurred. Class consciousness, i.e., awareness of class position and feelings of solidarity among class members, is limited. Cultural differences among classes are variations of the core culture.[3]

A caste system has strong support from religious institutions. Strata differentiations are on the basis of ascribed criteria; a person is born into a caste and remains there, as do his offspring. Personal accomplishments have no effect upon the rigidity of caste boundaries or upon caste placement. Thus, social mobility is virtually absent. Social relations with persons from other castes are narrowly prescribed. In general, associations among castes are minimal; especially taboo is marrying outside one's caste. All castes recognize the validity and rightness of the hierarchy. The system both expresses and sustains the mores of the society.[4]

CONCEPTIONS OF CLASS

The lines joining theories of social class to modern research methods lack the tangibility and clarity necessary for a well-developed science. From antiquity, scholars and essayists have used class themes to explain the conditions of society and the ubiquity of change within it. Their inquiries were prompted by a desire to understand such phenomena as authority and privilege, equality and inequality, and the survival of groups in a competitive environment. They drew

---

[3] Although we are principally concerned with class stratification in the United States, the selections in this volume deal with social stratification at various levels of generalization. Functionalist theory, for example, purports to make generalizations about stratification in all societies. Other papers in subsequent chapters focus on national, regional, or local stratification systems or on the stratification systems of ethnic groups. Awareness of the breadth of generalizations in particular studies is necessary for evaluations of their significance.

[4] Among the many fine monographs on caste systems, particularly with respect to India, see G. S. Ghurye, *Caste and Race in India* (London: Paul, Trench, Trubner, 1932) ; J. H. Hutton, *Caste in India: Its Nature, Function, and Origins* (London: Cambridge University Press, 1946) ; Andre Beteille, *Caste, Class and Power* (Berkeley, Calif.: University of California Press, 1965).

We deal with the nature of a caste society as it relates to the American stratification system in Chapter Five, which describes the Negro class structure.

their observations from the broad sweep of human events; they thought in historical periods and wrote of changes affecting millions of people.

By contrast, modern research on social classes usually refers to the activities of people in narrowly defined regions of society. It favors easily observable units, counting procedures, and sampling statistics. Its results are often based on ratings of individuals by individuals, and these results are customarily presented as measures of association between identifiable variables. For obvious reasons, then, conceptions of class and research methods rarely fall in neat correspondence. More often they meet obscurely or obliquely. And, when they seem to meet, each undergoes some alterations of meaning.[5]

Faced with these difficulties, how can we best describe the American system of stratification? Although sociologists provide somewhat different answers to this question, certain common threads in their interpretations stem, in part, from preferences for one or the other of the classical statements on the subject by Karl Marx and Max Weber.[6]

The writings of Marx[7] launched the modern study of class. Since Marx's time, few contributions have appeared on the subject that are not indebted to his conceptions. Marx's theory of class is an integral part of his fundamental thesis that economic conditions are the prime movers in the history of mankind. He conceives of classes as polarized manifestations of the relations of social aggregates to the means of production. One class (the bourgeoisie) owns these means; another class (the proletariat) provides labor, a primary instrument of production.[8] To Marx, the concept of class is far more than an abstraction constructed by the observer in order to make sense of the complexities of society and social behavior. Classes, grounded in material conditions, are tangible realities and decidedly real to class members. In addition to his focus on the objective economic situation, Marx places great emphasis on class consciousness—the sub-

---

5 In this situation, the sociologist speaks in broad generalities and of abstract concepts and applies them to a variety of descriptive events. However, the matching of concepts to events is largely arbitrary in the sense that the one does not consistently call forth the other. Thus, although this conjunction of abstract concepts and descriptive events is not entirely random, the connection between them is never constant enough to escape the influence of personal judgment. Since the conceptual responses to both the "same" and "different" events vary widely among observers, the possible meanings of same and different cannot, in their turn, be clearly specified.

6 This brief account of the conceptions of class by Marx and Weber leans heavily at several points on Reissman's fine analysis. Leonard Reissman, *Class in American Society* (Glencoe, Ill.: The Free Press, 1959), pp. 35–69.

7 While many references to class occur throughout much of Marx's voluminous writings, his basic statement is in *The Communist Manifesto* (New York: International Publishers, 1932). See also the interpretation of Marx's views on class by Reinhard Bendix and Seymour M. Lipset, "Karl Marx' Theory of Social Classes," in *Class, Status and Power*, eds. Reinhard Bendix and Seymour M. Lipset (Glencoe, Ill.: The Free Press, 1953), pp. 26–35.

8 Actually, Marx differentiates the bourgeoisie into several subclasses (e.g., petty bourgeoisie, landowners) and also distinguishes between the general proletariat and an element below this level, the *lumpenproletariat*, or dregs of society. For the most part, however, his analysis centers on the fundamental dichotomy of a two-class system rather than on a many-layered model.

jective awareness by class members of their objective position vis-à-vis the system of production and of their common interests. For Marx, the dynamic of class consciousness is an indispensable condition for the existence of viable classes. Class consciousness, arising from the objective conditions of the class situation, is the critical starting point for the class struggle, which will ultimately lead to the overthrow of those controlling the means of production, the ruling class.

Marx links his theory of class to a thesis of economic determinism. But, as Leonard Reissman[9] points out, he is not guilty of the simplistic kind of economic determinism so often attributed to him, for Marx gives considerable attention to other dimensions of class—the political and social realms—and their relationship to the economic factor. These aspects of his thinking anticipate Weber's conceptions of class.

In the opinion of many contemporary students of stratification, Weber rescues Marx's most important ideas from a "rut of economic monism."[10] Whereas Marx conceives of the ideological realm as a superstructure embedded in or emerging from an existential base (of which classes are one manifestation), Weber emphasizes and outlines the intricate interdependence of ideas, social structure, and motivation in a multidimensional scheme of social classes.

Weber takes Marx's conception of class and distinguishes three components, or orders: class, status, and party. His use of class is similar to Marx's without, however, the theme of class consciousness. The status order refers to communal aggregates differentiated from each other by estimation of social honor—or prestige—as expressed through a distinctive style of life. The third component— parties, or the political order—refers to groups which "live in a house of power [and whose] action is oriented toward the acquisition of social power, that is to say, toward influencing a communal action."[11]

To Weber, the differential distribution of power is the basis of class stratification. As several American scholars have emphasized, those who claim to follow Weber generally overlook the power theme, although it is the keystone of his theory of class stratification. Weber recognizes that, in reality, these three dimensions are closely intertwined, with any one capable of affecting or being affected by the others. Precisely because of this interaction, Weber stresses the need to

---

[9] *Op. cit.*, p. 50. See also Herbert Aptheker, *The World of C. Wright Mills* (New York: Marzani and Munsell, Inc., 1960), p. 31.

[10] Monism is an explanatory system based on single-factor determinism. This charge, so commonly used against Marx, can also be leveled against Weber. See Bernard Rosenberg, *The Values of Veblen* (Washington, D.C.: Public Affairs Press, 1956), p. 55.

It should be noted that, while homage is often paid to Marx, most American students of stratification esteem Weber more highly. Yet after paying due respect to Weber's ideas they do little toward translating his system into verifiable hypotheses or toward otherwise incorporating his contributions into empirical research. Perhaps part of the reason for the limited use of Weber's contributions is the fact that his views on stratification are restricted to about a dozen pages and most are expressed so ambiguously that it is difficult to agree upon what he is saying.

[11] Hans H. Gerth and C. Wright Mills, eds., *From Max Weber: Essays in Sociology* (Fair Lawn, N.J.: Oxford University Press, Inc., 1946), p. 194.

distinguish them analytically. Conceptual clarity, he feels, would enhance under-standing of the causal relationships between the social structure and the class system. Accordingly, his analytical distinctions are held to "offer the most mean-ingful framework for interpreting and understanding stratification in a modern industrial society."[12]

In reviewing the work of sociologists during the last several decades, Milton Gordon identifies five discrete variables associated with class concepts. Three of these variables—economic power, status ascription, and political power—are similar to Weber's class, status, and party. The two additional variables Gordon calls *group life* and *cultural attributes*. Group life refers to class as "an effective social system within which the class member has most or all of his intimate and meaningful social contacts."[13] In this conception, classes are more than social aggregates. Most of the significant life experiences of the individual may occur within the context of a given social class. The members of such a class view each other as equals and interact more with each other than with those outside their class. Cultural attributes refer to those "consistently different patterns of behavior and attitudes"[14] which may be associated with the several social classes. As Gordon puts it, "patterns of consumption, dress, speech, and participation in community life, attitudes and patterns relating to focal points of interest in the culture, such as sex, morality, religion, the family, patriotism, education, the arts, sports, etc., offer possible points of cultural differentiation by class."[15] In this sense, classes are subcultures involving a complex of attitudes, values, and beliefs, and a distinctive life orientation.

Gordon's classifications fall under two headings: stratification variables and associated variables. Stratification variables—economic power, status ascription, and political power—"refer by their very nature to hierarchical arrangement."[16] In contrast, associated variables (group life and cultural attributes) are "behav-ioral categories which are not, in themselves, hierarchical but which are produced by the operation of stratification variables and which, in turn, contribute to the dynamics of stratification."[17] The distinction between stratification and associated variables clarifies the nature of a class-stratification system and differentiates it from those class-related characteristics which are consequences of the basic vari-ables.

Gordon believes that for conceptual clarity the term *class* must be restricted to only one of the stratification variables—the social-status hierarchy.[18] One basis for this proposal is his belief that social class is conceptually more closely related to social status than it is to either political or economic power. Of greater im-

---

[12] Reissman, *op. cit.*, p. 69.
[13] *Social Class in American Sociology* (New York: McGraw-Hill Book Company, 1963), p. 18.
[14] *Ibid.*, p. 19.
[15] *Ibid.*
[16] *Ibid.*, p. 18.
[17] *Ibid.*
[18] *Ibid.*, p. 250.

portance in the support of class as a social-status level is the following hypothesis by Gordon.

> Of the three basic stratification dimensions, it is the social-status structure rather than the economic or political power dimensions which plays the largest immediate role in producing those social divisions, shifting and amorphous as they may be, of American communities which center around intimate friendships, clique life, association membership, and participation and intermarriage.[19]

Although Gordon gives precedence to social status because of its presumed predictive power, he suggests that "the role of economic power factors operating through time in conjunction with other factors to produce the crystallizing of the status structure should be kept to the fore at all times."[20]

This discussion of stratification variables highlights a basic question in the literature: Which of the three variables is most influential in determining the nature of class systems? Many sociologists, particularly those of the Warner school, see social status as the principal dimension of stratification. Some with Marxist orientations claim economic power to be the most important dimension of stratification. And still others favor political power. Gordon's remarks suggest one possible solution to this controversy, namely, the necessity of differentiating the variables which have an immediate effect upon behavioral categories from those which may have a long-term and indirect effect. Economic power, for example, may be a determiner in the first instance of the status hierarchy and thus, over an extended period of time, may have a significant effect upon a whole range of associated behavioral variables.

The conceptions discussed thus far view social classes as having a reality independent of feelings of group identification on the part of class members. A contrasting opinion is that classes are not meaningful without subjective class consciousness. The chief proponent of this approach is Richard Centers, who holds the following view.

> Classes are psychosocial groupings, something that is essentially subjective in character dependent upon class consciousness (i.e., a feeling of group membership), and class lines of cleavage may or may not conform to what seem to social scientists to be logical lines of cleavage in the objective or stratification sense. Class, as distinguished from stratum, can well be regarded as a psychological phenomenon in the fullest sense of the term. That is, a man's class is a part of his ego, a feeling on his part of belongingness to something and identification with something larger than himself.[21]

Researchers, such as Centers, who treat classes as subjective entities contend that, if classes make any difference and have any reality, they will be manifested

---

[19] *Ibid.*, p. 249.
[20] *Ibid.*, p. 250.
[21] *The Psychology of Social Classes* (Princeton, N.J.: Princeton University Press, 1949), p. 27.

in the attitudes and conceptions people hold. This view of class has its origins in the Marxian conception of class consciousness. We shall discuss Centers' approach to class as a social-psychological entity more extensively in Chapter Eight.

THE CONTINUUM-CATEGORY CONTROVERSY

The conceptions of class dealt with thus far bear upon such issues as the principal dimensions of class, the nature of their relationships, and the relative salience of objective and subjective judgments. Yet another problem is the structure of the American class system, or, as it has come to be known, the continuum-category controversy. Does the American class system consist of a set of discrete social groups or is it a continuous hierarchical order with no sharp breaks in the distribution of economic privilege, power, and prestige? Those who favor the first position—class as category—view social classes as *real groups*, i.e., sets of families and individuals who share common conditions of life and whose most meaningful associations occur within their own class. This conception of class (or perspectives compatible with it) has guided and been supported by the research of several investigators, including Robert and Helen Lynd, W. Lloyd Warner, and August Hollingshead,[22] and, at least until very recently, it has been favored in greater or lesser degree by the majority of American students of stratification.

Advocates of the continuum thesis argue that the conception of classes as distinct social groups does not match the realities of modern American society.[23] John Cuber and William Kenkel[24] have set forth the most extensive arguments. Assessing the methods and evidence of researchers favoring both positions, they

---

[22] Robert S. Lynd and Helen Merrell Lynd, *Middletown* (New York: Harcourt, Brace and Company, 1929); W. Lloyd Warner and Paul S. Lunt, *The Social Life of a Modern Community* (New Haven, Conn.: Yale University Press, 1941); August B. Hollingshead, *Elmtown's Youth* (New York: John Wiley & Sons, Inc., 1949).

[23] Gerhard Lenski reported the best-known empirical appraisal of this issue in 1952. "American Social Classes: Statistical Strata or Social Groups?" *American Journal of Sociology*, 58 (September 1952), 139–44. Using a method similar to Warner's reputational approach (discussed subsequently in this chapter), Lenski studied the stratification system of a small town in New England. Twenty-four residents ranked a sample of 150 families on community status. The extent and types of disagreement among these judges led Lenski to reject the hypothesis that social classes are discrete groups. The judges, for example, could not agree upon the number of strata or their boundaries. From remarks made to Lenski and requests for directions from him, it was also apparent that many of the judges "were not accustomed to thinking of the community as divided into discrete social strata" (p. 143). Lenski saw these results as "proof of the absence of any system of discrete social classes which are recognized by even the 'well-informed' members of the community" (*Ibid.*).

For supporting empirical assessments, see also Stanley A. Hetzler, "An Investigation of the Distinctiveness of Social Classes," *American Sociological Review*, 28 (October 1953), 493–97; William F. Kenkel, "Social Stratification in Columbus, Ohio," in *Social Stratification in the United States*, John C. Cuber and William F. Kenkel (New York: Appleton-Century-Crofts, 1954), 132–56; Thomas E. Lasswell, "A Study of Social Stratification Using an Area Sample of Raters," *American Sociological Review*, 19 (June 1954), 310–13.

[24] *Op. cit.*, Chap. iii and xiii.

give these reasons for rejecting the categorical theory and accepting the continuum theory:[25]

(1) There appear to be almost as many class systems as observers. Some describe a six-class system, others speak of two or four classes, and so on.

(2) Regardless of the criteria of classification many persons cannot be classified.

(3) The categorical approach seems to allow neither for changes in the bases for ranking nor for the fact that the class system itself is in flux.

(4) The criteria for ranking usually do not show significant correlations with each other. For example, a person may rank high in general prestige, medium in income, and low in occupational status.

(5) The methods used by those favoring the categorical view do not seem to support the claims that the population studied is differentiated into discrete classes.

(6) In general, all data, including findings from research carried out within a categorical framework, are compatible with a continuum theory. Whether the variable is income, education, power, attitudes, or prestige, measurement yields a continuous series of data.

Despite their firm rejection of the class-as-category position, Cuber and Kenkel do not object to the use of the term *social class* as a convenient label for facilitating communication as long as it is recognized as a statistical artifact. Thus, they recommend a nominalist[26] approach to the concept of social class. Those who support the categorical interpretation have seldom challenged this critique. The typical response simply reaffirms the contention that classes are real groups and holds that to treat them simply as statistical strata is to miss a significant reality of social life.

Gordon[27] has given the most important rebuttal of the continuum viewpoint. Focusing on the research utilized by Cuber and Kenkel (studies by Gerhard Lenski, Kenkel, and Stanley Hetzler), Gordon raises a number of questions about their procedures and findings, concluding that the empirical basis for the continuum model is ambiguous.

A key observation by Gordon concerns the undue significance attached to the

---

[25] Abbreviated from *ibid.*, pp. 25–26 and 306–7.

[26] Gerhard Lenski suggests that "conservative" writers have tended to favor a nominalist approach to the concept of class while "radicals" have generally taken the realist position. *Power and Privilege: A Theory of Social Stratification* (New York: McGraw-Hill Book Company, 1966), p. 23. Caution should be exercised in placing much weight on this differentiation; too many exceptions are at hand. W. Lloyd Warner, for example, strongly supports the realist position, but he cannot be labeled a radical.

[27] *Op. cit.*, pp. 183–87. Ellis also provides a significant criticism of the continuum theory. He claims that the empirical evidence for the continuum interpretation does not really comprise replications of the studies carried out by scholars such as Warner and that the evidence is marked by methodological inadequacies. Moreover, according to Ellis, advocates of the continuum approach have attempted to refute the class-as-category thesis with evidence irrelevant for that purpose. Robert A. Ellis, "Continuum Theory of Social Stratification: A Critical Note," *Sociology and Social Research*, 42 (March 1958), 269–73.

fact that variables such as occupational prestige, income, education, and rental values are distributed in a hierarchy with no discernible breaks. Gordon agrees that these variables usually form a continuum but emphasizes that it does not necessarily follow—as is often assumed—that other characteristics commonly associated with stratification are distributed in a corresponding series. Gordon is referring, although not explicitly, to his important distinctions between stratification variables and associated variables.[28] As he suggests, a common pitfall is to mix the two types and thus to obscure the nature of the relationship between them. This is true also in the context of the continuum-category controversy as well as in other contexts.

Of the several behavioral categories, which Gordon classifies under the rubric of associated variables, that which he refers to as *group life* may be most relevant to the category-continuum argument.[29] Systematic evidence on class-related group life is scanty. That which does exist certainly does not depict social interaction as rigidly circumscribed along class lines throughout the class hierarchy. On the other hand no research shows a strict continuum of finely graded social relationships which blur into each other in the way stratification variables are usually arrayed. Therefore, more research should be directed to the key issue of the interactional dimension[30] of the class system. We concur then with Gordon that neither the category nor the continuum framework is fully acceptable since at the present time the "nature of the American status order lies somewhere between these two extremes."[31]

While few students seriously object to the proposal that the category-continuum issue be seen as reflecting differences in degree rather than in kind, most re-

---

28 *Op. cit.*, Chap. 8. (See the previous section of this chapter for a summary of these distinctions.)

29 Gordon himself places considerable emphasis on the status dimension, which he describes as a psychological system of attitudes pertaining to superiority and inferiority. The continuum model, he suggests, is not clearly applicable to this dimension. *Ibid.*, pp. 186–87.

30 Goldthorpe and Lockwood find in recent years a pronounced neglect of the relational aspects of class, largely as a consequence of the preoccupation with the psychology of class. John H. Goldthorpe and David Lockwood, "Affluence and the British Class Structure," *The Sociological Review*, 11 (July 1963), 140. One of the very few studies focusing on the interactional dimension in a test of the continuum-category argument strongly supports the hypothesis of class as category. Robert A. Ellis, "Social Stratification and Social Relations: An Empirical Test of the Disjunctiveness of Social Class," *American Sociological Review*, 22 (October 1957), 570–78. Also bearing on this issue and lending some support to the categorical approach as it relates to occupational stratification is Edward O. Laumann and Louis Guttman, "The Relative Associational Contingency of Occupations in an Urban Setting," *American Sociological Review*, 31 (April 1966), 169–78.

31 *Op. cit.*, p. 188. At several levels of the class hierarchy, group life approximates the type of closure suggested by the categorical model. Consider, for example, the exclusive clubs and social circles of the upper set and the existence of working-class gangs.

This view is consonant with Landecker's conclusion that "neither the class-structure nor the status-continuum hypothesis takes precedence over the other, but rather that each is appropriate to a different portion of the total system of stratification." Werner Landecker, "Class Boundaries," *American Sociological Review*, 25 (December 1960), 877. The research by Laumann and Guttman, *op. cit.*, and Ellis, "Social Stratification and Social Relations," *op. cit.*, provides further support for this position.

searchers continue to utilize one or the other conception in their field studies. Llewellyn Gross examines below the consequences of this choice. This essay, an early analysis of the debate, examines several of the empirical problems considered by Cuber and Kenkel, but Gross's principal concern is with the logical structure of the two approaches—referred to as substantive and classificatory—and with their methodological consequences.

PROBLEMS IN THE CHOICE AND USE OF SUBSTANTIVE AND CLASSIFICATORY CONCEPTS IN CLASS RESEARCH*

Llewellyn Gross

State University of New York at Buffalo

SYSTEMATIC CRITERIA FOR EVALUATING RESEARCH

In studies of "social classes," two conceptual schemes, or usages are apparent or implied in the data and interpretations. Our objective is to clarify these schemes, to develop their methodological consequences, and to make explicit the larger framework of pluralistic contexts through which class concepts of all sorts may serve as useful scientific tools.

1. Class names are sometimes used as substantive concepts referring to separate and distinct social groups having identifiable characteristics. These groups are composed of individuals who are presumed to possess homogeneous social attributes. If the class concept is to be interpreted in this way, consistent scientific usage would seem to require a clear specification of (a) the number of classes used, (b) the kind of attributes defining each class, (c) the testable sensory basis of each attribute, (d) the operational steps taken to establish a constant conjunction between these attributes, (e) the attributes excluded from each class which serve to divide or "isolate" one class from another, and (f) the explanatory or predictive significance of the class-linked attributes.

2. Class names are sometimes used as classificatory concepts referring to the "arbitrary" subdivision of a population into class intervals constructed according to the degree to which individuals possess more or less amounts of a single quality. If the class concept is to be interpreted in this way, consistent scientific usage would seem to require a clear specification of (a) the number of classes used, (b) the single quality or *fundamentum divisionis* defining the classification, (c) the units of observation or measurement used to identify subdivisions of the quality in question, (d) the exhaustiveness of the classification in terms of the representativeness of members within the defined population, (e) the amount of

overlapping within the classification or between classes, and (f) the adequacy of the classification in terms of its explanatory or predictive significance. The latter point includes flexibility in the construction of classifications as evidenced by the possible utility of alternative classifications.[1]

The following are hypothetical models of the two schemes from which the operational procedures discussed above are probably derived.

Substantive Usage

1. *An attribute refers to a quality which has an all-or-none existence.*
2. *An attribute is not measurable; being a "constant," it is either present or absent.*
3. *A class is a combination of attributes, i.e., a category.*
4. *The units constituting a class are attributes; they designate kinds or occurrences of qualities.*
5. *Class boundaries are separated by a qualitatively differentiated region.*
6. *Classes are components of a heterogeneous totality.*

Classificatory Usage

1. *A variable refers to a quality which exists in varying degrees.*

2. *A variable is measurable; it can be ordered into amounts (of units) ranging from least to most.*
3. *A class is the subdivision of a variable, i.e., a class interval.*
4. *The units constituting a class are values; they designate the degrees or incidences of a single quality.*
5. *Class boundaries are coincident or adjacent to one another.*
6. *Classes are components of a homogeneous totality.*

The substantive usage implies an inescapable limitation; *viz.*, when each substantive class in a multiclass "system" is described in terms of attributes which are assumed to exist in constant conjunction with one another and to be absent from other classes which are composed of other attributes similarly related, classification in our explicit logical sense does not exist. For, as one multiplies the number of conjoined characteristics defining a class (or group), the number of members (or individuals) which can be included in that class decreases.[2] More specifically, if we define a given class in terms of five attributes, those individuals will be excluded who are lacking in the possession of one, two, three, four, or all five of these attributes. Nor will all these individuals be included in some one of an indefinite number of subsequent classes of five attributes, except when certain of the attributes of such classes overlap with those of the initially defined class. Given, then, a limited number of classes with which to work, a considerable proportion of individuals will remain unclassified (i.e., they will be members of no class or, if forced into the classification, will be members of more than one

---

[1] We do not wish to pose a logical dichotomy between these two usages or to reify and fix a conceptual antithesis. The term "classification" is not used in the Aristotelian sense of successive dichotomous subdivisions of the genus, each of which is a species of the order which precedes it. Such a usage assumes that things have stable and readily identifiable qualities which can be unambiguously placed within the various subdivisions of a logical classification. Instead, we propose to define the qualities which characterize things in terms of convenient fractional subdivisions of a continuous variable, each of which is a subclass which comprises the variable in question.

---

[2] Many sociologists seem to assume the reverse, i.e., that, by multiplying class attributes, they may increase the number of individuals that can be included.

class). The result is the contradiction of a basic principle of classification, *viz.*, that it must provide for a complete enumeration of *all* its members.[3] It is for this reason that the most adequate classification is one which approximates the ideal of a single basic principle or *fundamentum divisionis*.[4] In so far as this ideal is violated, there is overlapping or cross division of classes.[5]

The task of deciding upon which of the two usages of social class is most appropriate to a particular study does not revolve around the problem of discovering what essential properties they specifically designate but of determining which of their *provisionally assumed* properties will enable the researcher to realize his objective. If the objective is the prediction of social characteristics *ABC*, then whichever properties enable the researcher to predict these characteristics with the highest degree of probability will, by virtue of this fact,

become the essential properties which define and give meaning to class concepts. This implies that definitions are proposals for using certain concepts in certain ways for certain purposes and that, as purposes or objectives differ, the choice and definition of the essential properties of a concept will differ. Thus there is no absolutely true or correct meaning of "social classes." Failure to recognize this point may lead to the misappropriation of a definition—a definition constructed for an entirely different purpose from the one which the investigator has in mind.[6]

SOME CASE ANALYSES

Duvall's study.[7] In making her study, Duvall used four class levels—I, II, III, and IV—selected "on the basis of their participation in the status hierarchy." They are subdivided by six principal categories of "social characteristics"—"Occupation," "Source of Income," "Area Lived In," "Type of House," "Education and Literary Interests," and "Personal Appearance" (at home).[8]

A cursory inspection of her Table 2 suggests that social classes are used in a substantive sense, with each class being defined by certain qualitative attributes. Each class is found in specific residen-

---

[3] It is assumed that every member within the population group or universe of items being classified *should* find inclusion or representation (via sample theory) within one of the classes or subdivisions of the classification. Though the objective of an exhaustive classification has seldom been fully realized by the natural scientist, few students of the subject seriously doubt that genuine attempts to achieve this objective will usually lead to more fruitful results.

[4] It should be noted that the principle of a *fundamentum divisionis* is an ideal scientific norm whose realization in practice is rarely attained. Its existence merely guarantees that the number of basic qualities used and the degree of overlapping between classes will be reduced to a minimum.

[5] Notwithstanding what has been said in this paragraph, substantive classes must be related to one another in respect to at least one quality—else they could not be organized under the same heading. However, this relationship is usually only implicit; efforts are commonly directed toward demonstrating the *differences* between the classes in terms of their unique possession of certain functionally related qualities.

[6] Perhaps it should be added that the most obvious properties are not always the most significant for realizing a given objective. Moreover, people can sort and recognize things in terms of unrecognized purposes without knowing how they sort them or the respects in which they are alike and different. These contingencies may account for many of the irrelevant statements contained in the following studies.

[7] Evelyn M. Duvall, "Conceptions of Parenthood," *American Journal of Sociology*, LII (November 1946), 193–203.

[8] *Ibid.*, Table 2, p. 194.

tial areas labeled "smart," "good," "fair," and "poor"; each class reads specific magazines. But a closer inspection of the table indicates that in regard to "Type of House," Classes I and II overlap, the former living in medium to large apartments, the latter in medium-sized apartments; the same is true of Classes III and IV in respect to "poor conditions." In regard to "Source of Income," Classes II, III, and IV have "wages" but apparently in varying degrees. There are no units of observation or measurement for determining the presence or amount of any of the characteristics. Some of the class categories admit of overlapping; others do not, and yet there is no apparent explanation for this. There is little evidence of a functional relationship between the categories, and there is no way of knowing how representative the individuals included within each class are in terms of some larger population.[9]

Davis and Havighurst's study.[10] These authors used a two-class grouping, middle and lower social classes, with two subdivisions for each, white and Negro. They indicate that the principal factors used in making this grouping were "occupation of parents and their siblings, education of parents, their siblings and grandparents, property ownership, membership in churches and other associations, and section of the city."[11] Since no information is given as to precisely which occupations, which educational groups or degrees of education, etc., are included in each of the

social classes, there is no way of knowing whether these factors are treated as variables, as attributes, or both. If the social classes are distinguishable according to degrees of education, the result is a classificatory definition. If the social classes are distinguishable by the section of city in which their members reside, it seems that the meaning of social classes is best defined in substantive or qualitative terms, and, accordingly, specific constructs, such as type of housing, should be given.

Furthermore, since the authors fail to provide any unit of observation or measurement which would enable the reader to determine the degree of education of parents, parents' siblings, and grandparents possessed by each class or the attributes of the section of the city in which each class resides, there is no way of indicating which usage of social classes the authors have in mind. Because of their failure to present the kind of fundamental information called for by their study, there is no way of knowing whether each of the 200 mothers studied could be placed without ambiguity in only one social class. There is no evidence given to contradict the assumption that a number of mothers would fall into more than one class as the observer passed from one to another of the measures (attributes or variables?) determining class membership, and there is no description of the characteristics of the mothers whose omission or exclusion would define the hiatus between the classes. Functional interrelationships between the measures are not demonstrated, as would be necessary to sustain the substantive usage, and there is no way of knowing whether the four classes include either all the members in the defined population or a representative sample of it, as would be necessary for a valid classificatory usage.

---

9 Essentially the same criticisms can be made of Neugarten's study (Bernice L. Neugarten, "Social Class and Friendship Among School Children," *American Journal of Sociology*, LI [January 1946], 305–13).

10 Allison Davis and Robert J. Havighurst, "Social Class and Color Differences in Child-Rearing," *American Sociological Review*, XI (December 1946), 698–710.

11 *Ibid.*, p. 702.

Hollingshead's study.[12] This author's investigation of Elmtown indicated that the "social structure is composed of five strata whose members understand with varying degrees of precision how each ranks in the hierarchical order." "Stratification was accomplished by a rating procedure developed in the community." It was "based on the use of a standardized Control List of 20 families."[13] Since the criterion or criteria used in establishing the class groupings and in constructing the "Control List" are not discussed, we have no way of knowing whether the social classes are defined in substantive or in classificatory terms. It appears that Hollingshead's 735 cases were placed into one of five classes in proportion to their possession of some fairly well-recognized but undefined variable. Following this, a study was made of certain typical characteristics associated with each class.

If it is assumed that the author wished to use these typical characteristics as a basis for *defining* his social classes and he has successfully demonstrated that his five strata are found in varying but consistent proportions in all ecological areas, occupational groups, religious affiliations, and educational levels and each of the latter may be regarded as independent unilinear principles of division, he has correctly utilized the classificatory meaning of social classes. Suggestive of the classificatory use of social classes are the author's application of chi square as a measure of the degree of overlap between the classes and his offer of objective evidence regarding the exhaustiveness of the classification: All the adolescents in Elmtown are directly or indirectly included.

On the other hand, if it is assumed that all these characteristics combined are to be used in defining social classes, as is evidenced by his more informal analysis but contradicted by the fact that he gives coefficients of contingency for correlating them with class strata, then he is using the substantive meaning of class, and the kind of analysis described in the above paragraphs is inapplicable.

Mills's study.[14] At certain points Mills seems to exhibit some confusion between the classificatory and substantive usages of social classes. He writes: "When the occupations of a cross section of married men in Central City are coded in twenty-four groups and ranked according to average family income, five strata are crystallized out: Between each of them there is a "natural" break in average income, whereas the average income of the occupations making up each income stratum are relatively homogeneous."[15] On a first reading of this passage it appears that Mills has successfully combined our two meanings of class. He has taken a variable (incomes) and found "natural" breakages within it. But on a second reading of the passage it becomes apparent that he has done this by confusing class membership with class inclusion. The relation of class inclusion is transitive. The relation of class membership is intransitive; i.e., it does not follow that, if *A* is a member of *B* and *B* is a member of *C*, *A* is a member of *C*. Because Mills's married men can be classified into twenty-four occupational groups

12 August B. Hollingshead, "Selected Characteristics of Classes in a Middle Western Community," *American Sociological Review*, XII (August 1947), 385–95.

13 *Ibid.*, pp. 385–86.

14 C. Wright Mills, "The Middle Classes in Middle-sized Cities," *American Sociological Review*, XI (October 1946), 520–29.

15 *Ibid.*, p. 521.

and these occupational groups reclassified into five income strata, it does not follow that all his married men will find a place in one or another of these five income strata.

After having defined social classes in this way, Mills is concerned "with the *degree* and the *content* of political consciousness that they display and with whether they reveal any independence of policy or are politically dependent upon the initiative and ideologies of other strata."[16] As the above quotation implies, Mills combines variables (e.g., prestige ranking, amount of education, occupation of father) and attributes (e.g., characteristic attitudes and ideological contents). It is not surprising, then, that "of all the strata in the middle-size city, the small businessmen and the white-collar workers occupy the most ambiguous and least closely defined social position."[17] The fact that these strata are "the least homogeneous" and "make up the vaguer and 'somewhere in-between' strata" seems to us a logical consequence of the failure to distinguish between the classificatory and substantive usages of social classes.

Moore's study.[18] This author seems to use the substantive meaning of social classes more consistently than do most: "A social class is a group of persons of both sexes and all ages with a distinctive code of folkways and/or mores and to whom deference is given by other similar groups or from whom it is exacted by other similar groups."[19] The author is interested in finding the relationship between the presence or absence of class struggle (measured primarily in terms of hostile behavior) in a particular society and the stability of the economic structure of the society (measured in terms of the presence or absence of two attributes—stability in the distribution of economic goods and in the techniques of production for a generation or more). Thus qualitatively distinct and identifiable classes are dichotomized in terms of class struggle and correlated with qualitatively separable cultural attributes. It is unfortunate that space prohibited a precise description of the distinctive codes of folkways and mores which enabled the author to identify the social classes, the class struggle, and the economic stability of each culture. Without this information, confirmation of the substantive use of social classes must be withheld.

White's study.[20] In his study of low-income classes White seems to have closely followed the classificatory usage of social classes. His classes are in a certain sense subdivisions of a unilinear variable (income), though he introduces breakages in his income distribution.[21] These breakages serve to isolate one class from another and to define those individuals who are excluded from what might otherwise be an exhaustive classification. However, the result is in effect the presentation of sample sectors of a continuous variable rather than discrete substantive categories. The unit of measurement is dollars and the classification demonstrates the relevance of this variable for predicting expenditures.

Our analyses of these and other studies[22] suggest that much of the confusion found in the recent literature on

---

16 *Ibid.*, p. 521 (my italics).

17 *Ibid.*

18 B. Moore, "A Comparative Analysis of the Class Struggle," *American Sociological Review*, X (February 1945), 31–37.

19 *Ibid.*, p. 31.

20 R. Clyde White, "Low-Income Classes," *American Journal of Sociology*, XLVII (May 1942), 918–28.

21 *Ibid.*, p. 920.

22 The method that Form used in "determining the existence and shape of the status structure . . . was largely con-

social classes stems from an indiscriminate mixing of the two schemes or usages discussed above and to the absence of any serious attempt at realizing scientific criteria. It may be added, moreover, that these studies generally seem to misconstrue the function of sociology. Instead of seeking to find the "causative" factors and methods of classification which will enable them to predict specific social occurrences with the highest probability, they first select what they presume to be causative factors in the form of pseudosubstantive or pseudoclassificatory classes and then seek to predict their influences upon certain social occurrences. Perhaps, if these authors concentrated more upon the phenomena they wished to predict and less upon what seems to be a preconceived explanatory cause or principle, we believe that their work would be more in conformity with acceptable scientific procedures. Duvall, Davis and

---

cerned with the discovery of the existence, varieties, and directions of deference behavior." Upon this basis he describes eight main status groups each of which contains deference variables and a number of attributes not found in certain of the other groups (William H. Form, "Social Stratification in a Planned Community," *American Sociological Review*, X [October 1945], 605–13). Goldschmidt used substantive classes in the form of complexes of cultural traits which comprise denominational groups ("nuclear churches" and "outside churches") and subdivides each by a classificatory variable (occupation) (Walter R. Goldschmidt, "Class Denominationalism in Rural California Churches," *American Journal of Sociology*, XLIX [January 1944], 348–55). Schneider appears to have applied the classificatory usage. He demonstrates the relationship between social origins defined in terms of five occupational classes and activity-choice patterns defined in terms of three classes of activities (Joseph Schneider, "Class Origin and Fame: Eminent English Women," *American Sociological Review*, V [October 1940], 700–712).

Havighurst, Goldschmidt, Gordon, Neugarten, and others begin their definition of the problem with some kind of class analysis and then go on to investigate the effects or consequences of social classes upon some selected area of social phenomena.[23] This is putting the cart before the horse. Their implicit concern may be in demonstrating the ontological priority of social classes as a fundamental force in society. From the standpoint of an objective sociological science, social classes might be more appropriately regarded as heuristic groupings the variables or attributes of which are dictated by and adjusted to the kind of social phenomena being investigated.

A COMMON SUBSTANTIVE USAGE

We have suggested scientific criteria for identifying and evaluating the substantive and classificatory usages of social classes. Let us examine what is probably the most common substantive usage to be found—that which generally regards each class as possessing common interests and ideology and each individual in the society as identifying himself with one and being loyal to it.[24] This usage often assumes that the division between bourgeoisie and proletari-

---

23 Form's study is an exception to this generalization. Following a description of the status structure in a planned community, he attempts to "induct the principles along which it was based." These prove to be primarily organizational participation and secondarily occupation (*op. cit.*, p. 607).

24 "According to the subjectivists, classes are groups whose sources of income are similar and whose economic interests coincide. In this conception the subjective factor lies in a community of interest and outlook, rooted in the economic structure of any given period. . . . In such a view the common interests, common ideology, com-

at or between owners and managers, salaried employees and wage-earners, respectively, is fundamental for an understanding of society and must always be considered regardless of what may be the specific purpose of the researcher. For those who accept these assumptions there is no possibility that other subdivisions or cleavages within society may be of equal or greater importance *for certain purposes* and that in some instances it may be advantageous to dissect society along lines which cut across the more familiar class groupings. Before these assumptions can be widely accepted for social research, certain apparently contradictory observations must be shown to be inapplicable.

The assumption of class loyalty is contradicted and limited by the expressed desire of many individuals in the "lower classes" to move out of these classes into those of higher rank. Kornhauser found that people at the lower-income levels expect either themselves or their children to "get ahead."[25] These individuals are not likely to have consistently strong loyalties, personal identifications, or obligations toward those classes from which they would escape. The possibility that there are age and sex factors which mitigate against class loyalties should not be overlooked. Full awareness of one's position in the hierarchy of social stratification is not likely to be grasped before the period of early adolescence since it is only then that one's aspirations must give way to the circumstances limiting the realization of individual abilities. No doubt many youngsters are indoctrinated either to aspire to the symbols of a higher class or to react against the frustrations of low-class membership (particularly low income) by strong ambitions to enter a higher class. Likewise, since the class membership of young women is determined primarily by the class membership of their husbands and large numbers of young women hope to marry into a class above that of their origin, their class loyalties may be different from that of their fathers. Conceivably the influence of women who prime their daughters for higher-class marriages would tend to be antagonistic to their husbands' class interests.

A number of studies indicate that from one-fourth to one-third of the shifts in occupation are either up or down the scale. These groups cannot easily retain strong feelings of class identification. It is also possible that frequent shifts in occupation or vocation within the same status may produce an attitudinal set against strong loyalties. These shifts may, in turn, encourage other more durable group loyalties or identifications such as educational, national, ethnic, religious, geographical, and various personal-social allegiances which cut across class divisions. These allegiances may unite individuals of different classes and divide or estrange individuals of the same class.[26] Hence, for some investigators it will be a plausible hypothesis that the predominant attachments are found in relationships of person with person or group with group which cut across the more familiar class groupings.

There is considerable variety in the

mon consciousness of cohesion, come to the fore." Some subjectivists "conceive of social division according to rank and class as universal" (Paul Mombert, "Class," *Encyclopaedia of the Social Sciences* III, 531–36).

25 A. W. Kornhauser, "Analysis of 'Class' Structure of Contemporary American Society—Psychological Bases of Class Divisions," in *Industrial Conflict*, eds. G. W. Hartman and T. Newcomb (New York: Cordon Co., 1939), p. 241.

26 *Ibid.*, p. 244.

number of classes believed to be descriptive of comparable social structures. MacIver offers a five-class system; Warner and his collaborators, a six-class system; the Lynds, a two-class system; and so on. Such diversity of classification indicates a lack of consensus or consistency in what it is that is being observed. Moreover, the great variety of criteria or measures used to identify class members—economic, educational, religious, racial, or ethnic, etc.—attests to the absence of identifiable and determinate referents for the class names and to the presence of ambiguity in the use of class concepts. A representative list of connotations includes in-group and out-group feelings; special privileges and obligations; distinguishable customs, conventions, and ideologies; hierarchical social stratification; *esprit de corps;* common interests; characteristic ways of life; consciousness of the meaning and significance of class history; specific relations to a system of production; common attitudes, value sentiments, aspirations, or forms of behavior; and common descent. These connotations are not specific enough to lead to any kind of useful definition of the genus-species type. Furthermore, if they are to be taken as specific characteristics of the class of denotations designated by the symbols "social classes," they should be functionally correlated. That they are not correlated is evidenced by the fact that individuals who rank relatively high in one are often found to rank relatively low in another. It appears, then, that within the populations selected there are no clear and coincident referents that would indicate the presence of distinct and stable lines of division between population aggregates, typified by and differentiated in terms of specific social characteristics.

We offer the following propositions as criteria of scientific research:

1. The total number of social classes assumed should always be designated.

2. Social classes should be defined either in terms of subdivisions of a unilinear variable or in terms of a functional relationship between certain kinds of attributes but not in terms of both variables and attributes.

3. The units of observation used to measure or identify the variables or attributes constituting the social classes should be given regardless of which usage is accepted.

4. If social classes are defined in terms of subdivisions of a continuous variable, operational evidence of the probable exhaustiveness of the classification (i.e., the inclusion of all members of the defined universe or a representative sample of them) should be given; if they are defined in terms of a functional relationship between certain attributes, operational evidence of a constant conjunction between these attributes should be given.

5. If social classes are defined in terms of the logic of classification, an estimation of the continuousness of the classes and the extent to which one class overlaps with another should be given; if they are defined in terms of isolated groups of functionally related attributes, some description of those members excluded from the classes should be given.

6. Both usages of social class should be provisionally constructed and experimentally modified so as to best realize the objectives of science—the answering of questions or hypotheses which, it is hoped, arise out of systematic social theory. The identification of variable characteristics and the construction of a useful classification should develop *pari passu.* A classification is built upon the observation of an identifiable variable, common to a group of individuals be-

ing classified, and, in turn, the presence of a classification enables the observer to identify the existence of a common variable in a group of individuals.

Concepts pose, create, and re-create distinctions which serve as vantage points from which manifold social phenomena may be interpreted. The distinctions suggested by the words "social classes" have or may have had practical usefulness in respects which may be quite irrelevant for the realization of certain scientific or logical objectives. It is common knowledge to students of linguistics that primitive peoples classify their world in ways befitting their adjustment to what they find in it.[27] The same motives no doubt apply to the citizen and the scientist of a more complex society. In this connection it would be interesting to explore the likelihood that certain words, such as "social classes," were first used as "instruments of action" having volitional and emotional reference or as "keys to social attention" rather than as tools of conceptual analysis. It is even possible that for some people there may be something of the mythical in the class concept. Cassirer states that it is a familiar fact that all mythic thinking is governed and permeated by the principle of *pars pro toto*—"Whoever has brought any part of a whole into his power has thereby acquired power, in the magical sense, over the whole itself."[28]

By maintaining a clear distinction between substantive and classificatory usages of social classes and by offering criteria for each, we may seem to have assumed the presence of permanent gaps or cleavages in sociological data and thereby contradicted one of our main points, *viz.*, that a classification should be consistent with a particular research objective. However, our concern has been more with the adequacy of any and all usages rather than with the specific criteria which sustain a particular application of one of the usages. We believe that awareness of the differences between the two *general* usages discussed above will contribute toward the realization of a scientific sociology. To say that such differences are "real" means only that they have a certain stability or persistence in terms of verified human responses and that such differences make a difference in terms of realizing scientific objectives. We are reminded of other assumptions of fundamental cleavages in social phenomena useful to science: *viz.*, the limits placed upon a dimension or measure such as intelligence; the notion of limits in the statistics of chance variations; consensus in the separation of subject and predicate, terms and relations, and the "all-or-none" reactions of people to traumatic experiences.

We freely concede that more careful research may indicate that a given criterion of class membership may, in terms of certain specific scientific objec-

27 Cf. W. H. Werkmeister, *A Philosophy of Science* (New York: Harper & Bros., 1940), pp. 199 ff.; B. L. Whorf, "Science and Linguistics," *Readings in Social Psychology*, eds. Newcomb and Hartley, pp. 210–19; L. Thompson, "In Quest of an Heuristic Approach to the Study of Mankind," *Approaches to Group Understanding*, eds. L. Bryson, L. Finkelstein, and R. MacIver (New York: Harper & Bros., 1947), pp. 505–7.

28 Ernest Cassirer, *Language and Myth* (New York: Harper & Bros., 1946), p. 92

and *passim*. His example is that of the bird and butterfly that, having the characteristic of flight in common, are regarded as belonging to the same classification and become one in all respects. Is it not possible that, when a number of individuals are found to belong to the same social class in respect to a single criterion, there is a tendency for many people to regard them as being alike in respect to other criteria?

tives, be neither uniformly continuous nor subdivisible into discrete parts; rather, its distribution may be irregular. In certain social strata there may be heavy concentrations of individuals, while other strata may be occupied by as few as one individual. Moreover, a change from one social stratum to another may not be along the same vertical line defining a given criterion. A change from one occupation to another, for instance, may entail a considerable change in income status without any actual change in occupational status. Likewise, the same degree or amount of change at different strata within a given criterion may simultaneously entail different amounts of change in other criteria.

Gross's analysis deals with but a few of the many possible questions springing from the basic query: Are classes real groups or statistical strata? For example, are classes subdivisions on a homogeneous continuum of characteristics or are they combinations of heterogeneous attributes? If classes are subdivisions on a homogeneous continuum, is their distribution more like a continuous series with arbitrary points of demarcation or are they more like natural groupings with differentiating regions? If classes are natural groupings, must their characteristics necessarily be attributes? Even if all "reality" (defined by objective criteria) can be reduced to a continuous distribution of many variables, do people think this way? Or do people think and act in terms of class categories, thus eliciting categorical differences when responding to one another?

TOWARD THE CODIFICATION OF CLASS CONCEPTS

As with the basic concepts of social stratification and social differentiation, much variation exists in the conceptualization of class. The analytical essays and empirical studies presented in this chapter are ample evidence of the divergent ways in which class concepts are interpreted and employed in research. To mention one general source of confusion, different phenomena are often designated by the term *social class* and similar phenomena are referred to by such labels as *social stratum, social status,* and *social class.*

The following paper by John Coleman, "A Paradigm for the Study of Social Strata," examines some of the implications of the varying meanings and uses of class concepts. Through the device of a paradigm he presents six major stratification perspectives. Noting that different types of empirical categories are included in such perspectives, he indicates the kinds of methodological operations that should follow (but often do not) from them.

Coleman's contribution summarizes the issues dealt with so far in this chapter. These include the distinctions and relationships between stratification variables and associated variables, the continuum-category controversy, the significance of objective compared to subjective approaches to the study of class, and the general problem of the relationship between class concepts and research methods.

A PARADIGM FOR THE STUDY OF SOCIAL STRATA*

John A. Coleman, S. J.

Alma College, University of Santa Clara

.... Nowhere in sociological discourse is terminological ambiguity so apparent as in the area of social stratification. Thus, for example, social scientists debate whether social strata are real groups or statistical categories.[1] While some sociologists use the term *social stratum*—or *social class*—to refer to a prestige phenomenon, others employ the same term to speak about cultural, influence, psychological, or associational phenomena. The tacit assumption seems to be that, whatever perspective we take on social strata, we are converging on the same social reality. No wonder, then, that the terms social stratum and social class have come to be ambiguous, catch-all phrases. The proposed paradigm attempts to clear up this ambiguity by enumerating several different perspectives, noting both the different types of categories dealt with and the different ways stratification phenomena are made operational when perspectives are changed. Hopefully, once the necessary distinctions between these varying perspectives are defined, we can observe the extent to which they converge on the same social reality.

Table 1 presents a paradigm for the study of social strata. The reader is advised to glance over the paradigm at the outset, returning to it when he has concluded reading the article which explains it.

THE PERSPECTIVE OF PRESTIGE

I propose that status and prestige are equivalent synonyms in stratification research. These terms must be defined operationally. In general, all prestige studies assume that prestige "is estimable and that it lies in the opinions of others."[2] Prestige is not an innate quality of an occupation, clique, religious or ethnic group, or statistical category. Consequently, the method of operationalizing the perspective of prestige lies in polling the opinion of a selected group of raters concerning "the social standing" or individuals, occupations, or social groups in society....

What is the unit of analysis in prestige studies, real groups, or statistical categories? On this question, sociologists divide. Some, like Hollingshead and W. L. Warner, claim to have uncovered the real social structures of the communities which they studied.[3] On the other hand,

* From John A. Coleman, S. J., "A Paradigm for the Study of Social Strata," *Sociology and Social Research*, 50 (April 1966), 338–50.

[1] Gerhard E. Lenski, "American Social Classes: Statistical Strata or Social Groups?," *American Journal of Sociology*, 58 (September 1952), 139–44.

[2] Paul K. Hatt, "Occupation and Social Stratification," *American Journal of Sociology*, 55 (May 1950), 533–43.

[3] Hollingshead, *Elmtown's Youth* (New York: John Wiley & Sons, Inc., 1949); W. Lloyd Warner and Paul S. Lunt, *The Social Life of a Modern Community* (New Haven, Conn.: Yale University Press, 1941).

TABLE 1. A PARADIGM FOR THE STUDY OF SOCIAL STRATA

Perspective	Type of Category Studied	Principal Research Device	Nomenclature	Unit of Analysis
1. Prestige	Statistical category (reality is in the mind of the raters)	Use of raters	Prestige groups	Groups, real or statistical, ranked in a hierarchy of prestige
2. Culture	People who share symbolic meanings, ways of doing, thinking	Questionnaires, interviews, participant observation of behavior differences	Strata (culture)	Populations with demonstrably different symbolic systems of norms
3. Associational	Cliques, face-to-face groups	Sociometric techniques to measure interaction	Cliques	Real primary group in interaction
4. Influence: power/authority	Real interest groups in conflict	Re-creation of decision-making processes	Social classes	Interest groups in conflict
5. Demography	Statistical category (reality is in the mind of the sociologist)	Useful ordering of census data into discrete categories	Demographic categories	Whole populations divided into demographic categories
6. Social psychology	Reference groups to which I think that I belong (reality is in the mind of the self-rater)	Self-rating	Strata (reference group)	Perceptions of samples of the population

Lenski, in his study of a Connecticut community, found lack of consistency among his raters as to the number of strata and the criteria used to determine the divisions between strata in the community. Hence, he concluded that prestige studies only uncover statistical, not real, groups.[4] Similarly, Lasswell claimed that "his sample of residents did not conceptualize as rigid a pattern of social class stratification as researchers using selected raters have reported to exist in other communities."[5]

If we carefully analyze our method of operationalizing prestige (i.e., use of

[4] Lenski, *op. cit.*

[5] Thomas E. Lasswell, "Reply by T. E. Lasswell," *American Sociological Review*, 10 (February 1955), 83.

raters) we see that the perspective of prestige always uncovers a reality of social perception—what lies in the minds of raters. The units of analysis which are ranked according to relative estimation can be either real groups (cliques in a local high school, local families, the socioreligious communities of America) or statistical categories such as occupations, demographic classifications, etc. The hierarchy, however, into which raters rank these groups or categories tells us nothing directly about real qualities of these groups. Since the operational method yields subjective estimations of raters, even when raters rank real groups, the resultant prestige rankings are statistical categories, not real qualities of these groups. Indeed, as Lasswell and Lenski point out, the perception of prestige ranking varies as we vary our raters. Only when the sociologist abandons the perspective of prestige (i.e., the estimation of raters as to the perceived ordered hierarchy of disparate real groups or statistical categories), can he speak about real social structures. . . .

In the paradigm I suggest the term *prestige group* to refer to the units of analysis, whether real groups or statistical categories, when they are viewed from the perspective of prestige.[6]

THE PERSPECTIVE OF CULTURE

I take culture to mean an integrated system of norms or prescribed behaviors which a population shares.[7]

It is meaningless, from the perspective of culture, to rank on a scale demonstrably different symbolic systems of thinking and doing as if one culture were higher or better than another. In itself, one culture is simply different, not "better than" another. Whenever social stratification studies use cultural phenomena as a criterion for ranking strata, although their units of analysis are microcultures or stratacultures, their perspective is the perspective of prestige. A ranking of strata on the basis of cultural factors does not tell us anything about the cultural differences between strata, only about the prestige attached to proposed cultural units. Unfortunately, many social stratification studies confuse these two perspectives.

In order to demonstrate cultural differentiation between strata, the social scientist must first determine disparate populations and, then, demonstrate that they share different integrated systems of norms. It is to be noted, therefore, that the culture perspective in existing social stratification studies is always a dependent category. Only after the sociologist has identified discrete strata from a perspective other than culture—usually from the demographic perspective—can he ask whether these populations also differ culturally. A review of the journal articles on social stratification from the culture perspective bears out this point. Bernstein found that strata which he had already differentiated from a demographic perspective also exhibited distinct language traits.[8] Hol-

6 I have purposely avoided the term *status-group* since status is a term which is used for purposes other than its use in stratification research as in the correlative couplet, *status-role*.

7 For this definition of culture cf. J.

Milton Yinger, "Contraculture and Subculture," *American Sociological Review*, 25 (October 1960), 625.

8 B. B. Bernstein, "Language and Social Class," *British Journal of Sociology*, 21 (1960).

lingshead, differentiating his population on the basis of the I.S.P. (a two-factor demographic index), uncovered strata differences in family stability.[9] Assuming a difference between middle-class and working-class populations, neither term being carefully defined, Green spoke of class differences in child-raising practices.[10] Sociologists have asserted that strata differ in the use of leisure,[11] drinking mores,[12] fashion in clothes.[13] In each instance, discrete strata were first determined by some perspective other than culture, then viewed from a cultural perspective.

It is difficult to operationalize the culture perspective in stratification studies. Following Clark Wissler's "Universal Culture Patterns," categories of speech, material traits, family system, religious system may be employed. Random samples of populations drawn from demographic categories or real groups may be analyzed in terms of behavior either by questionnaires and interviews or by participant observation. Since the initial unit of analysis for the culture perspective may be either a statistical category or a real group, the paradigm suggests that this unit of analysis be described by the generic term *population*. To the extent that a population is shown to have a distinctive culture system, it ceases to be merely statistical in its reality. It may be termed "a people" and is so described in the paradigm under the heading "type of category studied."[14] The paradigm suggests the phrase *strataculture* to refer to populations viewed from the perspective of culture. This term is used both to point to the cultural perspective and distinguish stratacultures from the culture patterns which the larger society shares. It also avoids the loaded implications of dependency contained in the prefix of the more widely used term *subculture*.

THE ASSOCIATIONAL PERSPECTIVE

Are strata real groups or sociological constructs? The associational perspective tends to yield the answer, real groups. How is this perspective made operational? Some sociologists start by determining strata from some perspective other than association, again usually by means of demographic categories. They then analyze these strata to discover the extent to which members of a stratum intramarry and associate with one another.[15] On the other hand, the social scientist can take real cliques and friendship groups

[9] August B. Hollingshead, "Class Differences in Family Stability," *The Annals of the American Academy of Political and Social Sciences*, 272 (1950), 39–46.

[10] Arnold V. Green, "The Middle Class Male Child and Neurosis," *American Sociological Review*, 11 (February 1946), 31–41.

[11] R. Clyde White, "Social Class Differences in the Use of Leisure," *American Journal of Sociology*, 61 (September 1955), 145–50.

[12] John Dollard, "Drinking Mores of the Social Classes," *Quarterly Journal of Studies on Alcohol* (1945), 95–101.

[13] Bernard Barber and Lyle S. Lobel, "Fashion in Women's Clothes in the American Social System," *Social Forces*, 31 (December 1952), 124–31.

[14] For the distinction between a population and a people, see Robin M. Williams, Jr., *Strangers Next Door* (Englewood Cliffs, N.J.: Prentice-Hall, Inc., 1964), p. 18.

[15] George A. Lundberg and Lenore Dickson, "Selective Association Among Ethnic Groups in a High School Population," *American Sociological Review*, 17 (February 1952), 23–35; Floyd Dotson, "Patterns of Voluntary Association Among Urban Working-Class Families," *American Sociological Review*, 16 (October 1951), 687–93.

just as they exist in a community. Having discovered who associates with or marries whom, he ascertains the stratum level of individual members in the clique. Once again, this is done by using some perspective other than association.[16] It is evident, therefore, that the associational perspective is always a dependent category in stratification research. . . .

Two methodological cautions are necessary when using this perspective. First, although members of the same stratum tend to intermarry and associate with one another, association is never totally exclusive between strata. Some strata show higher rates of in-group preference than others. Indeed, Ellis found that populations of some strata actually associate more with members of other strata than with individuals drawn from their own stratum.[17]

Secondly, it is essential to remember that the units of analysis for the associational perspective are always much smaller than the units of analysis employed for other perspectives in stratification research. A clique of ten persons may be drawn entirely from a college graduate population. This clique, therefore, is a real group in interaction which happens to coincide with a sample of the demographic category, college graduates. It would be faulty logic to infer from one such sample or thousands of similar exclusively college graduate cliques that the demographic category of all college graduates is itself a real group in inter-

action. Some studies of social strata, by failing to clarify their varying perspectives, tend to mislead students into believing that whole demographic categories are associational, in the sense of whole real groups in interaction.

THE PERSPECTIVE OF INFLUENCE

Influence may be defined as the chances "of a man or group of men to realize their own will" even against opposition.[18] Influence is either legitimate or illegitimate. Individuals or groups who possess legitimate influence —the legitimation of which derives from law, constitutional grounding, custom, or consensus—have *authority*. Illegitimate influence is denominated as *power*. Authority and power, therefore, are subspecies of the generic term *influence*.

The sociologist, interested in group phenomena, is not concerned with individual authority or power as such. Rather, he is convinced that "individual power is always worked out within some larger framework of institutional power." He recognizes that "individuals of similar interests combine to achieve their ends, and such combinations of interlaced values and interests form subsystems of power." The power or authority disposed of by any given individual is "viewed less as an index of personal power than as an indicator of the existence of social subsystems of power to which he belongs and from which he derives his power."[19]

---

16 This is the way A. B. Hollingshead proceeded in his study of high school cliques in *Elmtown's Youth*, pp. 208–17.

17 Robert A. Ellis, "Social Stratification and Social Relations: An Empirical Test of the Disjunctiveness of Social Classes," *American Sociological Review*, 22 (October 1957), 570–78.

18 This is Max Weber's definition of power. Cf. H. H. Gerth and C. W. Mills, eds., *From Max Weber: Essays in Sociology* (New York: Oxford University Press, Inc., 1946), p. 180.

19 Robert Presthus, *Men at the Top*

How do we operationalize the perspective of influence? There have been two competing techniques proposed by sociologists as a means of converging on influence. Floyd Hunter in his pioneering work, *Community Power Structure*, strongly espoused the reputational technique to determine influence.[20] . . .

Polsby and his associates have uncovered major methodological flaws in the reputational method of determining influence. The reputational method assumes that a reputation for influence is synonymous with actual influence. A second faulty assumption of this technique is that the influence of leader-nominees is equal for all issues. Thirdly, the reputational method tends to rely on panels of nominators overdrawn from samples derived from the business community. Yet, businessmen have generally underestimated the extent of political power in community decision-making. Finally, a reputational scale is unable to indicate whether the "forty most powerfuls" are conspiring together or against one another.[21] . . .

The debate between Polsby and Hunter concerning the appropriate method for operationalizing the influence perspective in stratification research underscores again the need for a paradigm for the study of social strata. This debate need never have arisen if researchers maintained the distinctions between the varying perspectives presented in our paradigm. For, it is evident that the reputational technique in influence research is a variant of the method employed by prestige studies, i.e., use of raters. Consequently, the technique itself is designed to uncover a reality of prestige not of actual influence. What the reputational method yields, in fact, are subjective estimations of a panel of raters as to the perceived *prestige* of groups or individuals with respect to influence. The type of group analyzed by the method is a statistical category whose reality exists in the minds of raters. . . .

This author shares Ralf Dahrendorf's concern for rehabilitating the term *social class* from its morass of conflicting and multivariant usages by returning to the original heuristic purpose for which Karl Marx employed the term without, however, falling prey to the narrow ideology of doctrinaire Marxism. Marx was not so much interested in examining the many layered cross sections of society (the stratification perspective) as in uncovering the processes of social change due to social conflict. Dahrendorf distinguishes the two perspectives by stating that "class is always a category for purposes of the dynamics of social conflict and its structural roots, and as such has to be separated strictly from *stratum* as a category for purposes of describing hierarchical systems at a given point of time."[22] For Dahrendorf, society since Marx is organized into imperatively coordinated associations with defined chains of command and areas of legitimate influence. Legitimate influence or authority is by its nature a dichoto-

---

(New York: Oxford University Press, Inc., 1964), pp. 5–6.

[20] *Community Power Structure* (Chapel Hill, N.C.: University of North Carolina Press, 1953).

[21] For these criticisms of the reputational technique cf. Raymond Wolfinger, "Reputation and Reality in the Study of Community Power," *American Sociological Review*, 25 (October 1960), 636–41.

---

[22] *Class and Class Conflict in Industrial Society* (Palo Alto, Calif.: The Stanford University Press, 1959), p. 76.

mous concept: One either has it or he does not. Influence, of course, is not a dichotomous reality. Social change, to the extent that it arises out of conflict, is a process in which the major actors are interest groups. Conflict in decision-making, where it exists, takes place either between interest groups with authority and interest groups with power (legitimate vs. illegitimate influence) or between interest groups, none of which have authority, locked in a power battle to determine whose influence will be legitimated by continued *de facto* influence in community decision-making.

The "even against opposition" phrase in the definition of influence points to the fact that the perspective of influence is connected with conflict. The paradigm reserves the much abused term *social class* to refer to the units of analysis (interest groups in conflict) when viewed from the perspective of influence. This reservation of the term *social class* to refer to strata in conflict over community decision-making may seem too narrow, but it has the virtue of preserving the original Marxian heuristic intent for which the term was first, historically, employed.

The perspective of influence, just as the perspectives of culture and association, is often used as a dependent category. Sociologists should explore the extent to which demographic categories based on economics or education also represent conflicting interest groups. This is best done in the area of political sociology and the analysis of voting behavior.[23]

THE PERSPECTIVE OF DEMOGRAPHY

Demography is the most widely used and easily handled perspective in stratification research. Most community studies rely almost exclusively on demography to determine their strata.[24] The unit of analysis studied by the demographic perspective is some whole population (a small community, standard metropolitan area, the United States) divided into demographic categories based on income, educational achievement, occupation, intelligence, etc. In itself, the reality of a demographic category is always statistical. The very existence of discrete demographic categories depends on the constructual activity of the sociologist.

Of course, the means of operationalizing the demographic perspective is very easy. The social scientist merely decrees some useful ordering of census data into discrete categories. The dividing line between the categories is arbitrary. Thus, for example, if income categories are divided, it is impossible to determine a priori whether unit intervals of $1,000 per annum are superior to unit intervals of $1,500. Clarity, parsimony, and research utility are the only criteria which can determine whether one system of conceptualizing census data is superior to another. The Edwards index is perhaps the best known demographic scale used in strata research.[25] Most demographic scales suffer, in Bernard Barber's words, "from the coarseness of scaling

---

23 For an analysis of interest group behavior in voting cf. Seymour M. Lipset, *Political Man* (Garden City, N.Y.: Doubleday & Company, Inc., 1960), especially pp. 7–9.

24 Both Warner's I.S.C. and Hollingshead's I.S.P. are essentially demographic indices.

25 Alba E. Edwards, *Comparative Occupational Statistics for the United States, 16th Census, 1940* (Washington, D.C.: Government Printing Office, 1943).

that is inherent in their broad and overlapping categories."[26]

The paradigm suggests the nonpretentious term *demographic category* to refer to populations viewed from the perspective of demography. The term has the merit of protecting researchers from the danger of reifying their concepts. Demographic categories, as such, are always statistical, never real, groups. Demographic categories can be demonstrated to coincide with real groups if some perspective other than demography is employed in viewing them, e.g., culture, influence, associational. If, however, we limit our perspective in stratification research to demography, it is meaningless to ask whether strata are real or statistical groups.

THE PERSPECTIVE OF SOCIAL PSYCHOLOGY

Richard Centers has been most closely associated with the perspective of social psychology in stratification research. His units of analysis are perceptions of random samples of the population who are asked to rate themselves in terms of the social stratum to which they think they belong (upper, middle, working, lower). The type of group studied is a symbolic reference group whose reality and definition exists in the mind of the responding self-rater.[27]

Many of the same methodological problems encountered in prestige studies are also inherent in research by self-rating, especially inconsistency as to the number of strata and the criteria used to determine them. The perspective of social psychology is not simply identifiable with other stratification perspectives. John Haer compared the classification techniques used by W. Lloyd Warner—the demographic index, I.S.C., yielding an "objective" perspective on social strata—with the subjective, self-rating techniques of Centers. While the two perspectives relate statistically, they are not identical.[28]

Whether the researcher uses open-ended or forced-choice questions in his self-rating stratification pool, he must in some way define for his respondents what he means by strata or whatever synonym he chooses to point to stratification phenomena. His dependence on a definition of stratum drawn from some other perspective than the perspective of social psychology insures that the researcher's use of the social psychology perspective will be a dependent category in stratification research. The most basic flaw in most self-rating pools which take the perspective of social psychology is that they fail to define precisely in asking their questions what they mean by stratum or class. Unless they carefully define their terms in asking self-rating questions, sociologists can never be sure that the answers of any two respondents are commensurable. The term *strata reference group* is employed in the paradigm to refer to populations studied from the perspective of social psychology in stratification research.

---

[26] *Social Stratification: A Comparative Analysis of Structure and Process* (New York: Harcourt, Brace and Company, 1957), p. 173.

[27] *The Psychology of Social Classes: A Study of Class Consciousness* (Princeton, N.J.: Princeton University Press, 1949).

[28] "A Comparative Study of the Classification Techniques of Warner and Centers," *American Sociological Review*, 20 (December 1955), 689–92.

CONCLUSION

This article does not pretend to solve, with its proposed paradigm, all problems in stratification research. Its modest aim is to achieve some clarity in conceptualizing and speaking about strata. Throughout the article the term *stratum* has been used as a non-defined general term to refer to the hierarchically ordered levels of society viewed at a given point of time from any one of these six different perspectives. If further research shows that these different perspectives do verge on the same social reality, the use of a general term such as stratum to refer to this reality is valid. If, however, the varying perspectives do not converge on the same reality, a general term must be abandoned in favor of six specialized terms such as those listed in the paradigm under the heading *nomenclature*.

Our analysis of problems of terminology and methodology associated with each perspective makes evident the need to keep these perspectives distinct. Our further research task is the study of statistical correlations between these perspectives along the lines suggested by John Haer.[29] It should be helpful in pursuing this task to recall which perspectives are, by their nature, dependent categories and which not.

---

[29] *Ibid.*

RESEARCH OPERATIONS

Previously we noted that a major reason for sociological interest in class is the assumption that class variables play a causal role in behavior. This assumption is based on a large body of research which shows the association between position in the class system and a variety of phenomena of concern to sociologists. Although many students give principal attention to theories of the origins and general nature of stratification, the greatest interest is in the consequences of social class for the individual and the group.[1]

Since knowledge of the individual's place in the class system is commonly held to be significant for understanding social behavior, a key problem in stratification research is the determination of class position. Essentially what is required is a description of the social-class system by means of criteria that are adequate for determining the placement of individuals (or groups) within it. The remainder of this chapter reviews and illustrates alternative approaches to the implementation of such criteria.

---

[1] Most studies of the class concept treat it as an independent variable and use other behavioral characteristics as dependent variables. Although such studies at least implicitly assume that class "causes" certain forms of behavior, they seldom provide fully developed explanatory schemes.

Basic Methods of Class Placement

Three basic methods are used for determining the position of an individual in the class system: the objective, the self-placement, and the reputational. The *objective* approach calls for placement on the basis of criteria determined by the investigator. Typically, such objective indicators as occupation, income, and education are employed. The choice of criteria usually reflects the researcher's preferences and the nature of the research problem. A single criterion or multiple criteria may be the basis. (We discuss this approach further below.)

In the *self-placement* approach, individuals assess their own position in the stratification system. Some procedures use open-ended questions in which various classes are enumerated; the individual designates the one with which he identifies. The assumptions underlying this approach are that class consciousness exists at some level of awareness and that individuals are able to designate the class with which they identify. As we indicated in an earlier discussion of class concepts, Centers is the primary advocate of the self-placement approach. He and others see a strong association between an individual's subjective class identification and the kinds of beliefs, values, and attitudes he holds. According to this theory, the association between class based upon self-placement and various behavioral items is greater than the association between objective or other indices of class and behavioral items.

The *reputational* approach rests upon the following general procedure. Respondents known as prestige judges are selected from the community to be investigated. Selection is usually based upon the respondents' extensive knowledge of persons in the community. These informants then rank everyone in the community in as many class categories as they consider necessary. All persons placed in the same category are considered members of the same class. If the judges know everyone and agree on both the number of classes and the placement of persons, the class structure can be identified and the occupants of each class determined. Here the implied concept of class is simply that a social class is what people in the community say it is. The application of the reputational approach is limited to relatively small communities because it depends upon the selection of judges who know most of the people in the community.[2]

The reputational approach stems primarily from research carried out by Warner and his associates for the "Yankee City" series. In *Social Class in America* (essentially a manual for the empirical study of class) Warner describes in detail

---

[2] Although the subjective emphasis is more commonly associated with the self-placement method, both it and the reputational approach are based upon subjective evaluation. In the self-placement method subjectivity arises from the individual's evaluation of his own position, and in the reputational method it arises from a panel of judges who determine the class standing of others.

The reputational method, especially as it has been employed by the Warner school, has been subjected to great criticism over the past two decades. Of the many critiques perhaps the most thorough is Kornhauser's analysis of Warner's method. Ruth Rosner Kornhauser, "The Warner Approach to Social Stratification," in Bendix and Lipset, *op. cit.*, pp. 224–55.

the research procedures he employed. The excerpt below summarizes his method of Evaluated Participation.

THE METHOD OF "EVALUATED PARTICIPATION"*

W. Lloyd Warner

Michigan State University

The method of Evaluated Participation (E.P.), comprising several rating techniques, is posed on the propositions that those who interact in the social system of a community evaluate the participation of those around them, that the place where an individual participates is evaluated, and that the members of the community are explicitly or implicitly aware of the ranking and translate their evaluations of such social participation into social-class ratings that can be communicated to the investigator. It is, therefore, the duty of the field man to use his interviewing skill to elicit the necessary information and to analyze his data with the requisite techniques for determining social class, thereby enabling the status analyst to determine the levels of stratification present and to rank any member of the community. . . .

Each of the rating techniques combined in the E.P. method for stratifying a community and for placing families and individuals at their proper level in the status system of a community can play a decisive part in the process of determining the social strati-

* From W. Lloyd Warner, *Social Class in America* (New York: Harper & Row, Publishers, 1960), pp. 35–39.

fication of a community or determining the status of an individual or family.

The status analyst uses six techniques for rating an individual's social-class position. They are:

1. *Rating by matched agreements* (of several informants on the placement of many people in the several classes). In interviews with informants of diverse social background the status analyst obtains a Social-Class Configuration (rank order) of named social classes from each informant. He first examines the rank orders recognized in the several interviews to determine the degree of correspondence among them. When this is done and the correspondence is high (as it usually is), the next step is taken. Social-Class Configurations are ordinarily accompanied by lists of names of individual persons volunteered by the informants. The names on each list are always assigned to, and distributed through, the several classes. Many of the same names appear in two or more informants' interviews, thus making it possible for the analyst to match and count pairs of agreements and disagreements among the informants about the class positions of people in the community. When the correspondence between the ranking of classes by

different informants is complete or very high and when the count of matched agreements of informants on the class positions of a large number of people is also high, the analyst is assured that the class system he is studying has a given number of classes, is strong, and pervades the whole community; he also knows his class ratings of the individuals listed are likely to be highly accurate. For simplicity, this technique of matching class hierarchies and pairs of class assignments of subjects will be called *matched agreements*.

2. *Rating by symbolic placement.* An individual is rated by the analyst as being in a particular social class because he is identified with certain superior or inferior symbols by informants. We shall call this method of rating *symbolic placement*.

3. *Rating by status reputation.* An individual (or his family) is assigned to a given class by the analyst because (informants say) he has a reputation for engaging in activities and possessing certain traits which are considered to be superior or inferior. For convenience, this rating will be called *status reputation*.

4. *Rating by comparison.* The subject (or his family) is rated by the analyst as being in a particular class because informants assert he is equal, superior, or inferior to others whose social-class position has been previously determined. This technique of comparing the subject's status with the known class position of another will be called *comparison*.

5. *Rating by simple assignment to a class.* The subject (or his family) is rated by the analyst as being in a particular class because one or more qualified informants assign the individual to that particular class category; only one class is mentioned, and there

is no explicit reference to the other classes which compose the whole system. We distinguish this technique from matched agreements, first, because the analyst's operations are somewhat different from those used in matched agreements, and second, because the considerations of the informants are very different from those made in supplying information for matched agreements.

6. *Rating by institutional membership.* The subject is assigned to a particular status by the analyst because in the interviews of informants he is said to be a member of certain institutions which are ranked as superior or inferior. The institutions used for such a rating are families, cliques, associations, and churches. Hereafter, we will refer to this rating technique as *institutional membership* or *real interconnectedness*. The use of the latter term emphasizes the fact that memberships in these various institutions are interconnected and part of the class structure.

From the description of the six techniques of rating it is apparent that the analyst does not impose his ranking upon the people of the town but, on the contrary, must devise techniques of rating which will translate the criteria and judgments of the informants (townspeople) into explicit, verifiable results which will correspond with the class realities of the community. We must try to see the problem from the point of view of the informants for they are the final authorities about the realities of American social class. At the risk of appearing repetitive let us briefly review the questions that the people of a town think about (and which appear in their interviews) when they rate each other (by Evaluated Participation):

Is the person included in the membership of a particular family, clique, association, or church, or is he excluded?

Is the status of an individual superior, inferior, or equal to the status of some other individual or family whose status has been previously established?

Is the person (or family) identified with well-known (and easily used) symbols of superiority or inferiority (so that the attachment of the symbol to the individual places him in a particular social class)?

Is the person (or family) in activities or does he have traits that are superior or inferior which give him a superior or inferior reputation?

Those informants who are explicitly conscious of each social-class level and see all of them as a hierarchy of superior and inferior social levels ask: Which social class is the person in? Is it the upper, middle, or lower class? These are the questions which Americans ask and answer when they rate each other by Evaluated Participation.

Researchers have also used various combinations of the objective and subjective approaches in determining class placement. In some cases, the theoretical rationale for the use of one approach or another is relatively explicit, but often few clues indicate why the researcher is employing one type of class measure rather than another. A presumed basis for the selection of indexes is their predictive utility for the behavior of particular concern to the investigator. The selection below by Robert Ellis, W. Clayton Lane, and Virginia Olesen describes the rationale for and development of one of the very few indexes of class utilizing subjective as well as objective criteria. This paper is followed by John Haer's "Predictive Utility of Five Indices of Social Stratification."

THE INDEX OF CLASS POSITION*†

Robert A. Ellis, *University of Oregon*

W. Clayton Lane, *San Jose State College*

Virginia Olesen, *University of California, San Francisco Medical Center*

The Index of Class Position (ICP) described in this paper was developed

to provide an easily applied intercommunity measure of stratification

* From Robert A. Ellis, W. Clayton Lane, and Virginia Olesen, "The Index of Class Position: An Improved Intercommunity Measure of Stratification," *American Sociological Review*, 28 (April 1963), 271–75. Reprinted by permission of the American Sociological Association.

† Revised version of a paper read at the annual meeting of the Pacific Sociological Association, April 1962. The research has

been supported by grants from the Society for the Investigation of Human Ecology, the Social Science Research Council, Stanford University Research Funds, and the National Institute of Mental Health (M-4968). Appreciation is expressed to Kenji Ima and John Koval for their assistance in analysis of the data. The authors are also indebted to Robert Dubin and William Robinson for their helpful suggestions in the revisions of the manuscript.

that would improve upon the accuracy of estimating an individual's position in the class structure. The need for such a measure arose from research being done in the college setting, which often makes existing stratification procedures impracticable.

That college undergraduates characteristically establish residence on campus, often at a considerable distance from their homes, precludes employing a number of standard procedures. Eliminated by this consideration are: (1) the prestige rating technique in its various forms,[1] (2) Warner's Index of Status Characteristics,[2] and (3) socioeconomic status scales of the Chapin and Sewell prototype[3]—all of which require direct access to the community or home.

The methodological alternatives are further curtailed by the fact that lower-class students are a minority in the college setting[4] and are likely to have acquired many value and attitudinal characteristics of the middle class.[5] This poses a serious question about the feasibility of single-factor indexes inasmuch as their predictive utility in large part stems from the presence of a sizeable lower class sharply differentiated from the middle class.[6]

Hollingshead's two-factor Index of Social Position (ISP)[7] remains the

---

[1] Robert A. Ellis, "The Prestige Rating Technique in Community Stratification Research" in *Human Organization Research*, eds. Richard N. Adams and Jack J. Preiss (Homewood, Ill.: Dorsey Press, 1960). See also Milton M. Gordon, *Social Class in American Sociology* (Durham, N.C.: Duke University Press, 1958), pp. 135–51; Leonard Reissman, *Class in American Society* (Glencoe, Ill.: Free Press, 1959), pp. 125–34.

[2] W. Lloyd Warner, Marcia Meeker, and Kenneth Eells, *Social Class in America* (Chicago: Science Research Associates, 1949), pp. 121–230.

[3] F. Stuart Chapin, "A Quantitative Scale for Rating the Home and Social Environment of Middle Class Families in an Urban Community," *Journal of Educational Psychology*, 19 (February 1928), pp. 99–111; The *Measurement of Social Status by the Use of the Social Status Scale* (Minneapolis: University of Minnesota Press, 1933); William H. Sewell, *The Construction and Standardization of a Scale for the Measurement of the Socio-Economic Status of Oklahoma Farm Families*, Technical Bulletin No. 9 (Oklahoma Agricultural and Mechanical College Agricultural Experiment Station, 1940). See also George Lundberg, *Social Research* (2nd ed.) (New York: Longmans, Green & Co., 1943), pp. 288–309. For a critical survey of socioeconomic

status scales, see Gordon, *op. cit.*, pp. 210–20, and Reissman, *op. cit.*, pp. 117–25.

[4] There is, of course, considerable diversity among colleges and universities in the social composition of their student bodies. While in some schools, such as the one under study in the present report, the lower class represents only a small minority of the total enrollment, there are other institutions —particularly public junior colleges—where the lower class may in fact be in the majority. Cf. Burton R. Clark, *The Open Door College: A Case Study* (New York: McGraw-Hill Book Company, 1960), pp. 51–61; and Robert J. Havighurst and Bernice L. Neugarten, *Society and Education* (Boston: Allyn and Bacon, Inc., 1957), pp. 251–57.

[5] For a cogent discussion of the implications of reference group theory for social mobility, see Robert K. Merton, *Social Theory and Social Structure* (rev. ed.) (Glencoe, Ill.: Free Press, 1957), pp. 260–80, 288–97.

[6] Support for this interpretation is furnished by the frequent practice of dichotomizing stratification indices for tetrachoric correlation analysis without apparently seriously affecting the magnitude of the relationship under scrutiny. See, for example, Joseph A. Kahl and James A. Davis, "A Comparison of Indexes of Socio-Economic Status," *American Sociological Review*, 20 (June 1955), 317–25; Edwin D. Lawson and Walter E. Boek, "Correlations of Indexes of Families' Socio-Economic Status," *Social Forces*, 39 (December 1960), 149–52.

[7] August B. Hollingshead, *Two-Factor Index of Social Position* (privately mimeographed, 1957).

only procedure in common use possibly exempt from these deficiencies. Its two components of occupation and education can be applied on a society-wide basis, and the validity of the composite index score exceeds that yielded by either factor alone. Nevertheless, the utility of ISP is seriously reduced for our purposes by its inclusion of education as a component. One consequence is that the effect of education can no longer be analyzed independently of social class; this poses a serious limitation in the study of college students.[8] A second consequence is to exacerbate the tendency of most indices to elevate the prestige of the professional. For instance, the weight given education means that all college professors are operationally defined as class I. The ·result is a confounding of the upper and upper-middle classes which can be a source of significant measurement error, especially in those more selective institutions where a substantial proportion of the students are from the upper class.

DEVELOPMENT OF ICP

In developing the Index of Class Position, we used occupation as a major component variable because: (1) occupation is consistently the highest correlate of social status; (2) the *prestige* of occupations is judged by the general population with a high degree of consensus; and (3) the prestige of a particular occupation is attached to individual incumbents of that position—although a person's actual social status can fall considerably above or below the model prestige level of the occupation he holds.[9] The latter discrepancy can be attributed to the operation of other status evaluations.[10]

---

8 The confounding effect of education in class measurement has also been cited as an impediment to investigations of social class factors in mental illness. See Howard S. Freeman, "Attitude Toward Mental Illness Among Relatives of Former Patients," *American Sociological Review*, 26 (February 1961), 59–66, and S. M. Miller and Elliot G. Mishler, "Social Class, Mental Illness, and American Psychiatry," *Milbank Memorial Fund Quarterly*, 37 (April 1959), 174–99.

---

9 Cf. Paul K. Hatt, "Occupation and Social Stratification," *American Journal of Sociology*, 55 (May 1950), 533–43.

10 At least three different, though not mutually exclusive, explanations can be advanced for this variation.

A. The first involves the concept of multiple group membership. People participate in a number of different social structures during any one period. The prestige levels of the various positions held are not evaluated in isolation but rather as a totality —an holistic fact that is represented in Kingsley Davis' concept of "station," which is the total combination of prestige "scores" an individual receives for the cluster of positions occupied.

B. The second recognizes the existence of alternative modes of evaluation. An occupational incumbent is not judged exclusively in terms of the position he holds. He is also judged by the way he carries out the role mandates and by the extra-role personal qualities he possesses. These two additional modes of evaluation, which can be designated as *esteem* and *admiration* judgments, serve to reinforce or modify the initial *prestige* gained for incumbency of the occupation.

C. A third possible explanation is provided by the premise that social status is capable of being transferred among individuals (as well as positions). Status transfer can occur within a given generation, as for example when a wife's status within a community is higher or lower than her husband's, or it can occur intergenerationally in the form of lineage.

See John W. Bennet and Melvin M. Tumin, *Social Life: Structure and Function*

The next step was to locate a suitable auxiliary factor that would provide a cross-community measure of an individual's style of life but would be free from the disadvantages of education as a status indicator. Kahl and Davis' analysis of socioeconomic indices suggested the feasibility of substituting Centers' measure of class identification for that of education.[11] These two factors are highly correlated and, when processed by factor and cluster analysis, constitute a statistically distinct subgroup in which components can be treated as interchangeable. Kahl and Davis' data also allay some doubts about the validity of fixed categories for gaining information on "class identification."[12] They find not only that respondents can, and do, class-type themselves in meaningful and systematic fashion with Centers' question but also that such a closed-answer procedure proves superior to one that is open ended.[13]

Still another contribution of Kahl and Davis' research is their demonstration of the feasibility of relying on a more refined set of rating categories than Centers had done for distinguishing among the upper, middle, and lower levels of the middle class. This extension of Centers' procedure from a four-point to a six-point scale serves to increase the validity of class placement possible.

On the basis of these considerations, the decision was made to use occupation and class identification as the two components of the Index of Class Position. The first component is measured by Hollingshead's seven-point scale of occupational prestige, a rationally derived modification of the Alba Edwards' scale.[14] With college students, occupational data are gathered on the students' fathers—the assumption being made that the class status of a college undergraduate is at this stage of his career primarily ascribed by the family.[15]

Data on class identification are obtained by a procedure closely patterned

---

(New York: Alfred M. Knopf, Inc., 1949), pp. 108–9; Kingsley Davis, "Conceptual Analysis of Stratification," *American Sociological Review*, 7 (June 1942), 309–21; Kingsley Davis, *Human Society* (New York: The Macmillan Company, Publishers, 1949); Robert A. Ellis and Thomas C. Keedy, Jr., "Three Dimensions of Status: A Study of Academic Prestige," *Pacific Sociological Review*, 3 (Spring 1960), 23–28; Gordon, *op. cit.*, pp. 175–77, 245–46; Paul K. Hatt, "Stratification in the Mass Society," *American Sociological Review*, 15 (April 1950), 216–22; Albert J. Reiss, Jr., *Occupations and Social Status* (New York: The Free Press of Glencoe, Inc., 1961), pp. 140–51.

[11] Kahl and Davis, *op. cit.*

[12] Cf. Neal Gross, "Social Class Identification in the Urban Community," *American Sociological Review*, 18 (August 1953), 398–404.

[13] Kahl and Davis, *op. cit.*, p. 325.

---

[14] August B. Hollingshead, *op. cit.*, pp. 2–8; August B. Hollingshead and Frederick C. Redlich, *Social Class and Mental Illness: A Community Study* (New York: John Wiley & Sons, Inc., 1958), pp. 390–91.

[15] The task of gaining occupational information in adequate detail to insure reliable and reasonably accurate coding is more difficult than the stratification literature would indicate. Our experience has shown a minimum of fifteen questions need to be used. Even with these safeguards, some guesswork is involved in using Hollingshead's scale for occupational classification. While indicative of the need for still further refinement in occupational measurement, the objectivity of Hollingshead's procedure compares favorably with alternative scales. For example, for the Stanford data ($N = 194$) reported in this paper the percentage of instances guesswork was involved in occupational classification by four selected occupational scales was as follows:

Hollingshead	9 per cent
Centers	11 per cent
Warner	17 per cent
North-Hatt	36 per cent

after Kahl and Davis' modification of Centers' question, which, by its three-fold partition of middle-class status, allows a more refined series of class judgments. The class identification question is phrased as follows for use with college students:

An American social scientist has made a study of the United States which indicated that in this country there are four major social classes: the middle, the lower, the working, and the upper social classes. In which of these social classes would you say your family belongs?

[If answer is middle, then probe question is asked].

Would you say your family belongs to the upper-middle, middle-middle, or lower-middle social class?

Replies are numerically weighted so as to yield a five-point scale ranging from a score of 1 for upper class to a score of 5 for working class. No final decision has been reached concerning the weight to be assigned the sixth category of lower class since it has only been rarely used by college students in the researches we have done. Until such time as empirical evidence can be presented to corroborate Centers' thesis that a lower-class response is a distinct status level below that of working class, our suggestion is to treat the two as numerically equivalent.

Class identification and occupational scores are summated to yield a total ICP score ranging from 2 to 12.[16] These scores are divided to obtain the six class levels presented in Table 1.

The use of a total ICP score of 2 for designating a class I position means

---

16 A product moment correlation of 0.70 was obtained between the two scales in the present study.

TABLE 1.   CLASS LEVELS ARRANGED BY ICP SCORES

ICP Level	Range of Scores	Social Class
I	2	Upper
II	3–4	Upper-middle
III	5–7	Middle
IV	8–9	Lower-middle
V	10	Upper-lower
VI	11–12	Lower-lower

that for a person to qualify as class I with this index the head of household must be a proprietor of a large concern or must have a high-level managerial or professional position; and, in addition, his status circumstances must be perceived by the son or daughter (or, in theory, by himself) as upper class. On face validity, this seems a realistic requirement for upper-class status and far preferable to the situation in which all large proprietors and professional or high-level managerial people are automatically class-typed as being in the top social stratum.

At the lower range of ICP scores, the 9–10 division separates the lower class from the lower-middle. Thus, for a person to be categorized in the lower strata, he must be employed in a blue-collar occupation and must be perceived by the son or daughter (or, in theory, by himself) as working class. This offers a far more realistic basis for demarcating the lower class than is ordinarily the case. It considers the fact that in our society, with its high rate of geographic movement, its high standard of living, and a general faith in the intergenerational opportunity for success, the blue collar–white collar division is far from fixed and disparate. That a person is a blue-collar worker is not, by itself, sufficient grounds to place him in the lower stratum. In other respects he may have acquired a middle-class orientation to the world around him, so that other persons will view him as middle class, and, in turn, he will regard himself as such. Consequently, he would be distinguished from other blue-collar workers who perceive themselves as situated in lower- or working-class circumstances.

Thus, underlying the ICP procedure are two major assumptions. The first is that social status—and, hence, class position—is a perceptual phenomenon based on the mutual evaluations people make of each other's social importance in the community or society. The cues for these evaluations are provided by the symbolic manifestation of a culturally defined, group-shared style of life. Occupation is useful as a stratification indicator, but its invariability in the individual case needs to be offset by some additional factor sensitive to many other considerations that contribute to the overall social status a person is accorded. This, it would seem, is the merit of relying on class identification as the second component of ICP: It provides a means for estimating the respondent's own definition of his status situation, which, by the additional assumption of a "looking glass self" conception of status, should mirror the status assigned the individual by the larger community or society.

VALIDATION OF ICP

At the minimum, two conditions have to be satisfied before use of ICP as a stratification technique is empirically warranted. Evidence is needed, first, that ICP does measure the phenomenon of social class and, second, that it does so demonstrably better than the ISP procedure it was developed to replace.

Method. Data for these tests were gathered in the course of interviews with 194 Stanford freshmen soon after their matriculation in the fall of 1958. Of this total, 160 (ninety-nine males and sixty-one females) were selected by means of a standard probability sample. The remaining thirty-four students (twenty-seven males and seven females) represent an oversample taken of all other freshmen matriculants not included in the original sample who were in the three bottom class levels of ICP. The latter step was necessitated by the decided skewness of the Stanford population toward the upper-middle class. The oversample is included in the analysis to follow so as to provide a broader range of status inequalities.

Questions asked of the students about their family and themselves, as well as giving data for stratifying the sample by ICP and ISP, furnished six simply dichotomized stratification correlates that were used as validation criteria.[17] These attributes, stated in their positive form, are listed below:

---

17 Essentially, we are testing the construct validity of ICP. (Cf. Lee J. Cronbach and Paul E. Meehl, "Construct Validity in Psychological Tests," *Psychological Bulletin*, 52 [July 1955], 281–302.) This validity test does not require demonstrating a one-to-one correspondence between ICP and any single empirical indicator, but rather that there is a generally consistent relationship between ICP and the total of social, cultural, and economic correlates of class position which have been sampled. Without an agreed upon universe of stratification correlates, the choice of validating criteria is of necessity somewhat arbitrary, and the sampling, imperfect. Some justification for the specific choices made can be found in the stratification literature, but perhaps the best single evidence favoring their use is provided *post hoc* by the findings in Tables 3 and 4 that each criterion does bear a strong and systematic relationship to the two indices of social class.

1. Attending college on scholarship.
2. Having a mother who is employed outside the home.[18]
3. Clear expectations by student of having a job better than his father's.[19]
4. Affiliation with a high-status Protestant denomination (i.e., Congregational, Episcopal, or Presbyterian).[20]
5. Graduation from a nonparochial private secondary school.
6. Being a relative of a Stanford alumnus.

Results. Before analyzing the validation results, let us first turn to the relationship ICP and ISP bear to one another.[21] As might be expected from their common base in Hollingshead's

TABLE 2. FREQUENCY DISTRIBUTION OF ICP AND ISP*

	ISP Class				
ICP Class	I	II	III	IV	V
I	21	1	1	—	—
II	54	23	5	—	—
III	4	12	21	3	—
IV	—	—	7	13	1
V	—	—	—	20	—
VI	—	—	—	1	6

*$N=193$. On one subject, data on father's education were not available for computation of ISP.

---

[18] Students from broken homes were excluded from analysis since this factor, independently of social status, importantly contributed to the likelihood a mother would be working.

[19] This information was collected only from male respondents.

[20] The analysis of high-status Protestants was restricted to the Protestant members of the sample.

[21] An ISP score could not be computed for one student because of lack of information about the education of the student's father. For this reason, the sample N is reduced by one for all comparisons made between ICP and ISP.

occupational scale, the two are highly correlated ($r = 0.86$). But despite this close correspondence, the indices are far from identical. This can readily be seen by examination of Table 2, which presents the joint frequency distribution of ICP and ISP. The modification introduced in Hollingshead's procedure has resulted in a shift of class position for 109 of the 193 subjects.[22] The two main points of incongruency between the indices are found, as intended, at the upper and lower-middle class levels. Only 27 per cent of individuals class-typed as I by ISP are so classified by ICP, and only 35 per cent of the class IV students by Hollingshead's procedure are typed as Class IV by ICP. On the other hand, two-thirds of the students in the remaining class levels of ISP are similarly categorized by both indices.

While these changes are in the direction intended, it still remains to be demonstrated that the result is an improvement in stratification measurement. For this task, ICP and ISP were compared on their ability to predict the distribution of the six stratification correlates used as validating criteria. Each criterion, after being dichotomized, was cross-tabulated by each index and the level of association computed by Goodman and Kruskal's gamma (γ)—a coefficient that takes "distributed order" as well as statistical dependence into account.[23] The results are found in Table 3.

The uniformly high coefficients obtained throughout give ample evidence

---

[22] To facilitate comparison, classes V and VI by ICP were treated as a single unit.

[23] Leo A. Goodman and William H. Kruskal, "Measure of Association for Cross-Classifications," *Journal of American Statistical Association*, 49 (December 1954), 732–64.

Table 3. Gamma Coefficients Measuring Association of ICP and ISP with Six Selected Stratification Correlates

Students Who Are :

Stratification Index	On Scholarship	[Have] Mothers Who Are Working*	Expecting Job Better Than Their Father's**	High-Status Protestants***	Private School Graduates	Relatives of Stanford Alumni
ICP	−0.76	−0.54	−0.79	0.61	0.81	0.52
ISP	−0.59	−0.49	−0.80	0.54	0.60	0.50

*Students from broken homes were not included in the computation of γ. N of students from intact homes=166.
**Computed only for male students. N of males=125.
***Non-Protestants were not included in the computation of γ. N of Protestants=151.

that ICP scores do not represent an idiosyncratic combination of subscale scores but instead are tapping, along with their ISP counterparts, a general dimension of social stratification.

The data demonstrate some statistical advantage for ICP on four of the six validation criteria, the gamma coefficients for ICP being from five to nineteen points higher than for ISP. On the remaining two criteria (having relatives who are Stanford alumni and the student's expecting a job better than his father's), only negligible differences are found between the two indices.

The implications of relying upon ICP for class measurement are brought out more fully in Table 4, where percentage distributions of students by ICP and ISP are compared by selected stratification correlates. To the six already in use has been added a seventh, that of having a father with graduate training beyond the baccalaureate. This criterion differs from previous ones in that it can be premised on a priori grounds to bear a curvilinear relation to social class, its effect being concentrated in the upper-middle class. Because of this postulated curvilinearity,

it was not included in the statistical analysis above.

Examination of Table 4 indicates that in large part the superiority of ICP with the present data can be traced to the greater accuracy with which the upper class is delineated. Consistently, ICP prevents our drawing substantive conclusions contrary to present stratification knowledge. For example, the ICP data, unlike that obtained with ISP, show that private school preparation for college is a predominantly upper-class trait and that parental graduate training—the hallmark of the upper-middle class professional—is found concentrated in the upper-middle class. That only one out of twelve class I males, as measured by ICP, expects to have a job better than his father's would appear a "truer" upper-class response than the one-out-of-four figure yielded by Hollingshead's index. Similarly, the sharp differentiation ICP provides between class I and II students having Stanford alumni as relatives reflects more accurately than ISP's results the ascriptive basis of upper-class status.

Table 4 also reveals that the general superiority of ICP in differentiating the

TABLE 4. PERCENTAGE DISTRIBUTION OF STUDENTS BY ICP AND ISP
ON SELECTED CORRELATES OF STRATIFICATION

Per Cent of Students Who Are :	Class Level					
	I	II	III	IV	V	VI
1. On scholarship						
ICP	00	30	58	76	90	86
ISP	27	33	59	78	86	—
2. [Have] mothers who are working*						
ICP	05	20	35	58	44	60
ISP	12	36	35	52	40	—
3. Expecting a job better than their father's**						
ICP	08	45	67	94	93	100
ISP	26	61	72	96	100	—
4. High-status Protestants***						
ICP	74	71	41	40	13	00
ISP	69	62	56	15	14	—
5. Private school graduates						
ICP	43	16	00	05	00	00
ISP	20	19	00	03	00	—
6. Relatives of Stanford alumni						
ICP	70	39	25	24	05	14
ISP	49	44	18	16	00	—
7. [With] father's having graduate education						
ICP	39	51	28	05	00	00
ISP	63	31	09	00	00	—
Number of cases						
ICP	23	82	40	21	20	07
ISP	79	36	34	37	07	—

*Students from broken homes were excluded from analysis. Corrected N for ICP is: 22, 71, 31, 19, 18, 5; for ISP, corrected N is: 69, 33, 26, 33, 5.
**Computed only for males. N for ICP is: 12, 49, 26, 16, 15, 7; N for ISP is 43, 23, 25, 27, 7.
***Computed only for Protestants. Corrected N for ICP is 19, 68, 27, 15, 15, 7; corrected N for ISP is: 65, 26, 27, 26, 7.

upper class is gained without sacrifice of capacity to differentiate subordinate class levels. On all but one validating criterion, essentially comparable distributions of the lower strata are given by both indices. The one exception is that of being a high-status Protestant. On this criterion, ICP shows an abrupt break between classes IV and V—theoretically, the point demarcating the middle and lower classes—while ISP locates the point of disjuncture between classes III and IV. Except for the greater sharpness of the status cleavages yielded by ICP, little basis exists for choosing one point of demarcation over the other. These findings indicate that even at the lower range of the status order differentially interpretable results can be generated by the two techniques.

CONCLUSION

This paper has introduced an improved intercommunity measure of social stratification, offered a rationale for its development, and presented evidence confirming the validity of its use. While the discussion has focused on the college setting, where there has been a specific need for a class index that combines cross-community flexibility with a high degree of predictive utility, ICP may prove useful in other research areas.

PREDICTIVE UTILITY OF FIVE INDICES OF SOCIAL STRATIFICATION*

John L. Haer

Claremont Graduate School and University Center

The literature in the field of social stratification contains many disagreements over the suitability of various concepts of stratification and over the indices that may be employed to represent them. Some students have tried to lessen this confusion through studies of the logical and empirical foundations of the indices of social stratification. One useful approach involves the careful delineation of the characteristics of important indices.[1] Another line of inquiry investigates whether correlations exist among a variety of indices in current use.[2] A third approach, which serves as a guide in the present study, concerns the relationships between stratification indices and *other* phenomena. Findings of this kind may help to provide a basis for evaluating the relative utility of several indices in terms of their efficacy in providing predictions and generalizations.[3]

The present research is an attempt to assess the predictive efficacy of several well-known indices of social stratification. Assuming that there is no "real" index awaiting discovery, the question of the "best" index of stratification may be decided on the basis of *scientific utility*. From this point of view, a variety of concepts and indices

* From John L. Haer, "Predictive Utility of Five Indices of Social Stratification," *The American Sociological Review*, 2 (October 1957), 541–46. Reprinted by permission of the American Sociological Association.

[1] Theodore Caplow, *The Sociology of Work* (Minneapolis: University of Minnesota Press, 1954), pp. 30–58.

[2] J. A. Kahl and J. A. Davis, "A Comparison of Indexes of Socio-Economic Status," *American Sociological Review*, 20 (June 1955), pp. 317–25.

[3] This point is ably stated by Richard T. Morris in his review of three methods of class or status assignment. See Leonard Broom and Philip Selznick, *Sociology* (Evanston, Ill.: Row, Peterson and Company, 1955), p. 171.

may be equally feasible for particular purposes. The problem of correctly selecting from among them depends upon the degree to which they are reliably related to, and predictive of, other phenomena. It should be emphasized that this approach differs from previous research that has tested the adequacy of several indices only through a search for significant correlations among them. It is assumed here that, even in the case of correlations among indices, a further test of adequacy lies in their capacity for predicting other variables related to the stratification order.

THE PROBLEM AND DESIGN

The present research seeks to compare and evaluate five relevant and conventional indices of social stratification by examining their capacities for predicting variables that have been shown in previous studies to be related to measures of stratification. Both "objective" and "subjective" indices[4] are used so as to permit a variety of interpretations of the findings in relation to methodological and theoretical issues in the field of social stratification.

The data were collected from a sample of 320 adults representative of the white population of Tallahassee, Florida, a city of 38,000. The sample was selected in accordance with area-probability procedures and permits the application of statistical tests of significance. The respondents are classified on five indices of social stratification. The indices and the percentage of

respondents in their several categories are as follows:

1. Centers' class identification question. "If you were asked to use one of these names for your social class standing, which would you say you belong to: the middle class, lower class, working class, or upper class?"[5]

   Responses: middle class, 53.1 per cent; lower, none; working, 36.6 per cent; upper, 4.7 per cent; don't know, 1.0 per cent; other answers, 4.7 per cent.

2. An open-end question. After indicating whether they believed social classes exist in the United States, respondents were asked, "Which social class are you in?"

   Responses are classified in eleven categories: upper class, 1.6 per cent; middle, 43.1 per cent; white collar, 2.8 per cent; working, 6.3 per cent; lower, 1.9 per cent; white, 2.2 per cent; miscellaneous classes, 7.2 per cent; cannot name a class, 3.8 per cent; refused to answer, 6.3 per cent; don't know, 5.9 per cent; does not believe in class, 19.1 per cent.

3. Occupation. A classification of the main breadwinner in each respondent's family according to the definitions used by the U.S. census[6] results in the following: professional and managerial, 41.9 per cent; clerical and sales, 32.2 per cent; service, 4.4 per cent; agricultural, 1.0 per cent; skilled, 9.1 per cent; semi-skilled, 3.8 per cent; unskilled, 1.3 per cent; housewives, 2.2 per cent; students, 1.6 per cent; unclassified, 2.8 per cent.

4. Education. Twenty-three categories range from no schooling to 8 years of graduate training. The distribution of respondents by education can be found in Table 2 [p. 118].

---

[4] In the present study an "objective" index is defined as a criterion used *by an investigator* to divide a population into strata or categories; a "subjective" index is a ranking of a population in terms of positions in which the members *place themselves.*

[5] Richard Centers, *The Psychology of Social Class* (Princeton, N.J.: Princeton University Press, 1949).

[6] U.S. Employment Service, *Dictionary of Occupational Titles*, Vol. 2 (Washington, D.C.: Government Printing Office, 1949).

5. Index of status characteristics. Scores are based on the sum of weights for each respondent's type of occupation, dwelling area, house type, and source of income.[7] Forty-seven I.S.C. categories are obtained with scores ranging from 20 to 67. The mean I.S.C. score for the entire sample is 44.9, and the standard deviation is 9.5.

The above indices represent some of the most frequently used subjective and objective measures of social stratification. In addition to the subjective-objective distinction, there are differences between the indices in terms of the nature of the variable (qualitative vs. quantitative, single component vs. composite index) and the nature of the concept of stratification implied (categories vs. continuous ranking, subjective perspectives vs. objective position).

That the several indices reflect the same general order of social stratification seems indicated by the results of chi-square tests of association between them. Table 1 shows that the probability values for the several chi-square tests are significant beyond the 0.05 level of confidence in all cases but one. This finding suggests that each index does indeed tap the phenomena of social stratification and provides grounds for asking which particular indices are most closely associated with phenomena related to the stratification order.

The several behavioral and attitudinal variables cross-tabulated with the stratification indices consist of variables which, in previous studies, have been shown to be related to some measure of stratification or class. Twenty-two such variables are employed, and they are briefly described in the left-hand

---

7 W. L. Warner, M. Meeker, and K. Eells, *Social Class in America* (Chicago: Science Research Associates, 1949), Chaps. 8 and 9.

TABLE 1. PROBABILITY VALUES
RESULTING FROM CHI-SQUARE
TESTS OF ASSOCIATION
BETWEEN FIVE INDICES

	Open-End Question	Occupation	Education	I.S.C.
Centers' question	0.001	0.001	0.001	0.001
Open-end question		0.05	0.02	0.15
Occupation			0.001	0.001
Education				0.001

column of Table 3 [p. 119]. These twenty-two variables represent eight general areas of life experience:[8] (1) migrant experience, (2) membership in voluntary organizations, (3) religious experiences, (4) political behavior, (5) radio listening and reading habits, (6) travel outside the United States, (7) information and attitudes concerning a then pending U.S. Supreme Court decision on public school segregation, and

---

8 The relationships between these eight areas and various measures of social stratification have been documented extensively in the research literature of sociology in the last two decades. Most of these relationships are described in an extensive correlation table presented by Richard T. Morris in Broom and Selznick, *op. cit.*, pp. 189–92. The relationships between stratification indices and migrant experiences, religious experiences, and community satisfaction are documented, respectively, in the following sources: U.S. Bureau of the Census, "Population Characteristics," *Current Population Reports*, Series P-20, No. 36 (December 9, 1951), p. 1; Gerhard E. Lenski, "Social Correlates of Religious Interest," *American Sociological Review*, 18 (October 1953), 538-40; and John L. Haer, "Social Stratification in Relation to Attitude Toward Sources of Power in a Community," *Social Forces*, 35 (December 1956), 137–42.

Table 2. Relationship Between Educational Level and Travel

	Years of School Completed																							
Travel	0	3	4	5	6	7	8	9	10	11	12	13	14	15	16	17	18	19	20	21	22	23	24	Total
Outside United States	2				1	3	2	3	6	6	27	10	14	9	31	8	4	2	8		1	1		138
Not Outside United States		1	1	3	7	2	15	10	17	11	63	9	15	6	11	5	4			1			1	182

(8) attitudes indicative of relative satisfaction with the community.

The criterion employed to assess the relative utility of the several indices, *the coefficient of relative predictability,*[9] ascertains how much more effectively a given variable could be predicted through a knowledge of a stratification index than on the basis of a knowledge of the variable alone. Prediction of this type posits that for a given variable, which may be distributed in two or more categories, the best prediction that can be made for each subject or respondent is in terms of the modal category of the variable. After cross-tabulating a given variable with a presumed predictive index and predicting the distribution of the variable in terms of the new modal categories, a coefficient may be computed that states the percentage improvement in prediction. For example, Table 2 shows findings on whether respondents had traveled outside the United States. The modal prediction of this behavior based on the original marginal totals is that they did not travel outside the United States. Predicting on the basis of the modal category, there are 138 errors, constituting a total error of 43 per cent. When travel is predicted on the basis of modal categories for twenty-three education groups, however, the number of errors in prediction is ninety-six. The percentage by which the original prediction is improved through a knowledge of educational attainment may be computed as follows:

$$\frac{\text{Total error} - \text{error remaining}}{\text{Total error}}$$

$$= \frac{138 - 96}{138} = 0.30$$

Thus the coefficient of relative predictability expresses the percentage of error reduced in a gross modal category prediction through the introduction of a related index or other variable. The "prediction," in this case, is admittedly

9 Louis Guttman, "An Outline of the Statistical Theory of Prediction," in *The Prediction of Personal Adjustment*, eds. P. Horst *et al.* (New York: Social Science Research Council, 1941), pp. 253–313. For a practical application of the technique see Howard S. Swanson and John L. Haer, "The Application of Two Guttman Techniques in the Prediction of Some Political Activities," *Proceedings of the Pacific Sociological Society* (June 1952). The term "coefficient of relative predictability" seems to have been introduced by Sanford M. Dornbusch and Calvin F. Schmid, *A Primer of Social Statistics* (New York: McGraw-Hill Book Company, 1955), p. 215.

				Indices	
Variables	I.S.C.	Education	Occupation	Centers' Question	Open-End Question
Migrant experience					
Number of communities lived in 1 year or more	0.23	0.11*	0.05	0.02	0.07
Membership in voluntary organizations					
Total amount of participation	0.27**	0.08**	0.02	—	0.11**
Participation in civic groups	0.04	0.07**	—	—	—
Participation in fraternal groups	0.15**	—	0.03	—	0.05
Participation in political groups	0.28**	0.09**	0.05	0.01	0.10**
Religious behavior					
Frequency of church attendance	0.18	0.06	0.06	—	0.04
Frequency of prayer	0.19	0.05	0.03	—	0.05
Report on tithing	0.26*	0.13**	0.08**	0.04	0.07**
Attitude on importance of religion	0.22	0.11**	0.09*	0.01	0.06**
Political behavior					
Participation in campaigns by working or donating money	0.18*	0.07**	0.05	—	0.04
Listening and reading habits					
Listening to news broadcasts	0.18	0.15**	0.05	—	0.06*
Reading local paper	0.23	0.14	0.04	0.01	0.08**
Reading regional paper	0.26**	0.17**	0.18**	0.07*	0.06**
Reading news magazines	0.17*	—	0.02	—	0.02
Reading magazines containing no news	0.17**	0.07**	0.03	—	0.02
Travel experience					
Travel outside United States	0.38*	0.30**	0.14**	0.13**	0.09*
Knowledge and attitude regarding pending U.S. Supreme Court decision on desegregation					
Knowledge of pending decision	0.21**	0.12**	0.07*	—	0.02

(table continued on next page)

TABLE 3   (CONTINUED)

Indices

Variables	I.S.C.	Education	Occupation	Centers' Question	Open-End Question
Accuracy of information	0.24	0.15	0.09	—	0.04
Attitude toward possible results	0.21**	0.09**	0.23	0.02	0.04
Attitudes indicative of community satisfaction					
Toward local neighborhood	0.19	0.09	—	—	0.06
Toward future civic developments	0.25	0.10	0.07	0.03	0.29**
Toward wielding of power in city	0.03	—	—	0.04	—

* Chi square significant at the 0.05 level of confidence. Although at present there is no test for the reliability of the coefficient of relative predictability, chi-square tests were made to ascertain whether significant association existed between the indices and variables in the population studied.
** Chi square significant at the 0.01 level.

ex post facto and serves only to suggest the relative worth of several indices. This coefficient is used in the present study because it provides a *standard measure.* In view of the divergent nature of the variables employed in the cross-tabulations (qualitative-quali-tative, qualitative-quantitative, quanti-tative-quantitative, and quantitative-qualitative), it is felt that other possible statistical devices would not provide so satisfactory an answer to the question initially posed.[10]

THE FINDINGS

Table 3 shows the coefficients of re-lative predictability resulting from the cross-tabulations of the five indices with the other variables. An overall

---

10 Tetrachoric correlations also would provide a standard measure. They are not used, however, because the nature of some of the indices and variables does not con-form to the assumptions of the device—the necessity for a normal distribution and an underlying quantitative continuum.

comparison reveals that coefficients are higher for the Index of Status Char-acteristics than for other indices in eighteen out of twenty-two compari-sons. Occupation, the open-end ques-tion, and Centers' question each has the highest coefficient in only one cross-tabulation. The coefficients for educa-tion are higher than for all indices except the I.S.C. in twelve of twenty-two comparisons. The more effective relative predictability of the I.S.C. is demonstrated also by a comparison of the means for the coefficients of each index. The mean coefficient for the I.S.C. in the twenty-two cross-tabula-tions is 21 per cent; means for educa-tion, occupation, the open-end question, and Centers' question are, respectively, 10, 6, 6, and 2 per cent.

A comparison of the relative pre-dictability of the objective and subjec-tive indices (the open-end and Centers' question) shows that, with respect both to the magnitude of the coefficients and the number of successful comparisons, the objective indices have higher pre-dictability than the subjective. A comparison of only the three objective indices shows that the I.S.C. has higher coefficients than education or occupation twenty out of twenty-two times; a comparison of the relative predictability of education and occupation shows higher coefficients for education sixteen out of twenty-two times. Of the two subjective indices, the open-end question has a higher coefficient than Centers' question eighteen out of twenty-two times.

It is obvious that the magnitude of the coefficient of predictability is related to the frequency distributions of the variables that are cross-tabulated and the number of categories in the predictor. High coefficients are more likely when the original variable is evenly distributed throughout its categories and the predictor contains numerous categories. Parenthetically, this feature of the coefficient of predictability may be contrasted with a common measure of association, the chi-square test. Table 3 shows that several relationships resulting in high coefficients do not evidence chi-square values significant at the 0.05 level. In most cases this is because the numerous categories in a predictor afford new modal predictions that may reduce considerably the original error. In the chi-square test, however, a large number of categories increases the number of degrees of freedom, making necessary larger chi-square values for significance. More important, in chi-square tests adjacent categories in many cases must be combined in order to obtain acceptable theoretical frequencies, and this serves to reduce variations that may exist between the categories of different variables.[11]

In order to ascertain whether the high coefficients for the I.S.C. are due merely to the larger number of I.S.C. categories, the latter were combined into seven groups and new coefficients computed. The results showed that higher coefficients were obtained for the I.S.C. over the other indices in eighteen out of twenty-two comparisons, indicating that the superiority of the I.S.C. could not be accounted for simply on the basis of the numerous categories comprising it.

The validity of this conclusion is enhanced by a comparison of coefficients of predictability obtained for the several components of the I.S.C., taken separately, in relation to the twenty-two variables. In only four instances is a coefficient for an I.S.C. component higher than coefficients for other single-component indices—Centers' question, the open-end question, education, and occupation. The mean coefficients for the latter indices are 2, 6, 10, and 6 per cent, respectively; mean coefficients for the I.S.C. components—house type, dwelling area, occupation, and source of income—are 2, 2, 3, and 6 per cent, respectively. Thus it may be concluded that the superiority in prediction of the I.S.C. over the other indices is not due merely to the predictive efficacy of any one of its components.

CONCLUSIONS AND IMPLICATIONS

One methodological problem has been the question of the value of objec-

---

[11] As is pointed out in the footnote of Table 3, chi-square tests of association were undertaken because at present there is no test of the reliability of the coefficient of relative predictability. All chi-square tests were computed on the original cross-tabulations, except when it was necessary to combine categories in order to obtain suitable theoretical frequencies. Space limitations preclude the presentation of the 110 chi-square tables used, but the writer will supply these data upon request.

tive as contrasted with subjective indices in stratification research. In view of the striking disparity in coefficients for the two types of indices, it would seem that the objective indices provide by far the better research tools when predictability is desired. Subjective designations of class or status position may be forced through a Centers-type question or elicited by an unstructured inquiry, but at least in the present study such designations hold little significance in relation to other attitudes and behavior.

The obvious superiority of the I.S.C. over other indices suggests that its greater efficiency may be related to its distinguishing features. First, it is a composite index, and thus incorporates information pertaining to several areas of stratification; secondly, through the assignment of weights and scale scores to the various components, the I.S.C. provides a continuous series of ranks. Thus, I.S.C. scores represent summations of several components of stratification, and their arrangement in a continuous series makes it possible to discern minute variations in relation to other variables. It would appear that the single criterion and broad categories employed by subjective indices or by occupation and education may reduce predictability by blurring actual variations existing within a category.

Some conclusions seem warranted regarding the bearing of the findings on possible alternative concepts of stratification. Theorists have asked whether stratification is best conceived as continuous—consisting of a range of minute variations—or a relatively small number of discrete categories or strata.[12] Using predictability as a criterion, the former approach would seem the

more fruitful theoretical formulation. The conception of stratification in terms of discrete classes or strata may be logically entertained, of course, but the utility of the concept seems seriously questioned by the present findings.

A recurrent issue of theoretical concern has been the delineation of the several components or dimensions that comprise the stratification order. The present evaluation of indices does not permit suggestions concerning the appropriate components. The findings imply, however, that the more useful concept should embody several components rather than reflect only one aspect of behavior or attitude.

Methodologically, the findings of the present research suggest that attempts to resolve the question of the "best" indices of stratification may not be answered wholly on the basis of possible intercorrelations among them. The indices employed have been shown to be significantly associated yet to have a manifestly different relationship to other variables that presumably are linked to the stratification order. From the theoretical standpoint, these findings seem to bear out contentions that the stratification system of the United States is best perceived as an imprecise ordering of individuals, based on a number of related components, only generally and loosely related to numerous aspects of an individual's life activity,[13] rather than a small number of superimposed strata differing in terms of the objective characteristics and subjective perceptions and aspirations of the members of each strata.

---

12 This problem is one of the central issues discussed in a recent text on stratification. See John F. Cuber and William F.

Kenkel, *Social Stratification in the United States* (New York: Appleton-Century-Crofts, 1954).

13 See, for example, Gideon Sjoberg, "Are Social Classes in America Becoming More Rigid?" *American Sociological Review*, 16 (December 1951), 775–83.

THE USE OF SOCIOECONOMIC SCALES

By far the most frequently used measurements of social-class position are socioeconomic scales based chiefly on such indices as income, education, occupation, and residence. These "objective" indicators may be employed either singly or in combination. Described simply, they require the assignment of numbers to categories that can be ranked in order from greater to lesser. Persons belonging to the same category are assumed to have equivalent status. On this basis, each person's position can be compared with those of others in respect to different continua which may or may not be mutually exclusive. Gordon describes below the logic behind the use and methodology of socioeconomic scales.

THE LOGIC OF STRATIFICATION SCALES*

Milton M. Gordon

University of Massachusetts

The literatures of sociology and psychology are replete with studies which in one way or another stratify and sample a population and study the relationship of these stratified groups to some specific phenomenon such as birth rates, death rates, delinquency, illness, mental disease, education, intelligence, social participation, migration, and many others. Two principal "short-cut" techniques used in these studies for stratification purposes are "socioeconomic status" scales and occupational classifications which are declared to equate with social status. These scales and classifications have developed not only as a result of the demands of the research sociologists but also of the specialists in educational psychology, interested in studying the role of "home background" in children's lives, and the social workers, who face such practical problems as child placement. We turn now to an examination of the logic and "rationale" of these stratification techniques.

SOCIOECONOMIC STATUS SCALES

The construction of standardized multiple-factor scales or indexes of "socioeconomic status," or some similarly defined stratification variable, follows a rather definite pattern, although there are individual variations.[1] Basically,

* From Milton M. Gordon, *Social Class in American Sociology* (Durham, N.C.: Duke University Press, 1958), pp. 210–13, 218–20.

[1] For a good review of the historical development of these scales and their techniques of construction, see William H. Sewell, *The Construction and Standardization of a Scale for the Measurement of the Socio-Economic Status of Oklahoma Farm Families*, Technical Bulletin No. 9 (Oklahoma Agricultural and Mechanical College

there are eight steps involved in the process:

1. Socioeconomic status is defined, and its respective subareas are indicated.

2. A number of test items, or questions, are devised which are presumed to be connected with relative vertical position in each of these subareas. These items may be scored as either "present" or "nonpresent," or may be graded along a continuum.

3. These test items are tried out and scored on a sample of respondents, representing a cross section with regard to some objective factor commonly regarded to be associated with socioeconomic status (for instance, income or occupation).

4. Items are validated, or selected. That is, a selection of items from the original scale is made on the basis of statistical techniques which relate the items either to some external criterion or to an internal criterion (the test itself). The general goal is to obtain those items which show the greatest capacity to discriminate levels of socioeconomic status.

5. Weights for the items are derived by statistical techniques. Here, again, the choice of techniques depends on whether an external or an internal criterion is being used.

6. The reliability of the scale—that is, its ability to measure consistently that which it actually measures—is determined by certain standard techniques (test-retest, split-half correlation, etc.).

7. The validity of the scale—that is, proof that it really is measuring what it is designed to measure—is sought. The common procedure here is to correlate the results of the test with those obtained on the same group by some other "socioeconomic status" scale, or with occupational or economic divisions.

8. Norms, or group divisions, along the numerical status continuum may be established. This is an optional procedure and is sometimes performed arbitrarily, sometimes by examining the relationship of test scores to divisions along some external criterion of status.

It should be apparent that the first of the steps outlined, the definition of socioeconomic status, is of crucial importance for it determines specific procedure in nearly all of the subsequent steps and ultimately is the foundation on which the logic of the scale must rest. Essentially, there are two theoretically possible situations with regard to such a definition:

1. Socioeconomic status is a *known and demonstrable attribute*, in which case a sample of individuals or families representing different degrees of this attribute can initially be secured, and the subsequent steps in the construction of the scale or index, i.e., selection and weighting of test items, etc., are based on the degree of ability of the items to distinguish the respondents' possessing various degrees of this known attribute. Needless to say, the test population on which the items are originally administered is then the sample group, the "socioeconomic statuses" of whose members are already known, and valid-

---

Agricultural Experiment Station, 1940). See, also, for construction techniques, George A. Lundberg, *Social Research* (New York: Longmans, Green & Co., 1942), pp. 288–309.

For an excellent critique of the scales (and also occupational classifications) to which we are heavily indebted, see Genevieve Knupfer, *Indices of Socio-Economic Status: A Study of Some Problems of Measurement* (New York: privately published, 1946); also, Genevieve Knupfer and Robert K. Merton, "Discussion of Lundberg-Friedman Paper," *Rural Sociology*, VIII (September 1943), 236–39.

ation then becomes simply a matter of determining whether the final test items predict these various positions with a reasonable degree of accuracy.

2. Socioeconomic status is an *unknown but presumptive attribute*, *X*, in which case the test population is stratified with regard to some variable *presumed* to be highly correlated with *X* (such as income or occupation), and the selection and weighting of items is then usually based on the capacity of the items to distinguish various levels of scores on *the test itself*, which procedure is further predicated on the assumption that the test scores are highly correlated with *X*. Validity is then gauged by determining the ability of the final form of the test to distinguish various occupational or income levels, or by its correlation with other indices of "socioeconomic status" whose construction has been based on a similar series of assumptions. Since ultimate validation of *all* the indices, pending the isolation or discovery of *X*, eventually depends on their ability to distinguish groups differentiated by some external criterion, such as income or occupation, one might well ask why these more easily obtained criteria are not used in the first place, without bothering to construct an index. The only logical answer must be that these external criteria are highly but only imperfectly correlated with *X*. In reply to this, then, it must be pointed out that since the relative merits of the index and the external criterion as predictors of *X* are undetermined, the simpler, external criterion may be just as useful. A possible last resort answer of the Type 2 index maker might be that *X*, or "socioeconomic status," is a construct consisting of a combination of positions in the areas which the test differentiates—in other words, *X* is simply what the test measures. In such case, however, valid-

ation against some external criterion is obviously superfluous....

It should be obvious from the preceding discussion that until the concept of socioeconomic status is clearly defined, the construction and validation of scales designed to measure it must be based on theoretical inadequacies. Perhaps the key difficulty is illustrated by the nature of the descriptive term itself —*socioeconomic* status—a term which combines at once two dimensions of stratification, social and economic, in the unproved assumption either that they act as a unit as a stimulus for evoking responses or that they are perfectly correlated with one another. Throughout this entire work we have emphasized the need for isolating stratification variables, considering them separately, and studying their covariation empirically. This analytical framework applies with equal force to the concept of socioeconomic status. One dimension of stratification is social—that is, the evaluation of prestige position in the community; another dimension is economic power, as measured by wealth or income; another is political community power, in terms of ability to make decisions enforceable on other members of the community; another might be "cultural" quality of home, in terms of subjective standards agreed on by educators; and so on. If the data for the particular variable are easily obtainable, there is no need for a scale or index. If not, an index may be in order as a time-saving device for future researchers. But the framers of a scale must choose which of the stratification components they wish to measure. To lump them all together is justifiable neither on any theoretical basis nor on the basis of available research evidence considered in earlier chapters, which indicates that these stratification components do *not* vary perfectly with one another. At any rate, in the words of Knupfer, "the unity of status should ultimately be decided empirically.[2] Since there is little likelihood that this unity *can* be demonstrated, socioeconomic scales based on "buckshot" definitions must continue to wallow in the haze of theoretical uncertainty which so obviously surrounds them.[3] The roughly empirical usefulness of the scales, it should be noted, is not here being questioned. Since there probably are (on the basis of existing correlation studies of prestige, occupation, income, etc.) correlations of 0.5 and above among many stratification components, the scales undoubtedly serve as rough measures of position on any one of the standard stratification dimensions.[4] But

this is far from theoretical justification of their scientific adequacy and does not obviate the necessity for scale construction which is carefully based on that particular dimension of stratification pertinent to the problem at hand.

If recourse is had to the position that socioeconomic status is simply "what the scale measures," then the implications of this position must be faced. Briefly, these are that (a) the scale measures (granted, for the moment, the adequacy of its items) an artificial construct consisting of relative positions in two or more discrete areas, which raises the question of what the usefulness of the construct is for the researcher's problem; (b) validation of the scale against anything except itself is illogical; and (c) no two scales measure exactly the same thing, unless they use exactly the same items. These implications have not been recognized by the defenders of the scales, and one is not sure that they would be happy with them. Lundberg, for instance, in a vigorous defense of the "operationalist" position, declares that "the statement that socioeconomic status *is* what a scale for measuring socioeconomic status measures has therefore the same validity as to say that the conditions and the behaviors which any group calls high socioeconomic status *is* high socioeconomic status for that group."[5] But, if it is group judgments which constitute socioeconomic status, then the initial step in scale construction is to

---

[2] Knupfer, *op. cit.*, p. 28. This point is also well made by Knupfer and Merton, *op. cit.*, and by Jane Loevinger, "Intelligence as Related to Socio-Economic Factors," in the Thirty-Ninth Yearbook of the National Society for the Study of Education, *Intelligence: Its Nature and Nurture: Part I, Comparative and Critical Exposition* (Bloomington, Ill.: Public School Publishing Co., 1940), pp. 159–210.

[3] Kahl and Davis, in a factor analysis of intercorrelations among nineteen stratification variables, based on a sample of 219 residents of Cambridge, Mass., found that it was possible to control more variance by extracting two common factors rather than one. See Joseph A. Kahl and James A. Davis, "A Comparison of Indexes of Socio-Economic Status," *American Sociological Review*, XX (June 1955), 317–25. While they suggest that one common factor may be regarded "for rough purposes" as a single dimension, they go on to state that "a more precise statement would be that the battery of indices showed two common factors. The first was composed of the various measures of occupation, plus certain variables closely related to occupation, such as education, self-identification, and the interviewer's impressionistic rating of the subject. The second factor was composed of ecological measures plus those of the status of the parents of the subjects and his wife" (p. 325).

[4] Lazarsfeld has demonstrated the inter-

changeability of rough economic indices for obtaining approximately similar distributions of some attitude or behavior variable. See Paul F. Lazarsfeld, "Interchangeability of Indices in the Measurement of Economic Influences," *Journal of Applied Psychology*, XXIII (1939), 33–45.

[5] George A. Lundberg, "The Measurement of Socioeconomic Status," *The American Sociological Review*, 5 (February 1940), 36.

obtain these group judgments, distribute the community members accordingly, and then construct and validate the scale on the basis of this empirically established status distribution.

Occupational Scales

Occupation has become the most frequently used socioeconomic index. As Reissman notes, "Few studies omit a reference to occupation, and most of them incorporate occupational measures into the research design."[1] Two methodological features account in part for the popularity of occupational measures of social class. First, occupational information is objective data, obtainable without undue difficulty. Second, being a single-item index, it is relatively easy to scale and standardize.[2] These advantages have special appeal for students of social mobility and international stratification.

Theoretical considerations are also involved in the popularity of occupational scales and in findings from research gained by these instruments. At a common-sense level the pervasive influence of occupational roles in modern industrial society is most apparent. "To know that a person is a professional is to bring to mind an apperceptive mass about the kind of person he is—what he thinks, what he wants, and what his interests are."[3]

Perhaps too the dominant position of the functional school has been influential in the strong market for investigations of occupational prestige and in the search for improved procedures for obtaining this information. Particularly since the appearance of the Davis-Moore account of social inequality, sociologists have interpreted societal functions and rewards in occupational terms.

We can identify two general occupational indexes.[4] One consists of a classification of occupations into broad categories. Indexes of this kind are based upon the judgments of those ranking the occupations. In contrast to this "common-sense" classification the second kind of index, the occupational prestige scale, rests upon information gained directly from samples of the population on the standing of representative occupations.

The most influential classification scheme is that provided by Alba M. Edwards, formerly of the U.S. Bureau of the Census. In this system all occupations reported in the census are classified into six main groups:

1. Professional persons
2. Proprietors, managers, and officials
    2a. Farmers (owners and tenants)
    2b. Wholesale and retail dealers
    2c. Other proprietors, managers, and officials
3. Clerks and kindred workers

---

[1] *Op. cit.*, p. 145.
[2] Bernard Barber, *Social Stratification* (New York: Harcourt, Brace, 1957), p. 171.
[3] Reissman, *op. cit.*
[4] For a fuller discussion of these types see Gordon, *op. cit.*, pp. 222–28.

4. Skilled workers and foremen
5. Semiskilled workers
6. Unskilled workers
    6a. Farm laborers
    6b. Laborers, except farm
    6c. Servant classes

According to Edwards, "it is evident that each of these groups represents . . . a large population group with a somewhat distinct standard of life, economically, and to a considerable extent, intellectually and socially. In some measure, also, each group has characteristic interests and convictions. . . . Each of them is thus a really distinct and highly significant social-economic group."[5]

Edwards conceives of these occupational groups virtually as social classes—a conception readily shared by many researchers who seek a simple and seemingly plausible measure of class. Like earlier occupational classifications, this one also ranks the various groups according to the educated guesses of the author. As Gordon suggests, "Its correspondence to an economic or social hierarchy is largely assumed rather than empirically demonstrated."[6]

The second kind of occupational index is the prestige scale, which attempts to secure an empirical basis for its hierarchy of occupational positions by means of opinion surveys of samples of the population. The best scale of this type, and the one currently enjoying the widest usage, is that developed by C.C. North and Paul Hatt from data gathered by the National Opinion Research Center. The North-Hatt Scale is based upon ratings of relative prestige for ninety occupations. In 1946, approximately 3,000 adults, a cross section of the American population, rated the general standing of each occupation on a five-point scale: excellent, good, average, below average, and poor. North and Hatt then converted the ratings into a scoring system in which the occupation with the highest prestige received a maximum score of 100. A partial list of the occupations (together with their ranks and prestige scores) is on the following page.

As shown, the prestige scores range from a high of 96 for U.S. Supreme Court Justices (rank 1) to a low of 33 for shoe shiners (rank 90). It is to be remembered that these are composite scores and ranks based upon replies from all respondents.

While there was general agreement on occupational standing among the interviewees, intensive analyses of the data disclose some significant variations in replies. Region, size of community, occupation, education, and income, and, to a lesser degree, age and sex were associated with differences in respondents' evaluations. Nevertheless, as Albert J. Reiss emphasizes, "Despite the fact that

---

[5] Alba M. Edwards, *Comparative Occupational Statistics for the United States, 16th Census, 1940* (Washington, D.C.: Government Printing Office, 1943), p. 179.

[6] Gordon, *op. cit.*, p. 222. Gordon, among other critics, describes additional deficiencies of the Edwards type of index; most of these pertain to the rationale behind the choice of occupational categories. Questions are raised, for example, about the consistency of hierarchical arrangements, the distinctiveness of categories, and the breadth of occupational groupings.

North-Hatt Occupational Prestige Scale (Partial List)*

RANK	OCCUPATION	PRESTIGE SCORE
1	U.S. Supreme Court Justice	96
2	Physician	93
3	State governor	93
6	Mayor of a large city	90
7	College professor	89
8	Scientist	89
9	U.S. Representative in Congress	89
10	Banker	88
13	Head of a department, state government	87
14	Minister	87
16	Chemist	86
18	Lawyer	86
19	Member, board of directors of large corporation	86
20	Nuclear physicist	86
21	Priest	86
22	Psychologist	85
26	Owner of factory employing about 100 people	82
27	Sociologist	82
30	Musician in a symphony orchestra	81
32	Captain in the Regular Army	80
34	Economist	79
36	Public school teacher	78
39	Farm owner and operator	76
42	Newspaper columnist	74
44	Electrician	73
45	Trained machinist	73
46	Welfare worker for a city government	73
48	Reporter on a daily newspaper	71
50	Bookkeeper	68
53	Traveling salesman for a whole concern	68
55	Policeman	67
57	Mail carrier	66
58	Carpenter	65
59	Automobile repairman	63
61	Garage mechanic	62
63	Owner-operator of a lunch stand	62
64	Corporal in the Regular Army	60
65	Machine operator in a factory	60

* Reprinted in abridged form with permission from C. C. North and Paul K. Hatt, "Jobs and Occupations: A Popular Evaluation," *Public Opinion News*, 9 (September 1947), 3–13. Both authors deceased.

North-Hatt Occupational Prestige Scale (continued)

RANK	OCCUPATION	PRESTIGE SCORE
67	Clerk in a store	58
71	Restaurant cook	54
72	Truck driver	54
74	Filling-station attendant	52
75	Singer in a night club	52
76	Farm hand	50
80	Restaurant worker	48
82	Night watchman	47
85	Bartender	44
86	Janitor	44
88	Garbage collector	35
89	Street sweeper	34
90	Shoe shiner	33

the social position of a person has an effect on his ratings of some occupations, the prestige status of occupations is viewed in substantially the same way by major social groupings in American society."[7]

The methodological sophistication of the North-Hatt Scale probably accounts for its extensive use in empirical investigations of social stratification. Its appearance in 1947 gave impetus to a growing body of specialized research on occupational prestige, much of which either employs the North-Hatt Scale or consists of critical analyses aimed at its refinement. A replication study carried out in 1963 by Robert W. Hodge, Paul M. Siegel, and Peter H. Rossi[8] greatly enhanced the value of the scale. The correlation they obtained of 0.99 suggests that slight if any changes in occupational prestige have occurred since the original North-Hatt research of 1946. Furthermore, the authors conclude, from a review of other studies dating back to 1925, that no appreciable changes in the relative prestige of American occupations have occurred in the past four decades. Prior to their replication and their general assessment, the possibility of significant shifts in the statuses of occupations was unknown.

Many observers believe that the appeal of the North-Hatt Scale and related occupational measures has often led to the indiscriminate use of these tools in stratification research. Few take issue with the view that occupation is one of the most important indices of social class and that occupational measures, therefore, can be treated as shorthand appraisals of much that is encompassed by the concept of class. Doubts arise, however, with respect to the position, usually implied but

---

[7] *Occupations and Social Status* (Glencoe, Ill.: Free Press, 1961), p. 195. Chapter 8 of this work presents an extensive analysis of these sources of variations in ratings.

[8] "Occupational Prestige in the United States, 1925–63," *American Journal of Sociology*, 70 (November 1964), 286–302.

For further analyses and extensions of the North-Hall Scale, see Reiss, *op. cit.*

sometimes openly expressed, that few phenomena that are not occupational or controlled by occupation are involved in the concept of class. The objection, then, is to a conception of occupation that seems to equate it with social class.[9] To be sure, there is much overlap between occupational stratification and class stratification, but by no means does this overlap approach a level at which one can treat the two interchangeably. Depending on the phenomena one has in mind, occupation can be something more than or less than social class.[10]

Reissman[11] presents a more serious charge concerning the use of occupational measures in stratification research. Too often, he contends, the choice of occupation as an index of class is simply a matter of expedience, with little or no thought given to the implications of that choice for a theory of class. Findings from such research may indeed bear upon occupational stratification or cast light upon the relationship between occupation and behavior. However, their use in *ex post facto* "tests" of hypotheses stemming from stratification theory is of dubious value. In Reissman's words, those who employ the occupational variable as an index of class are unwittingly "using occupation as a synonym for class, which is a methodological step of vastly different order."[12]

Both of the following papers use the North-Hatt Scale as a point of departure for further inquiries into the sources and meaning of occupational prestige. Both are also concerned with the relationships between occupational prestige and theories of stratification. Their conclusions with respect to these concerns differ. The first selection, "Correlates and Estimation of Occupational Prestige," by Richard L. and Ida Harper Simpson, describes procedures for improving the precision and range of occupational indices such as the North-Hatt system. Their findings on the sources of differential occupational prestige lend support, they suggest, to the Davis-Moore explanation of stratification.

In the second selection, "The Meanings of Occupational Prestige," Joseph Gusfield and Michael Schwartz attempt to come to grips with several of the assumptions and unknowns in the rationale behind, and use of, the North-Hatt Scale. They contend that little is known about what prestige scales actually measure, and, consequently, findings gained through such methods are too ambiguous for the clarification of theoretical issues. Their substantive contribution—an

---

9 For some critics an even more questionable "reduction" of social class is the tendency to see a near identity between it and one dimension of occupation, namely, occupational prestige.

10 As Lasswell states, "No matter how high the correlation between occupational status and social class may be, they remain, at least in the mind of the writer, two different phenomena." Thomas Lasswell, *Class and Stratum* (Boston: Houghton Mifflin Company, 1965), p. 447.

Much of the rationale for relying so heavily upon the occupational factor rests upon findings of high correlations between occupations and other class variables such as income and education. However, as Reiss suggests, the high correlations commonly reported from research of small towns may not be representative of the situation in the general population. Reiss, *op. cit.*, p. 143.

11 *Op. cit.*, pp. 160–62.

12 *Ibid.*, p. 164.

exploration of the meanings of occupational prestige—poses problems for those who view studies of occupational ranking as supportive of functional perspectives.

CORRELATES AND ESTIMATION OF OCCUPATIONAL PRESTIGE*[1]

Richard L. Simpson, *University of North Carolina*

Ida Harper Simpson, *Duke University*

This paper reports an attempt to clarify the relationships between certain characteristics of occupations and their differential prestige and makes suggestions for an index of prestige based on judges' ratings of occupational characteristics.

In seeking to explain differential occupational prestige, writers have generally emphasized features intrinsic to

the work performed rather than extrinsic features, such as income, style of life, or working conditions. There appears to be good reason for this. Labor market conditions, class traditions, and management practices vary markedly from one locality to another and sometimes fluctuate greatly in brief spans of time. With these go variations in extrinsic correlates; yet rankings have shown a high degree of consistency in opinion polls taken at different times and places.[2] It seems likely that the intrinsic aspects of occupations do not change so rapidly or vary so much from place to place and that their stability helps to explain the consistency of prestige rankings found in the various studies.

The intrinsic correlates of prestige cited most often by recent writers fall under two general headings. One involves responsibility, authority, or control over others' behavior; the other, knowledge, specialized training, or skill required to perform the work ade-

* Reprinted from "Correlates and Estimation of Occupational Prestige," *American Journal of Sociology*, by Richard L. Simpson and Ida Harper Simpson by permission of The University of Chicago Press. Copyright 1960 by The University of Chicago Press.

[1] Revision of a paper presented at the meeting of the American Sociological Association, Chicago, September 1959. This research was financially supported by the University Research Council, University of North Carolina. We wish to thank the Duke University Computing Laboratory for its help in analysis; the Institute for Research in Social Science, University of North Carolina, for making its statistical facilities available; for suggestions, Charles E. Bowerman, W. Jackson Hall, David R. Norsworthy, Daniel O. Price, David M. Shaw, and Joel Smith; and David R. Norsworthy and Robert M. Rennick for statistical computation and other assistance.

[2] For a summary of some of these polls, see Bernard Barber, *Social Stratification* (New York: Harcourt, Brace & Co., 1957), pp. 101–8.

quately.[3] In addition, many high-ranking occupations possess in high degree personal autonomy, that is, a degree of power to decide one's own patterns of work and to work toward general objectives rather than toward assigned and specific tasks. Sociologists would probably agree that these considerations have some relation to prestige, but there has been no clear demonstration of their relative importance, nor has it been shown whether identical factors can account for gradations in prestige within all occupations—business, the professions, recreational and aesthetic occupations, manual work, and so on. Conceivably, one variable might account for differences in prestige within the professional situs[4] while another explains differences among business or recreational occupations.

---

[3] Barber, *op. cit.*, pp. 24–27; Theodore M. Caplow, *The Sociology of Work* (Minneapolis: University of Minnesota Press, 1954), pp. 52–56; Joseph A. Kahl, *The American Class Structure* (New York: Rinehart & Co., 1957), p. 71; Cecil C. North and Paul K. Hatt (National Opinion Research Center), "Jobs and Occupations: A Popular Evaluation," *Opinion News*, IX (September 1, 1947), 3–13. (Reprinted in Reinhard Bendix and Seymour Martin Lipset, eds., *Class, Status, and Power* [Glencoe, Ill.: Free Press, 1953], pp. 411–26.)

[4] The concept of "situs," a group of occupations distinguished by nature of work rather than by vertical level in a hierarchy, comes from Paul K. Hatt ("Occupations and Social Stratification," *American Journal of Sociology*, LV [May 1950], 533–43) and has been elaborated recently by Richard T. Morris and Raymond J. Murphy ("The Situs Dimension in Occupational Structure," *American Sociological Review*, XXIV [April 1959], 231–39). The notion of situs is similar to that of the occupational "field" or "group" as discussed by vocational psychologists (e.g., Anne Roe, *The Psychology of Occupations* [New York: John Wiley & Sons, Inc., 1956], pp. 143–250). Hatt's classification of situses is used in the present research.

Schemes for classifying occupations by general standing, rank, or prestige have generally made use of some of the intrinsic correlates of prestige, but the relative weighting of criteria has usually been implicit and vague. The census categories, for example, which are based on the nature of work, are often used as a scale of occupational rank; but the census must lump together occupations of dissimilar rank in the same category and is likely to reverse the actual order of prestige of some occupations in classifying them.[5] Schemes of this kind are useful for making gross distinctions among mass data but are not precise.[6] Another possible method is to use opinion polls, in which, as we have seen, occupations have been ranked with remarkable consistency. But what is one to do with occupations which have never been included in a poll and which may not even be known to the general public? Some progress toward solving the problem of measurement might result from greater knowledge of the correlates of prestige. If we knew to what extent various factors can account for differences in prestige among occupations, we could

---

[5] For example, the occupation "singer in a night club," which would be placed by the census in the top category of professional and semiprofessional occupations, ranked seventy-fifth among the ninety in the NORC study, while the skilled manual occupations "electrician" and "trained machinist" ranked forty-fourth and forty-fifth. Studies of mobility often use a twofold classification of manual versus nonmanual occupations to represent high and low status, but Blau's analysis of the NORC data shows that the average skilled occupation covered in this study outranks the average white-collar occupation (Peter M. Blau, "Occupational Bias and Mobility," *American Sociological Review*, XXII [August 1957], 392–99).

[6] For a discussion of occupational rating scales see Caplow, *op. cit.*, pp. 30–58.

construct from them an index of the prestige of occupations.

To this end we obtained ratings of three variables—responsibility; training, education, and skill; and personal autonomy—for the ninety occupations used in the North-Hatt NORC study.[7] Then by correlation and regression analysis we explored how well the three variables could explain and indicate occupational prestige as measured in the NORC study.

Twenty-one graduate students in social science evaluated the ninety occupations as to the three variables. They were instructed to give each occupation a score on a 100-point scale, in which "0 represents the smallest amount, 50 represents the average, and 100 the largest amount of each characteristic." The three variables were defined as follows:

> *Responsibility.* Number, difficulty, and scope of decisions. The more serious the consequences of a wrong decision, the greater is the responsibility.
> *Training, education, and skill.* Skill and training may differ both in degree and in generality (the surgeon's knowledge of anatomy is more general and

abstract than that of the butcher, even though they both cut up organisms).[8]

Personal autonomy. How free is the person to decide how he will behave in his job? The highest possible amount will be found where the worker has very general duties and obligations and decides for himself when, where, and how he will carry them out.

The reliability of ratings was judged satisfactory after analysis of variance showed that, for each of the three variables, the variance of occupational scores (between-class) exceeded that of different raters' scores assigned to specific occupations (within-class). Each distribution of ninety occupational scores by a single rater on a single variable was then converted to standard z-scores. This was for the purpose of equating the subjective rating scales employed by the twenty-one raters. Each occupation was then assigned a score, the mean of its z-scores, for each variable. Correlation and regression analysis was undertaken to show the relation between North-Hatt prestige scores and the three variables. Finally, separate correlations of prestige with the three variables were computed within each of six occupational situses. One purpose of the correlations within situses was to indicate indirectly whether the judges' ratings varied independently or merely reflected the halo of the occupations' general prestige; the former apparently was the case, as will be shown below.

Table 1 shows the correlations of the three variables with prestige and with each other. Our judges' ratings on the basis of three variables were highly correlated with NORC prestige

---

[7] North and Hatt, *op. cit.* In selecting the three variables for which to obtain ratings, we eliminated extrinsic aspects of occupations, such as income, for the reasons cited earlier in this paper. We combined training, education, and skill into a single variable on the ground that informal or on-the-job training in some occupations is equivalent in scope and difficulty to the formal education required in other occupations and that skill is a main objective of either kind of training. Caplow (*op. cit.*, p. 52) mentions another intrinsic occupational characteristic which is doubtless important: whether the person manipulates symbols, tools, and materials, or some combination of these. We did not include this as a variable because it did not seem susceptible to more than gross distinctions.

[8] The idea of "generality" of knowledge in an occupation and the example of surgeon vs. butcher are adapted from Barber (*op. cit.*, p. 25).

TABLE 1. CORRELATION MATRIX OF OCCUPATIONAL RATINGS
($N = 90$)

Basis of Rating	r	1 Confidence Limits*	r	2 Confidence Limits*	r	3 Confidence Limits*	r	4 Confidence Limits*
1. Prestige	—		0.933	0.956 / 0.872	0.949	0.970 / 0.913	0.811	0.887 / 0.693
2. Responsibility			—		0.915	0.950 / 0.857	0.815	0.889 / 0.699
3. Training-educa-tion-skill					—		0.852	0.912 / 0.756
4. Autonomy							—	

*Confidence limits of 99 per cent obtained by Fisher's Z transformation.

ratings. The correlations with prestige were 0.949, 0.933, and 0.811 for training-education-skill, responsibility, and personal autonomy, respectively. The three variables also showed high correlations with one another, but the highest of these, 0.915 between training-education-skill and responsibility, was less than the correlation of prestige with either of these two variables.

The multiple correlation of prestige with all three variables combined was 0.962. The multiple correlation of prestige with the two variables of training-education-skill and responsibility was also 0.962, and analysis of variance showed that the correlation of prestige with personal autonomy, after the effects of the other two variables had been removed, was not significant at the 0.05 level. The multiple-regression equation showed ß-coefficients of 0.612 and 0.406, and ß-coefficients of 10.321 and 7.097, for training-education-skill and responsibility, respectively: roughly a 3:2 ratio.

Table 2 shows correlations of the three variables with prestige within each six occupational situses. Among business, recreational-esthetic, manual, and service occupations, as among the ninety occupations as a whole, training-education-skill had the highest correlation with prestige. Within the political and professional situses, responsibility showed the highest correlation. Personal autonomy was the least correlated with prestige in every situs except recreational-esthetic, where responsibility showed the lowest correlation of any variable within any situs (0.301). Separate correlations were not computed within the agricultural and military situses, as they were represented by only four and two occupations, respectively.

With so few occupations represented in each situs, one should not attempt to draw firm substantive conclusions from the within-situs correlations. Nevertheless, this aspect of the findings is of interest for what it suggests about the method of rating. The fact that substantially different patterns appeared in the different situses indicates that the raters' judgments did not simply reflect a halo from the occupations' general prestige. It appears,

TABLE 2. CORRELATIONS OF PRESTIGE WITH THREE
VARIABLES WITHIN SIX OCCUPATIONAL SITUSES

Occupational situs	N	Responsibility r	Responsibility Confidence Limits*	Training-Education-Skill r	Training-Education-Skill Confidence Limits*	Personal Autonomy r	Personal Autonomy Confidence Limits*
			0.993		0.985		—†
Political	8	0.942		0.873		0.400	
			0.579		0.246		—
			0.946		0.927		0.887
Professional	20	0.822		0.767		0.654	
			0.453		0.370		0.157
			0.971		0.982		—†
Business	16	0.884		0.927		0.468	
			0.591		0.727		—
			—†		0.989		—†
Recreational-esthetic	8	0.301		0.903		0.470	
			—		0.375		—
			0.986		0.994		0.882
Manual	19	0.829		0.977		0.629	
			0.493		0.919		0.095
			0.981		0.986		—†
Service	13	0.902		0.926		0.522	
			0.555		0.649		—

*Confidence of limits of 99 per cent obtained by Fisher's Z transformation.
†Confidence limits show r not significantly different from zero at 0.01 level.

instead, that each set of ratings was to some extent independent of the others and of the occupations' overall standing—which gains credence from the fact that the deviations from the general pattern of highest correlation with training-education-skill and lowest with personal autonomy are of a kind which one might expect. It does not seem likely that they have arisen from random variability in raters' judgments. The extremely low correlation of prestige with responsibility in the recreational-esthetic situs appears reasonable —artists and performers may need great skill, but they do not ordinarily make important decisions affecting others. One might also have expected the high correlation with responsibility in the political situs since making decisions is the essence of politics and administration. With less confidence, the relatively low correlation with training-education-skill among the professions can be explained on purely statistical grounds. All professions have fairly high prestige and require extended training, and "if we are drawing a sample from a group which is restricted in range with regard to either or both variables, the correlation will be relatively low."[9]

---

[9] Quinn McNemar, *Psychological Statistics* (2nd ed.) (New York: John Wiley & Sons, Inc., 1955), p. 149.

Our main finding, that training-education-skill and responsibility, in conjunction, account for much of the variance in the prestige of occupations, supports the views of North and Hatt, Kahl, Barber, and others, who explain prestige in essentially these terms. It is also consistent with Davis and Moore's theory of stratification: They maintain that the high-ranking occupations will be those which "require the greatest training or talent" (training-education-skill, in our terms) and at the same time "have the greatest functional importance for the society."[10] To have responsibility may not be the same as to have functional importance; but the two seem related in most instances, and an evaluation of an occupation's responsibility may be as close as one can come to an estimate of its functional importance.

The significance of both responsibility and training or skill can be summed up by asking the question, "How serious will the consequences be if an inept individual enters the occupation?" Bad performance will not matter much if the job is unimportant and carries little responsibility. Similarly, if work requires almost no skill, nearly everyone can do it well enough to avoid serious harm. One might tentatively advance the hypothesis that the man in the street perceives this, however dimly, when he attributes prestige to occupations: He reserves the highest prestige for occupations which stand high in both characteristics and assigns less to those high in one but low in the other, such as the recreational and esthetic occupations, which require skill but lack responsibility. Likewise,

occupational groups which are trying to raise their professional standing, such as nursing, attempt to expand both their domain of responsibility and their repertoire of skills, apparently sensing that both are necessary for maximum prestige.

It this is true, it provides a link between the general theory of stratification and the factual implications of this paper. If we confine our attention to prestige alone rather than considering all forms of occupational reward, then some of the objections that have been raised against Davis and Moore's theory become less valid. Occupations which do not seem to fit their theory include those which receive rewards without contributing visibly to societal welfare, such as are found in the underworld, and those which receive higher rewards than appear necessary, such as acting in the movies; neither of these is placed near the top in the prestige polls. Their main rewards are money and transitory fame or notoriety. Thus the existence of such occupations is not inconsistent with Davis and Moore's theory if the theory is taken to refer only to prestige and not to all kinds of rewards.[11]

Our findings suggest that ratings of training-education-skill and responsibility could be used to form an index of occupational prestige. Since the correlations we obtained were based on ratings by graduate students in sociology, it seems likely that similar results would be obtained if other sociologists used the same method. This is why these particular raters were used. Applying regression weights to

---

[10] Kingsley Davis and Wilbert E. Moore, "Some Principles of Stratification," *American Sociological Review*, X (April 1945), 242–49.

[11] This interpretation concerns only the assertion by Davis and Moore that occupations possessing certain characteristics will receive certain rewards. It leaves aside their assertion that the pattern of rewards is functional for the society.

ratings of the two variables, one could arrive at a single score for each occupation. To determine the best weighting of the two would require additional research beyond the resources of the present study—for example, an opinion poll similar to the NORC's but covering a larger and more representative sample of occupations, on which ratings and regression analysis are undertaken. The NORC list of occupations, while it covers a broad range, overrepresents some kinds of occupations, especially those ranking high, such as professions and top governmental positions. It might be found that maximum predictability of prestige would result if different weights were used for different situses.

Several advantages would inhere in an index of this type: it would be explicitly linked to stratification theory in the manner described above; it would avoid the errors of gross and overlapping classificatory schemes such as the census categories; since it would involve scoring occupations, not merely classifying or ranking them, it would permit the use of more powerful statistical techniques in research using occupational status as a variable. Moreover, raters could evaluate new or little-known occupations, given a knowledge of their duties and requirements, and arrive at predictions of the prestige the occupations, were they to become better known, would enjoy.

THE MEANINGS OF OCCUPATIONAL PRESTIGE[*][1]

Joseph R. Gusfield, *University of Illinois*

Michael Schwartz, *Indiana University*

Many studies have attempted to measure, describe, or gauge the relative rankings of different occupations. Specialists in stratification have tried to find the various rungs of the occupational ladder in order to ascertain social mobility patterns. They have

sought to understand the bases of occupational choice, exit, and self-respect. Of the many studies labeled "occupational prestige" or "occupational evaluation" the one conducted in 1947 by the National Opinion Research Center has remained the most influential. But what is being asserted when respondents rate occupations?

To answer this we will report on the relation between the ranks of fifteen occupations on the NORC scale and the responses of the same respondents to a Semantic Differential form on which the same fifteen occupations were used as concepts and were judged

* From Joseph R. Gusfield and Michael Schwartz, "The Meanings of Occupational Prestige: Reconsideration of the NORC Scale," *The American Sociological Review*, 28 (April 1963), 265–71. Reprinted by permission of the American Sociological Association.

1 Revised from a paper read at the Mid-West Sociological Association Meeting, 1962.

on twenty-two scales of meaning. A modified NORC scale and the Semantic Differential were administered to 337 college students. Of course our empirical results cannot be generalized; however, the study does raise some doubts about the ways in which prestige rating scales had been used in stratification theory.

WHAT DO PRESTIGE SCALES SCALE ?

Many of our difficulties with the NORC and other occupational prestige scales arose from our failure to understand what respondents did when they were asked to rank occupations. How did the operations performed in scales of the NORC type support or reject or relate to the problems of ranked systems posited in stratification theory? Several theories of stratification suggest that it is important to distinguish between a normative and a factual order. A description of the distribution of unequal amounts of power, respect, and income according to social position is a description of the factual order of stratification. The system of norms by which such differentiation is made legitimate or rejected constitutes the normative order of stratification, the judgment of the justice or injustice of it all. Thus Barber makes the distinction when he writes: "Shared values are one source of . . . differential evaluations. . . . Social stratification is the product of the interaction of social differentiation and social evaluation."[2] It is on this basis that one of the major uses of rating scales emerges to determine the relation between social rank and evaluations of occupations.

If we assume that the hierarchy of occupations is institutionalized on a normative basis, then not only will some positions get more than others but the hierarchy will be legitimate. There will be a high level of consensus about the moral validity of the distributive system. In the Durkheimian conception of society, institutions rest on a moral consensus. Again to quote Barber, who uses this view of society in understanding stratification, "Social differentiation and social evaluation must have a certain degree of congruence with each other."[3] Are the factual and the normative orders indeed congruent, and which of these forms the subject matter of rating scales? We all recognize that no matter how random a sample of a society we question, they are seldom an adequate source of information about the factual order of distribution of tangible valued items. If we want to know the distribution of income in the United States, we will get a more accurate picture from economic data than by asking people for their perceptions of the income distribution pattern. However, if we are interested in how people perceive the distribution pattern or in how they evaluate it—that is, apply moral norms to it—then the best of economic data are worthless for our purposes. As an item of distribution, "prestige" inherently has a normative character. Respect, honor, status and deference all have reference to the evaluation which others place on a position or on action. Consider Johnson's definition of "prestige": "The approval, respect, admiration, or deference a person or group is able to command by virtue of

---

2 Bernard Barber, *Social Stratification: A Comparative Analysis of Structure and Process* (New York: Harcourt, Brace & Co., 1957), p. 2.

3 *Ibid.*, p. 3.

his or its imputed qualities or performances."[4] These are characteristics (respect, admiration, etc.) whose existence can only be determined by what the members of the society think about a position.

Furthermore, if the concept of prestige is to be used in the study of stratification it must occur as a separate, analytical dimension. We must mean something other than the fact that people perceive some jobs as getting more than others. Our usage of a prestige component in reward and in job choice implies that there are elements in work satisfaction and in social differentiation which are not completely determined by income or power. These relate to the pride or respect to which a given occupation entitles its incumbent. "Prestige" must be something other than the perception that a given job has a "better shake" than some other or else the term is useless and should be dropped. One could redefine "prestige" to imply only the recognition of differential distribution. Being a lawyer could be thought to be a "better job" than being a filling station attendant because the respondent perceives that the former earns more money than the latter. This usage, however, departs widely from the common historical usage of sociologists when speaking about occupational prestige. Rating scales, such as the NORC scale, can be focused upon at least four different dimensions of "occupational prestige." It is the major point of this paper (and the data that we will report) that rating scales have confounded these and have led to conclusions which assume that only one of the following dimensions has been used by the respondent.

4 Harry M. Johnson, *Sociology: A Systematic Introduction* (New York: Harcourt, Brace & Co., 1960), p. 469.

1. The respondent's perception of social differentiation: Here the respondent is telling the investigator that some jobs are perceived as "better" than others, as he sees it. Lawyers get more than filling station attendants and the respondent recognizes this factual order of things.

2. The respondent's perception of others: This is the posture of the natural sociologist. Here the respondent reports on the system of his society. He tells us that whatever his own views or judgments, this is how jobs are ranked in his society. He displaces the professional sociologist. As we have already indicated, this may be the case with prestige as well as with other items of reward.

In both of the above cases the emphasis is on the perception of the factual order—this is how things happen here. It is by no means normative. It tells us little about his evaluation of jobs. The respondent may admit that doctors earn more money or command more prestige than do janitors but he need not evaluate this as acceptable, good, or just. Veblen certainly saw that lawyers, clergymen, and businessmen occupied honorific positions in American life. His irony was a way of saying that he thought honor was unjustly bestowed on occupations not worthy of it.

3. The prestige dimension per se: Here we attempt to find out what relative amounts of honor or respect are bestowed by the respondent on occupations. The normative aspect of prestige attribution suggests that some jobs, though they bring money or power, are degrading; others dignifying. Here we would try to see if the respondent does indeed follow such a process with respect to specific occupations.

4. The attribution of justice: Here we

look at the normative order in its clearest form. This would represent the evaluation the respondent has of the rightness of the factual order and his conception of the just system. It would tell us whether or not respondents think doctors and lawyers *should* get more than machinists and salesmen.

It is worth noting that Centers found that approximately 45 per cent of the urban working class and of both rural middle and working classes felt that doctors and lawyers made too much money. These occupations, which ranked very high in "occupational standing," were the highest in being judged as instances of over-enrichment.[5] The question asked on the NORC study confuses several dimensions of "prestige." Look at the exact question asked of respondents:

For each job mentioned, please pick out the statement that best gives your own personal opinion of the general standing that such a job has. Excellent standing. . . .

The question is ambiguous with respect to which of the four dimensions of prestige or evaluation is being used. Even asking "What do you think is the one main thing about such jobs that gives this standing" (asked as a general question not in regard to each occupation) does not clear up the ambiguity of "general standing." In truth, the authors do not claim that they are studying prestige but rather job evaluation, and for purposes of predicting job choice the distinctions may well be unimportant. But for stratification the distinctions are crucial.

USE OF OCCUPATIONAL RATING SCALE

The NORC scale is used in many places where there is some need for "placing" jobs on a scale of differential respect; for example, to determine whether or not a respondent has undergone social mobility. It is also used in connection with the analysis of the relation of value systems to structural characteristics. This latter usage is especially our concern here. The problem has gained acute notice in respect to studies of occupational prestige and industrialization and the conclusions derived from these. Let us look at the most influential of these, the study by Inkeles and Rossi. They compared the occupational ratings in six studies from six different industrialized countries (using the NORC study for the United States). Although some differences in the comparative rank of certain occupations were found, the results were similar. Professional and business personnel ranked well above manual laborers. The authors concluded that "there exists among the six nations a marked degree of agreement on the relative prestige of matched occupations."[6] When we look at the operative terms in the questionnaire directives, we are left in real doubt as to whether we have learned the patterns of prestige conferral in those societies. The studies used the following directives for the subject

5 Richard Centers, *The Psychology of Social Classes: A Study of Class Consciousness* (Princeton, N.J.: Princeton University Press, 1949), p. 142.

6 Peter H. Rossi and Alex Inkeles, "National Comparisons of Occupational Prestige," *American Journal of Sociology*, 61 (January 1956), 329–39.

matter they sought from the respondents:

U.S.A. (NORC study): "general standing."

Japan: "general reputations they have with people, those which people think highly of . . . those not thought so well of."

Great Britain: "social standing."

New Zealand: "social standing."

USSR (emigrants): "very desirable—very undesirable."

Germany (original study did not specify its question form)

The authors use these findings to support a "structuralist" rather than a "cultural" interpretation. Industrial occupations have the same standing in each of the countries despite cultural differences between the nations. Barber uses the Inkeles-Rossi study as the primary empirical support for his perspective on stratification. It demonstrates, for him, the basis of a factual order of stratification in the value system of the society; it establishes the way in which functional needs are given moral support. In Barber's words, "functionally important roles are congruent with or partly determine a system of values."[7] On the basis of ambiguous findings, a complex theoretical conclusion has been shored up.

THE RELATION BETWEEN NORC SCALE RANKINGS AND SEMANTIC DIFFERENTIAL PATTERNS FOR FIFTEEN OCCUPATIONS

The above considerations set the stage for the study reported here. We wanted to find the imagery of the occupations and their relation to the NORC ratings. Specifically, we wished

7 *Op. cit.*, p. 6.

to determine whether occupations with high NORC ranks also received high ranks on (a) an evaluation scale, or (b) on a factual-normative, i.e., descriptive, scale, or (c) on both scales, or (d) on neither scale. The Semantic Differential[8] was selected as the most appropriate instrument since it eliminates verbal fluency of the respondents as an intervening variable while it measures connotative meanings that respondents attribute to word concepts. In general, it is the connotative meanings attributed to occupations that remain uncontrolled. The Semantic Differential permits the measurement of that aspect of meaning. We wanted to know whether the meanings attributed to occupations of varying ranks are evaluative meanings in the "good-bad," "base-honorific" sense, or whether they are essentially factual-normative, reality-based, descriptive meanings. The Semantic Differential is composed of scales of polar adjectives with seven points interposed between the adjectives, such as

Good: –: –: –: –: –: –: –: Bad

Respondents are asked to rate a word concept on each of these scales. Osgood has shown that different pairs of polarities are highly intercorrelated and that some of these pairs represent an evaluation dimension of meaning; other pairs, an activity dimension, and others, a potency, or strength, dimension. We selected six items that have high factor loadings on the evaluation dimension from Osgood's thesaurus study: honest-dishonest, useful-useless, successful-unsuccessful, dirty-clean, sweet-sour, secure-insecure. From the remaining

8 Charles E. Osgood, George J. Suci, and Percy H. Tannenbaum, *The Measurement of Meaning* (Urbana, Ill.: University of Illinois Press, 1957).

factors, we selected scales that are primarily reality-based descriptive ones. We have also constructed some new scale items for this purpose. These scales are: middle class–working class, sober-drunk, Democrat-Republican, rural-urban, poor-rich, Negro-white, unemotional-emotional, young-old, and things oriented–people oriented. Finally, we selected some items that are rather ambiguous in that they have both evaluative and descriptive aspects. We refer to these as "mixed items." They are: passive-active, religious-irreligious, masculine-feminine, foreign-American, strong-weak, light-heavy, and tough-tender.

The question with which we are concerned is the extent to which the rank of each mean scale value for each occupation is related to the rank of the occupation on the NORC scale, e.g., is the highest ranked occupation also highest on each of the twenty-two scales, on some of them (and if so, which ones), or on none of them. If respondents rank occupations in terms of prestige in the evaluative sense, we would expect only the evaluative items to be related to the occupational ordering. On the other hand, if the respondents are in fact assuming the posture of the natural sociologist and are ordering occupations in terms of the way others see it or are describing the factual order of things, then we would expect the group of descriptive items to be highly related to the occupational ordering. Finally, respondents may indicate that both sets of items, as well as the mixed type, are related to the occupational orderings, in which case we may speculate that "prestige" or "general standing" may be determined by more than one component.

An occupational rating questionnaire was administered to 337 students in sociology and architecture classes.

The questionnaire was identical to the one used in the NORC study, but it included thirty-four of the ninety occupations. Three weeks later a Semantic Differential was administered to the same groups, using fifteen of the thirty-four occupations as concepts to be judged on the twenty-two seven-point scales. The composition of the group of respondents is unimportant for our purposes here since our sole interest is in the consistency between rank order of the fifteen occupations on the NORC scale and rank order on the twenty-two scales. The fifteen occupations, in the order of their rank in the sample on the NORC scale, are as follows: scientist, lawyer, mayor, civil engineer, banker, building contractor, school teacher, radio announcer, farm owner, store manager, policeman, traveling, salesman, locomotive engineer, plumber, and machine operator.

As we can see from this order, the results were similar to those reported in 1947 by North and Hatt. Professionals and people in authority ranked higher than farmers, salesmen, and manual laborers. Each of the twenty-two scales yielded a rank order for the fifteen occupations which varied to some degree from the rankings on the administered NORC scale. For example, "manager of a store" ranked tenth among these fifteen occupations in "general standing." It ranked eighth on the dirty-clean scale, third on the passive-active scale, and ninth on the middle class–working class scale. (Read left hand as the first rank. Thus, on the passive-active scale, the machine operator ranked first. This means he had the highest score for passivity of the fifteen occupations. The entire rank order for each occupation and for each scale is reproduced in Table 1.) Spearman rank order coefficients were computed between the rank order on each scale and the rank order on the NORC modified scale. Twelve of these were statistically significant at the 0.05 level or less. These were also the twelve with the highest correlations, ranging between 0.47 (honest-dishonest) to 0.93 (middle class–working class). The entire table of coefficients is reproduced in Table 2. Among these twelve, six are from the factual-normative scales, five are evaluative scales, and one is a mixed type. The high correlations of the successful-unsuccessful and secure-insecure evaluative scales on the one hand and the middle class–working class and poor-rich descriptive scales on the other hand suggest circular reasoning may be at work. It is as if the respondent said, "In American society, lawyers, bankers, and scientists are successful people and in the middle class. Therefore, they have a high general standing or vice-versa." This leads us to believe that the NORC scale did not reflect only a set of values applied to occupations but rather a set of perceptions about the social status which the occupations receive in the society (factual-normative) as well as a set of values. In short, they may reflect a justified factual-normative order of stratification. This interpretation is not unqualified. The moral designations do appear related to occupational rating. Honesty and usefulness are imputed to highly ranked occupations with more intensity than they are to the lower ranked occupations, although these scales showed only the tenth and eleventh highest correlations (0.69 for useful-useless and 0.47 for honest-dishonest).

EVALUATION OF SPECIFIC OCCUPATIONS

Analysis of some specific occupations indicates the "mix" of different patterns tapped by the scaling instrument. Examining the scientist and the lawyer we can see some important differences between the occupations ranked first and second on our NORC scale. They both ranked among the top five in usefulness. The lawyer was identified as urban, while the scientist was somewhere in the middle. Both were viewed as among the five least religious occupations, the scientist being the most irreligious. The scientist was clearly things-oriented and the lawyer clearly people-oriented. The scientist was seen as the least emotional and the lawyer as ninth least emotional. While both were among the five most secure (lawyer second and scientist fifth), the lawyer was viewed second richest (the banker was first) and the scientist as seventh. There is very little that we can designate as a common evaluative framework for these two occupations. The lawyer ranks fifth most useful, while the scientist is seen as the most useful. The lawyer appears as a rich, powerful figure, while the scientist is much less so but is highly useful.

The fact that a high-ranking occupation can be comparatively disesteemed is certainly seen when we look at the banker as well as the lawyer. The lawyer is viewed as sixth most honest. The banker ranks fifth on the NORC rating but is only the eighth most useful. Similarly traveling salesmen and plumbers rank 12 and 14, respectively, but the salesman has the lowest score for honesty and usefulness while the plumber's ratings for honesty and for usefulness are above his NORC rank (10 and 9). The difference between descriptive and evaluative patterns is perhaps best seen in the case of the public school teacher. Here there is the sharpest contrast between elements of esteem and status on the one

TABLE 1. TOTAL SAMPLE SEMANTIC DIFFERENTIAL RANKS (LOW TO HIGH)

Semantic Differential Scales*

Occupation	NORC Rank	D-C	P-A	Y-O	R-I	Usf-Usl	F-M	F-A	To-Te	So-Sw	W-S	S-Un	Un-Em	H-D	T-Pe	Mc-Wc	L-H	R-U	D-R	P-R	N-W	So-Dr	In-Se
Scientist	1	11	9	12	15	1	4	1	13	5	5	5	1	2	2	5	3	9	11	7	8	1	11
Lawyer	2	14	15	8	11	5	8	14	8	10	8	2	9	6	14	1	6	14	14	14	13	6	14
Mayor	3	12	12	14	3	10	9	15	9	11	7	3	12	14	13	3	8	15	8	13	15	4	10
Civil engineer	4	7	14	4	10	3	11	8	7	6	10	4	3	5	1	4	9	6	13	12	7	9	13
Banker	5	15	5	15	7	8	6	12	10	8	6	1	2	4	9	2	7	13	15	15	14	3	15
Building contractor	6	5	13	6	8	6	13	6	4	4	12	6	8	9	7	6	10	13	15	11	11	10	9
School teacher	7	13	7	5	2	2	1	10	15	15	1	8	15	1	15	8	1	7	12	9	4	2	12
Radio announcer	8	10	6	2	2	2	10	13	14	14	4	9	14	8	11	7	3	11	7	6	9	12	3
Farm owner	9	4	11	1	13	14	3	7	3	9	15	7	10	8	5	11	4	1	9	10	6	5	8
Manager of store	10	8	3	9	8	13	2	4	12	12	3	10	11	3	8	9	5	10	5	5	10	8	5
Policeman	11	6	8	3	5	7	10	9	2	1	13	11	4	11	12	13	12	12	10	1	2	7	6
Traveling salesman	12	9	10	2	14	15	5	11	11	13	2	11	13	15	10	10	13	5	4	3	12	13	1
Locomotive engineer	13	2	4	13	4	11	15	5	1	7	14	13	3	7	6	14	2	2	6	8	3	11	7
Plumber	14	3	2	11	9	9	12	3	6	2	11	12	6	10	3	13	4	4	2	2	5	14	4
Machine operator	15	1	1	7	6	12	7	2	5	3	9	15	7	12	4	15	8	8	1	4	1	15	2

* The scale abbreviations and meanings are listed below:

D-C	= dirty-clean	To-Te	= tough-tender
P-A	= passive-active	So-Sw	= sour-sweet
Y-O	= young-old	W-S	= weak-strong
R-I	= religious-irreligious	S-Un	= successful-unsuccessful
Usf-Usl	= useful-useless	Un-Em	= unemotional-emotional
F-M	= feminine-masculine	H-D	= honest-dishonest
F-A	= foreign-American	T-Pe	= things oriented-people oriented

Mc-Wc	= middle class–working class
L-H	= light-heavy
R-U	= rural-urban
D-R	= Democrat-Republican
P-R	= poor-rich
N-W	= Negro-white
So-Dr	= sober-drunk
In-Se	= insecure-secure

145

TABLE 2. SPEARMAN RANK ORDER COEFFICIENTS BETWEEN
OCCUPATIONAL RANKS AND SEMANTIC DIFFERENTIAL RANKS

Scale Number	Description	Coefficient	Probability	Rank of Rho
1	D-C	−0.74	0.005	6
2	P-A	−0.70	0.005	8
3	Y-O	−0.20	0.10	19
4	R-I	−0.23	0.10	17.5
5	Usf-Usl	+0.60	0.01	10
6	F-M	+0.19	0.10	20
7	F-A	−0.40	0.10	14.5
8	To-Te	−0.40	0.10	14.5
9	So-Sw	−0.23	0.10	17.5
10	W-S	+0.24	0.10	16
11	S-Un	+0.92	0.0005	2
12	Un-Em	+0.13	0.10	22
13	H-D	+0.47	0.05	12
14	T-Pe	−0.18	0.10	20
15	Mc-Wc	+0.93	0.0005	1
16	L-H	+0.41	0.10	13
17	R-U	−0.48	0.05	11
18	D-R	−0.83	0.0005	3
19	P-R	−0.74	0.005	6
20	N-W	−0.62	0.01	9
21	So-Dr	+0.74	0.005	6
22	In-Se	−0.80	0.0005	4

Twelve Scales Significant at 0.05 or Beyond

Group I High ±0.93 to ±0.70	Group II Moderate ±0.69 to ±0.48
D-C (dirty-clean)	So-Dr (sober-drunk)
P-A (passive-active)	In-Sec (insecure-secure)
S-Un (successful-unsuccessful)	Use-Usl (useful-useless)
Mc-Wc (middle class–working class)	H-D (honest-dishonest)
D-R (Democrat-Republican)	R-U (rural-urban)
P-R (poor-rich)	N-W (Negro-white)

hand and those of power and income on the other. The teacher ranks as the second most useful occupation, the weakest, the most honest. He ranks seventh on the scale of general standing, a ranking close to his position on scales reflecting distribution of power and income—eighth most middle class and sixth richest.

CONCLUSIONS

The recent work of Reiss et al.[9] and of Kriesberg[10] also indicates the tenu-

[9] Albert J. Reiss, Jr., Otis Dudley Duncan, Paul K. Hatt, and Cecil C. North, *Occupations and Social Status* (New York: The Free Press of Glencoe, Inc., 1961), p. 41.

[10] Louis Kriesberg, "The Bases of Oc-

ousness of using NORC and other occupational rating scales in use as evidence of prestige or of the value accorded occupations. Using published and unpublished data from the original NORC study, Reiss found that considerations of "prestige" were seldom called into play in choosing an occupation, although respondents did report lack of prestige as one significant variable in deciding they might leave an occupation in the near future. They concluded, as Kriesberg also did, that "it is not clear that a 'prestige' component is consciously perceived as a reward attached to occupations." Respondents reported a number of criteria almost equally used as the "one main thing about such jobs that gives this standing." (Our results suggest there is far from one main thing.) In common with other studies, lower economic strata were more likely to emphasize the factual order and used income and security. Higher strata were more likely to focus on self-expression and "prestige" in the Weberian sense of a separate dimension. Kriesberg's evidence bolsters our suggestion that respondents often act like natural sociologists. In keeping with our findings of a general set of terms used in ranking (middle-working class and successful-unsuccessful), Kriesberg found that the variable of prestige accorded professionals was the most significant variable in explaining rating of dentists. Other perceived characteristics of the occupation, such as degree of skill or the utility of dentists, were not so crucial as knowledge of a hierarchy in which professionals had a high rat-

ing. As Kriesberg wrote, "It may be that a person accords an occupation high prestige because he knows *as a matter of fact* that most persons accord members of that occupation high prestige."

Both these findings and ours suggest there is a distinct possibility that in the study of occupational prestige we are not getting only the system of evaluations which respondents may use in judging occupations. Either we obtain the descriptions of a factual order, in which the existent fact that *A* is a "better" job than *B* is recognized, or we may be confronted with a "pluralistic ignorance" in which each respondent assumes that the factual order is a reflection of the normative order which others, not himself, possess. In either case the ratings emerge as descriptive rather than evaluative or ambiguously both. Kriesberg's suggestion that people learn prestige ratings apart from imputation of any qualities or moral judgments of specific occupations is in line with our reasoning. Our data lead us to conclude that future studies that require judgments of prestige be designed in a manner that will permit the investigator to designate the amount of variance explained by each of the component elements of the judgment.

But the point is more than peripheral and methodological. It cuts to the heart of a major issue in sociology. Recent criticisms of functional theory have pointed out the conflict between perspectives which emphasize the individual's adaptation to facts of power in institutional arrangements. If we assume that description is evaluation, we unwittingly approve or condemn rather than analyze. We find congruence where none has been displayed.

---

cupational Prestige: The Case of Dentists," *American Sociological Review*, 27 (April 1962), 238–44.

SELECTED BIBLIOGRAPHY

BECK, JAMES B., "Limitations of One Social Class Index When Comparing Races with Respect to Indices of Health," *Social Forces*, 45 (June 1967), 586–88.

BERGEL, EGON E., *Social Stratification*. New York: McGraw-Hill Book Company, 1962. Part 1.

BLALOCK, H. M., "Status Inconsistency, Social Mobility, Status Integration and Structural Effects," *American Sociological Review*, 32 (October 1967), 790–801.

BLAU, PETER M., and OTIS DUDLEY DUNCAN, *The American Occupational Structure*. New York: John Wiley & Sons, Inc., 1967.

BOTTOMORE, T. B., *Classes in Modern Society*. New York: Pantheon Books, Inc., 1966. Chaps. 2 and 3.

CASE, HERMAN M., "Marxian Implications of Centers' Interest-Group Theory: A Critical Appraisal," *Social Forces*, 33 (March 1955), 254–58.

CENTERS, RICHARD, *The Psychology of Social Classes*. Princeton, N.J.: Princeton University Press, 1949.

COX, OLIVER C., *Caste, Class and Race: A Study in Social Dynamics*. Garden City, N.Y.: Doubleday & Company, Inc., 1948.

———, "Max Weber on Social Stratification: A Critique," *American Sociological Review*, 15 (April 1950), 223–27.

CUBER, JOHN F., and WILLIAM F. KENKEL, *Social Stratification in the United States*. New York: Appleton-Century-Crofts, 1954. Chap. 3.

ELLIS, ROBERT A., "Continuum Theory of Social Stratification: A Critical Note," *Sociology and Social Research*, 42 (March 1958), 269–73.

———, "The Prestige-Rating Technique in Community Stratification Research," in *Human Organization Research*, eds. Richard N. Adams *et al.* Homewood, Ill.: The Dorsey Press, 1960.

———, "Social Stratification and Social Relations: An Empirical Test of the Disjunctiveness of Social Classes,"

American Sociological Review, 22 (October 1957), 570–78.

GARBIN, A. P., and FREDERICK L. BATES, "Occupational Prestige and Its Correlates: A Re-examination," *Social Forces*, 44 (March 1966), 295–302.

GLENN, NORVAL D., "Massification Versus Differentiation: Some Trend Data from National Surveys," *Social Forces*, 46 (December 1967), 172–80.

GORDON, MILTON M., *Social Class in American Sociology*. New York: McGraw-Hill Book Company, 1963. Chaps. 6–8.

GROSS, NEAL, "Social Class Identification in the Urban Community," *American Sociological Review*, 18 (August 1953), 398–404.

HAER, JOHN L., "Comparative Study of the Classification Techniques of Warner and Centers," *American Sociological Review*, 20 (December 1955), 689–92.

HATT, PAUL K., "Stratification in the Mass Society," *American Sociological Review*, 15 (April 1950), 216–22.

HETZLER, STANLEY A., "An Investigation of the Distinctiveness of Social Classes," *American Sociological Review*, 18 (October 1953), 593–97.

HODGE, ROBERT W., *et al.*, "Occupational Prestige in the United States, 1925–63," *American Journal of Sociology*, 70 (November 1964), 286–302.

HUGHES, EVERETT C., "Prestige," *Annals of the American Academy of Political and Social Science*, 325 (September 1959), 45–49.

KAHL, JOSEPH A., and JAMES A. DAVIS, "A Comparison of Indexes of Socio-Economic Status," *American Sociological Review*, 20 (June 1955), 317–25.

KORNHAUSER, RUTH R., "The Warner Approach to Social Stratification," in *Class, Status and Power*, eds. Reinhard Bendix and Seymour M. Lipset. Glencoe, Ill.: The Free Press, 1953.

KRIESBERG, LOUIS, "Bases of Occupational Prestige: The Case of Dentists," *American Sociological Review*, 27 (April 1962), 238–44.

LASSWELL, THOMAS E., "Social Classes as Affective Categories," *Sociology and*

Social Research, 46 (April 1962), 312–16.

———, "A Study of Social Stratification Using an Area Sample of Raters," *American Sociological Review,* 19 (June 1954), 310–13.

LAUMANN, EDWARD O., *Prestige and Association in an Urban Community.* New York: The Bobbs-Merrill Co., Inc., 1967.

LAWSON, EDWIN D., and WALTER E. BOEK, "Correlations of Indexes of Families' Socio-Economic Status," *Social Forces,* 39 (December 1960), 149–52.

LENSKI, GERHARD E., "American Social Classes: Statistical Strata or Social Groups?" *American Journal of Sociology,* 58 (September 1952), 139–44.

LEWIS, LIONEL S., "A Note on the Problem of Social Classes," *Public Opinion Quarterly,* 27 (Winter 1963), 599–603.

MARANELL, GARY M., "Stratification in a Small Town: An Attempt to Replicate," *Sociological Quarterly,* 8 (Spring 1967), 259–62.

MARSHALL, T. H., *Class, Citizenship and Social Development.* Garden City, N.Y.: Doubleday & Company, Inc., 1965.

MAYER, KURT B., "The Theory of Social Classes," *Harvard Educational Review,* 23 (Summer 1953), 149–67.

MONTAGUE, JOEL B., JR., "Class or Status Society," *Sociology and Social Research,* 40 (May 1956), 333–38.

NELSON, HAROLD A., and THOMAS E. LASSWELL, "Status Indices, Social Stratification, and Social Class," *Sociology and Social Research,* 44 (July 1960), 410–13.

OSSOWSKI, STANISLAW, *Class Structure in the Social Consciousness.* New York: The Free Press of Glencoe, Inc., 1963.

PFAUTZ, HAROLD W., and OTIS DUDLEY DUNCAN, "A Critical Evaluation of Warner's Work in Social Stratification," *American Sociological Review,* 15 (April 1950), 205–15.

REISS, ALBERT J., JR., *Occupations and Social Status.* New York: The Free Press of Glencoe, Inc., 1961.

STEINER, IVAN D., "Some Social Values Associated with Objectively and Subjectively Defined Social Class Memberships," *Social Forces,* 31 (May 1953), 327–32.

STOCKWELL, EDWARD G., "The Use of Socioeconomic Status as a Demographic Variable," *Public Health Reports,* 81 (November 1966), 961–66.

THOMAS, R. MURRAY, "A Five Dimension Anatomy of Stratification," *Sociology and Social Research,* 50 (April 1966), 314–24.

CHAPTER FOUR

The Upper, Middle, Working, and Lower Classes

For some time, controversy has existed over the question of whether Negro patterns of stratification approximate the class system of white society or are more nearly like those of a caste society. Whatever the viewpoint, the differences are sufficient to justify treatment of Negro stratification in a separate chapter. The present chapter, then, is devoted to descriptive studies of classes in the white sector of American society.[1]

The term *class* does not represent an abstract category but a group of people bound together by frequent interaction, equality of status, and similar life patterns. Sociologists assume that these conditions, shared and transmitted, give rise to characteristics that distinguish strata. However, many of the problems of class demarcation and placement discussed in Chapter Three are clearly evident in the attempts to make generalizations about social strata. We have noted that some researchers view the American stratification system as a continuum, while others see discrete social classes. Assuming a continuum, we may nevertheless find rela-

---

[1] To many sociologists, Negroes in American society represent a separate caste within which a distinctive class system has emerged. Although we could have considered other ethnic groups as part of a general treatment of the relationship between ethnic differentiation and social stratification, we have singled out the Negro class structure because of its importance in the American stratification system.

For extended analyses of the relationships between ethnic and class stratification, see Milton M. Gordon, *Assimilation in American Life* (Fair Lawn, N.J.: Oxford University Press, Inc., 1964); Tamotsu Shibutani and Kian M. Kwan, *Ethnic Stratification: A Comparative Approach* (New York: The Macmillan Company, Publishers, 1965).

tively distinctive characteristics of persons at different points. Thus salient features of people in different positions on the stratification ladder can be described as both attributes and variables.

We precede each selection of studies below on the upper, middle, working, and lower classes with a general profile of the condition and style of life of each class. These profiles are ideal-type constructions adduced from field research carried out at different times and places on various samples of the American population.[2] In addition to organizing the key findings from a variety of empirical investigations, the profiles provide a context for understanding the significance of the contributions.

All studies in this and the following chapter depict social classes as relatively distinct sociocultural entities. This orientation generally holds regardless of the researcher's theory of stratification or his views concerning the continuum-category controversy.

THE UPPER CLASS[3]

Most studies show that the upper class constitutes from 1 to 3 per cent of the population.[4] Upper-class families are among the top 5 per cent of the families which receive 18 per cent of the national income.[5] Among these people the dominant group (those more securely established) has possessed wealth for several generations, and, along with it, a distinctive life style. They are the primary carriers of upper-class culture. (Persons with newly acquired wealth are not fully accepted by the dominant group.)

Interest and dividends from investment of inherited wealth, often supplemented by income from the business or profession of the family head, are the

---

[2] The generalizations constituting these profiles are based upon studies of samples from cities, small towns, and rural communities taken principally from the late 1930s to the early 1960s.

[3] We deal with the upper class as a power elite group more extensively in Chapter Seven.

While this profile of the upper class draws generally upon the relevant literature, we utilized the following works especially. E. Digby Baltzell, *Philadelphia Gentlemen* (Glencoe, Ill.: The Free Press, 1958); W. Lloyd Warner and James Abegglen, *Big Business Leaders in America* (New York: Atheneum Press, 1963); C. Wright Mills, *The Power Elite* (Fair Lawn, N.J.: Oxford University Press, Inc., 1959); Cleveland Amory, *The Proper Bostonians* (New York: E. P. Dutton & Co., Inc., 1947); August B. Hollingshead, *Elmtown's Youth* (New York: John Wiley & Sons, Inc., 1949). We also used heavily the "Middletown" studies by Robert and Helen Lynd and W. Lloyd Warner's "Yankee City" series.

[4] This and the following estimates of class size are based largely upon a review of studies given in Egon E. Bergel, *Social Stratification* (New York: McGraw-Hill Book Company, 1962), pp. 274–77. Variations in estimates occur for many reasons. Among these are differences in the choice of cutting points for demarcating classes and in the selection of class dimensions, e.g., income, education, residence, and occupation.

[5] Herman P. Miller, *Rich Man, Poor Man* (New York: Thomas Y. Crowell Co., 1964), p. 7.

main sources of income. Upper-class families seek to keep their inherited wealth intact from one generation to the next. They see any reduction in the original inheritance as a threat to the family's position and to the status of future generations.

Membership in exclusive private clubs is one of the characteristic features of upper-class life. It provides an opportunity for interaction with persons of similar background and is an important symbol of upper-class standing. The metropolitan men's club is at the core of upper-class society. Here the powerful among the upper-class meet and make important decisions affecting the community and the nation. Along with the exclusive club, the exclusive residential area with distinctive homes is a feature of upper-class life. This physical separation of the upper class tends to limit social relations with other classes and increases the likelihood of interaction with those of similar position.

The upper-class person has sufficient leisure to cultivate varied interests. He usually has a smattering of knowledge of many subjects including music, art, and literature. His household possessions reflect interest in literary magazines, rare books, original paintings, and sculpture. The wealth and leisure of the upper-class person provide him with the opportunity to travel more widely than persons in other classes do. Distinctive clothing, speech, and manners constitute part of a way of life that differentiates the upper class from the remainder of society.

A strong sense of extended family solidarity is found in the upper class. Although each nuclear family maintains its own residence, loyalty to other families in the kinship network is expected. Solidarity is based upon common family heritage and the joint ownership of property, often in the form of estates held in trust. Authority in the family rests in an elderly patriarch or matriarch. He strongly influences important decisions, such as those relating to education, occupation, or the selection of a spouse. When control of income from the family estate is in his hands, his power over family members is decisive.

Parent surrogates are largely responsible for child-rearing. In the early years, the nurse and then the governess care for the young. School-age children attend first a private day school and then, at the secondary level, a boarding school. Parents choose each school on the basis of its reputation as a training establishment for the upper class. The boarding school prepares the adolescent for an Ivy League college or, more specifically, for an upper-class club in such an institution. His education plus etxensive travel and exposure to cultural activities make him more sophisticated than his contemporaries are. As a result of this exclusive and intensive socialization process, he develops a sense of self-confidence; he learns to accept high status as his birthright and to conduct himself in keeping with his station in life.

Upper-class persons tend to be strongly oriented to the past, particularly to family heritage. They usually esteem the ancestors from whom the family has derived its status. Reverence for the past and concern with maintaining the status quo are reflected in the political and economic conservatism of the class. This emphasis on the past and on following established principles produces a combination of the traditional and the inner-directed personality types.[6] Within the bounds of the central precepts of tradition, the upper-class person's sense of personal security allows him to express himself more freely than can those whose independence may be threatened by financial insecurity.

The excerpts from E. Digby Baltzell's *An American Aristocracy* describe the emergence of the upper class and some of its salient characteristics. Baltzell contends that, in America, the national metropolitan upper class is characterized by a "consciousness of kind" and a "common cultural tradition." In contrast to this metropolitan upper class, which is concentrated on the eastern seaboard, the upper class described by August Hollingshead (Class I) is located in a small, midwestern, rural community. Although there are some significant differences between these two groups, their status and life styles are in many respects similar.

The excerpt from *Big Business Leaders in America* by W. Lloyd Warner and James Abegglen describes the life style and personal characteristics of one member of the upper class. This account suggests the ease with which members of this group, given a modicum of ability, can perpetuate their high status.

---

6 See David Riesman *et al., The Lonely Crowd* (New Haven, Conn.: Yale University Press, 1952). We may expect, however, that, as old estates become part of larger organizational empires and as upper-class persons enter such organizations, transformation to the other-directed type will occur.

AN AMERICAN ARISTOCRACY*

E. Digby Baltzell

University of Pennsylvania

Conceived in a new world which was free of the traditional authority of an established church and a feudal nobility and born in a revolt from the tyranny of a centralized government symbolized in the British monarchy and mercantilism, American institutions have, virtually from the begin-

---

* Reprinted with permission of The Macmillan Company from *An American Business Aristocracy* by E. Digby Baltzell. © The Free Press, a Division of The Macmillan Company, 1962.

ning, been shaped in a laissez faire capitalist climate. The merchant, mining, manufacturing, railroad, and finance capitalists, each in their day, were the most powerful members of the elite in nineteenth- and early twentieth-century America. As "old family" is usually found to be synonymous with "old money," the leading capitalists in the pre-Civil War period were the "old-family" founders in America. In the 1870s, the families of these men and their descendants formed local business aristocracies in the older cities such as Boston, New York, and Philadelphia. Living near one another, on the gentle slope of Murray Hill in New York, on Beacon Street in Boston, or around Rittenhouse Square in Philadelphia, the members of these families knew "who" belonged within this formal and well-structured world of polite society.

In the last two decades of the nineteenth century, these provincial aristocracies of birth and breeding (old money) merged with a new and more conspicuously colorful world known as "Society." It was in the 1880s that New York Society with a capital "S," then moving uptown to the newly fashionable Fifth Avenue district, came under the tutelage of Mrs. Astor and her right-hand man, Ward McAlister. It was Mr. McAlister who coined the snobbish term "Four Hundred" and finally gave his official list to the *New York Times* on the occasion of Mrs. Astor's famous ball on February 1, 1892. During this same period, as millionaires multiplied and had to be accepted, as one lost track of "who" people were and had to recognize "what" they were worth, the *Social Register* became an index of a new upper class in America.

But this new upper class was soon to be organized on a national rather than a local scale. In an age which marked the centralization of economic power under the control of the finance capitalists, the gentlemen bankers and lawyers on Wall Street, Walnut Street, State Street, and La Salle Street began to send their sons to Groton, St. Mark's, or St. Paul's and afterwards to Harvard, Yale, or Princeton, where they joined such exclusive clubs as Porcellian, Fence, or Ivy. These polished young men from many cities were educated together, and introduced to one another's sisters at de-butante parties and fashionable weddings in Old Westbury, Mount Kisco, or Far Hills, on the Main Line or in Chestnut Hill, in Dedham, Brookline, or Milton, or in Lake Forest. After marriage at some fashionable Episcopal church, almost invariably within this select, endogamous circle, they lived in these same socially circumspect suburbs and commuted to the city, where they lunched with their fathers and grandfathers at the Union, Philadelphia, Somerset, or Chicago clubs. Several generations repeat this cycle, and a centralized business aristocracy thus becomes a reality in America. The *Social Register*, first published in 1888, lists the families of this business aristocracy and their relatives and friends in New York, Chicago, Boston, Philadelphia, Baltimore, San Francisco, St. Louis, Buffalo, Pittsburgh, Cleveland, Cincinnati-Dayton, and Washington, D.C. In 1940, approximately one-fourth of the residents of these twelve metropolitan areas who were listed in *Who's Who* in that year were also listed in the *Social Register*. Thus the members of this contemporary American upper class, descendants of leaders in American life from colonial times to the present, had considerable influence on the elite in 1940....

It is important to stress once again the fact that, while there are many middle and lower classes in America, and in Philadelphia, there exists one metropolitan upper class with a common cultural tradition, consciousness of kind, and "we" feeling of solidarity which tends to be national in scope. The origin and development of this intercity moneyed aristocracy in America quite naturally paralleled the rise of rapid communications and the national corporate enterprise. Moreover, just as economic control of the various local firms in the "Yankee Cities" and

"Middletowns" of America have gradually gravitated to such metropolitan centers as Boston, New York, or Chicago, so upper-class prestige has, over the years, become increasingly centralized in the fashionable metropolitan suburbs.

The growth and structure of this national upper class has, in turn, been supported by various institutions. First and most important, of course, are the New England boarding schools and the fashionable Eastern universities. Whereas the older generation of Proper Philadelphians were educated at home or in local schools and colleges, at the turn of the century, and especially after the First World War, these national upper-class family surrogates began to educate the children of the rich and well-born from all cities in ever-increasing numbers. At the same time, the Episcopal Church also developed into a national upper-class institution. By the end of the nineteenth century, the process of upper-class conversion, which had actually begun in the previous century, was virtually complete. In the twentieth century, the fashionable descendants of staunch New England Calvinists or pious Philadelphia Quakers almost invariably worshipped in the Episcopal churches in the metropolitan suburbs of America. And the Episcopal Church is also an important part of the summer social life at such fashionable resorts as Mount Desert which do so much to foster inter-city family alliances.

Several things follow from the development of this national upper class and its supporting institutions. On the whole, of course, the family is weakened and increasingly replaced by an associational aristocracy. The family firm gives way to the large and anonymously owned corporation with the attending consequences of declining family pride and responsibility. The entrepreneur who founded the family firm and fortune is replaced by the hired executive, and the corporation soon becomes an impersonal source of dividends which conveniently supports a suitable style of life. At the same time, the fashionable school, college, and club replace the family as the chief status-ascribing institutions: Often isolated geographically as well as socially from the rest of the community, these fashionable associations tend to make for less social contact between classes than was the case in an earlier day when the members of polite society, although undoubtedly protected by a formal social distance recognized by all classes, may well have interacted more frequently in the local community with the members of the middle and lower classes. George Wharton Pepper, for instance, met and befriended a Negro boy while he was growing up in the neighborhood of stiff and fashionable Rittenhouse Square; his grandsons, reared in the social homogeneity of the Main Line and a New England boarding school, were more geographically isolated even though born in a more egalitarian age. Finally, the Episcopalianization of the whole American upper class also tends to foster uniformity and class isolation. This is, of course, part of a general trend throughout Protestantism. The Catholic Church has traditionally been an altar before which men of all walks of life bow down together, but the various Protestant denominations have, almost from the beginning, been organized along class lines. Certainly most Protestant churches today are social centers where families of similar backgrounds assemble together for worship. One often wonders if fashionable Episcopalians, in their aversion to the middle-class drabness of the "Protestant ethic," have not thereby substituted a convenient conventionality for their ancestors' more rigid convictions. At any rate, these developments in upper-class institutions tend to make for an increasing conformity and uniformity, a decline in local color and originality, and perhaps, at the same time, a new snobbishness which inevitably follows the increasing importance now attached to proper associational affiliation.

ELMTOWN'S YOUTH*

August B. Hollingshead

Yale University

CLASS I[1]

Wealth and lineage are combined through the economic, legal, and family systems in such a manner that membership in class I is more or less stabilized from one generation to another. Consequently the members of class I tend to have their position ascribed through inheritance. In view of this, very few of its members have achieved their positions in the prestige structure through their own efforts. Because the station of the family is transferred to the children and because few persons achieve class I positions through their own efforts, only a very few persons are able to enter its ranks in any one generation. Although wealth is the prime requisite for achieving positions associated with class I, once such positions have been attained, they do not need to be reinforced by further pecuniary accumulation. In fact, there can be a decline in the amount of wealth possessed by a family through two or more generations without the loss of its class identification, providing it conforms to the approved social code. If some members show an inclination to do so, the family may recoup its fortunes through "brilliant marriages" or by the help of other families. It is generally assumed, both within and outside the class, that persons in this stratum have the "ability" to provide the material things customarily associated with a class I family. Class I persons strongly emphasize the inheritance of abilities and characteristics; they consider acquired traits the outward expressions of "hereditary qualities." This belief is expressed in the doctrine of "good blood" and "bad blood." It is assumed that class I families have "good blood" and that the lower ranking classes have "bad blood" in increasing potency as descent of the social scale occurs.

Marriage between social equals is desired but achieved only in about four cases out of five. Marriage with a family from a lower stratum is strongly disapproved—even the threat

---

* From August B. Hollingshead, *Elmtown's Youth* (New York: John Wiley & Sons, Inc., 1961), pp. 84–90.

[1] Although only four adolescents belonged to class I families the characteristics of this class are described here because of its importance in the control of Elmtown's institutions.

of one brings the force of gossip and personal pressures into play to "break the affair off" before "something happens." On the other hand, a potential marriage between equals is approved, and subtle pressures are brought to bear by relatives and friends to see it consummated, for a "successful" marriage will bring two estates together and assure the family of its station for another generation. Divorce is condemned in the strongest terms since it not only breaks a family but also brings disgrace upon the relatives. Moreover, it often results in the division of a family heritage, an undesirable consideration in this competitive economy. Children are desired, but only one or two and, at most, three; too many children break estates into too many pieces.

When children are born, they are delivered in a large city hospital, usually in Chicago, by a specialist recommended to the family by a local doctor to take the case during the lying-in period. Children are carefully attended and given every consideration due future scions of a proud "old family" whose reputation in future years will rest on their shoulders after the present generation has been borne to rest beneath the green sod of "Everest" in the shadow of majestic tombstones that signify prestige of a bygone era, or rolled into the marble crypts of the mausoleum to face eternity by the side of relatives and friends of this "exclusive 2 per cent" of the community's families to which Elmtowners refer as "the society class."

Accumulated wealth provided these families with the highest incomes in the community. The two banks, the large industries,[2] practically all the business buildings in town, as well as extensive farm lands, were owned by class I families. Although all but three or four families enjoyed an income estimated a number of times to be "at least $5,000," a few incomes "from $25,000 to $35,000 a year"[3] were reported. The men were almost exclusively engaged in large business or farming enterprises, but there were a few independent professionals who had either been born into this stratum or married into it; in two or three cases they had moved into it by personal effort.

Large tax bills accompany extensive ownership; consequently these families have a direct interest in keeping assessments and tax rates low. They accomplish this effectively, within the community and the county, through the control of the two major political party organizations on the township and county levels. The candidates for public office, except the district attorney and the judge, are generally not members of class I, but this does not mean they are free from controls exerted by class I interests. Money, legal talent, and political office are instruments used to translate interests into effective power. They are relied upon to implement decisions in contests which involve raising tax bills through public improvements, such as new public buildings, schools, roads, or welfare programs. This behind-the-scenes control results in the formulation of conservative policies and the election of officials who act in the capacity of agents for class I interests.

Although class I families have the highest standard of living, their level of consumption does not exhaust their incomes; so a sizable proportion is

---

2 Except the Mill and the largest strip mine, which were owned in part by four or five local families, though the majority of the stock was owned by outsiders.

3 Income figures given here and in succeeding sections are for 1941.

saved. All homes are owned; many have been inherited. They are located in two residential areas, but concentrated mostly in one. . . . Practically every family owns two or three cars. The "family car" is generally a Packard, Cadillac, or Buick, less than two years old. The "business car" may range from a Cadillac to a Ford; in age, it may be the latest model or an old "jalopy." Some of the older men have been running these "business cars" for twenty years without undue cost or trouble; their sentimental attachments to the car have replaced their earlier feelings about their saddle horses. The "young folks" usually have a late-model lightweight coupe or roadster as a personal car.

Leisure, not labor, is dignified; consequently as little time as possible is devoted to making a living. Wealth invested in lands, securities, and businesses assures the family a secure income with a minimum of effort. The wealthier families have managers who supervise their holdings, and only nominal supervision of these agents is necessary. The men may spend a few hours a day in the office, but most of the work is done by "the office girl." The remainder of the day may be spent in going out to the farm or farms "to see how things are going." A walk over the farms is always in order in good weather. There are fine, blooded cattle, either Angus or Herefords, to be admired, hogs to be inspected, and instructions to be given to the tenant or farm manager. Almost all families keep one full-time maid who does the daily chores of cooking, cleaning, washing, ironing, and keeping the house in order, and a considerable minority hires an additional woman part-time to do the heavy cleaning. Yard men do the gardening in the summer months and fire the

furnace in the winter. This hired help frees both the men and the women several hours each day from the confining requirements of making a living and keeping the household in order. The leisure time thus gained is consumed in many ways by different persons. In fall and early winter, the men spend several mornings each week in the duck blinds at the Hunt Club, owned and maintained by a select group of upper-class families. In spring and summer there is the thrill of fishing in local lakes or in the "game fish" lakes a hundred miles to the north. Practically all families belong to the Country Club, where they while away many pleasant hours during the summer months either on the golf course or lounging and visiting on the veranda over a coke, a beer, or a long highball. The women belong to the "Friday Morning Club"; they meet and listen to speakers or just visit and gossip.

Travel is an avidly followed leisure-time pursuit. Most families own or rent cottages near the northern lakes, and the women and children move to "the lake" for the summer. The head of the family makes trips there over a weekend that lasts from Friday afternoon to Monday evening. A trip to Florida, the Gulf Coast, or California during January or February is the order of the season.

In their leisure hours they associate almost exclusively with other class I persons who belong to the same clique. Sometimes cliques are composed of older women who play whist, 500, or bridge; middle-aged female cliques tend to confine their social activities to contract bridge and gossip. There are two or three younger women's cliques; these groups play bridge between discussions on child care and baby-rearing. Several are made up of couples of about the same age who have like interests (the Big Eight). It is difficult to generalize about what these mixed cliques do, as there is considerable variation from one to another.

Education is not highly regarded, either as a tool for a professional career or for knowledge in the traditional sense. Less than one-half of the men and women above 60 years of age attended college or university, and a very few were graduated. Practically all middle-aged persons were graduated from a public high school, and most attended either a good small college or a large middle-western university. A few of the women were graduated, but most dropped out after a year or two, either to stay home or to get married; some of the men were graduated, but only a few continued their education on a professional level. The younger people finish high school, and the majority attend good colleges or universities, but only about half of the men and a third of the women graduate. A considerable proportion of those who finish college do not return to the community to live their adult lives.

All class I families belong to a church; almost all are in the Federated, but they do not attend services with any marked frequency or regularity. However, they contribute freely to the church budget. Ten families from class I guaranteed and paid 71 per cent of the Federated Church budget in 1941. The year before one family spent more than $1,600 on the church parlors, but only one member came to services three or four times during the year. Some elderly persons and children from about 5 to 12 years of age are the only regular participants in religious affairs.

The ritual entailed in the social code is meticulously observed by the women; the men more or less ignore it or consider it "funny." Essential elements in the social ritual are clothes, stationary, good breeding, and self-assurance. Feminine apparel must be in accordance with the prevailing exclusive mode. It must be tailored by either an acceptable local dressmaker or by the lady herself in some cases, or it must come from an exclusive shop in a distant city. Its quality has to be excellent, exclusive in style, chic and smart, but not "popular" lest it lose its symbolic value. Absolute conformity in the use of note paper, personal cards, and invitations is stressed in the formal relations between the generations and between the new and the old families.[4] The women of a clique simply ignore the niceties of this convention in their informal relations with each other; however, the ritual is called upon when the occasion demands its use. Good breeding is observed at all times in the relations between men and women and those of different ages. Curiosity in any form by an outsider is considered to be the height of bad breeding and a violation of the social code. However, the women have no hesitation about inquiring into the affairs of people who rank lower than them-

---

[4] Two subdivisions are discernible in class I. The largest is composed of "old families," who have lived in Elmtown for generations and have been in the "society class" for at least two. The second section is made up of the "new rich," who have made "fortunes" through manufacturing and business enterprise. These families are not too well established in their positions, and the "old families" are rather dubious about their breeding and manners and are not on very intimate terms with them. The women in these families tend to wear dramatic clothes designed for stagy effects. Their charity and benefit activities, like their clothes, are means to one end—higher prestige.

selves in the prestige structure. An air of complete self-confidence and easy assurance may be observed among both men and women in their relations with equals. An occasional flash of hauteur is considered good form among the women "who have arrived" and a requisite to maintaining social distance in their relations with persons "who have not arrived." This pose— the velvet glove on the steel fist— sometimes is believed to be the only effective way to put "social climbers" in their place. Personal publicity in the local paper is avoided, because they believe notices in the social column advertise a person's "social weakness."

For the class I's, violation of the social code appears to be a vastly greater sin than violation of the Ten Commandments. High personal morals are prevalent, especially among older men and women, but middle-aged and younger men and women drink and gamble among themselves in a none too genteel manner. Some of them may not observe the laws of the community with care, yet there are no arrests. The prestige position a family enjoys appears to determine the light in which an act is interpreted by law-enforcement agencies.

BIG BUSINESS LEADERS IN AMERICA*

W. Lloyd Warner, *Michigan State University*

James Abegglen, *Boston Consulting Group*

The lives and careers of mobile leaders have been examined in previous chapters. In this we shall study the private and public worlds of the birth elite. Because the place of the family is of primary importance in understanding business leaders of this kind we shall pay particular attention to the relations of fathers and sons, husbands and wives, and other family members. The problems of men born to an "old" elite, three or more generations at the top, are different from those of the "recent" elite, those born to fathers who were the first generation to occupy this position; therefore,

* From pp. 144–48, *Big Business Leaders in America* by W. Lloyd Warner and James Abegglen. Copyright © 1955 by Harper & Row, Publishers, Incorporated. Reprinted by permission of the publishers.

we shall analyze both types. We shall also learn what we can about how and in what way their families influence occupational succession in American big business. Alton Dobson and his wife are excellent examples of the old elite. We will begin our inquiry by learning what kind of people they are and what part the family played in the career of this representative of the men who were born to position.

Alton Dobson's great-grandfather and his father's father before him were recognized as important figures in the business world. Socially the Dobson family has been prominent in New England for many generations. Since one-fourth of the business leaders are sons of big business men and only one-eighth are grandsons, Dobson represents a small but important group.

They, their careers, their families, and their social worlds contrast sharply with the world of mobile men. Dobson, throughout his life, has stayed in the *social* position given him by birth. The security of birth and family is of the utmost importance to him and his position.

Seemingly all men born to business leaders share a common position. Occupationally this is largely true, but socially it is not. The recent elite, the leaders who are sons of mobile men, are not in families with firmly established and consolidated positions; their family's place in the community is very different from that of the older families like the Dobsons. The new and old birth elites have different problems to solve—one is insecure socially, and the other firmly placed and secure.

We first see Alton Dobson through the eyes of the man who interviewed him.

"When I went into Alton Dobson's office," the interviewer wrote, "I felt a little let down. The quarters were almost cramped; his desk was a roll-top. There were indications of today's efficiency, yet all of it said that many men, generations before Alton Dobson, had ruled from these modest quarters and that he, the present occupant, would pass his empire on to a proper aspirant of the next generation, well trained to take command. His secretary, an elderly, spinsterish person, might have been a character in a Howells novel out of nineteenth-century Boston. Later when I saw the Beacon Street house I found its exterior somewhat dull and much like all of them on that street. But the interior was something else. It, too, was from the past. Despite some of the intrusive Victorian furniture, most of it went back to the classical elegance of the Georgian period. The house was quiet;

it had the stillness and unmoving quality of the past about it. A butler took me to the library where Alton Dobson was sipping a brandy with his after-dinner coffee. He looked small and insignificant against the background of the high walls, filled with tier upon tier of beautifully bound books.

"He told me of his family. Some time before the Revolution they started in the fishing trade, built ships, and sent them to the West Indies, to Africa, and China. This branch of the family gradually gave up shipbuilding and trade. From their financial knowledge gained as 'merchant princes' they moved into banking and soon owned one of the most powerful banks in the eastern United States. Now the stock is well distributed, but the Dobson name and the bank as an institution are often synonymous. He went to St. Mark's, to Harvard, 'got no more than a gentleman's C,' was coxswain on the crew (very proud of this), a member of a final club, spent a year abroad, another at the Harvard Law School, and then started as a clerk in another bank to learn the business. He learned to his astonishment that his business colleagues thought him a good business man and before long he was an employee 'of the bank my family has been associated with for so long, and after serving my time at the small desks I was promoted to a higher place and in time the bank made me president. The family name didn't hurt, but I know if I had not possessed ability I would never have been allowed to reach any position of importance in this bank. Perhaps I shouldn't say this. I know it's immodest, but to make my point—one of my cousins tried to do much what I've done. He just didn't have it. Finally, even he knew it, maybe because he got no place. He quit and is now living very modestly on a small inheritance in the south of France.'

"Outwardly he fitted the conventional role of the conservative bank president and the inheritor of social status well established by many generations of Dobsons. I was not prepared for his responses to the personality tests. They revealed something quite different.

"When he looked at the card of the athletic man on the rope, I expected the usual traditional and conventional answers, such as the man was a trapeze performer and, after prodding, to hear he was going up or coming down the rope. Mr. Dobson looked at the card, took his glasses off his nose, and turned to me with a big smile and a knowing look: 'That fellow on the rope is evidently escaping from someplace. Might be a fire although it's more apt to be—I could tell you something, but I wouldn't want you to put it down. He might have just heard the lady's husband come in the door. He's thrown his clothes out the window, and he's making a hasty descent out the fire escape. That would account for his being in the nude.'

"I was amused. I learned that Mr. Dobson was not the only one of his social class who seemed to have an inner freedom and an easy way of dealing with his 'impulse life.' True, they are conventional in manner, their business roles are exemplary, and their moral behavior without reproach, but some of them find joy in life and are capable of having fun.

"While we were having a drink before I left, the conversation turned to his civic and social life and the kinds of clubs and organizations to which he and his wife belonged. I told him I'd like to know what they were and

how he felt about them. He sighed:

"'I must belong to hundreds of associations. I'm constantly trying to weed them out. I've taken a pretty active part in some; sometimes I spread myself too thin. I belong to the National and State Chambers of Commerce, the NAM, American Banking Institute, and to the Harvard and Racquet Clubs. I belong to certain social clubs—you don't join one, you're born to it. I belong to some others but they don't amount to anything.' What philanthropic and public service organizations? He smiled. 'Do you really want them? Here are some that I'm active in. Mother and Infant Welfare Society, the Historical Society, the Geographic Society; I used to be on the board of directors of the national polio organization. I am on the board of the Art Museum; I'm on the boards of two prep schools. They take about as much time as my other extracurricular activities. The Historical Society is a closely knit organization tied up with New England. We publish our own histories. My mother was on the board of the Mother and Infant Welfare Society for some twenty-odd years. She got off, and they wanted me to come on.' Are you also interested in these groups? 'Oh, yes, I wouldn't be an officer unless I were interested. I've turned down many things that I thought would be nice, but I'm not personally interested in them or they have nothing to do with the company.'

"Political organizations? 'I've done very little in politics. That's just because I haven't taken the time, or I'm not a good enough citizen. But I contribute. I've voted the Republican ticket every time except in some local cases where I split my ticket.'

"'My friends? Basically, my good friends are from St. Mark's. My contact with them now is mostly social. A few friends are from college. Most of my friends are business executives, pretty much so. Loads of them turn out to be clients or lawyers, bankers —in that category. I'm not society minded at all, only my wife is. I'm usually involved in extracurricular activities so much that I don't gad about.

" 'My wife entertains our social and business friends. She takes an active part; she has to. She doesn't go on business trips, but she's active here. She wouldn't see me if she weren't. We entertain a lot at home.' "

Mr. Dobson and those who belong to the older birth elite participate in the community differently from those recently arrived. The birth elite are active in a greater variety of philan-

thropic and civic organizations and social clubs. Many of the outstanding and more prestigeful social clubs are not open to the newly arrived elite or to those whose fathers were the first to climb from social obscurity. Mr. Dobson had learned this at St. Mark's and Harvard; others of his kind grew up with such knowledge or gained it before going to Yale, Princeton, and other undergraduate, socially distinguished colleges. But mobile young men, striving to reach high position at such places, always learn sooner or later, as had Jake O'Flaherty, that "people like us are okay to know and be friends with, but it takes a great-great-grandfather to get you in the better clubs of Boston or New York."

THE MIDDLE CLASS[1]

Middle-class persons are distinguished from those above them by their more limited possession of wealth and power and from those beneath them by their occupational pursuits. Most investigators estimate the size of the middle class to be between 40 to 50 per cent of the population. Middle-class people have occupations requiring thinking rather than hand labor. Thus, they are concentrated pri-

---

[1] Although the generalizations constituting this profile are applicable to the middle class as a whole, they are more characteristic of the upper ranges of the group.

The following representative studies support this account of the middle class. Urie Bronfenbrenner, "Socialization and Social Class Through Time and Space," in *Readings in Social Psychology*, eds. Eleanor Maccoby *et al.* (New York: Henry Holt and Company, 1958), pp. 400–425; Daniel R. Miller and Guy E. Swanson, *The Changing American Parent* (New York: John Wiley & Sons, Inc., 1958); C. Wright Mills, *White Collar* (Fair Lawn, N.J.: Oxford University Press, Inc., 1956); Riesman, *op. cit.*; Robert R. Sears *et al.*, *Patterns of Child Rearing* (Evanston, Ill.: Row, Peterson and Co., 1957); John R. Seeley *et al.*, *Crestwood Heights* (New York: Basic Books, Inc., Publishers, 1956); William H. Whyte, Jr., *The Organization Man* (Garden City, N.Y.: Doubleday & Company, Inc., 1956); Richard F. Hamilton, "The Marginal Middle Class: A Reconsideration," *American Sociological Review*, 31 (April 1966), 192–99; Cyrus M. Johnson and Alan C. Kerckhoff, "Family Norms, Social Position, and the Value of Change," *Social Forces*, 43 (December 1964), 150–56; Melvin Kohn, "Social Class and Parent-Child Relationships: An Interpretation," *American Journal of Sociology*, 68 (January 1963), 471–80; Bernard C. Rosen, "The Achievement Syndrome: A Psychocultural Dimension of Social Stratification," *American Sociological Review*, 21 (April 1956), 203–11; Louis Schneider and Sverre Lysgaard, "The Deferred Gratification Pattern: A Preliminary Study," *American Sociological Review*, 18 (April 1953), 142–49.

marily in professional, technical, administrative, sales, and clerical jobs. Middle-class persons in positions requiring either extensive training and knowledge or the exercise of substantial power over others are the elites of their class. There is a considerable difference between this group and clerical and sales personnel, who have less training, power, and income. Nevertheless, the middle class as a whole share certain values, beliefs, and life styles which distinguish them from those above and below. While the following generalizations are applicable to the middle class as a whole, they are more clearly characteristic of the elite group.

Status advancement is important to middle-class people. Participation in community activities, including voluntary associations, is one of the chief means by which they enhance their prestige. Publicized community leaders are typically middle class, although in many cases they represent the upper-class people who make the final community decisions. Owning a home in one of the better residential areas of the city or, increasingly, in the suburbs is also an important validation of status. Home ownership is part of a general emphasis on the importance of property and the accumulation of capital goods.

Middle-class persons are the prime carriers of the success ethic in American society. They are strongly motivated to attain high socioeconomic position and believe that ability and ambition are rewarded by success. In line with this upwardly mobile orientation is their emphasis on competition in the occupational world. They place importance on higher education as a significant avenue of upward mobility and also as an end in itself.

The values pertaining to status advancement constitute the major motif of middle-class activity. Supporting beliefs include the conviction that achievement is a function of individual initiative and personal ability, that self-restraint and respectability are virtues, and that social opportunities are available to those who want to take advantage of them.

Middle-class persons are future-oriented. They are interested in long-term goals and are willing to defer immediate gratification in order to achieve such goals. In addition, their view of the world is a rational, purposeful, and manipulative one. The value they place on doing and achieving sets the tone for their social relationships and for their presentation and conception of self—as seen by their tendencies toward impersonality in social interaction and toward self-control. Rather than attributing responsibility to forces outside their control, they accept personal responsibility for what happens to them.

The middle-class family is a strong nuclear unit. Ties among husband, wife, and children are important, often to the exclusion of extended family relationships. Ties with more distant relatives are often severed also in the interest of maintaining social and geographical mobility. Husband and wife roles are closely interwoven. Thus, the husband often helps with household chores and cares for the children. In return, the wife is expected to be the "social director" of the family and to be of assistance to the husband in maintaining a social front.

Middle-class parents train their children from infancy to exhibit those characteristics which in later life will enable them to compete effectively for middle-class occupations. As previously mentioned, these characteristics include self-discipline, restraint of aggression, responsibility, initiative, and a high level of academic achievement. In recent years middle-class parents have moved away from adherence to rigid child-rearing practices such as early weaning and toilet training and toward more tolerance of the needs of the child. Nevertheless, they maintain high expectations for their children.[2] Thus, although methods of child-rearing have changed, the effect is the same: preparation of middle-class children for middle-class occupations and life styles.[3]

The selection from *Crestwood Heights* reflects the pattern of social and geographical mobility typical of the middle class. Career, meaning advancement up the occupational ladder, takes precedence over almost everything else. The excerpt from Arthur Vidich and Joseph Bensman's *Small Town in Mass Society* tells of the middle class in a small rural community. Despite its dissimilarity, in some respects, to the middle class in large urban areas, it displays some of the central features of this class, particularly a life style of individual competitiveness and disciplined effort. The participation of upper-middle-class people in organizations emphasizing self and community improvement is a salient feature of their way of life. The selection from *Democracy in Jonesville* highlights the extent of their involvement in this kind of associational activity.

---

2 With respect to the child-rearing practices of the modern middle class, Bronfenbrenner concludes that: "Middle-class families rely more on reasoning, isolation, appeals to guilt, and other methods involving the threat of loss of love. At least two independent lines of evidence suggest that the techniques preferred by middle-class parents are more likely to bring about the development of internalized values and controls. Moreover, the effectiveness of such methods should, at least on theoretical grounds, be enhanced by the more acceptant atmosphere experienced by middle-class children in their early years." Bronfenbrenner, *op. cit.*, p. 425.

3 Miller and Swanson have added a new dimension to the picture of middle-class child-rearing. They distinguish two types of families, the entrepreneurial and the welfare-bureaucratic. Heads of entrepreneurial families are engaged in the old middle-class occupations of independent businessmen and professionals. The welfare-bureaucratic type holds various middle-class positions in large bureaucratic organizations. Miller and Swanson found that middle-class parents in entrepreneurial occupations emphasize the themes of self-control and of an actively manipulative orientation toward the world. In contrast, middle-class parents who hold positions in bureaucratic organizations place emphasis on external controls and on an accommodative orientation toward the world. Each tends to emphasize the adaptation characteristics learned in his occupational world. Miller and Swanson, *op. cit.*

CRESTWOOD HEIGHTS*

John R. Seeley, *Center for the Study of Democratic Institutions*

R. Alexander Sim, *Canadian Department of Citizenship and Immigration*

Elizabeth W. Loosley, *University of Toronto Press*

The Crestwood child's environment includes, as earlier chapters have described, the very criteria by which the success of the career is measured. The conditions which make for comfort are in themselves the hallmarks of success in the career: harmonious surroundings keyed to the latest conception of beauty and elegance; the opportunity to consume food which is rich, yet approved by nutritionists as nourishing; the house, and the privilege of living, in a select area; superior opportunities for travel, education, entertainment, and training in special skills. These are the rewards of the father's capacity to earn, which is thus a major measure of a successful career.

The connections between the career and the symbols of success and the attendant attitudes and values are obvious. The child, who in more static social situations might be permitted to take certain aspects of the common life for granted, is in Crestwood Heights made to "appreciate" the close connection between effort and achievement: Where there has been rapid personal mobility (and will be more) one cannot take anything for granted. The past has been outmoded too recently. The present social and eco-

nomic status of the parent is too precarious. The goals ahead, higher up the ladder of achievement, beckon too invitingly for complacency. It seems that personal mobility develops a momentum of its own, which, until it is spent, carries the individual and his family from status to status. Yet it is inevitable that the child for whom so much is being done should also tend to "take everything for granted," including the inevitability of his own success. At the same time there is much uncertainty in Crestwood Heights as to whether the person who does *not* receive such a good start (like many of the adults who voice these doubts) does not really have the advantage; is he not more strongly oriented toward struggle and competition—and therefore more likely to achieve?

Various social interests have a stake in the development of career-oriented persons. We have said that the complex contemporary division of labor requires certain components at the professional and managerial level which become essential to the smooth operation of an industrial society. The maintenance of this group is, in turn, assured, it seems, by three conditions: mobility in space and in social class; occupational opportunity with commensurate rewards in material objects and class position; and finally, personal flexibility and adaptability within fairly well-defined limits respecting attitude, behavior, and occupational

* From *Crestwood Heights, A Study of the Culture of Suburban Life*, by John R. Seeley, R. Alexander Sim, and Elizabeth W. Loosley, © 1956 by Basic Books, Inc., New York. Canadian permission granted by University of Toronto Press.

techniques. These are the prerequisites of the successful career.

Mobility is, as we see it here, the highly developed pattern of movement from one job to another, from one place of residence to another, from one city to another, from one class position to another. To the individual, therefore, moving must not only hold the promise of material reward and added prestige, but, in spite of cost and labor, it should itself be "exciting." The chance to meet new friends, the known but as yet untried amenities in the distant city, together with the exhilaration of leaving behind the frustrations and jealousies of office, clique, and neighborhood, help to make moving more than tolerable. The man and woman of the Heights have few bonds that cannot be broken at the promise of a "promotion." They have been prepared for this from the cradle.

Mobility must be matched by opportunity: opportunity for training, employment, and advancement. Training must be available if the mobile person, bent upon a career, is to acquire the expected and necessary technical skills and social graces. He must have, of course, at least a minimum standard of intelligence, energy, and poise; but, more importantly, he must be drawn toward the enterprise around which skill, grace, intelligence, energy, and poise will play, and out of which his own career will develop. He must *wish* to manage or cure—and be prepared to *learn* to cure or manage.

The web of occupational opportunity for executive and professional which extends outward from Crestwood Heights to other upper-middle-class communities in an essential part of the career orientation of the individual. There must be posts to fill. It is best if there are more opportunities than men, but, even if the opposite is the case, the satisfactions which come from keen or even ruthless competition can be stressed. In either case, whether there is a buyers' market or a sellers', the experience is rationalized and justified.

The third prerequisite calls for a readiness in the professional and executive to abandon cherished usages and techniques as new ones arise. Of course the desire for change must not be so strong as to impair the individual's performance at the level presently occupied; the costs and risks of moving may help to bridle his ambition, but the job itself has its own satisfactions. Nevertheless, he must be willing to acquire new conceptions of life and organization and to revise constantly in later life his procedures within his chosen field. The differences between the career of the person who has risen by his own effort and the person who has been placed in Crestwood Heights by the parent have a relation to the flexibility which is so essential to the professional and executive person in a rapidly changing society since the individual who "gets a good start" is more likely to accept current techniques and practices than the individual who is struggling upward. The latter must challenge the very arrangements which give advantage to the former. Personal flexibility is a valued characteristic, whereas rigidity is generally condemned. "Flexibility" allows the person to accept innovation, to maneuver in difficult situations where precedent gives little guidance, and to seek by his own efforts new solutions to social and technological problems.

Careers are made within a structure of relationships, some of the elements of which have already been mentioned: incentives, checks and limitations to ambition, compensation for failure, and a delicate balancing between opposites. These elements and others are caught up in the notion of competition as it is understood and played out in the daily rounds of work and play in Crestwood Heights. In the Heights one encounters competition everywhere: in sport, in the classroom, at the dinner table ("Now let's see who will finish his vegetables first"), at the traffic light, in raising money for charity, in the mission work of the church.

SMALL TOWN IN MASS SOCIETY*

Arthur J. Vidich, *New School for Social Research*

Joseph Bensman, *City College of the City University of New York*

Independent entrepreneurs. The businessmen (all small in Springdale) are largely those whose business constitutes their sole source of income. The range of businesses includes grocery stores, restaurants, filling stations, household appliances, farm implements, feed mills, a hardware store, a television shop, and so forth. In an environment with a limited market, competition characteristically takes two forms: keeping the business establishment open for long hours, and the elaboration of overlapping inventories from store to store. A single operator in cooperation with his wife or another member of the family typically keeps his business open from ten to twelve hours daily.[1] The threat of buying elsewhere—in neighboring city stores—where prices may be cheaper and where service is more efficient is held over the merchant's head.

In response to his predicament the businessman engages in fewer and fewer risk ventures. He is geared to the maximum utilization of his existing facilities, eschews measures which would modernize his plant at capital expense and, instead, tries to develop a clientele whose loyalty is based on personal considerations. He conducts his business in an atmosphere of scarcity; he shies away from products which do not have an established market, fears large inventories, and avoids such merchandizing methods as "loss leaders."

The Better Business Bureau attempts to protect the limited market to which its members appeal. Transient peddlers and traders are resented and every effort is made to control their activities through licensing and other restrictive measures.

Although local competition is rigorous, the source of greatest competition lies in retail outlets in nearby cities and the surrounding region. As these large centers of retail distribution become more elaborate and efficient, the local merchant loses a greater share of the trade of the mobile segments of the population. His trade becomes more limited to the aged, the loyal, the infirm, and those who must buy on credit.

* From Arthur Vidich and Joseph Bensman, *Small Town in Mass Society: Class, Power, and Religion in a Rural Community* (Princeton, N.J.: Princeton University Press, 1958), pp. 53–61. Reprinted by permission of Princeton University Press. © 1958 by Princeton University Press.

[1] The psychological disposition to work is an important variable in distinguishing the life styles of the various classes. See Max Weber, *The Protestant Ethic and the Spirit of Capitalism* (New York: Charles Scribner's Sons, 1948).

The general business conditions of the merchant are largely determined by forces outside his control. The goods and commodities which he sells are provided by mass distributors who also set price scales. In the case of many commodities, profit margins are specified, and, in the case of franchise businesses, other business practices as well are more or less rigidly specified.

These circumstances lead the small businessman to a nonexpansive attitude toward his enterprise. Only six out of approximately fifty businessmen are in the process of investing capital. However, these are all new businessmen whose investment represents necessary expenditures toward establishing the business rather than a policy of continuous reinvestment and expansion. In the absence of efforts directed toward increasing his profits by increased capital investments and increased inventories (a more favorable merchandizing climate), he directs his efforts at a niggardly cutting of costs. This ideology is illustrated by the folklore of the business community which typically attributes the cause of local business failures to excessive spending for consumption and equipment and to the excessive utilization of potential labor for unprofitable leisure-time pursuits.

The businessman places a high value on the retention of money in the form of cash deposited in the bank or, as in some cases, hidden on his premises in a cigar box or the like. When he reaches a certain level of accumulation, he invests savings in real property or in mortgages on real property. Securities, bonds and the like are suspected where tangible property is not immediately visible.

The individual businessman is apt to be torn between maintaining the utmost secrecy about his net worth and a desire to boast about his financial well-being and success. In part he is afraid to let the community know how "rich he is," in the fear that jealousies aroused will affect his business; simultaneously, he wants to collect the esteem which he feels is his due.

In their relations with each other, businessmen are highly suspicious and distrustful. They scrutinize each other's business activities and practices so as to be able constantly to evaluate each other's standing and competition. All this is done with a minimum of social contact; businessmen do not socialize much with each other or with the rest of the community.

Their participation in community affairs is largely limited to supporting a great number of organizations without being active in any of them. The private life of the family tends to take place in the semipublic environment of the business premises, a fact which is frequently made possible by the absence of children (there is a high frequency of single-child families).

The only businessmen who deviate in any significant sense from this description are those involved in farm-connected businesses, grain and farm machinery sales, and milling operations. Since their business chances are closely linked to the farm economy, they along with the successful farmers exhibit quite different social characteristics.

Rational farmers. "Rational farmers" are those who conceive of and work at farming as a business. Costs, including labor and capital costs, are carefully calculated and related to the prices received, and costs and energy are distributed in such a way as to produce the maximum yield. Rationality rather than sentiment or tradition govern the work and mentality of rational farmers. The rationally operated farm requires at a minimum fifteen to twenty head of milking stock and is geared to maximum productivity. Each increase in size of herd (up to eighty head in Springdale) requires the farmer to recalculate all variables that enter into production efficiency. That is, the farmer must recalculate his total cost/gross income ratio as related to net income. The significant variables in this economic calculus are price levels of milk, additional labor and machinery required, the cost of building materials (he builds his own buildings), and additional feed costs since in Springdale it is relatively difficult to expand land holdings. Fifty milking cows and the machinery, land, and buildings required to support them have a total capital valuation ranging from $40,000 to $60,000 at price levels in 1953. Obviously, few independent farmers possess either the capital or the credit standing to enter farming at this level. Typically the farmer enters his enterprise at a much lower level of capital investment and over a period of time "builds his farm up." The last 10 years of agricultural prosperity have provided an ideal environment for the expansion of farm enterprise. Indeed, many of the farmers prosperous at the time of this study entered farming in Springdale within the last 10 to 15 years, while the rest include practically all the Polish farmers who entered the community 30 years ago.

It is the distinctive and typical feature of these farmers that they return their profits into the expansion of their enterprise. They do not save for the purpose of saving. Instead, they save for the purpose of reinvestment, i.e., modernization of equipment and plant expansion.

The farmer gears his enterprise to the production of fluid milk which is marketed in the New York Metropolitan Milk Marketing Area, a market controlled by law by a market administrator. He can determine his income from milk (the milk check) by his volume of production and its butter-fat content, the only two variables in the price structure which he is able to control directly. Depending on the price structure and on his calculation of his position in relation to it, the farmer may deliberately decide to increase volume at the expense of butter-fat content (poorer feed) or vice versa; or he may decide to decrease milk production by selling stock and investing feed in pigs. These suggest the level at which alternatives are open to him.

The rational farmer offsets his position of vulnerability and lack of power in relation to the determination of prices by concentrating on the reduction of production costs. However, his cost-cutting is not done at the expense of production efficiency; he cannot skimp on commercial fertilizers or machinery replacement, and it is to his perceived advantage to install labor-saving devices. The farmer cuts his costs by making the most efficient use of his own and his family's labor. In so doing, the style of living of the family of the rational farmer is linked to the productive enterprise.

The labor of children, especially boys, is highly valued and utilized. A child of 7 or 8 years is capable of operating a tractor in the organized work routine required for hay loading. A son in high school can be calculated as half-time labor—a farmer may plan an expansion program in coordination with the life cycle of his children. The farmer's wife, it is observed in Springdale, is capable of making or breaking a successful farm operation by whether she works in the barn, the fields, or garden at critical moments and in critical seasons.

The family as a productive unit has extensions into the home. Investments which will enhance the productive efficiency of the kitchen—modern appliances, modern kitchen plans, various labor-saving devices—are viewed on almost the same plane as investing in a new manure spreader. It is only after the productive plant has been expanded and the kitchen modernized that the external beautification and internal decoration of the farm home takes place. It is a commonplace to see shabby or neat but extremely modest farm dwellings attached to large-scale and prosperous farm enterprises. Personal or luxury consumption gives way to the investment of money in avenues which will yield further returns through production efficiency and the efficient utilization of labor. The emphasis on work and efficiency, using the clock as a standard, leaves little scope for rituals or ceremonials in the farmer's style of work. Social activities and participation, except in churches, play no or only a minor part in his life. At best, for him, such activities are a "waste of time."

The class position of the farmer relative to other segments of the middle class is most directly dependent on price structures and markets whose dynamics are determined in the society at large. Alterations in these dynamics affect him immediately and force him to respond to the alterations in both the operation of his business and his style of living. Within this dependence, he gears his style of living to economic mobility—economic expansiveness and hard work—but he achieves his mobility from a position of economic independence of the local community in which he lives.

Professionals and skilled industrial workers. Professionals, quasiprofessionals, managers, and skilled industrial workers, to be sure, do not constitute a class entity with a common social consciousness but, nevertheless, they exhibit a uniform and consistent style of living. Their central characteristic is their status as employees who have fixed ceilings on their incomes. Income is derived from the sale of professional services or a fixed number of hours of labor. The arbitrary fixing of the length of the work day by forces outside the individual's control makes this group the leisured section of the middle class. The manner in which this leisure time is allocated and expended separates them from the marginal middle class to be discussed below.

Their level of fixed income effectively prevents the accumulation of savings for investment purposes. Characteristically, total income is devoted to consumption purposes. In the absence of opportunities for capital expansion and the full utilization of labor, the central feature of their style of living may be described as a problem in consumption choices. The opportunity to spend thought and study in the expenditure of income is provided by the leisure available to them.

In rough order of priorities, income is devoted to home ownership, automobile ownership, children, home improvements and home decoration. Home ownership occupies a central place because it is viewed as a type of security and as the accumulation of equity. The gradual accumulation of equity over the course of a lifetime constitutes a major psychological substitute for an expansionist psychology.

The car, the home, and children are the main outlets for the expression of consumption and serve as a common basis for social competition, a fact which in this sense at least gives the group a psychological unity, although they may have little in common occupationally. They can and do, in their social intercourse, talk at length about consumption problems—comparing car models, furniture, rugs, color combinations, the dress and achievements of children, etc., etc.

Children, whatever other gratifications they may serve, are an important part of a *social* mobility calculus. Intellectual and competitive ability in school are highly esteemed, for the child is being groomed for higher education which will lead to a professional or at least a white-collar career. All manner of personal achievement is emphasized and rewarded in the hope that achievement will become a firmly fixed motive in the child. In a real sense parents project their own mobility strivings onto their children and in so doing perhaps minimize the conflicts that could arise from a conscious or unconscious perception of the limits placed on their own economic mobility.

Children, however, do not constitute a completely adequate substitute for mobility since they are at best a vicarious substitute and subliminally, at least, are recognized as such. The indirect drive for mobility has its corollary in a direct drive for security. In the case of the teacher, it is a tenure appointment; for the industrial worker, it is employment in a stable industry and the careful guardianship of his seniority; for other types of professionals, it is maintaining good personal relations with their professional superiors; for the fee professional, it is the protection of a clientele. In all instances retirement plans, unemployment insurance, sickness benefits, and all types of personal and medical insurance programs assume a central importance. Major decisions in the life plan are made with respect to assuring the possession of such deferred-

gratification contractual arrangements.

Taxation on income, contrary to the practice with farmers and businessmen, is automatically withheld by the employer and this system is passively accepted as a condition for receiving income. Their focus of attention is placed on the possibility of a tax rebate which, when received, is viewed as a windfall and stands as a symbol of what is perhaps the major degree of freedom in an otherwise totally allocated income. Viewed as unexpected income, it can be spent without regard to fixed plan on an "expensive night out," a weekend in New York City, or as a down payment on a household appliance. This stylization of attitude toward taxes is not found in any other group.

Like the businessmen and farmers, the fee professionals experience no technical ceiling on the utilization of labor. Their income is determined by the number of clients they are willing or able to accommodate. Characteristically, however, they make a conscious decision to underemploy themselves. That is, a high value is placed upon leisure-time activities. Their self-determination of their work/leisure ratio to accommodate for leisure is a decision which partly reveals their psychological orientation to economic mobility.

Teachers are accorded prestige because of the formal schooling they have completed, but their salary schedules in a small town are low. In Springdale their average salary is between $3,000 and $3,400, hardly sufficient to attain the level of consumption expected of them by themselves and by others. Typically this income is supplemented by secondary jobs. Due to the teachers' direct dependence on locally controlled resources (the attitude of the town that teachers are hirelings), the acquisition of capital holdings, except for a house (after tenure has been granted) and a car, arouses the hostility of other groups in the community. Hence the teacher is a total consumer not only by virtue of his income level but also by virtue of the purely social pressures which play upon him in the local community.

The leisure available to these middle-class segments enables them to provide the active support for many of the community's organizations. Whether or not they hold offices, they plan and execute most of the community's non-political organizational life, and it is in this context that the various occupational types who make up this class have an opportunity to meet. However, this does not mean that all participate equally in community organizations since level of activity is open to individual choice. It is here that industrial workers are socially differentiated. Because they work outside the community and because many live in the open countryside, they are relatively socially invisible to the rest of the community. By self-selection, however, some of them through social, religious, and organizational activities establish ties within the community. When these ties occur they connect these industrial participators with the professional group and not with the businessmen or farmers.

The social status of the professionals is based only partly on their education. All of the professionals gain status from the real or imputed connections which they are believed to have with the institutions and tastes of the outside society. The "college bred" are the culture carriers of the town and adhere to standards of taste and consumption which are not indigenous. Lawyers, teachers, ministers, etc., mediate between local institutions and those in the mass society to which they are connected. They are the functionaries who run the town. It is these facts, irrespective of size and source of income, which support their social position in the community.

The middle class more than any other class is concerned with social activities. Their concern with social activity is reflected in the one exclusive activity which is related to pretensions of social superiority—the book clubs. The book clubs are quite unique in Springdale because there is a definite implication that the Monday Club is superior to the Tuesday Club, which in turn is superior to the Wednesday Club, and all three by implication are superior, at least culturally, to everyone else. At the same time the more dominant ideology of social equality, defined in part as antisnobbishness, places the would-be snobs on the defensive and causes them to be resented by everyone else in the community, including members of the economically and politically more powerful classes. All of the book club *social aspirants* are drawn from the middle class, but specifically they are drawn from the wives of professionals and skilled workers and to a lesser extent from the wives of businessmen. Within the group of aspirants, ratings of superiority are made primarily on the basis of length of residence in the community. It is for this reason that the members of the Monday Club include the wives of the old aristocratic families. No wives of any rational farmers, the economically most successful group in the community, are members of book clubs. Moreover, since membership is restricted, not all wives of even the preferred segments of the middle class are members, though there are many who would like to be. Book-club membership serves to distinguish "social" status and prestige differences among middle-class women.

Although such *social* class does exist in the community, the numbers involved are relatively small and their importance is diminished by the public ideology of equality. This, however, does not mean that class is unimportant. Class, defined as differences in life styles rather than as differences in social snobbery, is all-important. In fact it is so important that to consider class only as social snobbery would grossly underestimate the importance of class in the community, particularly as it affects the dynamics of community life.

DEMOCRACY IN JONESVILLE*

W. Lloyd Warner

Michigan State University

The associational behavior of the upper-middle class resembles that of the upper class in many respects.... A large proportion of this class holds membership in associations dominated by the upper class. In addition, the clubs identified with the upper-middle class have programs and policies which imitate the manner of the superior stratum. The members of this class also participate almost as much in associations as do the members of the upper class: Every family holds membership in at least one organization and 86 per cent in more than one; the average number of memberships per family is 3.5 All but eight upper-middle-class families belong to either an upper- or an upper-middle-class association and three-quarters (74 per cent) belong to more than one.

In spite of these similarities, certain significant differences appear. In general, the associational participation of the upper-middle class is more diffuse than that of the upper class. They are found in the high-status organizations, but they tend to take a less active part in these groups and follow the leadership of the upper class. They are also found in organizations of low status; the men appear more frequently in the lodges, and a few of the women even belong to the auxiliaries, though they rarely take an active role. A few women support the satellite organizations of the "social church," and some also take an active part in the Methodist Church, which ranks second in the community.

The upper-middle class tends to be most closely identified with the civic and service clubs of the community. Clubs of this type—Rotary, the Woman's Club, and organizations designed to support the schools and the library —frequently have a wide class spread, but they tend to draw the majority of their members from the upper-middle class and to have the officers and other active members come primarily from that group.

Like the top clubs, these organiza-

* From pp. 134–38, *Democracy in Jonesville* by W. Lloyd Warner. Copyright 1949 by Harper & Row, Publishers, Incorporated. Reprinted by permission of the publishers.

tions are considered among the better associations of Jonesville. The members are said to be the important people or the prominent people of the community. In particular, membership in Rotary is a mark of status and a sign that a man has attained a degree of success in this competitive society. The members of the upper-middle class take pride in their associations and point to the prominent role that they play in the life of the community. These associations are highly regarded by the people of lower-middle or lower-class status, some of whom reveal a desire or hope that they may sometime join them. A woman of the lower-middle class, who had attained her goal of becoming a member of the Woman's Club, said:

. "When we first came to Jonesville I didn't think I was going to like it here. I didn't have any friends and at first I didn't meet anybody I liked. But just recently I've joined the Woman's Club, and I've met several people there that I would like for friends. They don't let just anybody join. You are supposed to be sponsored by somebody. It is a good way to get acquainted and meet sort of the—the better or the nicer people—I don't know how to say it but they don't let in the lower classes, the sort of common people, I mean. They are sort of the important people in town. I don't mean that they are always so wealthy, but you do meet the nicer people that way."

The members of the upper class do not reveal the same respect or admiration for these upper-middle-class groups; verbally they subordinate them, and they avoid membership in them. Even Rotary, for all its claims of prestige, boasts no more than a handful of upper-class men. Evaluation of these groups is frequently made by way of comparison with the organizations of

top status, and the members of the upper-middle as well as the upper class admit that there is a degree of difference and that those groups dominated by the upper class must be awarded the highest status. Particularly the Woman's Club is compared to those women's groups dominated by the upper class, and it is said to be "not *as* old," "not *as* nice," "not *as* exclusive."

While the upper-class clubs are exclusive clubs and even boast of being exclusive, many upper-middle-class clubs make claims to being "democratic" and "open to everybody." However, close examination indicates that this policy of democracy is fiction rather than fact. The president of the Woman's Club claims they will take in anybody who will be a good member, but the difficulty that the lower-middle-class woman, already quoted, experienced in becoming a member suggests that this is a policy which is not strictly adhered to. One all-male club, in certain respects most selective of all male groups in Jonesville, claims to be democratic and for evidence points to one member of lower status. This man is the son of an immigrant. He had a second-grade education and went to work on The Canal when he was 8 years old. In the course of years, he has built up a small business. He is pointed to as an example of the "truly democratic spirit of America." However, the democratic spirit" has not been extended sufficiently to accept him fully as an equal:

Perhaps the greatest differences between the upper-middle-class organizations and those dominated by the upper class is the emphasis by the former on active participation and accomplishment on the part of the members. The upper-middle-class associations are noted for their activity, achievement, and industry. They put demands upon their members, expecting them to take an active part in club affairs. Not content with arranging an endless round of speakers, the members present the programs, arrange tours, and organize special projects. There is an emphasis throughout on education and self-improvement. By way of contrast it might be said that the upper-class organizations are socially advancing while the upper-middle-class organizations are self-advancing; that the former require only proper family connection, while the latter, in addition, judge performance. The middle-class associations are interested in members with educational talents—musical, literary, dramatic, or artistic—talents which require training which, in turn, requires some wealth. They encourage the members to use these talents and even judge them by their ability to do so. Although the upper-class organizations show some interest in talented members, their primary interest is directed toward artists or speakers who have achieved excellence and fame on a much larger scale.

The upper-middle-class associations extend their influence beyond the immediate circle of members and take an interest in many civic problems. Both Rotary and the Woman's Club give their support to numerous community projects; the P.T.A. exerts its influence on the school system; the Band Parents support and sponsor the high school band; the Red Cross, in addition to raising money, organizes educational courses, influences the local relief office, and gives support to the county health officers. Taking part in these community affairs, the members of these associations perform functions which are necessary to the total community. Whereas upper-class organizations hold meetings on the arts, the theater, and all leisure-time activities, those dominated by the upper-middle

class grapple with the problems which face all segments of the community every day. The topics of their meetings include "Public Health and the Prevention of Tuberculosis," "The Future of Our Schools," "Safety in Traffic," "Our Responsibilities and Restrictions as to the War Program," "Personality Adjustment and How to Prevent Juvenile Delinquency," and "Helping Our Children to Be Better Citizens."

A good example of the difference in emphasis is seen in the relative attitude of the various organizations to the problems facing the high school. During the winter of 1941–42 the future of the high school was a critical issue in the community. The school was suffering from insufficient funds, which caused low salaries, poor teaching standards, and old overcrowded buildings, and the North Central Association was threatening to take it off the list of accredited schools. Following the general lecture on the school at the Woman's Club, reports were given by members of the school and members of the club on the conditions and needs of the school, and methods were discussed for raising taxes and building a new school. Groups of club members attended classes and observed the performances of teachers and students so that they would become better acquainted with the school system and the school personnel. In spite of the seriousness of the situation, none of the women's organizations of top status devoted a single meeting to this topic.

Through club activities the women of the upper-middle class come in contact with people of higher status and increase their own prestige in the eyes of the community. On the other hand, in spite of the fact that they deal with problems which affect the whole community, they restrict the membership in their associations, or at least do not permit active participation on the part of individuals of lower status. By this process of exclusion they increase the social distance between themselves and the people who rank below them in the class hierarchy.

THE WORKING CLASS[1]

The working class, consisting of skilled and semiskilled manual laborers, is the stable element of the blue-collar work force having a standard of living above subsistence. Most estimates of the size of the working class place it between 30 and 40 per cent of the population. In many cases the income of working-class people is equal to or surpasses that of persons in the lower reaches of the middle class, such as general clerical workers and some sales personnel.

Much of the social interaction of working-class people centers around the extended family, the informal work group, and the neighborhood peer group. They tend to avoid participation in voluntary associations, which are characterized by more formal and impersonal relationships. They have a feeling of family loyalty and obligation, even for distant relatives, and are likely to organize social and recreational activities within the extended family rather than with outside groups. Spending money on friends and relatives is a valued activity and necessary for the maintenance of status within the group. This involvement in primary groups protects the working-class man from the encroachments of an associational society with its impersonality and its stringent role requirements. At the same time, it lessens his ability to cope with modern complex society.

Confronted with obstacles to the attainment of the success ideal in American culture, working-class people do not discard this ideal but rather redefine it in achievable terms. Factors other than movement up the occupational ladder become, for the working class, symbols of success. These factors include ownership

---

1 The following studies are representative of those upon which this profile of the working class is based. Bennett M. Berger, *Working-Class Suburb* (Berkeley, Calif.: University of California Press, 1960); Alan F. Blum, "Social Structure, Social Class and Participation in Primary Relationships," in *Blue-Collar World: Studies of the American Worker*, eds. Arthur B. Shostak and William Gomberg (Englewood Cliffs, N.J.: Prentice-Hall, Inc., 1964); Richard Centers, *The Psychology of Social Classes* (Princeton, N.J.: Princeton University Press, 1949); Ely Chinoy, *Automobile Workers and the American Dream* (Garden City, N.Y.: Doubleday & Company, Inc., 1955); Floyd Dotson, "Patterns of Voluntary Associations Among Urban Working-Class Families," *American Sociological Review*, 12 (October 1951), 687–93; Herbert Gans, *The Urban Villagers* (New York: The Free Press of Glencoe, Inc., 1962); Hollingshead, *op. cit.*; Mirra Komarovsky, *Blue-Collar Marriage* (New York: Random House, Inc., 1964); Mark Lefton, "The Blue Collar Worker and the Middle-Class Ethic," *Sociology and Social Research*, 51 (January 1967), 159–70; Daniel B. Miller, Guy E. Swanson, *et al.*, *Inner Conflict and Defense* (New York: Holt, Rinehart & Winston, Inc., 1960); S. M. Miller and Frank Riessman, "The Working-Class Subculture: A New View," in Shostak and Gomberg, *op. cit.*, pp. 24–36; Lee Rainwater, Richard P. Coleman, and Gerald Handel, *Workingman's Wife* (New York: Oceana Publications, 1959); Charles R. Walker and Robert H. Guest, *The Man on the Assembly Line* (Cambridge, Mass.: Harvard University Press, 1952).

of a home, an automobile, and other personal possessions, and provision of educational opportunities for their children. In addition to being a sign of success, home ownership is the key to greater independence and escape from the limitations placed on those who rent.

The working class prefers economically secure jobs to those which are more congenial but involve greater risk. Consequently they cling to their present jobs rather than seeking other, possibly better, employment. In addition, they value manual skill because they define work in terms of the expenditure of physical energy. They do not believe that people who hold white-collar or supervisory positions are doing real work. For them, skilled manual work is the most desired form of employment.

In the working-class view, the world consists of concrete events and practical outcomes. Accompanying this view is a disrespect for intellectual activity and an inclination to use physical rather than conceptual modes of expression. Until recently, this anti-intellectual perspective was manifested in the working-class attitude toward higher education. They expected young people to go no further than high school before finding employment. Working-class parents now, however, increasingly express the desire that their children have a college education. This desire is less a result of changing attitudes toward education per se than it is of the increasing awareness of educational requirements for employment.

The working class, more than others, conforms to the traditional image of husband and wife roles. It is the wife's role to do housework and care for children; it is the husband's role to be a good provider. However, there is less tendency than in the past to feel that these roles must be adhered to under all circumstances. The husband, for example, may help his wife during an emergency period without seriously violating his male image. The working class also emphasizes traditional values in child-rearing. Respect for adults, neatness, honesty, and obedience are the central virtues which working-class adults seek to instill in their children. They want them to adhere to externally imposed standards and avoid trouble.

The passage from Herbert Gans's *The Urban Villagers* portrays working-class life as oriented around peer groups. The working-class man understands and is comfortable with the world of neighborhood, family, and friends. Robert Guest's study of assembly-line work depicts the boredom, lack of job satisfaction, and general meaninglessness which often characterize mass-production employment. In contrast, the selection from *Automation and the Worker* by Floyd Mann and L. Richard Hoffman describes the job enlargement that may occur with automation. It calls attention to the possibility that automation may bring greater responsibility and greater work satisfaction than are now found in assembly-line jobs.

Several scholars emphasize the many differences within the working class.[2] One of these differences is the extent to which family organization is patriarchal or equalitarian. The excerpt from Mirra Komarovsky's study *Blue Collar Mar-*

---

[2] For example, see Miller and Riessman, *op. cit.*

riage suggests that the tendency to accept a more equalitarian relationship is related to high school education.

THE URBAN VILLAGERS*

Herbert Gans

Center for Urban Education

The basis of adult West End life is peer-group sociability. By sociability I do not mean the entertaining and party-giving of the middle class. Nor do I mean the informal conversational activity that the middle class ranks well below occupational, familial, and self-improvement activities in importance. For the West Ender, sociability is a routinized gathering of a relatively unchanging peer group of family members and friends that takes place several times a week. One could almost say that the meetings of the group are at the vital center of West End life, that they are the end for which other everyday activities are a means.

Membership in the group is based primarily on kinship. . . . Brothers, sisters, and cousins of the husband and wife—and their spouses—are at the core. The group also includes godparents and friends who may come less regularly. Godparents are friends who, because of their closeness, are given quasifamilial status. Godparentage is awarded to best men at a wedding or to the children of one's godparents, as well as to true godparents; in short, to people who become "friends of the family" in middle-class American kinship terminology.[1] It is also used as a way of cementing relationships. For example, one West Ender asked his neighbors, with whom he had long been friendly, to be godparents for his newborn child, in order to maintain contact between the two families after redevelopment. In adult life, West Enders have little contact with their actual godparents since the older generation is not part of the peer-group social life.

Included among other unrelated individuals are friends of long duration, as well as more recent friends. Though the latter may be newcomers to the group, they are likely to have been known to the group before, because . . . everyone knows of everyone else. Consequently, nearly everyone is a potential friend who can join a peer group at any time. This happens most often after people have extended help to each other, met at ceremonial occasions, or have had prolonged contact, for example, as hospital patients. Recruitment is not deliberate, however, and self-conscious "mixing with peo-

---

* Reprinted with permission of The Macmillan Company from *The Urban Villagers* by Herbert Gans. © The Free Press of Glencoe, a Division of The Macmillan Company, 1962.

---

[1] This is one of the few instances in which West Enders still use an Italian term to describe a phenomenon. They refer to their "compares" (male) and "commares" (female), perhaps because the term godparents is not quite the same and because there is no other English word that quite describes the relationship.

ple" is explicitly rejected. A mobile woman who had left the West End suggested to West End relatives one night that women should get out of the house and mix with people. But her relatives, discussing it afterward, thought that this belief was a result of her being childless, for which they pitied her. Similarly, when a relocation official spoke to a West Ender about the new social experiences he would encounter in a new neighborhood, the West Ender replied angrily: "I don't want to meet any new people. I get out quite a bit all over Boston to see my brothers and sisters, and, when they come over, we have others in, like neighbors. You can't do that in the suburbs."

Neighbors also may be included in the group if they are friends, but they are not eligible merely because they live next door. As neighbors, they may have frequent physical contact that might facilitate the social contact prerequisite to friendship.[2] But it also might reveal differences in background and behavior that could preclude friendship.[3] In the West End, neighbors quite often were also socially close because of the . . . tendency of landlords to rent apartments to relatives or friends.

Potential peer-group members are many, but their number is effectively reduced by the requirement that people

must be relatively compatible in terms of background, interests, and attitudes: What they have to say and what they want to listen to must be of common interest. They also must hold somewhat similar attitudes toward marriage, child-rearing, religion, politics, taste, and other important issues, because West Enders cannot cope effectively with disagreement. . . . As a result, the group is limited to people of similar ethnic background and class. There is no formal exclusion, but since the conversation may be unkind to other ethnic groups, they do run the risk of being antagonized. Even within the Italian group itself, those who are more or less acculturated than the rest stay away. The former are uncomfortable because they are "too American"; the latter, because they become embarrassed when the group makes fun of old-fashioned people. A woman with old-fashioned ideas is more acceptable than a man since she is likely to keep quiet and not upset the group. Also, being old-fashioned is more of a virtue for women. The people who are mobile are kidded so much about their wealth that they come only rarely. Very mobile women are likely to be antagonized by references to wild or unwomanly ways or by scornful stories about "society ladies." Those of lower status than the rest of the group are not rejected unless they are "bums" but remain away because they may be weighed down by problems that do not concern the others.

Single individuals often are part of the group even if they do not meet the standards of compatibility. Included because they are alone—a dread scourge in Italian culture—they nevertheless remain on the fringes of the group's conversational and other activities even though they are likely to be present more often than people with

---

2 In most of the tenements, neighbors were residents of adjacent buildings who faced on a common fire escape or airshaft. In the building in which I lived, kitchens faced each other, thus giving housewives frequent opportunity for visual contact. There was less contact with people on other floors of one's own building, since they were seen only fleetingly when using the stairs.

3 The role of physical propinquity and background homogeneity in friendship is discussed further in Herbert J. Gans, "Planning and Social Life," *Journal of the American Institute of Planners*, 27 (1961), 134–40, at pp. 134–36.

familial responsibilities. Our own participation in one of the peer groups was due in part to the fact that we were new to Boston and, having few friends in the city, were thought to be isolated somewhat like the single people in the group. The initial invitation was extended, however, because we were neighbors and because the wives, who had met across the fire escape, took a liking to each other.

The peer group meets regularly in the kitchens and living rooms of innumerable West End apartments. There are no formal invitations or advance notifications; people arrive regularly one or more evenings a week. Generally speaking, the same people come the same days of the week. Certain evenings are thus reserved for being with the peer group, and the gathering is called off only for unusual events.

While a few people may come for dinner, the gatherings usually begin shortly afterward, and others may drop in all through the evening. The talk goes on for hours—often past midnight—even though the men have to be at work early the next morning. ... The sexes remain separate most of the evening, and, even when they gather around the kitchen table for coffee and cake, the men often sit at one end, the women at the other. Some people bring their children, especially if they do not have older ones who can stay home with the younger ones. The children sit and listen until they become sleepy and then are sent off to the bedrooms until their parents leave.

The peer-group conversation covers a relatively small number of topics: accounts of the participants' activities since the last gathering; news of people they all know; plans for special events such as weddings, showers, and other celebrations; current topics of interest; stories and anecdotes; and memories of younger days or highlights of the more recent past. Quite often, a current happening will set off talk about the past, and people contribute stories of parallel events that took place earlier. From there, it is easy to drift into talk about the good old days. The conversation also may turn to reports—and judgments—of deviant behavior. In addition, advice is exchanged, but there is little systematic attempt at problem-solving. Usually, people discuss problems encountered by others, especially those who are not present at the gathering. Problems common to the group as a whole also enter the conversation. I was always surprised, however, that what I thought to be the most pressing problem—redevelopment and relocation—received relatively little attention. Most West Enders felt that as there was not much they could do about this, there was little sense in discussing an unpleasant reality. This principle also covers the discussion of problems in general. The men talk about current happenings at work, in sports, in the area, and occasionally in the city and the country. But there is little concern with politics, except when events have occurred that illustrate once again the West Enders' belief that politics is corrupt. The women talk about housekeeping, child-rearing, and other subjects relevant to their occupational role.

MEN AND MACHINES: AN ASSEMBLY-LINE WORKER LOOKS AT HIS JOB*

Robert H. Guest

Dartmouth College

Of all occupations in modern industry none has aroused such controversial comment as that of the assembly worker, and especially the auto assembly worker on the "final line." The extraordinary ingenuity that has gone into the construction of automobile assembly lines, their perfected synchronization, the "all but human" or "more than human" character of the machines, the miracle of a car rolling off the conveyor each minute under its own power—all this has caught and held the world's imagination for a quarter of a century. On the other hand, the extreme subdivision of labor (the man who puts a nut on a bolt is the symbol) conjoined with the "endlessly moving belt" has made the assembly line the classic symbol of the subjection of man to the machine in our industrial age.

General Characteristics of the Mass-Production Method

But before considering man in relation to the machine, it would be advisable to define the general characteristics of the mass-production method.

Utilizing the two basic principles of standardization and interchangeability,

Ford was able to work out and apply the three following additional "principles" of progressive manufacture:

1. The orderly progression of the product through the shop in a series of planned operations so arranged that the right part always arrives at the right place at the right time.

2. The mechanical delivery of these parts to the operators and the mechanical delivery of the product from the operators, as it is assembled.

3. A breakdown of operations into their simple constituent motions.

The Mass-Production Job

Let us now look at these familiar principles or techniques as they are translated into the work experience of individual men and women in mass-production factories. The characteristics of the average mass-production job may be summarized in the following manner:

1. Mechanical pacing of work.
2. Repetitiveness.
3. Minimum skill requirement.
4. Predetermination in the use of tools and techniques.
5. Minute subdivision of product worked on.
6. Surface mental attention.

For the engineer, all the above characteristics are brought into focus in what is known as the *job cycle*. Each worker must perform a prescribed number of operations within a set time

* From Robert H. Guest, "Men and Machines: An Assembly-Line Worker Looks at His Job," *Personnel*, 31 (May 1955), 496–503.

185

limit, and, in the case of those working on moving conveyors, within a given distance along the assembly line.

HOW A TYPICAL ASSEMBLY-LINE WORKER FEELS

With these characteristics in mind, let us go right to a man on the assembly line and see how they affect him; but instead of a statistical summary of the findings from interviews with over 400 assembly-line workers in two plants, excerpts from a single interview will be given here and commented upon insofar as they hold true for the total sample.

The worker whose actual words are quoted below is, like many others, a graduate of a public vocational school in the United States. He is 36 years old and married; he has a couple of children, is buying his own home, and "takes home" just under $80 a week. Here, he is talking to me in his home:

In 1940 I heard that they were hiring people for the assembly plant. Must have been thousands of fellows lined up for the job. The word got around that they were paying real good money. It was a big outfit, too. No fly-by-night affair.

Figured I'd get any job and then, with a little electrician experience I had in vocational school, I could work my way up to a good job. And the idea of making automobiles sounded like something. Lucky for me, I got a job and was made a spot welder on the front cowling. There wasn't much to the job itself. Picked it up in about a week. Later I was drafted into the Army, and then in 1946 I came back. I tried to get into the Maintenance Department as an electrician, but there was no opening, so I went back to the line—we call it the iron horse. They made me a

welder again, and that's what I have been doing ever since.

WHAT HIS JOB IS LIKE

The worker then went on to describe his job:

My job is to weld the cowl to the metal underbody. I take a jig off the bench, put it in place and weld the parts together. The jig is all made up and the welds are made in set places along the metal. Exactly twenty-five spots. The line runs according to schedule. Takes me one minute and fifty-two seconds for each job. I walk along the line as it moves. Then I snap the jig off, walk back down the line, throw it on the bench, grab another just in time to start on the next car. The cars differ, but it's practically the same thing. Finish one —then have another one staring me in the face.

I don't like to work on the line—no man likes to work on a moving line. You can't beat the machine. Sure, maybe I can keep it up for an hour, but it's rugged doing it eight hours a day, every day in the week all year long.

During each day I get a chance for a breather 10 minutes in the morning, then a half hour for lunch, then a few minutes in the afternoon. When I'm working there is not much chance to get a breather. Sometimes the line breaks down. When it does we all yell "Whoopee!" As long as the line keeps moving I've got to keep up with it. On a few jobs I know, some fellows can work like hell up the line, then coast. Most jobs you can't do that. If I get ahead maybe ten seconds, the next model has more welds to it, so it takes ten seconds extra. You hardly break even. You're always behind. When you get too far behind, you get in a hole— that's what we call it. All hell breaks loose. I get in the next guy's way. The foreman gets sore, and they have to rush in a relief man to bail you out.

It's easy for them time-study fellows to come down there with a stop watch and figure out just how much you can do in a minute and fifty-two seconds. There are some things they can see and record with their stop watch. But they can't clock how a man feels from one day to the next. Those guys ought to work on the line for a few weeks and maybe they'll feel some things that they never pick up on the stop watch.

I like a job where you feel like you're accomplishing something and doing it right. When everything's laid out for you and the parts are all alike, there's not much you feel you accomplish. The big thing is that steady push of the conveyor—a gigantic machine which I can't control.

You know, it's hard to feel that you are doing a good quality job. There is that constant push at high speed. You may improve after you've done a thing over and again, but you never reach a point where you can stand back and say, "Boy, I done that one good. That's one car that got built right." If I could do my best I'd get some satisfaction out of working, but I can't do as good work as I know I can do.

My job is all engineered out. The jigs and fixtures are all designed and set out according to specifications. There are a lot of little things you could tell them, but they never ask you. You go by the bible. They have a suggestion system, but the fellows don't use it too much because they're scared that a new way to do it may do one of your buddies out of a job.

Interviewer: "Who do you talk to, Joe, when you're working?"

There's only three guys close by—me and my partner and a couple of fellows up the line a bit. I talk to my partner quite a lot. We gripe about the job 90 per cent of the time. You don't have time for any real conversation. The guys get along okay—you know the old saying, "misery loves company."

Interviewer: "What sort of a person is your foreman?"

Oh, I think as a man he is an all right guy. I see him once and a while outside, and he's 100 per cent. But in the shop he can't be. If I was a foreman nobody would like me either. As a foreman, he has to push you all the time to get production out so that somebody above won't push him. But the average guy on the line has no one to push— you can't fight the line. The line pushes you. We sometimes kid about it and say we don't need no foreman. That line is the foreman. Some joke.

The worker then discussed the general working conditions in the plant— the lighting, ventilation, safety conditions, housekeeping, cafeteria facilities, and the plant hospital. He thought these conditions were all good, and that in this respect at least the company had done all it could to make work as pleasant as possible for the workers. Then he added:

But you know it's a funny thing. These things are all good, but they don't make the job good. It's what you spend most of the time doing that counts.

His Chance of Promotion

The interview then turned to the subject of promotion opportunities:

My chances for promotion aren't so hot. You see, almost everybody makes the same rate. The jobs have been made so simple that there is not much room to move up from one skill to another. In other places where the jobs aren't broken down this way, the average fellow has something to look forward to. He can go from one step to another right up the ladder. Here, it's possible to make foreman. But none of the guys on the line think there's much chance to go higher than that. To manage a complicated machine like that, you need a college degree. They bring in smart college boys and train them for the better jobs.

Interviewer: "What does your wife think about your job?"

At this point his wife spoke up:

I often wish he'd get another job. He comes home at night, plops down in a chair, and just sits for about 15 minutes. I don't know much about what he does at the plant, but it does something to him. Of course, I shouldn't complain. He gets good pay. We've been able to buy a refrigerator and a TV set—a lot of things we couldn't have had otherwise. But sometimes I wonder whether these are more important to us than having Joe get all nervous and tensed up. He snaps at the kids and snaps at me—but he doesn't mean it.

The worker was then asked if he had considered working elsewhere:

I'll tell you honest. I'm scared to leave. I'm afraid to take the gamble on the outside. I'm not staying because I want to. You see, I'm getting good pay. We live according to the pay I get. It would be tough to change the way we live. With the cost of living what it is, it's too much of a gamble. Then there's another thing. I got good seniority. I take another job and I start from scratch. Comes a depression or something and I'm the first to get knocked off. Also they got a pension plan. I'm 37, and I'd lose that. Course the joker in that pension plan is that most guys out there chasing the line probably won't live 'til they're 65. Sorta trapped—you get what I mean?

His Views on the Union

The subject of the worker's relation-

ship to his union came up in the course of the interview:

The union has helped somewhat. Before they organized, it was pretty brutal. The bosses played favorites—they kept jacking up the speed of the line every time after they had a breakdown. But the union can't do much about the schedule and the way a job is set up. Management is responsible for that.

We had a walk-out last year. They called it an unauthorized strike. Somebody got bounced because he wouldn't keep up his job on the line. The union lost the case because it should have gone through the grievance procedure. The company was dead right to insist that the union file a grievance.

But it was one of those things it's hard to explain. When word got around that the guy was bounced—we all sort of looked at each other, dropped our tools and walked. Somehow that guy was every one of us. The tension on the line had been building up for a long time. We had to blow our top—so we did. We were wrong—the union knew it and so did the company. We stayed out a few hours and back we came. We all felt better, like we got something off our chests.

Some of these strikes you read about may be over wages. Or they may just be unions trying to play politics. But I sometimes think that the thing that will drive a man to lose all that pay is deeper than wages. Maybe other guys feel like we did the day we walked out.

Toward the end of the interview, the worker spoke of the company he worked for:

They are doing what they can—like the hospital, the safety, the pay, and all like that. And the people who run the plant I guess are pretty good guys themselves. But sometimes I think that the company doesn't think much of the individual. If they did they wouldn't have a production line like that one. You're just a number to them. They number the stock and they number you. There's a different feeling in this kind of a plant. It's like a kid who goes up to a grown man and starts talking to him. There doesn't seem to be a friendly feeling. Here a man is just so much horsepower. You're just a cog in the wheel.

Let's just take this interview apart for a moment.

Notice, first, that this worker's dissatisfaction was not due primarily to the things that are usually considered important to a job. People often say, "Pay a man enough, and he'll be satisfied." But this man's pay was good. His job was secure. He worked for a sound company. He had substantial seniority. He had a pension, hospitalization and disability benefits when he became sick, and a good boss; at least he did not hold the kind of job he had against the boss. Working conditions, heating, lighting, cafeteria facilities, and safety conditions were, I would say, as good as if not better than average.

Yet Joe despised his job.

The simple fact is that the impact of "sound" engineering principles had had a marked effect on his total outlook on the job.

What "Sound" Engineering Has Taken Away

For this man, and for hundreds of others with whom we have had experience, the engineer, in applying the principles of mass production to the extreme, had factored out virtually everything that might be of real, personal value to the worker. The sense of anonymity implicit in much of what this particular worker said can be traced back to some of the basic characteristics of his immediate job.

The conveyor belt determined the *pace* at which he worked. He had no control over his pace.

Because it was broken down into the simplest motions possible, the job was highly *repetitive*.

Simple motions meant that there was little or no need for *skill*.

The tools and the work procedure were predetermined. And when techniques changed, it was the engineer— not the worker—who controlled the change.

He worked on a *fraction of the product* and never got a sense of the whole. (He admitted that in 12 years of work he had almost never seen a finished car roll off the final line.)

Some attention was required. Too much to allow him to daydream or carry on any sustained conversation with others; but not enough to allow him to become really absorbed in his work.

The technical setup determined the character of his work relationships. This man identified himself with the partner who worked with him on the opposite side of the line, but beyond that he displayed almost no identification with a work group as such. Men on the line work as an aggregate of individuals with each man performing his operation more or less independently of the others. The lack of an intimate group awareness appeared to reinforce the same sense of anonymity fostered by the conveyor-paced, repetitive character of the job itself.

The worker's comments about promotion and job aspirations are interesting. He saw little hope for advancement because most of the production jobs paid about the same. By applying principles of work rationalization, the industrial engineer, in the best interests of efficiency, had simplified the tasks so that differences in skill from one job to the next were all but eliminated. It was difficult for the average worker to move vertically through a series of distinct steps in promotion. In this connection, it should be added that over the years the union itself, through collective bargaining, had encouraged the trend toward uniform wage standards by raising minimum levels without increasing the relative amounts between job classes.

From a careful examination of the actual work careers of over 200 workers we have found only a few who had experienced any substantial change in job classification during a period of from 12 to 15 years. Collectively, all the workers had improved their overall economic status; individually, few had experienced much change in their relative job status. The net effect of this condition was to increase the depersonalization of the job.

AUTOMATION AND THE WORKER*

Floyd C. Mann, *Institute for Social Research, University of Michigan*

L. Richard Hoffman, *University of Chicago*

JOB STRUCTURE IN POWER PLANTS

In the new power plant, Advance, through the integration of the boiler and turbine operations and the introduction of feedback and other automatic controls, the conversion to the unit system of production required management to reconsider the structure of the jobs. Since the division of labor used in the manning of the older plants could not be directly transferred to Advance, jobs in the new plant were designed by combining functions which had been performed by a single operator in the older plants. This made it possible to compare the attitudes and feelings of men with these enlarged jobs with those of the men in the older

plant who worked at more fractionalized jobs.

In the older plant, three major operating groups performed the three production functions—boiler, turbine and condenser, and electrical operations. The electrical switchboard operators' status and pay were higher than either the boiler or turbine groups. The "top-grade" wage rate for boiler and turbine men was three grades less —amounting to about twenty-five cents an hour less—than their counterpart in the electrical group. The men in the boiler and turbine rooms criticized this distinction as artificial and felt that it did not reflect true differences in either skill requirements or job responsibilities. Table 1 shows the point ratings assigned to each factor for each of the three jobs by a joint committee of representatives from the company and the union.

Within each of these operating groups there were a number of job

* From *Automation and the Worker: A Study of Social Change in Power Plants.* Copyright © 1960 by Holt, Rinehart and Winston, Inc. Reprinted by permission of Holt, Rinehart and Winston, Inc.

TABLE 1. JOB EVALUATION POINT RATINGS

Factor	Switchboard Operator First	Turbine Operator First	Fireman
1. Work experience required	28	26	26
2. Specialized education required	5	3	1
3. Physical skill required	5	5	5
4. Physical effort required	3	3	3
5. Complexity of duties	47	40	40
6. Seriousness of errors	9	9	9
7. Hazards	9	3	7
8. Adverse working conditions	1	2	2
9. Contacts with people outside the company	1	0	0
10. Contacts within the company	6	4	3
11. Responsibility for safety of other	13	5	8
12. Responsibility for company property	2	1	1
13. Amount of supervision received	5	5	5
14. Responsibility for work of others	6	6	2
Total points	140	112	112
Corresponding *T*-grade	16	13	13

gradations, especially in the boiler operations, where the simplest and dirtiest jobs existed. The following jobs were found in the boiler room, listed in the order of ascending skill requirements: flue blower-ash handler, fan operator, water tender, assistant fireman, and fireman. A similar division into more and less skilled jobs was made in the turbine and electrical groups.

Jobs in the low-pressure boiler operations largely involved the manual handling of equipment. The flue blower-ash handler had the assignment of directing the hoses inside the furnaces to clear the slag from the sides. He also operated the equipment for disposing of the ash at the bottom of the furnaces. The fan operator spent his working period in isolation at the top of the plant tending the operation of the induced-draft fans. The view of the production process, even by the highly skilled fireman, who was responsible for maintaining the proper boiler temperature, was restricted to the operation of his pair of boilers. The job responsibilities of the turbine and electrical operators were similarly limited to a small segment of the overall production process, although they included less manual work and more dial watching.

The operating jobs in the new plant were organized in an entirely different manner. Part of this change was the direct result of the technological changes, but a major part stemmed from a decision by management to develop operating personnel qualified in all aspects of the production process. The integration of the boiler and turbine functions and their controls meant that only operators with knowledge of both turbines and boilers could be employed and that the distinction between the turbine and boiler operators could no longer be maintained. This requirement led the company to examine the possibility of further enlarging the operating jobs to include knowledge of the electrical switching operations as well as those of the boilers and turbines. As a result, the distinctions among operators in the older plant according to the type of equipment they operated were eliminated in the new plant. Only one class of operators was established for the new plant: power-plant operators.

A skill hierarchy remained within the operating group, but it included only three skill classifications: power-plant operator A, power-plant operator B, and power-plant helper. The A operator was the most highly skilled classification. The men in this category were expected to have most of the skills and, especially, the knowledge previously held separately by the skilled boiler, turbine, and electrical operators. Their jobs now encompassed responsibility for the entire production process. The A operators, all of whom had transferred from specialized jobs in the older plants in the system, experienced a tremendous job enlargement.

In parallel fashion but at a slightly lower skill level, those men who transferred to Advance as B operators also experienced an enlargement of their jobs. Each B operator was paired with an A operator in his work, learning and receiving informal work direction from him. At the time of the study these pairings were made to ensure complementarity of skills and knowledge. These men worked on all aspects of operations.

The operator helper was the lowest skill classification among the operating jobs. The men in this category performed the few dirty and less desirable tasks which still remained in the new plant.

During each shift, pairs of A and B operators were assigned to the control stations and to a general utility position. One A-B pair was situated in each

of the three control stations—the two boiler-turbine control rooms and the electrical switchboard. A fourth pair was split up, the A operator patrolling the various portions of the plant and the mat, and the B operator serving as the work leader for the helpers in the condenser room. The fifth pair served as additional personnel to be assigned to whatever special jobs had to be done during the shift.

Rotation among these jobs was also originally instituted as part of the training program to prepare the men for the new jobs. This practice was continued past the end of the formal training period, with the men changing positions weekly. Thus, differences between the perceptions and attitudes of the Advance* operators about their new jobs and the Stand* operators about theirs-reflected both the differences between enlarged jobs and specialized jobs and between job rotation and fixed, permanent assignments.

In the rest of this chapter we shall report comparisons of the questionnaire responses of the operators in the two plants concerning perceptions of changes in their jobs, the training they received for these jobs, and the changes in and present state of their feelings about their jobs.

PERCEPTIONS OF JOB CHANGES

These job changes had striking effects on the men in the new plant. They reported that their present jobs were bigger in many ways than the ones held in the older plants (the following discussion is based on Table

---

* Editors' note: Advance is the name given in this study to the more fully automated power plant; Stand is an older plant used increasingly in a standby capacity.

TABLE 2. PERCEPTIONS OF CHANGES IN JOBS

Men Who Report:	Percentage of Men in Each Group Who Report			
	Advance Operators (N = 35)	Stand Operators (N = 109)	Advance Maintenance (N = 23)	Advance Coal Handling (N = 23)
General				
1–39. Much more responsibility on the job now	85	55*	26*	35*
1–47. Job requires much more training now	97	54*	57*	17*
Old skills				
1–46. Much or a little more time spent doing things skilled at now	63	49	48	35*
1–9. Very or fairly good chance to do things best at	77	44*	70	48*
1–40. Much or a little less time doing dirty work now	74	41*	13*	0*
New skills				
1–44. Learning much more on the job now	77	27*	61	13*
1–45. Much or a little more time spent doing things *not* skilled at	57	23*	48	39
Mobility				
1–42. Much or a little more moving around the plant	66	14*	48	25*
1–43. Many or a few more contacts with the men now	63	20*	52	13*

*Percentage is significantly different from the corresponding one for Advance operators of the 0.05 level of confidence, the level of confidence used in all statistical tests in this [article].

2). Eighty-five per cent of the operators who transferred from older plants reported that they had "much more responsibility" on their jobs now than they had had several years ago. . . . Also, almost all this group (97 per cent) reported that their jobs required more training now than earlier. Their present jobs were perceived by the men to be ones with increased responsibility requiring a greater amount of training than did their older jobs.

Two aspects of this enlargement of the operating jobs—the use of present skills and the development of new skills —deserve attention. Although they occurred in combination in this job change, the evidence from the data in Stand suggests that their independent occurrence can have different effects on the workers' attitudes toward their jobs.

The first facet of this change was that the new jobs made greater demands on the abilities, skills, and knowledge which the men already had when they transferred to the new plant. Almost two-thirds (63 per cent) of the men reported that they spent more time doing things they were skilled at than they had previously. There was a greater feeling that now their jobs really utilized their best abilities. More than three-quarters (77 per cent) of the Advance operators said that their jobs gave them a "very good" or "fairly good chance to do the things [they are] best at." Of the operators in Stand, only 44 per cent said that their jobs gave them a chance to do the things they were best at. The latter figure is characteristically found in most organizations where highly specialized, low-skilled jobs exist.

The second aspect of the change— and it was even more of a reversal of the trend toward job simplification— was the necessity for the operators to learn new things and acquire new knowledge and skills on the job. Seventy-seven per cent of the Advance operators said that they were learning much more on their jobs now than they were several years ago, and 57 per cent said they were spending more time now doing things they were not skilled at than they had previously. Thus, in addition to the jobs' providing a greater opportunity to use the skills and knowledge which the operators already had, these new jobs also demanded that the men expand their capabilities by acquiring new knowledge and skills on parts of the operations with which they had had no previous experience or training. Note again that 77 per cent of the Advance operators reported both that they had a "very" or "fairly good chance" to do the things they were best at and that they were learning "much" or "a little more" on their jobs now than they had before.

In addition to having the actual content of their jobs changed, the operators had the opportunity for greater physical mobility around the plant. The weekly rotation from position to position and the required patrol tours probably contributed to 66 per cent of the operators saying they moved around the plant much or a little more now than before. These men were no longer restricted to one part of the plant and to a limited range of activities connected with a highly specialized job. Moreover, most (63 per cent) of them said they made more contact with the other men now than they had done in the older plants.

Although these data show that a large proportion of the operators in the new plant had experienced major changes in their jobs, the question may be raised as to the extent to which this proportion merely represents changes which occurred in the normal promotion process. In an attempt to answer this question partially, a comparison of the perceptions of the operators at Advance with those at Stand is presented in Table 2. In columns 1 and 2 are shown the percentage of operators in each plant who reported particular changes in their jobs in the two previous years. Only one of these percentage differences fails to reach statistical significance. This lack of significance represents more the changes accompanying the promotions. of 44 per cent of the Stand operators rather than a lack of change in Advance.

As an attempt to control for the possibility of a general positive "halo" effect being associated with working in a new plant, with better working conditions, and at higher pay, comparisons on these questions were also made between the operating group and the two other major work groups in Advance: maintenance and coal handling. The percentage of men in these groups reporting recent changes in their jobs is presented in columns 3 and 4 of Table 2. On every question a greater percentage of operators than of either maintenance or coal-handling workers indicated that their jobs had been enlarged, that they had greater physical mobility around the plant, and that they were making many more contacts with other men.

BLUE-COLLAR MARRIAGE*

Mirra Komarovsky

Barnard College

WHO ARE THE DOMINANT MEN?

There were good reasons to expect that the better providers, the more skilled, and the better-educated men would enjoy more power in marriage than the men of lower socioeconomic status. The good providers can use money as a means of control. Higher occupational and economic status entails a higher social rank, which in turn tends to evoke deference. Better economic performance betokens a more effective personality, capable of exercising leadership. Past studies show that the husband's power rises with higher economic and occupational status.[1]

Contrary to the above expectations, however, the better providers in Glen-ton turn out to be the less powerful husbands. Of the men earning under $4,000 a year, 64 per cent are dominant in marriage, but only 41 per cent of men with incomes of $4,000 or over enjoy the superior power. Chances of dominance decline with better education: Forty-seven per cent of husbands with less than high school education, but only 35 per cent of the high school graduates, have the greater power in marriage. Eighteen skilled workers included only four dominant husbands, but there were sixteen such husbands among the thirty-four semiskilled and unskilled men. Moreover, the superior power of the less-educated husband persists when duration of marriage is taken into account.

These surprising results have been foreshadowed in one study which shows a curvilinear relationship between occupation and social status, on the one hand, and the husband's power, on the other. The low blue-collar men exercised *more* power than the high blue-collar men, and in white-collar occupations the power of the husband rose again. Similarly, white-collar men in the two lowest social status groups enjoyed *more* power than in the next higher status category, though less than in the highest status group. The authors

* From *Blue-Collar Marriage*, by Mirra Komarovsky. © Copyright 1962, 1964 by Random House, Inc. Reprinted by permission.

[1] Robert O. Blood, Jr., and Donald M. Wolfe, *Husbands and Wives* (Glencoe, Ill.: The Free Press, 1960); Fred L. Strodtbeck, "Husband-Wife Interaction over Revealed Differences," *American Sociological Review*, 16 (August 1951), 468–73; David M. Heer, "Dominance and the Working Wife," *Social Forces*, 36 (May 1958), 341–47.

of this study suggest that these low-status men may be older but otherwise do not explain the relatively high power of the men at the bottom of the occupational and social hierarchy.[2]

It is surely not their low achievement that gives Glenton's less-educated and unskilled husbands their relative power advantage. They must derive some compensating power from other sources. The explanation is suggested by the following comparison of two groups, the first consisting of the less-educated couples with both husband and wife with less than high school attainment and the second comprised of couples in which both spouses are high school graduates. Among the less-educated, patriarchal couples outnumber the matriarchal two to one; among high school graduates the percentages of husband-dominated and of wife-dominated couples are identical.[3]

IDEOLOGIES: PATRIARCHAL OR EQUALITARIAN

The traditional acceptance of masculine dominance has not disappeared in Glenton. The authority attached to the husband's status is certainly one source of his power in some of the families. This becomes especially visible when the husband takes selfish advantages of his position and the wife accepts frustrations as the normal lot of married women. The joyless mother of seven [described previously] is a case in point; she submits to her husband at least in part because she feels it to be her moral duty. She is an unhappy woman, but one of the happiest women in our sample is also the wife of a patriarchal husband. The traditional source of the latter's power is inferred from the manner in which this couple discussed marriage roles; the very question as to who should have the greater authority in marriage evoked surprise. Both husband and wife gave traditional answers on the male dominance schedule.

Patriarchal attitudes are more prevalent among the less educated. Men and women were asked to check one of four possible responses to the following statements: "Equality in marriage is a good thing, but by and large the husband ought to have the main say-so in family matters," and, "Men should make the really important decisions in the family." The responses ranged from "I agree a lot," "I agree," to "I disagree," "I disagree a lot."[4] Eighty per cent of the uneducated men and women agreed with these statements, and some 30 per cent checked "I agree a lot." On the other hand, only 57 per cent of the high school graduates endorsed these propositions, and only 17 per cent checked "I agree a lot." The comments of the high school graduates in answer to the schedule further supported equalitarian values: "The really important decisions should be discussed and a decision reached by both"; "Marriage is a fifty-fifty proposition"; "Both husband and wife should have equal say in important matters"; and the like.

---

2 Blood and Wolfe, *op. cit.*, pp. 31, 33.

3 The less-educated couples consist of fourteen patriarchal, six matriarchal, and six balance-of-power marriages, whereas the corresponding figures for high school graduates are four, four, and five.

4 These questions were adapted from the Male Dominance Ideology Scale of Lois Wladis Hoffman, "Effects of Employment of Mothers on Parental Relations and the Division of Household Tasks," *Marriage and Family Living*, 22 (February 1960), 31.

Some weak husbands, we noted, vociferously proclaimed patriarchal views, and others made use of equalitarian ideology to rationalize their own defeat. Similarly, some strong husbands accepted equalitarian ideals all the more readily because they were secure in their supremacy. If expressed values and actual behavior do not always coincide, in the group as a whole they do tend to be consistent. Moreover, in at least some cases, the internal evidence indicates that it is the ideals that influence behavior rather than the converse.

Related to their equalitarian attitudes is the further fact that the high school graduates do not grant males the privileges they enjoy as a matter of right among the less-educated couples. Masculine privilege is not identical with patriarchal authority. The latter refers to the sanctioned dominance of the husband, whereas privilege is a sanctioned advantage. The possession of a privilege removes an issue from the arena of possible contest by ensuring victory prior to any struggle. The high school wife expects and demands much of marriage. "This is not the kind of marriage I want," remonstrated one wife whose husband spent many nights in church work away from home. The husband told the interviewer that he felt that her complaint was justified and that he had reluctantly acceded to her demands. Standing on her rights, she was supported by her husband's sense of guilt. Another high school graduate is not always so helpful to his wife in the evenings as she would like him to be. "The worst of it," he confessed, "is that I don't feel right watching TV when she has all this work to finish." Thus, with respect to both patriarchal authority and masculine privilege, the less-educated men enjoy an advantage in comparison with the high school graduates.

PHYSICAL COERCION AS A SOURCE OF POWER

The threat of violence is another ground of masculine power. "Women got to figure men out," remarked a 23-year-old wife, "on account of men are stronger, and when they sock you, they could hurt you." Another woman said of her husband: "He is a big man and terribly strong. One time when he got sore at me, he pulled off the banister and he ripped up three steps." With the evidence of this damage in view, this woman realized, as she put it, what her husband could do to her if he should decide to strike her.

Superior physical strength is of little avail to the male when social norms prohibit the use of force. The outrage of the wife, if not the husband's own guilt, makes physical aggression too costly for the husband. This illustrates how the same attribute may either enhance or weaken an individual's power, depending upon his social environment. By the same token, a woman can grant or withhold sexual favors, but this "resource" cannot be "actualized" if the wife considers it her duty to submit sexually.

Some high school graduates in Glenton have been known to slap their wives, but wife-beating is less frequent than among the less educated. One educated woman married to a man with 9 years of schooling took him to court because he beat her. Superior masculine strength gives the less-educated man an advantage which the high school graduate cannot generally enjoy.

THE LOWER CLASS[1]

Much controversy has arisen over the characteristics of the lower class, a segment of American society comprising from 15 to 20 per cent of the population. In large measure this controversy is a consequence of the demarcation of this range of the class structure. Some writers refer to the lower class only as a general category and do not distinguish between upper and lower levels. Other writers do not use the term lower class but speak only of the working class. In some instances working class is synonymous with the general lower class; in others it is limited to the upper ranges of the lower class.[2]

Part of the problem stems from the tendency to treat the lowest range of the population as interchangeable with the working class. Most research in the past several decades on what is variously called *lower-status persons, the low-income group,* or *the lower class* has dealt with the working class. Findings from these studies are then taken to support views on the nature of life in the lower class. Another common practice is to lump together data on the working class (also known as the upper lower class) with data on the population below this level (the lower lower class) and to designate the combination the lower class. Since most studies are on the working class, characteristics of this class are given prominence in accounts ostensibly of the lower class.

While most persons in the lower strata of the class hierarchy share many characteristics in common, there are sufficient distinctions between those at the very bottom of the economic ladder and those directly above the poverty line (the working class) to warrant separate treatment.[3] We give a profile of this segment of society in terms of the stratification variables of income, education, and occupa-

---

1 Since the early 1960s the term *lower class* has been applied to the "poor" or the "poverty group." Prior to this period, at least since the Great Depression, the latter labels rarely appeared in the sociological literature. During the late 1940s and 1950s, sociological interest was directed principally to the middle and working classes. The lower class received relatively little attention, and scarcely more than passing reference was made to poverty.

We would agree that for purposes of discussion the range of the population referred to as the lower class can be called the *poor*. The attributes used to demarcate the one are the attributes commonly used to describe the other. In brief, this presentation and its related readings can also be viewed as a treatment of the poverty group. For further discussion of this issue see Jack L. Roach, "Sociological Analysis and Poverty," *American Journal of Sociology*, 71 (July 1965), 68–78.

2 This question is discussed at greater length in Jack L. Roach and Orville R. Gursslin, "The Lower Class, Status Frustration, and Social Disorganization," *Social Forces*, 43 (May 1965), 501–10. Others have noted this confusion. See Gans, *op. cit.*, Chap. 11, and Miller and Riessman, *op. cit.*

3 We recognize that the problem of differentiating between working and lower classes in terms of basic stratification variables (not to mention associated behavioral variables) is the subject of much controversy. We do not anticipate universal acceptance of our designation of the lower class as a population generally characterized by grammar school education, minimal job skills, and a living standard at or below the poverty line. These problems of demarcation, especially as they relate to the lower class, are incisively discussed in Howard E. Freeman and Camille Lambert, Jr., "The Identification of 'Lower-Class' Families in an Urban Community," in Shostak and Gombert, *op. cit.*, pp. 584–92.

tion below and follow it with a presentation of sociocultural and social-psychological characteristics.[4]

Persons in the lower class live at or below a subsistence level (the poverty line) throughout their lives. They exist in poverty as children and raise their own children under conditions of economic deprivation. Crowded, substandard housing; inadequate food and clothing; and lack of proper medical care are the significant facts of life. Marginal and erratic income forces these people to live on a day-to-day basis and to rely heavily on public welfare.

Few lower-class persons complete high school; they are high school dropouts as their parents were grammar school dropouts before them. Their education relegates them to poorly paying jobs requiring few or no skills. Unlike the income of the middle class (and to some extent also of the working class), which commonly increases up to middle age, the income of the lower-class person reaches a peak a few years after he starts employment and begins to decline by the time he has reached his late twenties. In a high proportion of lower-class homes the female works either full or part time and often is the only breadwinner. Even when her earnings, typically gained from domestic or service work, are combined with her husband's wages, the family's income seldom moves above the subsistence level.

Seen, then, in terms of basic socioeconomic variables this segment of the population is the lowest in the stratification system. It is a population generally characterized by grammar school education, by occupations requiring only minimal skills, nad by a standard of living at or below the poverty line.

The behavior of lower-class persons is usually outside the mainstream of cultural control. They exist in a milieu impoverished to the point where social learn-

---

[4] Extensive documentation for this description of the lower class is given in Jack L. Roach, "A Theory of Lower-Class Behavior," in *Sociological Theory: Inquiries and Paradigms*, ed. Llewellyn Gross (New York: Harper & Row, Publishers, 1967), pp. 294–315. The following studies are illustrative of those used to support the generalizations constituting this profile. (We have attempted to use only research in which the investigators give enough information to indicate that the group studied is the lower class not the working class. We have cited specific pages since in most of the relevant literature the researcher commonly reports data on both working and lower classes.)
Arthur Vidich and Joseph Bensman, *Small Town in Mass Society* (Garden City, N.Y.: Doubleday & Company, Inc., 1958), p. 296; James West, *Plainville, U.S.A.* (New York: Columbia University Press, 1945), p. 131; Frank Riessman, *The Culturally Deprived Child* (New York: Harper & Row, Publishers, 1962), p. 57; Earl H. Koos, *Families in Trouble* (New York: Kings Crown Press, 1946), p. xiii; John Spencer, "The Multi-Problem Family," in *The Multi-Problem Family*, ed. Benjamin Schlesinger (Toronto: University of Toronto Press), pp. 27–28; Daniel Wilner *et al.*, *The Housing Environment and Family Life* (Baltimore: The Johns Hopkins Press, 1962), p. 164; Herman Lantz, *People of Coaltown* (New York: Columbia University Press, 1958), p. 208; Hollingshead, *op. cit.*, pp. 178, 341; Lee Rainwater and Karol Weinstein, *And the Poor Get Children* (Chicago: Quadrangle Books, 1960), pp. 60–63; Albert K. Cohen and Harold M. Hodges, "Characteristics of the Lower-Blue-Collar Class," *Social Problems*, 10 (Spring 1963), 317; William Goode, *After Divorce* (Glencoe, Ill.: The Free Press, 1956), Chap. 4; Allison Davis, "Child Rearing in the Class Structure of American Society," in *Sourcebook in Marriage and the Family*, ed. Marvin Sussman (Boston: Houghton Mifflin Company, 1963), p. 230.

ing is retarded. Because impulse and immediate feelings rather than normative planning tend to control their behavior, their interest in educational or occupational achievements is very limited. Concerned primarily with subsistence rather than status advancement, they have few aspirations. In contrast to those in the working class, lower-class persons seek jobs that pay good money now. They do not seriously consider the potential for steady employment and advancement.

Lower-class persons are almost completely isolated from community activities whether these be formal organizations or cliques. This isolation is not simply a separation from the general outside world; typically they interact minimally and lack identification even with those of their own kind.[5] Men, in particular, have no clearly defined roles because of frequent unemployment and minimal involvement in group life.

Lower-class persons have little energy for, or interest in, new thoughts and ideas. Their knowledge of the outside world is hazy; they make critical decisions with little comprehension of the consequences or understanding of the alternatives. The self-systems of lower-class persons are poorly integrated; ego controls are weak. They are not inclined toward introspection, lack subleties in role-playing, and have difficulty in shifting perspectives.

The broken home is commonplace. In consequence, and also because of the high rate of illegitimacy, a large proportion of lower-class families have female heads. Of the homes that do remain intact the majority are strife-ridden and often on the verge of breaking up. Chronic quarreling marked by episodes of physical assault, child neglect, and bitter feelings characterizes family relations. Child-rearing in the lower-class home stands in sharp contrast to that in the middle-class home and also departs significantly from that in the working-class home. It has no plan or rationale other than an inconsistent attempt to keep the children under minimal control. Parents provide little guidance for everyday behavior, not to mention life goals. They may warn the children to do better in school, but this concern stems more from the wish to avoid trouble with school authorities than from valuation of education as the path to achievement. In general, discipline is erratic, swinging from harsh physical punishment to indifference.

Lower Class or Lower Aggregate?

In Chapter Three we outlined the continuum-category controversy. We suggested that strong insistence on the correctness of either view of social class as the only reality neglects claims in favor of the other, and we proposed that the issue of classes as "real groups" is a matter of degree. Depending on the choice of hierarchical levels, the class dimensions focused upon, and the phenomena to be predicted, either approach may prove suitable.

---

5 The reference here is to adults. Many writers rely upon studies of delinquent gangs to demonstrate group life among lower-class persons. Their conclusions appear to be tenuous in two respects. First, there is the problem of generalizing from adolescent behavior to adult life. Second, delinquent gangs are a very small fraction of the relevant population.

We have regarded the upper, middle, and working strata as classes since in varying degree they each include status equals who associate intimately with each other and have a relatively distinct culture. Is this usage of class appropriate to the population at the bottom of the socioeconomic ladder? Most writers appear to think so. Indeed they often have a greater disposition to treat this stratum rather than other levels in the socioeconomic hierarchy as a real group.[6] But this usage of the class concept assumes a strong group life and a distinct, integrated culture. The empirical research summarized above does not support these assumptions for the lower class. On the contrary it points to a low level of social interaction, a lack of viable group ties, and limited cultural regulation.[7] In brief, we must conclude that the group and cultural characteristics of the lower class are of such a nature that the class concept as customarily used may be particularly in appropriate for this population.[8]

While the paper below by Jack Roach and Orville Gursslin is addressed spe-

---

[6] Reasons for this treatment are complex, but the following factors appear to be involved. Empirical studies do not figure prominently in the recent return of interest in the lower class. Most of the current literature consists of speculative essays that cite empirical research carried out during the 1920s and 1930s. Notable changes in the sociocultural composition of the lower class have occurred since then. Immigrants, for example, constitute a negligible fraction of this segment of the population today, yet some accounts describe them as a sizable component. Misunderstanding arises, then, from the confusion of class groups with immigrant groups having a distinctive culture and group life. Paralleling this overlap between class and immigrant characteristics is the blurring of the lower class with ethnic or racial groups, especially Puerto Ricans and Negroes. The connections and distinctions between lower-class life and Negro or Puerto Rican culture is a moot point. In any event, the process of generalizing from these components to the lower class as a whole is open to serious question. We have already commented on what is probably the most important reason for the assumption that the lowest socioeconomic stratum is a real group—the failure to distinguish between the working class and the population at the bottom. This failure leads to the attribution of such working-class characteristics as a group life and a distinct culture to the lowest stratum.

[7] On theoretical grounds one could expect minimal or erratic cultural regulation because of the lack of effective social interaction.

[8] The remarks in footnote 6 should not be construed as support for the continuum thesis of stratification. To be sure, as advocates of this thesis maintain, such characteristics as education, occupation, and income may easily be seen as continuous variables. Viewed, however, from the standpoint of public practice, some equidistant intervals on the continua of education, occupation, and income are more productive of significant social distinctions than others. It is one thing to speak of persons with 11 years of school as only a notch below those with 12 years (high school graduates). But this apparently slight difference often leads to important occupational divisions. Previously, one or more years of high school education qualified a person for positions not open to those with grammar school education. Today, those without high school diplomas not only enter the occupational system at the lowest rung (unskilled factory hand, service worker, etc.) but also have a minimal chance of moving up to skilled blue-collar jobs (not to mention white-collar employment). Moreover, in contemporary America, educational and occupational barriers are increasingly associated with a subsistence income and a level of living at or below the poverty line. The significance of these conditions for lower-class life is obscured by an image of class structure which denies the importance of socially defined differences in education, occupation, and income. In short, while we seriously question whether the lower class should be treated as a "class" in the usual sense, it does not follow that the perspectives of the continuum school have meaning for the population at the bottom of the socioeconomic hierarchy.

cifically to the thesis of a culture of poverty, much of the discussion is relevant to the lower class since this population is generally described as living in poverty. The authors evaluate the claims that the poor have a distinct culture and strong group life and that these imputed characteristics are the major causes of their behavior. They propose an alternative explanation of the way of life of the poor, emphasizing the material conditions of economic deprivation.

Taped interviews with the Crawford family give glimpses of everyday life at the bottom of the socioeconomic ladder. The responses of the Crawfords to queries about their hopes, plans, and worries convey profound distrust of the world around them. Fears about the future and worries about money pervade their daily lives.

A sizable part of our social-scientific knowledge of the lower class comes from the work of Lee Rainwater. Excerpts from his *And the Poor Get Children*—a field study of sexual behavior, contraception, and family planning—provide another sketch of interaction between males and females in the lower class, especially as manifested in sexual attitudes and relationships.

AN EVALUATION OF THE CONCEPT "CULTURE OF POVERTY"*†

Jack L. Roach, *University of Connecticut*

Orville R. Gursslin, *Ohio University*

The recent awakening of American society to the fact that the poor are still with us has been followed by attempts of sociologists[1] and others to explain why poverty remains in the midst of abundance. Prominent among these explanations is the "culture of poverty" thesis.[2] Allowing for some

* From Jack L. Roach and Orville R. Gursslin, "An Evaluation of the Concept 'Culture of Poverty,'" *Social Forces*, 45 (March 1967), pp. 384–92.

† This is an enlarged version of a paper presented at the 1965 annual meeting of the Eastern Sociological Society. The authors wish to express their appreciation to Llewellyn Gross for his many helpful comments.

[1] Sociologists have become interested in poverty in contemporary America quite belatedly. See Jack L. Roach, "Sociological Analysis and Poverty," *American Journal of Sociology*, 71 (July 1965), 68–75.

[2] Among those who have contributed to the literature on the "culture of poverty" in American society are Frank Riessman, *The Culturally Deprived Child* (New York: Harper & Bros., 1962); Thomas Gladwin, "The Anthropologist's View of Poverty," in *The Social Welfare Forum, 1961* (New York: Columbia University Press, 1961), pp. 73–86; Jerome Cohen, "Social Work and the Culture of Poverty," in *Mental Health of the Poor*, eds. Frank Riessman *et al.* (Glencoe, Ill.: The Free Press, 1964), pp. 128–38; Roland Warren, *Multi-Problem Families: A New Name or a New Problem*

variation in wording, those who use the term "culture of poverty" usually hold that the poor share distinctive patterns of values, beliefs, and action, and exhibit a style of life which departs significantly from that of the core culture. Treated this way the concept of a culture of poverty corresponds to some of the general referents of the concept of subculture.[3]

The "way of life of the poor" is one of the latest additions to the list of phenomena to which the concept of subculture has been applied.[4] In the

past we have had accounts of the adolescent subculture, the suburban subculture, the delinquent subculture, and the prison subculture, to mention a few.[5] What is there about the poor to suggest that the subculture thesis would be a fruitful explanatory scheme for their behavior? Apparently, a major source of influence has been studies showing that the poor tend to live in enclaves, have similar socioeconomic characteristics,[6] and share a common set of life conditions. The use of the subculture concept in the field of social stratification has also helped to lay the groundwork for the claim that a culture of poverty exists. The majority of stratification students indicate their acceptance of the subcultural inter-

---

(New York: State Charities Aid Association, 1960); Michael Harrington, *The Other America* (New York: The Macmillan Company, Publishers, 1962); Lee Rainwater, "Marital Sexuality in Four Cultures of Poverty," *Journal of Marriage and the Family*, 26 (November 1964), 457–66; Robert E. Will and Harold G. Vatter, eds., *Poverty in Affluence* (New York: Harcourt, Brace & World, Inc., 1965). Although not all of these writers are sociologists, they are engaging essentially in a sociological argument. Numerous authors also refer in passing to the culture of poverty. So far as can be ascertained their conceptions of this culture are similar to more extended treatments. See, for example, Ronald G. Corwin, *A Sociology of Education* (New York: Appleton-Century-Crofts, 1965), p. 158.

3 For some general accounts and applications of the subculture concept, see Milton Gordon, "The Concept of the Sub-Culture and Its Application," *Social Forces*, 26 (October 1947), 40–43; Milton Yinger, "Contraculture and Subculture," *American Sociological Review*, 25 (October 1960), 625–35; Albert K. Cohen, *Delinquent Boys* (Glencoe, Ill.: The Free Press, 1955); Hylan Lewis, *Blackways of Kent* (Chapel Hill, N.C.: The University of North Carolina Press, 1955).

4 This is not to say that the conception of a "way of life of the poor" had not previously appeared in sociological writing, for it is clear that in many ways what is referred to as the "culture of poverty" today also came in for attention by sociologists during the Depression and in earlier periods. However there was no explicit attempt to apply the subculture framework.

5 As Reissman puts it, "The identification of subculture . . . can be carried to startling extremes. A subculture exists . . . whenever a definable criterion can distinguish any group of individuals from others." Leonard Reissman, *Class in American Society* (Glencoe, Ill.: The Free Press, 1959), p. 174. An example of "pushing too far" with the subculture concept is seen in Michael Schwartz and George Henderson, "The Culture of Unemployment: Some Notes on Negro Children," in *Blue Collar World*, eds. Arthur B. Shostak and William Gombert (Englewood Cliffs, N.J.: Prentice-Hall, Inc., 1964), pp. 459–69.

6 The reference here is to characteristics such as occupation, income, and education. Some authors virtually suggest a homogeneous racial or ethnic composition or they write as if immigrants still comprise much of the poor. Approximately one-fourth of the poor is nonwhite; immigrants are a negligible fraction. Other authors speak of the poor as made up of *heterogeneous* ethnic groups. This does not preclude the use of the subculture concept. The path taken is to refer to diverse *subcultures* of the poor rather than a general *subculture* of poverty. See, for example, Catherine S. Chilman, "Child-Rearing and Family Relationship Patterns of the Very Poor," *Welfare in Review*, 3 (January 1965), 9.

pretation by treating social classes as real entities having a separate group life as well as distinctive values, beliefs, and behavior. Given this orientation, it is not surprising that most sociological studies of the poor—commonly referred to as the lower class—start with the assumption of an existing subculture.

The subcultural theme has also been highly attractive to those engaged in mapping out plans for coping with poverty. Many of the current action programs focusing on the poor are based either explicitly or implicitly on the premise that a culture of poverty exists. These programs involve an attempt to interrupt this presumed cultural pattern.

PROBLEMS IN THE USE OF THE CONCEPT "CULTURE OF POVERTY"

The application of the concept of a culture of poverty involves many of the problems implicated in the general usage of the subculture concept. In a significant critique of the concept Milton Yinger comments that it is employed, "whenever a writer wishes to emphasize the normative aspects of behavior that differ from some general standard."[7] Among the numerous interpretations of subculture, Yinger distinguishes two general usages. One

refers to the normative systems of groups which simply differ from the larger society. This, he suggests, is the common use of subculture. The second prominent usage emphasizes conflict between a group and the larger society as seen by the presence of inverse or countervalues. This version he labels a contraculture.[8] Yinger asserts that the essential task for those using the subculture approach is to specify the conditions under which cultural or contracultural influences will be found in various empirical mixtures. Failure to differentiate between these two usages, especially failure to deal with differing origins and modes of relationship to the environing society, results in an inconsistent conceptual framework, weak in organizing and explanatory power.[9]

The problems noted by Yinger in his analysis of the subculture concept are evident in the conceptions of a culture of poverty. Indeed, a more complex typology than Yinger's is necessary in order to embrace the varying usages of the subculture concept as applied to the poor. The culture of poverty is seen either as a "derivative" of the main culture,[10] or as a traditional cultural system with a unique set of values developed over many generations.[11] Two versions of the "derivative" type

---

7 Yinger, *op. cit.*, p. 626. For other critiques of the subculture concept see Albert Cohen, *op. cit.*, Chap. 3; Reissman, *op. cit.*, pp. 173–77; William H. Sewell, "Social Class and Childhood Personality," *Sociometry*, 24 (August 1961), 352. More generally, see David Gottlieb and Jon Reeves, *Adolescent Behavior in Urban Areas* (Glencoe, Ill.: The Free Press, 1963), especially Sec. 2.

8 Yinger, *op. cit.*, pp. 627–30.

9 *Ibid.*, p. 633.

10 The concept of a derivative subculture is a more inclusive term than Yinger's concept of contraculture, which he reserves for subcultures where the conflict element is central. The idea of a derivative subculture implies only that the explanation for the emergence of the subculture is in terms of the group's relationship to the main sociocultural system.

11 For example, Walter Miller, "Implications of a Lower-Class Culture," *Social Service Review*, 33 (September 1959), 219–36.

of explanation are in common use. The culture of poverty is conceived of as either a natural *evolvement* from the main culture or as a *reaction* to it, that is, as an emergent stemming from the dynamism of conflict.[12] On the other hand, when the second major type, a traditional culture of poverty, is hypothesized, no assumption of a functional *derivation* from the core culture is made. In fact, the origins of the way of life of the poor are seldom dealt with. Changing from one version of the culture of poverty to another in the middle of a presentation is common, and some writers use a combination of several versions, apparently without recognizing that diverse explanatory schemes are implicated. Other deficiencies in the concept of a culture of poverty, most of which similarly reflect ambiguities in the concept of subculture, include the following:

1. *Generalizing from related subcultures to the culture of poverty.* Is the culture of poverty interchangeable with the lower-class Negro subculture? Much of the speculative writing on a culture of poverty draws heavily upon conjectures and limited empirical knowledge on this group.[13] There are

serious doubts that one can so readily generalize from the Negro poor to the vast majority of the poor who are white, native Americans.[14] A second questionable extrapolation, also frequently made, is from delinquent subcultures to the culture of poverty. In addition to the problem of generalizing from adolescent behavior to adult life, delinquent gangs comprise a very small fraction of the relevant population. Moreover, they consist of working-class as well as lower-class boys.

2. *Failure to indicate the purpose served by the concept.* Indiscriminate use of the concept of a culture of poverty is common. For many writers the concept appears to serve as a catch-all for covering gaps in knowledge about the poor. For others it seems useful both as a descriptive label and as an explanation in itself. Often it is impossible to determine what referents of the concept writers have in mind or why it is employed. If the purpose is explanation, what is to be explained: group life, personality processes, deviant behavior, the origins of poverty, or the perpetuation of poverty? Or is the term simply a convenient descriptive label for the behavior of the poor?

3. *Inadequate designation of subcultural characteristics.* Typically, a variety of social, cultural, and psychological traits (e.g., physical aggressiveness, mother-centered family, fatalism) are combined with descriptions of the *material* conditions of poverty and offered as a profile of the *culture* of poverty. If, as most writers hold, the

---

[12] Warren's account, for example, suggests derivation from or general linkage with the main culture (*op. cit.*). A conception of the culture of the poor as a conflict type is given in Peter Marris, "A Report on Urban Renewal in the United States," in *The Urban Condition*, ed. Leonard Duhl (New York: Basic Books, Inc., Publishers, 1963), pp. 123–27.

[13] References to the Negro group are commonly made by those attempting to demonstrate that the poor have many untapped abilities. These writers hold that the poor can be, and often are, militant activists on their own behalf. However, insofar as citations are given to support such claims they almost always pertain to the activities of the Negro poor not the white poor. . . .

[14] The basic problem is the unknown amount of overlap and subsequent confusion between racial or ethnic subcultures and poverty subcultures. Moreover, Negroes usually live in ghettos, which are comprised of the poor as well as the nonpoor. It is therefore difficult to generalize about the Negro poor as a discrete, isolated group.

term subculture basically refers to a normative system, then it is questionable that such characteristics as overcrowding, poor nutrition, and unemployment should be classified as normative elements. To some degree these physical facts of lower-class life might be seen as important antecedents to the emergence of norms as adaptive mechanisms. But such a view of cause and effect still requires an adequate conceptual distinction.

4. *Lack of specification of independent and dependent variables.* Causal relationships are often implied in descriptions of a temporal sequence and in expressions of primacy of factors, but explicit cause-effect statements are seldom put forth in discussions of the culture of poverty. When reference is made to causal relationships their implications are obscured, if not rendered empty, by tautological and circular explanations.[15] A common practice is to describe the culture of poverty in terms of regularities of behavior and thought-ways and then to treat a designated regularity as a contributing *cause* of the culture of poverty. For example, the belief of the poor that the future cannot be controlled may be treated as one of the causes of the culture of

poverty and, at the same time, as one *of its characteristics.*[16]

Most deficiencies in the concept of a culture of the poor can be traced to a failure to distinguish between culture as description and culture as cause. *Culture as description* places emphasis upon the common way of life of a group. Used in this way, culture is generally treated as a dependent variable rather than as an independent variable.

Culture as cause places emphasis on a shared pattern of living and transmitted social learning in a society. The primary cause of the younger generation's behavior is the socially transmitted culture of the older generation. It appears that most writers *intend* the latter, that is, culture as cause, when they use the concept "culture of poverty," for a major concern is with what is held to be the socially transmitted "culture of poverty" from the older generation.[17]

---

15. Basically, this difficulty comes from what many believe to be the inevitable circularity in most uses of the culture concept. See Edwin M. Lemert, "Social Structure, Social Control, and Deviation," in *Anomie and Deviant Behavior*, ed. Marshall B. Clinard (Glencoe, Ill.: The Free Press, 1964), pp. 59–60. More generally see Judith Blake and Kingsley Davis, "Norms, Values, and Sanctions," in *Handbook of Modern Sociology*, ed. Robert E. L. Faris (Skokie, Ill.: Rand McNally & Company, 1964), pp. 456–66. Nor can this problem be avoided by limiting analysis to the maintenance of poverty rather than to its emergence for circular reasoning is also present in the writings of those who are primarily concerned with the maintenance of a subculture.

16. Closely connected with the pitfall of tautology is the danger of one of the fallacies of functional analysis. With respect to the illustration given, this fallacy is the interpretation that the belief of the poor that the future cannot be controlled exists because it is essential to the persistence of a postulated culture of poverty. That is, this belief is treated as if it were caused by its alleged consequence—the culture of poverty. On this point, see Harry C. Bredemeier, "The Methodology of Functionalism," *American Sociological Review*, 20 (April 1955), 173–80. Furthermore, as Yinger cautions, "One should not assume, when the members of a group behave in similar ways, that cultural norms produce this result. Collective behavior theory and personality theory may also help to account for the similarities" (*op. cit.*, p. 628). As we shall indicate below there is a third possibility, namely, that to an important degree the behavior of the poor can be attributed to the physical conditions of poverty.

17. Gladwin, *op. cit.*, pp. 73–75; Leonard Schneiderman, "Value Orientation Preferences of Chronic Relief Recipients," *Social Work*, 9 (July 1964), 13. It should be noted

"CULTURE OF POVERTY" AS A CAUSAL EXPLANATION

If the thesis of a culture of poverty is used as a causal explanation two essential conditions must be present. The first condition, previously mentioned, is a demonstration that a culture of poverty is socially transmitted from one generation to the next. Moreover, this particular cultural pattern must be relatively uniform intragenerationally for the group concerned. The second condition, closely linked to the first, concerns the strength of the normative system of the poor. If it is claimed that the behavior of the poor is *primarily* determined by the culture of poverty, then it must be demonstrated that this culture is a *strong* normative system.

Most advocates of the thesis of a culture of poverty assume that these two conditions are met.[18] This presupposes the existence of various characteristics relative to the social life and psychological makeup of the poor of which the following appear to be most pertinent: (1) a similar socioeconomic background, (2) similar material con-

ditions of life, (3) physical proximity to each other, (4) requisite social-psychological properties, and (5) a high degree of social interaction within and across family lines.

As noted earlier, studies show that most of the poor do have a relatively homogeneous socioeconomic background, share a common set of life conditions, and live in close proximity in residential enclaves. The presence of these attributes has no doubt been instrumental in leading many writers to the conclusion of a culture of poverty. But these attributes are not in themselves sufficient for the emergence and maintenance of a viable subculture. Of more critical importance would be characteristics of the poor pertaining to their social psychology and the nature of their social relationships. Most writers, whether treating specifically the culture of poverty or other types of subcultures, appear to assume that these requisite characteristics are present.

Relevant empirical findings do not support this assumption as it relates to the poverty group. Evidence from many studies describes various social-psychological handicaps of the poor; notably, cognitive restrictions, limited role skills, apathy, and a general state of "psychic exhaustion."[19] Granting that knowledge

---

that, while these studies attempt to assess the value systems of the poor, they do not demonstrate an intergenerational transmission of the culture of poverty, a condition which is conventionally regarded as necessary for the perpetuation of culture. What exactly is transmitted from the "older poor" to the "younger poor" is not easy to ascertain. Paradoxically, according to this conjectural writing, what seems largely to be "transmitted" is the *absence* of a middle-class culture.

[18] A variety of terms are used by those writing on the culture of poverty, connoting an elaborate, intricate, strong culture. Yet one finds no descriptions of such characteristics as leadership, hierarchy of command, task differentiation—phenomena generally present in complex cultural systems—in accounts of the culture of poverty. On the transmision of the culture of poverty, see footnote 17.

[19] Much of this evidence is reviewed in Orville R. Gursslin and Jack L. Roach, "Some Problems in Training the Unemployed," *Social Problems*, 12 (Summer 1964), 86–98. There are a number of speculative accounts and empirical studies of the significance of cognitive abilities, an adequate self-system, and role skills for interpersonal functioning. For example, John D. Campbell and Marian R. Yarrow, "Perceptual and Behavioral Correlates of Social Effectiveness," *Sociometry*, 24 (March 1961), 12–19; A. Irving Hallowell, *Culture and Experience* (Philadelphia: University of Pennsylvania Press, 1955); Arthur L. Combs and Donald Snygg, *Individual Be-*

is limited concerning the requisites of an adequate social actor, it seems questionable that persons with such handicaps can form and maintain the types of cultural systems[20] implied in writings on the culture of poverty.

What is the nature of social interaction among the poor? A consideration of this question bears more directly on the issue of the social transmission of the culture of poverty. To be sure, cultural norms are transmitted via interaction between parents and children. But cultural norms by definition are group norms which must be additionally sustained by transmission through a system of *effective* social interaction involving a network of family units and other primary groups. Accordingly, it is not sufficient to demonstrate that adequate interaction takes place between parents and children. What is also required is evidence showing that the poor have an effective degree of interaction with others of their own kind

outside the family. Since it is widely held that innovative cultural forms require this kind of interaction for their persistence as well as for their emergence,[21] the absence of this condition would pose a much more serious question with respect to the tenability of the culture-of-poverty thesis.

Numerous studies have documented the marked degree of social isolation of the poor. This isolation is not simply a separation from persons of the outside world, for typically the poor interact minimally with those of their own kind.[22] Neither the quality nor the quantity of their social interaction would seem to qualify for the kind of effective social interaction posited in theoretical discussions of the genesis and maintenance of subcultures. These deficiencies in social interaction surely play a part in the social-psychological handicaps of the poor. Such a contention rests upon the assumption, fundamental in sociological thinking, that the

---

havior (New York: Harper & Bros., 1959); Daniel A. Rodgers, "Personality Correlates of Successful Role Behavior," *Journal of Social Psychology*, 46 (August 1957), 111–17; Urie Bronfenbrenner, "The Measurement of Skill in Social Perception," in *Talent and Society*, eds. David C. McClelland *et al.* (Princeton, N.J.: D. Van Nostrand Company, Inc., 1958).

More persuasive for most sociologists would be the argument that persons who are preoccupied with physical needs and are in a state of apathy and chronic psychic and physical exhaustion are scarcely in a condition to maintain "meaningful" social relationships. Relevant here is Levy's proposition that one of the four basic conditions that may terminate a society is "apathy of the members." Marion J. Levy, *The Structure of Society* (Princeton, N.J.: Princeton University Press, 1952), p. 492.

20 This issue of further discussed in Jack L. Roach and Orville R. Gursslin, "The Lower Class, Status Frustration and Social Disorganization," *Social Forces*, 43 (May 1965), 501–10.

21 A succinct statement of this requirement for the existence of a subculture is given in Cohen, *op. cit.*, especially p. 59.

22 Dorothea C. Leighton *et al.*, *The Character of Danger* (New York: Basic Books, Inc., Publishers, 1963), p. 384; Earl H. Koos, *Families in Trouble* (New York: Kings Crown Press, 1946), p. xiii; Daniel Wilner *et al.*, *The Housing Environment and Family Life* (Baltimore: The Johns Hopkins Press, 1962), p. 164; Jerome Myers and Bertram Roberts, *Family and Class Dynamics in Mental Illness* (New York: John Wiley & Sons, Inc., 1959), pp. 178–79; Jane Jacobs, *The Death and Life of Great American Cities* (New York: Random House, Inc., 1961), pp. 66–67; Harriet C. Wilson, *Delinquency and Child Neglect* (London: George Allen & Unwin, Ltd., 1962); Robert S. Lynd and Helen Merrill Lynd, *Middletown* (New York: Harcourt Brace & Co., 1929), pp. 272–73; David Caplovitz, *The Poor Pay More* (Glencoe, Ill.: The Free Press, 1963), pp. 133–34; August Hollingshead, *Elmtown's Youth* (New York: John Wiley & Sons, Inc., 1949), p. 219.

nature and functioning of the individual is largely shaped by his participation in group life.[23]

On such empirical grounds, then, it would appear that at least two crucial characteristics are not sufficiently present for an adequate transmission of a strong normative system comprising a culture of poverty. Inferentially, it can be concluded that a normative code which strongly induces and regulates behavior does not generally exist among the poor. This does not preclude the presence of distinctive folkways and customs which guide such aspects of daily living as food preference and dress.

This conclusion notwithstanding many writers refer to evidence which seems to support the contention that a strong culture of poverty does exist. What is the nature of this evidence? The contemporary sociological literature on poverty consists largely of speculative essays. A few empirical studies provide some basis for the claim that the poor exhibit a common life style, but seldom does the information go much beyond illustrative sketches.[24] Most references to the existence of a culture of poverty cite research on the lower socioeconomic ranges of the population as reported in the social-class

and social-problems literature. However, with few exceptions, research in the past several decades on what is variously called lower-strata or lower-status groups deals with subjects *above* the poverty line. Findings on the working class, also called the upper lower class, have been erroneously taken as data on those living *below* the poverty line, that is, the lower lower class. A typical practice is to lump together upper and lower segments, defining both as the lower class, or as the "poor."[25]

A recent work that has been used inappropriately in this respect is Herbert Gans' *The Urban Villagers.*[26] Gans emphasizes that his study is basically on the *working-class* subculture and is only peripherally concerned with what he calls the *lower class.*[27] Indeed, insofar as he speaks of a lower-class subculture, he depicts it as a *disintegrating* subculture.[28] Yet references to this book are used to support the contention of a lower-class subculture in the sense of a culture of poverty.[29]

Gans's remarks on the lower-class subculture are similar to findings from a number of other studies on the lower class which describe such characteristics as lack of group ties, hostility toward own kind, and minimal cultural regulation.[30] In general, empirical studies on

---

23 For analytical purposes there is the problem of where to cut into this seeming chicken-or-egg situation. With respect to the present case, while it is certainly desirable to study the effects of social deprivation upon the social-psychological functioning of the poor, there is the question of the sources or roots of this social deprivation. In our view, a reasonable causal sequence would be: material deprivation, social deprivation, social-psychological inadequacies.

24 Oscar Lewis has provided substantial descriptions of the "culture of poverty" in Mexico; there is little in the way of comparable material on the poor in contemporary America. To some extent the study by Schneiderman, *op. cit.*, is a contribution of this type.

25 Others have noted this confusion. See Herbert J. Gans, *The Urban Villagers* (Glencoe, Ill.: The Free Press, 1962); S. M. Miller and Frank Riessman, "The Working Class Subculture," *Social Problems*, 9 (Summer 1961), 88.

26 Gans, *op. cit.*

27 *Ibid.*, p. 349.

28 *Ibid.*, pp. 250–51, 267–68.

29 Harold M. Hodges, *Social Stratification* (Cambridge, Mass.: Schenkman Publishing Co., 1964), pp. 202–3.

30 Leighton *et al.*, *op. cit.*, pp. 388–89; Marris, *op. cit.*, p. 127; Myers and Roberts, *op. cit.*, pp. 66–255; Arthur Vidich and Joseph Bensman, *Small Town in Mass Society* (Garden City, N.Y.: Doubleday &

the *lowest* level of the population suggest *limited* or *marginal* subcultural characteristics, while studies of the upper segment (the working class) report the existence of a *strong* subculture. In short, the empirical case for a culture of the poor—particularly of the type described in the literature on poverty—rests on slim evidence.

THE NEED FOR ALTERNATIVE APPROACHES

There is no intent to dismiss summarily the subcultural approach. But if sociologists are to continue to employ the concept of a culture of poverty careful thought must be given to the type of population for which the thesis is appropriate. Certainly the concept of a culture of poverty, used as a causal explanation, is not applicable to all the poor. Those who are poor because of some life event such as sickness, accident, or old age but who have known "better times" are obviously not the product of a culture of poverty. The concept is clearly intended, by most writers, as an explanation of the behavior of those who have lived in poverty

_____

Company, Inc., 1958), p. 296; Hylan Lewis, "Child Rearing Practices Among Low-Income Families in the District of Columbia," paper presented at the National Conference of Social Welfare, Minneapolis, Minnesota, May 1961. See also the review of English and American studies of multiproblem families by Spencer, who concludes that the concept of subculture is of doubtful relevance to the behavior of such families. John Spencer, "The Multi-Problem Family," in *The Multi-Problem Family*, ed. Benjamin Schlesinger (Toronto: The University of Toronto Press, 1963), p. 28.

The picture of group life among the poor that emerges in these documents is closer in some ways to the concept of "near groups" as discussed in Lewis Yablonsky, *The Violent Gang* (New York: The Macmillan Company, Publishers, 1962).

for several generations. It would appear, then, that the culture-of-poverty thesis would be most relevant for subgroups of the long-term poor such as residents of regional enclaves (e.g., the Appalachian poor) or those living in ethnic and racial enclaves. Seen in this way it would be more appropriate to refer to several cultures of poverty rather than *a* culture of poverty.[31] Each type would require separate analysis in order to understand why it leads to the intergenerational perpetuation of poverty.

There remains, however, a large segment of the poor for which the culture-of-poverty thesis would be tangential if not inapplicable. Alternative schemes are needed for interpreting the behavior of this aggregate of the poor. As previously emphasized, insofar as one can speak of a culture of poverty it should be treated as a minimal culture characterized by rudimentary normative regulation. Such cultural determinants, it was contended, cannot be seen as a strong influence in the behavior of the poor. What might be the nature of other determinants and how are they to be conceptualized? Several writers have suggested a re-examination of the role of situational factors in analyses of the relationship between socioeconomic variables and behavior.[32] Kriesberg, for example, differentiates between a cultural and a situational explanation.[33] A cultural explanation basically involves the parental transmission of values and beliefs which in turn

_____

[31] For some comments along these lines see Chilman, *op. cit.*

[32] Louis Kriesberg, "The Relationship Between Socio-Economic Rank and Behavior," *Social Problems*, 10 (Spring 1963), 334–53; Ralph H. Turner, "Life Situation and Subculture," *British Journal of Sociology*, 9 (December 1958), 299–320.

[33] Kriesberg, *op. cit.*, pp. 334–35.

determine behavior. A situational explanation involves social conditions (e.g., patterns of interaction) or nonsocial conditions (e.g., differences in financial resources) which operate *directly* to determine behavior.

Kriesberg acknowledges that it is not easy to separate cultural from situational components. But the relative significance of one or the other sets of factors should be assessed since their differential effects will vary in different societies depending upon such conditions as the class structure, the analytical question being asked, and the kind of behavior under analysis.[34] He believes that increased attention to situational factors will "make it more likely that we explore the *bases* of the cultural differences which do exist rather than treat 'culture' as a residual factor which requires no further explanation."[35] It seems likely, however, that Kriesberg's conception of "situational factors" lacks sufficient distinctiveness from cultural factors to avoid the problems of tautology. This appears to be the case since he includes as part of the situation "patterns of interaction" which many social scientists conceive of as cultural phenomena.

Greater conceptual clarity is possible if more attention is directed to *nonsocial* aspects of the situation. In the present case this means a focus on material conditions of deprivation—a highly relevant emphasis since the physical circumstance of poverty appears to be one of the important factors contributing to the deterioration of behavior and attrition of social life of the poor.

A methodological advantage of using material conditions is that they meet several criteria for use as independent variables. For example, they are separable from the complex of characteristics usually encompassed under the rubric "culture of poverty." Several sophisticated schemes for assessing the material conditions of poverty are available which could be utilized for these purposes.[36] More importantly, the use of material conditions of poverty as independent variables allows for a framework in which intangible aspects of poverty are treated as intervening variables. In this framework the material conditions of poverty would be seen as affecting behavior *directly* as well as indirectly through their effects upon mediating conditions such as the *meaning* of poverty and, more pertinent to the present discussion, upon the general phenomena called the culture of poverty.[37]

Empirical support for such a focus upon material deprivation is present in findings from various types of studies. In recent research on mental illness, for example, there are many accounts of the destructive impact of prolonged poverty on family life and personal functioning. The research reported in the study *Mental Health in the Metropolis* suggests that material deprivation is heavily involved as a generating factor in the personal dis-

---

34 *Ibid.*, p. 336.
35 *Ibid.*, p. 352n.

36 A scale making use of "finite, observable criteria" of the conditions of poverty is given in Stanley A. Hetzler, "A Scale for Measuring Case Severity and Case Movement in Public Assistance," *Social Casework*, 44 (October 1963), 445–51. Probably the most rigorous definition to date of a "poverty line" is found in Mollie Orshansky, "Counting the Poor," *Social Security Bulletin*, 28 (January 1965), 3–26.

37 In addition to raising questions about the adequacy of the concept of the culture of poverty, several illustrations of the role of material determinants in the attitude and behavior of the poor are given in Alvin Schorr, "The Nonculture of Poverty," *The American Journal of Orthopsychiatry*, 34 (October 1964), 907–12.

organization of the poor.[38] Although usually confined to nominal remarks, references to the effects of material conditions on lower-class behavior are also seen in much of the social-stratification literature.[39] Similarly, some authors writing specifically on the topic of poverty allude to physical deprivation as having some causal bearing on the ways of the poor. But again the implications are not examined.[40]

So far, there is little indication in the current sociological literature on poverty that the role of tangible deprivation in behavior is receiving more than lip service.[41] Serious attention to material conditions of poverty requires greater flexibility by sociologists in their views concerning the causal significance of nonsocial factors. The de-emphasis on the role of nonsocial phenomena stems from a long tradition in sociology and was especially characteristic of the work of Max Weber and W. I. Thomas. While these two scholars are rightly regarded as major contributors to the school which excludes nonsocial conditions from sociological analysis both allowed for the possibility of nonmeaningful, objective events affecting social behavior.

To be sure, Weber distinguished between nonsocial and social behavior and clearly emphasized social behavior, but he did not summarily dismiss the nonsocial as "incidental" phenomena. In a seldom-noted observation on the possible role of nonmeaningful events Weber suggested:

> It is possible that things which appear to a given investigator as explicable in subjective terms will in the end turn out to be the product of the laws of nonsubjective systems, that is, the meaningful aspect may be epiphenomenal.[42]

Thomas' conception of the situation includes factors common to both the observer and the actor such as norms, the behavior of others, and the *physical* environment, as well as factors that exist only for the actors, i.e., the meaning of the situation to them.[43] In Thomas' original formulations, the definition of the situation was treated as an *adjunct* of the situation. Moreover, as he saw it, the character of the definition in any situation depended upon the "conjuncture of a variety of biological, physiological, social, and cultural factors."[44]

Sociologists writing on the topic of contemporary poverty are understandably concerned with the *definition* of

---

[38] Leo Srole *et al., Mental Health in the Metropolis* (New York: McGraw-Hill Book Company, 1962). Also, Leighton *et al., op. cit.*; Myers and Roberts, *op. cit.*

[39] A well-known illustration is Allison Davis, "The Motivation of the Underprivileged Worker," in *Industry and Society*, ed. William F. Whyte (New York: McGraw-Hill Book Company, 1946), pp. 84–106.

[40] Jerome Cohen, *op. cit.*, p. 10; Lewis, *op. cit.*, p. 9; Chilman, *op. cit.*, p. 15; Lola M. Irelan, "Escape from the Slums," *Welfare in Review*, 2 (December 1964), 21.

[41] Among the few sociologists who urge more attention to the effects of economic deprivation (and who recognize that more than status frustration is involved) are Herbert Gans and S. M. Miller.

[42] Talcott Parsons, *The Structure of Social Action* (New York: McGraw-Hill Book Company, 1937), p. 642. A similar observation is given in Max Weber, *The Theory of Social and Economic Organization*, trans. A. M. Henderson and Talcott Parsons (Fair Lawn, N.J.: Oxford University Press, Inc., 1947), p. 93.

[43] These brief remarks on Thomas' conceptions are based upon Edmund Volkart, ed., *Social Behavior and Personality—Contributions of W. I. Thomas* (New York: Social Science Research Council, 1951), pp. 2–7.

[44] *Ibid.*, p. 7.

the situation of poverty; that is, with its subjective dimensions. Since physical conditions are a significant part of the situation of poverty and are also involved in its definition, it is highly important that more attention be given to these conditions.

SUMMARY

Many of those who write on poverty in contemporary American life share the view that a viable culture of poverty exists. Some of the deficiencies of this approach have been indicated. The usage of the concept of a culture of poverty involves the application of a subculture framework and consequently reflects many of the same conceptual problems as other uses of this framework. An important distinction is that between the causal and descriptive conceptions of a culture of poverty. Many students of poverty tend to confuse these conceptions and conclude in effect that the traits of the poor are the cause of the traits of the poor.

The criteria were indicated for the usage of the culture of poverty as a causal explanation. It was suggested that these criteria hold for some elements of the poverty group but not for others. Empirical evidence indicates that an important segment of the poor does not have those characteristics which would make possible the emergence and persistence of a culture of poverty conceived of as a significant causal force in the behavior of the poor.

An alternative approach was suggested in which a wider range of factors would be considered, among them the material conditions of economic deprivation.

THE CRAWFORDS: LIFE AT THE BOTTOM*

Jack L. Roach

University of Connecticut

The Crawford family consists of Frank, age 30, his wife Viola, age 27, and their six children ranging from 11 years to 4 months. A premarital pregnancy resulted in a shot-gun marriage when she was 17 and he, 20. In addition to the six children Mrs. Crawford has had at least two miscarriages during the 10 years of their marriage. (She claims she has tried birth control but somehow slip-ups occur, for which she blames her husband.)

The family has a number of health problems. Most of the children badly need dental care. Both parents will probably require full extractions in a few years. The children seem to be constantly bothered by respiratory disorders. This condition is serious enough to warrant visits by the Public Health nurse. Mrs. Crawford is especially beset with health disorders. For several years she has needed corrective surgery for what she calls "female trouble" and for varicose veins. She appears to be chronically exhausted and looks closer to 40 than in her late twenties.

The Crawfords began marriage with

---

* From case files of Jack L. Roach.

no savings and with money owed for a car he purchased shortly before they wed. They set up housekeeping in a two-room, furnished apartment, remaining there until the second child was born, at which time they found a semifurnished flat. Although they have moved five times in the past 10 years (twice their dwelling was condemned by the health department; twice they were evicted for nonpayment of rent), they have remained within the same eight-block slum section. At present the Crawfords live in a five-room flat, haphazardly constructed from a former garage. Although they are cramped for space and the plumbing and heating are defective, better housing would be too costly for them.

Mr. Crawford is employed as a general laborer in an industrial plant. He has had a variety of jobs—assembly-line worker, truck driver, construction laborer, cab driver, gas-station attendant—none of which required much in the way of skill or training. He quit school when he was 17. Because of frequent unemployment, short work weeks, and marginal wages, Mr. Crawford's income has frequently been inadequate to cover the family's basic daily needs. Consequently the Crawfords have turned to public assistance several times in the past 10 years. One application was necessary when Mr. Crawford traveled to a neighboring city to find a better job and remained away from his family for several months. He was charged with desertion and placed on probation. The probation department in turn referred the Crawfords to a family agency for counseling.

Below are excerpts from three tape-recorded interviews with the Crawfords. These interviews were part of a larger study of lower-class families. The interviews were semistructured. Most questions were open-ended, allowing the Crawfords to enlarge upon their responses if they desired. The interview data are organized under question headings, phrased in the same way they were presented to the Crawfords.

What kind of work do you usually do? What kind of work would you like best?

Mr. Crawford. For about 6 months now I've been on the bullgang of the ironworks factory here. You know that's like a catchall job. We fill in, do the odd jobs ... the heavy work that the lift truck and that can't get at. We're like Chinese labor.

If I had a chance I would take a night watchman or guard job. That's steady work. No piecework where you break your back to make an extra buck. You know what you earn and that's that. It may not be the biggest pay, but it is always coming in and no more of this one week a big check and next week 2 days pay. I had a chance at a night watchman job a couple years ago, but I thought I'd be better off sticking it out with construction work. I thought maybe I'd get a chance at one of those big machines like a 'dozer or a power shovel, but I hurt my hand and couldn't do much of anything for a while. Then they laid off and I was out. And like I said before I've been mainly in factory work lately. You know, on the bullgang and things like that. Sometimes on the assembly line.

Since I got out of school when I was 17—I got sick of them teachers always yelling—I've done practically every kind of work. I've driven a truck, pick-up, dump, all kinds. I was a bartender for a while. I've been a kitchen helper. Been in business myself—haulin' things with a big pick-up truck. But that didn't pan out. No business. I've been in and out most of the factories here. Mostly on the assembly line or as a laborer. They hire and lay off. Once I told the foreman he could shove his job and walked off just when the line started. He begged me to stay, but I had it there. The longest I was at was the Rogers steel plant. I stayed there 3 years. I was set for a soft spot on the line when things got slack and they cut our hours down. I left for a dock-worker job and strained myself there. I was on sick leave for half a year from that. I must have had a dozen different jobs since I began working. Once I think I switched three or four times in 1 year. I got to watch myself now. I figure this is a good plant I'm in now. If I can stick it out on the bullgang till the end of the year, maybe I can switch over to a sweeper. Who knows, maybe a watchman job will come along. You gotta keep your eyes open and grab when the grabbin's good. I shoulda did that long time ago. Or else you gotta know some Big Wheel to suckhole around.

How are you doing as a family, with each other as well as raising the kids?

MRS. CRAWFORD. I do what I can with them. If they would just stay out of trouble. We have enough of that without them getting mixed up in something. The oldest boy—he's 11—he's a big mouth and always knows better. The school warned me they can't stand him. Well, I can't stand him either. I've told him I'll put him someplace if he doesn't straighten out. He even started to hit me back last week when I slapped him for lying. The others are bad enough, but they're younger and don't try that stuff. I can lock them in a room or something when they get on my nerves. I try to tell Frank to get after them more but he thinks all he has to do is to whip them once a month and then I'm supposed to take care of everything. If it wasn't for the way those kids are always at me, and Frank and his beer money, things would be a lot better.

How do you mean how are we getting along with each other? I get disgusted with things a lot but I guess we're gettin' by. Anyways we have stood it for 10 years now.

MR. CRAWFORD. It's up to the wife to keep them kids in line. What am I supposed to do, kill them everyday? I will too if any one of them ever raises a hand to me. I've got enough headaches without arguin' about those damn kids all the time. Whatta they care anyways. Even the 3-year-old all he knows is gimme, gimme! What do they care about their old man. All I ask is just give me a little peace and quiet when I come home. Why do I gotta listen to all that about the kids this and the kids that!

Except for naggin' about money all the time—what should I do, go rob a bank?—we get by. She's gotta put up with me, who else is she gonna find to put up with her and her temper like I do (said "jokingly" to his wife who gives him a sour look). Anyways, what do them marriage counselors know? We went there twice (his wife interjects: "You mean I did!"), and they couldn't find nothin' wrong. All I know is the wife's still the same. Still crab, crab, crab.

What sort of plans or hopes did you have when you first got married? What about now?

MR. CRAWFORD. For a long time now I've been wantin' to get into the junk business. I was thinkin' I could rent that empty lot around the corner. I would build a fence or something in the front so the city wouldn't squawk. There's a lot of junk and used stuff layin' around that people throw out or will sell for a buck or two. Like old stoves, washers, and things like that. Mostly metal things is what brings the money. Furniture you have to have a shed for. There's even some junk cars that are left here and there. I could rent a truck to haul things or maybe even buy an old one cheap. When I was 18 another guy and I were really going to do this and then . . . well, one thing led to another and we never got around to it. I still have that in my mind. All I need to do is get a few bucks ahead— then I think the finance place will let me take a hundred or so to get going. I've always wanted to be in some kind of business where you'd be your own boss. No one to keep telling you this or that and you can earn as much as you want to put time in. I know a guy who after the Korean War bought a couple of dump trucks. Now he's livin' in a big place of his own, got everything he wants, and he doesn't have any college degree either. In fact, I don't think he got finished with high school.

MRS. CRAWFORD. I've heard that junk business for how many years now? Anyways, we got no money to go buying a truck or renting some lot. I thought when we first got married that maybe somehow we could get our own place in a couple years. There's places around with empty grocery stores in front and a flat in back. You could buy something like that and pay it off with the grocery business. There's a need for a store like that here. The only one here now is that booky-joint place. All they got is rotten vegetables and they're always out of anything you want. Now we gotta go about eight blocks to the supermarket. And they don't give any credit.

I never looked into how much money they wanted for one of those stores. Anyways its too late now. We ain't got a dime, and the way I feel and with this bunch of kids how can I run a grocery business? I never did plan on all these kids I'll tell you! Sure I wanted some kids, anybody does. Why do you get married anyways? But I didn't want all these many. No more I say if I got something to say about it. I'm the one whose insides gotta be operated on. With the man, that's it, its fine and dandy. He don't have all this body trouble—afterwards.

I don't plan on nothing now. If you plan you just borrow trouble.

What would you say are your worst troubles, the things that bother you the most?

MRS. CRAWFORD. Money troubles! I get a headache thinking about it. I'm sick of bill collectors. Half the stuff I don't think we owe on anyways. Sometimes I feel like packin' up and clearing out. Now we even have the landlord squawking even though I told him there was a short pay and he'd have to wait. If he tries eviction, we'll tell the health department about his toilets leaking through the floor. And then they say I'm supposed to give the kids . . . how much more milk and things every day? On top of that we got a car that was driven less than a month and it broke down, and yet we have to pay through a garnishee on Frank's pay. But the company won't do right by the guarantee.

I'd say next to money the kids are the next big bother. They're gonna drive me to the bug house.

MR. CRAWFORD. I was figurin' I could rent a trailer for the car I bought last month and do odd jobs, carting and things. Now all I got is a clunker stittin' on the street which has to be moved or I get a fine. Why don't they bother some of those big deals with their big convertibles over on Rodney Street? Now either I take a bus to the plant and get up an hour early or I pay $4.50 a month for a car pool. It's the same old crap. You try to do something to save a buck and wind up all the worse. All I know is if there's going to be any clearin' outta here, I'm the one who'll do it. (The next remark is prompted by his wife's comment that the best way to save a dollar would be to stay away from the bars.) All I can say is that when it comes to a time when I can't have a few bucks a week for beer money then I've had it. I earn the money, what do I get—nothin'? (He ignores his wife's retort that $10 is a lot of beer money.)

Well, anyways, if I could put together two straight months of the pay I'm gettin' now, we might see our way clear and get rid of some of these bills and even get some more furniture and also a decent TV. I'm sick of that thing and its flip-flop picture. And I'm sick of this stinkin' chicken coop. Now the owner is coming around saying he has to raise the rent but he won't fix the damn toilet.

What about relatives, neighbors, and friends? Do you see much of them or visit often?

Mrs. Crawford. My sister lives over on Spring Avenue about three blocks from here. I see her once in a while at the A & P. She used to come around to the house every so often, but then she began to argue about the old man, my Dad, I mean. She was insistin' that I was supposed to give her some money because he was stayin' at her house. That's pretty good. She never gave us a dime when he stayed here a couple months last winter. Well, let her see how it is with his drinkin'. Anyways, she came around at Easter with her kids. I also got a brother someplace in Florida last

I knew. I guess he's just bumming around down there. He's 21. I also have a brother in the Stillwell School (an institution for the mentally retarded). He's 18 and I don't think he'll ever see the outside. I should go see him sometime.

I have a girl friend a couple doors up the street. She comes over a lot. Her husband took off in August. She's got two kids, and they're always sick with this or that. She's on welfare. She's got a raw deal from that rat husband of hers. She's about the only one I have over. The rest around here are a bunch of louses. They're always looking for trouble and looking for ways to get you mixed up in it. Two years ago one of them squealed to the welfare workers that we had money somewhere hidden in some bank or somethin'. They knew it was a lie, but they just did it to be miserable. So I stay away from them and mind my business.

Mr. Crawford. Her father is always comin' around trying to borrow a buck or sponge a meal. Why should I give him anything just for him to go booze it up? My parents live in Pennsylvania, where I come from. They split up a couple of years ago. I heard from my mother a while ago. She's working for some family there. I don't know what's going on with my old man. I also got a couple brothers and sisters in P.A. I don't hear from them. They're all married now so I hear.

I don't monkey much with the neighbors around here. Some of them think they're too good for anybody. It beats me why, they're nothin' and will never be nothin'. I go up to the gin mill every so often and have a couple beers and shoot the breeze with the bartender (as he is saying this his wife is shaking her head and making exasperated noises). I went to school with him. Once in a while I help him out, cleaning up and taking care of the bar sometimes. I don't like the place anymore though. They're gonna close up and get out, the owner says. The place is gettin' full of them Spics— you know, those Puerto Ricans. They stand around and jabber and act like they own the place. Why don't they go back where they came from? Who asked them around anyways? The place is getting dead anyways. There used to be some guys there I knew that hung around there before I was married. I dunno if they ain't got no money now or the wives make 'em stay home or they're dead or what. I don't see 'em around much anymore.

Can you see yourself in about 10 years? What do you think you will be like in 10 years?

MRS. CRAWFORD. I have enough trouble with things now without thinking about 10 years from now. Besides the Bible says take no thought for tomorrow. You never know if you are gonna be here tomorrow, to take thoughts for tomorrow. I don't even wanna bother about that sort of thing.

If you fret about something, sure enough it'll happen. So I keep my mind off the future. I suppose I'll have a bigger pack of kids by then. (Said with a grimace to her husband.) I'll be a wreck when I am 40 if I ain't already that. Things can't be no worse I know that. So maybe I'll just blow my top and they can drag me off someplace, and someone else can try to put two and two together around here.

MR. CRAWFORD. I don't believe in that day-dreamin' business. Anyways I'll be shot by then. I'm half shot now. At least maybe I won't have teeth trouble then, they'll be all gone by then. We got enough to worry about each day or maybe worry about a week ahead. How the bills are gonna get paid and all that. As my wife says, the Bible says let the future take care of itself. Who knows anyways about the future? I don't know, and I don't care. I've had enough bad luck now.

I suppose I will see myself as a bum in 10 years. They say I'm a bum now, so what's the difference? Anyways who knows if anybody will be around in 10 years. Maybe the Chinese or Russians will blow up the world.

AND THE POOR GET CHILDREN*

Lee Rainwater

Washington University

The typical lower-class pattern among men includes at most the

* Reprinted by permission of Quadrangle Books from *And the Poor Get Children* by Lee Rainwater, copyright 1960 by Social Research, Inc.

knowledge that men and women have sexual intercourse, that men enjoy it and women probably don't, that pregnancy results from having intercourse, and that contraception can be effected with a condom. The condom is useful especially before marriage to keep out of trouble if one is lucky enough to find a girl willing to have intercourse. Very little consideration seems to be given to family planning, and many lower-class men seem to have thought of the condom before marriage mainly as an appliance to be used in premarital intercourse as a protection against disease and the proverbial shotgun.

Only infrequently do lower—class couples discuss family planning or contraception before marriage. Sex is not discussed either; there may be some conflict over the man's desire for premarital intercourse, but it is an activity so surrounded with ambivalence and guilt that seldom does this problem lead to an explicit concern with sexuality or with family planning.

Common responses given by men to a question about premarital family planning and contraceptive information are these:

Oh, I knew the usual things, the kinds of things that men would know of like prophylactics. I hadn't ever used any; it was just common knowledge, I guess. Just the things that boys pick up as part of growing up, and in service.

I didn't know anything about it, and I didn't give it any thought. When we had two kids about a year apart and neither of us knew anything, I went in the army and I read quite a bit about it and discussed it with a good many fellows and learned a lot.

I didn't know nothing; I was 21 and my wife 18 when we married. The first child was an accident, you might say, because I didn't know nothing about it. After the second we started talking. I went to the hospital and talked to the social worker.

Well, I knew about rubbers and the Catholic way. The Catholic way I learned in church, the catechism and like that. I guess I learned about rubbers from the guys on the corner talking, you know, rubbers were the best

thing if you dated a girl. As I got older I learned for myself.

I knew very little before we got married, but right before we got a medical book, and I read it through quite a bit and learned quite a bit about it.

Working-class women, particularly those in the lower lower class, generally have even less information about sex and contraception than do the men, and the women seem to give relatively little thought to spacing and limiting their families until some time after marriage. Very often they say that they have learned what they do know (usually about condoms) from their husbands since their marriage. It is not unusual for women in this group to say that they have never discussed the subject with anyone. On the other hand, quite a few lower-class women have gotten information from female relatives *after* marriage: apparently discussions of sex and contraception are thought appropriate only among nonvirgins. This consideration also seems to apply to those cases where relatives first discuss these matters with a prospective bride just before her wedding day. In any case, such discussions seem oriented to an "emergency," in the sense that the woman is shortly going to be forced to deal with an issue she would really prefer to ignore. These various patterns of learning or not learning are illustrated in our interviews by comments like the following:

Girls talk about things like that—I knew about being careful before I was married. That's part of the reason I watch my girls so closely—more girls get themselves into troubles and expect the parents to get them out. I learned mostly after getting married, from my sisters-in-law, about douching and that. The rest I learned from the doctors and nurses at the clinic.

I didn't know anything before I was married. Then my sister told me about douching, and I don't remember who told me about rubbers, but it's something I never talked much about.

I knew nothing when I got married. I didn't even know how a baby was born and how you got pregnant. My mother told me the night before I got married.

I didn't know nothing about birth control before I got married. I learned from my husband. Just about the rubbers. He don't say nothing about any other stuff to me but that. He just uses rubbers. I haven't learned anything since. All my mother taught me ever was to not let boys get anywhere with me. She didn't explain nothing. She told me not to let boys be loving over me. She told me when I was about twelve; I didn't know what she meant. I guess she meant if they loved all over you what it would cause. I didn't know then, but now I do. I didn't know about it until I was married.

I knew nothing about babies or how to have or not have them before I was married. I didn't really know it. I heard it but didn't read no books. I learned by experience of being married. I always thought you had to see a doctor before you got pregnant. My husband never discussed it with me before we were married. I didn't know the act led to pregnancy.

Women who have a more thorough knowledge tend to be in the upper lower class rather than in the lower lower group, and they also more often have been reared in an urban environment. In general, those couples who manage to be effective at contracep-

tion before they have too many children know more about contraception and the facts of reproduction before they are married. Their behavior in marriage is based on information acquired before marriage and supplemented later. This is not to say that all the couples who have been effective were informed about contraception before marriage; a minority of the early-planner group learn later, as do many of those who become effective at contraception in desperation after having four or five children.

It is difficult to believe that a sizable minority of these women did not know at marriage that sexual intercourse leads to pregnancy. Perhaps it is rather that the whole question of sexuality was so anxiety-laden for them that they effectively pushed the issue aside in their minds and managed to ignore it completely, so that the relevance of sexual intercourse to their lives after marriage came as real shock to them. Actually, many lower-class men seem almost as effectively to isolate sexuality in the sense of a pleasurable "lay" from their thinking about a family and children. They do not so often repress the facts as do lower-class women, but they seem unable to use their knowledge constructively in considering the impending marriage. In any case, our data suggest that consciously usable knowledge is woefully lacking for most working-class couples and that a lack of consideration of the sex-planning-contraception constellation of issues results in tension and misunderstanding in the early period of marriage.

SELECTED BIBLIOGRAPHY

AMORY, CLEVELAND, *The Proper Bostonians*. New York: E. P. Dutton & Co., Inc., 1947.

BABCHUCK, NICHOLAS, "Primary Friends and Kin: A Study of the Associations of Middle Class Couples," *Social Forces*, 43 (May 1965), 483–93.

———, and C. WAYNE GORDON, *The Vol-*

untary *Association in the Slum*. Lincoln, Neb.: University of Nebraska Press, 1962.

BECK, BERNARD, "Bedbugs, Stench, Dampness and Immorality: A Review Essay on Recent Literature About Poverty," *Social Problems*, 15 (Summer 1967), 101–14.

BERGER, BENNETT, *Working Class Suburb*. Berkeley, Calif.: University of California Press, 1960.

BOEK, WALTER E., *et al.*, "Social Class and Child Care Practices," *Marriage and Family Living*, 20 (November 1958), 326–33.

CHILMAN, CATHERINE S., "Child-Rearing and Family Relationship: Patterns of the Very Poor," *Welfare in Review*, 3 (January 1965), 9–19.

CHINOY, ELY, *Automobile Workers and the American Dream*. Garden City, N.Y.: Doubleday & Company, Inc., 1955.

COHEN, ALBERT K., and HAROLD M. HODGES, JR., "Characteristics of the Lower-Blue-Collar-Class," *Social Problems*, 10 (Spring 1963), 303–33.

CUBER, JOHN F., and PEGGY B. HARROFF, "The More Total View: Relationships Among Men and Women of the Upper Middle Class," *Marriage and Family Living*, 25 (May 1963), 140–45.

DAVIS, ALLISON, "The Motivation of the Underprivileged Worker," in *Industry and Society*, eds. William F. Whyte *et al.* New York: McGraw-Hill Book Company, 1946.

DEUTSCH, MARTIN, "The Role of Social Class in Language Development and Cognition," *American Journal of Orthopsychiatry*, 35 (January 1965), 78–88.

DOBRINER, WILLIAM M., *Class in Suburbia*. Englewood Cliffs, N.J.: Prentice-Hall, Inc., 1963.

DOTSON, FLOYD, "Patterns of Voluntary Association Among Urban Working-Class Families," *American Sociological Review*, 16 (October 1951), 687–93.

FERMAN, LOUIS A., *et al.*, eds., *Poverty in America*. Ann Arbor, Mich.: University of Michigan Press, 1965.

FORM, WILLIAM H., and JAMES A. GESCHWENDER, "Social Reference Basis of Job Satisfaction: The Case of Manual Workers," *American Sociological Review*, 27 (April 1962), 228–37.

Fortune, The Editors of, *The Executive Life*. Garden City, N.Y.: Doubleday & Company, Inc., 1956.

FREEMAN, HOWARD E., and CAMILLE LAMBERT, JR., "The Identification of 'Lower-Class' Families in an Urban Community," in *Blue-Collar World*, eds. Arthur B. Shostak and William Gomberg. Englewood Cliffs, N.J.: Prentice-Hall, Inc., 1964.

GALLAHER, ART, JR., *Plainville 15 Years Later*. New York: Columbia University Press, 1961.

GOLDSTEIN, BERNARD, *Low Income Youth in Urban Areas: A Critical Review of the Literature*. New York: Holt, Rinehart & Winston, Inc., 1967.

GORDON, MARGARET S., *Poverty in America*. San Francisco: Chandler Press, 1965.

GROSS, LLEWELLYN, and ORVILLE R. GURSSLIN, "Middle Class and Lower Class Beliefs and Values: A Heuristic Model," in *Modern Sociology*, eds. Alvin W. Gouldner and Helen B. Gouldner. New York: Harcourt, Brace & World, Inc., 1963.

GURSSLIN, ORVILLE R., and JACK L. ROACH, "Some Issues in Training the Unemployed," *Social Problems*, 12 (Summer 1964), 86–98.

HALLER, ARCHIBALD O., and THOMAS SHAILER, "Personality Correlates of the Socioeconomic Status of Adolescent Males," *Sociometry*, 25 (December 1962), 398–404.

HANDEL, GERALD, and LEE RAINWATER, "Persistence and Change in Working Class Life Style," *Sociology and Social Research*, 48 (April 1964), 281–88.

HARRINGTON, MICHAEL, *The Other America, Poverty in the United States*. Baltimore: Penguin Books, Inc., 1963.

HAVIGHURST, ROBERT J., *et al.*, *Growing Up in River City*. New York: John Wiley & Sons, Inc., 1962.

HOLLINGSHEAD, AUGUST B., "Class and Kinship in a Middle Western Community," *American Sociological Review*, 24 (August 1949), 469–75.

JAFFE, FREDERICK S., "Family Planning

and Poverty," *Marriage and the Family*, 26 (November 1964), 467–70.

KAVALER, LUCY, *The Private World of High Society*. New York: David McKay Co., Inc., 1960.

KOHN, MELVIN L., "Social Class and Parent-Child Relationships: An Interpretation," *American Journal of Sociology*, 68 (January 1963), 471–80.

——, "Social Class and the Exercise of Parental Authority," *American Sociological Review*, 24 (June 1959), 352–66.

KRAUSS, IRVING, "Sources of Educational Aspirations Among Working-Class Youth," *American Sociological Review*, 29 (December 1964), 867–79.

KRONENBERG, LOUIS, *Company Manners*. Indianapolis: The Bobbs-Merrill Co., Inc., 1951.

LANTZ, HERMAN R., *People of Coal Town*. New York: Columbia University Press, 1958.

LARSON, RICHARD F., and SARA SMITH SUTKER, "Value Differences and Value Consensus by Socioeconomic Levels," *Social Forces*, 44 (June 1966), 563–69.

LEFTON, MARK, "The Blue Collar Worker and the Middle Class Ethic," *Sociology and Social Research*, 51 (January 1967), 159–70.

LYND, ROBERT S., and HELEN MERRELL LYND, *Middletown*. New York: Harcourt, Brace and Co., 1929.

——, *Middletown in Transition*. New York: Harcourt, Brace and Co., 1937.

McGUIRE, CARSON, "Family Life in Lower and Middle Class Homes," *Marriage and Family Living*, 14 (1952), 1–6.

McKINLEY, DONALD G., *Social Class and Family Life*. Glencoe, Ill.: The Free Press, 1964.

MILLER, DANIEL R., and GUY E. SWANSON, *The Changing American Parent*. New York: John Wiley & Sons, Inc., 1958.

——, *Inner Conflict and Defense*. New York: Henry Holt, 1960.

MILLER, S. M., "The American Lower Class: A Typological Approach," *Social Research*, 31 (Spring 1964), 1–22.

——, and FRANK RIESSMAN, "The Working Class Subculture," *Social Problems*, 9 (Summer 1961), 86–97.

MILLS, C. WRIGHT, *White Collar: The American Middle Classes*. Fair Lawn, N.J.: Oxford University Press, Inc., 1951.

PAVENSTEDT, ELEANOR, "A Comparison of the Child-Rearing Environment of Upper, Lower and Very Low Lower Class Families," *American Journal of Orthopsychiatry*, 35 (January 1965), 89–98.

RAINWATER, LEE, "Marital Sexuality in Four Cultures of Poverty," *Journal of Marriage and the Family*, 26 (November 1964), 457–66.

——, "A Study of Personality Differences Between Middle and Lower Class Adolescents," *Genetic Psychology Monographs*, 54 (1956), 3–86.

——, et al., *Workingman's Wife*. New York: Macfadden, 1962.

RIESMAN, DAVID, et al., *The Lonely Crowd: A Study of the Changing American Character*. New Haven, Conn.: Yale University Press, 1950.

RIESSMAN, FRANK, *The Culturally Deprived Child*. New York: Harper and Bros., 1962.

ROACH, JACK L., "A Theory of Lower-Class Behavior," in *Sociological Theory: Inquiries and Paradigms,* ed. Llewellyn Gross. New York: Harper & Row, Publishers, 1967.

RODMAN, HYMAN, "The Lower-Class Value Stretch," *Social Forces*, 42 (December 1963), 205–15.

——, "On Understanding Lower-Class Behavior," *Social and Economic Studies*, 8 (December 1959), 441–49.

SCHATZMAN, LEONARD, and ANSELM STRAUSS, "Social Class and Modes of Communication," *American Journal of Sociology*, 60 (January 1955), 329–38.

SCHORR, ALVIN L., *Poor Kids*. New York: Basic Books, Inc., Publishers, 1966.

SEARS, ROBERT R., et al., *Patterns of Child-Rearing*. Evanston, Ill.: Row, Peterson and Company, 1957.

SEXTON, PATRICIA C., *Education and Income*. New York: The Viking Press, 1962.

SHOSTAK, ARTHUR B., and WILLIAM GOM-

BERG, eds., *Blue-Collar World*. Englewood Cliffs, N.J.: Prentice-Hall, Inc., 1964.

STRAUS, MURRAY A., "The Influence of Sex of Child and Social Class on Instrumental and Expressive Family Roles in a Laboratory Setting," *Sociology and Social Research*, 52 (October 1967), 7–21.

TURNER, RALPH H., *The Social Context of Ambition*. San Francisco: Chandler Publishing Co., 1964.

WEISS, CAROL H., "Interviewing Low-Income Respondents," *Welfare in Review*, 4 (October 1966), 1–9.

WEST, JAMES, *Plainville, U.S.A.* New York: Columbia University Press, 1945.

WHYTE, WILLIAM F., *Street Corner Society*. Chicago: University of Chicago Press, 1943.

WHYTE, WILLIAM H., JR., *The Organization Man*. Garden City, N.Y.: Doubleday & Company, Inc., 1956.

WILLIE, CHARLES V., and JANET WEINANDY, "The Structure and Composition of 'Problem' and 'Stable' Families in a Low-Income Population," *Marriage and Family Living*, 25 (November 1963), 439–47.

YERACARIS, CONSTANTINE A., "Differentials in the Relationship Between Values and Practice in Fertility," *Social Forces*, 38 (December 1959), 153–58.

CHAPTER FIVE

The Negro Class System

CASTE OR CLASS?

An empirical account of the American stratification system would be incomplete without a description of the special position of the Negro. Because of the color barrier, Negroes often spend their lives in separate communities. Whether this barrier represents a caste differentiation is a matter of controversy. Arguments revolve around the definition of caste, with the Indian stratification system as the prototype. Gerald Berreman's article suggests the extent of the parallels between American and Indian society and hence the extent to which Negro-white interaction can be seen as a caste relationship.

CASTE IN INDIA AND THE UNITED STATES*[1]

Gerald D. Berreman

University of California at Berkeley

Many writers who have contributed to the vast literature on the caste system in India have emphasized its unique aspects and ignored or denied the qualities it shares with rigid systems of social stratification found in other societies. Others have claimed to find caste systems or caste groups in such widely scattered areas as Arabia, Polynesia, Africa, Guatemala, and Japan.[2] Some observers refer to Negro-white relations in the United States, and particularly in the South, as being those of caste,[3] a usage which others, including C. S. Johnson, Oliver C. Cox, and, more recently, G. E. Simpson and J. M. Yinger, have criticized. This paper will compare the relationship between "touchable," especially twice-born, and "untouchable" castes in India with that between Negroes and whites in the southern United States.

Caste can be defined so that it is applicable only to India, just as it is possible to define narrowly almost any sociocultural phenomenon. Indianists have traditionally held to specific, usually enumerative, definitions. Indeed, the caste system in India has several unique features, among which are its religious aspects, its complexity, and the degree to which the caste is a cohesive group that regulates the behavior of its members. Within India there is considerable variation in the characteristics of, and the relations among, the groups to which the term "caste" is applied.

However, caste can be accurately defined in broader terms. For many purposes similar social facts may be usefully categorized together, despite differences which, while not denied, are not crucial to the purposes at hand. For purposes of cross-cultural comparison this is necessary: For the study of social process, and with the aim of deriving generalizations, caste is a con-

* Reprinted from "Caste in India and the United States," *American Journal of Sociology*, by Gerald D. Berreman by permission of The University of Chicago Press. Copyright 1960 by The University of Chicago Press.

[1] Delivered in abbreviated form before the Fifty-eighth Annual Meeting of the American Anthropological Association in Mexico City, December 1959, and based partly on research carried out in India under a Ford Foundation Foreign Area Training Fellowship during 15 months of 1957–58 (reported in full in my "Kin, Caste, and Community in a Himalayan Hill Village" [unpublished Ph.D. dissertation, Cornell University, 1959]). I am indebted to Joel V. Berreman and Lloyd A. Fallers for their helpful comments.

[2] E. D. Chapple and C. S. Coon, *Principles of Anthropology* (New York: Henry Holt & Co., 1942), p. 437; S. F. Nadel, "Caste and Government in Primitive Society," *Journal of the Anthropological Society of Bombay*, New Series VIII (September 1954), 9–22; M. M. Tumin, *Caste in a Peasant Society* (Princeton, N.J.: Princeton University Press, 1952); J. D. Donoghue, "An Eta Community in Japan: The Social Persistence of Outcaste Groups," *American Anthropologist*, LIX (December 1957), 1000–1017.

[3] E.g., Allison Davis, Kingsley Davis, John Dollard, Buell Gallagher, Gunnar Myrdal, Kenneth Stampp, Lloyd Warner.

cept which might well be applied cross culturally. For these purposes a caste system may be defined as a *hierarchy of endogamous divisions in which membership is hereditary and permanent.* Here hierarchy includes inequality both in status and in access to goods and services. Interdependence of the subdivisions, restricted contacts among them, occupational specialization, and/ or a degree of cultural distinctiveness might be added as criteria, although they appear to be correlates rather than defining characteristics.

This definition is perhaps best viewed as describing an ideal type at one end of a continuum along which systems of social stratification might be ranged. There can be little doubt that the systems in India and the southern United States would fall far toward the caste extreme of the continuum.[4] It now becomes necessary to look at the differences cited as crucial by those who object to use of the term "caste" in both societies. The objections raised by those interested in structure, relationships, and interaction will be discussed here; the objections of those interested in specific content will be ignored—not because the latter objections are less cogent but because they are less relevant to the comparison of social systems.[5]

Johnson sees many similarities in the two systems but objects to identifying both as caste since "a caste system is not only a separated system, it is a stable system in which changes are socially impossible; the fact that change cannot occur is accepted by all, or practically all, participants. . . . No expenditure of psychological or physical energy is necessary to maintain a caste system."[6] Simpson and Yinger agree with Johnson and further object that, in the United States, "we lack a set of religious principles justifying a rigid system of social stratification and causing it to be willingly accepted by those at all levels."[7] Cox lists a number of features of a caste system (i.e., caste in India) which distinguish it from an interracial situation (i.e., Negro-white relations in America), important among which are its "nonconflictive," "nonpathological," and "static" nature, coupled with absence of "aspiration and progressiveness."[8]

Central to these distinctions is that caste in India is passively accepted and indorsed by all on the basis of religio-philosophical explanations which are universally subscribed to, while Negro-white relations in America are characterized by dissent, resentment, guilt, and conflict. But this contrast is invalid, resulting, as it does, from an

---

[4] The Tira of Africa, for example, would not fall so far toward this extreme (cf. Nadel, *op. cit.*, pp. 18ff.).

[5] As a matter of fact, ignorance of the details of content in the patterns of relations between whites and Negroes in the United States has prevented many Indianists from seeing very striking similarities. Two contrasting views of the cross-cultural applicability of the concept of caste have appeared since this paper was written: F. C. Bailey, "For a Sociology of India?" *Contributions to Indian Sociology*, No. 3 (July 1959), pp. 88–101, esp. pp. 97–98; and E. R. Leach, "Introduction: What Should We

Mean by Caste?" in *Aspects of Caste in South India, Ceylon and North-west Pakistan*, "Cambridge Papers in Social Anthropology," No. 2 (London: Cambridge University Press, 1959), pp. 1–10.

[6] C. S. Johnson, *Growing Up in the Black Belt* (Washington, D.C.: American Council on Education, 1941), p. 326.

[7] G. E. Simpson and J. M. Yinger, *Racial and Cultural Minorities* (New York: Harper & Bros., 1953), p. 328.

[8] O. C. Cox, "Race and Caste: A Distinction," *American Journal of Sociology*, L (March 1945), 360 (see also his *Caste, Class and Race* [Garden City, N.Y.: Doubleday & Company, Inc., 1948]).

idealized and unrealistic view of Indian caste, contrasted with a more realistic, pragmatic view of American race relations; Indian caste is viewed as it is supposed to work rather than as it does work; American race relations are seen as they do work rather than as they are supposed, by the privileged, to work. The traditional white southerner, asked to describe relations between the races, will describe the Negro as happy in his place, which he may quote science and Scripture to justify. This is similar to the explanations offered for the Indian system by the advantaged.

The point here is that ideal inter-caste behavior and attitudes in India are much like those in America, while the actual interaction and attitudes are also similar. Commonly, ideal behavior and attitudes in India have been contrasted with real behavior and attitudes in America—a fact which has led to a false impression of difference. Similarly, comparisons of race relations in the rapidly changing urban or industrial South with caste relations in slowly changing rural or agrarian India lead to erroneous conclusions. Valid comparison can be made at either level, but must be with comparable data. The impact on intergroup relations of the social and economic changes which accompany urban life seems to be similar in both societies. Recent literature on village India and on the changing caste functions and caste relations in cities and industrial areas presents a realistic picture which goes far toward counteracting traditional stereotypes of Indian caste.[9]

---

9 See, for example, the following community studies: F. G. Bailey, *Caste and the Economic Frontier* (Manchester: University of Manchester Press, 1957); Berreman, *op. cit.*; S. C. Dube, *Indian Village* (Ithaca, N.Y.: Cornell University Press, 1955); Oscar Lewis, *Village Life in Northern India*

In a study of caste functioning in Sirkanda, a hill village of northern Uttar Pradesh, India, I was struck by the similarity of relations between the twice-born and untouchable castes to race relations in the southern United States.[10] In both situations there is a genuine caste division, according to the definition above. In the two systems there are rigid rules of avoidance between castes, and certain types of

---

(Urbana, Ill.: University of Illinois Press, 1958); McKim Marriott, ed., *Village India*, American Anthropological Association Memoir No. 83 (Chicago: University of Chicago Press, 1955); M. E. Opler and R. D. Singh, "The Division of Labor in an Indian Village," in *A Reader in General Anthropology*, ed. C. S. Coon (New York: Henry Holt & Co., 1948), pp. 464–96; M. N. Srinivas *et al., India's Villages* (Development Department, West Bengal: West Bengal Government Press, 1955). See also, for example, the following studies of caste in the contemporary setting: Bailey, *op. cit.*; N. K. Bose, "Some Aspects of Caste in Bengal," *American Journal of Folklore*, LXXI (July–September 1958), 397–412; Leach, *op. cit.*; Arthur Niehoff, *Factory Workers in India*, "Milwaukee Public Museum Publications in Anthropology," No. 5 (1959); M. N. Srinivas, "Caste in Modern India," *Journal of Asian Studies*, XVI (August 1957), 529–48; and the several articles comprising the symposium on "Caste in India" contained in *Man in India*, XXXIX (April–June 1959), 92–162.

10 The following discussion is based not exclusively on the Sirkanda materials but on observations and literature in nonhill areas as well. The hill area presents some distinct regional variations in caste structure, important among which is the absence of intermediate castes—all are either twice-born or untouchable. This leads to a dichotomous situation, as in the United States, but one which differs in that there are important caste divisions on either side of the "pollution barrier" (cf. Bailey, *op. cit.*, p. 8; Berreman, *op. cit.*, pp. 389ff.). Relations across this barrier do not differ greatly from similar relations among plains castes, although somewhat more informal contact is allowed—pollution comes about less easily—in the hills.

contacts are defined as contaminating, while others are noncontaminating. The ideological justification for the rules differs in the two cultures, as do the definitions of the acts themselves; but these are cultural details. The tabooed contacts are symbolically rather than literally injurious as evidenced by the many inconsistencies in application of the rules.[11] Enforced deference, for example, is a prominent feature of both systems. Lack of deference from low castes is not contaminating, but it is promptly punished for it implies equality. The essential similarity lies in the fact that the function of the rules in both cases is to maintain the caste system with institutionalized inequality as its fundamental feature. In the United States, color is a conspicuous mark of caste, while in India there are complex religious features which do not appear in America, but in both cases dwelling area, occupation, place of worship, and cultural behavior, and so on are important symbols associated with caste status. The crucial fact is that caste status is determined, and therefore the systems are perpetuated, by birth: Membership in them is ascribed and unalterable. Individuals in low castes are considered inherently inferior and are relegated to a disadvantaged position, regardless of their behavior. From the point of view of the social psychology of intergroup relations, this is probably the most important common and distinct feature of caste systems.

In both the United States and India, high castes maintain their superior

position by exercising powerful sanctions, and they rationalize their status with elaborate philosophical, religious, psychological, or genetic explanations. The latter are not sufficient in themselves to maintain the systems, largely because they are incompletely accepted among those whose depressed position they are thought to justify. In both places castes are economically interdependent. In both there are great differences in power and privilege among, as well as class differences within, castes and elaborate barriers to free social intercourse among them.

Similarities in the two caste systems extend throughout the range of behavior and attitudes expressed in relations among groups. An important and conspicuous area of similarity is associated with competition for certain benefits or "gains" which are personally gratifying and/or socially valued and which by their nature or under the circumstances cannot be enjoyed by all equally. Competitive striving is, of course, not unique to caste organization; it is probably found to some extent in all societies. It is subject to a variety of social controls resulting in a variety of forms of social stratification, one of which is a caste system as defined here. However, the genesis of caste systems is not here at issue.[12]

The caste system in India and in the United States has secured gains for the groups established at the top of the hierarchy. Their desire to retain their position for themselves and their children accounts for their efforts to perpetuate the system. John Dollard, in his discussion of "Southerntown," identifies their gains as economic, sexual, and in prestige.

In the economic field, low-caste dependence is maintained in India as

---

11 The symbolic acts—the "etiquette" of caste relations—in India and in America are often remarkably similar. The symbolism in America is, of course, not primarily religious as much as it is in India, although the sacred aspects in India are often far from the minds of those engaging in the acts and are not infrequently unknown to them.

12 Cf. Nadel, *op. cit.*

in America by economic and physical sanctions. This assures not only greater high-caste income but a ready supply of free service and cheap labor from the low castes. It also guarantees the continuing availability of the other gains. In India it is the most explicitly recognized high-caste advantage.

The sexual gain for the southern white caste is defined by Dollard, quoting whom I will substitute "high caste" and "low caste" for "white" and "Negro," respectively. In this form his definition fits the Indian caste system equally well.

> In simplest terms, we mean by a "sexual gain" the fact that [high-caste] men, by virtue of their caste position, have access to two classes of women, those of the [high] and [low] castes. The same condition is somewhat true of the [low-caste] women, except that they are rather the objects of the gain than the choosers, though it is a fact that they have some degree of access to [high-caste] men as well as men of their own caste. [Low-caste] men and [high-caste] women, on the other hand, are limited to their own castes in sexual choices.[13]

This arrangement is maintained in the Indian caste system, as it is in America, by severe sanctions imposed upon any low-caste man who might venture to defy the code, by the toleration accorded high-caste men who have relations with low-caste women, and by the precautions which high-caste men take to protect their women from the low castes.

High-caste people gain, by virtue of their caste status alone, deference from others, constant reinforcement of a feeling of superiority, and a permanent scapegoat in the lower castes. Dollard has stated the implications of this gain in prestige, and, again substituting a caste designation for a racial one, his statement describes the Indian system perfectly:

> The gain here . . . consists in the fact that a member of the [high] caste has an automatic right to demand forms of behavior from [low-caste people] which serve to increase his own self-esteem.
>
> It must always be remembered that in the end this deference is demanded and not merely independently given.[14]

Ideally the high-caste person is paternalistic and authoritarian, while the low-caste person responds with deferential, submissive, subservient behavior. Gallagher might have been describing India rather than America when he noted: "By the attitudes of mingled fear, hostility, deprecation, discrimination, amused patronage, friendly domination, and rigid authoritarianism, the white caste generates opposite and complementary attitudes in the Negro caste."[15]

An additional high-caste gain in India is the religious tradition which gives people of high caste promise of greater rewards in the next life than those of low caste. People can increase their rewards in the next life by fulfilling their traditional caste duty. For high castes, this generally results

---

13 John Dollard, *Caste and Class in a Southern Town* (Garden City, N.Y.: Doubleday & Company, Inc., 1957), p. 135 (cf. Berreman, *op. cit.*, pp. 470ff.).

14 Dollard, *op. cit.*, p. 174. Nadel, speaking of caste in general, has noted that "the lower caste are despised, not only unhappily underprivileged; they bear a stigma apart from being unfortunate. Conversely, the higher castes are not merely entitled to the possession of coveted privileges, but are also in some way exalted and endowed with a higher dignity" (Nadel, *op. cit.*, p. 16).

15 B. G. Gallagher, *American Caste and the Negro College* (New York: Columbia University Press, 1938), p. 109.

in increasing the economic advantages and prestige acquired in this life, while it requires that the low castes subordinate their own economic gains and prestige in this life to the service and honor of high castes. Thus, for high-caste people, behavior leading to immediate rewards is consistent with ultimate rewards, while, for low-caste people, behavior required for the two rewards is contradictory.

These advantages are significant and recognized reasons for maintenance of the system by the privileged groups.[16] They are expressed in folklore, proverbs, and jokes; for instance, a story tells that, as the funeral procession of an old landlord passed two untouchable women going for water, one hand of the corpse fell from under the shroud and flopped about. One of the women turned to the other and remarked, "You see, Takur Singh is dead, but he still beckons to us." Other stories recount the avariciousness of Brahmins in their priestly role, the hardheartedness of landlords, and the like.

The compensatory gains for low-caste people are cited more often by high-caste advocates of the system than by those alleged to enjoy them. They are gains common to authoritarian systems everywhere and are usually subject to the will of the dominant groups.

As noted above, India is frequently cited as an example of a society in which people of deprived and subject

_____

16 Cf. Pauline M. Mahar, "Changing Caste Ideology in a North Indian Village," *Journal of Social Issues,* XIV (1958), 51–65, especially pp. 55–56; Kailash K. Singh, "Inter-Caste Tensions in Two Villages in North India" (unpublished Ph.D. dissertation, Cornell University, 1957), pp. 184–85; and M. N. Srinivas, "The Dominant Caste in Rampura," *American Anthropologist,* LXI (1959), especially p. 4.

status are content with their lot, primarily justifying it by religion and philosophy. This is the characteristic of caste in India most often cited to distinguish it from hereditary systems elsewhere, notably in the southern United States. On the basis of my research and the literature, I maintain that this is not accurate and therefore not a valid distinction. Its prevalence is attributable in part, as least, to the vested interests of the advantaged and more articulate castes in the perpetuation of the caste system and the maintenance of a favorable view of it to outsiders. The same arguments and the same biases are frequently presented by apologists for the caste system of the southern United States.

In both systems there is a tendency to look to the past as a period of halcyon amity and to view conflict and resentment as resulting from outside disturbances of the earlier normal equilibrium. Alien ideas, or large-scale economic disturbances, or both are often blamed for reform movements and rebellion. Such explanations may account for the national and regional reform movements which find their advocates and followers primarily among the educated and social elites; they do not account for the recurrent grass-roots attempts, long endemic in India, to raise caste status; for the state of mind which has often led to low-caste defections from Hinduism when the opportunity to do so without fear of major reprisals has presented itself; nor for the chronic resentment and tension which characterizes inter-caste relations in even so remote a village as Sirkanda, the one in which I worked.

Among the low or untouchable castes in Sirkanda, there was a great deal of readily expressed resentment regarding their caste position. Specific complaints revolved around economic, prestige, and sexual impositions by the high castes. Although resentment was suppressed in the presence of people of the dominant high castes, it was readily expressed where there was no fear of detection or reprisal.[17] Low-caste people felt compelled to express village loyalties in public, but in private acts and attitudes caste loyalties were consistently and intensely dominant when the two conflicted.

Caste, as such, was not often seriously questioned in the village. Objections were characteristically directed not at "caste" but at "my position in the caste hierarchy."

In the multicaste system of India, abolition of the system evidently seems impossible from the point of view of any particular caste, and a change in its rank within the system is viewed by its members as the only plausible means of improving the situation. Moreover, abolition would destroy the caste as a group, which is superior to at least some other groups, and, while it would give caste members an opportunity to mingle as equals with their superiors, it would also force them to mingle as equals with their inferiors. Abolition, even if it could be accomplished, would thus create an ambivalent situation for any particular caste in contrast to the clear-cut advantages of an improvement in rank.

In the dual system of the southern United States, where the high caste is clearly dominant, abolition of the caste division may be seen by the subordi-

nate group as the only plausible remedy for their deprived position. Furthermore, they have nothing to lose but their inferior status since there are no lower castes. There are, of course, Negroes and organized groups of Negroes, such as the black supremacist "Muslims" recently in the news in the United States, who want to invert the caste hierarchy; conversely, there are low-caste people in India who want to abolish the entire system. But these seem to be atypical viewpoints. The anticaste religions and reform movements which have from time to time appealed with some success to the lower castes in India, for example, Buddhism, Islam, Christianity, Skhism, have been unable, in practice, to remain casteless. This seems to be a point of real difference between Indian and American low-caste attitudes for in America objection is more characteristically directed toward the system as such.[18]

In Sirkanda those low-caste people who spoke most piously against high-caste abuses were likely to be equally abusive to their caste inferiors. However, no low caste was encountered whose members did not seriously question its place in the hierarchy. A sizable literature is accumulating concerning castes which have sought to alter their status.[19] Such attempts were made in Sirkanda. A more common reaction to deprived status on the part of low-caste people was what Dollard

---

[17] Elaborate precautions were often taken by informants to insure against any possibility that their expressions of feeling might become known to their caste superiors, which is very similar to behavior I have observed among Negroes of Montgomery, Alabama.

[18] Whether this difference in attitude is widely correlated with multiple, as compared to dual, caste systems or is attributable to other differences in the Indian and American situations can be established only by further comparative work.

[19] E.g., Opler and Singh, *op. cit.*, p. 476; B. S. Cohn, "The Changing Status of a Depressed Caste," in Marriott, ed., *op. cit.*, pp. 53–77; and Bailey, *op. cit.*, pp. 220–26.

calls "passive accommodation" coupled with occasional in-group aggression.[20]

In both America and India there is a tendency for the person of low caste to "laugh it off" or to become resigned. In Sirkanda low-caste people could not avoid frequent contacts with their superiors because of their proximity and relative numbers. Contacts were frequently informal, but status differences and the dangers of ritual pollution were not forgotten. An untouchable in this village who covered up his bitter resentment by playing the buffoon received favors denied to his more sullen caste fellows. The irresponsible, simple-minded untouchable is a widespread stereotype and one which he, like the Negro, has found useful. Similarly, sullen resignation, with the attendant stereotype of lazy shiftlessness, is a common response, typified in the southern Negro axiom, "Do what the man says." This, too, helps him avoid trouble, although it does little for the individual's self-respect. Aggression against the economically and numerically dominant high castes in Sirkanda was too dangerous to be a reasonable alternative. It was discussed by low-caste people in private but was rarely carried out. Even legitimate complaints to outside authority were avoided in view of the general belief that the high caste's wealth would insure an outcome unfavorable to the low castes—a belief well grounded in experience.

Since they harbored indignation and resentment, a number of rationalizations of their status were employed by low-caste people, apparently as mechanisms to lessen the sting of reality. Thus, they often attributed their caste status to relative wealth and numbers: "If we were wealthy and in the

majority, we would make the high castes untouchable."

Three more explanations of their caste status were consistently offered by low-caste people. These had the effect of denying the legitimacy of their low-caste position:

1. Members of the entire caste (or subcaste) group would deny that they deserved the low status to which they had been assigned. One example:

> Englishmen and Muslims are untouchables because they have an alien religion and they eat beef. This is as it should be. We are Hindus and we do not eat beef, yet we too are treated as untouchables. This is not proper. We should be accorded higher status.

No group would admit to being lowest in the caste hierarchy.

2. People might grant that the caste of their clan, lineage, or family was of low status but deny that their particular group really belonged to it. I have not encountered a low-caste group which did not claim high-caste ancestry or origin. Thus a typical comment is:

> Yes, we are drummers by occupation, but our ancestor was a Brahmin who married a drummer woman. By rights, therefore, we should be Brahmins, but in such cases the high castes here go against the usual custom and assign the child the caste of his low-caste parent rather than of his father, from whom a person inherits everything else.

3. A person might grant that his own caste and even his lineage or family were of low status, but his explanation would excuse him from responsibility for it. Such explanations were supplied by Brahmins who, as the most privileged caste and the recipients of religiously motivated charity from all castes, have a vested interest in

---

20 Dollard, *op. cit.*, p. 253.

maintenance of the system and its acceptance by those at all levels. An individual's horoscope would describe him as having been of high caste and exemplary behavior in a previous life and therefore destined for even greater things in the present life. However, in performing some religiously meritorious act in his previous existence, he inadvertently sinned (e.g., he was a raja, tricked by dishonest servants who did not give to the Brahmin the charity he intended for them). As a result he had to be punished in this life with a low rebirth.

Thus, no one said, in effect, "I am of low status and so are my family members and my caste fellows and justly so because of our misdeeds in previous lives." To do so would lead to a psychologically untenable position, though one advocated by high-caste people and by orthodox Hinduism. Rationalizations or beliefs such as these form a consistent pattern—they are not isolated instances. Neither are they unique to the village or culture reported here: The literature reveals similar beliefs elsewhere in North India.[21] They evidently indicate something less than enthusiastic acceptance of caste position, and, meanwhile, they perhaps alleviate or divert resentment.

That people remain in an inferior position, therefore, does not mean that they do so willingly or that they believe it is justified or that they would not do anything in their power to change it, given the opportunity. Rationalizations of caste status which are consistent and convincing to those who are unaffected or who benefit from them seem much less so to those whose deprivation they are expected to justify or explain. Adherence to a religious principle may not significantly affect the attitudes and behavior to which logic would seem or to which dogma attempts to tie it. A comparison of the realities of caste attitudes and interaction in India and the United States suggests that no group of people is content to be low in a caste hierarchy —to live a life of inherited deprivation and subjection—regardless of the rationalizations offered them by their superiors or constructed by themselves. This is one of many points on which further cross-cultural comparison and only cross-cultural comparison of caste behavior might be conclusive.

It should be evident that the range of similarities between caste in India and race relations in America, when viewed as relations among people, is wide and that the details are remarkably similar in view of the differences in cultural context. Without denying or belittling the differences, I would hold that the term "caste system" is applicable at the present time in the southern United States if it is applicable anywhere outside of Hindu India and that it can be usefully applied to societies with systems of hierarchical, endogamous subdivisions whose membership is hereditary and permanent, wherever they occur. By comparing caste situations, so defined, it should be possible to derive further insight, not only into caste in India, but into a widespread type of relations between groups—insight which is obscured if we insist upon treating Indian caste as entirely unique.

---

21 Cf. E. T. Atkinson, *The Himalayan Districts of the North-Western Provinces of India*, III (Allahabad: North-Western Provinces and Oudh Press, 1886), p. 446; B. S. Cohn, "The Camars of Senapur: A Study of the Changing Status of a Depressed Caste" (unpublished Ph.D. dissertation, Cornell University, 1954), pp. 112ff.; and D. N. Majumdar, *The Fortunes of Primitive Tribes* (Lucknow: Universal Publishers Ltd., 1944), p. 193.

From Berreman's argument, it is evident that many aspects of Negro-white relationships in American society are relatively close to those in a caste society. Although interaction between Negroes and whites in the South is more castelike than it is in the North, both relationships approximate a caste system.[1] Within this system a separate Negro class structure has developed.[2] Almost all empirical studies of this structure describe it as consisting of three levels: upper, middle, and lower.[3] Placement in these strata rests, as in white society, upon such criteria as income, education, occupation, and style of life.[4] Essentially, then, the point of reference for defining the Negro class structure is the dominant white structure. As Leonard Reissman puts it, "Negroes seek to apply to themselves the same criteria of prestige that whites use."[5] This does not mean, however, that Negro society is separate but equal to white society. With a few exceptions, the wealth and power of the Negro upper class are not comparable to those of the white upper class. Although the Negro middle class enjoys a decidedly more comfortable life than does the Negro lower class, its standard of living is seldom above that of the white working class. The distribution of the two populations in the total scheme of stratification gives a further perspective on the disjunction between the white and Negro classes. In white society the bulk of the population falls

---

[1] Probably the strongest argument against the caste thesis for American society is set forth by Cox, who emphasizes the role of economic exploitation and power in determining the position of the Negro group. Oliver C. Cox, *Caste, Class and Race* (Garden City, N.Y.: Doubleday & Company, Inc., 1948).

[2] It should be noted that class status can change without a corresponding change in caste status.

[3] As with the white class system, it is possible to give only rough estimates of the size of these three classes. While Lincoln emphasizes the lack of unanimous opinion on the proportion of Negroes in the upper, middle, and lower classes, he cites one appraisal which concludes that "not more than 25 per cent of the Negro population can be called middle class by any reasonable standards. And not more than 5 per cent can be called upper class." C. Eric Lincoln, "The Negro's Middle Class Dream," in *Minorities in a Changing World*, ed. Milton L. Barron (New York: Alfred A. Knopf, Inc., 1967), p. 341.

As Lincoln points out, "If one applies the full spectrum of criteria by which the white social structure is measured . . . the Negro middle class is reduced to 4 or 5 per cent of the Negro population, and the Negro upper class vanishes altogether." *Ibid.*

More evidence is available for appraising the size of the lower class. Many estimates indicate that close to 60 per cent of the Negro population live in poverty. (See, for example, St. Clair Drake, "The Social and Economic Status of the Negro in the United States," p. 779, and Daniel P. Moynihan, "Employment, Income, and the Ordeal of the Negro Family," p. 760, both in *Daedalus*, 94 (Fall 1965); Mollie Orshansky, "Counting the Poor: Another Look at the Poverty Profile," *Social Security Bulletin*, 28 (January 1965), 3–29. Reasonably, another 10 to 15 per cent of the Negro group—while not technically classifiable as "poor"—can be added to the lower class since they do not qualify as Negro middle class in view of their limited education and occupational skills. We suggest, then, that 70 to 75 per cent of the Negro population belong in the lower class.

[4] Skin color, too, plays a role in Negro class placement, although it is diminishing in importance. The emphasis of the "black-is-beautiful" theme is a conspicuous sign of this trend.

[5] "Social Stratification," in *Sociology: An Introduction*, ed. Neil J. Smelser (New York: John Wiley & Sons, Inc., 1967), p. 242.

Glenn, however, notes that education is increasingly becoming a more important basis of Negro than of white prestige. Norval D. Glenn, "Negro Prestige Criteria: A Case Study in the Bases of Prestige," *American Journal of Sociology*, 68 (May 1963), 645–57.

within the middle and working classes. By contrast, the vast majority of the Negro population falls in the lower class. While Negroes constitute only 11 per cent of the population, they make up nearly one-fourth of the group living in poverty.[6]

THE NEGRO UPPER CLASS[7]

The Negro upper class consists mainly of businessmen and professionals who serve the Negro community. A large section of the class initially accumulated its wealth in various illegitimate business activities and invested it in respectable business operations. By such means Negroes may achieve upper-class status in one generation. High occupational rank, a moderate amount of wealth, and a distinctive life style are class characteristics. Because light-skinned Negroes have had more educational and economic opportunities in a society dominated by whites, a larger proportion of the upper than of the middle or of the lower classes is light-skinned.

The Negro upper class has a comfortable existence, comparable to that of the white upper-middle class. Typically, members of this stratum live in the better residential areas of the Negro ghetto and occasionally in liberal upper-middle-class white neighborhoods in the urban North. Family incomes are sufficient for the usual appurtenances of high status: expensive homes and cars as well as manifest interest in art, music, literature, and travel. In some respects, upper-class Negroes live in an isolated world marginal to both white society and the main stream of Negro life.

The upper class has generally assumed leadership positions in the older civil rights and racial-advancement associations, such as the National Association for the Advancement of Colored People and the Urban League. Its members are chosen as token leaders of the Negro group and as officials and board directors with community-wide support. Participation in social clubs and in Negro fraternities or sororities occupies a large part of their leisure time. A puritanical code of conduct, including respectability and discreet behavior, is emphasized. In this

---

[6] As Drake suggests, "Negro class structure is 'pyramidal,' with a large lower class, a somewhat smaller middle class, and a tiny upper class (made up of people whose income and occupations would make them only middle class in the white society). White class profiles tend to be 'diamond shaped' with small lower and upper classes and a large middle class." *Op. cit.*, p. 785.

[7] This sketch of the Negro upper class is based largely on the following works. St. Clair Drake and Horace R. Cayton, *Black Metropolis* (New York: Harper & Row, Publishers, 1962); E. Franklin Frazier, *The Negro in the United States* (New York: The Macmillan Company, Publishers, 1957); G. Franklin Edwards, *The Negro Professional Class* (Glencoe, Ill.: The Free Press, 1959); Harold W. Pfautz, "The Power Structure of the Negro Sub-Community," *Phylon*, 23 (Summer 1962), 156–66; Daniel C. Thompson, *The Negro Leadership Class* (Englewood Cliffs, N.J.: Prentice-Hall, Inc., 1963); James Q. Wilson, *Negro Politics: The Search for Leadership* (Glencoe, Ill.: The Free Press, 1960).

way the upper class separates itself from lower-class Negroes and avoids the negative stereotypes associated with their life style.

Although upper-class Negroes favor interracial contacts, they tend to be suspicious of the motives of whites. They are ambivalent about the removal of caste barriers. Many recognize that their success is based on a caste system which has provided them with a clientele and a market free from white competition. Apart from their position on civil rights issues, they tend to be politically and economically conservative.

While the excerpt below from St. Clair Drake and Horace Cayton's *Black Metropolis* is based on research gathered during the late 1930s, the main themes in their portrait of the Negro upper-class style of life are still valid for this group today.

BLACK METROPOLIS*

St. Clair Drake, *Roosevelt University*

Horace R. Cayton, *University of California, Berkeley*

If one wished to ascertain just what people constitute Bronzeville's upper classs, it might seem practicable to group together those persons who have the most money, those with the greatest amount of education, those with the "best" family backgrounds, and those who wield the greatest political power—and attach to this group the label *upper class*. But this mélange, though including everyone whom the community calls "upper," would also include some persons not quite "in." So far as any single attribute entitles a person to this label, it is that he knows how to live with a certain definite "style." An income sufficient to maintain this style is taken for granted.

The general tone of upper-class life is conveyed by phrases used when people are explaining what they mean by "dicties," "hincties," "muckti-mucks" —i.e., "upper-class" people. Among such phrases are:

"...have money, culture, influence, and surplus money in the bank to go on..."

"...dress according to the latest styles and with quality..."

"...try to give their children the very best in life—education, luxuries, and things like that—according to their money..."

"...have reached their aim in life and become leaders of The Race..."

"...believe in taking life easy and taking trips wherever they want to without thought of work..."

"...secure recognition after they've made a trip abroad..."

"...go to church only to be seen and run the place..."

"...have received a high standing

by hard work and labor or inherited a lot of money..."

"...most of them are college-educated or have been up North a long time..."

"...travel a good bit..."

"...have money enough to give them a lot of leisure time..."

"...know the correct rules of etiquette even if they don't always observe them..."

"...the very top in the Negro neighborhood..."

WHO'S WHO IN BRONZEVILLE

When asked to name upper-class individuals, people of all levels will point out certain prominent doctors and lawyers, the editors of the major Negro newspapers, outstanding civic leaders, an occasional politician, and sometimes even a policy king. These are not necessarily the wealthiest persons in Bronzeville, but they have more than average education and usually are well known as Race Leaders.

One Dr. Cruikshank, whose name appeared very frequently in these community listings of upper-class persons, voluntarily submitted himself to study, averring that he was "pleased to be a guinea pig." Urbane and sophisticated, sure of his status, and interested in social research, he felt none of the objections to being studied that were expressed by many Bronzeville residents —perhaps quite justifiably. Dr. Cruikshank, in his early fifties, was at the top of most of Bronzeville's pyramids of power and prestige. A medical doctor, with a degree from an outstanding northern university, he was on the boards of several successful Negro-owned business enterprises and enjoyed extensive contacts with white philanthropists and wealthy "friends of the Negro."

Before the outbreak of the Second World War, the Cruikshank family lived comfortably on an income that ranged between $15,000 and $20,000 a year. The doctor owned a well-appointed house in the center of the Black Ghetto during the Fat Years and most of the Lean. Near the end of the Depression, he moved to an exclusive residential area outside of the Black Belt, where a small group of well-to-do Negroes were beginning to establish homes. His children had been sent to college and graduate school; the family owned two automobiles, took an annual vacation, and had traveled abroad. As in many of Bronzeville's upper-class families, however, all of the members of his family were employed. His wife and children were schoolteachers. When the Second World War began, Dr. Cruikshank received a very high commissioned officer's rating in a Jim-Crow army unit, as befitted a man of his stature.

Dr. Cruikshank was not born to wealth. His father had been a barber in a southern town, one of that older generation which derived considerable status from catering to a white clientele. At the age of 11 young Cruikshank could wield razor, shears, and clippers, but both he and his father realized that the colored barber's social pre-eminence was a southern-small-town kind of prestige, even then on the way out. So young Cruikshank was sent to college, where he received some aid from his family, though for the most part he was expected to earn his own way. He ran "on the road" in the summers as a Pullman porter while attending college and medical school. Even then he showed signs of becoming a Race Leader for he organized a union among the colored porters.

Dr. Cruikshank is light enough to pass for white, and his features and hair reveal the mingling of Negro and Indian strains with those of the English Cruikshanks and the Irish Mulligans. The doctor is proud of his distinguished English ancestors and at one time in his life considered "passing" permanently. When he finished medical school, he went to a Latin American country, thereby "resigning" temporarily from the American Negro group. But life as an émigré from American race prejudice did not satisfy him. His family and friends were in America; he had grown up in an atmosphere that stressed "race pride"; he felt confident that he could be successful within some Black Metropolis. So he came back to the States and finally settled down in Bronzeville. For over 30 years he has been a Race Leader in Midwest Metropolis and has gradually attained national prominence. After practicing medicine for a few years, he became

even more interested in "advancing The Race." Combining a career in medical education with business, Dr. Cruikshank emerged as a "leading citizen," respected by white political and civic leaders. Within Bronzeville, he won both the respect and the caustic criticism that Black Metropolis accords all its leaders.

Dr. Cruikshank is only one of Bronzeville's 300 doctors, all of whom are upper class or potentially so. Among them are men who have had training in the best medical schools in America and Europe. A few are distinguished practicing physicians: the city's leading dermatologist, two authorities on obstetrics and gynecology, and several widely known specialists in venereal diseases and tuberculosis. One or two are members of the medical faculties at the University of Chicago and Northwestern University—schools which, ironically

TABLE 1.   MEDIAN INCOMES OF NORTHERN URBAN MALE NEGRO COLLEGE GRADUATES FOR A SELECTED GROUP OF OCCUPATIONS*

Insurance officials	$4,250.00
Elementary school principals	3,750.00
Social work executives	3,750.00
Executive secretaries	3,000.00
High school principals	3,000.00
Physicians	2,750.00
Lawyers	2,666.67
Clergymen	2,421.05
Dentists	2,391.03
High school teachers	2,285.71
College professors	2,250.00
Vocational teachers	2,166.67
Post office clerks	2,193.18
YMCA workers	1,750.00
Druggists and pharmacists	1,750.00
Teachers, unspecified	1,714.28
Social workers	1,437.50
Businessmen	1,250.00

* Charles S. Johnson, *The Negro College Graduate* (Chapel Hill, N. C.: University of North Carolina Press, 1938), p. 155.

enough, do not welcome Negro medical students. These physicians and their wives, along with the majority of the dentists, lawyers, and the more prominent businessmen, social workers, schoolteachers, and public administrators, make up the core of Bronzeville's upper class. With family incomes ranging from $3,000 to $50,000 a year, their prestige is based not primarily on income (though in 1936 about 97 per cent of the residents of Bronzeville had family incomes of less than $3,000 a year) but rather on education and professional status and upon a definite way of life.

There are very few professional people in Bronzeville with an income from salaries of more than $5,000 a year, and very large incomes usually result from investments in real estate, Negro businesses, or securities to supplement salaries and fees. The . . . median incomes for Negro college graduates in the North are, in general, typical of Bronzeville [Table 1].

The white upper class in Midwest Metropolis is a wealthy leisure class. Bronzeville's upper class is a well-trained but only moderately well-to-do group, who have more leisure than the rank and file but who nevertheless must work for a living.

There are perhaps a thousand families in Bronzeville, probably comprising almost 5,000 individuals, who recognize each other as upper class. They consider themselves equal to each other in social status—fit associates for social affairs, marriage partners, and intimate friendships. Within this group are fewer than a hundred couples in their late fifties and sixties who constitute the social arbiters and status bearers for the upper class. Most of these people came to Bronzeville long before the Depression, although very few are Old Settlers. As they die off, the middle-aged pro-

fessional families assume their social position.[1] A list of the 106 Bronzeville celebrities mentioned in *Who's Who in Colored America* was submitted to some of these older social arbiters with the request that they check the names of persons who were "really upper" and not "just prominent people" or individuals who had bought their way into *Who's Who*. After the pruning, there were only thirty-one Chicagoans left on whom there was unanimous agreement.[2] Most of these were men over 40 years of age, though there were also five women. Twenty-six of the thirty-one were actively engaged in the professions, and one other had had some professional training. The others were either retired professional and businessmen or active business executives. All had attended college. In church affiliation, most were Congregationalists, Episcopalians, or Presbyterians. Only three were Baptists. One was a Christian Scientist, and one (who was re-

---

[1] Between the time in which field work for this study was begun and the date of publication, two of the key men in this group died. One was the founder of the Chicago *Defender* and the other was the president of an influential Negro insurance company.

[2] An elaborate analysis of the behavior pattern of this small group was made by the Cayton-Warner research staff. Using newspaper material and interview-observation records, social-participation charts were kept of most of the functions at which these people appeared over a 2-year period. They were then thoroughly interviewed as to their attitudes toward these events and the people who were present. Having defined the various cliques and associations to which these people belonged, a study was then made of the age, occupation, education, church affiliations, and associational connections of the clique members. Thus it was possible to describe *inductively* the traits of a large group of people who constantly associated together. The same procedure was used on other groups of cliques of various age levels within the upper class.

puted to have a white wife) belonged to the Bahai group. All were members of at least one professional association, and over half of the men were Masons. Nearly all reported membership in some social clubs or fraternities or sororities, and in the NAACP.

Interview-observation studies of these persons' families revealed extreme emphasis on maintaining "a good home," with fine furniture, linen, glassware, china, and silver much in evidence. Before the Second World War the majority kept at least a part-time maid, and a few had more than one servant, even during the Depression. The men dressed expensively but conservatively; the women, smartly but in good taste. All of the families carried accounts with exclusive downtown shops. The majority owned automobiles, and one family had three cars and a chauffeur. All were interested in real estate. All thought that Negroes should develop more business enterprises.

Politically, all of these persons were conservative, but they were tolerant even of extreme radical political activity on the ground that it might shock white America into awareness of the Negro's needs. Without exception these families were training their children for business or professional pursuits or reported that the children had already received such training.

These upper-class people took "respectability" for granted. They were concerned with "refinement," "culture," and graceful living as a class ideal, although many of them had never had the opportunity to cultivate an appreciation for music, art, and literature or had been so involved in the competitive struggle for professional advancement that they had ignored such interests. Twenty of the thirty-one were light-brown skinned or very fair in color, but they all talked like ardent Race Men and Race Women.

THE NEGRO MIDDLE CLASS[1]

The Negro middle class consists largely of clerical and stable blue-collar service workers. These occupations, together with a life style oriented to "bettering oneself," are the differentiating attributes of the group. Located primarily in the North and West, where opportunities for white-collar employment are greater, they have modest and relatively stable incomes. Many are home owners, but some live in apartments in the better Negro residential areas. Because their accumulated savings are not large, they always have some fear of losing their present status and especially of having to return to a lower-class area.

Middle-class Negroes tend to have an extensive organizational life. Membership in "established" churches[2] and recreational clubs typifies their interests. Such

---

[1] The major source for this depiction of the Negro middle class is E. Franklin Frazier, *Black Bourgeoisie* (Glencoe, Ill.: The Free Press, 1957). Representative of additional works utilized are Drake and Cayton, *op. cit.*; Frazier, *The Negro in the United States*; Lincoln, *op. cit.*; Seymour Parker and Robert Kleiner, "Status Position, Mobility, and Ethnic Identification of the Negro," *Journal of Social Issues*, 20 (April 1964), 85–102; Nathan Hare, *The Black Anglo-Saxons* (New York: Marzani and Munsell, Publishers, Inc., 1965).

[2] By established churches we mean those formally within the Negro Methodist and

disciplined activity distinguishes their behavior from the informal behavior of the lower class.

In many respects, the life style of the Negro middle class is an exaggeration of the life style of the white middle class. Their concern for getting ahead is even more intensified by the reality of Negro caste status. Their belief that they are important and prestigeful persons in the community guides their style of life. They consider owning one's home and having the latest furnishings and household equipment desirable goals and indications of a successful life. They emphasize an ostentatious display of wealth and conspicuous spending, and attempt to impress others with their influence in the community.

They value a college education as a significant avenue to upward mobility. Careful supervision of leisure-time activities, selection of playmates, and long-range planning for the future are consistent with the attempts of white middle-class parents to raise "successful" offspring. These background props plus polished behavior and putting on a front are the chief means of maintaining and enhancing one's prestige within this class.

The most widely known description of the Negro middle class is E. Franklin Frazier's *Black Bourgeoisie*. We reproduce below Frazier's conclusions to his study —including his controversial observations on the Negroes' "exaggerated, quasi-pathological" mimicry of middle-class whites.

Baptist denominations. They are different from the store-front churches attended by the Negro lower class. These are more or less informally organized and usually led by a part-time, self-ordained pastor. They are commonly referred to as Holiness sects. See Joseph H. Fichter, "American Religion and the Negro," *Daedalus*, 94 (Fall 1965), 1085–101. Alex Poinsett, "Negroes and the Christian Church," in *The Negro Handbook*, compiled by the editors of *Ebony* (Chicago: The Johnson Publishing Co., 1966), pp. 307–8.

BLACK BOURGEOISIE*

E. Franklin Frazier†

Howard University

When viewed in the broad perspective of the changes which are occurring in the western world, this study of the black bourgeoisie reveals in an acute form many of the characteristics of modern bourgeois society, especially in the United States. Hence it was difficult to resist the temptation to compare the black bourgeoisie with the same class among white Americans. However, it was not the purpose of this study to isolate and analyze the common characteristics of this class in the modern world. Our task was less ambitious and

* Reprinted with permission of The Macmillan Company from *Black Bourgeoisie: The Rise of a New Middle-Class in the United States* by E. Franklin Frazier. © The Free Press, a Corporation, 1957.
† Deceased.

therefore more restricted. Our purpose was to treat the black bourgeoisie as a case study of a middle-class group which had emerged during the changing adjustment of a racial minority to modern industrial society. From this standpoint our study may have a broader significance than the group which we have studied. It may have some relevance for the study of the emergence of a middle class in colonial societies, especially in African societies at present undergoing rapid changes. The characteristics of this class in the various societies will have to be studied in each case in relation to its history and the economic and social forces which are responsible for its development.

The black bourgeoisie in the United States is an essentially American phenomenon. Its emergence and its rise to importance within the Negro community are closely tied up with economic and social changes in the American community. Its behavior as well as its mentality is a reflection of American modes of behavior and American values. What may appear as distortions of American patterns of behavior and thought are due to the fact that the Negro lives on the margin of American society. The very existence of a separate Negro community with its own institutions within the heart of the American society is indicative of its quasipathological character, especially since the persistence of this separate community has been due to racial discrimination and oppression.

As the result of this fact, the black bourgeoisie is unique in a number of respects: First, it lacks a basis in the American economic system. Among colonial peoples and among other racial minorities, the bourgeoisie usually comes into existence as the result of its role in the economic organization of these societies. But the black bourgeoisie in the United States has subsisted off the crumbs of philanthropy, the salaries of public servants, and what could be squeezed from the meager earnings of Negro workers. Hence "Negro business," which has no significance in the American economy, has become a social myth embodying the aspirations of this class. Then, because of the position of the Negro in American life, it has been impossible for the black bourgeoisie to play the traditional role of this class among minorities. The attempt on the part of the Communist Party to assign to the black bourgeoisie the traditional role of this class in what the Party defined as the struggle of the "Negro people" for "national liberation" only tended to emphasize the unreality of the position of the black bourgeoisie. Moreover, the black bourgeoisie have shown no interest in the "liberation" of Negroes except as it affected their own status or acceptance by the white community. They viewed with scorn the Garvey Movement with its nationalistic aims. They showed practically no interest in the Negro Renaissance. They wanted to forget the Negro's past, and they have attempted to conform to the behavior and values of the white community in the most minute details. Therefore they have often become, as has been observed, "exaggerated" Americans.

Because of its struggle to gain acceptance by whites, the black bourgeoisie has failed to play the role of a responsible elite in the Negro community. Many individuals among the first generation of educated Negroes, who were the products of missionary education, had a sense of responsibility toward the Negro masses and identified themselves with the struggles of the masses to overcome the handicaps of ignorance and poverty. Their influence over the masses was limited, to be sure

—not, however, because of any lack of devotion on their part but because of the control exercised by the white community. Nevertheless, they occupied a dignified position within the Negro community and were respected. As teachers of Negroes, they generally exhibited the same sincere interest in education and genuine culture as their missionary teachers. Therefore they did not regard teaching merely as a source of income. On the other hand, today many Negro teachers refuse identification with the Negro masses and look upon teaching primarily as a source of income. In many cases they have nothing but contempt for their Negro pupils. Moreover, they have no real interest in education and genuine culture and spend their leisure in frivolities and in activities designed to win a place in Negro "society."

When the opportunity has been present, the black bourgeoisie has exploited the Negro masses as ruthlessly as have whites. As the intellectual leaders in the Negro community, they have never dared think beyond a narrow, opportunistic philosophy that provided a rationalization for their own advantages. Although the black bourgeoisie exercise considerable influence on the values of Negroes, they do not occupy a dignified position in the Negro community. The masses regard the black bourgeoisie as simply those who have been "lucky in getting money" which enables them to engage in conspicuous consumption. When this class pretends to represent the best manners or morals of the Negro, the masses regard such claims as hypocrisy.

The single factor that has dominated the mental outlook of the black bourgeoisie has been its obsession with the struggle for status. The struggle for status has expressed itself mainly in the emphasis upon "social" life or "society."

The concern of the Negro for "social" life and "society" has been partly responsible for the failure of educated Negroes to make important contributions within the fields of science or art. Educated Negroes have been constantly subjected to the pressures of the black bourgeoisie to conform to its values. Because of this pressure some gifted Negroes have abandoned altogether their artistic and scientific aspirations, while others have chosen to play the role of phony intellectuals and cater to the ignorance and vanities of the black bourgeoisie in order to secure "social" acceptance. Since middle-class Negroes have never been permitted to play a serious role in American life, "social" life has offered an area of competition in which the serious affairs of life were not involved. Middle-class Negroes who have made real contributions in science and art have had to escape from the influence of the "social" life of the black bourgeoisie. In fact, the spirit of play or lack of serious effort has permeated every aspect of the life of the Negro community. It has, therefore, tended to encourage immaturity and childishness on the part of middle-class Negroes, whose lives are generally devoted to trivialities.

The emphasis upon "social" life or "society" is one of the main props of the world of make-believe into which the black bourgeoisie has sought an escape from its inferiority and frustrations in American society. This world of make-believe, to be sure, is a reflection of the values of American society, but it lacks the economic basis that would give it roots in the world of reality. In escaping into a world of make-believe, middle-class Negroes have rejected both identification with the Negro and his traditional culture. Through delusions of wealth and power they have sought identification with the white America which continues to reject them. But these delusions leave them frustrated because they are unable to escape from the emptiness and futility of their existence. Gertrude Stein would have been nearer the truth if she had said of the black bourgeoisie what she said of Negroes in general, that they "were not suffering from persecution, they were suffering from nothingness," not because, as she explained, the African has "a very ancient but a very narrow culture."[1] The black bourgeoisie suffers from "nothingness" because, when Negroes attain middle-class status, their lives generally lose both content and significance.

[1] *The Autobiography of Alice Toklas* (New York: Harcourt, Brace & World, 1933), p. 292.

THE NEGRO LOWER CLASS[1]

The Negro lower class consists largely of unskilled farm and nonfarm laborers, domestic workers, and relief recipients. By far the largest percentage of all Negroes (70 to 75 per cent),[2] they are proportionally much larger than the white lower class. The essential attribute distinguishing them from the remainder of the Negro population is the fact that they live at or below the subsistence level. Lower-caste status and poverty combine to make them the most despised and disadvantaged group in American society.

The world of the Negro lower class is one of informal activities. Its members have neither the restraint nor the role-playing ability to establish and maintain task-oriented and leisure-time associations. For a segment of the lower class, mostly women, membership in the store-front church is an important exception to this general rule. While the street peer group is the center of activity for lower-class men, church and family are the centers of the women's activities. The churches are usually fundamentalist, offering salvation from the vices of drunkenness, sexual misconduct, family disruption, gambling, and fighting. Their otherworldly emphasis provides the lower-class Negro with an escape from the harsh realities of everyday life.

The Negro lower-class family is typically matrifocal; two or three generations of women and their children constitute one household. The tradition of the

---

[1] The following studies figure prominently in this profile of the Negro lower class. Robert R. Bell, "Lower-Class Negro Mothers' Aspirations for Their Children," *Social Forces*, 43 (May 1965), 493–500; Kenneth B. Clark, *Dark Ghetto* (New York: Harper & Row, Publishers, 1965); Allison Davis and John Dollard, *Children of Bondage* (New York: Harper and Co., 1940); Drake and Cayton, *op. cit.*; Frazier, *The Negro in the United States*; Joseph S. Himes, "Some Work-Related Cultural Deprivations of Lower-Class Negro Youths," in *Poverty in America*, eds. Louis A. Ferman *et al.* (Ann Arbor, Mich.: The University of Michigan Press, 1965), pp. 384–89; Herman P. Miller, *Rich Man, Poor Man* (New York: Thomas Y. Crowell Co., 1964), Chap. 6; Moynihan, *op. cit.*; Thomas F. Pettigrew, *A Profile of the Negro American* (Princeton, N.J.: D. Van Nostrand Company, Inc., 1964); Lee Rainwater, "Crucible of Identity: The Negro Lower-Class Family," *Daedalus*, 95 (Winter 1966), 172–216.

[2] See footnote 3 for a discussion of the basis of this estimate.

matriarchal family originated in the time of slavery, when males were sold separately from their families, leaving the mothers and children as the only stable family units. This tradition has persisted in the lower class largely because of the instability of male employment. The failure of Negro men to be good providers leads to marital discord and desertion. Since the presence of any one man in the family is short-lived, a woman commonly has more than one husband during her lifetime. In the extended family of two generations or more, the grandmother often assumes chief responsibility as well as decision-making authority.

The Negro lower class has no strong sanctions against extramarital sexual relations or out-of-wedlock children. Having sexual relations and begetting children are seen as being necessary to validate adult status. Thus social pressure and biological urge combine to make early child-bearing and large families a characteristic feature.

Living at or below the subsistence level, lower-class Negroes experience great anxiety over having enough of the bare necessities. Because of their sense of futility about directed effort, they generally limit their aspirations to the satisfaction of immediate needs. The pursuit of pleasure is a powerful motive since the only reality is the present with its problems and gratifications. They believe life to be controlled by fate, luck, and chance. The middle-class world of long-range planning and deferred gratification is incomprehensible to them, faced as they are with the task of surviving from day to day.

The similarities between the Negro and white lower classes are much greater than the differences. In both groups, the various manifestations of personal and family disorganization are responses to poverty and deprivation—the overriding forces for those at the bottom of the heap. The differences may be found in variations of adaptive techniques springing from differences in limited cultural traditions. (These techniques are related to the "strategies for living" discussed in the selection below by Lee Rainwater.)

For both Negroes and whites in this group, life is episodic, fluctuating between the search for excitement and routine activity. Although work is viewed as necessary for survival, it is transitory. Gravitating from one job to another with slight hope of permanency, members of the lower class have erratic work histories which stand in contrast to the stable employment pattern of the Negro middle class.

They teach their children to be aggressive. This characteristic is part of a broader pattern common to the lower class—an emphasis on toughness, which includes athletic skills, masculinity, absence of sentimentality, and bravery in the face of threats.

In some respects, the culture of the Negro lower class is more viable than that of the white lower class, in part because of the influence of Negro folk culture. Perhaps of greater significance, upward mobility has not taken away so many of the more intelligent and imaginative.

The extract below from Rainwater's *Crucible of Identity* describes some of the major characteristics of sexual and family relationships in the Negro lower class. It also discusses some of the origins of these characteristics and their consequences for family disorganization from the perspective of white society.

NEGRO LOWER-CLASS FAMILY LIFE*

Lee Rainwater

Washington University

We will outline below the several stages and forms of Negro lower-class family life. At many points these family forms and the interpersonal relations that exist within them will be seen to have characteristics in common with the life styles of white lower-class families.[1] At other points there are differences, or the Negro pattern will be

---

* From Lee Rainwater, "Crucible of Identity: The Negro Lower-Class Family," *Daedalus* (Winter 1966), pp. 182–91.

[1] For discussions of white lower-class families, see Lee Rainwater, Richard P. Coleman, and Gerald Handel, *Workingman's Wife* (Dobbs Ferry, N.Y.: Oceana Publications, Inc., 1959); Lee Rainwater, *Family Design* (Chicago: Aldine Publishing Co., 1964); Herbert Gans, *The Urban Villagers* (New York: The Free Press of Glencoe, Inc., 1962); Albert K. Cohen and Harold M. Hodges, "Characteristics of the Lower-Blue-Collar-Class," *Social Problems*, 10, No. 4 (Spring 1963), 303–34; 'S. M. Miller, "The American Lower Classes: A Typological Approach," in *Blue Collar World*, eds. Arthur B. Shostak and William Gomberg (Englewood Cliffs, N.J.: Prentice-Hall, Inc., 1964); and Mirra Komarovsky, *Blue Collar Marriage* (New York: Random House, Inc., 1964). Discussions of Negro slum life can be found in St. Clair Drake and Horace R. Cayton, *Black Metropolis* (New York: Harper & Row, Publishers, 1962), and Kenneth B. Clark, *Dark Ghetto* (New York: Harper & Row, Publishers, 1965); and of Negro community life in small-town and rural settings in Allison Davis, Burleigh B. Gardner, and Mary Gardner, *Deep South* (Chicago: University

seen to be more sharply divergent from the family life of stable working- and middle-class couples.

It is important to recognize that lower-class Negroes know that their particular family forms are different from those of the rest of the society and that, though they often see these forms as representing the only ways of behaving given their circumstances, they also think of the more stable family forms of the working class as more desirable. That is, lower-class Negroes know what the "normal American family" is supposed to be like, and they consider a stable family-centered way of life superior to the conjugal and familial situations in which they often find themselves. Their conceptions of the good American life include the notion of a father-husband who functions as an adequate provider and interested member of the family, a hard-working home-bound mother who is concerned about her children's welfare and her husband's needs, and children who look up to their parents and perform well in school and other outside places to reflect credit on their families. This image of what family life can be like is very real from time to time as lower-class men and women grow up and

---

of Chicago Press, 1944), and Hylan Lewis, *Blackways of Kent* (Chapel Hill, N.C.: University of North Carolina Press, 1955).

move through adulthood. Many of them make efforts to establish such families but find it impossible to do so either because of the direct impact of economic disabilities or because they are not able to sustain in their day-to-day lives the ideals which they hold.[2] While these ideals do serve as a meaningful guide to lower-class couples who are mobile out of the group, for a great many others the existence of such ideas about normal family life represents a recurrent source of stress within families as individuals become aware that they are failing to measure up to the ideals, or as others within the family and outside it use the ideals as an aggressive weapon for criticizing each other's performance. It is not at all uncommon for husbands or wives or children to try to hold others in the family to the norms of stable family life while they themselves engage in behaviors which violate these norms. The effect of such criticism in the end is to deepen commitment to the deviant sexual and parental norms of a slum subculture. Unless they are careful, social workers and other professionals exacerbate the tendency to use the norms of "American family life" as weapons by supporting these norms in situations where they are in reality unsupportable, thus aggravating the sense of failing and being failed by others, which is chronic for lower-class people.

Going together. The initial steps toward mating and family formation in the Negro slum take place in a context of highly developed boys' and girls' peer groups. Adolescents tend to become deeply involved in their peer-group societies beginning as early as the age of 12 or 13 and continue to be involved after first pregnancies and first marriages. Boys and girls are heavily committed both to their same sex peer groups and to the activities that those groups carry out. While classical gang activity does not necessarily characterize Negro slum communities everywhere, loosely knit peer groups do.

The world of the Negro slum is wide open to exploration by adolescent boys and girls: "Negro communities provide a flow of common experience in which young people and their elders share and out of which delinquent behavior emerges almost imperceptibly."[3] More than is possible in white slum communities, Negro adolescents have an opportunity to interact with adults in various "high life" activities; their behavior more often represents an identification with the behavior of adults than an attempt to set up group standards and activities that differ from those of adults.

Boys and young men participating in the street system of peer-group activity are much caught up in games of furthering and enhancing their status as significant persons. These games are played out in small and large gatherings through various kinds of verbal contests that go under the names of "sounding," "signifying," and "working game." Very much a part of a boy's or man's status in this group is his

---

2 For general discussions of the extent to which lower-class people hold the values of the larger society, see Albert K. Cohen, *Delinquent Boys* (New York: The Free Press of Glencoe, Inc., 1955); Hyman Rodman, "The Lower Class Value Stretch," *Social Forces*, 42, No. 2 (December 1963), 205ff.; and William L. Yancey, "The Culture of Poverty: Not So Much Parsimony," unpublished manuscript, Social Science Institute, Washington University.

3 James F. Short, Jr., and Fred L. Strodtbeck, *Group Process and Gang Delinquency* (Chicago: University of Chicago Press, 1965), p. 114. Chapter V (pp. 102–15) of this book contains a very useful discussion of differences between white and Negro lower-class communities.

ability to win women. The man who has several women "up tight," who is successful in "pimping off" women for sexual favors and material benefits, is much admired. In sharp contrast to white lower-class groups, there is little tendency for males to separate girls into "good" and "bad" categories.[4] Observations of groups of Negro youths suggest that girls and women are much more readily referred to as "that bitch" or "that whore" than they are by their names, and this seems to be a universal tendency carrying no connotation that "that bitch" is morally inferior to or different from other women. Thus, all women are essentially the same, all women are legitimate targets, and no girl or woman is expected to be virginal except for reason of lack of opportunity or immaturity. From their participation in the peer group and according to standards legitimated by the total Negro slum culture, Negro boys and young men are propelled in the direction of girls to test their "strength" as seducers. They are mercilessly rated by both their peers and the opposite sex in their ability to "talk" to girls; a young man will go to great lengths to avoid the reputation of having a "weak" line.[5]

---

4 Discussions of white lower-class attitudes toward sex may be found in Arnold W. Green, "The Cult of Personality and Sexual Relations," *Psychiatry*, 4 (1941), 343–48; William F. Whyte, "A Slum Sex Code," *American Journal of Sociology*, 49, No. 1 (July 1943), 24–31; and Lee Rainwater, "Marital Sexuality in Four Cultures of Poverty," *Journal of Marriage and the Family*, 26, No. 4 (November 1964), 457–66.

5 See Boone Hammond, "The Contest System: A Survival Technique" (Master's Honors paper, Washington University, 1965). See also Ira L. Reiss, "Premarital Sexual Permissiveness Among Negroes and Whites," *American Sociological Review*, 29, No. 5 (October 1964), 688–98.

The girls share these definitions of the nature of heterosexual relations; they take for granted that almost any male they deal with will try to seduce them and that given sufficient inducement (social not monetary) they may wish to go along with his line. Although girls have a great deal of ambivalence about participating in sexual relations, this ambivalence is minimally moral and has much more to do with a desire not to be taken advantage of or get in trouble. Girls develop defenses against the exploitative orientations of men by devaluing the significance of sexual relations ("he really didn't do anything bad to me"), and as time goes on by developing their own appreciation of the intrinsic rewards of sexual intercourse.

The informal social relations of slum Negroes begin in adolescence to be highly sexualized. Although parents have many qualms about boys and, particularly, girls entering into this system, they seldom feel there is much they can do to prevent their children's sexual involvement. They usually confine themselves to counseling somewhat hopelessly against girls' becoming pregnant or boys' being forced into situations where they might have to marry a girl they do not want to marry.

Girls are propelled toward boys and men in order to demonstrate their maturity and attractiveness; in the process they are constantly exposed to pressures for seduction, to boys "rapping" to them. An active girl will "go with" quite a number of boys, but she will generally try to restrict the number with whom she has intercourse to the few to whom she is attracted or (as happens not infrequently) to those whose threats of physical violence she cannot avoid. For their part, the boys move rapidly from girl to girl seeking to have intercourse with as many as they can and thus build up their "reps." The activity of seduction is itself highly cathected; there is gratification in simply "talking to" a girl as long as the boy can feel that he has acquitted himself well.

At 16 Joan Bemias enjoys spending time with three or four very close girl friends. She tells us they follow this routine when the girls want to go out and none of the boys they have been seeing lately is available: "Every time we get ready to go someplace we look through all the telephone numbers of boys we'd have and we call them and talk so sweet to them that they'd come on around. All of them had cars you see. (I: What do you do to keep all these fellows interested?) Well nothing. We don't have to make love with all of them. Let's see, Joe, J. B., Albert, and Paul, out of all them I've been going out with I've only had sex with four boys, that's all." She goes on to say that she and her girl friends resist boys by being unresponsive to their lines and by breaking off relations with them on the ground that they're going out with other girls. It is also clear from her comments that the girl friends support each other in resisting the boys when they are out together in groups.

Joan has had a relationship with a boy which has lasted 6 months, but she has managed to hold the frequency of intercourse down to four times. Initially she managed to hold this particular boy off for a month but eventually gave in.

Becoming pregnant. It is clear that the contest elements in relationships between men and women continue even in relationships that become quite steady. Despite the girls' ambivalence about sexual relations and their manifold efforts to reduce its frequency, the operation of chance often eventuates in their becoming pregnant.[6] This was the case with Joan. With this we reach the

[6] See the discussion of aleatory processes leading to premarital fatherhood in Short and Strodtbeck, *op. cit.*, pp. 44–45.

second stage in the formation of families, that of premarital pregnancy. (We are outlining an ideal-typical sequence and not, of course, implying that all girls in the Negro slum culture become pregnant before they marry but only that a great many of them do.)

Joan was caught despite the fact that she was considerably more sophisticated about contraception than most girls or young women in the group (her mother had both instructed her in contraceptive techniques and constantly warned her to take precautions). No one was particularly surprised at her pregnancy, although she, her boyfriend, her mother, and others regarded it as unfortunate. For girls in the Negro slum, pregnancy before marriage is expected in much the same way that parents expect their children to catch mumps or chicken pox; if they are lucky it will not happen, but if it happens people are not too surprised, and everyone knows what to do about it. It was quickly decided that Joan and the baby would stay at home. It seems clear from the preparations that Joan's mother is making that she expects to have the main responsibility for caring for the infant. Joan seems quite indifferent to the baby; she shows little interest in mothering the child, although she is not particularly adverse to the idea so long as the baby does not interfere too much with her continued participation in her peer group.

Establishing who the father is under these circumstances seems to be important and confers a kind of legitimacy on the birth; not to know who one's father is, on the other hand, seems the ultimate in illegitimacy. Actually Joan had a choice in the imputation of fatherhood; she chose J.B. because he is older than she and because she may marry him if he can get a divorce from his wife. She could have chosen Paul (with whom she had also had intercourse at about the time she became pregnant), but she would have done this reluctantly since Paul is a year younger than she and somehow this does not seem fitting.

In general, when a girl becomes pregnant while still living at home, it seems taken for granted that she will continue to live there and that her parents will take a major responsibility for rearing the children. Since there are usually siblings who can help out and even siblings who will be playmates for the child, the addition of a third generation to the household does not seem to place a great stress on relationships within the family. It seems common for the first pregnancy to have a liberating influence on the mother once the child is born in that she becomes socially and sexually more active than she was before. She no longer has to be concerned with preserving her status as a single girl. Since her mother is usually willing to take care of the child for a few years, the unwed mother has an opportunity to go out with girl friends and with men and thus become more deeply involved in the peer-group society of her culture. As she has more children and perhaps marries, she will find it necessary to settle down and spend more time around the house fulfilling the functions of a mother herself.

It would seem that for girls pregnancy is the real measure of maturity, the dividing line between adolescence and womanhood. Perhaps because of this, as well as because of the ready resources for child care, girls in the Negro slum community show much less concern about pregnancy than do girls in the white lower-class community and are less motivated to marry the fathers of their children. When a girl becomes pregnant the question of marriage certainly arises and is considered, but the

girl often decides that she would rather not marry the man either because she does not want to settle down yet or because she does not think he would make a good husband.

It is in the easy attitudes toward premarital pregnancy that the matrifocal character of the Negro lower-class family appears most clearly. In order to have and raise a family it is simply not necessary, though it may be desirable, to have a man around the house. While the AFDC program may make it easier to maintain such attitudes in the urban situation, this pattern existed long before the program was initiated and continues in families where support comes from other sources.

Finally it should be noted that fathering a child similarly confers maturity on boys and young men, although perhaps it is less salient for them. If the boy has any interest in the girl he will tend to feel that the fact that he has impregnated her gives him an additional claim on her. He will be stricter in seeking to enforce his exclusive rights over her (though not exclusive loyalty to her). This exclusive right does not mean that he expects to marry her but only that there is a new and special bond between them. If the girl is not willing to accept such claims, she may find it necessary to break off the relationship rather than tolerate the man's jealousy. Since others in the peer group have a vested interest in not allowing a couple to be too loyal to each other, they go out of their way to question and challenge each partner about the loyalty of the other, thus contributing to the deterioration of the relationship. This same kind of questioning and challenging continues if the couple marries and represents one source of the instability of the marital relationship.

Getting married. As noted earlier, despite the high degree of premarital sexual activity and the rather high proportion of premarital pregnancies, most lower-class Negro men and women eventually do marry and stay together for a shorter or longer period of time. Marriage is an intimidating prospect and is approached ambivalently by both parties. For the girl it means giving up a familiar and comfortable home that, unlike some other lower-class subcultures, places few real restrictions on her behavior. (While marriage can appear to be an escape from interpersonal difficulties at home, these difficulties seldom seem to revolve around effective restrictions placed on her behavior by her parents.) The girl also has good reason to be suspicious of the likelihood that men will be able to perform stably in the role of husband and provider; she is reluctant to be tied down by a man who will not prove to be worth it.

From the man's point of view the fickleness of women makes marriage problematic. It is one thing to have a girl friend step out on you, but it is quite another to have a wife do so. Whereas premarital sexual relations and fatherhood carry almost no connotation of responsibility for the welfare of the partner, marriage is supposed to mean that a man behaves more responsibly, becoming a provider for his wife and children, even though he may not be expected to give up all the gratifications of participation in the street system.

For all of these reasons both boys and girls tend to have rather negative views of marriage as well as a low expectation that marriage will prove a stable and gratifying existence. When marriage does take place, it tends to represent a tentative commitment on the part of both parties with a strong tendency to seek greater commitment on the part of the partner than on one's own part. Marriage is regarded as a fragile arrangement held together

primarily by affectional ties rather than instrumental concerns.

In general, as in white lower-class groups, the decision to marry seems to be taken rather impulsively.[7] Since everyone knows that sooner or later he will get married, in spite of the fact that he may not be sanguine about the prospect, Negro lower-class men and women are alert for clues that the time has arrived. The time may arrive because of a pregnancy in a steady relationship that seems gratifying to both partners or as a way of getting out of what seems to be an awkward situation or as a self-indulgence during periods when a boy and a girl are feeling very sorry for themselves. Thus, one girl tells us that when she marries her husband will cook all of her meals for her and she will not have any housework; another girl says that when she marries it will be to a man who has plenty of money and will have to take her out often and really show her a good time.

Boys see in marriage the possibility of regular sexual intercourse without having to fight for it or a girl safe from venereal disease or a relationship to a nurturant figure who will fulfill the functions of a mother. For boys, marriage can also be a way of asserting their independence from the peer group if its demands become burdensome. In this case the young man seeks to have the best of both worlds.[8]

---

7 Lee Rainwater, *And the Poor Get Children* (Chicago: Quadrangle Books, 1960), pp., 61–63. See also, Carlfred B. Broderick, "Social Heterosexual Development Among Urban Negroes and Whites," *Journal of Marriage and the Family*, 27 (May 1965), 200–212. Broderick finds that although white boys and girls and Negro girls become more interested in marriage as they get older, Negro boys become *less* interested in late adolescence than they were as preadolescents.

8 Walter Miller, "The Corner Gang Boys

Marriage as a way out of an unpleasant situation can be seen in the case of one of our informants, Janet Cowan:

Janet has been going with two men, one of them married and the other single. The married man's wife took exception to their relationship and killed her husband. Within a week Janet and her single boyfriend, Howard, were married. One way out of the turmoil the murder of her married boyfriend stimulated (they lived in the same building) was to choose marriage as a way of "settling down." However, after marrying, the new couple seemed to have little idea how to set themselves up as a family. Janet was reluctant to leave her parents' home because her parents cared for her two illegitimate children. Howard was unemployed and therefore unacceptable in his parent-in-law's home nor were his own parents willing to have his wife move in with them. Howard was also reluctant to give up another girl friend in another part of town. Although both he and his wife maintained that it was all right for a couple to step out on each other so long as the other partner did not know about it, they were both jealous if they suspected anything of this kind. In the end they gave up on the idea of marriage and went their separate ways.

In general, then, the movement toward marriage is an uncertain and tentative one. Once the couple does settle down together in a household of their own, they have the problem of working out a mutually acceptable organization of rights and duties, expectations and performances, that will meet their needs.

Husband-wife relations. Characteristic of both the Negro and white lower class is a high degree of conjugal role segregation.[9] That is, husbands and wives tend to think of themselves as having very separate kinds of functioning in the instrumental organization of family life and also as pursuing recreational and outside interests separately. The husband is expected to be a provider; he resists assuming functions around the home so long as he feels he is doing his proper job of bringing home a pay check. He feels he has the right to indulge himself in little ways if he is successful at this task. The wife is expected to care for the home and children and make her husband feel welcome and comfortable. Much that is distinctive to Negro family life stems from the fact that husbands often are not stable providers. Even when a particular man is, his wife's conception of men in general is such that she is pessimistic about the likelihood that he will continue to do well in this area. A great many Negro wives work to supplement the family income. When this is so the separate incomes earned by husband and wife tend to be treated not as "family" income but as the individual property of the two persons involved. If their wives work, husbands are likely to feel that they are entitled to retain a larger share of the income they provide; the wives, in turn, feel that the husbands have no right to benefit from the purchases they make out of their own money. There is, then, "my money" and "your money." In this situation the husband may come to feel that the wife should support the children out of her income and that he can retain all of his income for himself.

While white lower-class wives often are very much intimidated by their husbands, Negro lower-class wives come to feel that they have a right to give as good as they get. If the husband in-

Get Married," *Trans-action*, 1, No. 1 (November 1963), 10–12.

9 Rainwater, *Family Design*, pp. 28–60.

dulges himself, they have the right to indulge themselves. If the husband steps out on his wife, she has the right to step out on him. The commitment of husbands and wives to each other seems often a highly instrumental one after the "honeymoon" period. Many wives feel they owe the husband nothing once he fails to perform his provider role. If the husband is unemployed, the wife increasingly refuses to perform her usual duties for him. For example, one woman, after mentioning that her husband had cooked four eggs for himself, commented, "I cook for him when he's working, but right now he's unemployed; he can cook for himself." It is important, however, to understand that the man's status in the home depends not so much on whether he is working as on whether he brings money into the home. Thus, in several of the families we have studied in which the husband receives disability payments his status is as well-recognized as in families in which the husband is working.[10]

Because of the high degree of conjugal role segregation, both white and Negro lower-class families tend to be matrifocal in comparison to middle-class families. They are matrifocal in the sense that the wife makes most of the decisions that keep the family going and has the greatest sense of responsibility to the family. In white as well as in Negro lower-class families women tend to look to their female relatives for support and counsel and to treat their husbands as essentially uninterested in the day-to-day problems of family living.[11] In the Negro lower-class family these tendencies are all considerably exaggerated so that the matrifocality is much clearer than in white lower-class families.

---

[10] Yancey, *op. cit.* The effects of unemployment on the family have been discussed by E. Wright Bakke, *Citizens Without Work* (New Haven, Conn.: Yale University Press, 1940); Mirra Komarovsky, *The Unemployed Man and His Family* (New York: Dryden Press, 1940); and Earl L. Koos, *Families in Trouble* (New York: Kings Crown Press, 1946). What seems distinctive to the Negro slum culture is the short time lapse between the husband's loss of a job and his wife's considering him superfluous.

[11] See particularly Komarovsky's discussion of "barriers to marital communications" (Chap. 7) and "confidants outside of marriage" (Chap. 9), in *Blue Collar Marriage.*

SELECTED BIBLIOGRAPHY

BARTH, ERNEST A. T., and BAHA ABU-LABAN, "Power Structure and the Negro Sub-Community," *American Sociological Review*, 24 (February 1959), 69–76.

BELL, ROBERT R., "Lower Class Negro Mothers' Aspirations for Their Children," *Social Forces*, 43 (May 1965), 493–500.

BERNARD, JESSIE, *Marriage and Family Among Negroes.* Englewood Cliffs, N.J.: Prentice-Hall, Inc., 1966.

BLOOM, RICHARD, *et al.*, "Race and Social Class as Separate Factors Related to Social Environment," *American Journal of Sociology*, 70 (January 1965), 471–76.

BOWMAN, LEWIS, "Racial Discrimination and Negro Leadership Problems: The Case of 'Northern Community,'" *Social Forces*, 44 (December 1965), 173–86.

BROOM, LEONARD, and NORVAL D. GLENN, *Transformation of the Negro American.* New York: Harper & Row, Publishers, 1965.

BURGESS, M. ELAINE, *Negro Leadership in a Southern City.* Chapel Hill, N.C.: University of North Carolina, 1962.

CLARK, KENNETH B., *Dark Ghetto.* New

York: Harper & Row, Publishers, 1965.

Cox, Oliver C., *Caste, Class and Race.* Garden City, N.Y.: Doubleday & Company, Inc., 1948.

Davis, Allison, *et al., Deep South.* Chicago: University of Chicago Press, 1941.

Deutsch, Martin, "The Disadvantaged Child and the Learning Process," in *Education in Depressed Areas,* ed. Harry A. Passow. New York: Bureau of Publications, Teachers College, Columbia University, 1963.

Edwards, G. Franklin, *The Negro Professional Class.* Glencoe, Ill.: The Free Press, 1959.

Frazier, E. Franklin, *The Negro in the United States.* New York: The Macmillan Company, Publishers, 1949.

Gibbs, Jack P., "Occupational Differentiation of Negroes and Whites in the United States," *Social Forces,* 44 (December 1965), 159–65.

Glenn, Norval, "Negro Prestige Criteria: A Case Study in the Bases of Prestige," *American Journal* of Sociology, 68 (May 1963), 645–57.

Hare, Nathan, "Recent Trends in the Occupational Mobility of Negroes, 1930–1960: An Intracohort Analysis," *Social Forces,* 44 (December 1965), 166–73.

Harris, Edward E., "Some Comparisons Among Negro-White College Students: Social Ambition and Estimated Social Mobility," *Journal of Negro Education,* 35 (Fall 1966), 35–68.

Harris, Marvin, "Caste, Class and Minority," *Social Forces,* 37 (March 1959), 248–54.

Hill, Mozell C., and Bevode C. McCall, "Social Stratification in a Georgia Town," *American Sociological Review,* 15 (December 1950), 721–30.

Himes, Joseph S., "Interrelation of Occupational and Spousal Roles in a Middle Class Negro Neighborhood," *Marriage and Family Living,* 22 (November 1960), 362.

———, "Negro Teen-Age Culture," *Annals of the American Academy of Political and Social Sciences,* 338 (November 1961), 91–101.

———, "Some Work-Related Cultural Deprivations of Lower-Class Negro Youth," *Journal of Marriage and the Family,* 26 (November 1964), 447–49.

Kamili, Constance K., *et al.,* "Class Differences in the Socialization Practices of Negro Mothers," *Journal of Marriage and the Family,* 29 (May 1967), 302–10.

King, Charles E., "The Process of Social Stratification Among an Urban Southern Minority Population," *Social Forces,* 31 (May 1953), 352–55.

Lewis, Hylan, *Blackways of Kent.* Chapel Hill, N.C.: University of North Carolina Press, 1955.

———, "Culture, Class and Family Life Among Low-Income Urban Negroes" in *Employment, Race, and Poverty,* eds. Arthur M. Ross and Herbert Hill. New York: Harcourt, Brace & World, Inc., 1967.

Lieberson, Stanley, and Glenn V. Fugitt, "Negro-White Occupational Differences in the Absence of Discrimination," *American Journal of Sociology,* 73 (September 1967), 189–200.

Liebow, Elliot, *Tally's Corner: A Study of Negro Streetcorner Men.* Boston: Little, Brown and Company, 1967.

Mack, Raymond W., ed., *Race, Class, and Power.* New York: American Book Company, 1963.

Miller, S. M., "Poverty, Race and Politics," in *The New Sociology,* ed. Irving L. Horowitz. Fair Lawn, N.J.: Oxford University Press, Inc., 1964.

Monahan, Thomas P., and Elizabeth H. Monahan, "Some Characteristics of American Negro Leaders," *American Sociological Review,* 21 (October 1956), 589–96.

Moynihan, Daniel P., "Employment, Income, and the Ordeal of the Negro Family," *Daedalus,* 94 (Fall 1965), 745–70.

Myrdal, Gunnar, *et al., An American Dilemma.* New York: Harper and Bros., 1944.

Parker, Seymour, and Robert Kleiner, "Status Position, Mobility, and Ethnic Identification of the Negro," *Journal of Social Issues,* 20 (April 1964), 85–102.

Pettigrew, Thomas F., *A Profile of the*

Negro American. Princeton, N.J.: D. Van Nostrand Company, Inc., 1964.

PINKNEY, ALPHONSO, *Black Americans*. Englewood Cliffs, N.J.: Prentice-Hall, Inc., 1969.

QUEEN, STUART A., *et al.*, "The Contemporary American Negro Family," in *The Family in Various Cultures*. Philadelphia: J. B. Lippincott Co., 1967.

RAINWATER, LEE, and WILLIAM L. YANCEY, *The Moynihan Report and the Politics of Controversy*. Cambridge, Mass.: The M.I.T. Press, 1967.

ROSS, ARTHUR M., and HERBERT HILL, *Employment, Race and Poverty*. New York: Harcourt, Brace & World, Inc., 1967.

SCHMID, CALVIN F., and CHARLES E. NOBBE, "Socioeconomic Differentials Among Nonwhite Races," *American Sociological Review*, 30 (December 1965), 909–22.

THOMPSON, DANIEL C., *The Negro Leadership Class*. Englewood Cliffs, N.J.: Prentice-Hall, Inc., 1963.

WESTIE, FRANK R., and MARGARET L. WESTIE, "Social-Distance Pyramid: Relationships Between Caste and Class," *American Journal of Sociology*, 63 (September 1957), 190–96.

CHAPTER SIX

Concepts and Methods

CONCEPTIONS OF POWER[1]

The definitions and meanings of power vary widely. Moreover, the concept has been associated with a number of cognate terms such as authority, leadership, and prestige.[2] Two contrasting usages are discernible. In one, control, dominance, and manipulation are prominent, thus connoting processes of coercion. These terms apparently derive from Max Weber's conception of power as "the chance of a man or a number of men to realize their own will in a communal action even against the resistance of others who are participating in the action."[3]

---

[1] Important contributions to the vast literature on power have been made over the centuries not only by philosophers and social scientists but also by scholars from other fields. We are concerned with but a small portion of this literature, specifically, the place of power in the stratification of communities and societies. In sociology ·alone, this focus excludes a sizable segment of the literature. Studies of complex organizations, small groups, interpersonal relationships, and the processes of social control have yielded important insights into the dynamics of power. Our emphasis is on power at the macrosociological level.

For examples of research on other levels and types of power, see the studies in Robert K. Kahn and Elise Boulding, *Power and Conflict in Organizations* (New York: Basic Books, Inc., Publishers, 1964). Also, David Cooperman and E. V. Walter, eds., *Power and Civilization* (New York: Thomas Y. Crowell Co., 1962).

[2] See Robert Bierstedt, "An Analysis of Social Power," *American Sociological Review*, 15 (December 1950), 730–38. Also, Llewellyn Gross, "A Theory of Power and Organizational Processes," *The School Review*, 70 (Summer 1962), 149–62.

[3] H. H. Gerth and C. Wright Mills, eds., *From Max Weber: Essays in Sociology* (Fair Lawn, N.J.: Oxford University Press, Inc., 1946), p. 180.

259

The other usage of power is cast in somewhat more neutral language.[4] An example is Talcott Parsons' view of power as "the realistic capacity of a system-unit to actualize its 'interests' . . . within the context of system interaction and in this sense to exert influence on processes within the system."[5]

Students of stratification generally agree that power and stratification are closely related and that one cannot be discussed without considering the other. They disagree, however, on the specific nature of this relationship. In one view, power is a major dimension of social stratification and is positively correlated with economic status or prestige or both.[6] A second view subsumes stratification under power. Ralf Dahrendorf, for example, holds that "the category of social stratification belongs on a lower level of generality than that of power."[7] A third view sees the major dimensions of stratification as key elements in the differential possession of power. This approach is set forth by Weber, who postulates that his three orders of stratification—class, status, and party—are consequences of the distributions of power.[8]

Many writers expressly state or imply either that power is the major determinant in the differential distribution of other stratification variables[9] or that one or several of the other stratification variables are determinants in the differential distribution of power. Those expressing the latter view sometimes see economic or prestige factors or both as antecedents of or necessary conditions for the possession of power. Marxists, for example, believe that economic position is the prime factor in determining power distribution. On the other hand, functional writers, insofar as they deal with power in discussions of social stratification, often see the distribution of power as a result of the distribution of status or prestige. As put by Kingsley Davis, "the line of power corresponds roughly with

---

[4] While usually there is a correspondence between a writer's definition of power and his basic orientation, it should be emphasized that sometimes this generalization does not hold. Floyd Hunter, for example, refers to power as the "acts of men going about the business of moving other men to act in relation to themselves or in relation to organic or inorganic things." This relatively innocuous interpretation stands in contrast to Hunter's research on power, in which the themes of dominance and manipulation are conspicuous. *Community Power Structure* (Garden City, N.Y.: Doubleday & Company, Inc., 1963), p. 2. Published originally by The University of North Carolina Press, 1953.

[5] "A Revised Analytical Approach to the Theory of Social Stratification," in *Class, Status and Power*, eds. Reinhard Bendix and Seymour M. Lipset (Glencoe, Ill.: The Free Press, 1953), p. 95.
In a parenthetical phrase within this statement Parsons refers to "control of possessions," but it is clear that he relegates the coercive features of power to a minor role.

[6] For example, Kurt B. Mayer, *Class and Society* (New York: Random House, Inc., 1962), p. 26.

[7] "On the Origins of Social Inequality," in *Philosophy, Politics and Society*, eds. Peter Laslett and W. G. Runciman (New York: Barnes & Noble, Inc., 1962), p. 105.

[8] This is discussed further in Chapter Three of the present volume.

[9] For example, Lenski states that "the distribution of rewards in a society is a function of the distribution of power not of system needs." Elsewhere, he refers to prestige as being largely a function of power. Gerhard Lenski, *Power and Privilege* (New York: McGraw-Hill Book Company, 1966), pp. 63 and 45. A similar position is held by C. Wright Mills, *The Power Elite* (Fair Lawn, N.J.: Oxford University Press, Inc., 1956) ; and Leonard Reissman, *Class in American Society* (Glencoe, Ill.: The Free Press, 1959).

the hierarchy of prestige."[10] Milton Gordon, in contrast, emphasizes the long-run influence of power (political and economic) on the distribution of status or prestige.[11] These many-sided perspectives on power in studies of stratification highlight the need for research and analysis.

While our emphasis is on the treatment of power in conceptual, methodological, and empirical contributions by sociologists, we shall give some attention here to the views of political scientists. In recent years they have significantly increased their empirical research on power and decision-making at the community level. In large part this heightened interest is their reaction to the stratification theory of power—with its alleged assumption of identity between economic position and power and its consequent neglect of political processes in community life.[12] These and other conceptions and conclusions about community power by sociologists and political scientists are dealt with in this and the following chapter.

METHODS OF RESEARCH

Prior to World War II, sociologists confined their empirical research on power largely to explorations carried out as part of community studies in which the class concept was an organizing theme. In some of these investigations, notably the Middletown studies by Robert and Helen Lynd, issues of power were a major concern; in others, such as W. Lloyd Warner's Yankee City series, the power theme was not so prominent. With a few exceptions,[13] sociological attention to power continued along these lines throughout the 1940s and the early 1950s. A variety of factors no doubt accounted for the scarcity of empirical studies—especially of those in which power was a central concern. A tangible obstacle was the lack of systematic research methods.[14] Herbert Kaufman and Victor Jones's reference to the "elusiveness" of power and the seeming inability to measure it suggests the state of empirical research in this period. "There is an elusiveness about power. . . . We can tell whether one person or group is more powerful than

---

[10] *Human Society* (New York: The Macmillan Company, Publishers, 1949), p. 95. While many functionalists apparently make use of Weber's treatment of power and stratification, their emphasis on the prestige and status determinants of power and generally their conception that power follows from status suggest that their views are not in keeping with Weber's framework.

[11] *Social Class in American Sociology* (New York: McGraw-Hill Book Company, 1963), p. 250.

[12] Nelson W. Polsby, *Community Power and Political Theory* (New Haven, Conn.: Yale University Press, 1963), Chap. 1.

[13] Mills, for instance, pursued issues of power during this period. C. Wright Mills, *The New Men of Power* (New York: Harcourt, Brace & World, Inc., 1948); *White Collar* (Fair Lawn, N.J.: Oxford University Press, Inc., 1951).

[14] The scarcity of empirical studies may also have been part of the relative inattention generally to power during a period when the status, or prestige, dimension was the major concern (as it perhaps still is) of students of stratification.

another, yet we cannot measure power. It is as abstract as time yet as real as a firing squad."[15]

THE REPUTATIONAL APPROACH

A major innovation in sociological investigations of power came with the appearance in 1953 of Floyd Hunter's *Community Power Structure*.[16] Most of the many studies since that time have been strongly shaped by Hunter's work in the sense of being either replications or modifications of his research or of presenting alternatives to his procedures.[17] To many researchers, especially in the 1950s, Hunter's techniques represented a major step toward rigorous and objective analyses of the phenomenon of power.

Hunter based his conclusions about the power structure of Regional City (Atlanta, Georgia) upon field investigations of several years' duration. The first 18 months were spent acquiring background information on Regional City and perfecting methods of research via a pilot study elsewhere. The techniques developed in this study and employed by Hunter in Regional City constitute the reputational method.

Hunter used this method to identify power holders at various levels. His first step was to construct preliminary lists of leaders in community affairs from organizations such as the Community Council, the Chamber of Commerce, and the League of Women Voters, and from newspaper editors and various civic leaders. He then asked a panel of judges (mainly members of the business, political, and social circles he had chosen) to determine leadership rank. Through this process he designated forty persons as the top power holders among the more than 175 leaders named in the initial roster. The major part of the field investigation consisted of interviews with most of these men. Key questions elicited information on the degree of interaction of the respondents with each other and on the nature of their relationships. To discover the influentials at the apex of Regional City's power structure those interviewed were also asked to select five top leaders from

---

15 "The Mystery of Power," *Public Administration Review*, 14 (Summer 1954), 205.

16 *Op. cit.*

17 The following studies are only a few of the numerous empirical investigations which have used Hunter's approach as a point of departure—either for support or for refutation: Robert E. Agger *et al., The Rulers and the Ruled* (New York: John Wiley & Sons, Inc., 1964); Charles M. Bonjean, "Community Leadership: A Case Study and Conceptual Refinement," *American Journal of Sociology*, 68 (May 1963), 672–81; A. Alexander Fanelli, "A Typology of Community Leadership Based on Influence and Interaction Within the Leader Subsystem," *Social Forces*, 34 (May 1956), 332–38; William A. Form and William V. D'Antonio, "Integration and Cleavage Among Community Influentials in Two Border Cities," *American Sociological Review*, 24 (December 1959), 804–14; M. Kent Jennings, *Community Influentials: The Elites of Atlanta* (Glencoe, Ill.: The Free Press, 1964); William Miller, "Industry and Community Power Structure," *American Sociological Review*, 23 (February 1958), 9–15; Harry Scoble, "Leadership Hierarchies and Political Issues in a New England Town," in *Community Political Systems*, ed. Morris Janowitz (Glencoe, Ill.: The Free Press, 1961).

the forty names provided and to indicate the basis for their selections. Respondents could add names of their own choice if the ones listed did not meet their criteria for top leaders.

Hunter's approach to the study of power is a variation of the method used by Warner and his students in their research on community social-class systems. In those studies, as in Hunter's investigations of the power system of Regional City, the primary technique was the use of a panel of community judges. The personal knowledge, experiences, and general impressions of the judges provided the basic data for the class structure drawn by the investigators.

There are similarities in the reception generally accorded the reputational method in social-class research and that accorded its employment by Hunter. In each instance sociologists regarded the introduction of the approach as an important breakthrough and subsequently made it the object of much controversy. Indeed, several of the criticisms leveled at Hunter's techniques—for example, questions concerning the representativeness of panel members—are actually criticisms of the reputational approach in general. Hunter, his critics claim, not only chose his informants arbitrarily but also included a disproportionate number of businessmen.[18] Others inquire about the reliability of the judges' evaluations. As Raymond Wolfinger asks, "If people who are professionally involved in community decision-making cannot perceive accurately the distribution of political power, how can the rankings of less well-informed respondents be accepted . . . ?"[19] Any information about the structure of power in a community, these critics contend, is so heavily interwoven with folklore, misconceptions, and bias that separation of reality from fiction is impossible.

Closely related to these doubts is the more crucial charge that the reputational approach does not indicate *real* power but rather reputed *potential* for power. There is no simple correspondence between a reputation for possessing power and the overt use of power. In any event the reputational method provides no check on the translation of potential or inferred power into acts of power.[20] (This objection compares with the charge that Warner's reputational method never gets at objective classes but only at attitudes and beliefs, that is, the subjective impressions held by the panelists about what they feel to be the reality of social class.)

Additional criticisms, not related to the use of the reputational approach in social-class research, concern the way in which the reputational method predisposes the researcher toward the discovery of a monolithic power structure. Critics voicing this objection claim that elitist assumptions are built into the rationale of the reputational method (e.g., the assumption of a direct relationship between high socioeconomic status and power). Moreover, since influentials are

---

[18] Polsby, *op. cit.*, pp. 48–53; Kaufman and Jones, *op. cit.*

[19] "Reputation and Reality in the Study of 'Community Power,'" *American Sociological Review*, 25 (October 1960), 642.

[20] This charge is a central theme in critiques such as those by Polsby, *op. cit.*; Kaufman and Jones, *op. cit.*; Wolfinger, *op. cit.*; and Robert A. Dahl, "A Critique of the Ruling Elite Model," *American Political Science Review*, 52 (June 1958), 463–69.

used to rate influentials, critics hold that the procedures rest on circular reasoning.[21]

THE DECISIONAL APPROACH

Political scientists have been the most vociferous critics of the reputational method. Although they sometimes prefer the positional approach,[22] most use some variation of the method of decision analysis, or event analysis as it may be called.[23]

Advocates of the decisional approach claim it is the most realistic method for studying the overt use of power. It purports to give "more of the feel of precise, sociopolitical processes."[24] The focus is on those issues (past or pending) deemed important to the community by the investigator. He examines decisional processes in detail with reference both to the actions of specific individuals in a particular issue area and to the consequences of decision acts made and not made. The study of decisional behavior may consist of first-hand observations[25] or reconstructions based upon data from news media, speeches, formal releases and reports from organizations, and intensive interviews with informants, principally government officials.

The decisional approach is not without its critics.[26] At the procedural level a

---

21 Polsby, *op. cit.*, Chap. 1; Dahl, *op. cit.*

Several essays summarize and evaluate these and the aforementioned criticisms, together with additional points. For example, Thomas J. Anton, "Power Pluralism and Local Politics," *Administrative Science Quarterly*, 7 (March 1963), 425–57; Charles Bonjean and David M. Olson, "Community Leadership: Directions of Research," *Administrative Science Quarterly*, 9 (December 1964), 278–300; M. Herbert Danzger, "Community Power Structure: Problems and Continuities," *American Sociological Review*, 29 (October 1964), 707–17; William Spinrad, "Power in Local Communities," *Social Problems*, 12 (Winter 1965), 335–56.

There is no dearth of rebuttal of these criticisms of the reputational approach. See, for example, Anton, *op. cit.*; William V. D'Antonio and William H. Form, *Influentials in Two Border Cities* (South Bend, Ind.: University of Notre Dame Press, 1965), especially pp. 235–38; William Gamson, "Reputation and Resources in Community Politics," *American Sociological Review*, 72 (September 1966), 121–31.

22 The positional approach (often subsumed in the decisional method) assumes that occupants of high position in informal and formal organizations are key figures in decision-making and designates them as community leaders.

23 John Walton, "Discipline, Method, and Community Power: A Note on the Sociology of Knowledge," *American Sociological Review*, 31 (October 1966), 684–89.

24 Spinrad, *op. cit.*, p. 338.

25 Researchers may make such observations, for example, by attending public and unofficial meetings of organizations or by being present in an official's office while he is discussing his daily affairs. Dahl, a political scientist, based many of his conclusions upon an assistant's internship in the offices of the development administrator and the mayor of New Haven, Conn. Robert A. Dahl, *Who Governs?: Democracy and Power in an American City* (New Haven, Conn.: Yale University Press, 1961), pp. 335–36.

26 The following and additional criticisms are discussed in Anton, *op. cit.*; Bonjean and Olson, *op. cit.*; Spinrad, *op. cit.*, p. 343; William V. D'Antonio *et al.*, "Further Notes on

common objection is to the loose description of the techniques employed. Researchers rarely spell out operational steps, even to the modest degree found in accounts of the reputational method. Needless to say, the absence of such guidelines creates problems in replicability. And the criteria for the selection of issues usually are not explicit beyond the broad stipulation that they be important or significant for the community. This deficiency has prompted questions as to the representativeness of the issues selected, not only in terms of adequate samples of community issues but also with respect to their saliency for the small set of persons who control decision-making.

A more fundamental charge leveled at the decisional approach revolves around the general problem of where and what is reality. Those using this approach claim that the reputational method indicates the shadow rather than the substance of power and that the reality of power can best be uncovered by observing real acts of power. However, the equation of overt decisional acts by persons in recognized leadership roles with real power overlooks processes of covert decision-making.[27] In its own way this equation is a kind of subjectivism, comparable to the subjectivism of community judges in the choice of power holders.

RECENT TRENDS IN METHODOLOGY

The controversy over the respective merits of the reputational and decisional approaches is becoming an academic issue in view of the growing tendency to use both methods of investigation, sometimes in combination with additional procedures.[28] Much of the initial motivation for using a combination of techniques stemmed from a desire to show the validity or superiority of the researcher's own preferred approach. More recent attention to ends rather than means has led to methods that complement one another. The result is a more adequate picture of community power.

A second important trend in recent analyses of community power is the use of comparative research designs. A major criticism of most studies—regardless of techniques and concepts employed—is their confinement to a single community. While such studies usually add to substantive knowledge and refinement of methodology, they place serious constraints on the ability to generalize the findings. Comparative studies of communities having common features as well as dif-

---

the Study of Community Power," *American Sociological Review*, 27 (December 1962), 851–54; Linton C. Freeman *et al.*, "Locating Leaders in Local Communities: A Comparison of Some Alternative Approaches," *American Sociological Review*, 28 (October 1963), pp. 791–98.

[27] Bonjean and Olson, *op. cit.*, p. 287; Robert Prethus, *Men at the Top* (Fair Lawn, N.J.: Oxford University Press, Inc., 1964), p. 423.

[28] See, for example, D'Antonio and Form, *op. cit.*; Bonjean, *op. cit.*; Jennings, *op. cit.*; Presthus, *op. cit.*; Agger *et al.*, *op. cit.*

ferences make it possible to understand the variables which condition community power structures.[29]

The three selections below deal primarily with methodological problems of research in community power.[30] Charles Bonjean's essay describes ways of coping with some of the deficiencies of the reputational approach in order to improve its validity. His suggestions entail supplementing the standard method with "interaction data" and using the concept of leader in a more sophisticated way.[31]

The contributions by Robert Presthus and by Linton Freeman *et al.* appraise the consequences of using alternative methods for studying community power. Presthus' *Men At The Top* is one of the relatively few studies of community power employing a combination of methods within a comparative research design. In the following excerpt from this work Presthus describes his use of the decisional and reputational methods in the communities he studied and explains how these two techniques complement each other to form a more adequate methodology.

The research by Freeman *et al.* assesses the degree to which four methods of study agree or disagree in locating community leaders. Their results indicate that different types of leaders are disclosed by different procedures, pointing again to complexities in the concepts of leadership and community power and also to the undesirability of inflexible adherence to a single technique.

---

29 Walton, *op. cit.*, p. 689. Some examples of comparative studies are Delbert C. Miller, "Industry and Community Power Structure: A Comparative Study of an American and English City," *American Sociological Review*, 23 (February 1958), 9–15; Presthus, *op. cit.*; Agger *et al.*, *op. cit.*; D'Antonio and Form, *op. cit.* The last-named study employed a research design with a longitudinal as well as a comparative approach. This longitudinal dimension—also a most important feature for the development of community-power research—is part of the research framework employed by Jennings, *op. cit.*

30 Empirical findings are reported in two of the three papers reproduced in this chapter, but the main concern is with methodological issues.

31 Note should be taken of a study replicating Bonjean's research methods (a rarity in sociological research generally, not to mention the field of community power). Delbert C. Miller and James L. Dirksen, "The Identification of Visible, Concealed, and Symbolic Leaders in a Small Indiana City: A Replication of the Bonjean-Noland Study of Burlington, North Carolina," *Social Forces*, 43 (May 1965), 548–55.

COMMUNITY LEADERSHIP: A CASE STUDY AND CONCEPTUAL REFINEMENT*[1]

Charles M. Bonjean

University of Texas

The phenomenon of power-leadership decision-making at the community level has received a great deal of attention from both sociologists and political scientists during the past decade.[2]

Many of these investigations, especially those conducted by sociologists, have been criticized on the grounds that the method of investigation used—the reputational approach—is inadequate for several reasons.[3] (1) The approach

* Reprinted from "Community Leadership: A Case Study and Conceptual Refinement," *American Journal of Sociology*, by Charles M. Bonjean by permission of The University of Chicago Press. Copyright 1963 by The University of Chicago Press.

[1] This investigation involves one facet of community affairs in the Piedmont Industrial Crescent being studied by the Institute for Research in Social Science of the University of North Carolina under a grant by the Ford Foundation. The leadership studies are under the direction of E. William Noland, who suggested a number of revisions and modifications of this investigation. Revisions and useful suggestions were also made by Richard L. Simpson and Ernest Q. Campbell of the University of North Carolina.

[2] Including Floyd Hunter, *Community Power Structure: A Study of Decision Makers* (Chapel Hill, N.C.: University of North Carolina Press, 1953); Roland J. Pellegrin and Charles H. Coates, "Absentee-Owned Corporations and Community Power Structure," *American Journal of Sociology*, LXI (March 1956), 413–19; Charles Freeman and Selz C. Mayo, "Decision Makers in Rural Community Action," *Social Forces*, XXXV (May 1957), 319–22; Robert O. Schulze, "The Role of Economic Dominants in Community Power Structure," *American Sociological Review*, XXIII (February 1958), 3–9; Delbert C. Miller, "Industry and Community Power Structures: A Comparative Study of an American and an English City," *American Sociological Review*, XXIII (February 1958), 9–15; Ernest A. T. Barth and Stuart D. Johnson, "Community Power and a Typology of Social Issues," *Social Forces*, XXXVIII (October

1959), 29–32; Nelson W. Polsby, "Three Problems in the Analysis of Community Power," *American Sociological Review*, XXV (December 1959), 796–803; Orrin E. Klapp and L. Vincent Padgett, "Power Structure and Decision-Making in a Mexican Border City," *American Journal of Sociology*, LXV (January 1960), 400–406; Arthur J. Vidich and Joseph Bensman, *Small Town in Mass Society* (Garden City, N.Y.: Doubleday & Company, Inc., 1960); Robert A. Dahl, *Who Governs? Democracy and Power in an American City* (New Haven, Conn.: Yale University Press, 1961); and Benjamin Walter, "Political Decision Making in Arcadia," in *Urban Growth Dynamics*, eds. F. Stuart Chapin, Jr., and Shirley F. Weiss (New York: John Wiley & Sons, Inc., 1962).

[3] By reputational approach, of course, is meant asking certain members of the community under investigation to list and rank the most powerful and influential leaders in the community. The approach has also been termed the "snowball technique" since one informant's nominees become the next informants. Critics of this technique include Robert A. Dahl, "A Critique of the Ruling Elite Model," *American Political Science Review*, LII (June 1958), 463–69; Herbert Kaufman and Victor Jones, "The Mystery of Power," *Public Administration Review*, XIV (Summer 1954), 205–12; Nelson W. Polsby, "The Sociology of Community Power: A Reassessment," *Social Forces*, XXXVII (March 1959), 232–36; Raymond E. Wolfinger, "Reputation and Reality in the Study of Community Power," *American*

enables the investigator to find a mono-lithic power structure when, in fact, such a structure may not exist in the community. (2) Assuming there is a monolithic structure, this approach may lead to premature closure (not includ-ing all the leaders) or may lead to the inclusion of nonleaders. The problem is the cutoff point in the final list of nomi-nees. (3) If the reputational approach is used, we must take into consideration inaccuracies in respondent perceptions Private citizens, it is claimed, may be unreliable sources of information. (4) Interviewer and respondent may not agree on what is meant by "power." Certain questions used may not mean the same thing to both interviewer and respondent or there may be no con-sensus in regard to the meaning of the question among respondents.

The purpose of this investigation is to attempt to indicate how these short-comings may be overcome through an extension of method and a refinement of concepts. The collection of addi-tional data—sociometric and other—on a sample of community leaders so desig-nated by the reputational approach makes it possible to probe group char-acteristics and internal differentiations of the sample. Analysis of the data indi-cates that reputational leaders are, in fact, meaningful groups and not arti-facts of the operational measures in at least one community—Burlington, N.C. Because of the heuristic nature of this investigation, no specific hypotheses will be tested, but one general hypothe-sis of an exploratory nature will be entertained: A conceptual refinement of the term "community leader" based on the method of investigation itself will lead to greater agreement among investigators, will satisfy to some degree the basic criticisms listed above, and may serve as a useful basis for comparative studies in the future.

THE COMMUNITY

Burlington, located in north-central North Carolina, has a population of ap-proximately 33,000 (1960) and a subur-ban population of about 15,000 (1958 est.) Approximately 125,000 live in the city's trade area, which extends 8 miles to the west and 20 miles in all other directions. The population of the city increased slightly more than 33 per cent between 1950 and 1960, an increase due primarily to industrial expansion and new industries. Eighty-eight per•cent of the population is native-born white, and 11.4 per cent is Negro (1960).

Primarily an industrial community, Burlington ranks sixth in the nation in hosiery production and leads the South in the number of hosiery plants. Of the city's seventy-eight industrial establish-ments, thirty are hosiery mills and fif-teen others produce textile products. Among the 3,073 counties in the United States, Almance, of which Burlington is the largest city, ranks 216th in the number of manufacturing plants and 203rd in the number of industrial wage earners—well in the top 10 per cent on both items. A total of 19,000 persons are employed in Burlington's indus-tries.[4]

The city operates under the mayor-council type of government.

METHOD OF INVESTIGATION

The empirical objectives of the in-vestigation have already been stated: to isolate a group of community leaders

Sociological Review, XXV (October 1960), 636–44; and a number of the investigations listed in note 2.

[4] *Hill's Burlington and Graham City Directory* (Richmond, Va.: Hill Directory, Inc., 1958), pp. i–xiii.

according to standard methodology and to further delimit this group on the basis of other measures. A two-step reputational analysis supplemented with sociometric and interaction data was used to attempt to fulfil these objectives.

The executive secretary of an established community association was asked: "Who are the community leaders who really get things done around here?"[5] He was asked to rank up to twenty leaders in order of overall influence and to specify those leaders he had worked with as well as the areas of participation.[6] Using his list as a starting point, interviewers asked each individual named by him to do the same. This was continued until new lists yielded many more duplications than nominations. After forty-five interviews it was evident that there was relatively high agreement in regard to sixteen community leaders and little agreement on the remaining 100 nominations. Additional interviews would probably have had the same results—more nominations for the sixteen top leaders and more names to add to the remaining list of 100. According to Moreno, this assumption has general validity and may be termed the "sociodynamic effect":

It might be anticipated that increasing the chance probability of being chosen by allowing more choices within the same size population and thus lessening the chance probability to remain un-

chosen will gradually bring the number of unchosen to a vanishing point and likewise reduce more and more the number of comparatively little chosen.

However, in actuality, this does not take place. . . . The further choices allowed go more frequently to the already highly chosen and not proportionately more to those who are unchosen or who have few choices. The quantity of isolates and little chosen comes finally to a standstill, whereas the volume of choices continues to increase for those at the upper end of the range.

The sociodynamic effect apparently has general validity. It is found in some degree in all social aggregates.[7]

Thirty-eight of the forty-five respondents became informants by naming individuals and ranking them. Their 116 nominations were tabulated and weighted—a weight of 20 assigned to each first-place choice, 19 to a second-place choice, and so on down to 1 for a twentieth-place choice. The total leadership score assigned to each of the 116 individuals mentioned consists merely of the sum of the weighted choices.

Leadership scores ranged from 350.5 for Neal Allen, the top leader in the community, to 1 for Mrs. Robert Cain, who received one twentieth-place vote.[8] Fourteen of the 116 persons mentioned received scores of more than 100, and two received scores between 90 and 100. No other person received a total leadership score higher than 70, and most were far below this score.[9] Thus, be-

---

[5] This was but one question included in a standardized interview schedule consisting of seventy-eight questions (both poll type and open end) and requiring from 45 minutes to 4 hours to complete.

[6] Thirty specific activities were listed. They could be grouped into seven general participation areas: economic, welfare, livability, educational, political, philanthropic, and desegregational.

[7] J. L. Moreno *et. al., The Sociometry Reader* (Glencoe, Ill.: Free Press, 1960), p. 36.

[8] "Neal Allen" and "Mrs. Robert Cain" are pseudonyms as are the names and affiliations of the other leaders and nonleaders specifically referred to in this investigation.

[9] It is impossible to include the full data here because of space limitations. The investigator will provide mimeographed copies

TABLE 1. RANKING OF SIXTEEN LEADERS BY THEMSELVES
AND BY NONLEADERS

Leader	Total Sample ($N = 38$)	Leaders ($N = 10$)	Nonleaders ($N = 28$)	Difference	Leader Type*
Neal Allen	1	1	2	— 1	v
James Barton	2	2	3.5	— 1.5	v
George Welles	3	10	1	9	s
Mike Reynolds	4	3	5	— 2	v
Tom White	5	9	6	3	v
R. V. Daniels	6	4	11	— 7	c
Terry Jones	7	13	7	6	s
Percy Roberts	8	17	3.5	13.5	s
Charles Martin	9	11	12	— 1	v
Thomas Mintler	10	14	9.5	4.5	s
A. G. Curtis	11	7	13	— 6	c
Richard Murphy	12	16	8	8	s
Harold Smith	13	5	14	— 9	c
Harold B. Green	14	6	15	— 9	c
LeRoy Barton	15	8	16	— 8	c
Harvey Harris	16	15	9.5	5.5	s
Dan Morley	—	12	17	— 5	c

*Leader types: v, visible; s, symbolic; c, concealed.

cause of the high agreement regarding the selection of the first sixteen as leaders and because of the lack of consensus in regard to the remainder of the sample, it was assumed that, *if* a power elite existed in Burlington, these sixteen individuals would be the basic element of its membership.

Most power-structure studies stop here in regard to the reputational approach. (Two exceptions, studies conducted by Robert O. Schulze and A. Alexander Fanelli, will be discussed briefly below.) But using the same data and analyzing them from a different standpoint may yield additional valuable information. Thus a second step in the data analysis is incorporated. In Burlington, of the forty-five informants,

twelve were in the leader category (members of the top sixteen),[10] the other thirty-three were not. The second analysis utilizes only the choices and rankings of ten of the twelve "leaders."[11] When this is done, a new picture emerges—the "power elite" has gained new members (because of high agreement among these twelve but no or few of additional data or will answer more specific questions on request.

[10] Of the sixteen top leaders in Burlington, only twelve were interviewed. One died shortly after the study had started, one was not in the city during the time of the study, and, although the other two were interviewed, they asked to keep the schedule in order to complete some "difficult" questions and did not return it.

[11] Of the twelve leaders interviewed, two refused to rank leaders and to indicate those they interacted with. Thus, sociometric choices and actual information regarding interaction are available for ten of the sixteen leaders.

nominations from the remainder of the informants) and assigns much less power to other nominees (because of no or few choices from the elite). This modification of the reputational approach does not incorporate an arbitrary cutoff point, and, at the same time, it reduces the likelihood of inaccuracies in respondent perception (in that the "judges" are determined by the first analysis). The wording of the question and the additional requirement for judges to list the nominees' spheres of influence seem to overcome the problem of ambiguity. The possibility of ambiguity and the desirability of judges is indicated by comparing leader and nonleader rankings (Table 1). That there is little agreement between the two sets of rankings is supported statistically, as Spearman's rank correlation for the two groups is 0.012.

Two questions must be answered before further discussion. First, does this method imply an a priori assumption that a monolithic power structure does exist in the community? Second, have we really established a power elite?

In regard to the first question, it should be noted that this technique allows for disagreement as well as for agreement in regard to leadership choices. If there were no leadership elite in the community, we would expect little or no agreement in leadership selection. There is no reason to reject the assumption that the technique is able to indicate the absence of a power structure as well as its presence.

Obviously, all of Burlington's 48,000 residents (including suburbs) could not conceivably play leadership roles, strictly on the grounds of accepted role definition. When one starts cutting down a population of this size by factors of two for sex (excluding females), perhaps three for age bracket (excluding

those too old and those too young), X_1 for income sufficient to insure some leisure, X_2 for education, and so on, the result *is* a limited group. The size of this group is unknown in Burlington, but it is reasonable to assume that it is *at least* 116 (based on nominations alone). The 445 choices made by the 38 informants *could* have been distributed evenly, indicating a power vacuum. In fact, they were not. Of the 445 choices, 201 were directed to the top sixteen nominees ($X=12.6$); the other 224 were directed to the remaining 100 nominees ($\overline{X}=2.24$). Had there been the least possible agreement in leadership selection in regard to the leadership pool of 116, each nominee would have received almost four (actually 3.86) votes. Adopting 3.86 as the mean and 4.6 as the standard deviation (an estimate based on the range, which in this case is 22), an upper confidence limit of 4.97 (at the 99 per cent level) may be computed. In other words, we may assume that choices are no longer random if we are able to isolate a number of individuals, each receiving five or more choices. As a matter of fact, the number of choices assigned to the judges selected by the first step of the method ranges from six to twenty-two. No one in the remainder of the "leadership pool" has more than four choices and most have only one. An informal analysis of rankings (as opposed to sheer number of choices) seems to indicate, even more convincingly, that a power vacuum does not exist in Burlington.[12]

At least two validity checks may be

---

[12] These data were not subjected to the same sort of statistical analysis as described above because of time and cost limitations and because the first test was thought to be convincing enough to support the argument in question. The informal analysis was used merely as a quick check.

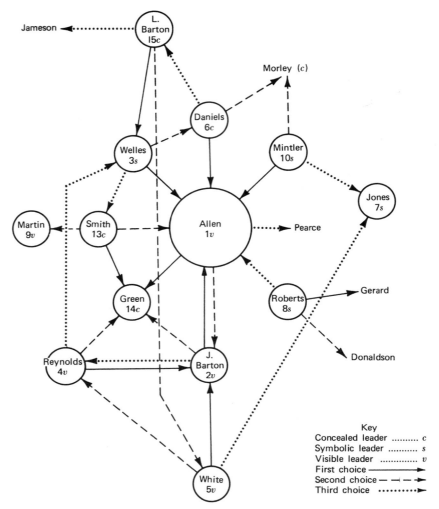

Fig. 1. Leadership Ranking by Ten Leaders. Uncircled Are Not Top Leaders.

employed to ascertain whether or not the technique actually has established a power elite.

First, if most top leaders also select one another as top leaders and, second, if, in fact, they actually indicate that they interact with one another, it seems reasonable to assume that a *group* has actually been discerned as opposed to a mere aggregate of individuals with similar characteristics.

By constructing a sociogram (Fig. 1) showing the first three leadership

choices of the ten top leaders completing this section of the interview schedule, an index of the degree to which these leaders form a group is available. Of the thirty possible choices (ten leaders times three choices each), twenty-four are within the elite designated by the entire sample. Thus, the *ratio of interest,* one aspect of group cohesiveness, is 0.80.[13] This statistic (the

13 For a discussion of the ratio of interest and other statistics of social con-

number of in-group choices divided by the total possible number of such choices) is meaningful only when compared with that of another group. The only group available for comparison at this point is the remainder of our sample of informants. Of their eighty-four possible choices, forty-five are directed to the top sixteen (ratio of interest= 0.53). Assuming the remainder of our informants do not form a group and are not a part of the elite group, we have a basis for comparison and consequently can test for statistical significance of differences between proportions. In this case, a *t*-test yields $P<0.001$.

A second validity check, "interaction," also indicates that Burlington's power elite resembles a group more than it does an aggregate. As was indicated above, after listing and ranking leaders, each informant was provided with a check list of thirty community activities (although not all were found to be salient in Burlington) and was asked to indicate those individuals he "worked with" on each of the thirty activities. Significant here is the fact that a number of interaction patterns could be noted that *were not* connected with formal memberships.[14] For example, a cross-tabulation of responses indicates that five of the ten leaders say they have worked with one another regarding "who gets elected to municipal office," yet none hold offices themselves nor do they hold formal positions in a political party. Eight of the power elite name one another in the area of attempting to attract new industries to the community. All in all, interaction patterns *within* the leadership elite are discernible in twenty-one of the possible community activities. In each case the patterns involve between three and eight of the ten interviewed leaders.

Thus, because the data indicate mutual choices between members of the power elite as well as interaction within the elite, most of the sixteen leaders uncovered by the reputational approach may be considered as a group rather than merely an aggregate. It should be noted, however, that four of the top sixteen leaders—ranks 8, 10, 11 and 12 (see Fig. 1)—received no first-, second-, or third-place choices within the power elite. It is apparent that their position in the leadership group is thus derived from one or both of two phenomena: Their leadership score was a consequence of rankings beyond three by members of the elite *or* their leadership score was a consequence of high ranking by nonleaders. Also, several other individuals, not originally identified as elite members, were given such choices. This brings us more directly to the second step in data analysis—an attempt to determine differentiations *within* the power elite.

---

figuration see Moreno *et. al., op. cit.,* pp. 19–51.

[14] This is not the first investigation conducted where interaction has been designated as a necessary "check." An "acquaintanceship scale" was used successfully by Schulze and described in a report published subsequent to the research described here (see Robert O. Schulze, "The Bifurcation of Power in a Satellite City," in *Community Political Systems,* ed. Morris Janowitz [Glencoe, Ill.: Free Press, 1961], p. 51).

TYPES OF LEADERS

Assuming that the sixteen persons uncovered by the first step in data analysis are the most qualified to perceive others of their kind, the next step should be to compare the leaders as perceived by one another with how they are perceived by that proportion of the sample not designated as part of the power elite. Such a comparison would yield three possible leadership types: (1) the leader who is assigned approximately the same amount of power by both other leaders and nonleaders, (2) the leader who is assigned more prestige by leaders than by nonleaders, (3) the leader who is assigned more prestige by nonleaders than by leaders.

Leaders of the first type will be termed *visible leaders* because they are playing roles in the community that are perceived and known by the community at large. Leaders of the second type will be termed *concealed leaders* because they have more influence within the leadership circle or power elite, and consequently in the community in general, than the community at large realizes. Leaders of the third type will be termed *symbolic leaders* because they probably do not wield so much influence in the community as the community at large thinks they do.

Looking at the comparison of leaders shown in Table 1, all three types may be distinguished. Arbitrarily setting a rank variation of 5 (true limits of 4.5 or greater) as the point where leaders are classified as concealed or symbolic rather than as visible, there are five visible leaders, six concealed leaders, and six symbolic leaders. Sixteen of the leaders, of course, were uncovered by the general reputational approach; but a seventeenth was located by the modification described here. Leader types are indicated on both the sociogram and Table 1 by the symbols *v* (visible), *c* (concealed), and *s* (symbolic).

For this differentiation to be meaningful, the next step is to determine whether or not there is a relationship between leader type and other variables. In attempting to locate differences between symbolic and concealed leaders, there are no patterns or trends in regard to age, type of business, num-

ber of employees, types of activities engaged in, memberships (including religion), or education.

There is, however, one basic difference betwen the two extreme types of leaders—symbolic and concealed. Four of the six symbolic leaders are members of prominent Burlington families—familes that have lived in the city for several generations, that are wealthy, and that have passed the family business on to the person listed as a leader. Murphy (12), before his death, was the top officer in a hosiery mill that had been in his family for three generations; Roberts (8) is the second-generation administrator of his family's hosiery mill; Jones (7) inherited his father's automobile dealership; and Harris (16) is the member of a family possessing all of the characteristics except the last (inheritance of family business). Only Welles (3) and Mintler (10) differ in this respect from the other symbolic leaders. Welles's symbolic placement may be explained by the fact that he is paid by the city businessmen for work in community affairs. Thus he occupies a position highly visible to the community in general but one of perhaps less importance in the sphere of policy formation and decision-making than in the actual execution of policy. Thus, this deviant case analysis seems to further validate the method proposed here. Only Mintler's placement as a symbolic leader is unexplainable. This may indicate a necessary change in method. The arbitrary rank variation set forth for classification as a concealed or symbolic leader was 5 (4.5 true limit). Mintler was a borderline case. The difference between leader and nonleader ranking was exactly 4.5. This may indicate that the arbitrary difference is set too low—perhaps, for example, the true limit should be raised to 5.

The concealed leaders differ markedly from the symbolic leaders. Only one of the six concealed leaders *owns* a large business or industry and this leader, Congressman Green, founded his businesses himself, rather than inheriting them. In other words, his wealth is at least a generation newer than is the wealth of most of the symbolic leaders. His concealed status may also be due to the fact that he is the local power structure's link with a larger, more influential power structure at the state or national level.[15] As such, perhaps he would be more closely connected to the elite personnel and consequently more visible to them at the community level than to the remainder of the sample, who perhaps have a more macroscopic conception of his role. It is interesting to note that Allen, the leader receiving the greatest number of choices and highest ranks, ranked Green first. The other five concealed leaders do not own businesses—two are professionals and three are the local administrators of subsidiaries of state or national corporations. Five of the concealed leaders spent their childhood or longer outside of Burlington and thus, compared with the symbolic-leader group, are relative newcomers. The outstanding observation is that none is from a traditionally prominent Burlington family. This suggests that nonleaders perhaps think more in terms of the status or class dimensions of stratification when asked to name community leaders, whereas leaders themselves are more apt to think in terms of the power dimension. It suggests further that nonleaders may not recognize changes in the leadership base or power elite but think instead that those that have always been powerful will probably continue to be so. In other words, individuals who have formerly ranked high on all three dimensions of social stratification—class, status, and power—may through time have lost, to some degree, one of these characteristics, but for several years a "halo effect" will operate to influence the general viewpoint. Schulze's Cibola findings lend some credulity to this hypothesis (economic dominants exerted sociopolitical power as well as economic power in the past but currently have relinquished the former in that community).[16]

Critics of stratification studies continually remind us of the necessity to distinguish between class and status.[17] Studies of the third major aspect of stratification—power—face the same problem. High status or class position may lead to the assumption by informants of high power positions. Thus it becomes necessary to differentiate between three different types of community leaders—class (economic) leaders, status (reputational) leaders, and true power leaders. The *hypothesized* relationship between the methodological distinction of visible, concealed, and symbolic leaders to class, status, and power leaders, as suggested by this

---

[15] See Floyd Hunter, *Top Leadership U.S.A.* (Chapel Hill, N.C.: University of North Carolina Press, 1959) for a discussion that supports this tentative hypothesis.

[16] Schulze, in Janowitz, *op. cit.*, pp. 40–41.

[17] Including Paul K. Hatt, "Stratification in the Mass Society," *American Sociological Review*, XV (April 1950), 216–22; Harold F. Kaufman, Otis Dudley Duncan, Neal Gross, and William H. Sewell, "Problems of Theory and Method in the Study of Social Stratification in Rural Society," *Rural Sociology*, XVIII (March 1953), 12–24; Kurt Mayer, "The Theory of Social Classes," *Harvard Educational Review*, XXIII (Summer 1953), 149–67; Gregory P. Stone and William H. Form, "Instabilities in Status: The Problem of Hierarchy in the Community Study of Status Arrangements," *American Sociological Review*, XVIII (April 1953), 149–62; and others.

TABLE 2. HYPOTHESIZED
RELATIONSHIP BETWEEN
METHODOLOGICAL TYPES AND
STRATIFICATION COMPONENTS

	Class	Status	Power
Symbolic	High	High	Low
Visible	High	High	High
Concealed	Low	Low*	High

* The concealed leader may rank high in
either class or status position but not
in both.

sensitizing exploratory investigation, is
summarized in Table 2. Two important relationships should be noted: (1)
The traditional reputational approach
uncovers symbolic leaders who are
actually not members of the power
elite. (2) It may *not* uncover actual
members of the power elite if these
members rank low in either class or
status.[18]

Thus, a second step needs to be
added to the reputational approach if
its use is to be continued in this type of
study. The second step, of course, is the
one that has been outlined here—the
comparison of rankings by leaders and
nonleaders and the classification of
leaders into three types based on rank
differences. This method itself is a useful heuristic device at the single case-
study level of investigation. When

[18] A. Alexander Fanelli ("A Typology
of Community Leadership Based on Influence Within the Leader Subsystem," *Social Forces*, XXXIV [May 1956], 332–38)
sets forth a method that enables the investigator to distinguish between the symbolic and visible leaders (he calls them
prestige influentials and active influentials)
but that ignores the possibility of concealed
leaders. Schulze's distinction between economic dominants and public leaders (in
Janowitz, *op. cit.*, pp. 19–80) has the same
shortcoming, but obviously the economic
public leader distinction has other merits
and is thus not so comparable to the method
being discussed as is the Fanelli distinction.

power studies reach the comparative
level (examining two or more leadership
structures simultaneously), it should be
even more useful as it is one means of
assessing one of the most controversial
and central characteristics of such structures—their visibility. Are leaders and
leadership behavior overt or covert?
Furthermore, is this characteristic, the
structure's visibility, related to community attributes?

The first question may be answered
in regard to the case at hand. The second answer must be delayed until a
uniform methodological approach is
applied to the study of other communities. In Burlington, the leadership
structure is partly visible and partly
concealed. The structure's "star," Neal
Allen, is visible. Although it is a subjective impression, it seems that one
factor coinciding with Allen's number
one rank in the community may be that
he is a coordinator of community affairs. In other words, because so many
of the other top leaders, each with his
own specialized community interests,
select Allen as the top leader, his function may be that of assigning priority
to various projects (some visible and
some concealed) and attempting to in-
tegrate and interrelate them. Supporting evidence is that he is a member of
all important civic organizations but
holds formal offices in none of them.
Informants furthermore remarked, for
example, "He really isn't active himself
as far as *doing* things goes, but he certainly has more influence than anyone
else in town." On the other hand, most
of the other top leaders (both visible
and concealed) direct their activities
toward only one or two institutional
spheres of the community—usually economic plus one other. Other than Allen,
only two leaders, Welles (3) and Rey-
nolds (4), are active in more than two
institutional areas of participation. In

summary, Burlington's leadership structure may be seen as a network of overlapping subgroups, some visible and some concealed, coordinated by one central visible figure. This structure is not too unlike the smaller and simpler power structure described by Arthur J. Vidich and Joseph Bensman in Springdale and is similar to the structure described by Schulze in Cibola—three groups of dominants linked by two individuals occupying "dual statuses."[19]

CONCLUSION

Adding a second step in data analysis, interaction checks, and statistics of social configuration to the traditional reputational approach used in the study of community power-leadership decision-making and distinguishing between three types of leaders (1) takes account of and, to varying degrees, answers the criticisms of the traditional reputational approach, (2) serves as a heuristic device leading to more penetrating modes of analysis in itself, (3) emphasizes that structural characteristic —visibility—that has been a major source of disagreement and discussion, and (4) suggests interrelationships between the concepts "class," "status," and "power" that may later contribute to a more general theory of stratification.

The fact that all generalizations discussed above are based on, and derived from, only one case study obviously requires cautious interpretation. They are offered here only as material for hypotheses—hypotheses to be tested by this investigator in the near future in other communities and to be modified, improved, or rejected by other interested investigators.

[19] Vidich and Bensman, *op. cit.*, pp. 110–230, and Schulze, in Janowitz, *op. cit.*, p. 52.

IDENTIFYING THE COMMUNITY POWER STRUCTURE*

Robert Presthus

Cornell University

THE DECISIONAL METHOD

Essentially, three discrete methods of measuring community power have been used in the research, each of which has certain advantages and disadvantages.[1]

There have been firstly attempts to identify individuals who have a *potential* for power because of their statuses in community organizations.[2] Other re-

* From *Men at the Top: A Study in Community Power* by Robert Presthus. Copyright © 1964 by Robert V. Presthus. Reprinted by permission of Oxford University Press, Inc.

[1] These methods are discussed by W. H. Form and D. Miller, *Industry, Labor and Community* (New York: Harper & Row, Publishers, 1960), pp. 517–33.

[2] Examples include R. J. Pellegrin and C. H. Coates, "Absentee Ownership and Community Power Structure"; R. O. Schulze and L. U. Blumberg, "The Determination of Local Power Elites," *American Journal of*

searchers have focused on individuals who have a reputation for power and influence.[3] And finally, the roles played by different individuals and organizations in selected community decisions have been used as the basis for identifying power.[4] Power in Edgewood and Riverview was determined using a combination of the second and third methods.

To measure overt power, five important decisions were selected in each community and active participation in one or more of these became the basic criterion of individual power. Insofar as the decisions were concerned, the criteria of "importance" included the sum of money involved in the decision; the number of people affected by the decision, i.e., whether it engaged the attention and interest of most citizens or it was germane to only a segment of the community; and the need to obtain a roughly "representative" and comparable panel of decisions.[5] After initial

interviews which identified a number of recent community issues, we selected a panel of decisions that best met these criteria. In the end, we were confident that all the decisions were in fact "important," partly because the number of decisions involving community-wide interests and expenditures of from \$100,-000 to \$1,000,000 was so few that there was a virtual consensus about them. A survey of local newspapers indicated that our panel included almost all the important decisions made by the communities during the last decade. The five decisions in Edgewood included a new school building program; a flood-control project; a new industry; a new hospital building program; and a new community center. All but the last of these also occurred in Riverview, whose unique issue was the construction of a public-housing project.

Our conception of a "decision" requires comment. Obviously, any important decision has several dimensions. Each is typically composed of a number of *stages*, some of which are relatively more crucial than others. Different individuals may participate at various stages as the strategic and skill requirements of the decision evolve. Making a theoretical distinction between the *initiation* and the *implementation* of the various decisions, we assumed that the most critical of these stages was the *initial*, to-do or not-to-do stage. For example, the action of one or a few prestigeful men in lending their names and their support to a project is usually a critical element in this "take-off" stage. Once this commitment has been secured, participation broadens to include the "legmen" and the activists required to carry out the decision. We found that this

---

Sociology, 63 (November 1957), 290–96; and C. Wright Mills, *The Power Elite* (Fair Lawn, N.J.: Oxford University Press, Inc., 1956).

[3] For example, Floyd Hunter, *Community Power Structure* (Chapel Hill, N.C.: University of North Carolina Press, 1953); and A. Fanelli, "A Typology of Community Leadership Based on Influence and Interaction Within the Leadership Subsystem," *Social Forces,* 34 (May 1956), 332–38.

[4] For example, Robert Dahl, *Who Governs?* (New Haven, Conn.: Yale University Press, 1961); Linton Freeman *et al., Local Community Leadership* (Syracuse, N.Y.: Syracuse University Press, 1960); and C. Banfield, *Political Influence* (Glencoe, Ill.: Free Press, 1961).

[5] Strictly speaking, the ten decisions are not "representative" of all decisions made in the two communities during the recent past. They are too important to occur very frequently and consequently are unusually salient and visible. For these very reasons, however, they are most likely to evoke the

interest and participation of the most powerful members of the community.

process characterized almost every decision in both communities. A nice example is seen in the comments of a prominent Edgewood influential who, in explaining his corporation's contribution to a community hospital fund drive, said, "We made an early contribution at a level [$50,000] which would avoid a situation where other people might be inclined to give less than they should." Such a commitment was secured during the initial stage of this particular decision and was a necessary step in the decision to launch the fund drive. Here, an analogy with the human reproduction process seems useful: We focused mainly on the act of conception and were somewhat less concerned with the period of gestation. Our "decision-makers," however, include those who were directly active in either stage, including those in opposition. . . . The "veto power" is built into our criteria of the relative power exercised by leaders.

Participation and power were determined mainly by an individual's activity in one or more of these decisions. The following criteria were used to define "participants" in the ten decisions and hence to determine who had power in terms of its *overt* use.[6]

6 Some community researchers have included *formal membership* on boards, councils, and committees as a criterion of "participation" and power. Although we initially planned to do the same, it soon became apparent that this criterion lacks discriminatory power, in the sense that several members of such boards did not play an active role in some of the decisions for which their boards were nominally responsible nor were they nominated by participants as having been active. Although many decision-makers are in fact members of such boards or committees, to have defined *all* their members as "powerful" would have been unwarranted. This procedure was used by Dahl in establishing leadership "pools," i.e., membership was based upon formal

(1) Those who (a) were named as being "active participants" or "opponents" in a decision by others who were themselves active participants in response to the question, "Could you give me the names of several other people in the community whom you know of first-hand who also participated in (or were actively opposed to) the———decision?" and (b) nominated *themselves* as being active participants or opponents.

(2) Those who were nominated as having been "active participants" by at least three other individuals selected in terms of (1) above, *whether or not* they also nominated themselves.

A "decision-maker," in effect, was an individual nominated by another active participant as having been active in a given decision and who, when interviewed, also nominated himself as an active participant. Alternatively, he could have been nominated by three or more other participants, whether or not he nominated himself. Each individual so nominated was interviewed and asked for additional nominations. Initially, a tentative list of individuals who were active in each decision was prepared, based upon an analysis of newspaper accounts of each decision and preliminary discussion with such local figures as the mayor and the director of the Chamber of Commerce. Each individual was then interviewed and asked

office rather than upon demonstrated activity. Unfortunately, this useful preliminary classification was subsequently used as the basis of an attempt to demonstrate the limited *power* of New Haven's social and economic "notables," despite the fact that the "pools" themselves were initially based on essentially "reputational" rather than upon "decisional" criteria. See Thomas J. Anton, "Rejoinder," *Administrative Science Quarterly*, 8 (September 1963), 260–61.

to name the decisions in which he had played an "active" role. Specific questions asked to ascertain the timing and extent of his participation included the following: *How and when did you become aware of this problem? In what specific ways did you participate?* Criteria of participation included active membership on a committee selected to handle the problem; contacting others on behalf of (or against) the proposed decision; speaking before interested groups about the decision; and contributing funds to publicize or otherwise support (or defeat) the proposed decision. Respondents were also asked to indicate how they became aware of the decision, how it evolved, and how they evaluated the outcome. This helped us specify the time, extent, and weight of their involvement.

All interviews with those nominated as "decision-makers," as well as those with our sample of organizational leaders, were carried out by the author and his colleague, Vaughn Blankenship. The interviews took place either in the respondent's office or in our hotel rooms. Each interview with those nominated as decision-makers lasted from one-and-one-half to three hours. A structured interview schedule was used in each case. . . . After a brief explanation of the objectives of the study and a guarantee of confidence as to answers, the respondent was handed five cards, each listing one of the five decisions. He was then asked to read through the cards and indicate which decisions he had played an "active" part in. Often, we were asked to define "active," but in most cases individuals were able to specify the character of their participation without difficulty. We gradually became so well versed in the background and evolution of each decision that we felt confident in our ability to judge accurately the extent of the

respondent's participation. We did not, however, determine participation on this basis.

Each participant was asked to name "several" individuals who had played an active role in the decision. Every effort was made to avoid prompting or any reaction to such nominations. Finally, each respondent was asked to name the two or three persons who, in his opinion, were "most influential" in determining the outcome of the decision. He was then asked to specify exactly why he attributed so central a role to these nominees. Every individual nominated as having played an active part in the decision was interviewed to determine his role in the decision. In this way we cross-checked participation and secured data which helped us differentiate *relative* degrees of participation and influence in each decision. We soon found that there was a virtual consensus as to those who had been actively involved in the various decisions, and within a brief period no new names were forthcoming. When these lists were later checked against newspaper accounts of the decisions and other documents, no new names that had not appeared in the initial interviews were found.

THE REPUTATIONAL METHOD

In order to check overt power as measured above with *potential* power, we asked the following question: "Suppose a major project were before the community, one that required decision by a group of leaders whom nearly everyone would accept. Which persons would you choose to make up this group—regardless of whether or not you know them personally?" This is the "reputational" question used by Hunter and also by Schulze to determine power by reputation in his study of

Cibola, a midwestern industrial city of 20,000.[7] Our decision to identify leaders in Edgewood and Riverview by both the reputational and the decisional methods is in line with experiences which "strongly suggest the advisability of studying a community's power structure from at least two methodological perspectives. . . ."[8] Every individual nominated as an "influential" was interviewed until, finally, we reached the point where no new names were being suggested. As always, a cutoff point had to be established: For an individual to be included in the "influential" category, it was decided that he must receive at least 20 per cent of the total nominations.

In the context of the criticism that Hunter's reputational method measured only potential power, rather than its overt use, it is noteworthy that Schulze found considerable difference between power measured by reputation and that measured by *formal position*. However, he found a virtual consensus as to those in "the uppermost range of community power" among three panels of judges representing the heads of voluntary associations, public leaders, and economic dominants. Our two methods similarly enabled us to compare potential with overt power, as well as to throw some light on methods used earlier. By comparing the extent of the overlap among "decision-makers" (i.e., the extent to which each leader was active in two or more decisions), as well as the degree of consensus about "influentials," we were able to make judgments about the nature of the power structure in each community. As will be shown later, extensive (and in some cases extreme) differences were found between power measured by the two methods. More-

over, as the evidence came in, we were obliged to modify our initial perspective about their relative utility and precision.

RESOLVING THE METHODOLOGICAL ISSUE

Initially, we had assumed that the decisional method would prove to be superior to the reputational in identifying "real" community power. On the surface, it seemed highly probable that the more behaviorally oriented method would provide more accurate evidence of participation and would help solve the vexing problem of the difference between potential and overt power. The severe criticisms of Hunter's use of the reputational method by fellow political scientists also contributed to this perspective, as did my own intellectual revolt against a traditional political science education in which normative and objective analyses were often uncritically intermixed. In sum, we were conditioned to assume that the decisional method would provide a bench mark against which the reputational evidence could be checked to determine, in effect, how close it came to the revealed truth about the distribution of community power.

An analysis of all the evidence led (not without some resistance) to a reformulation of this initial perspective. *We decided that the two methods were better conceived as mutually supportive means of ascertaining power.* In Vidich and Bensman's terms, an initial perspective was "exhausted" and modified once it no longer seemed able by itself to interpret the empirical data.[9] Each method, in effect, became

---

[7] Schulze and Blumberg, *op. cit.*

[8] *Ibid.*, p. 296.

[9] J. Bensman and A. Vidich, "Social Theory in Field Research," *American Journal of Sociology*, 45 (May 1960), 577–84.

a foil against which the evidence provided by the other could be tested and modified. It soon became clear that the reputational method had a great deal to contribute in refining the somewhat gross power ascriptions provided by the decisional technique. A particularly disturbing tendency of the latter (shared by the formal-board-membership criterion) was to assign high power ranks to individuals largely on the basis of merely formal or ministerial participation in several decisions. In the case of one political-legal official, for example, overtly active in four decisions, we were for some time unable to account for his failure to appear on the reputational list or to receive any other empirical power ascriptions. It finally became clear that his role had been limited to the formal legitimation of these decisions as a part of his official responsibilities. Both reputational and other evidence made clear that his power ranking was inflated by the decisional method. But this insight could only occur after our theoretical commitment to the decisional method had been undercut by other empirical findings and analyses. Obviously, some safeguards against this kind of skewing are built into the decisional method, e.g., by items which ask activists to nominate the "most influential" participants. Moreover, further refinement of the decisional instrument will no doubt reduce such analytical problems.

On the other hand, the reputational method also revealed certain shortcomings, including the tendency of respondents to mix personal preferences with objective judgments in attributing power to community leaders. A related and well-known tendency was to equate potential with overt power. The reputational method, as the term nicely suggests, tends to identify individuals who by typical, marketplace criteria "should" be powerful in any community. For many reasons, however, some of them do not choose to use their power, or they use it in ways that are not picked up by the researcher who is bound to this method. The decisional instrument provided a useful check against such inadequacies of the reputational method. In effect, by playing one method against the other and by abandoning our initial assumption concerning the superiority of one over the other, we are able to obtain a somewhat more penetrating analysis of power in the two communities.

In combining the decisional and reputational techniques, we have engaged the method of *Verstehen*,[10] in contrast to complete dependence upon the rigorous application of a single empirical method. As Max Weber noted, *Verstehen*—the use of a combination of intellectual and subjective frames of thought in interpreting an actor's "state of mind" and in understanding the meaning of events from a functional point of view—is required for the analysis of social behavior.[11] In synthesizing, weighing, and modifying the evidence provided by the two methods, we have obviously brought to bear composite judgments about the meaning of events, regardless of the behavior and the intentions of certain leaders and despite our original intention of confining ourselves exclusively to evidence produced by a single method. Nevertheless, we are confident that the final result is a truer picture of the distribution and use of power in the two communities.

---

10 For a critical analysis of the meaning and utility of *Verstehen* as a method in the social sciences, see Theodore Abel, "The Operation Called *Verstehen*," *American Journal of Sociology*, 54 (November 1948), 211–18.

11 *The Theory of Social and Economic Organization*, trans. A. M. Henderson and T. Parsons (Glencoe, Ill.: The Free Press, 1947), Chap. 2 and pp. 87–88, 94–115.

Certainly, in addition to suggesting the desirability of using both the decisional and the reputational methods, we have indicated that the distinction between overt and potential power, however precise it may be logically, is extremely difficult to preserve operation-ally. We have also questioned whether overt power, as measured by the decisional method, is really a more critical index of community power than potential power, which may provide a situational framework that conditions greatly the exercise of overt power.

LOCATING LEADERS IN LOCAL COMMUNITIES*†

Linton C. Freeman, *University of Pittsburgh*

Thomas J. Fararo, *University of Pittsburgh*

Warner Bloomberg, Jr., *University of Wisconsin at Milwaukee*

Morris H. Sunshine, *Syracuse University*

Most investigators would probably agree that leadership refers to a complex process whereby a relatively small number of individuals in a collectivity behave in such a way that they effect (or effectively prevent) a change in the lives of a relatively large number. But agreement on theoretical details of the leadership process or on how it is to be studied is another matter. Much of the recent literature on community leadership has been critical.[1] Gibb has suggested that there are a great many *kinds* of leadership—many different ways in which changes may be effected. He has proposed that leaders be assigned to various types including "the initiator, energizer, harmonizer, expediter, and the like."[2] Banfield has stressed the importance of the distinction between intended and unintended leadership.[3] And both Dahl and Polsby have called attention to the desirability

---

* From Linton C. Freeman, Thomas J. Fararo, Warner Bloomberg, Jr., and Morris H. Sunshine, "Locating Leaders in Local Communities: A Comparison of Some Alternative Approaches," *American Sociological Review*, 28 (October 1963), 791–98. Reprinted by permission of the American Sociological Association.

† Support for this study was provided by a grant from the Fund for Adult Education to the University College of Syracuse University.

[1] Cecil A. Gibb, "Leadership," in *Handbook of Social Psychology*, Vol. 2, ed. Gardner Lindzey (Reading, Mass.: Addison-Wesley Publishing Co., Inc., 1954), pp. 877–920; Edward C. Banfield, "The Con-cept 'Leadership' in Community Research," paper read before the Annual Meeting of the American Political Science Association, St. Louis, Mo., 1958; Robert A. Dahl, "A Critique of the Ruling Elite Model," *American Political Science Review*, 52 (June 1958), 463–69; Nelson W. Polsby, "The Sociology of Community Power: A Reassessment," *Social Forces*, 37 (March 1959), 232–36; Nelson W. Polsby, "Three Problems in the Analysis of Community Power," *American Sociological Review*, 24 (December 1959), 798–803; Raymond E. Wolfinger, "Reputation and Reality in the Study of 'Community Power,'" *American Sociological Review*, 25 (October 1960), 636–44.

[2] Gibb, *op. cit.*

[3] Banfield, *op. cit.*

of considering the *extent* of the effect a given leader has in expediting a particular change and the *range* of changes over which his effect holds.[4] It seems evident, then, that although these critics might agree with the minimum definition presented above, they would all like to see some additional factors included within its scope.

Polsby has translated the comments of the critics into a set of operational guides for research.[5] He has suggested that a satisfactory study of community leadership must involve a detailed examination of the whole decision-making process as it is exhibited over a range of issues. Here we should have to specify each issue, the persons involved, their intentions, and the extent and nature of their influence if any. Such a program represents an ideal that might be used to think about the process of community leadership. But as a research strategy, this plan raises many problems.

In the first place, both influence and intention are concepts presenting great difficulty in empirical application. Both require that elaborate observational and interviewing procedures be developed, and both raise reliability problems.[6] May we, for example, take a person's word concerning his intentions, or must they be inferred from his behavior? And even when two persons interact

and one subsequently changes his stated position in the direction of the views of the other, it is difficult to *prove* that influence has taken place. But even if these questions were eliminated, a practical problem would still remain. To follow the prescriptions listed above would be prohibitively expensive, requiring detailed observation of hundreds (or thousands) of individuals over an extended period. To record all interaction relevant to the decisions under study, it would be necessary to observe each person in a large number of varied situations, many of them quite private. Even then it would be difficult to evaluate the impact of the process of observation itself. Given these considerations, Polsby's ideal has never been reached. All existing studies of community leadership represent some compromise.

Most authors of community leadership studies would probably agree that the critics are on the right track. But most have been willing (or perhaps forced by circumstances) to make one or more basic assumptions in order to achieve a workable research design. Four types of compromise have been common. They will be discussed below.

Perhaps the most realistic of the compromise studies are those based on the assumption that active participation in decision-making *is* leadership. Typically, in such studies, one or a series of community decisions are either observed or reconstructed. In so doing, an attempt is made to identify the active participants in the decision-making process. These decision-making studies frequently are restricted to a small number of decisions, and they usually fail to present convincing evidence on the questions of intent and amount of impact. But they do provide a more or less direct index of participation. If they err it is by including

---

[4] Polsby, "The Sociology of Community Power: A Reassessment," *op. cit.*, and Dahl, *op. cit.*

[5] Polsby, "The Sociology of Community Power," *op. cit.*

[6] Herbert A. Simon, "Notes on the Observation and Measurement of Political Power," in his *Models of Man* (New York: John Wiley & Sons, Inc., 1957); James G. March, "An Introduction to the Theory and Measurement of Influence," *American Political Science Review*, 49 (June 1955), 431–51; James G. March, "Measurement Concepts in the Theory of Influence," *Journal of Politics*, 19 (May 1957), 202–26.

individuals who, though present, had little or no impact on the decision. On the face of it this seems preferable to the likelihood of excluding important influentials.[7]

A second compromise approach is to assume that formal authority *is* leadership. Aside from arbitrarily defining which positions are "on top," these studies underestimate the impact of those not in official positions on the outcomes of the decision-making process.

The third approach assumes that leadership is a necessary consequence of social activity. This assumption leads to studies of social participation. Such studies have used everything from rough indexes of memberships in voluntary associations to carefully constructed scales of activity in such associations. In each case it is reasoned that community leadership results from a high degree of voluntary activity in community affairs. The social-participation approach is thus the converse of the study of position. While the former stresses activity, the latter is concerned only with formal authority. But to the extent that activity in voluntary associations leads to having an impact upon community change, activists are leaders.

The final approach assumes that leadership is too complex to be indexed directly. Instead of examining leadership as such, proponents of this approach assess reputation for leadership. Their reasoning suggests that all of the more direct approaches neglect one or another key dimension of the leadership process. They turn, therefore, to informants from the community itself.

Often rather elaborate steps have been taken to insure that the informants are indeed informed. For example, positional leaders may be questioned in order to develop a list of reputed leaders or influentials; then the reported influentials are polled to determine the top influentials. In such cases it is reasonable to suppose that the grossly uninformed are ruled out.

Various critics have condemned the indeterminancy and subjectivity of this procedure.[8] But its defenders reason that the reputational approach is the only way to uncover the subtleties of intent, extent of impact, and the like in the leadership process. What, they ask, but a life-long involvement in the activities of a community could possibly yield sophisticated answers to the question "Who are the leaders?" The reputational approach, then, assumes the possibility of locating some individuals who unquestionably meet the criteria of community leadership and who in turn will be able to name others not so visible to the outside observer.

Currently, the controversy continues. Proponents of one or another of these competing points of view argue for its inherent superiority and the obvious validity of its assumptions. Others take the view that all of these approaches get at leadership. But these are empirical questions; they can be answered only on the basis of comparison, not by faith or by rhetoric. A number of partial contrasts have been published, but so far no systematic overall comparison of these procedures has been reported. The present report represents such an attempt. An effort is made to determine the degree to which these several procedures agree or disagree in locating community leaders.

---

[7] Numerous examples of this and other approaches to the study of leadership may be found in Wendell Bell, Richard J. Hill, and Charles R. Wright, *Public Leadership* (San Francisco: Chandler, 1961).

[8] See the articles by Dahl, Polsby, and Wolfinger cited above.

The data presented here represent a part of a larger study of leadership in the Syracuse, N.Y. metropolitan area. Two reports have been published,[9] and several additional papers are forthcoming.

DECISION-MAKING

The study of participation in the decision-making process was of central concern in the Syracuse study. The first major task of the project team was to select a set of community problems or issues which would provide a point of entry into a pool (or pools) of participants in the decision-making process. Interviews were conducted with twenty local specialists in community study and with fifty informants representing diverse segments of the city's population. Care was taken to include representatives of each group along the total range of interest and institutional commitment. These seventy interviews provided a list of about 250 community issues. The list was reduced to a set of thirty-nine issues according to the following criteria:

1. Each issue must have been at least temporarily resolved by a decision.
2. The decision must be perceived as important by informants representing diverse segments of the community.
3. The decision must pertain to the development, distribution, and utilization of resources and facilities

which have an impact on a large segment of the metropolitan population.
4. The decision must involve alternative lines of action. It must entail a certain degree of choice on the part of participants; and the outcome must not be predetermined.
5. The decision must be administered rather than made by individuals in "the market." For the purpose of this study, an administered decision was defined as one made by individuals holding top positions in organizational structures which empower them to make decisions affecting many people.
6. The decision must involve individuals and groups resident in the Syracuse Metropolitan Area. Decisions made outside the Metropolitan Area (e.g., by the state government) were excluded even though they might affect residents of the Metropolitan Area.
7. The decision must fall within the time period 1955–1960.
8. The set of decisions as a whole must affect the entire range of important institutional sectors, such as governmental, economic, political, educational, religious, ethnic, and the like.[10]

The next step in the research process required the determination of positional leaders or formal authorities for each of the set of thirty-nine issues. The study began with those individuals who were formally responsible for the decisions. The element of arbitrary judgment usually involved in the positional approach was thus avoided. Here, the importance of a position was derived from its role in determining a choice among alternative lines of action rather than of being the consequence of an arbitrary assumption.

[9] Linton C. Freeman, Warner Bloomberg, Jr., Stephen P. Koff, Morris H. Sunshine, and Thomas J. Fararo, *Local Community Leadership* (Syracuse, N.Y.: University College of Syracuse University, 1960); Linton C. Freeman, Thomas J. Fararo, Warner Bloomberg, Jr., and Morris H. Sunshine, *Metropolitan Decision-Making* (Syracuse, N.Y.: University College of Syracuse University, 1962).

[10] The entire set of thirty-nine issues is described in the earlier publications of the study group, *op. cit.*

The responsible formal authorities were determined on the basis of documents pertinent to the thirty-nine decisions. In addition, several attorneys were consulted to insure that correct determinations were made. The number of authorities responsible for making each of these decisions ranged from two to fifty-seven.

The interviews started with authoritative persons. Respondents were presented with a set of thirty-nine cards, each of which identified a decision. They were asked to sort the cards into two piles: (1) "Those in which you participated; that is, where others involved in this decision would recognize you as being involved," and (2) "Those in which you were not a participant." For those issues in which they claimed participation, individuals were then asked to name all the others who were also involved. Here they were instructed to report on the basis of first-hand knowledge of participation rather than on hearsay. Respondents were also given a questionnaire covering their social backgrounds.

When the interviews with authorities were completed, their responses for those decisions on which they possessed authority were tabulated. Then, any person who had been nominated as a participant by two authorities for the same issue was designated as a first-zone influential. Two nominations were deemed necessary in order to avoid bias due to accidental contacts, mistakes of memory, or a tendency to mention personal friends. In the final tabulations this same rule of two nominations was applied to authorities also. Therefore, no person is counted as a participant unless he has two nominations by qualified nominators.

As the next step, all first-zone influentials were interviewed using exactly the same procedures as those used for authorities. Their responses were tabluated for the decisions in which they had been involved, and any person nominated by one authority and one first-zone influential was also classified as a first-zone influential and interviewed. Then any person nominated by two first-zone influentials was designated a second-zone influential—two steps removed from formal authority but still involved. We did not interview beyond these second-zone influentials. We might have continued with third and fourth zones and so on; but on the basis of qualitative data gathered during the interviews, we suspected we were moving well into the periphery of impact on the outcome of decision making.

In all, 628 interviews were completed. Of these, 550 qualified as participants. These participants, then, are the leaders as determined by the decision-making phase of the Syracuse study. They were ranked in terms of the number of decisions in which they were involved. For the present analysis the thirty-two most active participants are considered.

SOCIAL ACTIVITY

Each of the 550 participants uncovered by the decision-making study was asked to complete a questionnaire covering his social background and current activities. These questionnaires were returned by 506 informants. The answers included responses to a set of questions designed to elicit as much information as possible about voluntary association memberships. Specific questions were included to determine memberships in the following areas:

1. Committees formed to deal with community problems.

2. Community service organizations.
3. Business organizations.
4. Professional organizations.
5. Union organizations.
6. Clubs and social organizations.
7. Cultural organizations.
8. Religious organizations.
9. Political parties, organizations and clubs.
10. Veterans' and patriotic organizations.
11. Other clubs and organizations.

Memberships in these organizations were tabulated, and a rough overall index to voluntary activity was calculated by simply summing the number of memberships for each person. The respondents were ranked in terms of number of memberships, and the thirty-two most active organizational members were included in the present analysis.

REPUTATION

Each questionnaire also invited the respondent to list the most influential leaders in the community. Eight spaces were provided for answers. Nominations were tabulated and, following traditional procedures, the top forty-one reputed leaders were listed. The responses of those forty-one respondents were then tabulated separately. The top thirty-two were derived from their rankings. This was done in order to maximize the chances that our nominators would be informed. As it turned out, however, the top thirty-two nominations of the whole group and the top thirty-two provided by the top forty-one were exactly the same persons and in the same order. For Syracuse these nominations showed remarkable consistency all along the line.

POSITION

In determining the top positional leaders it seemed desirable to avoid as much as possible making the usual arbitrary assumptions. Traditional usage of the positional approach dictated the determination of the titular heads of the major organizations in business, government, the professions, and the like. Within each of these institutional areas choice could be made in terms of size, but it was difficult to determine how many organizations should be selected in each area.

An empirical resolution for this problem was provided in a recent report by D'Antonio et al.[11] These authors provided data on the proportions of reputed leaders representing each of the seven relevant institutional areas in ten previous studies. Since agreement on these relative proportions was reasonably close for the six middle-sized American communities reported, they were used to assign proportions in each institutional area in the present study. The proportions derived from D'Antonio and those used in the present study are reported in Table 1. In this case positional leaders are the titular heads of the largest organizations in each of the institutional areas, and

TABLE 1. PERCENTAGE OF LEADERS IN EACH INSTITUTIONAL AREA

Institution	Six Cities	Syracuse
Business	57	59
Government	8	9
Professions	12	13
Education	5	6
Communications	8	6
Labor	4	3
Religion	5	3
Total	99	99

11 William D'Antonio, William Form, Charles Loomis, and Eugene Erickson, "Institutional and Occupational Representatives in Eleven Community Influence Systems," *American Sociological Review*, 26 (June 1961), 440–46.

each area is represented according to the proportion listed in Table 1. Thirty-two organizations were chosen in all. As a check on its validity, the list of organizations was shown to several local experts in community affairs. They were in substantial agreement that the organizations listed seemed consistent with their perceptions of the "top" organizations in Syracuse. The heads of these organizations might be expected to have formal control over much of the institutional system of the community.

These, then, are the raw materials of the current study. An attempt was made to determine the degree to which these several procedures would allocate the same persons to the top leadership category.

RESULTS

The several procedures for determining leaders did not converge on a single set of individuals. Top leaders according to one procedure were not necessarily the same as those indicated by another. An index of agreement for each pair was constructed by calculating the ratio of the actual number of agreements to their total possible number. Results are listed in Table 2.

It is possible that any of the methods used, if modified enough, would have yielded significantly different results.[12] The procedures we followed seem in their essentials to be like those followed in most of the studies so far published. (Those who believe they have altered the use of positions, nominations, memberships, or other indexes

---

12 The choice of the top thirty-two leaders in each category is, for example, somewhat arbitrary. When another number is used, the absolute percentages of agreement vary, but their standings *relative* to one another remain stable.

TABLE 2. PERCENTAGE OF AGREEMENT IN DETERMINING LEADERS BY FOUR TRADITIONAL PROCEDURES

Participation			
25	Social Activity		
33	25	Reputation	
39	22	74	Position

in such a way as to obtain a major difference in the output of the technique have only to demonstrate this by empirical comparisons.) Our impression is that most versions of each approach represent only vernier adjustments of the same device and thus can have only marginally differing results.

Table 2 suggests that there is far from perfect agreement in determining leaders by means of these four methods. In only one case do two of these methods concur in more than 50 per cent of their nominations. Reputation and position seem to be in substantial agreement in locating leaders. To a large degree, therefore, reputed leaders are the titular heads of major community organizations. They are not, however, themselves active as participants in decision-making to any great extent.

Reputation for leadership seems to derive primarily from position not from participation. But it appears unlikely that position itself constitutes a sufficient basis for reputation. The reputations, however, might belong to the organizations and not the individuals. In such a case, when an informant named John Smith as a leader, what might have been intended was the fact that the Smith Snippel Company (of which John Smith was president) is influential in community decisions. Smith would thus have been named only because we had asked for a person's name. Our hypothesis, then, is that reputation should correspond with the participation rate of organizations rather than the participation rates of individuals.

On the basis of this hypothesis, the data on participation were retabulated. Each participant was classified according to his organization or place of employment. Then the head of each organization was credited not only with his own participation, but with the sum of the participation of his employees. In this manner an index of organizational participation was constructed and the top thirty organizational leaders were determined. Individuals so nominated were compared with those introduced by the earlier procedures. The results are shown in Table 3.

TABLE 3. PERCENTAGE OF AGREEMENT BETWEEN ORGANIZATIONAL PARTICIPATION AND FOUR TRADITIONAL PROCEDURES

Traditional Procedure	Percentage of Agreement
Participation	33
Social activity	25
Reputation	67
Position	80

The proportions shown in Table 3 support our hypothesis. Organizational participation seems to uncover substantially the same leaders as reputation and position. The top reputed leaders, therefore, though not active participants themselves, head up the largest organizations, and the personnel of these organizations have the highest participation rates.

This result accounts for a great deal of participation in community decision-making. Since organizational participation provides a workable index, many participants must be employees of large community organizations. But this does not explain the most active class of in-

TABLE 4. PERCENTAGE OF LEADERS ACCORDING TO FOUR TRADITIONAL PROCEDURES WHO ARE GOVERNMENT OFFICIALS OR EMPLOYESS OR PROFESSIONAL PARTICIPANTS

Traditional Procedure	Percentage of Government Personnel or Professional Participants
Participation	66
Social activity	20
Reputation	20
Position	28

dividual participants—those who were picked up by the individual participation index. These people seem to be virtually full-time participants in community affairs. We know that they are not organizational heads, but we have not determined who they are.

In view of the sheer amount of their participation, the top participants must be professional participants of some sort. And, as a class, professional participants in community affairs should be government officials and employees or full-time professional executives of non-governmental agencies formally and primarily committed to intervention in community affairs. With this as our hypothesis, the individuals nominated as leaders by the four traditional indexes were all classified into either government and professional or non-professional categories. Then percentages of government personnel and professionals were calculated for all four indexes. The results are shown in Table 4.

Again the results support our hypothesis. The most active individual participants are typically government personnel.

The participation index thus gets at

personnel quite different from those selected by reputational or positional indexes, or by social activity. These differing cadres of people seem to represent *different kinds* of leadership behavior with respect to the local community.

SUMMARY AND DISCUSSION OF RESULTS

These results indicate that at least in Syracuse "leadership" is not a homogeneous category. Which "leaders" are uncovered seems in large part to be a function of the mode of study. The several traditional indexes allow us to locate one or another of three basic types of "leaders."

First, there are those who enjoy the reputation for top leadership. These are very frequently the same individuals who are the heads of the largest and most actively participating business, industrial, governmental, political, professional, educational, labor and religious organizations in Syracuse. They are uncovered by studies of reputation, position, or organizational participation. In view of their formal command over the institutional structure and the symbolic value of their status as indexed by reputation, these individuals may be called the *Institutional Leaders* of Syracuse.

These Institutional Leaders, however, are for the most part not active participants in community affairs. There is no evidence that they have any direct impact on most decisions which take place. Their activity may be limited to that of lending prestige to or legitimizing the solutions provided by others. They might conceivably be participating decision-makers in secret, but more likely they serve chiefly to provide access to the decision-making structure for their underlings: the *Effectors*.

The Effectors are located by studying participation. They are the active workers in the actual process of community decision-making. Many of the most active Effectors are government personnel and professional participants, and the others are the employees of the large private corporations directed by the Institutional Leaders. In some cases, the Effectors are in touch with their employers, and it seems likely that their activities are frequently guided by what they view as company policy; but, judging from our data, they are often pretty much on their own. At any rate, these men carry most of the burden of effecting community change.

The third type of leader might be called the *Activists*. These people are active—and often hold office—in voluntary organizations, community service organizations, and clubs. Although they are not involved as often as the Effectors, the Activists do participate in decision-making. For the most part they seem to lack the positional stature to be Institutional Leaders. Furthermore, they often work for or direct smaller organizations in the community. They lack the power base provided by association with government or one of the major industrial or business firms. Yet, seemingly by sheer commitment of time and effort to community affairs, these Activists do help shape the future of the community.

In conclusion, the various differing approaches to the study of community leadership seem to uncover different types of leaders. The study of reputation, position or organizational participation seems to get at the Institutional Leaders. Studies of participation in decision-making, on the other hand, tap the Effectors of community action.

And studies of social activity seem to seek out the Activists who gain entry by dint of sheer commitment, time, and energy.

In part, our results are dependent upon the Syracuse situation. It is likely that twenty-five years ago, when Syracuse was smaller and less diversified, the Institutional Leaders and the Effectors were the same people.[13] And

---

[13] For an interesting discussion of the development of a community leadership

twenty-five years from now this description will probably no longer hold. Other communities, in other stages of development and diversification will probably show different patterns. But until more comparative studies are done, conclusions of this kind are virtually guesses.

---

structure, see Robert O. Schulze, "The Bifurcation of Power in a Satellite City," in *Community Political Systems*, ed. Morris Janowitz (Glencoe, Ill.: Free Press, 1961).

SELECTED BIBLIOGRAPHY

Abu-Laban, Baha, "The Reputational Approach in the Study of Community Power: A Critical Evaluation," *Pacific Sociological Review*, 8 (Spring 1965), 35–42.

Agger, Robert E., "Power Attributions in the Local Community: Theoretical and Research Considerations," *Social Forces*, 34 (May 1956), 322–31.

Anton, Thomas J., "Power, Pluralism, and Local Politics," *Administrative Science Quarterly*, 7 (March 1963), 425–54.

Bachrach, Peter, and Morton Baratz, "Two Faces of Power," *American Political Science Review*, 51 (December 1962), 947–52.

Bierstedt, Robert, "An Analysis of Social Power," *American Sociological Review*, 15 (December 1950), 730–38.

Blankenship, Vaughn, "Community Power and Decision-Making: A Comparative Evaluation of Measurement Techniques," *Social Forces*, 43 (December 1964), 207–16.

Bonjean, Charles M., and David M. Olson, "Community Leadership: Directions of Research," *Administrative Science Quarterly*, 9 (December 1964), 278–300.

Booth, David A., and Charles R. Adrian, "Power Structure and Community Change: A Replication Study of

Community A," *The Midwest Journal of Political Science*, 6 (August 1962), 277–96.

Clark, Terry N., "The Concept of Power: Some Overemphasized and Underrecognized Dimensions," *Southwestern Social Science Quarterly*, 48 (December 1967), 271–86.

D'Antonio, William V., et al., eds., *Power and Democracy in America*. Notre Dame, Ind.: University of Notre Dame Press, 1961.

D'Antonio, William V., Howard J. Ehrlich, and Eugene C. Erickson, "Further Notes on the Study of Community Power," *American Sociological Review*, 27 (December 1962), 848–54.

D'Antonio, William V., and Eugene C. Erickson, "The Reputational Technique as a Measure of Community Power: An Evaluation Based on Comparative and Longitudinal Studies," *American Sociological Review*, 27, No. 3 (June 1962), 362–76.

Danzger, M. Herbert, "Community Power Structure: Problems and Continuities," *American Sociological Review*, 29 (October 1964), 707–17.

Dick, Harry R., "Method for Ranking Community Influentials," *American Sociological Review*, 25 (June 1960), 395–99.

Ehrlich, Howard J., "The Reputational Approach to the Study of Community Power," *American Sociological Review*, 26 (December 1961), 926–27.

GAMSON, WILLIAM A., "Reputation and Resources in Community Politics," *American Journal of Sociology*, 72 (September 1966), 121–31.

GROSS, LLEWELLYN, "A Theory of Power and Organizational Processes," *The School Review*, 70 (Summer 1962), 149–62.

HERSON, LAWRENCE J., "In the Footsteps of Community Power," *American Political Science Review*, 55 (December 1961), 817–30.

KAUFMAN, HERBERT, and VICTOR JONES, "The Mystery of Power," *Public Administration Review*, 14 (Summer 1954), 205–12.

LASSWELL, HAROLD D., and ABRAHAM KAPLAN, *Power and Society*. New Haven, Conn.: Yale University Press, 1960.

MARCH, JAMES G., "The Power of Power," in *Varieties of Political Theory*, ed. David Easton. Englewood Cliffs, N.J.: Prentice-Hall, Inc., 1966.

PARTRIDGE, P. A., "Some Notes on the Concept of Power," *Political Studies*, 11 (June 1963), 107–25.

POLSBY, NELSON W., *Community Power and Political Theory*. New Haven, Conn.: Yale University Press, 1963.

———, "The Sociology of Community Power: A Reassessment," *Social Forces*, 37 (March 1959), 232–36.

SCHERMERHORN, RICHARD A., *Society and Power*. New York: Random House, Inc., 1961.

SCHULZE, ROBERT O., and LEONARD U.

BLUMBERG, "The Determination of Local Power Elites," *American Journal of Sociology*, 63 (November 1957), 290–96.

SIMON, HERBERT, "Notes on the Observation and Measurement of Political Power," *Journal of Politics*, 15 (November 1953), 500–516.

SNYDER, RICHARD C., *et al.*, "The Decison-Making Approach," in *Political Behavior*, eds. Heinz Eulau *et al.* Glencoe, Ill.: The Free Press, 1956.

STRAUSZ-HUPE, ROBERT, *Power and Community*. New York: Frederick A. Praeger, Inc., Publishers, 1956.

SWANSON, BERT E., ed., *Current Trends in Comparative Community Studies*. Kansas City, Mo.: Community Studies, Inc., 1962.

TANNENBAUM, ARNOLD S., "An Event Structure Approach to Social Power and the Problem of Power Comparability," *Behavioral Science*, 7 (July 1962), 315–31.

WALTON, JOHN, "Substance and Artifact: The Current Status of Research on Community Power Structure," *American Journal of Sociology*, 71 (January 1966), 430–38.

WOLFINGER, RAYMOND E., "A Plea for a Decent Burial," *American Sociological Review*, 27 (December 1962), 841–47.

———, "Reputation and Reality in the Study of Community Power," *American Sociological Review*, 25 (October 1960), 636–44.

CHAPTER SEVEN

Studies of Community and National Power

Of the large body of research on power which has accumulated over the past 15 years, only a small part is explicitly relevant to the subject of social stratification. Most studies have been directed by investigators whose major interests lie elsewhere, such as in urban sociology, political sociology, or community organization, and who see issues of power as central to these areas. Although the majority of these studies have not been carried out expressly within a stratification framework, their findings often bear on the role of power in social stratification.[1]

---

1 Polsby, a political scientist, suggests that stratification theory strongly influences most sociologists' research on community power. Based upon an examination of eight investigations (four of which are studies of stratification in communities and four specifically of community power), Polsby claims that both types employ "basic axioms of stratification theory." These axioms, he claims, underlie a number of assumptions about community power, namely that the upper class rules in the community, that economic and status elites control political leaders, and that indices of high status are also indices of high power. While Polsby overstates his case (for example, the studies of functionalists such as those of the Parsons school, including Davis and Moore, could not be so categorized), on the whole his critique highlights the various relationships often presumed to exist between stratification and power. Nelson Polsby, *Community Power and Political Theory* (New Haven, Conn.: Yale University Press, 1963), Chaps. 2 and 3.

COMMUNITY POWER

Floyd Hunter's influential study of the power structure of Atlanta, Georgia, is a prime example of sociological research on community power which relies heavily upon the concepts and perspectives of social stratification.[2] On the basis of his research, Hunter concludes that a small group of men, through behind-the-scenes activities, controlled the significant community decisions. Drawn largely from the ranks of business and finance, these top influentials formed social and economic cliques and tended to act together. Hunter found that the possession of economic resources was instrumental in gaining access to the top echelons of power. Admission to the inner circle of influentials rested almost wholly upon high position in the business community. While this was a study of power at the community level, Hunter's research disclosed that the influence of many of the top leaders extended much beyond the boundaries of their own community. As Hunter emphasizes, "Regional City cannot be isolated from state, national, and international affairs."[3] In brief, Hunter's findings point to a relatively closed power system controlled by business elites. On a continuum of power extending from a monolithic structure to a pluralistic one, the model suggested by Hunter falls near the monolithic end.

Although the results of most studies of community power are not consonant with Hunter's, it is incorrect to conclude that such studies "tend to substantiate a pluralistic interpretation of American community power."[4] Research does not support either the view that the typical community is led either by a small group of powerful individuals or the view that it is led by a simple pluralistic majority. As Robert Presthus emphasizes, what passes for pluralism today is close to some interpretations of elitism; it bears slight resemblance to traditional notions of pluralism, which envision the participation or adequate representation of the common man.[5] Such traditional images run counter to the view of community power which holds that "pluralism exists if no single elite dominates decision-making in every substantive area."[6]

---

2 *Community Power Structure* (Garden City, N.Y.: Doubleday & Company, Inc., 1963). Published originally by the University of North Carolina Press, 1953.

3 *Ibid.*, p. 167.

4 William Spinrad, "Power in Local Communities," *Social Problems*, 12 (Winter 1965), 354. We must emphasize, however, that this is a debatable assessment. Walton, for example, suggests that a substantial number of studies are congruent with Hunter's findings. (We discuss Walton's views subsequently.) John Walton, "Substance and Artifact: The Current Status of Research on Community Power Structure," *American Journal of Sociology*, 71 (January 1966), 430–38.

5 *Men at the Top* (Fair Lawn, N.J.: Oxford University Press, Inc., 1964), pp. 17–22.

6 *Ibid.*, p. 21. Presthus proposes an updating of the concept of pluralism for it to serve as an adequate framework for research on power. He lists five necessary conditions of pluralism against which research findings on the contemporary scene can be interpreted. These conditions are stated in propositional form: (1) that competing centers and bases of power and influence exist within a political community; (2) that the opportunity for individual and organizational access to the political system is present; (3) that individuals actively participate in and make their will felt through organizations of many kinds; (4) that elec-

Increasingly, researchers are moving away from the all-or-none argument on the existence of power elites and are examining the degree to which power is concentrated or dispersed along a continuum. While the growing variety of findings reported in the literature does not lend itself readily either to classification or to hard and fast generalizations, most studies fit the typology of power structures proposed by John Walton,[7] who identifies four general types: *pyramidal* (monolithic, monopolistic, or with a single concentrated leadership group); *factional* (with at least two durable factions); *coalitional* (with fluid coalitions of interest usually varying with issues); and *amorphous* (with no persistent pattern of leadership).

In a review of thirty-three studies of fifty-five communities, Walton classified nineteen as exhibiting a pyramidal power structure, seventeen as factional, fourteen as coalitional, and five as amorphous. This is, of course, a rough classification. Not all the investigators of the nineteen communities designated as pyramidal by Walton would regard this descriptive label as satisfactory especially since its prime referent appears to be the type of power system reported by Hunter. More acceptable would be the view that these communities fall within that range of the continuum nearest to low pluralism.

POLITICAL VERSUS ECONOMIC POWER

A critical issue cutting across problems of degree and form of concentration of power is that of the key groups or figures who wield power. Of several strategic groups which one usually prevails? While some may object to the connotations of labels such as elites, top leaders, and chief decision-makers, most writers agree that not all those who possess or exercise power are in the innermost circles. Within the higher echelons certain sets of individuals have more power than others.

The two groups most frequently identified as salient in community power structures are business elites and political leaders, especially local government officials. As William Spinrad comments, "The pattern of American community power observed is mostly a matter of the respective positions of these two groups and their relation with the residual 'all other groups'."[8] Sociologists have typically concluded that the business faction tends to possess and exercise greater control over community decisions.[9] While they perhaps do not see this control in such

---

tions are viable instruments of mass participation in political decisions, including those on specific issues; (5) that a consensus exists on what may be called the *democratic creed. Ibid.*, pp. 22–24.

[7] *Op. cit.*

[8] *Op. cit.*, p. 354.

[9] One of the strongest proponents of this view of business dominance is Delbert C. Miller. He discusses his own research and conclusions from supporting studies in "Democracy and Decision-Making in the Community Power Structure," in *Power and Democracy in America*, eds. William V. D'Antonio and Howard J. Ehrlich (South Bend, Ind.: University of Notre Dame Press, 1961), pp. 25–71.

oligarchical terms as Hunter does, their view is roughly congruent with his conclusions concerning the dominance of business. An opposing conception rests on studies showing either that the business group shares power more or less equally with government officials or that, if either is ascendant, it is the latter.[10]

Several factors produce these contrasting findings. Some are related to the nature of the community; others are connected with the ideological proclivities of the researcher.[11] One or more studies have designated community variables, such as size, complexity, socioeconomic composition, type of economy, locus of business ownership, and region, as affecting the relative strength of the economic and political groups in the community. For most of these variables, however, the relationships are tenuous and often inconsistent.[12] For example, all investigations may not confirm conclusions regarding the association between absentee ownership or economic complexity and business dominance.

The greatest concern has focused on the part played by ideology in interpretations of the primacy of political or business factions. The most noticeable cleavage in this regard is that between sociologists and political scientists. Most sociological studies of community power conclude in favor of the pyramidal or factional power structure.[13] Studies which find a pyramidal type usually describe the business group as occupying the apex of the hierarchy. Studies which discover vying factions most often report that the balance of power is in the hands of the business elite.

In keeping with a general thesis of pluralism, most political scientists are inclined to argue, at least in the abstract, that no one group is dominant in a community.[14] M. Kent Jennings takes a common stance in his contention that "ranking economic position is only one of a number of factors related to political power and, by itself, is unlikely to be the decisive factor."[15] In addition to expressing pluralistic perspectives on power, this observation reflects the conception that power cannot be treated as a subsidiary aspect of the social structure, especially of the economic institution. Even stronger objections arise against the view that "governmental institutions and officials are derivative of and subordinate to economic and social institutions."[16] Most political scientists claim that the political

---

[10] The study now taken as the prototype for this kind of conclusion is Robert A. Dahl's *Who Governs?* (New Haven, Conn.: Yale University Press, 1961). See his essay "Equality and Power in American Society," in D'Antonio and Ehrlich, *op. cit.*, pp. 73–89, in which he takes specific exception to Miller's conceptions of community power.

[11] A third source of influence upon findings is the methodology used. We discussed such influences in Chapter Six.

[12] Walton, *op. cit.*; Donald A. Clelland and William H. Form, "Economic Dominants and Community Power: A Comparative Analysis," *American Journal of Sociology*, 69 (March 1964), 511–21.

[13] John Walton, "Discipline, Method, and Community Power: A Note on the Sociology of Knowledge," *American Sociological Review*, 31 (October 1966), 687.

[14] Dahl, *Who Governs?*; Polsby, *op. cit.*

[15] *Community Influentials: The Elites of Atlanta* (Glencoe, Ill.: The Free Press, 1964), p. 199.

[16] *Ibid.*, p. 201.

sector functions, at a minimum, as an effective countervailing force to economic elites. Furthermore, although usually expressed circumspectly, the opinion is fairly widespread among political scientists that the balance of power tends to be in the hands of local government officials.

We emphasize that not all political scientists and sociologists agree with these divergent views concerning pluralism and elitism, including those on the salience of the business or political factions.[17] The conceptions of power and research reported by Presthus[18] and Robert Agger *et al.*,[19] for instance, have much more in common with sociological views than with those of political science. Linton Freeman *et al.*,[20] Peter Rossi,[21] and Robert Schulze,[22] on the other hand, present studies of power somewhat at variance with the writings of the majority of sociologists and compatible with many of the perspectives of political scientists.[23]

The following two selections are illustrative of research findings proceeding from divergent conceptions of community power and employing alternative techniques of study. Using the reputational approach in both instances, Delbert Miller compares the structure of community power in an American and an English city. Much as Hunter concludes on the nature of power in Regional City, Miller finds in Pacific City a pyramidal system dominated by business leaders. In contrast, in English City the business group plays a less significant role in community decision-making; key influentials represent a broad area of community life.

While not specifically intended as such, Jennings' study of community influentials in Atlanta, Georgia, is tantamount to a replication of the research Hunter carried out a decade earlier in that city. Using a modification of the reputational technique plus elements of the decisional and positional approaches, Jennings gives a portrayal of community power in Atlanta which differs from Hunter's. Jennings' data suggest a relative lack of power of economic dominants. His findings point to a dispersal of power and a tendency for government officials to play the significant role in community decisions.

---

[17] As Walton notes, the results obtained are more closely associated with the method used for conducting research on power than with academic discipline. He concludes, however, that "the disciplinary background of the investigator tends to determine the method of investigation he will adopt...." "Discipline, Method, and Community Power," p. 688.

[18] *Op. cit.*

[19] *The Rulers and the Ruled* (New York: John Wiley & Sons, Inc., 1964).

[20] "Locating Leaders in Local Communities," *American Sociological Review*, 28 (October 1963), 791–98.

[21] "The Organizational Structure of an American Community," in *Complex Organizations*, ed. Amitai Etzioni (New York: Holt, Rinehart & Winston, Inc., 1962), pp. 301–12.

[22] "The Role of Economic Dominants in Community Power Structure," in *Political Sociology*, ed. Lewis A. Coser (New York: Harper & Row, Publishers, 1966), pp. 167–80.

[23] In general, see the assessment of divergences and similarities between political scientists and sociologists in Walton, "Substance and Artifact," especially pp. 431–32. Also, Polsby, *op. cit.*, p. 13.

INDUSTRY AND COMMUNTY POWER STRUCTURE*†

Delbert C. Miller

Indiana University

The role of business leaders[1] within a local community poses some challenging questions about the on-going processes of community decision-making. Why do business leaders take an active interest in community affairs? What is the extent of their influence in the community? How do they exercise this influence?

These questions have been asked by sociologists who have sought answers by conducting research on both the community[2] and the national level.[3] However, community power structure as a field of knowledge still

* Reprinted from "Industry and Community Power Structure: A Comparative Study of an American and an English City," *American Journal of Sociology*, by Delbert C. Miller by permission of The University of Chicago Press. Copyright 1958 by the University of Chicago Press.

† I am indebted for research assistance to Stuart D. Johnson, William Wilkinson, Esther Hirabayashi, and Anthony Baker, all of the University of Washington. Financial support by the Graduate School of the University of Washington is gratefully acknowledged. This report is one of a series describing tests of twelve hypotheses of community power structure in Pacific City (studied 1952–54; 1956–57) and English City (studied 1954–55). Other published work includes Delbert C. Miller, "The Seattle Business Leader," *Pacific North West Business*, 15 (February 1956), 5–12; and "The Prediction of Issue Outcome in Community Decision Making," Proceedings of the Pacific Sociological Society, *Research Studies of the State College of Washington*, 25 (June 1957), 137–47.

This study is now part of a larger comparative work: *International Community Power Structures: A Comparative Analysis of Four World Cities: Seattle, Washington; Bristol, England; Córdoba, Argentina; and Lima, Peru* (Bloomington, Ind.: Indiana University Press, 1968).

[1] Cf. Howard R. Bowen, *Social Responsibilities of the Businessman* (New York: Harper and Bros., 1953), especially Chaps. 8 and 9; William H. Whyte, Jr., *Is Anybody Listening?* (New York: Simon & Schuster, Inc., 1952), Chap. 1.

[2] Robert S. Lynd and Helen M. Lynd, *Middletown in Transition* (New York: Harcourt Brace, 1937); Floyd Hunter, *Community Power Structure* (Chapel Hill, N.C.: University of North Carolina, 1954); James B. McKee, "Status and Power in the Industrial Community: A Comment on Drucker's Thesis," *American Journal of Sociology*, 58 (January 1953), 364–70; Roland J. Pellegrin and Charles H. Coates, "Absentee-Owned Corporations and Community Power Structure," *American Journal of Sociology*, 61 (March 1956), 413–17; Donald W. Olmsted, "Organizational Leadership and Social Structure in a Small City," *American Sociological Review*, 19 (June 1954), 273–81; Peter R. Rossi, J. L. Freeman, and James M. Shiften, *Politics and Education in Bay City* (forthcoming); Floyd Hunter, Ruth C. Schaffer, and Cecil G. Sheps, *Community Organization* (Chapel Hill, N.C.: University of North Carolina Press, 1956).

[3] Robert S. Brady, *Business as a System of Power* (New York: Columbia University Press, 1939); C. Wright Mills, *White Collar, The American Middle Classes* (Fair Lawn, N.J.: Oxford University Press, Inc., 1951); C. W. Mills, *The Power Elite* (Fair Lawn, N.J.: Oxford University Press, Inc., 1956); Karl Mannheim, *Freedom, Power, and Democratic Planning* (Fair Lawn, N.J.: Oxford University Press, Inc., 1950).

has wide areas in which research data are lacking.[4]

The purpose of this paper is to describe and analyze the characteristics of decision-makers in an American and an English city. It has been repeatedly asserted that business men (manufacturers, bankers, merchants, investment brokers, and large real estate holders) exert predominant influence in community decision-making. This is the central hypothesis under test. Hunter has recently demonstrated this hypothesis in his study of a large regional city of southern United States.[5] This paper applies Hunter's basic methods to two cities of similar size and economic structure. The research design has been altered only to refine the conceptual framework and provide for more extensive data to test the hypothesis.

RESEARCH DESIGN

Two cities with similar economic, demographic, and educational characteristics were selected. "Pacific City" is located in the Pacific Northwest, U.S.A.; "English City" in southwestern England. Both are comparable in many features with Hunter's Southern City. All of the cities qualify under the Harris classification as "diversified types."[6] The following summary shows the close similarity of the three cities.

Southern Regional City in 1950 had a population of 331,000. It serves as the commercial, financial, and distributive center for the Southeastern section of the United States. It manufactures aircraft, textiles, and cotton waste products; is a transportation center of rail, air, bus, and truck lines; and is a center of education possessing a large university and many small colleges.

Pacific City had a population of 468,000 in 1950. It is the commercial, financial, and distribution center for the Pacific Northwest. Major transportation lines are centered in the city and it has a fine port. The city is the largest educational center of the region with a state university and many small colleges.

English City, also a regional city, serves as the commercial, financial, and distributive center of the West of England. Its population in 1950 was 444,000. The major manufactures are airplanes, ships, beer, cigarettes, chocolate, machinery, and paper. It possesses an ocean port. The city houses a provincial (state) university and many private grammar schools.

The community power structure[7] is composed of key influentials, top influentials, the community power complex, and those parts of the institutionalized power structure of the community that have come into play when activated by a community issue. When not active, the community power

---

4 Ralph B. Spence, "Some Needed Research on Industry Within the Community," *The Journal of Educational Sociology*, 27 (December 1953), 147.

5 Hunter, *op. cit.*, p. 113.

6 Employment in manufacturing, wholesaling, and retailing is less than 60 per cent, 20 per cent, and 50 per cent, respectively, of total employment in these activities. See Chauncey D. Harris, "A Functional Classification of Cities of the United States," *Geographical Review*, 22 (January 1943), 86–89.

7 Cf. Albert J. Reiss, Jr., "Some Logical and Methodological Problems in Community Research," *Social Forces*, 33 (October 1954), 51–57; Gordon W. Blackwell, "A Theoretical Framework for Sociological Research in Community Organization," *Social Forces*, 33 (October 1954), 57–64; Conrad W. Arensberg, "The Community Study Method," *American Journal of Sociology*, 60 (September 1954), 109–24. The theory and concepts used in this paper were developed jointly with William H. Form of Michigan State University.

structure remains in a latent state. In this paper attention is centered upon the role of the top influentials and the key influentials as representative of a significant part of the community power structure.

The top influentials (T.I.) are persons from whom particular members are drawn into various systems of power relations according to the issue at stake.

The key influentials (K.I.) are the sociometric leaders among the top influentials.

Lists of leaders were secured from organizations and informants in nine institutional sectors: business and finance, education, religion, society and wealth, political and governmental organization, labor, independent professions, cultural (aesthetic) institutions, and social service. The initial lists included a total of 312 names in Pacific City and 278 in English City.

Ten expert panel raters were selected on the basis of the following qualifications: (1) knowledge of the leaders in one institutional sector with special thoroughness, (2) broad knowledge of the community, (3) many contacts with T.I. but not themseleves K.I. Raters meeting these qualifications are commonly found among public relations officials, newspaper reporters, and some government officials. Raters were asked to designate each person as *most influential, influential, or less influential* on the specific criterion: "Person participates actively either in supporting or initiating policy decisions which have the most effect on the community." Those nominated most frequently as most influential were selected for interviewing.[8]

Personal interviews were held with a 50 per cent stratified random sample of forty-four T.I. in Pacific City and thirty-two T.I. in English City. The sample had been stratified according to the nine institutional sectors enumerated above, and corresponding proportions of leaders from each sector were interviewed. During the interview each top influential was asked the following question: "If you were responsible for a major project which was before the community that required decision by a group of leaders—leaders that nearly everyone would accept—which ten on this list would you choose, regardless of whether they are known personally to you or not? Add other names if you wish."

Each respondent was asked to check a social acquaintance scale for each T.I. by don't know, heard of, know slightly, know well, know socially (exchange home visits). He was also asked to check each T.I. with whom he had worked on committees during the past two years.

The interview included questions on current issues, role played by respondent, persons and organizations that worked for and against issues. Ratings were also secured of influential organizations and associations in the community. The interview concluded with the question: "There are several crowds in (Pacific City) that work together and pretty much make the big decisions. Is this true or false? The responses were probed.

A questionnaire was left with each respondent at the time of interview. The questionnaire called for background data, career history, business participation (other than own business), social, civic, and professional

---

[8] A valuable test of this technique has been conducted by Foskett and Hohle. See John M. Foskett and Raymond Hohle, "The Measurement of Influence in Community Affairs," *Research Studies of the State College of Washington*, 25 (June 1957), 148–54.

participation. These questionnaires were later collected through the mail or by a personal visit.

Newspaper accounts during the period of the study were used to record activities of T.I., committee appointments of T.I., activities of their wives, community issues, and interactions between institutions of the community.

Informants were interviewed to validate findings on clique behavior, and to describe activities of top influentials and the community power complex in the resolution of current issues.

TEST OF THE HYPOTHESIS

Evidence for a test of the hypothesis that business men exert a predominant influence in community decision-making was secured from three major sources: from *interviews:* (1) Degree of sector representation based on panel selection of T.I., (2) Sociometric rank of each T.I., (3) Committee participation score of T.I.; from *questionnaires:* (1) Participation scores in business, social, civic, and professional organizations of T.I.; from *newspapers:* (1) Participation mentions (acts and opinions) of T.I., (2) Current committee appointments of T.I. for community activities.

In each of the three cities a panel of representative judges from various institutional sectors designated the most influential leaders in the community. Table 1 shows the institutional affiliation of the T.I. selected by the panels in the three cities. Business has the largest representation among the T.I. but there is a considerable spread over the other institutional sectors. A chi square test applied to the frequency distribution in the three cities failed to reveal any significant variation in the panel selections. However, a different

TABLE 1. TOP INFLUENTIALS BY INSTITUTIONAL AFFILIATION AS SELECTED BY EXPERT CITIZEN PANELS

Institutional Affiliation	Pacific City (N=44), Per Cent	English City (N=32), Per Cent	Southern City (N=40), Per Cent
Business	33	34	58
Labor	14	19	5
Education	10	9	5
Government	17	9	5
Independent professions*	12	13	15
Religion	7	9	0
Society and wealth	0	7	12
Social welfare and cultural leaders (combined)	7	0	0
Total	100	100	100

* Hunter says that both of the lawyers in Southern City are corporation lawyers. I have been inclined to classify them as part of the business representation, but I have not because they are lawyers of independent law firms. Lawyers are classified under independent professions unless they were reported as salaried employees in a business firm.

pattern emerged when the K.I. were selected by the T.I. themselves.

The K.I. are a significant feature of any community power structure for they are the sociometric leaders. The initiation and sanction of policy tends to be centered about them so that they may greatly influence the values which dominate in decision-making. The K.I. are those persons who were most often chosen by the T.I. as the ten leaders they would want if they were responsible for a major project before the community and they were seeking leaders nearly everyone would accept.

TABLE 2. KEY INFLUENTIALS AS SELECTED BY TOP INFLUENTIALS
AND RANKED BY STATUS AS INFLUENTIAL POLICY-MAKERS

Pacific City	English City	Southern City
1. Manufacturing executive	1. Labor party leader	1. Utilities executive
2. Wholesale owner and invester	2. University president	2. Transport executive
3. Mercantile executive	3. Manufacturing executive	3. Lawyer
4. Real estate owner—executive	4. Bishop, Church of England	4. Mayor
5. Business executive (woman)	5. Manufacturing executive	5. Manufacturing executive
6. College president	6. Citizen party leader	6. Utilities executive
7. Investment executive	7. University official	7. Manufacturer owner
8. Investment executive	8. Manufacturer owner	8. Mercantile executive
9. Bank executive—investor	9. Labor leader	9. Investment executive
10. Episcopalian bishop	10. Civic leader (woman)	10. Lawyer
11. Mayor (lawyer)	11. Lawyer	11. Mercantile executive
12. Lawyer	12. Society leader	12. Mercantile owner
Business representation : 67 per cent	Business representation : 25 per cent	Business representation : 75 per cent

The twelve influentials with the highest sociometric choice status are shown in Table 2 for the three cities. In Pacific City and Southern City of the United States business representation predominates among the K.I. A comparison of the proportions of business representation within the T.I. (Table 1) and the business representation within the K.I. (Table 2) reveals that the T.I. chose business men more frequently as K.I., in the two American cities.[9] In contrast, English City retains a representation of business among its K.I. (25 per cent) that corresponds closely to the business representation among its T.I. (34 per cent). Moreover, English City reveals a more even representation from the various institutional sectors of the community among its K.I.

This marked difference between the American cities and English City raises questions about community organization. Why should two labor leaders be among the outstanding leaders in English City while not one labor leader appears among the key influentials of the two American cities? These and other questions will be explored later when

---

[9] A test of the significance of the difference between the proportions of business representation in Pacific City showed that the difference was significant at the 0.02 level. No statistically significant difference was found for Southern City, although the direction toward increased business representation among its key influentials is indicated. If the two corporation lawyers were classified as business, the business representation would be 92 per cent and a significant upward difference.

the findings of further analysis have been presented.

Evidence for the influence of the

TABLE 3. SPEARMAN RANK-ORDER CORRELATIONS DERIVED FROM POLICY COMMITTEE-CHOICE RANKINGS OF TOP INFLUENTIALS AND RANKING ON VARIOUS MEASURES OF COMMUNITY BEHAVIOR

Policy Committee-Choice Rank Compared With:	Pacific City (N = 44)	English City (N = 32)
Committee appointments accepted during past 2 years, as shown by newspaper reports	0.51	0.43
Committee participation for 2-year period, as designated by T.I. on the interview schedule	0.84	0.67
Newspaper mentions of community activities and statements	0.15	−0.31
Participation in other businesses as owner or director	0.53	0.33
Participation in social clubs	0.51	0.47
Participation in civic organizations	0.58	0.43
Participation in professional organizations	0.45	0.34
Total social participation in business, social, civic, and professional organizations	0.59	0.48

K.I. was sought by establishing measures of actual behavior for all the T.I. These measures included the activity of T.I. in committee work as reported in the newspapers over a 2-year period, and by their own statements of committee participation. Likewise, we sought evidence of their activity as spokesmen in community life as reported by the newspapers. Participation scores were derived from adapted Chapin Social Participation scales for social, civic, professional, and other business affiliations.

Table 3 shows the Spearman rank-order correlations of the top influentials for these various forms of community behavior in Pacific City and English City. These correlations indicate that there is a definite correspondence between the policy committee choices designating K.I. and actual behavior patterns in both Pacific City and English City. The highest correlation is shown to be that between policy committee-choice rank and the committee participation for a 2-year period as designated by the T.I. on the interview schedule. K.I. are very active in community affairs. However, this activity may not be reflected in newspaper accounts. There is no significant correlation in Pacific City between committee-choice status and newspaper mentions of community activities; in English City there is a low negative correlation indicating that K.I. have received less newspaper publicity than T.I. This lack of publicity is in keeping with two features of civic activity as engaged in by K.I.: (1) much of their activity is policy-making and is carried on quietly, and (2) there is a social convention that "key" leaders do not seek publicity. In England, a deliberate effort is made by some K.I. to keep their names from the newspaper as a role requirement of their social class. The similarities exhibited by K.I. in the two cities suggest that there are many common role patterns. The influentials participate widely in social, civic, and professional organizations. Based on his research contacts, the writer believes that key community leaders develop skills and influence that enable them to originate action for others. It would appear that such leaders could exchange positions with comparable influentials in other American or English cities and soon come to function effectively as K.I. in another community. However, marked differences may be discerned between Pacific City and English City. In general, there is more participation of all kinds by Pacific City K.I., and especially in other businesses. This is because the K.I. in Pacific City have a much higher business composition and because they rely more heavily on voluntary organizations for influence in community decision-making.

CONCLUSION

Validity of the K.I. as identified is now assumed to be demonstrated with sufficient confidence to validate the hypothesis for Pacific City. Business men do exert a predominant influence in community decision-making in Pacific City and Southern City. However, in English City the hypothesis is rejected. The K.I. come from a broad representation of the institutional sectors of community life. Why should this difference exist between the two American cities and the English city? Two major factors seem to explain much of this difference. The first is the difference in occupational prestige values between the United States and England. In contrast to the United States "the social status of industry in England, and so of its captains is low by

comparison with the law, medicine, and the universities."[10] Top business managers are recruited from the universities (and upper-class families) where the tradition of a liberal education predominates, and this kind of education emphasizes humanistic values and minimizes the business orientation that characterizes the social climate of the typical American university campus. Many top business leaders, educated at Oxford and Cambridge, reported during interviews that they regarded business life as a very useful activity but did not view it as occupying the whole man. They expressed a respect for scholarly pursuits. Indeed, specialized courses in business administration in the university are very few, and the tradition continues that business management is learned by experience within the firm. This value system plays a role in the selection of community leaders in English City just as the larger emphasis and prestige of business leadership influences the selection of community leaders in the two American cities.

A second major factor is the structure of city government. In Pacific City the city council is composed of nine members elected at large on a non-partisan ballot. These nine members have the following occupational affiliations:

Newspaper owner-editor	*Business*
Merchant	*Business*
Merchant	*Business*
Newspaper owner-editor	*Business*
Merchant	*Business*
Merchant	*Business*

---

[10] Bosworth Monck, "How to Make a Captain of Industry," *The Listener* (January 13, 1955), 57. Cf. C. J. Adcock and L. B. Brown, "Social Class and the Ranking of Occupations," *British Journal of Sociology*, 8 (March 1957), 26–32.

*Housewife (formerly
   teacher)*
*Jeweler (and labor
   officer)*
Bus operator

Professional

Skilled worker
*Semi-skilled
   Worker*

A background of small business predominates. None of the council members was chosen as a top influential by our panel raters or by top influentials. There is every indication that the top community leaders do not regard the council as a strong center of community power. The council tends to make decisions on community issues after a relatively long period of debate and after power mobilization has taken place in the community. During this period such groups as the Chamber of Commerce, the Labor Council, Municipal League, Parent-Teachers Association, and Council of Churches take stands. Council members may be approached and appeals made to them. Newspaper editors write articles. K.I. may make open declarations for or

against the current issues and use their influence with the "right persons or groups." The mayor, as administrative head and an elective official, is both relatively powerful as patronage dispenser, and, at the same time, exposed to pressure from citizens to whom he may be indebted for his position either in the past or in the future.

In contrast to this pattern, English City has a city council composed of 112 members drawn from twenty-eight wards. Each ward elects four members. When the council is organized, members are appointed to committees that meet once or twice a week. Issues that arise in any part of the community are quickly brought to the Council's attention. The city clerk is the administrative head of the city government. He is a civil servant appointed by the council on the basis of his administrative ability and serves under a requirement of impartiality as elections come and political parties change in power. The members of the Council are released by

TABLE 4. OCCUPATIONAL COMPOSITION OF ENGLISH CITY
COUNCIL IN 1955

32 Per Cent Trade Union Members, N = 37	30 Per Cent Business Group Members, N = 33	37 Per Cent Other Community Sectors, N = 40
2 Foremen	4 Manufacturers	2 Solicitors
16 Skilled workers	7 Wholesale and retail owners	1 Doctor
5 Semiskilled workers		1 Dentist
8 Clerical workers	1 Cinema owner	1 Engineer
4 Trade union officials	4 Contractors	1 Accountant
2 Unskilled workers	8 Company directors and secretaries	1 Auctioneer
	1 Bank official	1 Teacher
	8 Insurance officials	2 Ministers
		3 Political party organizing secretaries
		3 National government officials
		12 Housewives
		12 Retired workers

their employers from work at the time of meetings. They are paid a stipend by the local government for time lost from work and for any personal expenses incurred in attending meetings within or outside the city. Table 4 shows the occupational composition of 110 members (two vacant seats) of English City Council in 1955.

The council is composed of three major groups, trade union members (32 per cent), business members (30 per cent), and other community members (37 per cent). Five of the twelve K.I. of the community are members and play major roles in their respective parties. The council is the major arena of community decision. Issues reach it directly, are investigated by Council committees, and are decided upon by a vote taken in the full council. Com-

munity organizations play important roles in debating the issues, but these are definitely secondary or supplementary activities. The community values system condemns any pressure tactics on the Council as "bad taste." However, in the council a caucus of elected party leaders is held before any important vote and a position is taken by the leaders for the party. The "whip" is applied and members are expected to vote as instructed. Such action is rationalized as necessary for responsible party government.

Two factors, a different occupational prestige system and a different council-community power complex, seem to explain the variation in the composition of key influentials who come to power in Pacific City and English City.

COMMUNITY INFLUENTIALS: THE ELITES OF ATLANTA

M. Kent Jennings

University of Michigan

DISCUSSION OF CONFLICTING FINDINGS*

This material indicates how Atlanta's nominal ruling elite was subjected to a test of the ruling-elite model, a model which emerged from Hunter's original investigations. Viewed out of context and not in comparison with

other actors, this group, especially its top echelon, seems to fit the configuration of a general elite. When other actors and the specifics of issue resolution are introduced into the analysis, however, the validity of the ruling-elite model appears more doubtful. That is not to say that the power structure of Atlanta is not perhaps more highly structured and less fragmented than those of some other communities.[1] In

---

---

[1] For two journalistic accounts that suggest high concentrations of influence in Atlanta, see Douglass Cater, "Atlanta: Smart Politics and Good Relations," *The*

general, the upper echelons of Atlanta's power structure may be described as a number of slightly to moderately competitive coalitions, *not dominated by economic notables*, exercising determinative influence in their own policy areas. There is, in turn, a moderate amount of overlapping membership among these coalitions, with some actors performing interstitial roles in linking the coalitions.

Despite this *caveat*, a discrepancy clearly exists between our more recent findings and Hunter's original ones. There are at least three possible major causes for the discrepancy: change in the structure over time; different study orientations to the decision-making process; and questions of validation of the sociometric techniques. The most obvious possibility is that the configuration of power has changed in the approximately eight years that elapsed between the two research efforts.[2]

Reporter (July 11, 1957), pp. 18–21; and Seymour Freedgood, "Life in Buckhead," *Fortune* (September 1961), pp. 108ff.

2 In one of the few instances in the literature of the social sciences of the empirical re-examination of reported findings, the time factor was found to explain some, but by no means all, of the discrepancies. Our reference is to Robert Redfield, *Tepoztlan: A Mexican Village* (Chicago: University of Chicago Press, 1930); and to Oscar Lewis, *Life in a Mexican Village: Tepoztlan Restudied* (Urban, Ill.: University of Illinois Press, 1951). For a discussion of these two studies, see Horace Miner, "The Folk-Urban Continuum," *American Sociological Review*, XVII (October 1952), 1952), 529–37. More relevant to our work are two studies of Syracuse, New York. Wayne Hodges, in *Company and Community* (New York: Harper & Row, Publishers, 1958), found that industrialists in locally owned firms were at the apex of the power structure and government officials and politicians were subordinate. A later study— Roscoe C. Martin, Frank J. Munger, *et al.*, *Decisions in Syracuse* (Bloomington, Ind.: Indiana University Press, 1961)—encom-

There is some support for this explanation, especially in the increasing importance of local government officials in Atlanta and surrounding Fulton County. As federal programs in such fields as urban renewal, highway construction, housing, and airport development assume increasing importance in Atlanta's economic and political life, government officials speak more authoritatively on these subjects and are more often those who deal directly with state and national officials. They assume the role of influential specialists and help to fragment the distribution of power.

Developments in the field of race relations have also altered the distribution of power in recent years. Since the 1954 Supreme Court decision, Atlanta officials have been expected to take the lead in defining the ground rules of the local racial struggle. By the same token, Negroes have obtained increasing leverage in community decision-making. Negro voters have cast the "decisive" ballots in recent elections. The militant Negro student-protest movement in Atlanta has coincided with other developments to alter the patterns of influence in the larger community, as well as within the Negro community itself.

Of the possible reasons for discrepancies between the two pictures of Atlanta's power structure, change over time is the hardest to refute since precise reconstruction of the power structure of eight years ago is a difficult feat. The time explanation is at least questionable, however, because there have been no dramatic, overt changes in the

passed part of the time period covered by Hodges. The conclusions were quite different, with a variety of actors and institutions appearing as power wielders. Differences in methodology and orientation appear to account for the variance between the two studies.

structure similiar to that in northern cities like Philadelphia and New Haven and no radical policy innovations outside the race-relations area. The major institutions of the community are basically the same. The configuration of the current power structure seems based on the same sources as that in the past. Internal analysis of Hunter's work[3] and reliance on the informed opinion of participants and observers[4] provide other arguments against acceptance of Hunter's original formulations. On the basis of these arguments, it does not appear that the power structure has changed so much as the discrepancy between the two sets of findings suggests.

A second possible explanation for the inconsistency is that Hunter's orientation to decision-making and power is basically different from our own. Although his meaning is somewhat unclear, he seems to designate one pivotal stage in the decision-making continuum as determinative of all future events.[5] This stage is similar to our own second stage —fixing priorities. This orientation tends to emphasize the importance of dinner gatherings, telephone conversations, and office conclaves that are *presumably* necessary to make projects "go," to veto others, and to hold the status quo on still others. This orientation tends to overlook other phases and actors in the decision-making process— phases like initiation, planning, long range conditioning of attitudes, persuasion, bargaining, promotion, and implementation; and actors like civic-staff personnel, government officials, lay leaders, controllers of mass media, and episodic participants. By emphasizing one particular phase of decision-making, Hunter highlighted the importance of the attributed influentials. Our orientation placed no a priori emphases on any particular point in community decision-making (but did assume a continuum). Our study therefore highlights other roles performed by actors who are not necessarily perceived as influentials.

Third, the question arises about the validity of Hunter's portrayal of a unidimensional power structure. His severest critics charge that he committed the sin of reifying his concepts of power, influence, leadership, and decision-makers without actually demonstrating that the perceived influentials did exert pervasive influence on the resolution of vital issues in Atlanta. Specifically, it has been suggested that Hunter used one or more variants of three false tests of a ruling elite that Robert Dahl has suggested:

> The first improper test confuses a ruling elite with a group that has a high *potential for control*. . . . The second improper test confuses a ruling elite with a group of individuals who have more influence than any others in the system. . . . The third improper test . . . is to generalize from a single scope of influence.[6]

---

[3] See particularly Raymond Wolfinger, "Reputation and Reality in the Study of Community Power," *American Sociological Review*, XXV (October 1960), 636–44; Herbert Kaufman and Victor Jones, "The Mystery of Power," *Public Administration Review*, XIV (Summer 1954), 205–12. For a detailed dissection of the famous Middletown studies, parts of which resemble Hunter's, see Nelson Polsby, "Power in Middletown: Fact and Value in Community Research," *Canadian Journal of Economics and Political Science*, XXVI (November 1960), 592–603.

[4] Although no systematic effort was made to gather such opinion, several respondents questioned the validity of the ruling-elite model for Atlanta.

[5] Floyd Hunter, *Community Power Structure* (Chapel Hill, N.C.: University of North Carolina Press, 1953), pp. 95–100.

[6] Robert A. Dahl, "A Critique of the Ruling Elite Model," *American Political Science Review*, LII (June 1958), 645.

Textual criticism of *Community Power Structure* yields evidence that Hunter did indeed use these false tests.[7] Certainly Atlanta's attributed elite, both then and now, lends itself to such improper tests. Virtually all its members occupy positions that vest incumbents with potential power; most do have more influence than most other people in the community; and most are influential in at least one policy area of community life. Our research attempted to avoid these three misleading tests by gaining more exact data on involvement and exercise of power-oriented behavior through detailed interviewing and case analysis. Perhaps, then, the differences in the two studies' conclusions arise from differences in the techniques of validating the nomination-attribution approach to identifying community decision-makers.

Our findings about Atlanta's power structure point toward a revision of Hunter's ruling-elite model. There is more specialization and therefore less generalization of decision-making among the reputed elite. Second, influentials are not restricted to the perceived elite. We do not reject, however, the claim that some actors are influential in more than one issue area in the community. Influentials do overlap issue areas in Atlanta, but the overlap is less extensive than Hunter implied, and actors other than the reputed elite play key roles in decision-making.

From a methodological point of view, our findings show that the nomination-attribution technique is neither so infallible as its supporters claim nor so misleading as its attackers insist. Most of the perceived influentials at both levels were indeed influential in one or more issue areas. Those considered most influential tended to en-

gage in more deliberately influential behavior and appeared actually to be more influential than those reputed to be less influential. The technique measures more than simply respect, popularity, or social status. It serves to locate people of consequence in community decision-making.

Two results of our study illustrate the limitations of the technique, however. First, few deductions can be made about the scope, nature, and employment of the influence of the attributed influentials. Few were found to be actively engaged in a majority of the issues and issue-areas cited and a few were mostly inactive. The researcher cannot conclude that, because others perceive them as generally influential, they actually are generally influential. In fact, it appears that they are usually engaged in a restricted number of areas. Second, the finding that actors other than those perceived as community influentials also become involved in and play key roles in issue resolution disproves the claim that the reputed elite monopolizes community decision-making. After such an elite has been defined, it remains an empirical question whether its members "run" the community.

THE PLACE OF THE ECONOMIC DOMINANTS

If, indeed, there is no general ruling elite in Atlanta, the question of whether the economic dominants constitute this elite is eliminated. Even though we reject the notion of a ruling elite composed of economic notables, however, it is still worthwhile to re-examine Hunter's conclusion that the economic giants are the linchpins of Atlanta's power structure.

Taking only those economic domi-

---

[7] See note 3.

nants who were not also attributed influentials—twenty-six of the forty-one identified—the data clearly show them to be less politicized than the attributed and prescribed influentials on virtually all measures. More significantly, almost none appeared as key actors in the resolution of our two minor and three major issues. Surely, if they composed even a modest ruling elite, they would have emerged as key actors in at least one and preferably all of these issues.

This test is a bit unfair since it excludes those fifteen economic dominants who were also among the fifty-seven attributed influentials. Their behavior can be summarized as reflecting the general behavior of the attributed influentials as a whole. For example, if one-third of the attributed influentials exhibited a certain behavioral characteristic, then probably about one-third of the fifteen economic dominants within that group would exhibit the same characteristic. This statement is, of course, a rough rule of thumb that would not apply in all instances. An examination of the evidence, however, provides no clues to suggest a consistent differentiation between the economic dominants among the attributed influentials and the attributed influentials as a whole.

Where, then, is the place of the economic dominants in the power structure? The answer is in two parts. First, the economic dominants of Atlanta are only one of several key groups that play significant roles in community decision-making. Both elective and appointive government officials, both professional and amateur civic-staff personnel, and a variety of other actors form the total dramatis personae of most community issues. There is no evidence to suggest that the economic dominants who do exercise power consistently or often prevail over other actors.

Second, the economic dominants are by no means a monolithic group in terms of their behavior. This point is most apparent in the tremendous differences in the power-oriented activities they engage in. As the evidence shows, this behavior falls at the lower end of the continuum among those not perceived as influential but edges into the upper end among those who are perceived as influential. Far less than a majority of the economic dominants are key actors in community decision-making in Atlanta, but those who are share power with other elites.

Having established that the economic dominants as a class do not form a ruling group, nevertheless we cannot deny the importance some of them have for decision-making in Atlanta. It is apparent, for example, that economic interests and leaders are more influential in Atlanta than in Chicago, New York, and New Haven, to mention three cities that have been thoroughly explored in the literature.[8] Their influence is more akin to that reported in such cities as Detroit, Seattle, Pittsburgh, Dallas, and perhaps Syracuse.[9]

---

[8] See Edward C. Banfield, *Political Influence* (New York: The Free Press of Glencoe, Inc., 1961); Wallace S. Sayre and Herbert Kaufman, *Governing New York City* (New York: Russell Sage Foundation, 1960); and Robert A. Dahl, *Who Governs?* (New Haven, Conn.: Yale University Press, 1961) for reports on Chicago, New York, and New Haven, respectively.

[9] For a report on Detroit's business leaders, see [author anonymous] in David Greenstone, *A Report on Politics in Detroit*, Part V (Cambridge, Mass.: Joint Center for Urban Studies of the Massachusetts Institute of Technology and Harvard University, 1961), pp. 1–19. Two studies of Seattle are Delbert C. Miller, "Industry and Community Power Structure: A Comparative Study of an American and an English City," *American Sociological Review*, XXIII (February 1958), 9–15; and William J. Gore and Robert L. Peabody, "The Functions of

Why are economic dominants more influential in Atlanta than in some other American cities? Very briefly, we may sketch in three possible reasons.[10] First, the governmental and partisan structure of Atlanta is conducive to civic-political activity on the part of economic interests. There is an absence of political party organization and control at the local level. Elections are, in effect, nonpartisan, so that the business leaders whose tendencies are Republican at the national level are not bothered by supporting candidates who in most instances are Democrats. More important, since they do not have to work through a party apparatus that might be repugnant to them, the economic leaders are able to enter the fray of candidate selection and support directly, if often covertly. The absence of strong partisanship not only encourages initial engagement, but it also means that the presence of a strong coalition of partisan interests—like that of Chicago—is not present as a competitor for power and influence in the day-to-day issues facing the community. Economic interests are thus more likely to have an influential voice, and are thereby encouraged to participate still further. The presence of a formally weak and decentralized city and county government has also

the Political Campaign: A Case Study," *Western Political Quarterly,* XI (March 1958), 55–70. Pittsburgh is referred to in Peter B. Clark, "Civic Leadership: The Symbols of Legitimacy" (paper delivered at the 1960 meeting of the American Political Science Association, New York, September 1960). A recent account of Dallas is found in Carol Estes Thometz, *The Decision-Makers* (Dallas: Southern Methodist University Press, 1963). See Martin, Munger, *et al., op. cit.,* for data on Syracuse.

10 The organization of the following pages draws on [author anonymous] in Greenstone, *op. cit.*

proved conducive to the exertion of economic power.

The second reason is related to the characteristics of the firms with which many of the leading economic notables are associated. . . . Economic dominants who are perceived as influentials (and who in fact tend to *be* influential) most often come from locally owned, downtown firms with a locus of consumption in the immediate metropolitan area. The futures of their firms are thus tied firmly to the future of the community. There is, in short, a tremendous incentive to participate. Nor should we discount the incentives coming from more altruistic and traditional sources. Many of these economic dominants come from families and firms for which service to the community has been a responsibility for decades. To some extent, today's actors have internalized these civic-obligation norms.

Such incentives would not be sufficient, however, were the "climate" for business influence less favorable in Atlanta. One of the factors here is the prevailing ideology in the community, an ideology that has served to heighten the hospitality of the decision-making structure to action by economic interests.

The absence of a strong working-class movement and organization, the exclusion of "redneck" and "woolhat" elements from the upper levels of decision-making, and the aforementioned absence of party operations have all served the cause of the business ethic and business spirit in the community. Furthermore, leading economic institutions have not treated the community and its inhabitants badly. If a spirit of *noblesse oblige* has guided some of their actions, it has not caused resentment. Partly because they have developed some imposing economic giants of their own, the Negroes of the community have, until recently, directed little of their fire against the business elements of the community.

While there are incentives and a favorable climate for some economic notables, still a third ingredient is essential: relatively high cohesion among diverse economic enterprises. Financial, real-estate, construction, and retail firms have often acted with an unanimity rare in other communities. If industry has seldom been part of this alliance, it is not from opposition so much as from disinterest. One factor producing cohesion lies in institutional arrangements like the strong Chamber of Commerce and satellite organizations. There are no competing civic-business organizations, although some trade organizations may find themselves at odds from time to time. Cohesion is also based on personal ties, many of them stretching back over two or three generations. "Gut-fighting" is not likely to flourish in this environment.

Another source of cohesion is the role of a half-dozen or so economic firms as pace setters and opinion leaders for other members of the large business interests. Thanks to their resources, the efficiency with which they use them, and their generally good personal relations with others, these opinion leaders help weld the business community into a united front. Finally, for a complex series of reasons, Atlanta business leaders seem to feel that all will profit in the long run from benefits that may not be apparent for any one given firm. There is a feeling that another firm's gain is not necessarily one's own loss.

Some of these explanations of why some economic leaders are quite influential in Atlanta could be applied, with certain changes, to explaining why Atlanta has a more pluralistic power structure than the one Hunter attributed to it. Economic dominants, elective and appointive government officials, lay and professional civic leaders, and minority group leaders—especially from the Negro community—all have some say in who rules and what is decided in Atlanta.[11]

---

[11] The reader will notice that little attention has been paid the average citizen and his part in decision-making. Obviously, the scope and design of the study did not permit any extensive work in this area. On the basis of what has been observed about the masses in Atlanta, however, it appears that they are probably no better or worse off than citizens of other metropolises when it comes to political participation, access to decision-making posts, and having their preferences anticipated by influentials.

NATIONAL POWER

A criticism often raised against the literature on community power is the disproportionate amount of attention it gives to empirical studies which appear to have slight bearing upon broad theoretical and conceptual problems of power. The opposite charge is appropriate with respect to sociological writings on national power since most are of a speculative nature and are only tangentially connected with empirical research.[1] (Over the past decade sociologists have given primary

---

[1] Some suggest that most of the literature on national power is theoretical, given a very liberal interpretation of theory.

attention to community power; relatively few publications deal with power at the national level.)

The central issues debated in studies of community power parallel those in the literature on national power. Is there a national power elite, or is there a dispersal of power comparable to that which many find at the local level? Is power fundamentally in the hands of economic leaders? What constitutes appropriate empirical methods and adequate data against which conflicting claims concerning national power can be assessed?

From the casual observations made by some writers, it appears, at first glance, that considerable empirical knowledge exists on the nature of national power. To a large extent this erroneous conclusion arises from the tendency of many analysts of power (including some of those who carry out field research) to transfer information about power at the community level to the national level. Some make this transfer directly; others imply a continuity between local and national power.[2]

Some critics have expressed strong reservations about the a priori assumptions of correspondence between these two realms. Spinrad suggests that to extrapolate the findings from community studies to the national scene is to engage in reductionism: The operations of the society at large and of its smaller units are considered identical.[3] Other factors may also be operative, but the reason most commonly given for the incommensurability between local and national power is the magnitude and complexity of the political and economic institutions at the national level.[4] Indeed, the scope of the economy and the government at the federal level—presumptively two strategic loci of power—is no doubt a major reason for the scarcity of studies on national power.

THE THESIS OF THE POWER ELITE

The most widely known and controversial analysis of power at the national level is C. Wright Mills's study *The Power Elite*.[5] Since its appearance in 1956 most writers have found it impossible to discuss the subject of national power without taking Mills's thesis into account, by either refuting or adding substance to it.

According to Mills, a relatively small number of men—rulers of the big corporations, top figures in government, and those in the higher echelons of the military —occupy key posts in the social structure and are thus able to make interlocking decisions having critical import for society and the common man. Mills cites "the size and shape of the national economy, the level of employment, the pur-

---

[2] Hunter, *op. cit.*, p. 167.

[3] Spinrad, *op. cit.*, p. 342. Also, Suzanne Keller, *Beyond the Ruling Class: Strategic Elites in Modern Society* (New York: Random House, Inc., 1963), pp. 110–11.

[4] Leonard Reissman, *Class in American Society* (Glencoe, Ill.: The Free Press, 1959), p. 192.

[5] C. Wright Mills, *The Power Elite* (Fair Lawn, N.J.: Oxford University Press, Inc., 1956).

chasing power of the consumer, the prices that are advertised, the investments that are channeled"[6] as types of consequences importantly influenced by the three sets of elites in the economic, political, and military domains. The essence of Mills's thinking is in the following essay, "The Structure of Power in American Society," which incorporates the main thesis from his monograph *The Power Elite*.

[6] *Ibid.*, p. 125.

THE STRUCTURE OF POWER IN AMERICAN SOCIETY*

C. Wright Mills†

Columbia University

I

Power has to do with whatever decisions men make about the arrangements under which they live, and about the events which make up the history of their times. Events that are beyond human decision do happen; social arrangements do change without benefit of explicit decision. But in so far as such decisions are made, the problem of who is involved in making them is the basic problem of power. In so far as they could be made but are not, the problem becomes who fails to make them?

We cannot today merely assume that in the last resort men must always be governed by their own consent. For among the means of power which now prevail is the power to manage and to manipulate the consent of men. That we do not know the limits of such power, and that we hope it does have limits, does not remove the fact that much power today is successfully employed without the sanction of the reason or the conscience of the obedient.

Surely nowadays we need not argue that, in the last resort, coercion is the 'final' form of power. But then, we are by no means constantly at the last resort. Authority (power that is justified by the beliefs of the voluntarily obedient) and manipulation (power that is wielded unbeknown to the powerless) —must also be considered, along with coercion. In fact, the three types must be sorted out whenever we think about power.

In the modern world, we must bear in mind, power is often not so authoritative as it seemed to be in the medieval epoch: ideas which justify rulers no longer seem so necessary to their exercise of power. At least for many of the great decisions of our time—especially those of an international sort—mass 'persuasion' has not been 'necessary'; the fact is simply accomplished. Furthermore, such ideas as are available to the powerful are often neither taken up nor used by them. Such ideologies usually arise as a response to an effective debunking of power; in the United

* Chapter I of *Power Politics and People: The Collected Essays of C. Wright Mills*, edited by Irving Louis Horowitz, New York and London, Oxford University Press, 1963, pp. 23–28.
† Deceased.

States such opposition has not been effective enough recently to create the felt need for new ideologies of rule.

There has, in fact, come about a situation in which many who have lost faith in prevailing loyalties have not acquired new ones, and so pay no attention to politics of any kind. They are not radical, not liberal, not conservative, not reactionary. They are inactionary. They are out of it. If we accept the Greek's definition of the idiot as an altogether private man, then we must conclude that many American citizens are now idiots. And I should not be surprised, although I do not know, if there were not some such idiots even in Germany. This—and I use the word with care—this spiritual condition seems to me the key to many modern troubles of political intellectuals, as well as the key to much political bewilderment in modern society. Intellectual 'conviction' and moral 'belief' are not necessary, in either the rulers or the ruled, for a ruling power to persist and even to flourish. So far as the role of ideologies is concerned, their frequent absences and the prevalence of mass indifference are surely two of the major political facts about the western societies today.

How large a role any explicit decisions do play in the making of history is itself an historical problem. For how large that role may be depends very much upon the means of power that are available at any given time in any given society. In some societies, the innumerable actions of innumerable men modify their milieux, and so gradually modify the structure itself. These modifications—the course of history—go on behind the backs of men. History is drift, although in total 'men make it.' Thus, innumerable entrepreneurs and innumerable consumers by ten-thousand decisions per minute may shape and re-

shape the free-market economy. Perhaps this was the chief kind of limitation Marx had in mind when he wrote, in *The 18th Brumaire*: that 'Men make their own history, but they do not make it just as they please; they do not make it under circumstances chosen by themselves. . . .'

But in other societies—certainly in the United States and in the Soviet Union today—a few men may be so placed within the structure that by their decisions they modify the milieux of many other men, and in fact nowadays the structural conditions under which most men live. Such elites of power also make history under circumstances not chosen altogether by themselves, yet compared with other men, and compared with other periods of world history, these circumstances do indeed seem less limiting.

I should contend that 'men are free to make history', but that some men are indeed much freer than others. For such freedom requires access to the means of decision and of power by which history can now be made. It has not always been so made; but in the later phases of the modern epoch it is. It is with reference to this epoch that I am contending that if men do not make history, they tend increasingly to become the utensils of history-makers.

The history of modern society may readily be understood as the story of the enlargement and the centralization of the means of power—in economic, in political, and in military institutions. The rise of industrial society has involved these developments in the means of economic production. The rise of the nation-state has involved similar developments in the means of violence and in those of political administration.

In the western societies, such transformations have generally occurred gradually, and many cultural traditions have restrained and shaped them. In most of the Soviet societies, they are happening very rapidly indeed and without the great discourse of western civilization, without the Renaissance and without the Reformation, which so greatly strengthened and gave political focus to the idea of freedom. In those societies, the enlargement and the co-ordination of all the means of power has occurred more brutally, and from the beginning under tightly centralized authority. But in both types, the means of power have now become international in scope and similar in form. To be sure, each of them has its own ups and downs; neither is as yet absolute; how they are run differs quite sharply.

Yet so great is the reach of the means of violence, and so great the economy required to produce and support them, that we have in the immediate past witnessed the consolidation of these two world centers, either of which dwarfs the power of Ancient Rome. As we pay attention to the awesome means of power now available to quite small groups of men we come to realize that Caesar could do less with Rome than Napoleon with France; Napoleon less with France than Lenin with Russia. But what was Caesar's power at its height compared with the power of the changing inner circles of Soviet Russia and the temporary administrations of the United States? We come to realize—indeed they continually remind us—how a few men have access to the means by which in a few days continents can be turned into thermonuclear wastelands. That the facilities of power are so enormously enlarged and so decisively centralized surely means that the powers of quite small groups of men, which we may call elites, are now of literally inhuman consequence.

By concern here is not with the international scene but with the United States in the middle of the twentieth century. I must emphasize 'in the middle of the twentieth century' because in our attempt to understand any society we come upon images which have been drawn from its past and which often confuse our attempt to confront its present reality. That is one minor reason why history is the shank of any social science: we must study it if only to rid ourselves of it. In the United States, there are indeed many such images and usually they have to do with the first half of the nineteenth century. At that time the economic facilities of the United States were very widely dispersed and subject to little or to no central authority.

The state watched in the night but was without decisive voice in the day.

One man meant one rifle and the militia were without centralized orders.

Any American as old-fashioned as I can only agree with R. H. Tawney that 'Whatever the future may contain, the past has shown no more excellent social order than that in which the mass of the people were the masters of the holdings which they ploughed and the tools with which they worked, and could boast . . . 'It is a quietness to a man's mind to live upon his own and to know his heir certain.'

But then we must immediately add: all that is of the past and of little relevance to our understanding of the United States today. Within this society three broad levels of power may now be distinguished. I shall begin at the top and move downward.

II

The power to make decisions of national and international consequence is now so clearly seated in political, military, and economic institutions that other areas of society seem off to the side and, on occasion, readily subordinated to these. The scattered institutions of religion, education, and family are increasingly shaped by the big three, in which history-making decisions now regularly occur. Behind this fact there is all the push and drive of a fabulous technology; for these three institutional orders have incorporated this technology and now guide it, even as it shapes and paces their development.

As each has assumed its modern shape, its effects upon the other two have become greater, and the traffic between the three has increased. There is no longer, on the one hand, an economy, and, on the other, a political order, containing a military establishment unimportant to politics and to money-making. There is a political economy numerously linked with military order and decision. This triangle of power is now a structural fact, and it is the key to any understanding of the higher circles in America today. For as each of these domains has coincided with the others, as decisions in each have become broader, the leading men of each—the high military, the corporation executives, the political directorate—have tended to come together to form the power elite of America.

The political order, once composed of several dozen states with a weak federal-center, has become an executive apparatus which has taken up into itself many powers previously scattered, legislative as well as administrative, and which now reaches into all parts of the social structure. The long-time tendency of business and government to become more closely connected has since World War II reached a new point of explicitness. Neither can now be seen clearly as a distinct world. The growth of executive government does not mean

merely the 'enlargement of government' as some kind of autonomous bureaucracy: under American conditions, it has meant the ascendency of the corporation man into political eminence. Already during the New Deal, such men had joined the political directorate; as of World War II they came to dominate it. Long involved with government, now they have moved into quite full direction of the economy of the war effort and of the postwar era.

The economy, once a great scatter of small productive units in somewhat automatic balance, has become internally dominated by a few hundred corporations, administratively and politically interrelated, which together hold the keys to economic decision. This economy is at once a permanent-war economy and a private-corporation economy. The most important relations of the corporation to the state now rest on the coincidence between military and corporate interests, as defined by the military and the corporate rich, and accepted by politicians and public. Within the elite as a whole, this coincidence of military domain and corporate realm strengthens both of them and further subordinates the merely political man. Not the party politician, but the corporation executive, is now more likely to sit with the military to answer the question: what is to be done?

The military order, once a slim establishment in a context of civilian distrust, has become the largest and most expensive feature of government; behind smiling public relations, it has all the grim and clumsy efficiency of a great and sprawling bureaucracy. The high military have gained decisive political and economic relevance. The seemingly permanent military threat places a premium upon them and virtually all political and economic actions are now judged in terms of military definitions of reality: the higher military have ascended to a firm position within the power elite of our time.

In part at least this is a result of an historical fact, pivotal for the years since 1939: the attention of the elite has shifted from domestic problems—centered in the 'thirties around slump—to international problems—centered in the 'forties and 'fifties around war. By long historical usage, the government of the United States has been shaped by domestic clash and balance; it does not have suitable agencies and traditions for the democratic handling of international affairs. In considerable part, it is in this vacuum that the power elite has grown.

(i) To understand the unity of this power elite, we must pay attention to the psychology of its several members in their respective milieux. In so far as the power elite is composed of men of similar origin and education, of similar career and style of life, their unity may be said to rest upon the fact that they are of similar social type, and to lead to the fact of their easy intermingling. This kind of unity reaches its frothier apex in the sharing of that prestige which is to be had in the world of the celebrity. It achieves a more solid culmination in the fact of the interchangeability of positions between the three dominant institutional orders. It is revealed by considerable traffic of personnel within and between these three, as well as by the rise of specialized go-betweens as in the new style high-level lobbying.

(ii) Behind such psychological and social unity are the structure and the mechanics of those institutional hierarchies over which the political directorate, the corporate rich, and the high military now preside. How each of these hierarchies is shaped and what

relations it has with the others determine in large part the relations of their rulers. Were these hierarchies scattered and disjointed, then their respective elites might tend to be scattered and disjointed; but if they have many interconnections and points of coinciding interest, then their elites tend to form a coherent kind of grouping. The unity of the elite is not a simple reflection of the unity of institutions, but men and institutions are always related; that is why we must understand the elite today in connection with such institutional trends as the development of a permanent war establishment, alongside a privately incorporated economy, inside a virtual political vacuum. For the men at the top have been selected and formed by such institutional trends.

(iii) Their unity, however, does not rest solely upon psychological similarity and social intermingling, nor entirely upon the structural blending of commanding positions and common interests. At times it is the unity of a more explicit co-ordination.

To say that these higher circles are increasingly co-ordinated, that this is *one* basis of their unity, and that at times—as during open war—such co-ordination is quite wilful, is not to say that the co-ordination is total or continuous, or even that it is very sure-footed. Much less is it to say that the power elite has emerged as the realization of a plot. Its rise cannot be adequately explained in any psychological terms.

Yet we must remember that institutional trends may be defined as opportunities by those who occupy the command posts. Once such opportunities are recognized, men may avail themselves of them. Certain types of men from each of these three areas, more farsighted than others, have actively promoted the liaison even before it took its truly modern shape. Now more have come to see that their several interests can more easily be realized if they work together, in informal as well as in formal ways, and accordingly they have done so.

The idea of the power elite is of course an interpretation. It rests upon and it enables us to make sense of major institutional trends, the social similarities and psychological affinities of the men at the top. But the idea is also based upon what has been happening on the middle and lower levels of power, to which I now turn.

III

There are of course other interpretations of the American system of power. The most usual is that it is a moving balance of many competing interests. The image of balance, at least in America, is derived from the idea of the economic market: in the nineteenth century, the balance was thought to occur between a great scatter of individuals and enterprises; in the twentieth century, it is thought to occur between great interest blocs. In both views, the politician is the key man of power because he is the broker of many conflicting powers.

I believe that the balance and the compromise in American society—the 'countervailing powers' and the 'veto groups', of parties and associations, of strata and unions—must now be seen as having mainly to do with the middle levels of power. It is these middle levels that the political journalist and the scholar of politics are most likely to understand and to write about—if only because, being mainly middle class themselves, they are closer to them. Moreover these levels provide the noisy content of most 'political' news and gossip; the images of these levels are more

or less in accord with the folklore of how democracy works; and, if the master-image of balance is accepted, many intellectuals, especially in their current patrioteering, are readily able to satisfy such political optimism as they wish to feel. Accordingly, liberal interpretations of what is happening in the United States are now virtually the only interpretations that are widely distributed.

But to believe that the power system reflects a balancing society is, I think, to confuse the present era with earlier times, and to confuse its top and bottom with its middle levels.

By the top levels, as distinguished from the middle, I intend to refer, first of all, to the scope of the decisions that are made. At the top today, these decisions have to do with all the issues of war and peace. They have also to do with slump and poverty which are now so very much problems of international scope. I intend also to refer to whether or not the groups that struggle politically have a chance to gain the positions from which such top decisions are made, and indeed whether their members do usually hope for such top national command. Most of the competing interests which make up the clang and clash of American politics are strictly concerned with their slice of the existing pie. Labour unions, for example, certainly have no policies of an international sort other than those which given unions adopt for the strict economic protection of their members. Neither do farm organizations. The actions of such middle-level powers may indeed have consequence for top-level policy; certainly at times they hamper these policies. But they are not truly concerned with them, which means of course that their influence tends to be quite irresponsible.

The facts of the middle levels may

in part be understood in terms of the rise of the power elite. The expanded and centralized and interlocked hierarchies over which the power elite preside have encroached upon the old balance and relegated it to the middle level. But there are also independent developments of the middle levels. These, it seems to me, are better understood as an affair of intrenched and provincial demands than as a center of national decision. As such, the middle level often seems much more of a stalemate than a moving balance.

(i) The middle level of politics is not a forum in which there are debated the big decisions of national and international life. Such debate is not carried on by nationally responsible parties representing and clarifying alternative policies. There are no such parties in the United States. More and more, fundamental issues never come to any point or decision before the Congress, much less before the electorate in party campaigns. In the case of Formosa, in the spring of 1955, the Congress abdicated all debate concerning events and decisions which surely bordered on war. The same is largely true of the 1957 crisis in the Middle East. Such decisions now regularly by-pass the Congress, and are never clearly focused issues for public decision.

The American political campaign distracts attention from national and international issues, but that is not to say that there are no issues in these campaigns. In each district and state, issues are set up and watched by organized interests of sovereign local importance. The professional politician is of course a party politician, and the two parties are semifeudal organizations: they trade patronage and other favours for votes and for protection. The differences between them, so far as national issues are concerned, are very narrow and very mixed up. Often each seems to be forty-eight parties, one to each state; and accordingly, the politician as campaigner and as Congressman is not concerned with national party lines, if any are discernible. Often he is not subject to any effective national party discipline. He speaks for the interests of his own constituency, and he is concerned with national issues only in so far as they affect the interests effectively organized there, and hence his chances of reelection. That is why, when he does speak of national matters, the result is so often such an empty rhetoric. Seated in his sovereign locality, the politician is not at the national summit. He is on and of the middle levels of power.

(ii) Politics is not an arena in which free and independent organizations truly connect the lower and middle levels of society with the top levels of decision. Such organizations are not an effective and major part of American life today. As more people are drawn into the political arena, their associations become mass in scale, and the power of the individual becomes dependent upon them; to the extent that they are effective, they have become larger, and to that extent they have become less accessible to the influence of the individual. This is a central fact about associations in any mass society: it is of most consequence for political parties and for trade unions.

In the 'thirties, it often seemed that labour would become an insurgent power independent of corporation and state. Organized labour was then emerging for the first time on an American scale, and the only political sense of direction it needed was the slogan, 'organize the unorganized'. Now without the mandate of the slump, labour remains without political direction. Instead of economic and political struggles it has become deeply entangled in administrative routines with both corporation and state. One of its major functions, as a vested interest of the new society, is the regulation of such irregular tendencies as may occur among the rank and file.

There is nothing, it seems to me, in the make-up of the current labour leadership to allow us to expect that it can or that it will lead, rather than merely react. In so far as it fights at all it fights over a share of the goods of a single way of life and not over that way of life itself. The typical labour leader in the U.S.A. today is better understood as an adaptive creature of the main business drift than as an independent actor in a truly national context.

(iii) The idea that this society is a balance of powers requires us to assume that the units in balance are of more or less equal power and that they are truly independent of one another. These assumptions have rested, it seems clear, upon the historical importance of a large and independent middle class. In the latter nineteenth century and during the Progressive Era, such a class of farmers and small businessmen fought politically—and lost—their last struggle for a paramount role in national decision. Even then, their aspirations seemed bound to their own imagined past.

This old, independent middle class has of course declined. On the most generous count, it is now 40 per cent of the total middle class (at most 20 per cent of the total labour force). Moreover, it has become politically as well as economically dependent upon the state, most notably in the case of the subsidized farmer.

The *new* middle class of white-collar employees is certainly not the political pivot of any balancing society. It is in no way politically unified. Its unions, such as they are, often serve merely to incorporate it as hanger-on of the labour interest. For a considerable period, the old middle class *was* an independent base of power; the new middle class cannot be. Political freedom and economic security *were* anchored in small and independent properties; they are not anchored in the worlds of the white-collar job. Scattered property holders were economically united by more or less free markets; the jobs of the new middle class are integrated by corporate authority. Economically, the white-collar classes are in the same condition as wage workers; politically, they are in a worse condition, for they are not organized. They are no vanguard of historic change; they are at best a rear-guard of the welfare state.

The agrarian revolt of the 'nineties, the small-business revolt that has been more or less continuous since the 'eighties, the labour revolt of the 'thirties—each of these has failed as an independent movement which could countervail against the powers that be; they have failed as politically autonomous third parties. But they have succeeded, in varying degree, as interests vested in the expanded corporation and state; they have succeeded as parochial interests seated in particular districts, in local divisions of the two parties, and in the Congress. What they would become, in short, are well-established features of the *middle* levels of balancing power, on which we may now observe all those strata and interests which in the course of American history have been defeated in their bids for top power or which have never made such bids.

Fifty years ago many observers thought of the American state as a mask behind which an invisible government operated. But nowadays, much of what was called the old lobby, visible or invisible, is part of the quite visible government. The 'governmentalization of the lobby' has proceeded in both the legislative and the executive domain, as well as between them. The executive bureaucracy becomes not only the center of decision but also the arena within which major conflicts of power are resolved or denied resolution. 'Administration' replaces electoral politics; the manœuvring of cliques (which include leading Senators as well as civil servants) replaces the open clash of parties.

The shift of corporation men into the political directorate has accelerated the decline of the politicians in the Congress to the middle levels of power; the formation of the power elite rests in part upon this relegation. It rests also upon the semiorganized stalemate of the interests of sovereign localities, into which the legislative function has so largely fallen; upon the virtually complete absence of a civil service that is a politically neutral but politically relevant depository of brain-power and executive skill; and it rests upon the increased official secrecy behind which great decisions are made without benefit of public or even of Congressional debate.

IV

There is one last belief upon which liberal observers everywhere base their interpretations and rest their hopes. That is the idea of the public and the associated idea of public opinion. Conservative thinkers, since the French Revolution, have of course Viewed With Alarm the rise of the public, which they have usually called the masses, or something to that effect. 'The populace is sovereign,' wrote Gustave Le Bon, 'and the tide of barbarism mounts,' But surely those who have supposed the masses to be well on their

way to triumph are mistaken. In our time, the influence of publics or of masses within political life is in fact decreasing, and such influence as on occasion they do have tends, to an unknown but increasing degree, to be guided by the means of mass communication.

In a society of publics, discussion is the ascendant means of communication, and the mass media, if they exist, simply enlarge and animate this discussion, linking one face-to-face public with the discussions of another. In a mass society, the dominant type of communication is the formal media, and publics become mere markets for these media: the 'public' of a radio programme consists of all those exposed to it. When we try to look upon the United States today as a society of publics, we realize that it has moved a considerable distance along the road to the mass society.

In official circles, the very term, 'the public', has come to have a phantom meaning, which dramatically reveals its eclipse. The deciding elite can identify some of those who clamour publicly as 'Labour', others as 'Business', still others as 'Farmer'. But these are not the public. 'The public' consists of the unidentified and the nonpartisan in a world of defined and partisan interests. In this faint echo of the classic notion, the public is composed of these remnants of the old and new middle classes whose interests are not explicitly defined, organized, or clamorous. In a curious adaptation, 'the public' often becomes, in administrative fact, 'the disengaged expert', who, although ever so well informed, has never taken a clear-cut and public stand on controversial issues. He is the 'public' member of the board, the commission, the committee. What 'the public' stands for, accordingly, is often a vagueness of policy (called 'open-mindedness'), a lack of involvement in public affairs (known as "reasonableness'), and a professional disinterest (known as 'tolerance').

All this is indeed far removed from the eighteenth-century idea of the public of public opinion. That idea parallels the economic idea of the magical market. Here is the market composed of freely competing entrepreneurs; there is the public composed of circles of people in discussion. As price is the result of anonymous, equally weighted, bargaining individuals, so public opinion is the result of each man's having thought things out for himself and then contributing his voice to the great chorus. To be sure, some may have more influence on the state of opinion than others, but no one group monopolizes the discussion, or by itself determines the opinions that prevail.

In this classic image, the people are presented with problems. They discuss them. They formulate viewpoints. These viewpoints are organized, and they compete. One viewpoint 'wins out'. Then the people act on this view, or their representatives are instructed to act it out, and this they promptly do.

Such are the images of democracy which are still used as working justifications of power in America. We must now recognize this description as more a fairy tale than a useful approximation. The issues that now shape man's fate are neither raised nor decided by any public at large. The idea of a society that is at bottom composed of publics is not a matter of fact; it is the proclamation of an ideal, and as well the assertion of a legitimation masquerading as fact.

I cannot here describe the several great forces within American society as well as elsewhere which have been at work in the debilitation of the public. I want only to remind you that publics,

like free associations, can be deliberately and suddenly smashed, or they can more slowly wither away. But whether smashed in a week or withered in a generation, the demise of the public must be seen in connection with the rise of centralized organizations, with all their new means of power, including those of the mass media of distraction. These, we now know, often seem to expropriate the rationality and the will of the terrorized or—as the case may be—the voluntarily indifferent society of masses. In the more democratic process of indifference the remnants of such publics as remain may only occasionally be intimidated by fanatics in search of 'disloyalty'. But regardless of that, they lose their will for decision because they do not possess the instruments for decision; they lose their sense of political belonging because they do not belong; they lose their political will because they see no way to realize it.

The political structure of a modern democratic state requires that such a public as is projected by democratic theorists not only exist but that it be the very forum within which a politics of real issues is enacted.

It requires a civil service that is firmly linked with the world of knowledge and sensibility, and which is composed of skilled men who, in their careers and in their aspirations, are truly independent of any private, which is to say, corporation, interests.

It requires nationally responsible parties which debate openly and clearly the issues which the nation, and indeed the world, now so rigidly confronts.

It requires an intelligentsia, inside as well as outside the universities, who carry on the big discourse of the western world, and whose work is relevant to and influential among parties and movements and publics.

And it certainly requires, as a fact

of power, that there be free associations standing between families and smaller communities and publics, on the one hand, and the state, the military, the corporation, on the other. For unless these do exist, there are no vehicles for reasoned opinion, no instruments for the rational exertion of public will.

Such democratic formations are not now ascendant in the power structure of the United States, and accordingly the men of decision are not men selected and formed by careers within such associations and by their performance before such publics. The top of modern American society is increasingly unified, and often seems wilfully coordinated: at the top there has emerged an elite whose power probably exceeds that of any small group of men in world history. The middle levels are often a drifting set of stalemated forces: the middle does not link the bottom with the top. The bottom of this society is politically fragmented, and even as a passive fact, increasingly powerless: at the bottom there is emerging a mass society.

These developments, I believe, can be correctly understood neither in terms of the liberal nor the marxian interpretation of politics and history. Both of these ways of thought arose as guidelines to reflection about a type of society which does not now exist in the United States. We confront there a new kind of social structure, which embodies elements and tendencies of all modern society, but in which they have assumed a more naked and flamboyant prominence.

That does not mean that we must give up the ideals of these classic political expectations. I believe that both have been concerned with the problem of rationality and of freedom: liberalism, with freedom and rationality as supreme facts about the individual; marxism, as supreme facts about man's role in the political making of history. What I have said here, I suppose, may be taken as an attempt to make evident why the ideas of freedom and of rationality now so often seem so ambiguous in the new society of the United States of America.

Many social scientists[1] have strenuously objected to Mills's depiction of power at the national level. The most frequently voiced criticism concerns the empirical basis for Mills's conclusions. Too often, it is held, Mills engages in sweeping generalizations which lack adequate empirical grounds.[2] Furthermore, much of his data appears to support a pluralistic rather than an elitist image of national power. One critic suggests that many readers have confused the examples and illustrative data given by Mills with an empirical analysis, when in reality *The Power Elite* is neither empirical nor an analysis but a scheme for analysis.[3]

---

[1] Among the essentially negative appraisals of Mills's thesis are Daniel Bell, "The Power Elite Reconsidered," *American Journal of Sociology*, 64 (November 1959), 238–50; Robert A. Dahl, "A Critique of the Power Elite Method," *American Political Science Review*, 52 (June 1958), 463–69; Keller, *op. cit.*, pp. 110–11; Talcott Parsons, *Structure and Process in Modern Societies* (New York: The Free Press of Glencoe, Inc., 1960), pp. 199–225; Alexander Heard, "Review of Power Elite," *The Annals* (May 1957), 169–70; Arnold Rose, *The Power Structure* (Fair Lawn, N.J.: Oxford University Press, Inc., 1967), pp. 15–42.

Some of these critics have reacted with diatribes of their own in arguing that *The Power Elite* should be viewed as a polemical exercise rather than as a scholarly work.

[2] Keller, *op. cit.*, p. 111.

[3] Bell, *op. cit.*, p. 238.

While no systematic attempt has yet been made to assess the picture of power given in *The Power Elite*, a few empirical studies of national power bear upon several of Mills's propositions. The most relevant supporting research[4] is Hunter's *Top Leadership, U.S.A.*, a field investigation designed to locate the elites who shape national policy. Employing a method similar to the reputational approach used in his Regional City research, Hunter developed a list of 100 top leaders reputedly highly influential in national affairs. Hunter then proceeded to document the network of relationships among this group of key figures. He found that "the politicians, the men of wealth, and the military elite" tended to know one another personally and had close social, political, and business connections. He discusses these findings below.

---

[4] While differing from Mills's position on the role and function of elites in society, Baltzell, in his study of a metropolitan upper class, supports several themes in *The Power Elite*. E. Digby Baltzell, *Philadelphia Gentlemen* (Glencoe, Ill.: The Free Press, 1958).

Another line of support for some of Mills's conceptions of power at the top is presented by Hacker, who emphasizes the burgeoning power of the corporation in America. Hacker notes several convergences between Mills's views and the consequences of what he refers to as the *corporation takeover*. Andrew Hacker, "Power to Do What?" in *The New Sociology*, ed. Irving L. Horowitz (Fair Lawn, N.J.: Oxford University Press, Inc., 1964), pp. 134–45. See also, Hacker's edited collection *The Corporation Take-Over* (Garden City, N.Y.: Doubleday & Company, Inc., 1965).

Further empirical substance for certain aspects of the power elite thesis is given in Domhoff's study, which places heavy emphasis on the significance of the corporation complex in American life. G. William Domhoff, *Who Rules America?* (Englewood Cliffs, N.J.: Prentice-Hall, Inc., 1967).

TOP LEADERSHIP, U.S.A.*

Floyd Hunter

Social Science R & D

During the course of this study, it may be repeated, I was seeking to learn whether there was a definable national power structure decisive in shaping the general policy course of the country. With modifications that will be made later, I have found that there is such a power superstructure, generally with a coordination of goals and a resolution of unavoidable conflicts by the same types of individuals in roles and status positions similar to those found in communities. Utilizing the familiar sociological concepts of role and status analysis, together with questions related to group action patterns, I found it increasingly clear that the formulation of national policy and its ultimate execution by these individuals also were processes in a structure of action not unlike that found in community-power situations. The broad framework of action

---

* From Floyd Hunter, *Top Leadership, U.S.A.* (Chapel Hill, N.C.: The University of North Carolina Press, 1959), pp. 160–61, 163–67, 173, 176, 179–81.

can be outlined as power elements:

1. Establishment by power group of claims of status

2. Use of selected personnel to put forward ideas on new policy or to reinforce existing policy claims

3. Use of quasiformal organization to shape policy

4. Use of formal organization to promote policy

5. Use of institutional organization to sanction and execute policy

In thinking of these elements it is necessary to recognize that we are dealing with people acting in relation to policy direction. Thus one must hold in mind conflicting ideas—fluidity and stability, specifics and generalities. Let me illustrate the meaning of this by taking element number one, the establishment of claims of status.

The social roles that a man plays and the importance of the roles determine a man's status. If his roles are generally power-oriented, the man becomes a power figure. This is true first locally and then nationally. The habitual assumption of a policy-making role where vital subjects are under consideration gives a man power prestige. It also gives him an expertness in handling policy problems and, through recognition gained by his activities, opens for him further opportunities for utilizing his skills. Social responsibilities are delegated to those deemed trained and qualified to handle them. Power exercised according to determined policy is effective when it is localized, whether the localization be from the national scene to a county or town or from a corporate board chairman to an operating field supervisor. Policy must be translated into the living activities of individuals moving in accord with the requirements and directives of higher authority. Social organizations devoted to controlling the activities of their members develop gradations of status for the implicit or express purpose of exacting obedience of all individuals within them. By custom, regulation, and law, men become habituated to following the patterns of activities agreed upon by the directors of an organization. These patterns of action are, then, structured. They give form and stability to organization operations. In a very real sense, those who top the various pyramids of power in society are status symbols. They stand as points of localization of power direction. . . .

Prestige from local status and power is a vital element in national power status. This does not mean that a man cannot become a national power figure without a local following, but without exception the men with whom I talked and who were designated by their peers as national power leaders were men quite stable in their positions as key figures in a localized configuration of activities. According to interests and capabilities, individuals are tapped from such positions for wider service in the cause of policy development. Few, indeed, are rootless men. Top leaders within basic, local power organizations are drawn into ever-widening circles of associations devoted to policy development.

For this study to nail down the fact of recognition in status evaluations, three things were necessary to establish. First, men designated as top policy-makers should know each other. I did not consider that knowing about others would be sufficient to contend that a power structure of top policy-makers exists. Consequently, I asked those who were chosen by association groups as leaders to tell how many persons they knew on a list provided them. Secondly, they were to rate, by status, the persons they knew. And last, but most important, they must have acted with these others in developing specific policies. I have devoted a separate chapter to the last point and I deal here with the question generally.

An analysis of the results of cross-country interviews, mailed questionnaires, and leadership polls conducted during the course of study showed that by 1956, out of several hundred persons named from all sources, between 100 and 200 men consistently were chosen as top leaders and were considered by all informants to be of national policy-making stature. One hundred of these received more votes proportionately than all others. These were also judged in the status-rating process as number-one power leaders. A second hundred were designated by the same informants as second raters. The remainder were either third raters or did not count at all in the opinion of the persons polled.

Utilizing a one-in-three sample of persons for test purposes, I demonstrated that number-one leaders were generally personally known to each other . . . , and second and third raters knew fewer and fewer of the number-one group. . . . Again, a mere personal knowledge between persons does not prove a power structure, but it was considered axiomatic that if persons presumed to wield power were unknown to one another, it would be very difficult to have said that any sort of structure existed. Correspondence or hearsay knowledge hardly would be the basis of power activities. It must be remembered here that all questions related to leaders in the various polls were aimed at selecting top policy-making leaders in the many categories of persons polled. Thus, such national organizations as the American Association of Social Workers contributed names, along with the National Asso-

ciation of Manufacturers. Consequently, when the next questions were asked, such as "Pick the top policy-making group in the nation from our list" or "Rate the names on the list on a one-two-three power scale," many of the lesser power-potent figures fell by the wayside. It should be repeated too that the 100 number-one leaders do not represent the total power structure of the nation. Nor do the second and third raters necessarily represent an understructure of the number-one policy-makers. These facts are stressed to avoid the charge that I believe that these 100 men ever act in total concert. It is incontrovertible, however, that a nucleus of a power structure is contained in the 100 number-one leaders, and their activities fan out in various ways that I have continued to describe as fully as my facts have warranted.

The structure of top number-one leaders tended toward closure. The number-one men knew number-one men. They recruited rising number-one leaders into their orbit and excluded those who did not fit. They knew generally the pattern of policy development, and they knew well and specifically how to go about getting what was good for them and for their individual enterprises. Their names appeared repeatedly in the national press.[1] (Only twelve on a research list of 100 top leaders did not receive one or more press notices during the course of study up to 1956. It is likely that these twelve may have received notices that were missed.) They knew and were known by elected and appointed officials, from whom they tended to hold themselves somewhat superior and aloof. They represented a cross section of national civic

---

[1] Some of these objected to local publicity but did not resist national news releases about them.

life. They belonged to clubs and associations in common membership across the nation. Their operating bases were located essentially in the large cities. They included the politicians, the men of wealth, and the military elite of whom Professor Mills speaks.[2] None of these things can be said about the second and third raters nor about all leaders examined in this study. In the cities, small towns, and states studied, connections between the upper leadership structures could be made, but the little fellows were excluded from the top leadership structure. The exclusion was made on a power-status basis, not primarily on the basis of class position or institutional status. Inclusion in the top group of number-one leaders was, then, a rough measure of a man's power potential.

Let it be clearly understood again that I am not suggesting that the top leaders in the nation ever sit face to face around a table and decide in solemn judgment what will or will not be good for the nation. Such a view would deny the whole notion of process that is contained in the social power-structure concept. Nor do I believe that much policy is ever wholly decided in smoke-filled rooms, nor in club-leadership outings of the Aspen, Hot Springs, or Bohemian groups. No one-factor analysis is ever satisfactory, even though some articles that suggest this may appear from time to time in the sensational press. Yet, there is a selective process of agreement and habit patterns related to leadership recognition that can be observed. There is a kind of reservoir of leadership on tap from which men are chosen to perform the important tasks of policy-making

[2] C. Wright Mills, *The Power Elite* (Fair Lawn, N.J.: Oxford University Press, Inc., 1956).

and/or to give status to any major policy proposal. As one said, "Of course there is a group that's recognized as national leaders. They quietly put their stamp of approval on most of the things that go on. They're big men. You don't send a boy to do a man's job, you know."

I probed the notion that the men of family, wealth, and society prestige might be the true leaders of power in American society. I asked whether the managers had taken over. I questioned concerning the status of professional politicians in power-wielding. I wanted to know whether the country is run by powerful lobbies of labor and other special interest groups. I was interested in determining again whether the narrowed circle of men about whom I questioned represented a conspiracy of interests bent on doing the nation out of its birthright.

The answers to all of these questions were qualified. "Yes, there is a definite number of men looked upon as being more powerful than others, but that answer is too simple. It does not explain power as a total thing." "Yes, some men of family and wealth are included, but there's more to a man's inclusion than being born on the right side of town." "Yes, managers have taken over in many areas of influence, but they never act alone." "Yes, professional politicians and their political parties are important factors in policy-making and power, but they are a part of something bigger than pure politics." "Lobbies and their professional secretaries are very meaningful in decisions, but they are not always useful." "No, there is no conspiracy of interests. It is just natural that some men act the way they do, and most have the good of the country in mind.". . .

It was abundantly clear that the men interviewed did not think of gov-

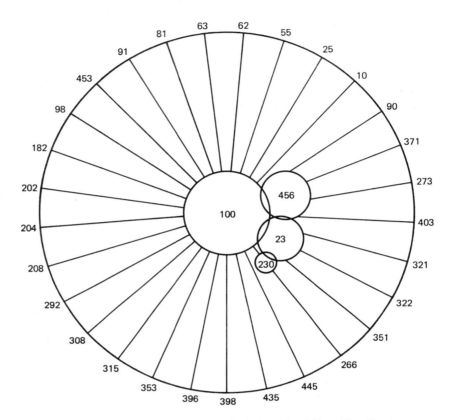

Fig 1. Communication Net Showing Relationship of Four Top Leaders to Twenty-Nine Other Top Leaders, 1954. Numbers are Code Numbers Used in This Study to Refer to Top Leaders.

ernment officials exclusively as top policy-makers in the country. This does not say they did not recognize the important roles played by politicians in the process of getting things done, but, universally, government was thought of as an instrument of extending policy rather than a primary source of policy development. It was taken for granted that government is extremely important. It was also taken for granted that organized government was but one of many power structures with which the men of national influence worked. Key men in government represent an apex

of power, but in general it was assumed that these key men would act in concert and in accord with one or more other power groupings to formulate and extend policy. . . .

The larger power interests had direct contact with government through the placement of dollar-a-year executives in key government spots. The same interests tended to find their way to key government committees, and there were close ties between these interests and the key cabinet posts.

A 1958 analysis of ninety-nine number-one leaders in terms of their business and government connections showed that seventeen of them had made a career of politics, thirty-six had never held either appointive or elective political office, but forty-six had been in both business and government during their careers. The interchange between business and government was apparent, and the statistical findings were borne out by qualitative data. . . .

The top policy-makers can communicate with each other easily enough. In testing the fact of communication among the number-one leaders I found that four men knew and could close a communications net with twenty-nine others. Their mutuality of acquaintance was such that at one time or another all had been in contact with approximately two-thirds of the circle. The four, shown by center circles in Fig. 1, could communicate directly with nearly any man in the larger circle.

The nation's power system is a series of interlaced and coordinated power structures. Those at the apexes of power in communities, states, regions, service organizations, and industrial complexes become generally known to each other. Some of the leaders in the larger units of power become symbolic power figures in the nation. When such leaders think of policy directions and alternatives, they think of interrelated and weighted factors. Although individual units within the power system may appear to act in isolation, it is well known that major changes in pace and direction of any single power unit have profound effects on the whole.

Most attempts to refute Mills's thesis consist of critiques of the rationale of his argument or the validity of his evidence. However, only a minimal amount of empirical data supports alternative interpretations. An important exception is Suzanne Keller's *Beyond the Ruling Class.* Her sanguine portrayal of elites in contemporary American society stands in marked contrast to Mills's. Her strategic elites include moral, cultural, and scientific leaders as well as the political, economic, and military elites discussed by Mills. This core group ("specialists in excellence") is responsible for the material and moral well-being of society and is increasingly effective in meeting this responsibility. In contrast to Mills's power elite Keller speaks of a proliferation of independent yet interdependent strategic elites which have eclipsed the "ruling class" and are recruited from an increasingly broad base.[1]

---

[1] As seen by one reviewer, the adequacy of Keller's own evidence for her conceptions of national elites is a moot question. John C. Leggett, "Review of *Beyond the Ruling Class*," *American Journal of Sociology*, 70 (November 1964), 391–92.

BEYOND THE RULING CLASS*

Suzanne Keller

Princeton University

Increasingly, the topography of the American social structure appears to consist of a number of peaks, each scalable by highly specialized methods adapted to the social and organizational terrain. The decline of the hereditary transmission of elite status is manifested in all leadership groups except that of high society. Privileged groups still predominate in some elites, but privilege is not a prerequisite for success, and although wealth and high social status are very advantageous in some elites, they no longer determine access to the top echelons in business, politics, and culture. Recruitment of elite members, however, is not as yet a random process. The link between material means and education persists, and the appeal of various types of success is unequally distributed in the different strata of society. Yet, even the elites least open to lower class and lower status aspirants are becoming more accessible. At the highest pinnacles, the boy of privilege, no less than the "poor boy who made good," must achieve and maintain his elite position by hard work, competitive merit, and intensive application of effort throughout most of his adult life. This trend weakens and may eventually break the age-old link between elite status and upperclass status.

The family system—the major link between social classes and the genera-

tions—will likely play a diminished role in elite recruitment in the future. In the past, the family was the chief school for both kings and carpenters, and thereby contributed to the continuity of the social order, even as it inhibited the adaptability of this order. The family could only teach what it knew, and much of what it knew were the class codes and ideals by which it lived. It was not necessarily the best nor the most efficient school, and in allowing little leeway to the young it was even tyrannical, but for centuries it was almost the only school.

Today, social and technological changes have deprived the family of the capacity to prepare the future generations for the lives they are to lead. This function is gradually being transferred to other agencies, still in process of formation, whose knowledge and resources are more up to date. Parents are separated from their children not merely by the natural course of the biological life cycle, but also by the accelerating tempo of the sociological life cycle. Once, a goal of most children was to know as much as their parents; today, having only this knowledge would condemn children to ignorance about large and important areas of life. Understandably, more and more parents know less than their children, and this affects not only the psychology of family relations, but the structure of the institution as a whole.

Historically, the influence of the family in class-stratified societies stemmed not only from its power in socializing the young, but also from its powers to reward them later in life with status, property, education, or access to important positions in society. Now, elite positions, though bringing high rewards to their possessors, some of which may be passed on to their children, are usually neither secure nor transferable. Upper and upper middle-class individuals, along with their less fortunate peers, must win such positions through their own efforts. No matter how much this principle may be violated in practice, it is more genuinely observed today than it was 100 years ago. And once the link between social position and the family system has been broken, the perpetuation of inequality along fixed generational lines may be abolished.

Current patterns of recruitment can hardly be expected to mirror all of these changes equally. These must be perceived rather as part of a shifting balance of social forces—including tradition, self-selection, objective requirements, and public (which includes elite) expectations—each acting on and reacting to the others. The recruitment of elites in American society today reflects the pull of social class, the push of individual merit, and the invisible hand of tradition.[1]

Of course, the suggested trend in elite recruitment in advanced industrial societies may be no more permanent than parallel trends during other expanding epochs in history. Writing of the eighteenth-century Prussian civil service and the heterogeneous origins of its elite members, Rosenberg could be referring to our own day:

> It was indeed an unusual melange of individuals who managed to enter the evolving elite of "public law bureaucrats."... Drawn from many walks of life, these social stragglers, when thrown together into the hierarchy of commissioned Hohenzollern servants, suddenly faced each other as professional associates in a joint enterprise. Collectively they formed a distinct functional status group. As individuals, however, they differed sharply among themselves in class origins, education, and occupational background, personal ability and achievement, the amount and sources of income, and, consequently, also in their tastes, attitudes, loyalties, and modes of living.[2]

But he also notes that the most noteworthy component of this service class consisted of "indigenous nobles." Reminiscent of our own day is the fact that even "titled aristocrats were now impelled, before they were entrusted with definite duties, to give the impression of competence."[3] Soon, however, the merit system became linked to a new form of spoils system. Although the permanent hereditary rights to particular offices had been broken at least in principle, family hold on positions and on special branches of the service prevailed, along with other forms of nepotism. In practice, the new emphasis on professionalization and competence became overshadowed by the old stress on family obligations. However, the ideas and ideals had been transformed, and this left its mark on the new system. In time, the Prussian

---

[1] Sjoberg has argued that the class system at present is both rigid and fluid and that both are necessary—rigidity for the sake of integration in a highly specialized industrial order and fluidity for meeting the ever growing need for trained specialists. Gideon Sjoberg, "Contradictory Functional Requirements and Social Systems," *Journal of Conflict Resolution*, IV, No. 2 (1960), 198–208.

[2] Hans Rosenberg, *Bureaucracy, Aristocracy and Autocracy. The Prussian Experience 1660–1815* (Cambridge, Mass.: Harvard University Press, 1958), pp. 60–61.

[3] *Ibid.*, p. 72.

aristocracy was effectively displaced by professional middle-class bureaucrats.

The likelihood of a relapse to some form of hereditary privilege in the modern industrial world is tempered by one important new difference between that time and ours: the nature of the skills and knowledge demanded. Today, these skills can only be acquired individually, and the knowledge on which they are based is ever-changing. With the spread of science, men and their leaders are beginning to learn that knowledge is proximate rather than final, that the discoveries of today may be anachronisms tomorrow. With the institutionalization of this kind of social change, entrenched classes or groups will be less able to monopolize elite positions in the future.

The prevalence of achievement and performance standards and the rise of new patterns of socialization also signifies the decline of the amateur and the rise of the expert—not merely as an adjunct of, or an auxiliary to, those in power, but as a wielder of power.[4]

And since experts are made, not born, the circulation of elites increases, along with the variety of individual and of social types recruited into each elite. This consequence of changing social and moral conditions decisively alters the principles of social cohesion and of social balance, not only in the society at large, as Mannheim anticipated, but also, and perhaps especially, at the top.[5]

The almost legendary cohesiveness of British upper-class sons raised and educated by gentry families and public schools has never been characteristic of a society like the United States whose class system is of recent vintage and whose aristocratic traditions were slight from the start. However, the American equivalent—a more or less unified wealthy upper middle class tied by ancestry, property, race, religion, and national descent—has provided a sense of cohesion that should not be underestimated in a mobile, rapidly expanding society. This type of cohesion is difficult to sustain, not to say create, under modern conditions. As Mannheim has vividly shown,[6] with the de-

---

[4] The expert is a specialist in a particular field. Of course, as Janowitz and others have shown, such specialists need not be narrowly defined. Morris Janowitz, *The Professional Soldier* (New York: The Free Press of Glencoe, Inc., 1960), Chap. ii.

Samuel Grafton, TV comment on the news, December 17, 1962, Channel 13, made the following observation: "One caught a glimpse of the President as what, I am convinced, history will some day call him—a kind of artist of decisions. He has objectified the decision-making process. He looks at it with an amazing detachment, as a sculptor, perhaps, looks upon the carving process. He talked of how 'mistaken' decisions abroad started both world wars and of how a mistaken interpretation of our intentions by China started the Korean war. Time and again he used the word 'decision,' and in his use of it, it is not a word denoting *power* but a word denoting skill....Mr. Kennedy seemed tonight, more than ever, the cool, clear-headed, professional of de-

cision-making. No wonder he bulks so large in a country in which the word 'executive' has come to have so many golden and glamorous meanings." Quoted by permission of the author in a personal communication to me, January 5, 1963.

[5] Note, however, that Mannheim emphasizes the negative impact of this phenomenon. "Indeed, the more elites there are in a society the more each individual elite tends to lose its function and influence as a leader for they cancel each other out." Karl Mannheim, *Man and Society in an Age of Reconstruction* (New York: Harcourt, Brace & World, Inc., 1940), p. 86. This need not be the case however for, if one views these elites as linked to the tasks of the social system and proliferating in number and kinds as these do, then the elites do not cancel each other out but supplement each other.

[6] Karl Mannheim, *Ideology and Utopia* (New York: Harcourt, Brace & World, Inc., 1949), p. 58.

cline of the medieval church in western Europe, the idea of one absolute truth was replaced by that of relative truth, varying with the social vantage point of the observer. This phenomenon, which can lead to a sense of anomie described by Durkheim,[7] is now affecting the very heights of the social structure. Elites, in participating in a common enterprise, need a common set of binding moral principles, but, being specialized, they also need an ethic of separateness. This ethic is no longer created *for* them in the homes and schools of their childhood, but *by* them in the corporations and laboratories, the party hierarchy and studios, of the modern industrial world.

Common values among otherwise disparate elites—no longer joined by race or caste pride, nor by ethnic, economic, or religious exclusiveness—may perhaps be furthered by their experience in a society whose culture stresses achievement of that great and rare unifier, *success*. Most members of most elites approve of ambition, self-discipline, and hard work because this is their common lot. And the awareness that theirs is an uncommon destiny contributes to their appraisals of men and events, and enters, though does not determine, their decisions and conduct. The sheer fact of elite membership entails certain similar experiences: the necessity to supervise subordinates, the responsibilities of power and influence, the temptation to self-indulgence, the enjoyment of similar privileges. But this community of experience does not lead to a community of interests. The latter demands a self-assurance which helps elites accept their existence, instead of, as seems the case in the United States,

denying or camouflaging it.[8] It also calls for a set of articulated beliefs and ideals justifying the social superiority required by elites to perform their functions. Today, when individual achievement is supposed to determine such superiority, the possession of ascribed attributes, such as race, sex, or descent, while pertinent, is no longer morally relevant.[9] New factors must take the place of these earlier promoters of elite identity.

Elites must be capable of developing self-images that stress their communality and their uniqueness. They must consolidate their identities, images, and aims around ideologies that justify and at the same time illumine their specialized, autonomous roles in a joint

---

[7] Emile Durkheim, *The Division of Labor in Society*, Book III (New York: The Free Press of Glencoe, Inc., 1947), Chap. i.

[8] Daniel Bell, *The End of Ideology* (Glencoe, Ill.: The Free Press of Glencoe, 1960), p. 89.

[9] But recruitment on the basis of individual merit rather than ascription will not alter the elite unless these individuals also are permitted to bring new ideas and new moral values along with them. If new men are inculcated with old principles, however, the net result will not be very different from what it was. Such a situation is vividly described by an observer of the recruits at Sandhurst, the British training ground for the military elite. He was shocked by what he calls the "feudal" attitude among the officers and the sense of caste pride coupled with a personal belief in the individual "right to command." "Where I had expected to find a professional officer corps, I found a caste rooted in its own conception of superior, God-given status." Simon Raven, "Perish by the Sword," in *The Establishment*, ed. Hugh Thomas (New York: Clarkson N. Potter, 1959), p. 79. Earlier, however, the author had indicated that the virtues which the new Army "wished its new entries to possess were of a long-established nature." *Ibid.*, p. 56. Since the ideals had not changed along with new methods of recruitment, these new men were soon turned into old-type military officers. One wonders, however, whether and for how long these ideals can survive the modern conditions of military life in peace and war.

destiny.[10] Only in this way will they be able to "transmit and safeguard the best elements of tradition," and "develop dynamic ideas" to promote their own claims—which increasingly transcend national boundaries—as well as those of their nation and of humanity.[11] The "end of ideology" may well be the beginning of ideology, for "the end is where we start from."[12]

---

10 Daniel Bell argues that as a result of the "new nature of decision-making, its increased technicality," the older elites are being displaced. He mentions the "managerial executive class," the old-style military leaders, and Southern traditionalists. "The Dispossessed—1962," *Columbia University Forum*, V, No. 4 (Fall 1962), 12. I think this is partly true but somewhat exaggerated. It seems more likely that instead of being altogether displaced these elites are merely being asked to move over and make room for some newcomers. They may of course react to this as Bell describes, but then he is diagnosing not the facts of the situation but their fears about it.

11 Karl Mannheim, *Freedom, Power, and Democratic Planning* (Fair Lawn, N.J.: Oxford University Press, Inc., 1950), p. 106.

12 In the current period of transition between the old and the new, the formation of informal coteries and operational cliques in politics, and perhaps in other spheres, provides a partial sense of community and continuity of interest. These should increasingly be challenged and supplemented by countercliques and coteries, equally well organized, if the outcome is to lead to more than the preservation of established vested interests.

Richard H. Rovere, "The American Establishment," *Esquire* (May 1962), seems to be referring to just such a unifying clique whose attitudes seem regularly to prevail in important national affairs, although he caricatures them.

Richard Rose, in "Anatomy of British Political Factions," *New Society* (October 11, 1962), pp. 29–31, refers to "operational parties" composed of a "group of individuals with representation in Parliament which seeks to further a broad range of policies through political action." These operational parties are "elitist, London-based, and concerned primarily with the small political world of Westminster.... The functional requirements of a major operational party seem to be: leadership, an ideology, technical expertise, cadres, and a communication network."

In contrast to these two elitist versions of national power by Mills and Keller is yet a third stance, one that shares some of the perspectives of those who see the structure of power in pluralistic terms. A leading exponent of this view, David Riesman, contends that no one group or set of groups holds power. Indeed, in Riesman's estimation, if there is a controlling sector or level of society, it is the middle class.[1] William Kornhauser[2] has assessed the two versions of power given by Riesman and Mills. The major characteristics of each as he summarizes them are in Table 6.1.

TABLE 6.1.   TWO PORTRAITS OF THE AMERICAN POWER STRUCTURE

Power Structure	Mills	Riesman
Levels	(a) Unified power elite	(a) No dominant power elite
	(b) Diversified and balanced plurality of interest groups	(b) Diversified and balanced plurality of interest groups
	(c) Mass of unorganized people	(c) Mass of unorganized people

1 *The Lonely Crowd* (New Haven, Conn.: Yale University Press, 1951), pp. 242–55.

2 " 'Power Elite' or 'Veto Groups'?" in *Culture and Social Change*, eds. Seymour M. Lipset and Leo Lowenthal (New York: The Free Press of Glencoe, Inc., 1961), pp. 252–67.

See also Reissman's comparison of the two images of power and his criticisms of David Riesman's views. Reissman, *op. cit.*, pp. 193–203.

TABLE 6.1 (CONT'D)

Power Structure	Mills	Riesman
	who have no power over elite	who have some power over interest groups
Changes	(a) Increasing concentration of power	(a) Increasing dispersion of power
Operation	(a) One group determines all major policies	(a) Who determines policy shifts with the issue
	(b) Manipulation of people at the bottom by group at the top	(b) Monopolistic competition among organized groups
Bases	(a) Coincidence of interests among major institutions (economic, military, governmental)	(a) Diversity of interests among major organized groups
	(b) Social similarities and psychological affinities among those who direct major institutions	(b) Sense of weakness and dependence among those in higher as well as lower status
Consequences	(a) Enhancement of interests of corporations, armed forces, and executive branch of government	(a) No one group or class is favored significantly over others
	(b) Decline of politics as public debate	(b) Decline of politics as duty and self-interest
	(c) Decline of responsible and accountable power—loss of democracy	(c) Decline of effective leadership

SELECTED BIBLIOGRAPHY

AGGER, ROBERT E., *et al.*, *The Rulers and the Ruled.* New York: John Wiley & Sons, Inc., 1964.

ANTON, THOMAS J., "Power, Pluralism and Local Politics," *Administrative Science Quarterly*, 7 (March 1963), 425–54.

BARTH, ERNEST A. T., "Community Influence System: Structure and Change," *Social Forces*, 40 (October 1961), 58–63.

BELKNAP, GEORGE M., and RALPH SMUCKLER, "Political Power Relations in a Midwest City," *Public Opinion Quarterly*, 20 (Spring 1956), 73–81.

BELL, DANIEL, "The Power Elite Reconsidered," *American Journal of Sociology*, 64 (November 1958), 238–50.

BERLE, ADOLF A., *Power Without Property*, New York: Harcourt, Brace & World, Inc., 1966.

BONJEAN, CHARLES M., "Class, Status and Reputation," *Sociology and Social Research*, 49 (October 1964), 69–75.

———, and LEWIS F. CARTER, "Legitimacy and Visibility: Leadership Structures Related to Four Community Systems," *Pacific Sociological Review*, 8 (Spring 1965), 16–20.

BONJEAN, CHARLES M., and DAVID M. OLSON, "Community Leadership: Directions of Research," *Administrative Science Quarterly*, 9 (December 1964), 278–300.

CLARK, TERRY N., ed., *Community Structure and Decision Making: Comparative Analyses.* San Francisco: Chandler Publishing Co., 1968.

———, "Who Governs, Where and

When," *The Sociological Quarterly*, 8 (Summer 1967), 291–316.

CLELLAND, DONALD A., and WILLIAM H. FORM, "Economic Dominants and Community Power: A Comparative Analysis," *American Journal of Sociology*, 69 (March 1964), 511–21.

"Community Politics" (special issue on community power), *Southwestern Social Science Quarterly*, 48 (December 1967).

CONNOLLY, WILLIAM E., *Political Science and Ideology*. New York: Atherton Press, 1967.

COSER, LEWIS A., *Political Sociology*. New York: Harper & Row, Publishers, 1966.

CRAIN, ROBERT L., and DONALD B. ROSENTHAL, "Community Status as a Dimension of Local Decision-Making," *American Sociological Review*, 32 (December 1967), 970–84.

D'ANTONIO, WILLIAM V., and WILLIAM H. FORM, *Influentials in Two Border Cities*. Notre Dame, Ind.: University of Notre Dame Press, 1965.

DAHL, ROBERT A., "Critique of the Ruling Elite Model," *American Political Science Review*, 52 (June 1958), 463–69.

———, *Who Governs?* New Haven, Conn.: Yale University Press, 1961.

DOMHOFF, G. WILLIAM, *Who Rules America?* Englewood Cliffs, N.J.: Prentice-Hall, Inc., 1967.

———, and H. B. BALLARD, eds., *C. Wright Mills and the Power Elite*. Boston: Beacon Press, Inc., 1968.

FORM, WILLIAM H., and DELBERT C. MILLER, *Industry, Labor and Community*. New York: Harper & Row, Publishers, 1960.

GILBERT, CLAIRE W., "Some Trends in Community Politics: A Secondary Analysis of Power Structure Data from 166 Communities," *Southwestern Social Science Quarterly*, 48 (December 1967), 373–81.

HUNTER, FLOYD, *The Big Rich and the Little Rich*. Garden City, N.Y.: Doubleday & Company, Inc., 1965.

———, *Community Power Structure*. Chapel Hill, N.C.: University of North Carolina Press, 1953.

JANOWITZ, MORRIS, ed., *Community Political Systems*. Glencoe, Ill.: The Free Press, 1960.

KOLKO, GABRIEL, *Wealth and Power in America*. New York: Frederick A. Praeger, Inc., Publishers, 1962.

KORNHAUSER, ARTHUR, ed., *Problems of Power in American Democracy*. Detroit, Mich.: Wayne State University Press, 1957.

KORNHAUSER, WILLIAM, *Politics in Mass Society*. New York: The Free Press of Glencoe, Inc., 1959.

LAMPMAN, ROBERT J., *The Share of Top Wealth Holders in National Wealth*. Princeton, N.J.: Princeton University Press, 1962.

McCONNELL, GRANT, *Private Power and American Democracy*. New York: Alfred A. Knopf, Inc., 1966.

MARTIN, ROSCOE C., *et al.*, *Decisions in Syracuse*. Bloomington, Indiana: Indiana University Press, 1964.

MERRIAM, CHARLES, *Political Power*. New York: Collier Books, 1964.

MILLS, C. WRIGHT, *The Power Elite*. Fair Lawn, N.J.: Oxford University Press, Inc., 1956.

NOSSITER, BERNARD D., *The Mythmakers: An Essay on Wealth and Power*. Boston: Houghton Mifflin Company, 1964.

PARSONS, TALCOTT, "The Distribution of Power in American Society," *World Politics*, 10 (October 1957), 123–43.

PELLEGRIN, ROLAND J., and CHARLES H. COATES, "Absentee Owned Corporations and Community Power Structure," *American Journal of Sociology*, 61 (March 1956), 413–19.

POLSBY, NELSON W., *Community Power and Political Theory*. New Haven, Conn.: Yale University Press, 1963.

ROSE, ARNOLD, *The Power Structure*. Fair Lawn, N.J.: Oxford University Press, Inc., 1967.

ROSSI, PETER H., *Community Social Structure*. Englewood Cliffs, N.J.: Prentice-Hall, Inc., 1968.

SCHULZE, ROBERT O., "The Role of Economic Dominants in Community Power Structure," *American Sociological Review*, 23 (February 1958), 3–9.

SPINRAD, WILLIAM, "Power in Local Communities," *Social Problems*, 12 (Winter 1965), 335–56.

SWEEZEY, PAUL M., "Power Elite or Ruling Class," *Monthly Review*, 8 (September 1956), 138–50.

WALKER, JACK L., "A Critique of the Elitist Theory of Democracy," *American Political Science Review*, 60 (June 1966), 285–95.

WALTON, JOHN, "Discipline, Method and Community Power: A Note on the Sociology of Knowledge," *American Sociological Review*, 31 (October 1966), 684–89.

———, "The Vertical Axis of Community Organization and the Structure of Power," *Southwestern Social Science Quarterly*, 48 (December 1967), 353–68.

WILDAVSKY, AARON, *Leadership in a Small Town*. Totawa, N.J.: Bedminster Press, 1964.

PART FOUR

SPECIAL AREAS

CHAPTER EIGHT

Class Consciousness

Students of stratification agree that class factors can function as determinants of group action only to the extent that members subjectively experience the operation of these class factors in their group life.[1] As Leonard Reissman puts it, "Theory is not complete unless the conclusions on the level of structure can be reinterpreted in social-psychological terms as referring to individual behavior."[2] Indeed, without some form of subjective state associated with objective class conditions, we could not speak of a social class in the sense of a real group.[3]

Most investigations dealing with the social-psychological aspects of class closely follow traditional sociological paths. From such a standpoint the basic concern is with processes which are assumed to mediate between society and the individual. How does society get into the individual? How does social structure become transformed into personality structure? How does the individual conceive of himself and his milieu, and how are his actions guided by his conceptions? Such questions are implicit if not expressed in studies of the social psychology of class, just as they are generally in social-psychological investigations.

In the main, research into the social psychology of class consists of inquiries

---

[1] While most sociologists would agree that objective conditions of class can affect behavior directly, their primary concern is with behavior mediated by group action as structured by social class.

[2] *Class in American Society* (Glencoe, Ill.: The Free Press, 1959), p. 270.

[3] As MacIver and Page state, "Whatever objective criteria we use, we do not have a social class unless consciousness is present." Robert M. MacIver and Charles H. Page, *Society* (New York: Rinehart, 1949), p. 350.

343

about the influences of social class upon values and beliefs and upon class consciousness. A large part of the former type of inquiry is directed to the interaction among stratification, values, and a variety of dependent variables such as family life and child-rearing, achievement motivation, and political behavior.[4] In this framework, the value concept is an intervening or dependent variable. Studies of class consciousness of this type then are special versions of research on the influences of class upon values, notably political and economic values.[5]

CONCEPTIONS OF CLASS CONSCIOUSNESS

While most sociologists would agree that "the study of class consciousness is at the core of stratification theory and research,"[6] such agreement probably rests upon a loose interpretation of class consciousness[7]—i.e., the tendency to equate class consciousness with any indicator of subjective feelings about class. Regarded this way, class conciousness has always been an integral part of much of the literature on social class.[8]

However, in terms of awareness of class situation and associated politicoeconomic attitudes and action to satisfy mutual interests, sociological attention to class consciousness has fluctuated markedly. Much early writing consisted of speculative and often polemical conclusions about the Marxist conception of class consciousness and its applicability to American society.[9] The essential characteristics of

---

[4] Much of Chapter Four, on the way of life of the classes, and of Chapter Ten, on social mobility, concerns class-conditioned values and beliefs.

[5] While there is often considerable overlap between the two types of research—studies of the relationship between class and values and studies of class consciousness—the tendency is to treat class consciousness as a separate topic.

[6] Richard T. Morris and Raymond J. Murphy, "A Paradigm for the Study of Class Consciousness," *Sociology and Social Research*, 50 (April 1966), 297.

[7] As put by Lewis, "the concept of class consciousness seems to mean many things to sociologists, perhaps because they have not always agreed on the meaning of one of its elements—*class*." Lionel S. Lewis, "Class Consciousness and Inter-Class Sentiments," *The Sociological Quarterly*, 6 (Autumn 1965), 325.

[8] This is particularly so with community studies which measure social-class phenomena by means of the reputational approach. Such techniques—whether self-placement methods or placement by others—presuppose class consciousness in varying degree or type.

Class consciousness in these studies generally corresponds to what Lewis refers to as class identification: manifestation of (1) an awareness that a system of stratification exists in society, (2) a willingness to designate where one feels he belongs in the system, and (3) interests in common with others who feel they belong in the same aggregate. *Op. cit.*, p. 325.

[9] Most of the fathers of American sociology wrote on the existence of class consciousness in America around the turn of the century, but typically they rejected a Marxist explanation in favor of a more sanguine portrayal of the sources and meaning of the phenomenon. See especially the discussions of Giddings and Cooley in Charles Page, *Class and American Sociology: From Ward to Ross* (New York: The Dial Press, Inc., 1940).

For a markedly different assessment of this period in American history as it relates to class consciousness, see Powell's excellent historical research. Elwin H. Powell, "Reform, Revolution and Reaction: A Case of Organized Conflict," in *The New Sociology*, ed. Irving Louis Horowitz (Fair Lawn, N.J.: Oxford University Press, Inc., 1964), pp. 321–56.

class consciousness in the Marxist view are (1) realization by members of a class of their common economic interests, (2) hostility to other classes, and (3) collective commitment to political ideology for the attainment of economic interests.

In this preoccupation with the Marxist controversy the tendency was to view class consciousness as an all-or-none attribute. One either had class consciousness or not. Such views presupposed a relatively unequivocal, undifferentiated phenomenon. Those supporting the Marxist interpretation were quick to infer the existence of class consciousness from tenuous evidence. Their critics, observing that the conditions of Marxist class consciousness were not fully satisfied, often concluded that class consciousness was virtually nonexistent.[10]

These comments suggest why Richard Morris and Raymond Murphy state that the designation and use of class consciousness is characterized by "vagueness, unclarity, and disagreement." Their paper is an important step in the direction of conceptual order. In addition to presenting a theoretical scheme for classifying the types of class consciousness possible in a society, they offer several propositions concerning the conditions under which class consciousness may be fostered or impeded. Their contribution is helpful not only in appraising the different meanings and uses of class consciousness in empirical studies but also in facilitating such research.

---

[10] A good example is the research carried out by Jones in the late 1930s on the Akron rubber strike. Both Marxists and their critics have used his findings to support their respective positions concerning the extent of class consciousness during the Great Depression. Alfred W. Jones, *Life, Liberty and Property* (Philadelphia: J. B. Lippincott Co., 1941).

A PARADIGM FOR THE STUDY OF CLASS CONSCIOUSNESS*

Richard T. Morris, *University of California, Los Angeles*

Raymond J. Murphy, *University of California, Los Angeles*

The study of class consciousness is certainly at the core of stratification theory and research. In fact, the very term "social class" is often based on an assumption of the presence of class consciousness. MacIver and Page, for example, insist that "Whatever objective criteria we use, we do not have a social class unless consciousness is present. If white collar workers, for example, do not regard themselves as belonging to the same class as industrial workers, then they do not together form one social class."[1] It is generally agreed that

---

* From Robert T. Morris and Raymond J. Murphy, "A Paradigm for the Study of Class Consciousness," *Sociology and Social Research*, 50 (April 1966), 298–313.

[1] Robert M. MacIver and Charles H. Page, *Society* (New York: Rinehart, 1949), p. 350.

without such consciousness or awareness on the part of the members of a society we are dealing only with "statistical classes" or strata.[2]

Yet, despite the central importance of stratification as a field of study in sociology[3] and despite the central position of class consciousness in the study of stratification, there is a great deal of vagueness, unclarity, and disagreement as to what class consciousness is as a theoretical construct, and as to how it can be measured empirically. It is the purpose of this paper to propose a paradigm [Fig. 1] for the study of this basic sociological idea, and to outline several of the major theoretical and methodological positions on the definition and measurement of class consciousness.

Through the use of the paradigm the authors attempt to bring some order to the definitional phase of the problem and to pose some very tentative hypotheses about the formation of class consciousness, its determinants and its results.[4] The paradigm has three uses: (1) first as a classification scheme for variant definitions and research methodologies already employed in this area; (2) second, as a set of social-psychological propositions about the way in which class consciousness develops in an individual member or group in a society; and (3) third, a set of propositions about the way in which class consciousness develops, can be made to develop, or can be impeded, in a society.

The paradigm can be most readily presented as a social-psychological model. The first ingredient necessary for class consciousness in an individual is some sort of perception of differences in status, of a status range or hierarchy in his society. It is possible that some people do not perceive any stratification phenomena in their view of society, but rather assume and operate as though all individuals or groups are equal in value. Although we would expect this situation to be rare, we have designated Box 1 of the paradigm to represent this lack of status perception.

Once status differences are perceived, they can take the form of a continuous range of gradations from high to low prestige. (In all of the discussion which follows, our usage of the term status refers to positions arranged in a rank order of evaluation, not simply any position defined by a role.) Some students of stratification maintain that this is the perception of most Americans. The equalitarian value system of this country, the lack of a feudal past, the relative absence of the more obvious symbols of class distinction (titles, dress, manners, etc.), the high rate of mobility, abundant economy, and other factors are thought

---

2 See for example, Gerhard Lenski, "American Social Classes: Statistical Strata of Social Groups?" *American Journal of Sociology*, 58 (September 1952), 139–44; Richard T. Morris, "Social Stratification," in *Sociology*, eds. Leonard Broom and Philip Selznick (Evanston, Ill.: Row, Peterson, 1958), pp. 165–88; Hans Speier, "Social Stratification in the Urban Community," *American Sociological Review*, 1 (April 1936), 192–202.

3 The subject of stratification is included routinely in introductory text books; a number of specialized texts and readers have appeared in recent years; a special issue of *The American Journal of Sociology* published in 1953 listed a bibliography of 333 items dealing with the topic, 58 (January 1953), 391–418. See also Richard L. Simpson, "Expanding and Declining Fields in American Sociology," *American Sociological Review*, 26 (June 1961), 458–66.

4 For a somewhat parallel discussion of class consciousness and related types of awareness, see Milton M. Gordon, "A System of Social Class Analysis," *The Drew University Bulletin*, 39 (August 1951), 1–19.

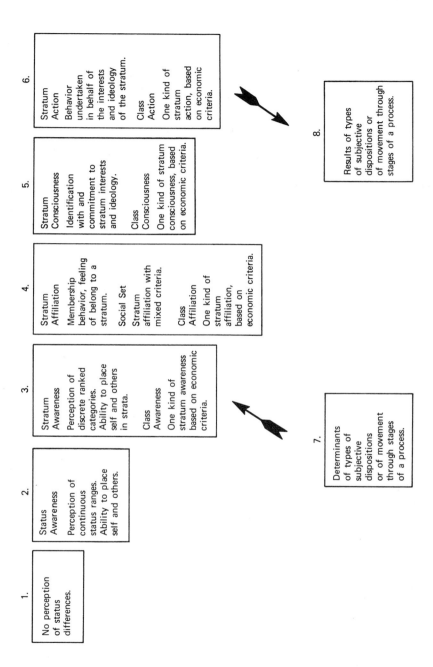

Fig. 1. *A Paradigm for the Study of Class Conciousness.*

to contribute to a perception of the stratification structure as a more or less complete series (or several parallel series) of status positions hierarchically ordered, but without clear dividing points, or strata.[5] The perception of this hierarchy, and the ability on the part of members of a society to place self and others on this kind of status continuum we should like to term "status awareness" (Box 2). According to this definition, the usual occupational rating scales, even though they may show a great deal of consistency, are not evidences of class consciousness, but of uniformity in status awareness.[6]

It is also possible that people in a society, when they perceive status differences, see discrete categories instead of a continuum of status positions. Such categories are also ordered in a hierarchy of evaluation. The practice of perceiving self and others in ranked categories of status we will term "stratum awareness" (Box 3).[7]

The most commonly perceived strata in industrial societies are probably

those based upon the criteria of educational attainment, occupation, economic rewards and life style, religious affiliation, political orientation, genealogical, ethnic, and racial ancestry. In our view, class is a particular kind of stratum based upon the exclusively economic criteria of ownership and control of goods and services as expressed in the operation of the market economy.[8] The perception of such economic strata, and the ability to place self and others in them we will term class awareness, which is but one kind of stratum awareness.

It could be argued, as illustrated at the beginning of this paper, that class cannot exist without class awareness, i.e., that economic strata without stratum awareness on the part of the members of society cannot be called classes, but must be termed strata. We have chosen, however, in order to make the terminology consistent, and in order to be able to talk about other kinds of strata (racial, religious, etc.), with or without stratum awareness, to speak of class in these terms also. Objectively described economic strata are herein called classes; classes may or may not be accompanied by class awareness on the part of members of society.

A number of theoretical approaches and empirical findings relate to this type of stratification perception.[9] In

---

5 See Stanley Hetzler, "An Investigation of the Distinctiveness of Social Classes," *American Sociological Review*, 18 (October 1953), 493–97; and William F. Kenkel, *An Experimental Analysis of Social Stratification in Columbus, Ohio* (unpublished Ph.D. dissertation, The Ohio State University, 1952), summarized in John F. Cuber and William F. Kenkel, *Social Stratification* (New York: Appleton-Century-Crofts, 1954), pp. 132-56.

6 For an excellent summary and analysis of the NORC occupational prestige material, see Albert J. Reiss, *Occupations and Social Status* (New York: The Free Press of Glencoe, Inc., 1962).

7 We could also speak of *situs awareness*, the ability to place self and others into discrete categories which are not differentially evaluated. See Richard T. Morris and Raymond J. Murphy, "The Situs Dimension in Occupational Structure," *American Sociological Review*, 24 (April 1959), 231–39.

---

8 We have chosen to take this restricted economic definition of class in order to avoid confusion with other kinds of strata, also to avoid contradiction with the large, established body of literature which uses the term in the economic sense, e.g., Marx, Weber, Schumpeter, etc.

9 The "functionalist" school of stratification would presumably fit into this category. See Kingsley Davis, "Conceptual Analysis of Stratification," *American Sociological Review*, 7 (June 1942), 309–21; Kingsley Davis and Wilbert E. Moore, "Some Principles of Stratification," *Ameri-*

these approaches the investigators use the term "class consciousness" to refer to our definition of class awareness. They seem to assume that if class consciousness is present in society, the best way to find out about its extent and other properties is to ask the members of society directly what their perceptions of class are. The problem is usually investigated in one of two ways: (1) The respondent is asked to comment about the structure of the community or society, so as to reveal his perceptions, if any, of the stratification dimension, or, (2) he is asked the direct question, "What class are you in?" In this latter technique, the structural category is supplied by the investigator and the respondent is asked to fit himself (and sometimes others) into this structure. There are a number of variations in technique, the study may be made nationally, or within a community; the investigator may ask a random sample of members or use judges to make placements of others; the number and names of classes may be specified in advance by the investigator, or the information may be drawn from the opinions of the respondents in order not to prestructure their perceptions.[10] In all of these tech-

niques, however, the assumption seems to be that unless and until a number of the members of a community or society, especially important members, e.g., community leaders, are able to say that there are classes, are able to say how many there are, what the names of the classes are and are able to place themselves and others in these classes, class consciousness does not exist. According to these writers, class consciousness is present in the society to the degree that there is a common perception of such ranked categories.

Both the ability to perceive strata and the number of strata perceived seem to be a function of the positional location of the individual in his social and occupational spheres. Popitz has shown that in Germany, for example, the socioeconomic position of the individual plays an important role in determining whether he perceives society as a status or stratum arrangement.[11] Similarly, Hoggart describes the image of the British working class member as a dichotomous one, with little propensity to view society as composed of a series of infinitely graded statuses.[12] Dahrendorf suggests that these differing models of society distinguished by individuals represent a commitment to ideology. Those with a perception of status gradations represent an ideology of satisfaction and conservativism,

---

can Sociological Review, 10 (April 1945), 242–49; and Talcott Parsons, "An Analytical Approach to the Theory of Social Stratification," in *Essays in Sociological Theory: Pure and Applied* (New York: The Free Press of Glencoe, Inc., 1949), pp. 166–84, for representative examples.

[10] For examples of this methodology see Richard Centers, *The Psychology of Social Class* (Princeton, N.J.: Princeton University Press, 1949); Neal Gross, "Social Class Identification in the Urban Community," *American Sociological Review*, 18 (August 1953), 398–404; Harold F. Kaufman, *Prestige Classes in a New York Rural Community*, Memoir 260 (Ithaca, N.Y.: Cornell University Agricultural Experiment Station, March 1944); and F. M. Martin, "Some

Subjective Aspects of Social Stratification," in *Social Mobility in Britain*, ed. D. V. Glass (New York: The Free Press of Glencoe, Inc., 1954), pp. 51–75.

[11] Heinrich Popitz *et. al.*, *Das Gesellschaftsbild des Arbeiters* (Tübingen, 1957), pp. 237, 252, quoted in Ralf Dahrendorf, *Class and Class Conflict in Industrial Society* (Stanford, Calif.: Stanford University Press, 1959), pp. 283–84.

[12] Richard Hoggart, *The Uses of Literacy* (Boston: Beacon Press, Inc., 1961), especially pp. 62–77.

while those who see society stratified into discrete strata (the dichotomous image) are more likely to be dissatisfied and express a wish for change in the *status quo*.[13]

It should be noted again at this point that we still are not talking about or defining class consciousness. Most of the studies referred to above are, from our point of view, studies of stratum awareness (or sometimes class awareness) rather than of class consciousness. They are basically measures of the ability of members of a society or community to place themselves and others into a set of categories; they say nothing at all of membership identification, interaction patterns, or commitment to an ideology, as criteria.[14]

Moving on to Box 4 of the paradigm, it may be proposed that the next step in the development of stratum consciousness is the emergence of group membership properties. The category (whether it be racial, economic, religious, etc.) takes on the characteristics of a *group* (or a series of related groups) of interacting individuals who share feelings of belonging, identification with and practice of common norms, expectations, sentiments and activities.[15] This feeling of belonging

and the participant behavior which it induces we will term stratum affiliation. As before, we consider class affiliation as one kind of stratum affiliation, based solely on economic criteria. Many investigators use the term "class consciousness" to refer to our definition of class affiliation. They seem to assume that individual perception of structure is not a sufficient indicator of class consciousness, but that group membership behavior must be added. It is not enough to perceive class differences, the members of a society must act in accordance with this perception by maintaining patterns of association and dissociation, inclusion and exclusion, in their daily lives. The outstanding proponents of this view are, of course, W. Lloyd Warner and his associates.[16] Although the precise methodology may be rather unclear at times, the general procedure seems to be to combine measures of stratum awareness with an analysis of the actual interaction patterns of the members of a community, such as organizational memberships, attendance at social gatherings and events, intermarriage and dating regularities, and the like. Again, although there are variations in technique, the studies are usually carried out in small communities, but may be investigated in a large metropolis;[17] or

---

13 Dahrendorf, *op. cit.*, p. 284.

14 A number of different criteria are used or discovered in these studies. "Class" may refer to occupational strata, ethnic strata, educational strata, as well as to economic strata. Some of these studies demonstrate that people are thinking in terms of class simply by supplying the word to them, without specifying what they or the investigator means by it. See Gross, *op. cit.*

15 Our meaning of the concept "group" here is similar to that employed by Smith: "A unit consisting of a plural number of organisms (agents) who have collective perception of their unity and who have the ability to act, or who are acting, in a unitary manner toward the environment." M. Smith, "Social Situation, Social Behavior, Social

Group," *Psychological Review*, 52 (1945), 224–29.

16 See especially, W. Lloyd Warner and Paul S. Lunt, *The Social Life of a Modern Community* (New Haven, Conn.: Yale University Press, 1941), pp. 81–126; W. Lloyd Warner and associates, *Democracy in Jonesville* (New York: Harper, 1949); and W. Lloyd Warner, Marchia Meeker, and Kenneth Eels, *Social Class in America* (Chicago: Science Research Associates, Inc., 1949).

17 See the study of the upper class in Philadelphia by E. Digby Baltzell, *Philadelphia Gentlemen* (New York: The Free Press of Glencoe, Inc., 1958); and the journalis-

on an intercommunity, national or even international level.[18] The investigators may use a combination of ratings by judges, comments from community members, organizational membership lists, "blue books" of various kinds, sociometric techniques, and other methods to arrive at the composition of classes. The investigator who supplies class names to his respondents may "synthetically" arrive at the membership variable by asking respondents to list the organizations they belong to. He then classifies as class conscious those individuals who identify with a class category and who belong to an organization (usually economic or political) thought by the investigator to be class linked. For example, those who check "working class" from a list of classes and who belong to labor unions may be classified by the researcher as class conscious. "Inappropriate" group memberships serve to identify the non-class conscious or the "false" class conscious.[19] In all of these techniques there seems to be the assumption that in a society, or a community, class consciousness is expressed through differential interaction patterns and identification and membership in groups reflecting some order of social evaluation, from high to low prestige. The degree of class consciousness varies with the clarity of the differential in-

teraction patterns, e.g., exclusion and inclusion, and with the clarity of and agreement upon, the prestige ranking of these groups.[20] Anderson and Davidson make explicit this meaning of class and class consciousness:

[A self-conscious class] means a social group distinguishable from all other groups by the intimacy of its relationships, aware of its distinction and regardful of its position in the social scale, resisting intrusion from below, fearful of intrusion from above, having a like scale of living, its individual members "going with" and intermarrying in the group, sharing group rituals and ceremonies, possessing a sense of "belonging" and for the most part not expecting and perhaps not eager to alter its status.... When such a group acquires a sense of permanence, continuing through successive generations, it may be considered a "class." When this class becomes aware of its distinct character, develops a ritual and ceremony of membership and class taboos, and is regardful of itself as a distinct entity in the community, then it may be said to have acquired "class consciousness."[21]

It should be noted that not all group or organizational affiliation is stratum affiliation and that stratum awareness seems logically to be a necessary pre-

---

tic but relevant work by Cleveland Amory, especially *The Proper Bostonians* (New York: E. P. Dutton & Co., Inc., 1947).

[18] See for example, Thomas Bottomore, "Social Stratification in Voluntary Organizations," and Rosalind C. Chambers, "A Study of Three Voluntary Organizations," both in Glass, *op. cit.*, 349–406.

[19] This logic is followed (along with a measure of allegiance) by Oscar Glantz in "Class Consciousness and Political Solidarity," *American Sociological Review*, 23 (August 1958), 375–83. See also, Centers, *op. cit.*

[20] A closely related approach is the subcultural view which assumes that classes are composed of groupings of the population with different ways of life, values, behavior patterns, norms, and the like. See Milton M. Gordon, "The Concept of Sub-Culture and Its Application," *Social Forces* 26 (October 1947), 40–42; and Joseph A. Kahl, *The American Class Structure* (New York: Rinehart, 1957), especially Chap. VII, "Classes as Ideal Types: Emergent Values," pp. 184–220.

[21] H. Dewey Anderson and Percy E. Davidson, *Ballots and the Democratic Class Struggle* (Stanford, Calif.: Stanford University Press, 1943), pp. 211–12.

condition for stratum affiliation. In other words, the groups or membership units have to be stratified subjectively, have to be seen by the members of society as ordered in a hierarchy of evaluation before we can speak of stratum affiliation, as distinct from group affiliation. Again, there are many varieties of stratum affiliation: racial stratum affiliation; occupational stratum affiliation; religious stratum affiliation; and class affiliation. Perhaps the most commonly discussed stratum affiliation in American sociology is the community set portrayed by Warner and others. Although these are usually called social classes in the literature, we prefer the term "social set" to refer to these strata made up of mixed criteria, usually genealogy, life style, geographical location, as well as income, and restrict the use of the term class affiliation to mean membership in and identification with exclusively economic strata. The existence of social sets in a community, or in society generally, does not necessarily imply or mean that there is class consciousness or even class affiliation in that community or society. In fact, the existence of such sets may be a factor precluding or impeding the development of class affiliation, particularly in the sense that any affiliation with stratum groups other than economic may indicate a higher priority of other values and a more meaningful identification with noneconomic aspects of social life. Thus Weber explains the lack of class antagonism and consciousness in the American South by pointing to the importance of the racial affiliation dimension in stratifying the population along noneconomic lines.[22] To speak properly

of class affiliation, the stratum criterion must be exclusively economic;[23] to speak properly of class consciousness there must be a commitment to an ideology.

Stratum consciousness (Box 5) is identification with, or commitment to, the interests and ideology of the stratum. It is not enough to perceive the stratification system as being divided into strata and to be able to place self and others in it. It is not enough to feel and behave as a member of the stratum. There must be a knowledge of and a commitment to the interests, aims, and goals of the stratum before we can speak about the presence of stratum consciousness. Again, as above, we consider class consciousness as one kind of stratum consciousness, based solely on economic criteria. Many investigators seem to agree with this definition, and assume that class consciousness is not merely a matter of perception of structure or of group membership and prestige arrangements. They argue that it is essential to the very idea of class consciousness that some sort of commitment to class interest or ideology be present, together with participation in a program of action to forward these interests in the name of the class. Class consciousness often represents a political awareness and orientation. As C. Wright Mills puts it:

> Class consciousness has always been understood as a political consciousness of one's own rational class interests and their opposition to the interests of other

---

[22] Max Weber, "Social Stratification and Class Structure," in Weber, *The Theory of Social and Economic Organization*, trans. Parsons and Henderson (New York: The Free Press of Glencoe, Inc., 1947), pp. 425–26.

[23] See the distinction drawn between competitive class feeling and "corporate class consciousness" by MacIver and Page, *op. cit.*, pp. 359–60, for a similar view.

classes. Economic potentiality becomes politically realized: 'a class in itself' becomes a 'class for itself.' Thus for class consciousness there must be (1) a rational awareness and identification with one's own class interests; (2) an awareness of and rejection of other class interests as illegitimate; and (3) an awareness of and a readiness to use collective political means to the collective political end of realizing one's political interests.[24]

This approach is one which most closely articulates with that of Marx in its emphasis on class action and conflicting interests as essential components of a "mature" class consciousness. Proponents of this orientation, too, place greater stress on structural factors producing class differences. Instead of focusing primarily on the subjective perception of classes or strata and from such psychological data investigating or deducing structural correlates, these investigators analyze broad socioeconomic trends in the structure and analyze or deduce their psychological expression or consequences. Lockwood, for example, analyzes the psychological and behavioral resistance of the British "black-coated" worker to the Labor party in terms of broad historical trends in the work situation, the status structure of British society, and the changing pattern of economic rewards in the English labor force.[25] Similarly, Mills investigates the "social-historical" structure of the United States to account for the apolitical mentality of the white-collar class.[26] A parallel, though usually less

broad approach involves the study of the political economic, of social reform attitudes or behavior of individuals located at different points in the social structure, e.g., in different occupations, in unions vs. management positions, at different income levels, in different political parties.[27] Here a typical finding and conclusion might be that if members of unions or those in unskilled occupations favored economic reforms, while those in managerial or professional occupations did not, this is prima facie evidence of class consciousness. In such investigations frequently the respondent is not asked to describe his subjective views about stratification, nor is he required to place himself or others in the system. Rather, he is asked to supply information on his objective status (e.g., occupation, income, education) and asked for his attitudes about political and/or economic issues or for his voting preferences. Thus Glantz, for example, classifies his respondents as class conscious if they are business or white collar people who say they owe allegiance to business (rather than to labor) and if their responses to six attitude items, derived from AFL-CIO and NAM statements show a "business orientation." In such investigations, then, the researcher rather than the respondent, describes on the existence of and expression of class consciousness.[28]

The ideological approach to the study of class consciousness varies in

---

[24] C. Wright Mills, *White Collar* (Fair Lawn, N.J.: Oxford University Press, Inc., 1951), p. 325.

[25] David Lockwood, *The Blackcoated Worker* (London: George Allen & Unwin, Ltd., 1958).

[26] Mills, *op. cit.*

[27] For an example of this kind of analysis, see Angus Campbell *et. al., The American Voter* (New York: John Wiley & Sons, Inc., 1960), especially Chap. 13, "The Role of Social Class," pp. 333–80. See also, Bernard R. Berelson, Paul F. Lazarsfeld, and William N. McPhee, *Voting* (Chicago: University of Chicago Press, 1954), pp. 56–60.

[28] Glantz, *op. cit.*

its theoretical assumptions as well as in its techniques. Some theorists maintain that true class consciousness (as opposed to false) must involve a revolutionary ideology, a clear idea of an enemy class and the desire to destroy it as a necessary part of the action program for the class.[29] This view, of course, stems from the writings of Marx who defined classes as economic groups in opposition: "Individuals form a class only insofar as they are engaged in a common struggle with another class."[30] Others do not hold that revolutionary action or the ideology of inevitable class war are essential, but rather insist that class conscious persons are those who have internalized the interests and aims of their class, and are fully committed to their achievement. Weber seems to have taken this position with regard to property classes:

> The differentiation of classes on the basis of property alone is not 'dynamic' that is, it does not necessarily result in class struggle or class revolutions. It is not uncommon for very strongly privileged property classes such as slave owners to exist side by side with such far less privileged groups as peasants or even outcasts without any class struggle. There may even be ties of solidarity between privileged property classes and unfree elements.[31]

Another point about which opinions may differ concerns whether or not real as opposed to intended or hypothetical action must be demonstrated before class consciousness can be said to exist. The proper aim of action also may be disputed. For the more orthodox Marxist, economic issues may be paramount and only political action directed to changes in the basic economic issues may be viewed as indicative of true class consciousness. Others might view actions aimed at "exclusion of undesirables" or aims of union organizations to increase bargaining strengths as indicative of class consciousness.

In the face of these disagreements, in order to provide for a more flexible use of the concept with strata other than classes, we have chosen to use a rather broad definition of the content of the ideology or interests of the stratum. Very generally, by ideology we refer to any set of programmatic goals which involve the use of any means to ensure the maintenance, protection, or improvement of the position of a particular stratum relative to other strata.

More specifically, in order to separate stratum ideology from more general stratum attitudes or values for operational purposes (e.g., middle-class values vs. middle-class ideology), it may be proposed tentatively that stratum ideology must include the following component elements: (a) an understanding of the present position of the stratum in relation to other strata (e.g., higher, lower, exploited, in power, out of power, superior, inferior, elect, despised, etc.); (b) an explanation or rationale accounting for the present position (e.g., God's will, the nature of man or society, the machinations of another stratum, historical accident, inevitable evolution, etc.); (c) an evaluation or justification of the present position (e.g., legitimate,

---

[29] See, for example, Nikolai Bukharin, *Historical Materialism* (New York: International Publishers, 1925): "A class interest arises when it places one class in opposition to another. The class struggle arises when it throws one class into active conflict with the other.", p. 297.

[30] Karl Marx and Friedrich Engels, *The German Ideology*, II (London: Lawrence & Wishart, 1939), p. 59.

[31] Weber, *op. cit.*

illegitimate, justified, unfair, intolerable, functionally necessary, threatened, promising, etc.) ; (d) a proposal of action to be taken in order to maintain, protect, or improve the present position (e.g., political activity, cooperation or conflict with other strata, economic changes, passive acceptance or resistance, educational improvement, legal or illegal action, etc.) ; and (e) a statement of a desirable ultimate future position and role for the stratum (e.g., as coequals, as the only existing stratum, national or international betterment, amalgamation, disappearance, a return to the past position, etc).

It is implied in the present discussion that, similar to stratum affiliation, it is possible to discover many varieties of *stratum consciousness*, of which class consciousness is but one type. We can speak of race-strata consciousness, occupational-strata consciousness, religious-strata consciousness, etc., to the extent that the groupings are stratified and the members are identified with and committed to the ideology of the stratum.

An old problem in the literature on class consciousness concerns the issue of whether or not class action is an essential ingredient in consciousness. This difficulty rests in part with the problem of differentiating commitment from activity. It is possible to imagine individuals who are sympathetic to the causes of their class, but who are unable or unwilling to act in its behalf. Is the person who "mans the barricades" more class conscious than the one who wishes him well in his fight? This issue has methodological consequences for us in that it raises the question (almost as ancient in our literature) as to whether attitudes are a form of behavior. Does the respondent who expresses discontent in his replies to an attitude scale, have as much class

consciousness as the person who indicates membership participation and activity with others in the cause of his class? We have chosen to separate the concept of class action from class consciousness in the belief that it makes sense, that it is theoretically useful to speak of class consciousness with or without class action on the part of individual members, and that the separation clarifies the nature of class action itself.

Stratum action (Box 6) is behavior undertaken by an individual or group on behalf of the interests of the stratum. This implies that class consciousness (awareness and commitment to the interests) is logically a necessary precondition for class action. By action we mean some form of overt behavior explicitly motivated by what are thought to be class (or stratum) interests on the part of the participants. This may mean proselytizing friends, distributing propaganda, organizing and joining in strikes, supporting political candidates, boycotting stocks, "sit in" demonstrations, participating in passive resistance programs, etc. In each case, the behavior must, according to our definition, be based upon and directed toward the satisfaction or resolution of class (or other stratum) interests. Not all behavior that looks like class or stratum action actually is. Studies which correlate voting behavior with occupation, or attitudes toward picketing with union membership usually have *not* by our definition, demonstrated the presence of class action (or in many cases class consciousness) for two reasons: (1) There is no demonstration that the behavior is based on and motivated by an awareness of and commitment to class or stratum. (2) A set of attitudes or predispositions to act in a hypothetical situation do not constitute action per se (although they may be useful devices for predicting potential actors). It is true, that in actual tactics, a person may become engaged in class or stratum action without being class conscious, and he may find out "why" his actions were significant at a later date, e.g., in a well-organized student riot. Subjectively, the person is not engaged in class action, if he goes along for the excitement, the satisfaction of a personal interest or motive (e.g., a share of the rewards of looting), or simply because he happened to be present when the activity was taking place and he is forced to "choose sides."[32] From the point of view of the group organizing the riot, it may well be class action perhaps consciously involving the use of "dupes" to swell the ranks of participants. Here again, we can speak of a variety of *stratum actions* insofar as persons engage in behavior directed toward the achievement of stratum interests.

The remaining elements of the paradigm involve the determinants and results of being in a given box, i.e., having a certain subjective disposition (perception, attitude, behavior) at a given point in time, or in moving as part of a process from one box to another.

It is impossible within the limits of this discussion to do more than make a bare and merely suggestive list of possible determinants of the predominant mode of stratum attitude or behavior in a given society, group, or individual, or of the determinants which facilitate or deter the movement from one type of stratum attitude to another.

_____

32 An interesting example of this involuntary involvement in collective behavior is provided by Alfred McClung Lee and Norman D. Humphrey, *Race Riot* (New York: Dryden Press, 1943).

The first problem is whether or not in a given society the attitudes toward economic strata (or classes) are more highly developed or salient than attitudes toward other kinds of strata or status hierarchies, e.g., racial, religious, kinship, age, etc. Davis and Moore, and Parsons, among others, seem to agree that the salient criteria for stratification are closely related to the predominant value system of the society. As values change, the importance of various stratification (according to new, or newly important) criteria may emerge. In other words, differential evaluation by economic criteria may become less important or irrelevant, as the value system changes in certain ways. In addition to value determinants, there are structural determinants, e.g., a compression of the range of economic differences, a mixture of racial characteristics, or universal compulsory education through college, which may make certain stratification systems less important, irrelevant, or impossible to apply. There of course may be discrepancies between the rates of change of value determinants and structural determinants, e.g., the need for artificial labelling of some Jews in Nazi Germany; the difficulty in shifting from a racial stratification system to an economic stratification system in some African nations.

The second problem, given the relative salience of various social hierarchies, is the extent to which these systems are seen as continuous ranges or as vertical arrangements of discrete categories. In our terminology, is there status awareness or stratum awareness among the various hierarchies? Class awareness cannot exist unless the economic criterion is salient, and is used in such a way as to create discrete categories. The chief determinants of perceptive posture in this sense are probably social psychological, and structural. The concepts of ambiguity tolerance, rites of passage, role clarity, stereotype, and the embedding process are relevant here. The structural determinants may involve such factors as availability of knowledge about, or visibility of, criteria; the degree of demarcation and formalization of symbols of achieved or ascribed rank; and the overlap and discrepancy of multiple, coexistent status hierarchies. It is possible that within this list of determinants, for example, we might find reasons why income and occupation are seen as continuous status ranges in our society, why education, and race are divided into discrete stratum categories, and why ownership vs. nonownership is very difficult to use as a criterion at all.

The third problem, given salience of criteria and the perception of strata, is whether or not the strata take on group characteristics. The determinants of the transformation of a collectivity into a group, such as the emergence of interaction patterns, norms, division of labor, roles, etc. are too complex—and at the same time too familiar—to be described here. Suffice to say that many of the preconditions for the formation of classes as groups which were suggested by Marx are still applicable, e.g., communication, interaction, organization, common experience, leadership.

The fourth problem, once the stratum becomes a group, whether it be an economic group, an occupational group, a racial group, or an educational group, is to establish the extent to which the stratum is committed to some ideology or programmatic goal of action. The determinants of the establishment of an ideology have been outlined by Marx and include such elements as a sense of injustice, unwarranted deprivation, dissatisfaction with

the system, placement of blame, loyalty and responsibility to group goals, and overthrow as the only successfuul solution. Viewed from the top, we might add such elements as fear of losing identity, protection against intrusion from below, fear of failing, desire to maintain position for next generation, desire to expand or gain more control, and the like. Propaganda, education, a rationale and explication of present conditions, goals and appropriate action are important factors—such determinants should help explain the development of ideologies in professionalization, unionization, or the action programs of racial organizations.

The final problem, once the goals have been set and organized action proposed, is to establish the conditions under which such action is actually carried out.

Again, within these limits we can only suggest such broad factors as financing, leadership, organization, pressure or aid from the outside, critical incidents, etc.

In closing we would like to summarize what seem to us to be the major contributions of the paradigm to the study of subjective aspects of stratification and to pose some of the questions which the scheme has raised as we have worked on it. The model's most apparent use is in conceptual clarification, both in the differentiation between class consciousness and other types of consciousness, and between class consciousness and other types of subjective perception and identification. While our particular definition of class consciousness may seem unduly restricted to some, particularly since the empirical facts of American life seem to preclude its existence, this narrowness may prevent us from trying to fit a Marxian concept developed to explain 19th Century European social structure to the 20th Century conditions of highly bureaucratized society. If Weber's analytical distinction among class, status, and power have any heuristic significance at all, and the majority of sociologists seem to think they do, then it behooves us to carry out these distinctions in matters of the subjective meanings of stratification. In our distinction between stratum consciousness and class consciousness we have attempted to follow out the implications of this distinction.

Another contribution of the paradigm, as we see it, is its use as an orientation to the analysis of the subjective aspects of social stratification. As has already been suggested, the paradigm can be used as a model for investigating the development of differing states of subjective awareness concerning stratification phenomena. The implication here is that class consciousness (or any other form of stratum consciousness) is a *processual* emergent and that it must be studied in a dynamic framework, either historical or biographical, rather than as a characteristic which is either present or absent among a population at a given time.[33]

A third potentially useful function of the paradigm is in the application as a framework for the comparative analysis of differing kinds of awareness and commitment to social groups or categories which exhibit rank characteristics. We have called attention to the fact that class consciousness is but one kind of stratum consciousness which may be expressed by the members of a society. The paradigm is constructed in such a manner as to invite

the analysis of different types of perception and commitment, i.e., those related to racial characteristics, occupational groups, religious denominations, age groups, educational attainment, etc. It would seem to us fruitful for those interested in race relations, for example, to use the paradigm as a model for the study of the development (or disappearance) of race consciousness in a population. Furthermore, many of the studies which have been made of the development of racial prejudice should be classifiable in terms of our categories. The examination of such material might well suggest underlying similarities in the process of perception and identification with race and class. Such comparisons have often been impeded in the past because we have lacked a framework for including both kinds of interests and due to increasing specialization of fields within sociology and social psychology we have had little opportunity to exchange views. A comparative study of subjective perceptions might lead us to ask (and hopefully to answer) such questions as: Under what, if any, conditions does race consciousness lead to class consciousness? Does a preoccupation with race inhibit a commitment to class ideology? Are there "functional equivalents" for class consciousness in a society?[34]

The paradigm is a suggestion for a

[33] See Rudolph Heberle, "Recovery of Class Theory," and Robert A. Nisbet, "The Decline and Fall of Social Class," *Pacific Sociological Review*, 2 (Spring 1959), 11–24.

[34] The recent study of the Muslim movement in the United States by E. U. Essien-Udom is most suggestive of the relationship between race consciousness and class awareness. It is the author's hypothesis that the lower class urban Negro has become estranged both from the white society and the middle-class Negro group. "This estrangement suggests the beginning of class consciousness and conflict among the Negro masses, directed not against whites but against the Negro middle and upper classes." See E. U. Essien-Udom, *Black*

way of bringing some order to a field of inquiry which continues to fascinate, but which, unfortunately, is still accurately described by Morris Ginsberg's conclusion of 1937:

> The psychology of class differentiation has not been studied with sufficient thoroughness and there is as yet no

Nationalism (Chicago: University of Chicago Press, 1962), especially pp. 326–39.

generally accepted technique for the observation, analysis, and record of the behavior of groups in relation to one another. Accordingly it is extremely difficult to say what exactly one is conscious of when one is class conscious.[35]

[35] Morris Ginsberg, "Class Consciousness," in *The Encyclopedia of the Social Sciences*, Vol. III, eds. Edwin R. A. Seligman and Alvin Johnson (New York: The Macmillan Company, Publishers, 1937), p. 538.

SUBSTANTIVE RESEARCH

The appearance in 1949 of Richard Centers' monograph *The Psychology of Social Class*[1] was an important turning point in research on class consciousness. Not only was his investigation the first large-scale national study of class consciousness, but it also spurred interest in a variety of issues beyond the boundaries of the earlier, largely fruitless debate over Marxist conceptions.

Centers saw classes as essentially subjective phenomena, as psychosocial groupings dependent upon class consciousness.[2] This concept of class guided his nationwide opinion survey, in which a cross section of adult white males were questioned about their political and economic attitudes. Information on the respondent's self-placement in the class system was elicited by the following question: "If you were asked to use one of these four names for your social class, which would you say you belonged in: the middle class, lower class, working class, or upper class?"[3] Other data were obtained, but the core of Centers' research rests upon findings of class consciousness as indexed by the respondent's subjective identification with a class and his expression of politicoeconomic orientations. While Centers acknowledges his indebtedness to Marxist views, he sees his own approach to class consciousness as superior in two ways. First, he does not assume class consciousness but demonstrates its existence and nature through an empirical test. Second, he suggests, many of the ideas which are implicit and often ambiguous in Marxist thinking are rendered more explicit by their inclusion within an "interest-group theory." The following statement summarizes this theory:

> A person's status and role with respect to the economic processes of society impose upon him certain attitudes, values, and interests relating to his role and status in the political and economic sphere. It holds, further, that the status and role of the indi-

[1] *The Psychology of Social Class* (Princeton, N.J.: Princeton University Press, 1949).
[2] *Ibid.*, p. 27. See also the discussion of Centers' approach to the study of class in Chapter Three of the present volume.
[3] *Ibid.*, p. 76.

vidual in relation to the means of production and exchange of goods and services give rise in him to a consciousness of membership in some social class which shares those attitudes, values, and interests.[4]

For close to a decade after Centers' contribution much of the literature on class consciousness consisted of critical analyses, replications, and extensions of the methods of study and findings reported in *The Psychology of Social Class.* Critics have expressed a variety of reservations about Centers' research. Some challenge his conceptualization of class consciousness. Others doubt that his hypotheses follow from a Marxist framework and suggest that his conclusions are not warranted by his data. The strongest criticisms concern Centers' methodology, particularly the system of self-placement he used to ascertain class. To many critics the use of a structured question, in which a respondent is asked to classify himself as middle class, lower class, working class, or upper class, makes it uncertain that Centers was really tapping the subjective identifications of his respondents. These doubts regarding the adequacy of Centers' methodolgy were highlighted in 1953 by Neal Gross,[5] who replicated Centers' method and compared the results with those obtained by open-ended questions. He found much disparity in the responses. Gross concludes that the open-ended system is preferable since it minimizes structuring of the respondent's subjective state by the investigator and thus more truly elicits self-identification.

Centers' investigation still serves as a major point of reference for many contemporary studies of class consciousness, but recent research is increasingly more sophisticated than Centers'. The studies presented below illustrate such developments.

To most researchers, the significance of class consciousness lies in its implications for politicoeconomic orientation and behavior: how one views the political and economic system, the political values and beliefs one holds, one's participation in political movements, and one's voting behavior. As treated by some writers politicoeconomic values and activities per se constitute the essence of class consciousness and are not simply its possible consequences. The selection by Oscar Glantz deals with this central question. His study also is an empirical inquiry into the relevance of some aspects of the Marxist thesis for the American scene.

---

[4] *Ibid.*, pp. 28–29.

[5] "Social Class Identification in the Urban Community," *American Sociological Review*, 18 (August 1953), 398–404. See also Herman Case, "Marxian Implications of Centers' Interest Group Theory," *Social Forces*, 23 (March 1955), 254–58; Arthur W. Kornhauser, "Public Opinion and Social Class," *American Journal of Sociology*, 55 (January 1950), 333–45; Milton Gordon, *Social Class in American Sociology* (New York: McGraw-Hill Book Company, 1963), pp. 193–202.

CLASS CONSCIOUSNESS AND POLITICAL
SOLIDARITY*

Oscar Glantz

Brooklyn College

Is a class a class because "thinking makes it so," or is a class a class purely on objective grounds? If the first view is correct, it must be extended logically to include the proposition that class consciousness is necessarily antecedent to the existence of classes,[1] and this proposition in turn carries with it the notion that an individual's subjective self-placement is the determinant of his class position. Thus, sociologists who hold this view may entertain such images as "business class" assembly-line workers and "laboring class' corporation executives, both of which are encountered in field surveys which depend upon a subjective conceptualization of classes.[2]

To the writer, the subjective approach is a form of solipsism in which objective conditions are either neglected or negated.[3] The view here is that the existence of an objective class is one of the prior conditions to class consciousness. Accordingly, class is not the product of its consciousness but develops into a self-conscious class when its members become aware of their objective conditions. From this viewpoint, when an assembly-line worker, say, claims allegiance to the business class, he is not therefore a member of that class. Such claims may have their place in social reality, but we would do well to view them as examples of false consciousness. Following Durkheim, an individual can never recruit himself into a class by psychological invention.[4]

---

* From Oscar Glantz, "Class Consciousness and Political Solidarity," *American Sociological Review*, 23 (1958), 375–82. Reprinted by permission of the American Sociological Association.

[1] It would be discursive in the current paper to examine the literature on this problem, but it might be noted that the subjective approach has been dominant in recent decades. For an early example, see R. M. MacIver, *Society* (New York: Farrar and Rinehart, Inc., 1937). MacIver suggests that "the concept of class loses its sociological significance if it is defined by any purely objective criterion, such as ... occupational function." Moreover, he argues that "unless class consciousness is present, then no matter what criterion we take, we have not a social class but a mere logical category or type" (p. 167).

[2] For example, Richard Centers, *The Psychology of Social Classes* (Princeton, N.J.: Princeton University Press, 1951). Among the blue-collar workers in his sam-

ple, 21 per cent claimed membership in the upper or middle class, while 23 per cent of his business, professional, and white-collar respondents claimed membership in the working class. To account for these claims, he referred to them in the following way: "The manual workers identifying themselves with the middle class are thus a *minority group*, in a sense, within it. Likewise, ... businessmen, professional people, and white collar workers ... constitute a *minority* within the working class" (p. 125, emphasis added).

[3] This is not to say that the subjective approach does not have heuristic value in some types of research, e.g., in studies of vertical mobility.

[4] Emile Durkheim, *The Rules of Sociological Method*, trans. S. A. Solovay and J. H. Mueller (Chicago: University of Chicago Press, 1938).

This is not to say that the study of class consciousness should attach any significance to self-identifications which are consistent with objective position, particularly if such identifications are responses to a forced-choice question.[5] If class consciousness is supposed to mean more than a simple awareness of economic position, one should expect this awareness to be accompanied by class related politicoeconomic values.[6] Indeed, it would appear that class consciousness can emerge only when an individual is aware of his politicoeconomic interests, and in such a way that he recognizes his unity with other and the general nature of class opposition.[7]

Class consciousness, so construed, can be observed when an individual responds to appropriate politicoeconomic situations, stories, or statements by accepting the values of his own class and rejecting the values of an antagonistic class,[8] particularly if he claims initially

(even in reply to a forced-choice question) that he owes his allegiance to his occupational fellows. In the research reported in this paper, an approach of this sort was used.

In addition to the related problems of the meaning and measurement of class consciousness, there is the question of whether "class-conscious" individuals in a given in-group are motivated similarly in responding to political events. More specifically, *does class consciousness lead to political cohesiveness at the ballot box, not only in party preference but also in the motivational basis for that preference?* This is the question to which this paper is addressed.

The importance of this question derives from a well-known theory of political behavior. If common action can serve as a mechanism of social change when it challenges the social system or as a mechanism of social rigidity when it defends the system, we ought to know whether there is a firm relationship between common action and class consciousness. In the event that an accumulation of empirical evidence indicates that such consciousness does not lead inevitably to cohesiveness in political behavior, we should re-examine the theoretical problem of the dynamic elements in mass society.

PROCEDURE

This paper is part of a larger study of political behavior and motivation in

---

[5] For a demonstration of the inadequacies of forced-choice questions on class identification, see Neal Gross, "Social Class Identification in the Urban Community," *American Sociological Review*, 18 (August 1953), 398–404.

[6] On this point, see Llewellyn Gross, "The Use of Class Concepts in Sociological Research," *American Journal of Sociology*, 54 (January 1949), 409–21; and H. J. Eysenck, "Social Attitude and Social Class," *The British Journal of Sociology*, 1 (March 1950), 56–66.

[7] Along this line, we would suggest that any "loss" of awareness can affect the dynamics of class relations but not the existence of objective classes.

[8] For an excellent example of a study which utilized stories to detect attitudes toward corporate property, see Alfred W. Jones, *Life, Liberty and Property* (Philadelphia: J. B. Lippincott Co., 1941). Jones was not concerned explicitly with class consciousness, but he measured an aspect of it by asking respondents in Akron whether they approved or disapproved of the action portrayed in a series of nonfictional stories

which had one feature in common, namely "that each of them describes a struggle or antagonism in which one of the sides is working to protect the interests of corporate property. . . ." (p. 21).

Philadelphia.[9] To collect the necessary data, 400 white males of Protestant (201) or Catholic (199) background, selected in a disproportionately stratified sample from fourteen precincts throughout the city, were interviewed in their homes during the winter of 1952—1953.[10] Of the 400, 388 were

classified as follows: forty-three big businessmen, sixty-three professionals, sixty-five small businessmen, sixty-one salesmen and clerical workers, seventy-four skilled craftsmen, and eighty-two semiskilled and service workers.[11] Of the 156 workers in the latter two groups, ninety-three were union members in various AFL, CIO, or independent locals; sixty-two were nonunionists; and one could not be classified. With the exception of the big business stratum, in which Catholics were somewhat underrepresented, there was at least a 60–40 distribution of Protestants and Catholics, or Catholics and Protestants, in all strata and in the union and nonunion divisions. More than 90 per cent of the informants in each group were native-born.

To sharpen the focus of this report, it was decided to concentrate on the responses of four groups: big and small businessmen, and union and nonunion workers. Moreover, the big business and union groups receive primary attention in the analysis.

"Class conscious" persons were designated on the basis of a combination of "allegiance" and "orientation." The question on allegiance, administered as part of the interview schedule, read: "To which one of these groups do you feel you owe your allegiance—business or labor?" Some respondents, of course, claimed allegiance to both groups, others to neither group, and a few stated that they did not know. Answers such as "both," "neither," and "don't know" are treated alike as middle-of-the-road responses.

In a separate questionnaire, respon-

---

[9] For a report on a different aspect of the study, see Oscar Glantz, "Unitary Political Behavior and Differential Political Motivation," *Western Political Quarterly*, 10 (December 1957), 833–46.

[10] As a stratified sample, a set of seven predominantly Protestant precincts, each somewhat different in occupational composition, and a set of seven predominantly Catholic precincts, similarly marked by occupational diversity, were selected on the basis of census tract data on occupational distributions in various neighborhoods, information in a directory of churches, and political maps. Each set was supposed to yield 210 males evenly distributed in seven occupational groups, but the final sample was inadequate in one cell (fourteen Catholics in the big business stratum) and far below a usable number in two cells (four unskilled Protestants and eight unskilled Catholics). The selection of precincts was followed by the preparation of lists of households so that fourteen subsamples could be drawn on a random basis. The sample proportions varied in size, with the smallest including every sixteenth household in one of the larger precincts and every twelfth household in another, and the largest including every sixth household in one of the smaller precincts. Every eighth unit was selected in seven precincts, and every tenth in four others. With some allowance for refusals and households without adult males, the total sample was designed to yield 420 interviews, preferably with the male head of the house. As it happened, the male head of the house was obtained in 387 of the 400 completed cases, the remaining interviews taking place with sons, one father-in-law, and one boarder. The refusal rate was lower than expected (10 per cent) but the number of households without adult males was larger than expected, particularly in two precincts selected as upper occupational areas, In addition, a small number of dwellings were lost because they were vacant, the family was on vacation, or were oc-

cupied by persons who were neither Protestant nor Catholic.

[11] For a detailed examination of the types of occupations included within each stratum, see Glantz, *op. cit.*, Table 1, p. 835.

dents were asked to agree or disagree with six partisan statements culled from the literature of two organizations of opposite politicoeconomic viewpoints— three from the National Association of Manufacturers and three from the Congress of Industrial Organizations,[12] which were unidentified in the questionnaire. Interviewees were not required to agree or disagree if they found it impossible to do so, but could indicate that they were undecided or uninformed on any given issue. The following statements were used:

> Industry-wide bargaining in the coal industry has fostered one of the strongest [union] monopolies . . . ever experienced.[13]
>
> Federal ownership and operation of electric power facilities . . . [is] the spearhead of our advance into socialism.[14]
>
> The demand for an excess profits tax is always based on emotional and political considerations. . . .[15]
>
> If your senators or your congressmen voted to end rent control, they voted to take money out of your pocket.[16]

A national health insurance program to provide . . . medical care for all the people [should be enacted by Congress].[17]

The Taft-Hartley law is a legalized attack on the basic human rights of wage earners. . . .[18]

To gain some notion of the extent to which informants in the various groups were consistently oriented in responding to the total set of items, a technique for organizing qualitative data on an essentially qualitative basis was used. Agreement with the NAM or disagreement with the CIO was scored as a *business-oriented* response, while disagreement with the NAM or agreement with the CIO was scored as a *labor-oriented* response. In the case of indecision (or "don't know"), the answer was scored as an *indeterminate* response. Interviewees who gave at least three more business-oriented than labor-oriented responses to the six statements were classified as consistently business-oriented; those who gave at least three more labor-oriented than business-oriented responses were listed as consistently labor-oriented. All other combinations or responses were categorized as inconsistent or indeterminate combinations.[19]

---

12 The statements were selected after a search through business and labor literature had produced an abundance of suitable items. The writer judged these items as to their relative importance, intelligibility, and incisiveness. Some attempt was also made to balance the quality of formulation on each side, but this task was complicated by the fact that the literature was originally addressed to different audiences.

13 National Association of Manufacturers, *The Economic Impact of an Industry-Wide Strike,* Economic Policy Division Series, No. 27 (July 1950), p. 1.

14 NAM, *Cut Non-Defense Spending Now,* Economic Policy Division Series, No. 40 (February 1951), p. 10.

15 NAM, *A Federal Tax Program for the Period of Defense and Partial Mobilization,* Economic Policy Division Series, No. 34 (October 1950), p. 15.

16 Congress of Industrial Organizations, Political Action Committee, *How To Cut Your Rent* (1952), p. 2.

17 Congress of Industrial Organizations, Political Action Committee, *The Platforms: Here's How They Stack Up* (1952), no pagination.

18 *Ibid.*

19 That the six statements belong together as a meaningful matrix was established by an item-analysis test in which the phi coefficient was utilized as a measure of the correlation between each item and total score for persons in top-score versus bottom-score criterion groups, each containing 27 per cent of the sample. To obtain the criterion groups, a total score for each person in the sample was developed by assigning 3, 2, and 1 points, respectively, for business-oriented, indeterminate, and labor-oriented responses to eight statements in the original set. Inasmuch as the phi coefficient

Table 1 shows that a majority of persons in three of the four occupational groups were marked off as inconsistently oriented persons. The business-oriented and labor-oriented categories could have been inflated considerably by including combinations in which there was a preponderance of two responses of a given type over its opposite, thereby deflating the large percentages of inconsistently oriented persons. But such a procedure clearly would invalidate the idea of consistency and might impair the meaning of the several categories.[20]

On the assumption that the six NAM and CIO statements were appropriate representations of business and labor values at the time of the interviews, consistent orientation was taken as a sign of contemporary "class consciousness' when it accompanied ingroup allegiance. In these terms, loyal business-oriented businessmen and loyal labor-oriented workers were designated as "class-conscious" persons.

There is no suggestion here, however, that such "consciousness" on the part of a wage worker carries with it a Marxian determination to smash the wage system. A latent tendency toward radicalism undoubtedly exists among some workers, but there is little or no historical evidence to indicate that it has recently been developing into a conscious ideology.[21] The more realistic view is that American workers, in the main, have not been receptive to political or economic radicalism. This situation may be, in part, the consequence of the nonmilitancy of labor leaders, but it probably also reflects the seductive combination of mass consumer goods, mass advertising, and mass credit.

Nonetheless, spokesmen for organized business and labor engage continuously in a conflict which reflects immediate politicoeconomic interests, illustrated by the literature of the NAM and CIO at the time of this study. The NAM and CIO did not represent all of business and labor in the winter of 1952–53, of course, but both were prominent in the on-going contest between the two factions.[22]

"CLASS CONSCIOUSNESS"

Distribution of business-labor orientations. The data show, in the first

---

measures the correlation of a fourfold distribution, dichotomous classifications are necessary. In the case at hand, the computations for each item were in terms of agree-disagree dichotomies in which indeterminate responses were divided proportionately. The coefficients for the six items retained in the politicoeconomic battery are located within a range from 0.54 to 0.79, while both of the excluded statements had coefficients of 0.37. For a discussion of this method, see, e.g., P. H. Kriedt and K. E. Clark, "'Item Analysis' Versus 'Scale Analysis'," *Journal of Applied Psychology,* 33 (April 1949), 114–21.

[20] For a study involving six items from which conservative and radical categories were established by including combinations in which there was a lead of *two* responses of a given type over its opposite, see Centers, *op. cit.,* pp. 40–41.

[21] On this point, an interesting methodologically derived fiction is presented by Centers, *op. cit.,* Table 8, p. 57. As a result of the criterion discussed in footnote 20, no less than 50 per cent of the semiskilled workers in a national sample were labeled "radicals" or "ultraradicals."

[22] On the leadership of the NAM, see, e.g., Robert A. Brady, *Business as a System of Power* (New York: Columbia University Press, 1943), p. 191 *et passim*; and Alfred S. Cleveland, "NAM: Spokesman for Industry?" *Harvard Business Review,* 26 (May 1948), 353–71. On the CIO, it should be noted that by 1952 the eventual AFL-CIO merger was already visible in various parts of the country, including Philadelphia. For example, Labor's League for Political

place, that there was less out-group antipathy on the part of union members in responding negatively to individual NAM statements than there was on the part of big businessmen in so responding to individual CIO statements.[23] In addition, unionists were more indecisive in responding to the total set of items. For example, approximately one-fourth of the union members expressed neither a positive or negative position on two prominent issues, the excess profits tax and the Taft-Hartley law. Thus the percentage of consistently labor-oriented unionists was substantially below the percentage of consistently business-oriented businessmen (Table 1). Whereas almost two-thirds of the big businessmen were definitely business-directed, less than half of the union members were labor-directed.[24] Notwithstanding union newspapers, pamphlets, meetings, and resolutions, it appears that unionism in Philadelphia had not been especially effective as an in-group educational agency.

At the same time, the influence of unionism (or other factors) was apparently sufficient to counteract the development of consistent pro-business attitudes. Although many union mem-

---

Education (AFL) and the Political Action Committee (CIO) cooperated extensively in the presidential campaign that year.

[23] On the other hand, it should be noted that there was as much in-group solidarity on the part of unionists in responding affirmatively to CIO statements as there was on the part of big businessmen in responding affirmatively to NAM statements.

[24] The writer has suggested elsewhere that some persons may have reduced the consistency of their total response by rejecting the emotionalism inherent in partisan statements with which they might have otherwise agreed. "An Appraisal of Protestant-Catholic Differences in Voting Behavior," *Public Opinion Quarterly*, 23 (Spring 1959), 73–82.

TABLE 1. DISTRIBUTION OF BUSINESS-LABOR ORIENTATIONS

	N	Business-oriented, Per Cent	Labor-oriented, Per Cent	Indeterminate, Per Cent
Big businessmen	(43)	63	2	35
Small businessmen	(65)	35	5	60
Nonunion workers	(62)	13	22	65
Union workers	(93)	4	43	53

bers revealed indeterminate or wavering attitudes toward the selected values of business and labor, only 4 per cent expressed attitudes which were definitely incongruous with their objective occupational class.

Allegiance and orientation. The immediate question here is the extent to which in-group allegiance is accompanied by in-group orientation. But the basic problem is to determine whether "class consciousness," defined as integrated allegiance and orientation, can be viewed as an intervening variable which leads to political cohesiveness.

Table 2 shows that business allegiance was accompanied by business orientation in about three-fourths (77 per cent) of twenty-two big business cases and in half of thirty-two small business cases, thereby indicating that 40 per cent of all big businessmen in the sample (17/43) and 25 per cent of all small businessmen (16/65) were "class conscious." The 40 per cent figure for big businessmen, however, may be an underassessment. The percentage of big business persons who were actually business-oriented (63 per cent) was higher

TABLE 2. BUSINESS-LABOR ORIEN-
TATIONS, BY ALLEGIANCE
GROUPS

	N	Business-oriented, Per Cent	Labor-oriented, Per Cent	In-determinate, Per Cent
Business allegiance*				
Big businessmen	(22)	77	0	23
Small businessmen	(32)	50	3	47
Middle-of-the-road				
Big businessmen	(19)	47	0	53
Small businessmen	(23)	26	4	70
Nonunion workers	(22)	18	23	59
Union workers	(29)	7	38	55
Labor Allegiance**				
Nonunion workers	(27)	7	30	63
Union workers	(52)	2	50	48

* Among workers who claimed allegiance to business, business orientation was limited to two of thirteen nonunionists and one of twelve unionists. There were ten indeterminates in the former group, and eight in the latter.

** Of two big businessmen who claimed allegiance to labor, one was labor-oriented, the other business-oriented. Labor orientation among ten small businessmen who claimed allegiance to labor was limited to one person, while eight were in the indeterminate category.

than the percentage of those who claimed allegiance to business (51 per cent). By disclaiming (perhaps self-consciously) singular allegiance to the group toward which they were clearly oriented, some big businessmen did not meet the requirements for "class consciousness" used in this study. Nonetheless, "class consciousness" was found most markedly in the big business unit.

For wage workers, labor allegiance was accompanied by labor orientation in 50 per cent of fifty-two union cases and 30 per cent of twenty-seven non-union cases(indicating that 28 per cent of all unionists (26/93) and 13 per cent of all nonunionists (8/62) were "class conscious." The 28 per cent figure for the union group is consistent with the findings of other recent studies, not of class consciousness as such, but of attitudes which seem to reflect a strong working-class predisposition. In a study of UAW members (auto workers), for example, 26 per cent were found to be "very strongly" pro-labor.[25] An investigation of IAM members (machinists) reports that 22 per cent agreed that the union "should tell members whom to vote for."[26] And, in a study of unionists in a large local of steelworkers, 25 per cent of the active members stated without qualification that slowdowns are justified.[27] If these figures are representative, they suggest that roughly 20 to 30 per cent of the rank-and-file are militants, the hard core of the union movement.[28]

[25] A. Kornhauser, H. L. Sheppard, and A. J. Mayer, *When Labor Votes* (New York: University Books, 1956), p. 117.

[26] Hjalmar Rosen and R. A. Rosen, *The Union Member Speaks* (Englewood Cliffs, N.J.: Prentice-Hall, Inc., 1955), p. 37.

[27] R. S. Hammett, J. Seidman, and J. London, "The Slowdown as a Union Tactic," *Journal of Political Economy*, 65 (April 1957), 131.

[28] However, note the view of Seymour M. Lipset and Reinhard Bendix that militancy varies considerably from one group of workers to another, depending on the type of work, their relative isolation in society, and other factors in their working

POLITICAL COHESIVENESS

Party preference. Additional questions in the interview schedule requested information on how the interviewee had voted in the Truman-Dewey election of 1948 and the Eisenhower-Stevenson election of 1952. A final question on the 1952 election was phrased as follows: "May I ask you why you voted for your candidate? *Your most important reason or reasons?"*

When big businessmen are divided between "class-conscious" individuals and others, the voting data show, for the former, a solid "class" vote in both elections, as well as very large majorities for the Republican candidates for other big businessmen. Thus: [29]

PERCENTAGE
REPUBLICAN:

	1948	1952
"*Class conscious*" big businessmen	(16) 100	(16) 100
Other big businessmen	(23) 78	(23) 87

When unionists are similarly divided, the data show that the "class-conscious" segment voted overwhelmingly for Truman in 1948 (91 per cent) and Stevenson in 1952 (86 per cent). Other unionists displayed less solidarity in voting, particularly in 1952, but the probable influence of unionism is still apparent in their 64 per cent vote for Stevenson. This is strongly suggested when the Democratic vote among nonunionists is examined. Thus: [29]

PERCENTAGE
DEMOCRATIC:

	1948	1952
"*Class-conscious*" union workers	(22) 91	(21) 86
Other union workers	(59) 75	(56) 64
All nonunion workers	(49) 59	(48) 35

Although the foregoing data indicate that "class consciousness" is associated with voting behavior, they do not establish a causal nexus. The latter requires independent evidence that "class consciousness" is related causally to political action. Such evidence would be available, for example, if "class-conscious" businessmen claimed that they voted Republican because they *believe* that "the Democrats pursue policies which are inimical to the prosperity of business," or if "class-conscious" unionists claimed that they voted Democratic because they *believe* that they were "backing a labor party." In these terms, if "class consciousness" does in fact lead to solidarity in voting, one should expect a greater concentration of such motives in "class-conscious" groups than among their occupational peers who voted the same way.

Motives. In answering the question about why they voted for a given candidate in 1952, Republican and Democratic voters made various positive and negative comments concerning parties, issues, and personalities. Most of these comments were classified under general captions designed to convey the major motivational tendencies, while a small number were regarded as miscellany. [30] These captions (except a few, considered to be unimportant) are listed in Table 3 for Republicans and Table 4 for Democrats.

---

environment. *Social Status and Social Structure: A Re-Examination of Data and Interpretations,* Reprint No. 35 (Berkeley, Calif.: Institute of Industrial Relations, University of California, 1952), pp. 243–44. This paper is an excellent analysis of theoretical and methodological problems in stratification research.

[29] *N*'s exclude nonvoters.

[30] For a detailed discussion of the procedure used to classify Republican motives, see Glantz, "Unitary Political Behavior ...," *op. cit.*, pp. 836–38.

TABLE 3. REASONS FOR VOTING
REPUBLICAN IN 1952*

	Big Businessmen	
	"Class-Conscious" (16), Per Cent	Others (20), Per Cent
Vs. policies and record of Democratic Party (including association of Democrats with -isms of the left)	56	20
Republican principles and policies	25	15
Always Republican	44	25
Vs. corruption in government	19	25
Time for a change	13	45
To end Korean war; improve international situation	13	15
Eisenhower as a personality (organizer, leader, honest)	6	10

* Does not include miscellaneous reasons. Percentages total more than 100 because some respondents gave more than one major reason.

The data for big businessmen who voted Republican are more difficult to interpret than the data for wage workers who voted Democratic. Note in Table 3 that larger percentages of "class-conscious" big businessmen, in comparison with other big businessmen, claimed that it was a matter of perennial Republicanism, that they were commited to Republican principles and policies, and that they viewed the Democratic Party in various unfavorable ways. These three reasons were offered by 88 per cent of the "class-conscious" segment and 45 per cent of the others. Thus, the two groups differed to some extent in their approach to Republicanism, but the factors creating the difference were not always explicitly class-related. References to perennial Republicanism, unless associated with Republican business principles, can have several meanings. References to Republican principles, unless specifically associated with business principles, can leave the issue in doubt. Similarly, negative references to the Democratic Party are difficult to evaluate in some cases.

This is not to say that all of the comments were difficult to interpret. Some comments, in fact, contained implicit class-related meanings. For example, one informant explained that he voted Republican "for the salvation of the country, to get us out of the clutches of the crazy Democratic economic pattern." Another put it this way: "I'm bitterly opposed to the New Deal. I think it is un-American." In the writer's opinion, in these cases, "class consciousness" did in fact lead to political solidarity, not only in political preference but in the motivational basis for it as well.

A similar conclusion for wage workers who voted Democratic is drawn with much less hesitancy. Note in Table 4 that approximately three-fourths of the "class-conscious" unionists, in comparison with one-third of the other wage workers, associated the Democratic Party or Stevenson with the interests of labor. To illustrate the explicitly class-related nature of their remarks a composite quotation is presented below. It contains key comments of the thirteen "class-conscious" unionists who are included in the 72 per cent

TABLE 4. REASONS FOR VOTING
DEMOCRATIC IN 1952*

	Wage Workers	
	"Class-Conscious" Unionists (18), Per Cent	Others** (53), Per Cent
Democratic Party and Stevenson associated with interests of labor	72	34
Vs. influence of Taft	11	15
Vs. policies and record of Republican Party (including association of Republicans with depression)	11	11
Democratic Party associated with prosperity	11	32
Vs. military man as president	6	30
Stevenson as a personality (experienced, bright, like F.D.R.)	22	23
Liberal principles of Democratic Party	6	4

* Excludes miscellaneous reasons. Percentages total more than 100 because some respondents gave more than one major reason.
** Includes other unionists and all nonunionists.

figure in Table 4. They voted Democratic for the following reason:

Labor. It comes down to labor. I was backing a labor party. Because the Democratic Party is more for the working class. I felt the Democrats was more or less in favor of the working class—they proved this in the past 20 years with favorable laws. I got more under them than I did under anyone else—I got collective bargaining. Things were all right for labor under the Democratic Party. Generally, I felt as though Stevenson had more sympathy for unions. Well, he was for the labor man. For his prolabor policy. To me, he seemed to be more for the working class of people. Because he's for the working party. He seemed to be in back of labor, which the Democrats have proven the years they've been in power.

DISCUSSION

A series of empirical observations have been presented based upon some in-group responses to partisan statements on politicoeconomic issues. Inasmuch as the statements must be regarded as mere fragments of business and labor "lines" at the time of the interviews, it is conceivable that a different set of items might have produced different results. In the current study, however, the leading observations can be summarized as follows:

(1) Unionists displayed less out-group antipathy than big businessmen in responding negatively to out-group statements.

(2) Consequently, the percentage of consistently labor-oriented persons in the ranks of organized labor (43 per cent) was substantially below the percentage of consistently business-oriented persons in the business elite (63 per cent).

(3) On the basis of integrated in-group allegiance and in-group orientation, 40 per cent of all big businessmen in the sample and 28 per cent of all union members were designated as "class-conscious" persons.

(4) "Class consciousness" was related *empirically* to political solidarity

in voting. "Class-conscious" big businessmen gave a 100 per cent vote to Dewey and Eisenhower in 1948 and 1952, respectively, while "class-conscious" unionists gave 91 per cent of their vote to Truman in 1948 and 86 per cent to Stevenson in 1952.

(5) Moreover, "class consciousness" was related *intrinsically* to solidarity in voting. Much more often than not, and more often than their occupational peers who voted the same way, "class-conscious" persons had class-related motives for voting as they did.

It is not necessary to belabor the point that interest-group propaganda, when effective, is one of the conditions which can create class consciousness. But it is important here to recall that the characteristics of such propaganda tend to vary from one historical situation to another. At the time of the current study, in a period of excellent business profits and full employment, in a period when social forces were more conducive to intergroup harmony than to intergroup conflict, the prevailing business and labor "lines" were characterized by immediate and limited politicoeconomic interests. The organizational literature of business and labor for the period under review shows that these interest groups were not engaged in an ideological conflict of durable consequences for long-range class dynamics. Thus, the research procedure was designed to discover the presence or absence of immediate and limited "class consciousness."

Within this limited historical context, the findings suggest that the big businessmen were much more alert than the unionists to the advantages of a common politicoeconomic front. This disparity was primarily a function of differential out-group hostility. Readiness to stand in opposition may be typical of dominant groups in periods of relative quiescence.

On the other hand, "class-conscious" persons in both groups seemed to be equally alert to the advantages of common political action. To be sure, "the numerical strength of the business and industrial community...is such that complete group solidarity at the polls is of little significance."[31] But solidarity obviously would augment the power of the elite to manipulate the political situation. It would provide, for example, additional opportunities to "sell" their program to the general community. In contrast, if working-class consciousness were highly developed, the numerical strength of that class could have direct influence on the political situation.

One final remark concerns a problem which was not treated in this study but should be examined in the future. Why were some unionists "class conscious," while others were not? An approach to this problem designed to measure diverse aspects of the individual's class-related experiences might turn up an index of some predictive value.

---

[31] Cleveland, *op. cit.*, p. 354.

John Leggett's continuing research on working-class consciousness is in the foreground of a renewal of interest in this subject.[1] His study "Economic In-

---

[1] In large measure the renewed interest in class consciousness in the lower ranges of the population reflects the return of attention to the lower class following the "rediscovery" of poverty. In addition, the rising incidence of Negro unrest, as represented in the Black Power movement, has played a supporting role. See, for example, John C. Leggett, *Class, Race and Labor* (Fair Lawn, N.J.: Oxford University Press Inc., 1968); Harold Wilensky, "Class,

security and Working-Class Consciousness" is reproduced below. Utilizing a revised Marxist framework, he presents data which challenge the commonly held assumption of a low level of working-class consciousness.[2] In addition, Leggett's research bears upon the complex issue of the relationship between racial consciousness and class consciousness.[3]

Class Consciousness and American Workers," *Institute of Industrial Relations*, Reprint No. 283 (Berkeley, Calif.: University of California, 1966); Lewis Lipsitz, "Working-Class Authoritarianism: A Re-Evaluation," *American Sociological Review*, 30 (February 1965), 103–9; Robert Blauner, *Alienation and Freedom* (Chicago: University of Chicago Press, 1964). Data and observations on working-class consciousness can also be found in Arthur B. Shostak and William Gomberg, eds., *Blue-Collar World* (Englewood Cliffs, N.J.: Prentice-Hall, Inc., 1964).

[2] The following authors are among those who hold that class consciousness in the working class either is a misnomer (that is, a misinterpretation of some other phenomenon—e.g., "job consciousness") or is minimally present: Daniel Bell, *The End of Ideology* (Glencoe, Ill.: The Free Press, 1960); Seymour Lipset, *Political Man* (Garden City, N.Y.: Doubleday & Company, Inc., 1960); Arnold M. Rose, *Sociology* (New York: Alfred A. Knopf, Inc., 1965), pp. 330–39; Robert L. Faris, "The Middle Class from a Sociological Viewpoint," *Social Forces*, 39 (October 1960), 1–5; Robert A. Nisbet, "The Decline and Fall of Social Class," *Pacific Sociological Review*, 2 (Spring 1959), 11–17.

In general, advocates of the continuum theory of stratification support the view of limited class consciousness in the working class.

[3] He gives further findings and views on this problem of class-racial consciousness in his "Working-Class Consciousness, Race, and Political Choice," *American Journal of Sociology*, 69 (September 1963), pp. 171–84; See also, S. M. Miller, "Poverty, Race, and Politics," in Horowitz, *op. cit.*, pp. 290–312; E. U. Essien-Udom, *Black Nationalism* (Chicago: University of Chicago Press, 1962), pp. 326–40; Harold R. Isaacs, *The New World of Negro Americans* (New York: The Viking Press, 1963).

ECONOMIC INSECURITY AND
WORKING-CLASS CONSCIOUSNESS*†

John C. Leggett

University of Connecticut

Early industrial society is characterized by endemic economic insecurity, considerable struggle between classes, and many indications of working-class consciousness. As industrial capitalism matures, the incidence of serious eco-

* From John C. Leggett, "Economic Insecurity and Working-Class Consciousness," *American Sociological Review*, 29 (April 1964), 226–34. Reprinted by permission of the American Sociological Association.

† I am indebted to the Social Science Research Council, the Horace H. Rackham School of Graduate Studies, the Department of Sociology of the University of Michigan, and the Department of Political Science of Wayne State University for their assistance. In addition, I would like to thank Gerhard Lenski, Morris Janowitz, Daniel Katz, Werner Landecker, and Robert Mowitz for

nomic crisis lessens, the class struggle abates, and class consciousness wanes.[1] Despite these long-term changes, extensive economic insecurity may still exist in the advanced industrial community. Indeed, whether it persists and is related to class militance is problematic.

If one observes the modern industrial town, one cannot help but note that many advances in technology and economic organization have helped to establish a high standard of living for workers as a whole but at the same time have created occupational havoc for large sections of the working class. The new prosperity is accompanied by structural alterations and deficiencies that threaten the sources of sustenance for many workmen who had hitherto benefited by technological progress. Automation, plant closures, occupational obsolescence, as well as cyclical recessions continue to generate short- and long-term unemployment, especially among workmen in primary and secondary industries.[2]

Numerous writers have observed both early and late industrial societies and commented on the relation between tenuous economic position and working-class consciousness. Marx argued that successive economic crises would heighten the *élan* of the working class,[3] while Engels in his later years took a modified stance: A mature industrial capitalism even though subject to periodic dips in economic activity would nevertheless provide an overall prosperity that would dull the militance of workmen.[4] Indeed, Engels was perhaps less "orthodox" on this matter than Michels, who wrote some time after the death of Engels that condemnation to life-long membership in the working class constituted one of the greatest sources of anticapitalism in the modern world, precisely because of the precarious nature of capitalist economy.[5] Michels' position is consistent with conclusions drawn by many contemporary observers. Lipset, Lazarsfeld, Barton, and Linz, for example, have effectively argued that occupational groups (such as miners, lumbermen, fishermen, one-crop farmers) subject to great fluctuations of income have traditionally supported leftist parties all over the world.[6]

---

their provocative criticisms and suggestions.

[1] A number of analysts have commented on the demise of the class struggle. Eduard Bernstein described the transformation of the German socialist movement from revolutionary organization to bureaucratic mass party and related it to the upward trend of productivity and standard of living under capitalism. See Peter Gay's excellent treatment of his analysis, *The Dilemma of Democratic Socialism, Eduard Bernstein's Challenge to Marx* (New York: Collier Books, 1962), pp. 121–51, 184–98.

[2] Automation and other forces mentioned have had a deleterious impact on many workmen in Detroit and elsewhere in Michigan. See William Haber, Eugene C. McKean, and Harold C. Taylor, *The Michigan Economy, Its Potentials and Its Problems* (Kalamazoo, Mich.: The W. E. Upjohn Institute for Employment Research, 1959). Also, see Harold S. Sheppard, Louis A. Ferman, and Seymour Faber, *Too Old to Work—Too Young to Retire, A Case*

Study of Permanent Plant Shutdown (Washington, D.C.: Special Committee on Unemployment Problems, United States Senate, 1960).

[3] Karl Marx, "Communist Manifesto," in *Selected Writings in Sociology and Social Philosophy*, eds. T. B. Bottomore and Maximilien Rubel (London: Watts, 1956), pp. 184–85.

[4] Engels' comments on this subject can be found in "Letter to Karl Kautsky," November 8, 1884, in Karl Marx and Friedrich Engels, *Correspondence, 1846–1895* (New York: International Publishers, 1946), p. 422.

[5] Robert Michels, *First Lectures in Political Sociology* (Minneapolis: University of Minnesota Press, 1949), pp. 80–82.

[6] Seymour M. Lipset, Paul F. Lazarsfeld,

On the other hand, not a few social scientists prefer to characterize the structural dislocations of advanced industrial society as minor and without consequence. From this optimistic point of view, economic insecurity, while present in an "affluent society," diminishes in importance through time, and hence the related question of incidence of working-class consciousness should provide lean pickings for a "young man with questionnaire." What the optimists fail to note, however, are the economic forces that promise, first, to eliminate many of the material gains of workmen and, second, to generate discontent and consciousness within at least some sections of labor.[7] Few economists or sociologists have turned to these problems even when structural conditions have failed to correspond to the popular image of the affluent community.

In spite of the paucity of recent research on these matters, the argument presented and past research cited strongly suggest that *the advanced industrial community generates economic insecurity which in turn is directly related to working-class consciousness.* Indeed, if one assumes the obvious, namely, that unemployed workers are structurally less secure in the economic realm than the employed, then one can hypothesize that the former should be more class conscious than the latter. I shall consider the applicability of this

hypothesis to a modern community after describing the population studied and the measure of working-class consciousness devised.

PROCEDURE

To gauge the impact of economic insecurity on class consciousness, 375 male blue-collar residents of the city of Detroit were interviewed during the spring and early summer of 1960, a period of moderate prosperity for the community as a whole. The 1957—58 recession had ended and the percentage of unemployed had dropped from 20 per cent of the total labor force to slightly less than one-third of that figure. But even though unemployment had declined considerably, many men laid off during the 1957—58 recession had failed to find work after the automobile industry recovered. The sample, then, was drawn from a population of workmen many of whom had faced considerable economic distress during the late 1950s. It should be noted that unemployment during this period struck hardest at Negro workers, one of the principal groups included in this study.

Ethnically, the workers studied were heterogeneous, and most of them belonged to industrial unions. Those interviewed were selected from seven districts of high ethnic concentration, i.e., locales known to be quite homogeneous in terms of ethnic social organization. A list random-sample procedure was used to select male respondents from these districts, three of which were predominantly Negro, three Polish, and one northwest European. Only Negroes, Poles, Ukrainians, Germans, and Britons (non-Southern-born) of blue-collar background were interviewed.[8] Of these workers three-quarters belonged to a labor union. In-

Allen M. Barton, and Juan Linz, "The Psychology of Voting: An Analysis of Political Behavior," in *The Handbook of Social Psychology*, Vol. 2, ed. Gardner Lindzey (Reading, Mass.: Addison-Wesley Publishing Co., Inc., 1954), pp. 1124–75.

7 Several exploratory studies have dealt with the sources and consequences of deprivation in Detroit. See Harold Sheppard *et al., op. cit.*; also see David S. Street and John C. Leggett, "Economic Deprivation and Extremism: A Study of Unemployed Negroes," *American Journal of Sociology*, 67 (July 1961), 53–57.

8 For a more detailed statement on sam-

cluded were members of the CIO, AFL, Teamsters, and several other unions, but over 80 per cent of the union members belonged to the CIO, a union with a relatively militant history in Detroit politics.[9]

DEGREE OF WORKING-CLASS CONSCIOUSNESS

Working-class consciousness was defined as a cumulative series of mental states, running from class verbalization through skepticism and militance to egalitarianism. *Class verbalization* denotes the tendency of working-class individuals to discuss topics in class terms. They need not do so consistently; in fact, only an occasional use of class symbols designates some facility in their usage. *Skepticism* describes the belief that wealth is allocated within the community so as to benefit primarily the middle class. *Militance* refers to a predisposition to engage aggressively in a course of action, the purpose of which is to advance the interests of one's class.[10] *Egalitarianism* denotes favoring a distribution of wealth so that every individual would have (1) the same amount once the wealth was reallocated

and (2) the material basis thereby for the full development of his natural talents.[11]

To measure *class verbalization,* a battery of eight unstructured questions was used. Each question deliberately made no reference to class, so as not to prejudice the answers of the respondent. He was asked whom he had voted for in the last election and why, who was his favorite president and why, and so forth. If the respondent used class terms in just one of these instances, his comment constituted class verbalization. *Skepticism* was operationally defined by asking: "When business booms in Detroit, who gets the profits?" If the respondent used categories such as "rich people," "upper class," "big business," and similar class references, he was treated as class conscious in this regard. *Militance* was defined by asking the respondent whether he would join a group of workers who were about to take action against a landlord in a series of activities, including picketing. If he would take part in the latter, the study classified him as militant. *Egalitarianism*, the final item considered, was defined as agreement with the no-

---

ple design, see John C. Leggett, *Working-Class Consciousness in an Industrial Community* (unpublished Ph.D. dissertation, University of Michigan, 1962), pp. 54–72.

9 Of these CIO members, 83 per cent belonged to the UAW.

10 My definition of militance resembles Marx's notion of a class acting for itself. Marx argued that in the long run the class struggle would generate not only a common sense of class identity but a high degree of class solidarity. Awareness of class position would be later supplemented by the determination to act as a class, one of the highest forms of consciousness: "Economic conditions had in the first place transformed the mass of the people into workers. The domination of capital created the common situation and common interest of this class. Thus, this mass is already *a class in relation to capital* but not yet a class for itself. In

the struggle, of which we have only indicated a few phases, the *mass unites* and forms itself into a class *for itself*. The interests which it defends become class interests." (Emphasis my own.) See excerpts from Karl Marx, "The Poverty of Philosophy," in eds. Bottomore and Rubel, *op. cit.,* p. 200.

11 My conception of egalitarianism combines entrepreneurial and socialist ideas. The content of this conception is similar to Marx's position in that it does not specify commitment to full and perpetual equality. Some writers (such as Max Nomad, *Aspects of Revolt* [New York: Bookman Associates, 1959], pp. 19–20), have argued that Marx's famous pledge of "from each according to his ability, to each according to his needs," under conditions of communism, did not specify complete equality and stemmed from Marx's need to undercut the appeal of the anarchists.

DIAGRAM 1. IDEAL CLASSIFICATION OF RESPONDENTS, FOUR
ASPECTS OF CLASS CONSCIOUSNESS

Individuals Typed According to Class Perspective	Egalitarianism	Militance	Skepticism	Class Verbalization
Militant egalitarians	+*	+	+	+
Militant radicals	−**	+	+	+
Skeptics	−	−	+	+
Class verbalizers	−	−	−	+
Class indifferents	−	−	−	−

* "+" refers to class consciousness.
** "−" refers to non-class consciousness.

tion that the wealth of our country should be divided up equally so that people would have an equal chance to get ahead.

The various aspects of class consciousness were linked to one another so as to measure the degree to which each worker had developed class consciousness. Ideally, workers thereby fell into one of the following five categories: militant egalitarians, militant radicals, skeptics, class verbalizers, and class indifferents. Diagram 1 indicates how workmen were typed.

Approximately three-quarters of the respondents held opinions corresponding either exactly or consistently with this model; the others expressed a point of view that was inconsistent with this configuration. Although they were clearly "error types," they were nevertheless categorized like the rest on the basis of a point system suggested by Guttman. Of the 375 workers thereby classified, thirty-eight qualified as militant egalitarians, eighty-seven as militant radicals, 114 as skeptics, ninety-eight as class verbalizers, and thirty-eight as class indifferents.[12]

This treatment of consciousness, although original, rests on several formulations found in sociological literature. Not only the ideas of Marx[13] and Guttman,[14] but those of Manis and Meltzer,[15] as well as Alfred Jones,[16] were used to define the various aspects of consciousness.

FINDINGS

It is not surprising that the unemployed are more class conscious than those with work. As Table 1 indicates, 46 per cent of the unemployed as opposed to 31 per cent of the employed are either militant egalitarians or militant radicals.[17] (The findings in Table

---

12 The Menzel coefficient of reproducibility for this measure of class consciousness was 0.77. For a detailed statement of construction of these ideal types and empirical categories, see Leggett, *op. cit.*, pp. 73–135.

13 Some of Marx's most provocative notions on class consciousness appear in his *German Ideology* (New York: International Publishers), 1960.

14 Guttman's presentation of a useful measurement technique can be found in Samuel Stouffer *et al.*, *Studies in Social Psychology in World War II*, Vol. 4 (Princeton, N.J.: Princeton University Press, 1950), pp.3–90, 172–212.

15 Jerome G. Manis and Bernard N. Meltzer, "Attitudes of Textile Workers to Class Structure," *American Journal of Sociology*, 60 (July 1954), 30–55.

16 *Life, Liberty, and Property* (Philadelphia: J. B. Lippincott Co., 1941), pp. 250–80.

17 Economic insecurity might also be

TABLE 1. EMPLOYMENT STATUS AND CLASS CONSCIOUSNESS*,
IN PERCENTAGES

Employment Status	Militant Egalitarians	Militant Radicals	Skeptics	Class Verbalizers	Class Indifferents	Total
Employed	9	22	31	27	11	100 (274)
Unemployed	16	30	30	16	8	100 (51)

* This table does not include the forty-nine retired workers.

1 are statistically significant at the <0.05 level.)

If the assumption that lack of sound sustenance base engenders consciousness is correct, then not only marginal individuals but racial subcommunities similarly situated should express a high degree of militance. In our society, Negroes on the whole hold more tenuous occupational positions than whites. Working-class Negroes generally stand at the edge of the labor force, particularly in northern industrial communities, where automation and plant closures have eliminated hundreds of thousands of jobs traditionally held by Negroes in the steel, auto, rubber, meat-packing, and related industries. Given these developments, Negro workmen should be more class conscious

TABLE 2. RACIAL GROUP MEMBERSHIP AND CLASS CONSCIOUSNESS,
IN PERCENTAGES

Racial Group	Militant Egalitarians	Militant Radicals	Skeptics	Class Verbalizers	Class Indifferents	Total
Negroes	23	36	28	12	1	100 (120)
Whites	5	17	31	33	14	100 (255)

measured in terms of occupational skill, assuming that blue-collar skill level is inversely related to tenuous quality of economic position. Occupational skill proves to be related as expected to working-class consciousness. Eighteen per cent ($N = 110$) of the skilled, 39 per cent ($N = 251$) of the semiskilled, and 46 per cent ($N = 13$) of the unskilled workers studied were classified as militant. If one takes race into account, this relationship holds for both skilled and semiskilled, but the lack of sufficient cases does not allow the same comparison for the unskilled.

Paucity of respondents also precludes detailed analysis of the impact of length of unemployment. A crude distinction between short (0–6 months), medium (6–13 months), and long-term unemployment (more than 1 year) fails to uncover any notable differences. Marie Lazarsfeld Jahoda and Hans Zeisel's classical study of Marienthal found that long-term and very widespread unemployment contributed to collective lethargy, political disengagement, and, presumably, a diminution of working-class militance. Conditions comparable to the economic malaise of Marienthal during the height of the Great Depression, however, did not exist in Detroit when my study was conducted. See Marie Lazarsfeld Jahoda and Hans Zeisel, *Die Arbeitslosen Von Marienthal* (Leipzig: Verlag Von S. Hirzel, 1933).

than whites, and this study indicates that they are (see Table 2).[18]

Further, let us assume that insecure economic status and affiliation with an economically marginal racial group constitute complementary forces which togethers accentuate the formation of working-class consciousness. If this formulation is correct, then unemployed Negro workers should be more class conscious than their employed counterparts. Table 3, however, fails to support this hypothesis. If anything, the Negro unemployed are slightly *less* class conscious than the employed, while the whites are distributed as expected. Clearly, unemployment, considered by itself, is not a source of class consciousness among Negroes. One question raised by this interesting finding is ob-

vious: Is employment status unrelated to the militance of *all* Negro workers?

The question cannot be adequately answered unless one considers the additional impact of union membership for Negroes living in many northern cities are heavily concentrated in industrial unions, themselves a traditional source of class consciouness.[19] Among the Negroes in our sample, the combination of unemployment and union membership clearly heightens class consciousness, as Table 4 shows. *Eighty* per cent of the unionized unemployed, as opposed to 27 per cent of the nonunion workmen found in this cheerless position, are class militants.[20] Admittedly, the number of cases in each category is small, and hence any conclusions based upon them are at best tentative. Never-

TABLE 3.   RACIAL GROUP MEMBERSHIP, EMPLOYMENT STATUS, AND CLASS CONSCIOUSNESS, IN PERCENTAGES

Racial Group	Employment Status	Militant Egalitarians	Militant Radicals	Skeptics	Class Verbalizers	Class Indifferents	Total
Negroes	Employed	23	34	30	10	3	100 (86)
	Unemployed	20	36	28	16	0	100 (25)
Whites	Employed	3	17	30	35	15	100 (188)
	Unemployed	12	20	32	16	20	100 (25)

[18] A discussion of the existential bases of class consciousness among Negroes can be found in Leggett, *op. cit.*, pp. 162–71. Other observers have found a relatively high degree of militance among Negro workmen who are heavily concentrated in industrial unions. See Theodore V. Purcell, *The Worker Speaks His Mind on Company and Union* (Cambridge, Mass.: Harvard University Press, 1953), pp. 79–101, 111–17, 137–42, 146, 148, 152–57, 160–62, 196.

[19] See Jones, *op. cit.*; Leggett, *op. cit.*, pp. 175–212; Robert F. Brooks, *When Labor Organizes* (New Haven, Conn.: Yale

University Press, 1942).

[20] Not only union membership but size and condition of workplace undoubtedly contributed to these differences. Unionized workmen in Detroit are disproportionately concentrated in large plants, where relations tend to be impersonal and in many other ways conducive to the development of class consciousness. Unfortunately, lack of sufficient cases prevents simultaneous evaluation of the importance of union membership, employment status, and size of plant among Negro workers. For a general discussion of impact of size of workplace, see

TABLE 4. UNION MEMBERSHIP, EMPLOYMENT STATUS, AND CLASS
CONSCIOUSNESS (NEGROES ONLY), IN PERCENTAGES

Union Membership	Employment Status	Militant Egalitarians	Militant Radicals	Skeptics	Class Verbalizers	Class Indifferents	Total
Union Member	Employed	26	29	30	12	3	100 (69)
	Unemployed	27	53	13	7	0	100 (15)
Nonmember	Employed	12	53	29	6	0	100 (17)
	Unemployed	9	18	46	27	0	100 (11)

theless, one cannot overlook the impact of the union.

INTERPRETATION

At least two important problems emerge from consideration of these findings: (1) Why does economic insecurity contribute to class consciousness, and (2) why does union membership help to engender militance among unemployed Negro workers?[21]

Security and consciousness. Several interrelated conditions common to many industrial towns facilitate the formation of working class consciousness: (1) denial of full employment opportunity to many workmen, (2) spatial concentration of large numbers of these and other workers, and (3) their informal and formal channels of communication.[22] The modern industrial community creates medium and high levels of working-class unemployment, as many firms continue to discharge and lay off many workmen when markets contract, plants mechanize, factories relocate, and businesses fail. At the same time, large numbers of both employed and unemployed workmen are concentrated in relatively small, culturally homogeneous residential districts.[23] There, neighborhood organizations often deal with class and race questions, such as unemployment, edu-

Seymour M. Lipset, *Political Man* (Garden City, N.Y.: Doubleday & Company, Inc., 1960), pp. 230–32.

[21] Two other relevant questions are: (1) How does the widespread unemployment within the Negro community help to increase the militance of all Negro unionists? (2) Why is there little difference between unionized and nonunionized Negroes who are employed? The latter question is partially explained by the disproportionately large concentration of "uprooted" workers in the nonunion, employed category. Uprooted workers are generally quite class conscious. See John C. Leggett, "Uprootedness and Working-Class Consciousness," *American Journal of Sociology*, 68 (May 1963), 682–92.

[22] These ideas have many sponsors. Marx was probably one of the first to recognize their importance. See Karl Marx, "The Poverty of Philosophy," in eds. Bottomore and Rubel, *op. cit.*, pp. 186–88. Of course, it would be foolish to discount the many forces working against the development of class consciousness in the modern community. For an excellent discussion of several of the more important considerations, see Morris Rosenberg, "Perceptual Obstacles to Class Consciousness," *Social Forces*, 32 (October 1953), 22–27.

[23] Racial and ethnic ghettoes still exist in many northern industrial towns, certainly in the one studied. See *ibid.*, pp. 54–72.

cational facilities, and similar matters.[24] In many instances, however, discussions among workers who later become unemployed may occur within racially mixed work groups and unions.[25] Under

these circumstances, racial heterogeneity and associated interracial hostility no doubt curtail, but certainly fail to eliminate, activities that generate working-class consciousness.[26]

The union, Negro unemployment, and class consciousness. To discuss the importance of labor-union membership for unemployed Negroes is to speculate on the impact of industrial unions since almost all unemployed Negro unionists belong to these organizations. Industrial unions have often perceived unemployment as a problem that workmen must continually and collectively face with little or no employer support. Time and again they have emphasized employer opposition to political legislation and union contracts that would increase full-employment opportunity not only for workers in general but for

---

[24] For a discussion of block-club organization and activities in Detroit, see Melvin Ravitz, "The Sociology of the Block Club" (unpublished paper, Department of Sociology, Wayne State University). Also pertinent is George Henderson's "The Block Club Movement Within the Detroit Tenth Police Precinct" (unpublished paper, Community Services Department, Detroit Urban League). My own participant observation in Detroit block clubs during 1961–62 indicated that they pursue a wide variety of functions. Under certain conditions they also contribute to a collectivistic, militant point of view. See Street and Leggett, *op. cit.*, pp. 56–57.

[25] Pertinent are the general remarks of Arthur Kornhauser and his colleagues on the official policy of the UAW. This policy reflects, to some degree, grass-roots sentiment within this industrial union.

> The Union (UAW) has initiated and vigorously supported measures which, according to its view, will insure stable economic growth and full employment; it has steadily worked for extensions of social security and unemployment compensation (along with its drive for pension plans and guaranteed annual wages from companies) and improvements of governmental provisions for health, education, and welfare....

Arthur Kornhauser, Albert J. Mayer, and Harold L. Sheppard, *When Labor Votes* (New York: University Books, 1956), pp. 16–17. James Stern, Staff Consultant of the UAW–CIO Automation Committee, has commented on the consequences of automation for blue-collar employment opportunity: "To the extent that we have not expanded total output commensurate with the productivity gains of automation, automation will heighten the insecurity of all workers and other disadvantaged groups." "Possible Effects of Automation on Older Workers," an address given at the 8th Annual Conference on the Aging, the University of Michigan, Ann Arbor, Michigan, June 28, 1955.

My comments on class issues as salient for the unions should not be misconstrued. It would be foolish to portray the unions as working to support the "class struggle," but they often do use class appeals, especially during contract negotiations and elections to state and national office.

[26] Dissension among workers based on nationality or racial differences is not peculiar to the American scene. Otto Bauer, one of the first to deal with this question, pointed out that German workers in Czechoslovakia held greater prestige than Czechs. Mutual dislike based on this prestige difference was partially responsible for acts that simply widened the ethnic breach. For example, Czech workers often acted as strikebreakers when German workers went out on strike. As a result of these incidents, workmen who belonged to antagonistic nationality groups could not develop a strong sense of working-class solidarity. See Otto Bauer, *Die Nationalitätenfrage und die Sozialdemokratie* (Vienna: Brand, 1907), pp. 187–234. Earlier, Engels noted that nationality differences in the United States impeded the formation of a genuine American labor movement. See his "Why There Is No Socialist Party in America," in *Basic Writings on Politics and Philosophy*, ed. Lewis S. Feuer (Garden City, N.Y.: Doubleday & Company, Inc., 1959), p. 458.

Negro workers in particular.[27] Labor organizations taking this position can claim a large audience among working-class Negroes for, since the early 1940s, the overwhelming majority of Detroit Negro unionists have belonged to, and provided considerable leadership within, industrial unions.[28] On the

---

[27] Full-employment opportunity is obviously only partially a function of employer policy. Equal educational opportunity is also important, and Detroit working-class groups, such as Negroes, have generally been denied facilities of the sort found in middle-class neighborhoods. See Patricia Cayo Sexton, *Education and Income* (New York: The Viking Press, 1961), pp. 3–136.

[28] James Q. Wilson has provided us with an excellent but brief analysis of Negro participation in the Detroit CIO during the late 1950s. See *Negro Politics* (Glencoe, Ill.: The Free Press, 1960), pp. 21–48.

In explaining the militance of Detroit Negro union members, one must also take into account the past (and to a far less degree, the present) influence of the Communist Party, even though a number of writers have dismissed it as having no significant influence among Negroes. (For example, see Wilson Record, *The Negro and the Communist Party* [Chapel Hill, N.C.: University of North Carolina Press, 1951].) During the formative stages of the CIO, the Communists were particularly powerful in large auto locals containing a disproportionate number of Negroes. The best known example was, of course, UAW Local 600. During the 1950s, however, Party popularity and influence in such locals waned considerably. Today, the Party has little influence.

A relatively new organization, the all-Negro Trade Union Leadership Council (TULC), constitutes a "black caucus" of approximately 9,000 Negroes, functions largely within the UAW, enjoys considerable member participation, and undoubtedly contributes to the class and racial consciousness of Negro workmen throughout Detroit. The TULC stresses working-class solidarity among Negroes and between races as partial means to solving class-racial problems such as unemployment. Politically, the TULC works with the block clubs and other organizations. See interview with Robert Battle,

other hand, these particular working-class associations have little contact with unemployed *nonunion* Negroes. Consequently, the latter are less likely to develop and use a class frame of reference to appraise their circumstances.

Yet, certain policies pursued by *part* of organized labor have undoubtedly detracted from its overall impact. Of these, racial discrimination is perhaps one of the most important. As is well known, most craft unions have systematically discriminated against Negroes, especially on the question of admittance, and the craft unions in the community studied have adhered to this tradition. To the extent that some Negro workers have mistakenly generalized the policies of craft unions so as to ascribe their racism to *all* labor groups, class standards and recommendations made by both craft and industrial unions have perhaps less impact than might otherwise be the case. In short, the policies of racial discrimination followed by these craft organizations through the years may well have decreased the class consciousness of many Negro workmen, including some who belong to industrial unions.[29]

An additional consideration. Even if this explanation appears feasible, one might still question the data for, after all, none of the items used to measure class consciousness refers to class identification, perhaps the most popular measure of class consciousness. This is

---

III and Horace Scheffield, "Trade Union Leadership Council: Experiment in Community Action," *New University Thought*, 3 (September–October 1963), 34–41.

[29] Negro unionists who belonged to the CIO proved to be more class conscious than their AFL counterparts. The small number of AFL members precluded systematic analysis of this category. See Leggett, *Working-Class Consciousness in an Industrial Community, op. cit.*, pp. 197–98.

TABLE 5. DEGREE OF CLASS CONSCIOUSNESS, EMPLOYMENT STATUS,
AND RACIAL GROUP MEMBERSHIP, IN PERCENTAGES

Variable Considered	Militant Egalitarians	Militant Radicals	Skeptics	Class Identifiers	Class Indifferents	Total
(1) Employment status						
Employed	8	19	31	31	11	100 (274)
Unemployed	12	33	29	22	4	100 (51)
(2) Racial group						
Negroes	18	37	32	10	3	100 (120)
Whites	4	15	32	36	13	100 (255)

a reasonable objection, but, when a closed-ended measure of awareness of class position is substituted for class verbalization and linked to other measures of consciousness,[30] the evidence (presented in Table 5) proves to be almost identical with informaton presented in Tables 1 and 2. Moreover, the joint impact of union membership and unemployment (among Negroes only) remains the same as in Table 4.[31]

---

[30] Five types based on a Guttman scale comparable to the one already presented in this paper have been devised. The "class identifiers" replace the "class verbalizers" shown in Tables 1–4, while the measure remains valid. The Menzel coefficient of reproducibility is 0.75. See Leggett, *Working-Class Consciousness in an Industrial Community, op. cit.*, pp. 111–13.

[31] An alternative measure of militance was also devised, based on workers' reactions to the following story situation: "Back in 1938 negotiations took place between the Utility Workers' Organizing Committee and the Consumer's Power Company of Michigan. The union wanted a renewal of its contract with the company and a year's guarantee against wage cuts. The company refused this and negotiations broke down at the same time as the contract expired. A strike followed, in which the workers took possession of the company's power plants in the Saginaw Valley area and expelled the company's superintendents and foremen.

CONCLUSIONS

Employment insecurity continues to be a source of working-class consciousness in the industrial community. The unemployed prove to be more militant than the employed, while a disproportionately large number of Negro workers take militant positions on class matters. On the other hand, Negroes without out work do not acquire unusually mili-

---

During the several days that this stay-in strike lasted, the property of the company was not damaged in any way. Nor was it a sitdown strike since the workers continued to operate the power plant, so that the interests of the consumers did not suffer. Although the company officials were strongly opposed to this strike action, they settled with the union after a time and it is safe to say that the union won better terms by this action than they would have won in any other way. How do you feel about the actions of the workers? I will read you five different choices. You tell me which one of the five is closest to your feeling."

Class-conscious responses
  1. Approve.
  2. Approve, but with qualifications.
Nonclass-conscious responses
  3. Cannot decide.
  4. Disapprove in general, but find points in favor of this action.
  5. Disapprove.

tant perspectives unless they belong to unions. Indeed, industrial labor organizations appear to have considerable impact upon unionized, unemployed Negroes, partly because of the behavior of these unions on class and race questions such as unemployment and partly because the overwhelming majority of Negro unionists belong to these non-craft unions.

Structural dislocations in the economy today, however, cannot be described as generating new waves of class consciousness of comparable magnitude to those in communities experiencing severe economic crises. More appropriate would be a prognosis of verbal aggressiveness, limited to a certain segment of the working class. Yet, the sources and presence of this militance should not be overlooked if only because of the potential political consequences. Indeed accelerated automation, occupational obsolescence, and cyclical recessions may foster both the accentuation of consciousness and a related political program designed to deal with problems largely unforeseen a decade ago.

Unfortunately, I was unable to interpret the answers to the story question so as to determine whether a favorable response meant (1) support of the stay-in when it took place 25 years ago, *plus* endorsement of any such action if taken today; (2) approval of this direct action when taken in 1938, *but* opposition to such behavior if it were to occur today; or (3) approbation of such action if taken today, *but* disapproval of this method when used 25 years ago. Intuitively, the latter alternative seems unpopular, but whether workmen favored the first or the second choices remains unclear. Nevertheless if one assumes that the question has *some* validity, the results might be of interest.

For example, the unemployed favored the "stay-in" more than the employed; a disproportionate number of Negroes did so as well; unemployed Negro unionists proved to be particularly militant in this regard. When the "stay-in" measure was substituted in place of the landlord question within the larger empirical indicator of class consciousness, predictable results remarkably similar to those already presented were obtained.

The story question was taken from Jones, *op. cit.*

We have noted that most studies of class consciousness concern its role as an independent variable influencing attitudinal or behavioral phenomena, particularly those pertaining to politicoeconomic ideology and action. Werner Landecker's paper is like Leggett's in viewing class consciousness as a dependent variable. He explores the sources and types of class consciousness and examines its relationship to an important aspect of class structure—class crystallization.

CLASS CRYSTALLIZATION AND CLASS CONSCIOUSNESS*†

Werner S. Landecker

University of Michigan

Given a social system whose population is simultaneously distributed in a number of specific rank systems, such as those of income, occupation, education, or racial and ethnic origin, *class crystallization*[1] exists as a property of the entire social system insofar as its several rank systems correlate with one another. The analysis of social systems reveals, however, that the class structure often lacks uniformity in its degree of crystallization. This variable aspect of social stratification can be envisaged by means of G. D. H. Cole's model of a nucleated class system. The core of such a system consists of persons whose respective class membership is clearly established and beyond question. Those for whom this is not true stand outside the core; their distance from it grows as their class affiliation becomes increasingly doubtful, until a point is reached where they can hardly be assigned to any class at all.[2] In terms of class crystallization, class systems of this kind have a core of highly crystallized class statuses; the core shades off into a less and less structured fringe, along a gradient of diminishing class crystallization.

Moreover, different locations on this gradient tend to give rise to different images which people hold of the class system and of their own relationship to it. The crystallized core of a class system provides support for a strong class consciousness, while more blurred impressions should result from weaknesses in class crystallization.[3] A major basis for this hypothesis is the truism that consciousness varies with experience.

* From Werner S. Landecker, "Class Crystallization and Class Consciousness," *American Sociological Review*, 28 (April 1963), 219–29. Reprinted by permission of the American Sociological Association.

† This study is part of a larger project conducted jointly with Gerhard E. Lenski within the framework of the Detroit Area Study at the University of Michigan. Grants from the Social Science Research Council and from the Faculty Research Fund of the University of Michigan are gratefully acknowledged. Helpful suggestions were made by Robert C. Angell, Gerhard E. Lenski, Robert H. Somers, and Guy E. Swanson.

1 Ronald Freedman *et al.*, *Principles of Sociology* (New York: Henry Holt, 1952), Chap. 7; and Werner S. Landecker, "Class Crystallization and Its Urban Pattern," *Social Research*, 27 (Autumn 1960), 308–20. For a correlative concept see Gerhard E. Lenski, "Status Crystallization: A Non-Vertical Dimension of Social Status," *American Sociological Review*, 19 (August 1954), 405–13; and Gerhard E. Lenski, "Social Participation and Status Crystallization," *American Sociological Review*, 21 (August 1956), 458–64.

2 *Studies in Class Structure* (London: Routledge & Kegan Paul, Ltd., 1955), p. 1.

3 This hypothesis is consistent with some French data, which show that self-identifications with a class become distorted by discrepancies among diverse status criteria pertaining to the same occupation. Natalie Rogoff, "Social Stratification in France and in the United States," *American Journal of Sociology*, 58 (January 1953), 347–57, especially p. 354. See also Bernard Barber, *Social Stratification* (New York: Harcourt, Brace, 1957), p. 215.

Thus, images of a given phenomenon will differ, depending on which of its facets is the most salient object of experience. For the incumbent of a highly crystallized class status, the structured core of the class system is likely to be the immediate and salient environment. Here he will find others whose similar status characteristics provide him with a basis for intimate contacts. By the same token, he has little or nothing in common with those whose respective statuses are strongly crystallized on either a higher or a lower status level than his. It may be assumed then, that the experience of clear-cut equalities with some and inequalities with others tends to evoke an acute consciousness of class.

On the other hand, a person who combines within himself a set of disparate statuses has a basis for interaction with others whose status constellations show a similar degree of internal disparity. His closest ties will probably lie in an area of the class system where crystallization is particularly weak, and his impressions regarding the whole system will be formed largely in that relatively unstructured area. Furthermore, because his own statuses are distributed over a wide range of the social scale, neither he nor others should readily see him as personally identified with any particular social level.

THE CRYSTALLIZATION GRADIENT IN THE COMMUNITY

The empirical setting of this investigation was the metropolitan area of Detroit. The data were gathered through interviews with 749 adult residents selected by means of an area sampling technique.[4] Some interviews did not meet the requirements of this study, either because the subject did not participate in the labor force or because information about his status characteristics was insufficient. After elimination of these interviews the sample consisted of 613 cases.

On the basis of interview data about the head of every household, cumulative percentage distributions of these 613 cases were computed separately by income, occupation, education, and ethnic-racial origin. Within each distribution, its respective categories were arranged in accordance with their amount of prestige. These distributions may be thought to represent four major rank systems.

To determine a person's location on the crystallization gradient of the community, it was necessary to gauge the degree to which his class status is crystallized. For this purpose he was assigned a status score in each rank system, indicative of his place in the cumulative percentage distribution of that rank system. The degree to which a person's four rank statuses are crystallized into a class status is expressed by an inverted measure of the amount of dispersion among them, which is designated as "crystallization score."[5]

A score of 100 would indicate a fully crystallized class status. The actual scores ranged from 98 to 10. This range represents the class-crystallization gradient of the community. The problem, then, is whether different segments of this gradient tend to induce different degrees of class consciousness.

---

[4] For particulars on this and other methodological points mentioned below see Lenski, "Status Crystallization: A Non-Vertical Dimension of Social Status," *op. cit.*; and Landecker, *op. cit.*

[5] A detailed description of this measure can be found in Lenski, "Status Crystallization . . . ," *op. cit.*, pp. 407ff.

TYPES OF CLASS CONSCIOUSNES

"Class consciousness" has been used to refer to a large number of social phenomena, probably because social classes have many different properties which can be singled out as possible objects of consciousness. The various meanings of the concept which have evolved in the literature seem to fall into three major categories: "class-status consciousness," "class-structure consciousness," and "class-interest consciousness."[6]

The "class-status consciousness" of a person has as its object his actual position in a class system and his relationship to others who share that position. This type of class consciousness includes a person's self-identification with a particular class, if corroborated by some kind of reality check; a preference for members of one's own class as friends and leisure-time associates (Berelson *et al.*), manifestations of allegiance to one's class (Glantz), and conceptions of one's class as a local, regional, or national entity (Haer), or as cutting across national boundaries (Buchanan and Cantril).[7]

"Class-structure consciousness" has as many facets as does class structure itself. Questions as to whether there are different classes in a given community or society, asked in a number of opinion surveys, provide limited evidence of this kind. Other aspects of class-structure consciousness are: a recognition of the class positions charactertistic of various occupations (Centers); the belief that there are class barriers which keep some men of personal ability from getting ahead (Berelson *et al.*); knowing the location of boundary lines between different classes (Martin); a sense of class differences in power or privilege (Manis and Meltzer); and conceptions of a class structure as a system of two, three, or more strata (Oeser and Hammond).[8]

By "class-interest consciousness" we mean a series of beliefs, ranging from an identification of personal interests with class interests and a distinction between the interests of different classes to the extreme view that class conflict is the necessary result of conflicting class interests. The following items from earlier studies are relevant here: the belief that the class affiliation of a person has much to do with the way he votes (Oeser and Hammond); the ability to recognize the class of which a socioeconomic or political point of view is characteristic (Centers); explicitly

---

6 Elements representing these categories are distinguishable in the discussion of "corporate class consciousness" by R. M. MacIver, *Society* (New York: Rinehart, 1937), pp. 174ff. Similar is the classification of meanings of "subjective identification" by Leonard Reissman, *Class in American Society* (Glencoe, Ill.: Free Press, 1959), p. 143.

7 Bernard R. Berelson, Paul F. Lazarsfeld, and William N. McPhee, *Voting* (Chicago: University of Chicago Press, 1954), pp. 57ff.; Oscar Glantz, "Class Consciousness and Political Solidarity," *American Sociological Review*, 23 (August 1958), 375–83, especially p. 376; John L. Haer, "An Empirical Study of Social Class Awareness,"

Social Forces, 36 (December 1957), 117–21, especially p. 119; William Buchanan and Hadley Cantril, *How Nations See Each Other* (Urbana, Ill.: University of Illinois Press, 1953), p. 17.

8 Richard Centers, "Social Class, Occupation, and Imputed Belief," *American Journal of Sociology*, 58 (May 1953), 543–55, especially p. 545; Berelson *et al.*, *op. cit.*, p. 58; F. M. Martin, "Some Subjective Aspects of Social Stratification," Chap. III in *Social Mobility in Britain*, ed. D. V. Glass (London: Routledge & Kegan Paul, Ltd., 1954), pp. 58–64; Jerome G. Manis and Bernard N. Meltzer, "Attitudes of Textile Workers to Class Structure," *American Journal of Sociology*, 60 (July 1954), 30–35, especially p. 31; O. A. Oeser and S. B. Hammond, eds., *Social Structure and Personality in a City* (London: Routledge & Kegan Paul, Ltd., 1954), pp. 270–76.

favoring big business or labor (Berelson *et al.*); the belief that the interests of one's own class are contradictory to those of other classes (Inkeles); the desire for a political movement specifically dedicated to the interests of one's own class (Berelson *et al.*); and the view that different classes are each other's enemies (Manis and Meltzer).[9]

As a point of departure for research, this threefold classification of class consciousness calls for a corresponding variety of indicators because, like any other typology, it implies the possibility that different types behave dissimilarly under similar conditions. For example, a comparison of scattered findings allows the tentative inference that social status varies directly with class-status consciousness[10] but inversely with class-interest consciousness.[11] In this study an attempt is made, therefore, to examine the relation between class crystallization and three variables, each chosen from a different type of class consciousness. While none of these variables is coextensive with, and fully representative of, the category from which it is selected, their very diversity should help in forestalling overgeneralizations from data limited to a single type.

CLASS-STATUS CONSCIOUSNESS

The area of class-status consciousness was tapped by a self-identification question. Each respondent was asked whether he thought he belonged to the upper, upper-middle, lower-middle, or lower class. As distinguished from this self-appraisal, his actual standing was expressed by the arithmetic mean of his four rank status scores, designated as "general status score." The range of these scores was split at its midpoint into an upper and a lower status level.[12]

The analysis of these data rests on the premise that in a highly class-conscious population self-ratings of class affiliation will differ markedly from one status level to another; these differences should be less pronounced where consciousness of class status is blurred. With this assumption, the general hypothesis that class consciousness varies directly with class crystallization can be rendered in operational terms as follows: In their frequency of choosing the upper or upper-middle class label, respondents on the upper status level should exceed those on the lower level by a larger margin under conditions of strong rather than weak crystallization; the lower or lower-middle class label should be chosen more often on the lower than on the upper status level, the main point being again that this difference should be enhanced by strong crystallization. For purposes of these comparisons, the total crystallization range was divided into a "strong" and a "weak" segment, the former comprising three-fourths of the respondents. This cutting point was chosen[13] because

---

[9] Oeser and Hammond, *op. cit.*, p. 304; Centers, *op. cit.*, pp. 553–55; Berelson *et al.*, *op. cit.*, p. 58; Alex Inkeles, "Images of Class Relations Among Former Soviet Citizens," *Social Problems*, 3 (January 1956), 181–96, especially pp. 185–89; Berelson *et al.*, *op. cit.*, p. 57; Manis and Meltzer, *op. cit.*, p. 33.

[10] Buchanan and Cantril, *op. cit.*, pp. 20 and 22; and Haer, *op. cit.*, p. 119.

[11] Inkeles, *op. cit.*, p. 188; and Oeser and Hammond, *op. cit.*, pp. 304ff.

[12] A larger sample would have permitted distinctions among proportionately more limited categories. Earlier findings suggest that a comparison between a small elite range, limited to the highest decile, and the remainder of all status scores would have been especially discriminating. See Werner S. Landecker, "Class Boundaries," *American Sociological Review*, 25 (December 1960), 868–77.

[13] Lenski found a very similar cutting point to be the most discriminating; "Status Crystallization," *op. cit.*, p. 408.

it divided the entire scale of crystallization into equal portions.[14]

This research design, however, introduced a statistical artifact which gave spurious support to the hypothesis. Since a composite measure of status can yield extremely high or low values only in those ·cases where its component scores are either consistently high or consistently low, strong crystallization is necessarily associated with a larger proportion of relatively extreme status scores than is weak crystallization. To cancel out this bias, the range of general status scores in the "strong-crystallization" category was reduced by the successive elimination of the most extreme scores, until the upper status levels of both crystallization categories had identical means of general status scores and until the lower status levels were equalized in the same manner.[15]

The decrease in the number of cases by which these controls were accomplished had the effect of remedying one problem at the price of aggravating another. It diminished the "upper-class" and "lower-class" choices, whose frequency had been small in the first place, to a point where their examination fails to yield significant evidence.[16] It was decided, therefore, to limit this phase of the analysis to the distribution

of the "upper-middle class" and "lower-middle class" identifications, which jointly constitute the bulk of all responses.

An inspection of "upper-middle class" choices in Table 1 indicates that in the "strong-crystallization" category this type of choice was made by 20 per cent more respondents on the upper than on the lower status level. In the "weak-crystallization" category the two percentages differ by 13.4 points.[17] The findings regarding "lower-middle class" identifications further contribute to this picture; in the category of strong crystallization the percentages for the two status levels differ by 15.6 points, while in the category of weak crystallization the percentages are identical with one another.[18] There is, then, some support

---

would have been not more than eight cases in any cell. Furthermore, it is hard to tell what the term "upper class" may have signified to respondents who chose it; the mean of their general status scores was lower than for those who placed themselves into either of the two middle classes.

[17] For strong crystallization, the difference between upper and lower status responses is significant at the 0.01 level, while for weak crystallization the corresponding difference is significant at the 0.05 level. The greater significance of the former than of the latter difference is consistent with the hypothesis, but a more crucial question is whether the difference between these two differences is significant. A test geared to this type of problem has been provided by Leo A. Goodman, "Modifications of the Dorn-Stouffer-Tibbitts Method for 'Testing the Significance of Comparisons in Sociological Data,'" *American Journal of Sociology*, 66 (January 1961), 355–63. It is used in this study as the most nearly appropriate procedure, although there may be doubt whether the data treated conform strictly to all of its requirements. By this test, the difference between the two differences is not significant.

[18] Strong crystallization: $P < 0.01$; weak crystallization: n.s.; difference between differences: $P = 0.056$.

---

[14] This explanation suggests the advisability of selecting a cutting point on the basis of its location on the crystallization scale, as distinguished from its location in the percentage distribution of a particular population.

[15] In the "strong-crystallization" category the interval range of general status scores was reduced from 0–99 to 30–79, while it remained 20–79 in the "weak-crystallization" category. The mean of general status scores, equalized for both crystallization categories, was 61.3 on the upper and 39.3 on the lower status level.

[16] If their distribution had been examined in the manner of Table 1, there

for the hypothesis that assertions of class membership become more discriminating, suggesting an increase in consciousness of class status, as class status becomes more crystallized.

CLASS-INTEREST CONSCIOUSNESS

Two questions were used with reference to class-interest consciousness. In one, the respondent was asked whether he thought that most businessmen would agree or disagree with his views on such issues as price control or national health insurance. In the other, he was asked whether most working-class people would agree or disagree with him in these matters. The "class-interest choices" shown in Table 2 are based on answers to both questions. A respondent was classified as sharing the interests of businessmen if his reaction was positive to businessmen and negative or neutral to working-class people or if it was negative to the latter and neutral to the former. If his response pattern reversed any of these combinations, he was classified as sharing the interests of working-class people.

The questions used in this part of the study were asked of approximately one-half of all respondents, this subsample being selected at random from the total sample. To compensate for the reduction in the number of cases, the cutting point between the two segments of the crystallization range was moved up by a few points, so that the proportion of subjects in the "weak-crystallization" category was raised from one-fourth to one-third.[19] The

[19] The change in dichotomizing did not seriously impair the comparability among the several parts of the study since the cutting point was moved only from 50.5 to 54.5.

TABLE 1. PERCENTAGE DISTRIBUTION OF SELF-IDENTIFICATION WITH CLASS, BY STATUS AND BY CRYSTALLIZATION

Status Level	Identifies with Upper-Middle Class		Identifies with Lower-Middle Class		Other		Totals			
	Strong Crystallization	Weak Crystallization	Strong Crystallization	Weak Crystallization	Strong Crystallization	Weak Crystallization	Strong Crystallization		Weak Crystallization	
							Number	Per Cent	Number	Per Cent
Upper	45.0	42.7	34.4	38.7	20.5	18.5	151	99.9	75	99.9
Lower	25.0	29.3	50.0	38.7	25.0	31.9	136	100.0	75	99.9
Differences	20.0	13.4	15.6	00.0						

TABLE 2. PERCENTAGE DISTRIBUTION OF "CLASS INTEREST" CHOICES, BY STATUS AND BY CRYSTALLIZATION

Status Level	Choice: Businessmen		Choice: Working-Class People		Inconsistent Choices		Other		Totals			
	Strong Crystal-lization	Weak Crystal-lization	Strong Crystal-lization	Weak Crystal-lization	Strong Crystal-lization	Work Crystal-lization	Strong Crystal-lization	Weak Crystal-lization	Strong Crystallization		Weak Crystallization	
									Num-ber	Per Cent	Num-ber	Per Cent
Upper	26.1	6.6	36.9	42.2	27.7	42.2	9.2	8.9	65	99.9	45	99.9
Lower	5.7	5.3	50.9	49.2	22.6	36.8	20.8	8.8	53	100.0	57	100.1
Differences	20.4	1.3	14.0	7.0								

previously noted difference between the two crystallization categories in their distribution of general status scores was canceled out again, as in the total sample.

The material shown in Table 2 is amenable to two ways of examining the effect of the crystallization factor. One of these is the "greater difference vs. smaller difference" test used before. In applying this procedure to "businessmen" choices, one finds that in the "strong-crystallization" column the percentages for the two status levels differ by 20.4 points, as compared with a difference of only 1.3 in the "weak" column.[20] The crystallization factor has a similar, although less pronounced effect on the "working-class" choices: In the "strong-crystallization" column the difference is 14.0; in the "weak" column it is 7.0.[21]

A second approach is concerned with cases where a person's statement regarding businessmen is inconsistent with his statement regarding working-class people. If he indicated that most businessmen as well as most working-class people are in agreement with his own views, this seemed to be an inconsistency, reflecting a lack of consciousness of discrepant class interests. It also was thought inconsistent for a person to claim that not only most businessmen but also most working-class people would disagree with his views. In this type of inconsistency, one's personal involvement in either set of class interests seemed to be denied.

If status discrepancies represented in weak crystallization contribute to in-

---

[20] Strong crystallization: $P < 0.01$; weak crystallization: n.s.; difference between differences: $P < 0.01$.

[21] Strong crystallization: $P = 0.06$; weak crystallization: n.s.; difference between differences: n.s.

consistent responses, one should be able to observe this by comparing the percentages of inconsistent answers in the two crystallization categories, while using each status level as a control device. The results are very similar on both status levels: In the frequency of inconsistent answers, the "weak-crystallization" category exceeds the other by about 14 percent.[22]

If this finding is combined with those based on the consistent answers to the same questions, there is mutual reinforcement between two strands of evidence which separately have but limited credibility. Both suggest that crystallization of class status contributes to consciousness of class interests. Furthermore, as reported earlier, data pertaining to class-status consciousness permit analogous conclusions.

CLASS-STRUCTURE CONSCIOUSNESS

None of the data in this study can be presumed to represent every aspect of a given type of class consciousness. This point needs special emphasis in the present context because of the specialized character of the data to be discussed. The particular variety of class-structure consciousness to which they are relevant may be designated as "class-barrier consciousness." Its object is the role played by structural divisions as impediments to the upward mobility of persons in the class system.

An attempt was made to probe class-barrier consciousness by means of two questions, both of which were used with the total sample. In one of these, the respondent was asked what the chances are that children of workingmen can become well-to-do and important businessmen. In the other, he was asked whether the men who are getting to be important people in the community are getting there mainly because of their own ability or their family connection.

The results of the second question suggest that the belief in the prevalence of individual opportunities is diffused among Americans and bears little relationship to status variables. Comparable evidence has come from Elmira, New York, where a similar question was asked; on every status level at least 74 per cent of the respondents said that most of the successful people had "gotten ahead" because of their own ability.[23] Even in Detroit, a community characterized by a less traditional outlook, the corresponding minimum was 70 per cent. In the present context, the significance of this interview question is to show that, on the whole, the degree of class-barrier consciousness in the community is very low.[24] However, since it discriminated neither by status level nor by crystallization, it was omitted from the remainder of the analysis.

The general belief in the prevalence of individual opportunities had a less pervasive impact on the outcome of the other question, regarding the chances which workers' children have of rising to a high social level. Relatively few persons gave clearly pessimistic answers, and their distribution apparently is not affected by any of the factors considered here. Substantial variations occur, however, among answers which are basically optimistic but differ in the degree of their optimism.[25] Thus the

---

[22] Upper status level: $P = 0.058$; lower status level: $P < 0.05$.

[23] Berelson *et al., op. cit.,* p. 58.

[24] Berelson *et al.* draw a similar conclusion, *ibid.,* p. 58.

[25] Answers to the interview question were coded on a five-point scale, ranging from the most optimistic to the most pessimistic responses. The first two major

TABLE 3. PERCENTAGE DISTRIBUTION OF OPINIONS ON "CHANGES TO RISE," BY STATUS AND BY CRYSTALLIZATION

Status Level	Highly Optimistic		Moderately Optimistic		Other		Totals			
	Strong Crystallization	Weak Crystallization	Strong Crystallization	Weak Crystallization	Strong Crystallization	Weak Crystallization	Strong Crystallization		Weak Crystallization	
							Number	Per Cent	Number	Per Cent
Upper	24.5	30.7	39.1	26.7	36.3	42.7	151	99.9	75	100.1
Lower	19.1	8.0	40.4	49.3	40.4	42.7	136	99.9	75	100.0
Differences	5.4	22.7	1.3	22.6						

prevailing ideology, as well as the facts observed from its perspective, apparently leaves room for a limited range of socially acceptable controversy; within that range, strong optimism can be taken as a denial of class barriers, and guarded optimism as an admission that there are minor barriers. This interpretation is supported by the greater frequency of the somewhat restrained kind of optimism on the lower than on the upper status level, while the reverse is true for strong optimism (Table 3).

Therefore, in line with the hypothesized relationship between class crystallization and class consciousness one should have expected that on both status levels the proportion of highly optimistic answers would increase in the direction from strong to weak crystallization and that moderately optimistic answers would increase in the opposite direction. Table 3 indicates, however, that neither prediction is sustained on the lower status level. Nor can the data be interpreted in terms of the familiar hypothesis that the subculture of a higher class will be more conservative than that of a lower class, much as it would make sense to consider the belief in virtually unlimited chances of rising as a politically conservative view. To demonstrate the presence of a class differential it would be necessary to show a greater difference between status levels under conditions of strong rather than weak crystallization. The findings do not meet this requirement.

In fact, if one looks at Table 3 in anticipation of the same pattern which was observed in earlier tables, one is faced with an apparent reversal. While

columns of Table 3 represent the two categories on the optimistic side of the scale, while the three remaining categories and the code item "not ascertained" are combined in the residual column of the table.

strong crystallization was found to accentuate the distinct effect of each status level on those responses which were treated in Tables 1 and 2, the opposite seems to be the case here. Highly optimistic answers differ between status levels by only 5.4 percentage points in the "strong-crystallization" column but by as much as 22.7 points in the "weak-crystallization" column.[26] The same pattern is slightly more pronounced in the case of moderately optimistic answers, with differences of 1.3 for strong crystallization and 22.6 for weak crystallization.[27]

In view of these results, it is not possible to retain the basic hypothesis of this study with as high a degree of generality as stated at the outset. While the hypothesis seems to have some validity for the data selected from other areas of class consciousness, in the present case the findings suggest a more complex connection among the variables. At least as an internal gradient of the community, class crystallization does not account for differences in class-barrier consciousness; however, a low degree of crystallization appears to be a condition favorable to an inverse relation between that type of class consciousness and the social status of the respondent.

Being unanticipated, this finding is not explained by the rationale underlying the original hypothesis. Perhaps it was too broad an assumption, not true for all types, to think of class consciousness as a mental manifestation of a class system, reflecting in its strength or weakness a corresponding aspect of that system. One may wonder also whether

the initial typology of class consciousness might have been too simple for heuristic purposes. Therefore, by way of conclusion, these premises of the investigation will be re-examined in the light of its findings.

COGNITION AND AFFECTIVITY IN CLASS CONSCIOUSNESS

An assumption implicit in the hypotheses of this study has been that class consciousness is a cognitive response, varying in accuracy with the degree that the object of experience is structured. Among the three measures of class consciousness used, there are two—those pertaining to class status and class interests—whose reaction to the crystallization factor is consistent with that assumption. This is not to say that affectivity is completely absent from these responses but merely that their cognitive element is sufficiently strong to account for their distribution.

On the other hand, the pattern of class-barrier responses does not permit the same explanation and thus raises the question whether these responses have a larger admixture of affectivity. Indeed, if one grants the cultural salience of the "American dream" of unlimited opportunities, it becomes possible to interpret denials of class barriers or their affirmations, cautious as they may be, in terms of positive or negative affectivity; that is, as manifestations of satisfaction or dissatisfaction. The problem posed by this interpretation is, then, how to explain the effect of weak class crystallization on either type of affectivity.

The answer to this problem is both a tentative inference from the reported findings and a hypothesis for further research. It is predicated on the fact

---

[26] Strong crystallization: n.s.; weak crystallization: $P<0.01$; difference between differences: $P<0.05$.

[27] Strong crystallization: n.s.; weak crystallization: $P<0.01$; difference between differences: $P<0.05$.

that a poorly crystallized class status is, by definition, a combination of disparate rank statuses. While a highly crystallized class status will tend to give the incumbent a unified image of his status as a whole, weak crystallization is likely to draw his attention to the distinctness of each rank status and to invite comparisons between one and another.

It is probable, furthermore, that such comparisons will influence the incumbent's judgment of a given rank status and the amount of satisfaction or dissatisfaction derived from it. He may say, for example, regarding two discrepant rank statuses: "I can be proud of how I rate in one respect, considering how little I amount to in the other." Or: "I am doing rather poorly in one respect, considering how well I am doing in the other." It would appear from Table 3 that favorable comparisons tend to occur more often if high rank statuses outweigh low ones, and unfavorable comparisons if the contrary is the case.

It is not known whether the observed pattern of responses is affected equally by all status disparities involved or whether it represents the influence of some varieties more than others. For example, the evidence does not make it possible to assess the relative importance of disparities due to vertical mobility in one or another rank system, as compared with disparities due to other factors. Another question which remains unanswered is concerned with the extent that a given response is induced by one rather than another combination of disparate statuses, such as the combination of high achieved and low ascribed status or the converse.

Although lacking in such specifications, the hypothesis has relevance in theoretical respects, particularly in its relation to the theory of "relative deprivation." Both assume that feelings of deprivation or gratification, seemingly evoked by a given object of experience, are based on a comparison between that object and other units of a framework which has direct significance for the individual. In the past, "relative-deprivation" theory has treated as the framework for such comparisons a person's so-called "reference group," that is, a set of other individuals with whom he identifies himself.[28] It appears now that a person's framework of comparison may take different forms; his reference group is one of these, while his status constellation is another. Hence, "relative-deprivation" theory seems to require a formulation of sufficient generality to include both instances and others which might be encountered in future research.

A REVISED TYPOLOGY OF CLASS CONSCIOUSNESS

Research on class consciousness should distinguish between cognitive and affective modes[29] from the very outset. To do so requires a modification of the threefold typology of class consciousness which has served as an organizing principle for this study. Although the assumption of a largely

---

[28] For an illustrative statement of "relative-deprivation" theory, see Robert K. Merton and Alice Kitt, "Contributions to the Theory of Reference Group Behavior," in *Continuities in Social Research: Studies in the Scope and Method of "The American Soldier,"* eds. Robert K. Merton and Paul F. Lazarsfeld (Glencoe, Ill.: Free Press, 1950), pp. 40–105, especially pp. 42–53.

[29] In a similar manner Geiger has distinguished between "cognitive" and "active" class consciousness. See Theodor Geiger, *Die Klassengesellschaft im Schmelztiegel* (Cologne: Gustav Kiepenheuer, 1949), p. 126.

cognitive response was compatible with findings in two among the three areas of investigation, while an interpretation in terms of affectivity seemed needed in the third area, none of the three major types can be considered as identified exclusively with either the cognitive or the affective mode of class consciousness.

If one looks for evidence on this point by examining diverse instances of class consciousness, primarily cognitive as well as primarily affective cases are found in each of the three substantive areas. This observation is documented in Table 4, which is intended to replace the earlier typology by a more detailed scheme. This scheme is based on the use of modes as well as objects of class consciousness as criteria of classification. The simultaneous application of these criteria results in the formation of two-dimensional categories, such as "cognitive class-structure consciousness" or "affective class-status consciousness." The proposed typology thus consists of six broad categories, as distinguished from their more specific and potentially more numerous examples also shown in Table 4.

One of the functions of a typological scheme is to pose problems of relationship among its units. It is possible, for instance, that the considerable diversity among the affective responses listed in Table 4 is not accidental but that, as a matter of regularity, different objects of class consciousness tend to elicit different kinds of affectivity. Furthermore, one could seek to establish developmental connections among different types of class consciousness; there may be conditions under which some types tend to evolve in regular succession. If it were observed that one type provides a foundation for another it should then be possible to show that their respective

TABLE 4. CLASS CONSCIOUSNESS CATEGORIZED BY OBJECT AND MODE, WITH EXAMPLES

Object	Cognitive Mode	Affective Mode
Class status	Self-placement by class	Solidarity with class
Class structure	Discernment of different classes	Assertion of class barriers
Class interests	Identification of personal interests with class interests	Hostility toward other classes

expressions constitute a single scale of responses.[30]

For research involving other factors, whether sociostructural or psychological, the scheme implies that a given factor may be related differently to different types of class consciousness. The present study illustrates this insofar as expressions of class consciousness in the role of dependent variables are concerned. The same general assumption would call for a corresponding differentiation in their use as independent variables; for example, in hypotheses regarding the particular effect of each on voting behavior[31] or on class conflict.[32]

In a more methodological vein, one would treat the boundary between any two types as a limit for inductive con-

[30] John C. Leggett has constructed an index of working-class consciousness, composed of scalable interview questions. See his *Working Class Consciousness in an Industrial Community* (unpublished Ph.D. dissertation, University of Michigan, 1962).
[31] Glantz, *op. cit.*, pp. 380–82.
[32] Geiger, *op. cit.*, pp. 106, 110, and 123.

clusions; inferences further extended should be considered as highly tentative. These boundaries are only provisional in character since future investigations may show a need for finer distinctions and suggest additional aspects of class consciousness which ought to be taken into account. In the meantime it would seem, as a minimal rule of caution, that findings representing one category of the proposed scheme should not be generalized to variables in other categories.

SELECTED BIBLIOGRAPHY

AIKEN, MICHAEL, et al., *Economic Failure, Alienation and Extremism.* Ann Arbor, Mich.: University of Michigan Press, 1968.

ALFORD, ROBERT R., *Party and Society.* Skokie, Ill.: Rand McNally & Company, 1963.

ALMOND, GABRIEL A., *The American People and Foreign Policy.* New York: Harcourt, Brace, 1950.

ARCHIBALD, KATHERINE, "Status Orientations Among Shipyard Workers," in *Class, Status and Power,* eds. Reinhard Bendix and Seymour M. Lipset. Glencoe, Ill.: The Free Press, 1953.

BAKKE, E. W., *The Unemployed Man.* New York: E. P. Dutton & Co., Inc., 1934.

BELL, DANIEL, *The End of Ideology.* Glencoe, Ill.: The Free Press, 1960.

BERELSON, BERNARD R., et al., *Voting: A Study of Opinion Formation in a Presidential Campaign.* Chicago: University of Chicago Press, 1954.

BLAUNER, ROBERT, *Alienation and Freedom.* Chicago: University of Chicago Press, 1964.

BOTT, ELIZABETH, "The Concept of Class as a Reference Group," *Human Relations,* 7 (August 1954), 259–85.

BROTZ, HOWARD M., "Social Stratification and the Political Order," *American Journal of Sociology,* 64 (May 1959), 571–78.

CASE, HERMAN, "Marxian Implications of Centers' Interest Group Theory," *Social Forces,* 23 (March 1955), 254–58.

CENTERS, RICHARD, "The Intensity Dimension of Class Consciousness and Some Social and Psychological Correlates," *Journal of Social Psychology* (August 1956), pp. 101–14.

———, *The Psychology of Social Classes: A Study of Class Consciousness.* Princeton, N.J.: Princeton University Press, 1949.

CHINOY, ELY, *Automobile Workers and the American Dream.* Garden City, N.Y.: Doubleday & Company, Inc., 1955.

DAHRENDORF, RALF, *Class and Class Conflict in Industrial Society.* Stanford, Calif.: Stanford University Press, 1959.

DEGRE, GERALD, "Ideology and Class Consciousness in the Middle Class," *Social Forces,* 29 (December 1950), 173–79.

EULAU, HEINZ, *Class and Party in the Eisenhower Years.* New York: The Free Press of Glencoe, Inc., 1962.

———, "Identification with Class and Political Perspective," *Journal of Politics,* 18 (May 1956), 232–53.

———, "Identification with Class and Political Role Behavior," *Public Opinion Quarterly,* 20 (Fall 1956), 515–29.

HAER, JOHN L., "An Empirical Study of Social Class Awareness," *Social Forces,* 36 (December 1957), 117–21.

HALBWACHS, MAURICE, *The Psychology of Social Class.* New York: The Free Press of Glencoe, Inc., 1958.

HAMILTON, RICHARD F., "The Marginal Middle Class: A Reconsideration," *American Sociological Review,* 31 (April 1966), 192–98.

HETZLER, STANLEY A., 'Social Mobility and Radicalism-Conservatism," *Social Forces,* 33 (December 1954), 161–66.

HOULT, THOMAS F., "Economic Class Consciousness in American Protestantism," Part I, *American Sociological Review,* 15 (February 1950), 97–100; Part II, 17 (June 1952), 349–50.

KORNHAUSER, ARTHUR W., "Public Opinion and Social Class," *American Jour-*

nal of Sociology, 55 (January 1950), 333–45.

KORNHAUSER, WILLIAM, *Politics in Mass Society*. New York: The Free Press of Glencoe, Inc., 1959.

LASSWELL, THOMAS E., *Class and Stratum*. Boston: Houghton Mifflin Company, 1965. Especially Parts 2 and 3.

———, "Orientations Toward Social Classes," *American Journal of Sociology*, 65 (May 1960), 585–87.

———, "Perception of Social Status," *Sociology and Social Research*, 45 (January 1961), 170–74.

———, "Social Classes as Affective Categories," *Sociology and Social Research*, 46 (April 1962), 312–16.

LEGGETT, JOHN C., "Uprootedness and Working-Class Consciousness," *American Journal of Sociology*, 68 (May 1963), 682–92.

———, *Class, Race and Labor*. Fair Lawn, N.J.: Oxford University Press, Inc., 1968.

———, "Working-Class Consciousness, Race, and Political Choice," *American Journal of Sociology*, 69 (September 1963), 171–76.

LEWIS, LIONEL S., "Class and the Perception of Class," *Social Forces*, 42 (March 1964), 336–40.

———, "Class Consciousness and Inter-Class Sentiments," *The Sociological Quarterly*, 6 (Autumn 1965), 325–38.

———, "A Note on the Problem of Classes," *Public Opinion Quarterly*, 27 (Winter 1963–64), 55–59.

LIPSET, SEYMOUR M., "Democracy and Working-Class Authoritarianism," *American Sociological Review*, 24 (August 1959), 482–501.

———, *Political Man*. Garden City, N.Y.: Doubleday & Company, Inc., 1960.

LIPSITZ, LEWIS, "Work Life and Political Attitudes: A Study of Manual Workers," *American Political Science Review*, 58 (December 1964), 951–62.

———, "Working-Class Authoritarianism: A Re-Evaluation," *American Sociological Review*, 30 (February 1965), 103–9.

LOCKWOOD, DAVID, "Sources of Variation in Working-Class Images of Society,"

Sociological Review, 14 (November 1966), 249–68.

MANIS, JEROME G., and BERNARD N. MELTZER, "Attitudes of Textile Workers to Class Structure," *American Journal of Sociology*, 60 (July 1954), 30–35.

———, "Some Correlates of Class Consciousness Among Textile Workers," *American Journal of Sociology*, 69 (September 1963), 177–84.

MILLER, S. M., and FRANK RIESSMAN, "Working-Class Authoritarianism: A Critique of Lipset," *British Journal of Sociology*, 12 (September 1961), 268–81.

MITCHELL, ROBERT E., "Class-Linked Conflict Between Two Dimensions of Liberalism-Conservatism," *Social Problems*, 13 (Spring 1966), 418–27.

MURPHY, RAYMOND J., and RICHARD T. MORRIS, "Occupational Situs, Subjective Class Identification, and Political Affiliation," *American Sociological Review*, 26 (June 1961), 383–92.

OSSOWSKI, STANISLAW, *Class Structure in the Social Consciousness*. New York: The Free Press of Glencoe, Inc., 1963.

PARSONS, TALCOTT, "Social Classes and Class Conflict in the Light of Recent Sociological Theory," in *Essays in Sociological Theory*. Glencoe, Ill.: The Free Press, 1954.

PECK, SIDNEY, *The Rank and File Leader*. New Haven, Conn.: College and University Press, 1963.

PINARD, MAURICE, "Poverty and Political Movements," *Social Problems*, 15 (Fall 1967), 250–63.

ROSENBERG, MORRIS, "Perceptual Obstacles to Class Consciousness," *Social Forces*, 32 (October 1953), 22–27.

RUSH, GARY B., "Status Consistency and Right-Wing Extremism," *American Sociological Review*, 32 (February 1967), 86–92.

SARGENT, S. STANSFELD, "Class and Class-Consciousness in a California Town," *Social Problems*, 1 (June 1953), 22–27.

STREET, DAVID, and JOHN C. LEGGETT, "Economic Deprivation and Extremism: A Study of Unemployed Negroes," *American Journal of Sociology*, 67 (July 1961), 53–57.

WESTBY, DAVID L., and RICHARD G. BRAUNGART, "Class and Politics in the Family Backgrounds of Student Political Activists," *American Sociological Review*, 31 (October 1966), 690–92.

WILENSKY, HAROLD, "Class Consciousness and American Workers," *Institute of Industrial Relations*, Reprint No. 283. Berkeley, Calif.: University of California, 1966.

ZEIGLER, HARMON, *Interest Groups in American Society*. Englewood Cliffs, N.J.: Prentice-Hall, Inc., 1964.

CHAPTER NINE

Social Stratification and Social Pathology

Stratification variables are frequently used to explain the phenomenon variously called *deviant behavior, social disorganization,* or *social pathology.*[1] For the student of stratification, research on the relationship between stratification and pathology—beyond its potential value in contributing to an explanation of social pathology—can facilitate understanding of the processes through which stratification affects individual and group behavior.[2]

In every society, members of the upper strata have ample opportunities to accumulate the wealth and other physical resources necessary for individual development and well-being. By contrast, personal stress and frustration, the "troubles of a people," as C. Wright Mills would say, are often traceable to the disadvantages sustained by those who are less well situated. Lacking sufficient power and status the lower strata are unable to utilize opportunities that might otherwise be available to them. Their only recourse, it would seem, is some form of the behavior which has come to be identified as pathological, deviant, or disorganized. This interpretation bears on the controversy over the functional view

---

[1] The high interest in the relationship between stratification and deviant behavior probably stems from a general concern with the topic of deviance in sociology.

[2] Seen this way, interest in the connections between stratification and pathology is an instance of the general thesis that one can learn about fundamental processes of social organization through the study of social disorganization, not to mention the thesis that disorganization is a form of organization. Cf. Albert K. Cohen, "The Study of Social Disorganization and Deviant Behavior," in *Sociology Today,* eds. Robert K. Merton, Leonard Broom, and Leonard S. Cottrell (New York: Basic Books, Inc., Publishers, 1959).

399

of social stratification. If stratification is a major source of deviant behavior or social disorganization, can it at the same time fulfill such societal needs as integration, coordination, cohesion, and social control? In short, can the pathological consequences of stratification be adequately accounted for within a functionalist framework?[3]

Early research at the University of Chicago on the role of socioeconomic factors in social pathology served as a foundation for modern investigations in which social class is employed as an independent variable.[4] Like those of the Chicago school, contemporary studies generally show an inverse correlation between various indices of socioeconomic rank and nearly every type of personal and social pathology. They present a strong case for the contention that social stratification plays a significant role in the etiology, forms, and distribution of pathology.[5] However, they do not answer the problem of how stratification variables are *causally* linked to social pathology. The following are among the possible reasons for the absence of specific knowledge of this kind.[6]

(1) Most of the research on social pathology gives limited attention to the concepts and theory presumably guiding the choice of stratification indices.[7] Consequently, research may bear upon a theory of pathology but have little relevance for a theory of stratification.

(2) Few researchers recognize that the particular social pathology under investigation may be significant in determining the appropriateness of a given

---

3 The so-called *dysfunctions* of social stratification (discussed in terms of various personal and societal problems) and how to consider them are among the chief issues in the debate over the Davis-Moore thesis. (See Chapter Two.) Further observations on this issue are in the following chapter, on social mobility, where we present research on the dysfunctions of mobility.

Most students of stratification, who are of functional persuasion, make use of Merton's essay on manifest and latent functions in accounting for the dysfunctional consequences of stratification. See Robert K. Merton, *Social Theory and Social Structure* (Glencoe, Ill.: The Free Press, 1957), Chap. 1.

4 As we indicated in Chapter One, the primary interest of the Chicago school of the 1920s was in an ecological approach to problems of social disorganization. Within this framework, however, they prominently featured socioeconomic variables. See, for example, Edward W. Burgess, ed., *The Urban Community* (Chicago: University of Chicago Press, 1926); Robert E. L. Faris and H. Warren Dunham, *Mental Disorders in Urban Areas* (Chicago: University of Chicago Press, 1939); E. Franklin Frazier, *The Negro Family in Chicago* (Chicago: University of Chicago Press, 1932); Clifford R. Shaw *et al., Delinquency Areas* (Chicago: University of Chicago Press, 1929); Frederick M. Thrasher, *The Gang* (Chicago: University of Chicago Press, 1927); Harvey W. Zorbaugh, *The Gold Coast and the Slum* (Chicago: University of Chicago Press, 1929).

5 Some sociologists hold that, while a plausible case exists for the causal involvement of stratification factors in the form of a given social pathology, little evidence indicates that stratification is significantly involved in the etiology or distribution of that pathology. See Edwin Lemert, "Social Structure, Social Control, and Deviation," in *Anomie and Deviant Behavior*, ed. Marshall B. Clinard (Glencoe, Ill.: The Free Press, 1964), pp. 57–97.

6 To be sure, most of the following points are symptomatic of problems surrounding interpretations of the relationship between theory and empirical research, including that of causal analysis generally in sociology.

7 The employment of differing indices of stratification, based on varying concepts or dimensions, adds to the problem of constructing a systematic body of research.

concept or theory of stratification. For example, delinquency is usually a group act, but suicide and mental illness are "acts" of individuals. Suicide is usually a single act; delinquency and mental illness are complex sequences of many acts. Moreover, all types of pathology, except suicide, occur in a variety of forms. It is unlikely, then, that a single concept or theory of stratification is equally appropriate for explaining all pathological manifestations.

(3) Some researchers employ stratification variables as historically determined social structures impinging directly upon behavior (the dependent variable) and either ignore or take minimal note of the problem of intervening social-psychological variables.[8] Other researchers focus upon the social-psychological dimensions of stratification as the independent variable, but commonly they only superficially connect this emphasis with a theory of stratification. In either case, stratification is inadequately dealt with as a causal phenomenon.

(4) In general, researchers almost never detail the variables and mechanisms of stratification at a variety of levels and in various subsystems of social disorganization. How are particular variables in diverse strata manifested in the differentiation of atypical or deviant social roles? What are the particular combinations of stratification variables in different classes and subclasses of pathological behavior, their genesis, and course of historical development? What is the significance of culturally diverse patterns of stratification for definitions of pathology?

The empirical studies reprinted in this chapter are examples of research on the role of stratification in mental illness, family disorganization, suicide, and delinquency. The general finding, supporting a disproportionate occurrence of pathology in the lower class, holds despite variations in the operational use of the class variable and in the measurement of pathology. In addition to providing some understanding of findings on different forms of social pathology, the selections illustrate the kinds of theoretical frameworks utilized in attempts to explain the associations between stratification and pathology.

MENTAL ILLNESS

The classic study by Robert Faris and H. Warren Dunham, *Mental Disorders in Urban Areas*,[9] carried out in the 1930s, began contemporary sociological interest in the phenomenon of mental illness. Much current research is still addressed to one of their chief concerns: the nature of the relationship between socioeco-

---

[8] A case in point is the use of concepts of anomie in research on the relation of social stratification to pathology. Some researchers use these concepts as intervening variables; others employ them as independent or causal variables and treat social class as an ancillary or contributing factor. Further variations in the use of anomie concepts in causal schemes hinge upon whether they are conceived in social-structural or social-psychological terms. For examples of the various ways in which anomie is used in stratification research see Clinard, *op. cit.*

[9] *Op. cit.*

nomic factors and mental illness. In general, these investigations, along with those of Faris and Dunham, indicate a concentration of psychopathology in the lower economic ranges; that is, they show a rough inverse relationship between class level and most forms of mental disorder.[10] Several writers maintain however that this relationship cannot be so simply expressed, that the effects of class variables are uneven and complex, and that this diversity is especially evident when attention is directed to specific forms of psychopathology. For example, the relatively consistent finding over the past several decades of an inverse relationship between socioeconomic status and schizophrenia often does not hold with most other types of psychoses, and the evidence is also not clear with neuroses.[11] These exceptions and cautions notwithstanding there is agreement that a basis does exist for describing the association between class and mental illness as inverse when *all forms* of mental illness or psychopathology are combined with respect to *severity* or *intensity*.[12]

While epidemiological and etiological concerns continue to guide the bulk of research in mental disorders, increasing attention has been directed to the role of class influences in the processes and effects of therapeutic programs for the

------

[10] For example, Robert E. Clark, "Psychoses, Income, and Occupational Prestige," *American Journal of Sociology*, 54 (March 1949), 433–40; Robert M. Frumkin, "Occupation and the Major Mental Disorders" in *Mental Health and Mental Disorder*, ed. Arnold Rose (New York: W. W. Norton & Company, Inc., Publishers, 1955), pp. 136–60; August B. Hollingshead and Frederick Redlich, *Social Class and Mental Illness* (New York: John Wiley & Sons, Inc., 1958); Charles C. Hughes *et al.*, *People of Cove and Woodlot* (New York: Basic Books, Inc., Publishers, 1960); Bert Kaplan, Robert Reed, and Wyman Richardson, "A Comparison of the Incidence of Hospitalized and Non-Hospitalized Cases of Psychosis in Two Communities," *American Sociological Review*, 21 (August 1956), 472–79; William H. Sewell, "Social Class and Childhood Personality," *Sociometry*, 64 (August 1961), 340–56; Leo Srole *et al.*, *Mental Health in the Metropolis* (New York: McGraw-Hill Book Company, 1962); Bruce P. Dohrenwend and Barbara S. Dohrenwend, "The Problem of Validity in Field Studies of Psychological Disorder," *Journal of Abnormal Psychology*, 70 (February 1965), 52–69.

[11] S. Kirson Weinberg, "Urban Areas and Hospitalized Psychotics," in *The Sociology of Mental Disorders*, ed. S. Kirson Weinberg (Chicago: Aldine Publishing Co., 1967); S. M. Miller and Elliot G. Mishler, "Social Class, Mental Illness and American Psychiatry: An Expository Review," *Milbank Memorial Fund Quarterly*, 37 (April 1959), 1–26; Robert J. Kleiner and Seymour Parker, "Goal-Striving, Social Status, and Mental Disorder: A Research Review," in Weinberg, *op. cit.*, pp. 55–66; Raymond G. Hunt, "Socio-Cultural Factors in Mental Disorders," *Behavioral Science*, 4 (April 1959), 96–106; Bruce P. Dohrenwend, "Social Status and Psychological Disorder: An Issue of Substance and an Issue of Method," *American Sociological Review*, 31 (February 1966), 14–34.

Indeed, some researchers contend that the sequence of cause and effect may often be the reverse, with mental illness determining class position rather than class position influencing mental illness. See, for example, H. Warren Dunham, Patricia Phillips, and Barbara Srinivasan, "A Research Note on Diagnosed Illness and Social Class," *American Sociological Review*, 21 (April 1966), 223–27.

[12] The strongest case for this contention rests on the research reported in Srole *et al.*, *op. cit.*

Note, however, that the reference is to an *association* between class and mental illness. The *causal* connections between class and mental illness are yet another matter, of which we know little. Much of the literature cited in the preceding footnote concerns the problem of explaining the reported statistical associations.

mentally ill. Many of these studies demonstrate that lower-class patients tend to receive less intensive forms of therapy, hesitate more to use psychiatric facilities, and appear to benefit less from care than do patients from higher classes. Such findings are valuable in themselves, but, of more importance, they bear directly on inquiries aimed at determining the incidence and the prevalence of mental illness.[13]

The excerpts from *Mental Health in the Metropolis*[14] illustrate large-scale epidemiological research on mental illness. This work, known as the Midtown Manhattan Study, is one of the very few investigations which has attempted to assess the total occurrence of mental illness in both a sample of the general population and a patient group. Of special note is the use of socioeconomic status as an independent variable. The investigation differentiates the socioeconomic status of the individual from that of his parents. Only parental socioeconomic status, the authors claim, can be considered *etiologically independent*—that is, "not open to reciprocating influence from, or choice by, the individual and the psychological process subsumed under the independent variable, i.e., his mental health."[15] Such reciprocating or interdependent influences affect the individual's *own* socioeconomic status and pose difficulties in discriminating antecedent from consequence. By concentrating on the social class and other demographic characteristics of the respondent's childhood family and their linkages to adult mental health, the researchers felt they had "converted the Midtown investigation from a synchronic kind of study into one that is at least partially of the general longitudinal-retrospective type."[16]

Two major findings from this research—the distribution of mental illness in the community at large by parental and own socioeconomic statuses—are reproduced here. These findings along with other results from the Midtown study support the interpretation of a rough inverse correlation between socioeconomic status and mental illness.

---

[13] Several studies bearing on these aspects of the relationship between stratification and mental illness are given in Frank Riessman, Jerome Cohen, and Arthur Pearl, eds., *Mental Health of the Poor: New Treatment Approaches for Low Income People* (New York: The Free Press of Glencoe, Inc., 1964). See also, Hollingshead and Redlich, *op. cit.*; Orville Gursslin, Raymond G. Hunt, and Jack L. Roach, "Social Class, Mental Hygiene and Psychiatric Practice," in *Sociology in Use*, eds. Donald Valdes and Dwight Dean (New York: The Macmillan Company, Publishers, 1965), pp. 212–20; Gerald Gurin, Joseph Veroff, and Sheila Feld, *Americans View Their Mental Health* (New York: Basic Books, Inc., Publishers, 1960).

[14] *Op. cit.*

[15] *Ibid.*, p. 18.

[16] *Ibid.*, p. 25; footnote 42.

MENTAL ILLNESS IN THE METROPOLIS*

Leo Srole, *Columbia University*

Thomas S. Langner, *New York University*

Stanley T. Michael, *Cornell Medical College*

Marvin K. Opler, *State University of New York at Buffalo*

Thomas A. C. Rennie,† *Cornell Medical College*

PARENTAL SES: MENTAL HEALTH DISTRIBUTIONS

During childhood, the individual shares the socioeconomic status of his parents and its many fateful consequences. This factor of SES origin we postulate to be an independent precondition related inversely to variations in adult mental health. We look to the Midtown Home Survey and its sample, representing some 110,000 adult, "in-residence" Midtowners, for a test of this hypothesis. . . . Respondents' SES origins are distributed among six strata according to composite scores derived from their fathers' schooling and occupational level. With the SES-origin strata designated *A* through *F* in a sequence from highest to lowest position, Table 1 arranges the Midtown sample adults in each stratum as they are distributed on the gradient classification of mental health assigned by the Study psychiatrists.

Reading Table 1 horizontally from left to right in order to discern the nature of the trends, we might direct first attention to the Mild and Moderate categories. It is readily apparent that the frequencies of these two mental-health conditions are remarkably uniform across the entire SES-origin range. These categories, it will be remembered, encompass more or less adequate functioning in the adult life spheres, although some signs and symptoms of mental disturbance in presumably sub-clinical forms are present. Equally prevalent along the entire continuum of parental SES, these two mental-health types emerge here as generalized phenomena. . . .

We also note in the above table that around these numerically stable mental-health categories the Well and Impaired frequencies vary on the SES-origin scale in diametrically opposite directions. From the highest (*A*) to the lowest (*F*) of the status groups the Well proportions recede gradually from 24.4 to 9.7 per cent, whereas the Impaired rate mounts from about one in every six (17.5 per cent) to almost one in every three (32.7 per cent).

These countertrends can be more efficiently communicated by converting them into a single standard value that expresses the number of Impaired cases accompanying every 100 Well people in a given group. In the Midtown sample as a whole, this Sick-Well ratio emerges with a value of 127, a norm available for comparative uses in the

* From Leo Srole, Thomas S. Langner, Stanley T. Michael, Marvin K. Opler, and Thomas A. C. Rennie, *Mental Health in the Metropolis* (New York: McGraw-Hill Book Company, 1962), pp. 212–14, 230–36.

† Deceased.

404

TABLE 1. HOME SURVEY SAMPLE (AGE 20-59), DISTRIBUTIONS OF
RESPONDENTS ON MENTAL HEALTH CLASSIFICATION
BY PARENTAL-SES STRATA

Mental Health Categories	Parental-SES Strata, per cent					
	A (Highest)	B	C	D	E	F (Lowest)
Well	24.4	23.3	19.9	18.8	13.6	9.7
Mild symptom formation	36.0	38.3	36.6	36.6	36.6	32.7
Moderate symptom formation	22.1	22.0	22.6	20.1	20.4	24.9
Impaired*	17.5	16.4	20.9	24.5	29.4	32.7
Marked symptom formation	11.8	8.6	11.8	13.3	16.2	18.0
Severe symptom formation	3.8	4.5	8.1	8.3	10.2	10.1
Incapacitated	1.9	3.3	1.0	2.9	3.0	4.6
$N=100$ Per Cent	(262)	(245)	(287)	(384)	(265)	(217)

* $x^2=28.81$, $5df$, $p<0.001$

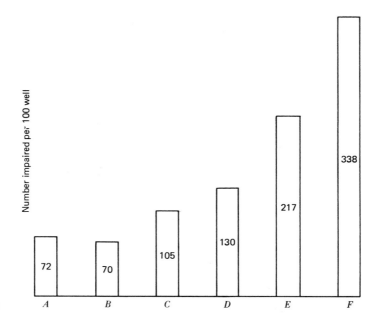

Fig. 1. *Home Survey Sample (Ages 20 to 59). Sick-Well Ratios of Parental-SES Strata.*

pages to come. In bar chart form Fig. 1 presents the Sick-Well values translated from Table 1.

With the top SES-origin levels (*A* and *B*) as our points of comparison, we observe in Fig. 1 that the Sick-Well ratio is half again larger in the adjoining group *C*, almost twice higher in the *D* stratum, three times greater in the *E* level, and at a point of five-power magnification in the bottom (*F*) group. Phrased somewhat differently, the two highest strata (*A* and *B*) taken together

constitute about 30 per cent of the sample but account for 40 per cent of the Well and for only 22 per cent of the Impaired. On the other hand, the two lowest strata (*E* and *F*) taken together constitute 29 per cent of the sample but account for only 19 per cent of the Well and for fully 39 per cent of the Impaired. Through these variously expressed data a connection seems to be apparent between parental SES and mental health in Midtown's adults. . . .

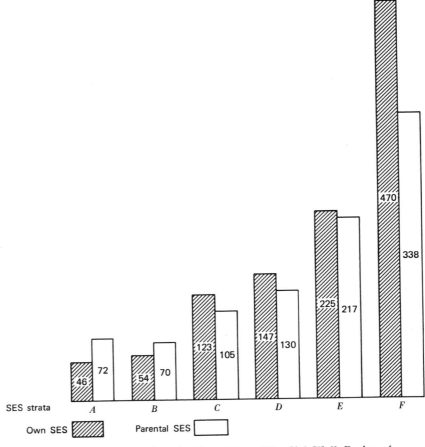

Fig. 2. Home Survey Sample (Ages 20 to 59). Sick-Well Ratios of Own-SES and Parental-SES Strata.

OWN SES AND MENTAL HEALTH

From the unraveling of father-son occupational changes we can better grasp the results when the entire Midtown sample of adults is examined for mental-health composition as classified on the scale of own socioeconomic status. In Fig. 1 we charted the Sick-Well ratios of the sample arranged by SES origin as indexed by father's schooling and occupation. These are reproduced in Fig. 2, but they now accompany bars representing the Sick-Well values of the entire sample when sorted by own SES as indexed by respondent's own education and own occupation.

Reflecting the greater tendency of the Well to move upward and the Impaired downward, Fig. 2 for the first time reveals that own SES stands to adult mental health in a relationship even more sharply accentuated than does parental SES. In other words, if parental socioeconomic status plays any contributory part in mental-health determination, own SES tends to overstate the magnitude of that contribution.

For purposes of strict comparison of SES origin and own SES, we were compelled to apply to respondents the same two socioeconomic indicators as were available for their fathers. In order to obtain a more refined differentiation of respondent's own SES, we inquired about his family income and household rent as well as his education and occupation. From the sum of the scores on these four indicators, the sample was divided into twelve own-SES strata, as nearly equal in numbers of respondents as possible.

In the strata at the top and bottom extremes of this expanded range are 7.0 and 6.5 per cent of the sample, respectively. Table 2 gives the complete distributions of these two sets of respondents on the Study psychiatrists' classification of mental health.

The Moderate and Mild categories of symptom formation aside, the mental-health contrast between the top and bottom strata could hardly be more sharply drawn. The story is partially told in their Severe and Incapacitated totals (5.8 and 30.6 per cent, respectively) and above all in their Sick-Well ratios.

Of even larger interest perhaps is the shape of the Sick-Well trend line across the entire range of the expanded own-

TABLE 2. HOME SURVEY SAMPLE (AGE 20–59), RESPONDENT DISTRIBUTIONS ON MENTAL HEALTH CLASSIFICATION OF TOP AND BOTTOM STRATA IN EXPANDED OWN-SES RANGE

Mental Health Categories	Highest Stratum	Lowest Stratum
Well	30.0 per cent	4.6 per cent
Mild symptom formation	37.5	25.0
Moderate symptom formation	20.0	23.1
Impaired	12.5*	47.3*
Marked symptom formation	6.7	16.7
Severe symptom formation	5.8	21.3
Incapacitated	0.0	9.3
$N=100$ per cent	(120)	(108)
Sick-Well ratio	42	1,020

* $t=6.0$ (0.001 level of confidence)

SES continuum. This is profiled in Fig. 3.

Confronting the data that yielded Fig. 3, some investigators would defer to a statistical device (like chi square) for a yes-or-no dictum about the existence of a relationship between two variables, beyond that producible by

chance, and consider their work done if the answer is "yes" at a given level of confidence. Since such an answer conveys nothing whatever about the relative strength or weakness of the relationship so affirmed, other investigators apply more specialized statistical devices to measure closeness of the correlation.

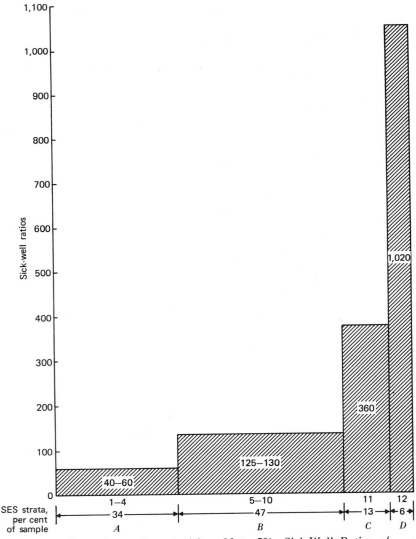

Fig. 3. Home Survey Sample (Ages 20 to 59). Sick-Well Ratios of Expanded Own-SES Strata.

However, both kinds of statistical yardsticks are completely insensitive to something potentially important in the data which are given in Fig. 3. That is, on the overall spread of the trend there is a wide socioeconomic span (strata 1–4) devoid of any notable differences in mental-health composition until a line of change is crossed. Rising to the 125 to 130 level at this crossing point, the Sick-Well ratio next remains in a flat trend across another broad span of own-SES differences (strata 5–10). These two large plateaus are followed toward the bottom of the own-SES range by two Sick-Well peaks (strata 11 and 12).

The precise extent to which Midtown's mental-health distributions statistically vary with differences in own socioeconomic status is of negligible moment compared to this demand of sheer curiosity: Given that each of the graph's four SES zones has its own inner similitude of mental-health composition, how can these segments be concretely identified? We have already seen that the adult own-SES groupings are the residues of rise and fall of status around the parental-SES points of departure. However, our immediate interest in identifying the four own-SES zones is directed not to their past but rather to their present life circumstances. These are large contemporary "worlds," we can assume, that are the scene or the source of morbidity-precipitating events for the more vulnerable people in their midst. On the basis of data culled for this volume we can indicate the approximate boundaries of these four worlds only in the most elementary economic terms.

In order of size, the largest is zone *B*, embracing strata 5 to 10 and roughly half of the entire sample. These six strata are quite uniform in mental-health composition, with Sick-Well ra-

tios that stand near the whole sample's value of 127. They are broadly spread across the lesser ranks of the middle managerial and semiprofessional occupations, through the lower white-collar, the skilled blue-collar, and the higher-wage ranks of the semiskilled factory workers. The family income span, in 1954 dollars, was in the main from $3,000 to $6,000, permitting a tolerable but hardly ample standard of consumption and certainly not permitting the accumulation of any significant reserve funds. With this "tightrope" living standard as the foundation of their claim to respectability, these respondents are close to the line of insecurity. When family crises jeopardize the economic supports of this way of life, the strain placed upon personality resources may be great.

Since these people are numerically the dominant and psychosocially the pivotal segment in the Midtown population, they have a potentially large influence on the mental-health climate of the community, above all at times of collective crisis.

Noteworthy also is the large representation of blue-collar respondents in this zone. In recent decades they have caught up with the lower white-collar class in both income and level of consumption and now also match their mental-health composition. A tantalizing question they pose is this: Has their documented economic and social progress through these decades been accompanied by an unobserved improvement in mental health, i.e., improvement sufficient to close what had previously been an unfavorable difference? A ready source of evidence to answer the question is not directly apparent. However, the historical implications of a positive answer *are* immediately apparent. . . .

Second in sample representation (34

per cent) are zone *A*'s own-SES strata 1 to 4, covering the more affluent managerial and professional classes. Here we cross into a world characterized by a more secure, expansive, and ego-nurturing style of life with larger buffers or cushions against the inevitable abrasions and hard knocks of human existence. It is striking that above roughly $6,000 annual income, further increments toward $15,000 and far beyond, with all the accompanying socioeconomic corollaries, do not appear to register any further gains in group mental-health composition. However, it can be hypothesized that without the common-denominator "prophylactics" of these strata their latent store of mental pathology would probably emerge in more overt and impairing forms.

At the other side of the own-SES range we find that zone *C* absorbs a relatively narrow 13 per cent segment of the Midtown sample. Occupationally they are semiskilled workers in the City's newer, marginal low-wage industries and workers in the more stable forms of unskilled labor, e.g., domestics, sweepers, window washers, and janitors. Weekly family income may at times reach the $60 point but more often hovers around $50. Here, we move into a zone of "struggle to keep head above water." The entire style and tone of life bear the marks of strain from constant struggle at the edge of poverty. The mental-health situation here is suggested by the spike in the Sick-Well ratio to the 360 point.

In zone *D* there is breakthrough to still another psychosocial realm, namely, poverty itself. Stemming in the main from parents in unskilled and semiskilled manual occupations, people in zone *D* are in or near the bottom bracket on every one of our four status indicators. Probably of first significance is that most of them did not complete elementary school. For some respondents this default doubtless was determined by such exogenous barriers as extreme poverty, a disabled or departed parent, or an otherwise acutely deprived family; for other respondents the default may reflect childhood endogenous disabilities, physical or mental.

Whatever the specific source of the barrier, subminimal schooling on its own account sets off a chain of other restrictions: (1) restriction largely to marginal, temporary forms of unskilled labor; (2) restriction to a low, unstable income that at best is beneath the minimal necessary to shelter, clothe, and feed a family (total income in zone *D* households almost without exception was in a range between $15 to $40 weekly); (3) restriction to cramped quarters in the most deteriorated slum tenements.

Such noxious life burdens, together with inadequate or vulnerable personalities developed in childhood, often combine to produce a break in the intolerable struggle. Chronic poverty has brought almost all zone *D* respondents to the City Welfare Department for financial assistance; and many belong to "multiproblem" families that are known to the police, courts, private social agencies, and mental hospitals.

From this group's mental-health distribution reported in Table 2 above, it is seen that exceedingly few are Well (4.6 per cent) and nearly half (47.3 per cent) are Impaired. Segregated with others in like circumstances and mental-health conditions, the numerically dominant Impaired of zone *D* doubtless help to create a "sick" slum community that often carries its own pathogenic "contagion," in particular for the children in its midst. It is hardly surprising, therefore, to hear of a 1956 New York City Youth Board Survey that covered 825 children of needy families and reported that 40 per cent of these children manifest "serious behavior problems." It was predicted that another 10 per cent, principally in the youngest segment of the sample, would likely develop such problems.

Here the frequency of adult mental pathology is probably of unprecedented proportions. And here the environmental contamination of children very likely ensures that the epidemic shall continue to reproduce itself in the generation ahead, as it apparently has from the generation preceding.

Reviewing the four zones observed in Fig. 3, we can infer that certain turning points in the quality and weight of adult life conditions emerge along the status continuum represented in our expanded own-SES scale.

SUMMARY

In this sweep across the front defined by socioeconomic status with its multiform salients, we probed a number of discrete hypotheses with the following returns:

1. On the parental-SES range the frequency of impairment varies inversely and the Well rate varies directly.

2. This trend in Impaired-Well balance also characterizes those in the sample's youngest age group, who only recently have crossed the threshold from adolescence. It was thus possible to reject the hypothesis that SES-origin differentials in mental health had almost entirely been generated during adult life.

3. Among the several SES-origin groups no significant differences appear in the frequency of schizophrenic signs, anxiety-tension symptoms, or excessive

intake behaviors. In all other pathognomonic dimensions covered, however, there is an *inverse* correlation with parental SES. These dimensions included disturbances in intellectual, affective, somatic, characterological, and interpersonal functioning.

4. Simultaneous analysis of age and status origin against respondent mental health revealed that *both* demographic variables are related to mental health, each in its own right. This suggested first that parental-SES differences had implanted varying mental-health potentialities among sample respondents during childhood; and second, that, during the temporal course of adolescence and adulthood, precipitating factors had provoked overt morbidity among the more vulnerable people from all SES-origin strata. The combined power of these two demographic variables, as reflected in the index of Sick-Well magnitudes, is substantial.

5. The hypothesis was suggested that this triad of age, parental SES, and adult mental health was specific to the kinds of people who choose to live in an area like Midtown. That is, the identified nexus lacked wider currency in the American population. Evidence from three radically different populations indicated rejection of this hypothesis. Positively stated, the complex triad isolated in the Midtown sample may well characterize larger reaches of the American people.

6. Intergeneration status mobility, as read in a single point-of-time study, is a reciprocal factor relative to adult mental health. In the Midtown sample's coverage of three mobility types, the climbers had the smallest Sick-Well values and the descenders had the largest by far. For prospective longitudinal studies these data suggested the two-part hypothesis: (a) Preadult person-

ality differences partially determine directions of status change in adulthood; (b) *on the whole,* upward status mobility is rewarding psychically as well as materially, whereas downward status mobility is depriving in both respects.

7. Reflecting the selective escalator effects of status mobility, own-SES shows an even stronger relationship to adult mental health than does respondent status origin.

8. Using four status indicators it is possible to divide the own-SES range into twelve finer strata. Revealed in these strata are four mental-health zones, or contemporary worlds, seemingly marked at their boundaries by breakthrough points of differences in the size and security of economic underpinnings, in styles of life, in ego nurturance, and in their psychosocial atmospheres. In zones *C* and *D,* at or near the poverty level, we discern particularly heavy pathogenic weights currently bearing on these especially vulnerable people.

For targeting of social policy, Midtown zones *C* and *D,* and likely their psychosocioeconomic counterparts elsewhere on the national scene, convey highest priority claims for milieu therapy in its broadest sense. Ultimately indicated here may be interventions into the downward spiral of compounded tragedy, wherein those handicapped in personality or social assets from childhood on are trapped as adults at or near the poverty level, there to find themselves enmeshed in a web of burdens that tend to precipitate (or intensify) mental and somatic morbidity; in turn, such precipitations propel the descent deeper into chronic, personality-crushing indigency. Here, we would

suggest, is America's own displaced-persons problem.

For basic research, the joint evidence of this chapter and of several collateral studies of general populations here reviewed highlights the status system as an apparatus that differentially sows, reaps, sifts, and redistributes the community's crops of mental morbidity and of sound personalities.

In no way have we claimed that the mental health effects produced by this apparatus are determined by sociocultural processes alone. Nevertheless, in line with our field of professional competence and responsibility to future investigators, we have advanced a number of hypotheses that implicate certain specific forms of sociocultural processes operating within the framework of the social-class system. These hypotheses focus on the four mental health zones we have found dividing Midtown's SES range. Distinguishing these zones, the hypotheses suggest, are economic factors linked to mechanisms of invidious discrimination that pervade the zones' respective way-of-life constellations. These postulates hold that toward one pole of the status range, in both preadult and adult life, such processes tend to penetrate the family unit with eugenic or prophylactic effects for personality development, whereas toward the opposite pole they more often work with pathogenic or precipitating effects.

These hypotheses chart paths of further necessary exploration. They can thereby lay reasonable claim to the attention of the several sciences that are joined in the "crash" research program of social psychiatry.

Most investigations of the relationship between stratification and social pathology deal with stratification variables in the structural sense. The study by R.

Jay Turner and Morton Wagenfeld presents an alternative way of conceptualizing the influence of social class by inquiring into the consequences of social mobility for pathology. In keeping with typical findings they report a disproportionate number of schizophrenics in the lowest occupational category. They attribute this overrepresentation primarily to downward mobility. By employing the alternative hypotheses of social selection and social drift, they carry their analysis of the effects of downward mobility a step further than do other students of this phenomenon.

OCCUPATIONAL MOBILITY AND
SCHIZOPHRENIA*†

R. Jay Turner, *New York State Mental Health Research Unit*

Morton O. Wagenfeld, *Western Michigan University*

One of the most discussed and least understood issues in social psychiatry is the relationship between social class or socioeconomic status and mental illness—particularly schizophrenia. There is little doubt that a disproportionate number of schizophrenics are in the lower socioeconomic strata, whatever the measure of social rank.[1] The area of contention revolves around the role played by social class: Are the stresses and rigors attendant to existence at these levels *etiologically* associated with the disorder, or do schizophrenics tend to collect in the lower strata *as a result* of their illness? The former interpretation is generally known as the "social causation" hypothesis, while the latter is usually referred to as the "social selection" or "social drift" explanation.[2]

The pioneering work of Faris and Dunham[3] and similar investigations by others[4] have generally assumed a social

* From R. Jay Turner and Morton O. Wagenfeld, "Occupational Mobility and Schizophrenia: Assessment of the Social Causation and Social Selection Hypotheses," *American Sociological Review*, 32 (February 1967), 104–13. Reprinted by permission of the American Sociological Association.

† This paper derives from a study supported by Grant #MH–09204 from the National Institute of Mental Health, R. Jay Turner, Ph.D., John Cumming, M.D., and Elmer Gardner, M.D., principal investigators. Computer analysis was supported, in part, by the National Science Foundation, under Grant GP–1137.

[1] An outstanding review and critique of some of the major issues in the field may be found in Elliot G. Mishler and Norman A. Scotch, "Sociocultural Factors in the Epidemiology of Schizophrenia," *International Journal of Psychiatry*, 1 (April 1965), 258–305.

[2] Bruce P. Dohrenwend, "Social Status and Psychological Disorder: An Issue of Substance and an Issue of Method," *American Sociological Review*, 31 (February 1966), 14–34.

[3] Robert E. L. Faris and H. Warren Dunham, *Mental Disorders in Urban Areas* (Chicago: University of Chicago Press, 1939).

[4] See, for example, E. H. Hare, "Mental Conditions and Social Conditions in Bristol," *Journal of Mental Science*, 102 (April 1956), 349–57; R. Lapouse, M. A. Monk, and M. Terris, "The Drift Hypothesis and Socioeconomic Differentials in Schizophrenia," *American Journal of Public Health*, 46

causation frame of reference. In contrast, psychiatric critics have contended that the phenomenon is explainable in terms of a "social selection" hypothesis.[5] One approach toward the resolution of the "selection vs. causation" problem has been studies of social or occupational mobility—both intergenerational and intragenerational—of schizophrenics. The rationale behind these studies is that, if schizophrenics display downward mobility, whether within their own career or in relation to their fathers, and if the social class distribution for their fathers does not differ from that of the general population, this would constitute evidence for the social drift or social selection hypothesis. If, on the other hand, little downward mobility is observable and the occupations of the patients' fathers, like those of the patients themselves, are overrepresented at the lower levels, the social causation explanation would be supported.

Unfortunately, studies of social mobility and schizophrenia have produced ambiguous and contradictory findings. Two *intra*generational studies are illustrative. Lystad, using a sample of first admission schizophrenics in New Orleans, found that the patients were more downwardly mobile than their controls.[6] In contrast, approximately equal mobility between schizophrenics

and controls was found by Clausen and Kohn.[7]

In New Haven, Hollingshead and Redlich noted that 91 per cent of the schizophrenics were in the same class as their families of origin, while only 1–3 per cent were in a lower class.[8] Similarly, Tietze, Lemkau, and Cooper have concluded that the differential distribution of schizophrenics by social class cannot be explained by the downward movement of those who were already ill.[9] A recent study in England, however, using both documentary and case history material and measuring both intergenerational and intragenerational occupational mobility, strongly supported the social drift hypothesis.[10] It was observed that while schizophrenics were found disproportionately in the lowest occupational rank (Class V), the distribution of their fathers' occupations did not deviate appreciably from that of the general population. They also showed that schizophrenics displayed more downward intragenerational mobility in comparision with their male siblings. They noted that,

Selected Groups of Schizophrenic Patients," *American Sociological Review*, 12 (April 1957), 288–92.

[7] John Clausen and Melvin Kohn, "Relation of Schizophrenia to the Social Structure of a Small City," in *Epidemiology of Mental Disorder*, ed. Benjamin Pasamanick (Washington, D.C.: American Association for the Advancement of Science, 1959), pp. 69–86.

[8] August B. Hollingshead and Frederick C. Redlich, *Social Class and Mental Illness* (New York: John Wiley & Sons, Inc., 1958), pp. 246–47.

[9] C. Tietze, P. Lemkau, and M. Cooper, "Schizophrenia, Manic Depressive Psychosis, and Socioeconomic Status," *American Journal of Sociology*, 47 (September 1941), 167–75.

[10] E. M. Goldberg and S. L. Morrison, "Schizophrenia and Social Class," *British Journal of Psychiatry*, 109 (November 1963), 785–802.

(1956), 978–86; and Leo Srole, Thomas S. Langner, Stanley T. Michael, Marvin K. Opler, and Thomas A. C. Rennie, *Mental Health in the Metropolis* (New York: McGraw-Hill Book Company, 1962), especially Chap. 12.

[5] O. Ødegaard, "The Incidence of Psychoses in Various Occupations," *International Journal of Social Psychiatry*, II (1956), 85–104; A. Myerson, "Review of Mental Disorders in Urban Areas," *American Journal of Psychiatry*, 96 (1940), 995–97.

[6] Mary Lystad, "Social Mobility Among

"If we had classified the patients on an index in which place of residence and education were included, as Hollingshead and Redlich (1958) have done, the process of drift caused mainly by the illness would have been obscured."[11]

This criticism is in line with one of several made by Mishler and Scotch in enumerating possible sources of error inherent in the studies of social class and schizophrenia. The latter note:

Among the many sources of potential error, three in particular deserve attention: the case finding procedures are not independent of social class, and the diagnostic procedures are not independent of social class, and the measurement of social class is unreliable.[12]

An ongoing study of social correlates of community tenure and work performance among schizophrenics appeared to afford a unique opportunity to investigate this important issue under conditions that minimize the objections raised by Mishler and Scotch.[13] The sample for this study was drawn from the Monroe County (New York) psychiatric case register.[14] Since its inception in January, 1960, the register has recorded almost all (95%) of the psychiatric contacts, whether diagnostic or treatment, inpatient or outpatient, public or private, that occur within the county. The psychiatric register thus provides a broad and representative sampling base and, therein, a case-finding procedure for the diagnosed population that is quite independent of social class.

From the psychiatric case register, a random sample of white male schizophrenics, ages 20 to 50, was drawn, of whom 214 were later interviewed. The sample was limited to those patients who had been reported to the register for the first time between January 1, 1960 and June 30, 1963, had no history of psychiatric hospitalization prior to the initial reported contact, and had received a diagnosis of schizophrenia on one or more psychiatric contacts during the three and a half year period.

The question of whether the diagnostic procedures applied to this population were independent of social class was assessed in relation to diagnosis at first reported psychiatric contact and, for each subject, the proportion of schizophrenic diagnoses to the total number of diagnoses received. Chi-square analysis of social class by category of first diagnosis offered no evidence for any relationship. Since the majority of included subjects had been diagnosed on between three and nineteen separate occasions, and by a variety of facilities and individuals, it was reasoned that any differential propensity to assign the label of "schizophrenic" would be reflected in the proportion of times that such a diagnosis was made. Again, the chi-square technique was employed to compare social class groupings on the proportion of schizophrenic diagnoses received. The result provided no suggestion of any relationship. These findings allow the assumption of independence between diagnostic tendency and the patients social-class position.

The measure of socioeconomic status

---

[11] *Ibid.*, p. 800.

[12] Mishler and Scotch, *op. cit.*, p. 270.

[13] This study, entitled "Predicting Social Functioning and Psychiatric Status," is being conducted by the New York State Mental Health Research Unit in cooperation with the University of Rochester Department of Psychiatry.

[14] Elmer A. Gardner, Harold C. Miles, Howard P. Iker, and John Romano, "A Cumulative Register of Psychiatric Services in a Community," *American Journal of Public Health*, 53 (August 1963), 1269–77.

employed in the general study is the Hollingshead Two-Factor Index of Social Position,[15] consisting of a weighted score of occupation and education. However, based on Goldberg and Morrison's experience,[16] the present paper utilizes only the occupational prestige level, in preference to the two-part index, in order to avoid any obscuring of mobility by levels of educational attainment. The classification of occupations —often one of the most difficult problems in sociological investigation—was facilitated by the gathering of detailed information on title, work situation, and the characteristics of each subject's job. To allow assessment of intragenerational mobility, patients' work histories were recorded in some detail. In addition, subjects were queried on their father's last or current job, his usual occupation, if different, and his occupation at about the time the subject was 16 years old.

Explication of terms. As noted above, two major opposing hypotheses have generally been invoked to explain the observed rate variations according to socioeconomic position. Briefly, the issue is whether social position is to be viewed as a *consequence* or as a *cause* of psychological disorder. While "social drift" and "social selection" are often used interchangeably to denote the "social-position-as-a-consequence-of-disorder" approach, it seems useful to distinguish between these terms. In the present paper, "social drift" refers to the drifting of individuals from higher- to lower-status occupations following the onset or intensification of symptoms.[17] "Social selection," on the other

hand, refers to the failure of eventually diagnosed individuals to achieve the occupational status that might reasonably have been expected, given their class of origin.

In addition, it is worth keeping clearly in mind that the social causation interpretation proposes not only that environmental variables are etiologically related to schizophrenia, but that such variables covary strongly with social position. In other words, those environmental conditions associated with the occurrence of the disorder are, in large measure, functions of socioeconomic status. The dual character of this hypothesis suggests a need for caution when interpreting the results of mobility studies.

RESULTS

Our first step was to determine whether the distribution of occupations among this broadly sampled, and therefore relatively heterogeneous, schizophrenic population was consistent with the common finding of an inverse relationship between social position and psychological disorder. Table 1 presents the observed and expected[18] occupational distributions for the schizophrenic sample and for their fathers' usual jobs and jobs at about the time when the patient was 16 years old.

individuals from higher to lower socioeconomic areas of residence. Area of residence, however, is not a variable in the present paper and the referent of "social drift" should be carefully distinguished from its more traditional usage.

[18] In the absence of a control sample, the expected frequencies were based, for patients, upon the distribution of occupations provided by the 1960 U.S. Census of Monroe County and, for fathers, upon the distribution provided by the 1950 U.S. Census of Monroe County, with corrections for age and sex.

---

[15] August B. Hollingshead, "Two Factor Index of Social Position," mimeographed, New Haven, 1952.

[16] *Op. cit.*, p. 800.

[17] The term "social drift" has often been used to refer to the geographic movement of

TABLE 1. OBSERVED AND EXPECTED OCCUPATIONAL PRESTIGE LEVEL DISTRIBUTIONS FOR SCHIZOPHRENIC PATIENTS AND THEIR FATHERS

Occupational Prestige Level	Patients' Current or Last Job				Fathers of Patients							
					Usual Job				Job When Patient Was 16 Years Old			
	Observed	Per Cent	Expected	Per Cent	Observed	Per Cent	Expected	Per Cent	Observed	Per Cent	Expected	Per Cent
Major and lesser professional (1–2)	13	6.2	32.5	15.4	13	6.5	22.1	11.0	13	6.5	22.1	11.0
Minor professional and managerial (3)	18	8.5	23.2	11.0	20	10.0	23.1	11.5	18	9.0	23.1	11.5
Clerical-sales (4)	48	22.7	35.2	16.7	25	12.4	31.2	15.5	26	12.9	31.2	15.5
Skilled manual (5)	45	21.3	51.5	24.4	80	39.8	51.9	25.8	81	40.3	51.9	25.8
Semiskilled manual (6)	55	26.1	58.2	27.6	38	18.9	62.5	31.1	39	19.4	62.5	31.1
Unskilled (7)	32	15.2	10.3	4.9	25	12.4	10.2	5.1	24	11.9	10.2	5.1
Subtotal	211	100.0	211.0	100.0	201	100.0	201.0	100.0	201	100.0	201.0	100.0
Occupation unknown	3*				13				13			
Total	214				214				214			
Goodness of fit tests	$\chi^2=64.3$; $p<0.001$				$\chi^2=51.7$; $p<0.001$				$\chi^2=49.6$; $p<0.001$			

* Patient never worked.

In summarizing what they consider to be the nine studies most relevant to the relationship at issue, Mishler and Scotch[19] point to two highly consistent findings. First they note that the highest incidence is associated with the lowest social grouping used in each study and that the rates for this category are much higher than for the adjacent occupational group. The second finding is that the lowest rate is observed within what amounts to the highest occupational category. As Table 1 clearly indicates, the data on our schizophrenic sample are highly consistent with these two findings. While, for the four middle categories, the observed frequencies probably do not differ significantly from expectation, the highest occupational category is two-and-one-half times under-represented and the lowest is more than three times over-represented.

Table 1 also shows the distributions of fathers' occupations to be somewhat at variance with expected values. Although to a less marked degree than their offspring, they are somewhat under-represented in the highest prestige category and are substantially overrepresented in the lowest prestige category. This remains true whether the point of reference is usual job or job held at about the time the patient left school.[20] These findings, while at least superficially consistent with those of Hollingshead and Redlich, directly contradict two British investigations[21] and

a recent study in this country by Dunham[22] that report the social position distribution for fathers of schizophrenics to approximate that of the general population.

Addressing the issue of social causation vs. social selection or social drift, these data appear to clearly favor the social causation explanation. However, examination of the recruitment sources of those patients in the lowest occupational category, i.e., their class of origin, indicates that the question is by no means so simply resolved. Table 2 shows the prestige level of patients' occupations against those of their fathers at the time the patient left school.[23]

Only six of the twenty-three patients whose fathers were level 7 themselves remain in this lowest occupational category. These nonmobile individuals represent only 20.7 per cent of the patients in the lowest category, the great majority having originated in higher-status families. Thus, although a disproportionate number of our schizophrenics grew up within families of very low status, a fact that clearly supports the social-etiology argument, this observation does not provide us with a satisfying explanation for the extreme overrepresentation of low-status individuals among the schizophrenic population.

While Table 2 provides an estimate of the upward and downward movement of patients relative to their fathers, the meaningful interpretation of these data in terms of the social-selec-

19 *Op. cit.*, pp. 268–69.

20 The distribution of "father's last or current job," as well as those of "usual job" and "job when patient was 16 years old," were also run against expected values based upon the 1960 census. Observed departures from expectation, although somewhat sharper, remained in each instance the same as those noted above.

21 Goldberg and Morrison, *op. cit.*; J. N. Morris, "Health and Social Class," *Lancet* (February 1959), pp. 303–5.

22 H. Warren Dunham, *Community and Schizophrenia* (Detroit: Wayne State University Press, 1965), p. 196.

23 A tabling of patients' occupations against fathers' usual jobs will not be shown in the present paper. As a comparison of the two distributions for fathers in Table 1 suggests, this table varies so slightly from the one presented that, for the purpose of interpretation, they can be considered as equivalent.

tion or social-drift hypotheses required a comparison population. Although such father-son occupational data were not available for the geographical area of our study, some data provided by Blau[24] appeared to offer a suitable alternative. Based upon a 1962 census survey, Blau presents a table for a sample representing the 45 million American men between the ages of 20 and 64 in the civilian noninstitutional population.[25] The data considered are the same as those already presented on our schizophrenic sample: respondents' current occupation and occupation of father when the respondent was about 16 years old.

Table 3 presents Blau's national sample data, adjusted to conform to the Hollingshead prestige level categories. A comparison of the general mobility characteristics of the two populations is shown in Table 4. While the percentages that are nonmobile in the two populations are nearly identical, it is clear that in the schizophrenic group a substantially smaller number are upwardly mobile, and a substantially greater number downwardly mobile, relative to their fathers, than is true of the general population. The table also indicates the mean number of steps moved by the upwardly and downwardly mobile for the two samples. While the degree of movement is greater among the upwardly mobile in the general sample, the

---

[24] Peter M. Blau, "The Flow of Occupational Supply and Recruitment," *American Sociological Review*, 30 (August 1965), 475–90.

[25] For a description of procedures used in the survey and some findings, see Bureau of the Census, "Lifetime Occupational Mobility of Adult Males," Series P–23, No. 11, *Current Population Reports* (1964). This report excludes men between the ages of 20 and 25, while Blau includes them in his analysis.

TABLE 2. PRESTIGE LEVEL OF PATIENT'S CURRENT OR LAST JOB BY PRESTIGE LEVEL OF FATHER'S WHEN PATIENT WAS 16 YEARS OF AGE

Occupational Prestige Level of Father	Occupational Prestige Level of Patient														Total N
	1–2		3		4		5		6		7			
	N	Per Cent	N	Per Cent	N	Per Cent	N	Per Cent	N	Per Cent	N	Per Cent		
1–2 (high)	6	50.0	1	5.7	3	7.0	1	2.4	1	1.8	1	3.4		13
3	2	16.7	3	16.6	4	9.3	1	2.4	8	14.6	0	0.0		18
4	1	8.3	2	11.1	7	16.3	3	7.3	7	12.7	6	20.7		26
5	3	25.0	7	38.9	17	39.5	23	56.1	20	36.4	10	34.5		80
6	0	0.0	3	16.6	9	20.9	8	19.6	12	21.8	6	20.7		38
7 (low)	0	0.0	2	11.1	3	7.0	5	12.2	7	12.7	6	20.7		23
Total	12	100.0	18	100.0	43	100.0	41	100.0	55	100.0	29	100.0		198*

*Thirteen cases—fathers' occupations unknown. Three cases—patient never worked.

TABLE 3. PRESTIGE LEVEL OF SON'S CURRENT OR LAST JOB BY FATHER'S JOB WHEN SON WAS 16 YEARS OF AGE, FOR GENERAL SAMPLE

Occupational Prestige Level of Father	Occupational Prestige Level of Son													Total N
	1–2		3		4		5		6		7			
	N	Per Cent	N	Per Cent	N	Per Cent	N	Per Cent	N	Per Cent	N	Per Cent		
1–2 (high)	722	17.1	303	6.7	320	7.7	156	2.7	260	4.0	40	2.4		1801
3	940	22.3	1380	30.7	770	18.6	618	10.8	529	8.2	98	5.8		4335
4	651	15.4	643	14.3	575	13.9	409	7.2	437	6.7	86	5.1		2801
5	912	21.6	1081	24.0	922	22.2	1993	34.8	1715	26.5	466	27.6		7089
6	850	20.1	918	20.4	1275	30.7	2016	35.3	2671	41.2	616	36.5		8346
7 (low)	149	3.5	176	3.9	285	6.9	524	9.2	867	13.4	381	22.6		2382
Total	4224	100.0	4501	100.0	4147	100.0	5716	100.0	6479	100.0	1687	100.0		26754

opposite is true for downward moves —the downwardly mobile schizophrenics showing, on the average, a more severe drop. Thus in terms of both the number of movers and the extent of movement, the broad trend is one of relatively less upward movement and more downward movement within the schizophrenic population.

To determine whether this general trend accounts for the specific observation of a threefold overrepresentation in the lowest occupational category, we refer again to Tables 2 and 3. Inspection of the last column of each table indicates that, for both the patient and the general sample, approximately 20 per cent of the level 7 subjects are individuals who remained at the level of their fathers. For the general sample, then, like the patient sample, nearly 80 per cent of those sons at level 7 got there by moving downward relative to their fathers.

This similarity between the samples is however much more apparent than real. Their substantial disparity becomes obvious through two simple comparisons (Tables 2 and 3). First, of those who originated at level 7, 26 per cent of the schizophrenics remained at that level as compared to less than 16 per cent of those in the general sample. Second, of the total general sample, only 4.9 per cent had moved downward into the lowest occupational level while 11.6 per cent of the total schizophrenic sample reside at level 7 as a result of downward movement. Given the two preceding observations, it is not surprising that, over the single generation considered, the general sample shows about a 30 per cent *decrease* in the total number at level 7, as compared to about a 25 per cent *increase* for the patient sample.

TABLE 4. DIRECTION AND MAGNITUDE OF OCCUPATIONAL MOBILITY FOR
THE SCHIZOPHRENIC AND GENERAL SAMPLE

Direction and Movement	Schizophrenic		General Sample	
	Per Cent Mobile*	Mean Number of Steps Moved	Per Cent Mobile*	Mean Number of Steps Moved
Up	34.8	1.667	45.6	1.957
None	28.8	—	28.9	—
Down	36.4	1.806	25.5	1.667

*$P < 0.001$ (χ^2 test).

SOCIAL SELECTION OR SOCIAL DRIFT

The data presented to this point leave little doubt that social selection and social drift contribute heavily to the substantial overrepresentation of the lowest occupational category among schizophrenics. Earlier we distinguished between social selection, referring to intergenerational downward mobility, and social drift, referring to intragenerational downward movement. Since it seemed of both theoretical and practical importance, an attempt was made to assess the relative prevalence of these differential modes of movement.

To evaluate the extent of intragenerational movement, prestige levels were assigned for all jobs held by each patient during the ten years preceding the interview. Each profile of prestige levels was then inspected and coded as upward or downward whenever such movement could be detected. If the same job was held throughout most of the ten-year period, or if the subject held a series of jobs at about the same level, he was coded as nonmobile. In some instances both upward and downward movement had occurred but no clear trend could be detected. To distinguish these individuals from the non-

mobile group, they were coded as "irregular." These data are shown in Table 5.

This table shows clearly that, within their own careers, the sample schizophrenics have been surprisingly stable in terms of the character of jobs held. Fully 82 per cent of the group either remained at the same level during the 10 year period or definitely moved from lower to higher prestige jobs, while less than 7 per cent evidenced a decline in the prestige level of jobs held. A comparison of these figures with those for total mobility, shown in Table 4, indicates the relative contributions of social selection and social drift. Three specific comparisons are pertinent. These are: (1) Although 36.4 per cent of the total schizophrenic sample were downwardly mobile relative to their fathers, only 6.8 per cent showed downward movement within their own work histories; (2) While almost 80 per cent of the patients at the lowest occupational level had moved downward, relative to their father's levels into that category, only 9.7 per cent had experienced downward movement intragenerationally; (3) While 11.66 per cent of the total schizophrenic sample had moved downward, relative to their fathers, into level 7, only 1.4 per cent of the total sample

TABLE 5. INTRAGENERATIONAL OCCUPATIONAL MOBILITY OVER PRECEDING TEN YEARS BY OCCUPATIONAL PRESTIGE LEVEL OF PATIENT'S LAST OR CURRENT JOB

Direction of Movement	Occupational Prestige Level of Patient													
	1-2		3		4		5		6		7		Total	
	N	Per Cent	N	Per Cent	N	Per Cent	N	Per Cent	N	Per Cent	N	Per Cent	N	Per Cent
Upward	3	23.1	6	35.3	9	19.1	15	33.3	2	3.7	0	0.0	35	16.9
No mobility	7	53.8	11	64.7	28	59.6	24	53.4	39	72.2	26	83.9	135	65.2
Downward	1	7.7	0	0.0	4	8.5	2	4.4	4	7.4	3	9.7	14	6.8
Irregular	2	15.4	0	0.0	6	12.8	4	8.9	9	16.7	2	6.5	23	11.1
Total	13	100.0	17	100.0	47	100.0	45	100.0	54	100.0	31	100.0	207*	100.0

* Three cases never worked; two cases refused information regarding post 1955 work history; two cases were students.

moved downward into level 7 within their own working careers.

It seems clear that although social drift, presumably following the onset or intensification of symptoms, is observable in the present study, its contribution to the resulting occupational distribution is relatively minor. The relatively lower occupational structure generally and the threefold overrepresentation in level 7, specifically, appear to derive, in the largest measure, from social selection—the failure of pre-schizophrenic individuals to achieve the level which, given both their point of origin and the changing occupational distribution, could be anticipated.

TWO SAMPLE CONSIDERATIONS

Although our data favoring the social selection explanation are consistent with one of Dunham's recent conclusions[26] our findings in general appear to diverge importantly from those of most prior studies. To place these results into a perspective that will allow appropriate comparisons with those of prior and future studies requires discussion of two issues. These issues are those of "heterogeneity of sample" and "the lost population."

Heterogeneity of sample. The character of the samples that have been utilized in investigating the present topic has varied widely. Some studies have simply used a state hospital population while, at the other extreme, some have attempted a more representative base by sampling from public and private hospitals, private outpatients and clinic patients.

Whatever the sampling procedures that have previously been used, it seems unlikely the resulting sampling

26 *Op. cit.*

pools were quite as complete or varied as that provided by the Monroe County Psychiatric Case Register. More important, the diagnostic criterion for inclusion in our study was not very stringent. To be included, a subject need only have been diagnosed as schizophrenic on at least one occasion by any facility or private psychiatric or psychological practitioner. The number of separate diagnoses that had been received by patients in our sample ranged from one to nineteen, and the proportion of schizophrenic diagnoses to total diagnoses received varied from as little as 10 per cent to 100 per cent. These factors suggest that the present sample may be considerably more heterogeneous than those typically used in such research, and raises the question of whether all included subjects can be confidently regarded as schizophrenic in fact.

To assess the possible effect of such heterogeneity upon the findings presented, an index was constructed to distinguish the "possibly schizophrenic" from the "definitely schizophrenic." For those who had been diagnosed on three or more separate occasions, a patient was categorized as "definitely schizophrenic" only if he was diagnosed as schizophrenic 75 per cent or more of the time, or exhibited to our interviewing psychiatrists one or more classically schizophrenic symptoms. The symptom criterion required definite evidence of hallucinations, delusions, or disturbances of thought processes.

Based upon this index, 152 subjects were classified as "definitely schizophrenic." Table 6 shows the prestige levels of patients by those of their fathers for this refined population. Although a greater proportion of this group are downwardly mobile than for the total group (42.7 per cent as compared to 36.4 per cent), a repeat of all previous

TABLE 6. PRESTIGE LEVEL OF PATIENT'S CURRENT OR LAST JOB BY PRESTIGE LEVEL OF FATHER'S JOB, FOR PATIENTS CLASSIFIED AS DEFINITELY SCHIZOPHRENIC

Occupational Prestige Level of Father	Occupational Prestige Level of Patient													Total N
	1–2		3		4		5		6		7			
	N	Per Cent	N	Per Cent	N	Per Cent	N	Per Cent	N	Per Cent	N	Per Cent		
1–2 (high)	4	50.0	0	0.0	3	8.7	0	0.0	1	2.2	1	3.8		9
3	1	12.5	3	33.3	4	11.8	2	6.8	5	11.1	0	0.0		15
4	1	12.5	0	0.0	4	11.8	4	13.3	7	15.6	5	19.2		21
5	2	25.0	3	33.3	14	41.2	16	53.3	17	37.8	10	38.5		62
6	0	0.0	1	11.2	5	14.7	4	13.3	10	22.2	6	23.1		26
7 (low)	0	0.0	2	22.2	4	11.8	4	13.3	5	11.1	4	15.4		19
Total	8	100.0	9	100.0	34	100.0	30	100.0	45	100.0	26	100.0		152

analyses using this population indicates no need for any revision in the findings already presented. In other words, the results based upon our rather heterogeneous sample do not differ materially from those that would have been derived had a more limited and homogeneous population been utilized.

The lost population.[27] A total of eighty-two cases (27.7 per cent of the total sample) that met all sample criteria were lost to interview. Of these, fifty-nine were counted as refusals, six of which resulted from the psychiatrist withholding permission to contact and fifty-three of which resulted from direct refusal by the patient or interference by a family member. The remaining twenty-three cases (7.7 per cent of the total sample) simply could not be traced.

TABLE 7. OCCUPATIONAL PRESTIGE
LEVEL DISTRIBUTION FOR LOST
PATIENT SAMPLE

Prestige Level	N	Per Cent
1–2 (high)	7	10.2
3	3	4.3
4	12	17.4
5	15	21.7
6	17	24.6
7 (low)	15	21.8
Unknown	13	—
Total	82	100.0

27 A detailed evaluation of the characteristics of our lost population is currently in preparation by Elmer Gardner, M.D., and the senior author of this paper. The evaluation will benefit from an unusually large amount of data on lost cases provided by the psychiatric register and other Monroe County facilities. The intended paper will also consider cases that are known to have moved out of the area. These cases are not considered in the present paper and are not represented in the percentage of lost cases shown above.

Although data on fathers' occupations were not available for the lost group, information on last or current job was obtained for all but thirteen of the lost patients. Table 7 presents the occupational prestige distribution for this lost population. Comparison of these data with that for the interviewed sample in Table 1 shows the two distributions to be quite similar. It appears that the only significant discrepancy occurs at the lowest occupational level. While level 7 is about three times overrepresented in the interviewed population, it is more than four times overrepresented in the lost group. Although some of the specific figures reported would no doubt be slightly modified by inclusion of these cases, it seems highly unlikely that the basic findings would, in any way, be altered. We take the position, therefore, that the 27.7 per cent sample mortality does not attach appreciable doubt to the conclusions of this paper.

SUMMARY AND CONCLUSIONS

An ongoing study of schizophrenic males provided an opportunity to study factors associated with the presumed relationship between social class and schizophrenia under conditions that minimized the objections often raised against such investigations. Analysis of patients' occupations supported the typical finding of a substantially disproportionate number of schizophrenics in the lowest occupational category.

In attempting to uncover the source of this overrepresentation, it was determined that the fathers of the patients were also overrepresented at the lowest prestige level, although to a lesser degree. This finding is consistent with the social causation hypothesis regarding the etiology of schizophrenia. Although this observation lent some general support to the view that social factors contribute to the occurrence of the disorder, it appeared to make only a minor contribution to the overrepresentation we sought to explain.

The detailed analysis of the occupational movement of patients relative to the position of their fathers clearly indicated that subject overrepresentation results primarily from downward mobility. Following this conclusion, an effort was made to distinguish the relative contributions of social selection (the failure of patients to ever attain expected levels) and social drift (the movement from higher-level to lower-level jobs within one's own career) to the observed downward mobility. These analyses led to the conclusion that social selection accounts, in largest measure, for the downward shift, with social drift making a relatively minor contribution.

Raymond Hunt, Orville Gursslin, and Jack Roach describe the influence of social class in determining who gets what kind of psychiatric care. Using another type of population, they attempted to replicate some aspects of the series of investigations by August Hollingshead and Frederick Redlich which show an inverse relationship between class and quality of psychiatric help.[1]

[1] Hollingshead and Redlich, *op. cit.*

SOCIAL STATUS AND PSYCHIATRIC SERVICE IN A CHILD-GUIDANCE CLINIC*

Raymond G. Hunt, *State University of New York at Buffalo*

Orville Gursslin, *Ohio University*

Jack L. Roach, *University of Connecticut*

The present investigation is an exploration of the relationship between psychiatric service and social class. It is an attempt to test the general findings of a number of previous studies[1] in a different treatment setting—a child-guidance clinic. The authors have also attempted to deal more directly with the status dimension in the case of practitioners than has been done here-

---

* From Raymond G. Hunt, Orville Gursslin, and Jack L. Roach, "Social Status and Psychiatric Service in a Child-Guidance Clinic," *American Sociological Review*, 23 (February 1958), 81–83. Reprinted by permission of the American Sociological Association.

[1] F. Auld and J. Myers, "Contributions to a Theory for Selecting Psychotherapy Patients," *Journal of Clinical Psychology*, 10 (1954), 56–60; A. B. Hollingshead and F. Redlich, "Social Stratification and Psychiatric Disorders," *American Sociological Review*, 18 (April 1953), 163–69; J. Myers and L. Schaffer, "Social Stratification and Psychiatric Practice," *American Sociological Review*, 19 (June 1954), 307–10; H. A. Robinson, F. C. Redlich, and J. K. Myers, "Social Stratification and Psychiatric Treatment," *American Journal of Orthopsychiatry*, 24 (1954), 307–16; A. E. Winder and M. Hersko, "The Effect of Social Class on the Length and Type of Psychotherapy in a Veteran's Administration Mental Hygiene Clinic," *Journal of Clinical Psychology*, 11 (1955), 77–79; W. S. Williams, "Class Differences in the Attitudes of Psychiatric Patients," *Social Problems*, 4 (January 1957), 240–44.

tofore. Factors other than degree of training were taken into consideration in determining their status rank. Included among these factors are seniority in the clinic; implicit evaluations of competency within the clinic; and "traditional" prestige differences among psychiatrist, psychologist, and social worker. Thus the status dimension employed here is largely specific to the particular treatment setting, thereby affording an opportunity more directly to assess the significance of this factor.

In addition, a second proposition was tested—that there is a relationship between the social status of the client and the length of treatment given.

PROCEDURE

Data relevant to the variables under investigation were obtained from records of those presently closed cases serviced in any capacity at a community child-guidance clinic during the period 1954–56. The clinic which provided the data offers complete psychiatric services to community residents through an open-referral system. Fees are charged according to a sliding scale based primarily upon income. Any dif-

ferential utilization of clinic services may thus be considered to be a function of variables other than fees.

The total patient population serviced at the clinic during the time period noted provided a subject pool of 246 cases. Every case for which necessary information was available is represented in the data reported below.

Each case was classified along a seven-point scale of social status according to the Occupational Scale of Hollingshead's Two-Factor Index of Social Position.[2] Similarly, members of the professional staff at the clinic were classified along a seven-point scale of professional status. The scale positions and their corresponding professional categories are as follows: (1) chief psychiatrist, (2) chief psychologist, (3) chief psychiatric social worker, (4) senior psychiatric social worker, (5) junior psychiatric social worker and junior psychologist, (6) intern psychologist, and (7) student psychiatric social worker.

Each case was entered in a five-step-interval frequency distribution according to total number of interviews. All interviews were then plotted independently against patient social status and worker professional status. Finally, cor-

TABLE 1. RELATIONSHIPS BETWEEN TOTAL NUMBER OF INTERVIEWS
AND WORKER AND PATIENT STATUS LEVELS

	Number of Interviews							
Status Levels	1–9		10–19		20 or More		Totals*	
1–3	100	75	4	7	9	10	113	92
4–7	101	113	6	12	11	10	118	135
Totals	201	188	10	19	20	20	231	227

Note: Italicized figures refer to total interviews $\times$ parent's worker status ($\chi^2 = 0.48$) and other figures to total interviews $\times$ client status ($\chi^2 = 0.91$).
* Variations in total Ns are a function of lack of relevant information in case records.

2 August B. Hollingshead, *Two Factor Index of Social Position* (New Haven, Conn.: August B. Hollingshead, 1957).

relations between the social status of patient and the professional status of worker were calculated.

RESULTS

Two general propositions were tested in the present study. First, it was postulated that simple amount of service (as reflected by number of interviews) would vary directly with the social status of the patient and/or the professional status of the worker. Secondly, it was postulated that the professional status of the worker active in a given case would vary directly with the social status of the client.

On the assumption that differences between adjacent intervals on either of the status scales would tend to be slight and probably variable it was decided that the most meaningful analysis of interview data could be obtained by calculating a χ^2 from the data classified into broad categories. These data are reported in Table 1. The analysis yielded χ^2s of 0.91 between client status and number of interviews and 0.48 be-

tween practitioner status and number of interviews. (For two degrees of freedom, neither of these was significant at the 0.05 level of confidence.)

Thus, for the population included in this study there appears to be no significant relationship between either social status of the client or professional status of the worker and amount of psychiatric service, as measured by total number of interviews.

In assessing the postulated relationship between the social status of the client and the professional status of the worker on the case, three independent correlations were obtained by calculation of coefficients of contingency. The first is a correlation betwen the social status of the client and the professional status of that worker handling the parent. The second is between the social status of the client and the professional status of that worker handling the child. It should be noted that, among child-guidance clinics, therapy is generally conceptualized as work with the child rather than with the parent. In addition, a coefficient of contingency was calculated between the social status of the client and the combined status

TABLE 2. RELATIONSHIPS BETWEEN STATUS LEVELS OF CLIENTS AND OF CLINIC STAFF WORKING WITH PARENT AND WITH CHILD

Worker Status Levels	Client Status Levels														
	1		2		3		4		5		6		7		Σf*
1	9	*7*	0	*5*	7	*2*	7	*0*	5	*3*	0	*1*	1	*2*	29 *20*
2	7	*7*	1	*6*	13	*0*	4	*1*	1	*3*	0	*0*	1	*0*	27 *17*
3	2	*5*	0	*5*	10	*1*	12	*1*	13	*8*	0	*1*	3	*1*	35 *22*
4	3	*2*	0	*10*	14	*1*	11	*0*	5	*9*	0	*0*	1	*1*	34 *23*
5	6	*0*	0	*7*	10	*2*	16	*5*	7	*6*	0	*0*	1	*1*	40 *21*
6	1	*1*	0	*4*	10	*2*	16	*4*	6	*9*	0	*1*	3	*0*	36 *21*
7	0	*0*	0	*3*	3	*0*	3	*0*	7	*4*	0	*3*	3	*1*	16 *11*
Σf	28	*22*	1	*40*	67	*8*	69	*11*	39	*42*	0	*6*	13	*6*	217 *135*

Note: Italicized figures refer to client status $\times$ parent's worker status ($C = 0.28$) and other figures to client status $\times$ child's worker status ($C = 0.48$).
* Variations in total Ns are a function of lack of relevant information in case records.

TABLE 3. RELATIONSHIP BETWEEN CLIENT STATUS LEVEL AND
MEDIAN STATUS RATINGS OF CLINIC STAFF WORKING
WITH BOTH PARENT AND CHILD

Median Worker Status Levels	Client Status Level							
	1	2	3	4	5	6	7	Σf
1–2	11	8	3	5	6	1	0	34
2.5–3.5	9	21	10	14	10	10	6	75
4–5	7	2	17	16	22	20	5	89
5.25–5.75	1	0	2	1	2	3	2	11
6–7	2	1	2	1	0	1	4	11
Σf	30	27	34	37	40	35	17	220

$C = 0.50$

of the workers handling both parent and child. In obtaining this last rating the median status rating of the two practitioners in the case was taken as reflecting their combined status. The results of these correlations are presented in Tables 2 and 3. When tested against the null hypothesis[3] each of these contingency coefficients is significant beyond the 0.05 level of confidence. Thus, while the relationship between the status level of the client and the professional status of the worker assigned to the parent is only slight, it must be remembered that work with the parent does not represent a "prestige" aspect of therapy in most child-guidance clinics. On the other hand, the relationship between status of client and worker in the case of the child is marked. In addition, it may be noted that these results indicate that when a client is of high social status, both parent and child are likely to work with professional workers of high status level. Hence, it may be concluded that a fairly strong, significant relationship exists between the social status of the client and the professional status of the worker handling the case, especially when a therapeutic function is involved. Thus the results of this investigation confirm the second postulate cited above, at least within the patient population studied.

CONCLUSIONS

The failure to confirm the hypothesis with reference to length of service is at variance with the results of previous studies. However, the present findings (that length of service varied independently of either client or worker status) are far from conclusive because of a marked skewness in the distribution of number of interviews. Better than 50 per cent of the cases were seen for fewer than five interviews, and were about evenly distributed among the status categories. Thus a peculiarity of the treatment setting supplying the data prevents unequivocal analysis of the length-of-service factor. It is of passing interest that the mean length of service

---

3 H. E. Garrett, *Statistics in Psychology and Education* (New York: Longmans, Green & Co., 1947).

in the clinic was between six and seven interviews—not particularly lengthy as psychiatric treatment goes.

With respect to the relationship between client and practitioner statuses the results are consistent with previous investigations. The modification of prior researches with regard to the assignment of practitioner status intervals seems to support the hypothesis that status dimensions per se are important determinants in the assignment of cases.

Whatever the importance of these factors, it may be concluded that the professional status of members of psychiatric clinic staffs working with particular clients tends to vary directly with the social status of those clients. The factors determining this relationship remain a matter for intensive investigation.

FAMILY DISCORD AND MARITAL DISRUPTION

The Great Depression sparked much interest in the effects of economic deprivation on family life.[1] Following World War II, concern shifted to the middle-class family. Although most community studies of the past several decades presented findings on class-linked variations in family stability, prior to 1950 comparatively little writing by family specialists dealt with cross-class comparisons. Since that time they have used social stratification more frequently as a variable in research on family pathology. The two most characteristic findings are: (1) a rough inverse correlation between socioeconomic level and all forms of marital dissolution[2] and (2) significant differences in the nature of family discord—e.g., types of problems, forms and intensity of conflict—between lower-class families and families of the middle and upper ranges.[3]

The selections by William Kephart and by Karen Hillman illustrate research in which indices of social stratification are found to be inversely related to marital dissolution. While Hillman's study supports Kephart's findings, the former's approach suggests the need for adequate controls of demographic variables to avoid spurious correlations.

[1] For example, Robert C. Angell, *The Family Encounters the Depression* (New York: Charles Scribner's Sons, 1936); Reuben Hill and Elsie Boulding, *Families Under Stress* (New York: Harper, 1949); Ruth S. Cavan and Katherine Ranck, *The Family and the Depression* (Chicago: University of Chicago Press, 1938); Earl H. Koos, *Families in Trouble* (New York: Kings Crown Press, 1946).

[2] William Goode, *After Divorce* (Glencoe, Ill.: The Free Press, 1956), Chaps. 4 and 5; J. Richard Udry, "Marital Instability by Race, Sex, Education, and Occupation Using 1960 Census Data," *American Journal of Sociology*, 72 (September 1966), 203–9.

[3] John C. Cuber and Peggy B. Harroff, *Sex and the Significant Americans* (Baltimore: Penguin Books, Inc., 1966); Orville G. Brim *et al.*, "Relations Between Family Problems," *Marriage and Family Living*, 23 (August 1961), 219–26; August B. Hollingshead, "Class Differences in Family Stability," in *Class, Status, and Power*, eds. Reinhard Bendix and Seymour M. Lipset (Glencoe, Ill.: The Free Press, 1953), pp. 284–92; Earl L. Koos, "Class Differences in Family Reactions to Crisis," *Marriage and Family Living*, 12 (Summer 1950), 77–99; Jerome K. Myers and Bertram H. Roberts, *Family and Class Dynamics in Mental Illness* (New York: John Wiley & Sons, Inc., 1959); Lee Rainwater, *And the Poor Get Children* (Chicago: Quadrangle Books, 1960).

OCCUPATIONAL LEVEL AND MARITAL DISRUPTION*

William M. Kephart

University of Pennsylvania

BACKGROUND

Because of the absence of a centralized federal collection of marriage and divorce records, "family" statistics are discouragingly few. Through the establishment of a national registration area for births and deaths, a wealth of statistical information has accrued in these areas, in contrast to the dearth of national statistics in the significant areas of marriage and divorce. While the sociological literature abounds with factual material relating to birth rates, death rates, infant mortality, morbidity, and life expectancy, some of the most basic facts about divorce remain unknown. For example, there are no *national divorce statistics* to indicate whether the Negro divorce rate is higher or lower than that of whites, whether the remarriages of divorced persons are more or less stable than first marriages, whether divorce is more prevalent among the educated or the uneducated, or whether the age (or relative age differences) at the time of marriage is related to marital stability.

In the absence of national divorce data, researchers in the family field have utilized other sources in an attempt to supply the missing information: Kephart and Monahan compared the racial and nativity proportions in county divorce cases with comparable population figures derived from U. S. Census tabulations;[1] Jacobson explored relationships between presence of children and divorce by analyzing data collected from county and state vital statistics offices;[2] working with divorce records of Iowa and Missouri, Monahan analyzed the relationship between remarriages and divorce;[3] Christensen and Meissner, examining county birth, marriage and divorce records, reported on premarital pregnancy as a factor in divorce;[4] Kephart and Strohm, utilizing local divorce records and newspaper marriage listings, investigated the stability of "Gretna Green" marriages;[5] on the basis of his own interview-study with divorcees, together with data derived from previous studies, Goode

* From William M. Kephart, "Occupational Level and Marital Disruption," *American Sociological Review*, 20 (August 1955), 456–65. Reprinted by permission of the American Sociological Association.

[1] William M. Kephart and Thomas P. Monahan, "Desertion and Divorce in Philadelphia," *American Sociological Review*, 17 (December 1952), 719–27.

[2] Paul H. Jacobson, "Differentials in Divorce by Duration of Marriage and Size of Family," *American Sociological Review*, 15 (April 1950), 235–44.

[3] Thomas P. Monahan, "How Stable Are Remarriages?" *American Journal of Sociology*, 57 (November 1952), 280–88.

[4] Harold T. Christensen and Hanna H. Meissner, "Premarital Pregnancy as a Factor in Divorce," *American Sociological Review*, 18 (December 1953), 641–44.

[5] William M. Kephart and Rolf B. Strohm, "The Stability of Gretna Green Marriages," *Sociology and Social Research*, 36 (May–June 1952), 291–96.

reexamined the relationship between economic factors and divorce.[6] There are other examples, and the foregoing list is merely illustrative of the areas that have been studied. These studies have been published within the last few years, and nearly all have a common motivating factor; i.e., they were undertaken primarily because of the absence of national divorce data bearing upon the specific area that was investigated. And in the foreseeable future it is probably through these segmental studies that our statistical knowledge of the factors associated with marital discord will be increased to a fund of respectable proportion. The purpose of the present paper is to shed additional light on the relationship between occupational factors and marital disruption.

In passing, it might be mentioned that the whole area of marital stability and socioeconomic status has received little attention from research sociologists. Students of the class structure, for example, have shown little or no interest in relative class frequencies of divorce and separation. And while the major marital adjustment surveys have all included an analysis of socioeconomic variables, for very practical reasons all of these surveys—with the exception of Harvey Locke's[7]—have centered attention largely or entirely on the upper-middle and upper classes. In the smaller psychological or sociological studies reporting on specific phases of marital adjustment, sexual factors and personality patterns have been investigated extensively while socioeconomic variables are largely ignored. Goode pinpointed the discrepancy when he said:

It is an interesting commentary on recent sociological history that while we have tended to reject economic factors partly because they are on another emergent level, we have not done the same with so-called personality factors. Rather, we have used the latter as standard tools in our sociological analyses of the family, although they are as clearly on a different emergent level as economic or political variables. This has led us to stress the "causative" character of personality and psychodynamic variables in the shaping of economic processes, and to gloss over the real possibility that economic variables may equally well be important in the shaping of personality structures.[8]

It is hoped that the following analysis will focus sociological attention on the need for a wider examination of the role of socioeconomic factors in marital adjustment.

DIVORCE

The last attempt by the Census Bureau (or by the National Office of Vital Statistics) to secure occupational information from *divorce records* was for the period 1887–1906. For this period the occupational distribution of divorced husbands was compared to that of married males in the population, the latter being derived from census data for the year 1900. The tabular comparisons indicated that actors, musicians, commercial travelers, and doctors had the greatest over-representation in divorce, although no discernible socioeconomic pattern emerges when the divorce ratios are arranged by major occupational categories.[9] In any case, these early data

6 William J. Goode, "Economic Factors and Marital Stability," *American Sociological Review*, 16 (December 1951), 802–12.

7 Harvey J. Locke, *Predicting Adjustment in Marriage: A Comparison of a Divorced and a Happily Married Group* (New York: Henry Holt and Co., 1951).

8 Goode, *op. cit.*, p. 803.

9 Bureau of the Census, *Marriage and Divorce, 1887–1906,* Bulletin 96 (2nd ed.) (Washington, D. C.: Government Printing Office, 1913), pp. 46–51.

were routinely incorporated and interpreted by writers of family texts. It became habitual for text writers, basing their conclusions on the 1887–1906 data, to state, in effect, that "divorce characterized persons whose occupations call for contact with the opposite sex under conditions conducive to familiarity." Divorce rates, for example, were said to be high among doctors "not merely because the physician has numerous contacts with attractive women, but also because the physician's wife is forced to lead a restricted social life." There is no reason to list the texts nor to parody the sometimes ingenious interpretations. It is true, though, that uncritical acceptance of these early divorce data was characteristic of practically all of the most widely used family texts and indicates an almost blind faith in the Census tabulation.

In a paper read at the March, 1951, meeting of the Eastern Sociological Society, the writer cautioned against the wholesale acceptance of the data published in the 1887–1906 Census Report. Actually such a caution should have been unnecessary inasmuch as the limitations of the data are clearly stated in the Report itself. The very first paragraph dealing with occupations begins as follows:

> An attempt was made to secure a statement of the occupation of the husbands involved in the divorce suits, but the effort cannot be characterized as successful. An occupation was reported for but 226,760 divorced husbands, only 24 per cent of the total number divorced during the period covered by this investigation. . . .
> Returns so incomplete can hardly be accepted as typical, or as indicating the proportion of divorced men in the different occupations. . . . The comparison would not be so unreliable and unsatisfactory if the degree of incompleteness had been the same for all parts

of the country. This, however, was not the case. In some states a return of occupation was received for 50 per cent or more of the total number of divorces. In New Jersey the percentage reached 81.1. In other states practically no returns were received. . . . Moreover, it is probable that the occupation is more apt to be recorded in those cases where alimony is asked than in other cases. . . . Perhaps the only safe conclusion that could be deduced from the above [occupational] table, is that a large proportion of the persons obtaining divorces come from those occupations in which a large proportion of the population are engaged.[10]

Partly because of textbook acceptance and interpretation of this early material, and perhaps also because of the "drawing room manner" of depicting divorce by Hollywood and by fiction writers, the impression grew that divorce was largely a middle- and upper-class phenomenon. Contrary findings—ecological studies by Bossard[11] and Schroeder,[12] and an occupational study by Weeks based on the children of divorced and nondivorced parents[13]—went largely unnoticed until William Goode's recent survey.[14] After a recapitulation of the previous studies, together with a presentation of occupational data drawn from his own study of divorcees, Goode concludes that "there is a rough inverse correlation be-

---

10 Bureau of the Census, *op. cit.*, pp. 46–48.

11 James H. S. Bossard and Thelma Dillon, "Spatial Distribution of Divorced Women," *American Journal of Sociology*, 40 (1935), 503–7.

12 Clarence W. Schroeder, *Divorce in a City of 100,000 Population* (Peoria, Ill.: Bradley Polytechnic Institute Library, 1939).

13 H. Ashley Weeks, "Differential Divorce Rates by Occupations," *Social Forces*, 21 (March 1943), 334–37.

14 Goode, *op. cit.*

tween economic status and rate of divorce."[15] His conceptual analysis of the interrelatedness of marital stability and economic patterns appears to be one of the most definitive yet made on the subject.

The Weeks study,[16] based on the responses of Spokane school children, showed the following relationship between occupation and divorce rate (number of divorces per 100 families):

Professional	*6.8*
Proprietors	*8.4*
Clerical	*10.4*
Skilled	*11.6*
Semiskilled	*13.4*
Unskilled	*7.3*

The April, 1949, Sample Census Survey[17] contained occupational data "by sex and marital status," and by dividing the "married, wife present" per cent into that of "other marital status," Goode computed an occupational index of what he termed "proneness to divorce."[18] His figures are as follows:

Professional	*67.7*
Proprietors	*68.6*
Clerical and sales	*71.8*
Skilled	*86.6*
Semiskilled	*94.5*
Service	*254.7*
Unskilled	*180.3*

On the basis of his own study of divorced mothers, Goode's corresponding figures are as follows:[19]

Professional, proprietors	*62.6*
Clerical, sales, service	*63.6*

15 *Ibid.*, p. 803.
16 Weeks, *op. cit.*
17 Bureau of the Census, *Current Population Reports, Labor Force*, Series P–50, No. 22 (April 19, 1950), Table 5, pp. 11–12.
18 Goode, *op. cit.*, p. 805.
19 *Ibid.*

Skilled	*89.9*
Semiskilled	*142.4*
Unskilled	*166.7*

All of the above studies have certain weaknesses which were unavoidable because of the nature of the project design. The Weeks and Goode studies dealt with the occupations of *parents*, whereas a large proportion of divorced couples are childless. Such studies may contain a systematic error. The Sample Census Survey classified a divorced-but-remarried-person as married, not as divorced. Since most divorcees remarry, the Survey computations may contain a residual bias.

In spite of their limitations, however, these studies offer valuable clues to a hitherto clouded issue. Moreover, they are in general agreement, and, as Goode has pointed out, when they are analyzed in conjunction with the previously mentioned ecological surveys by Bossard and Schroeder, the evidence all points in the same direction; i.e., toward a rough inverse relationship between frequency of divorce and occupational level.

The writer's occupational data, based on a study of 1,434 Philadelphia divorces[20] has the advantage of being derived directly from a random sample of *divorce records*, the first such transcription since the often-interpreted 1887–1906 Census data. Major occupational groupings for males in the divorce sample were compared with male occupational categories for the City of Philadelphia, and these data appear in Table 1.

It can be seen that the upper occupation levels—the professional and managerial (proprietors) categories—are clearly underrepresented in divorce

20 For an account of the methodology employed in the Philadelphia study, see Kephart and Monahan, *op. cit.*, pp. 722–23.

TABLE 1. PERCENTAGE DISTRIBUTION
BY OCCUPATIONAL CATEGORIES OF
TOTAL MALES AGED 14 AND OVER
IN PHILADELPHIA IN 1940 AND
1950, AND A SAMPLE OF MALE
DIVORCEES IN PHILA-
DELPHIA, 1937–1950

Occupational Category	Total Males 1940*	Total Males 1950†	Males in Divorce Sample 1937–1950‡
Professional	6.3	7.9	4.3
Proprietors	10.6	10.8	5.0
Clerical and sales	19.3	17.5	19.6
Skilled	20.6	22.3	20.4
Semiskilled	24.5	23.9	35.4
Labor-service	18.7	17.6	15.3

Sources: 1940 figures—*Sixteenth Census
of the United States, 1940 Population,*
Vol. III, The Labor Force, Part 5,
Reports by States: Pennsylvania-Wyo-
ming, Table 20, p. 121. 1950 figures—
Seventeenth Decennial Census, 1950, Vol.
II, Part 38, Pennsylvania, Table 35, pp.
38–135.
* $N = 485,086$, including 3,704 occupations
not reported.
† $N = 552,711$, including 6,500 occupations
not reported.
‡ $N = 1,434$.

actions; the middle groups—clerical,
sales, and skilled workers (craftsmen,
foremen)—are represented to the degree that would be expected on the
basis of their population ratios, while
the semiskilled (operatives) occupations
are overrepresented. Thus, the Philadelphia findings are in general agreement
with the previous studies which point
to a rough inverse correlation between
occupational level and frequency of
divorce. The slight underrepresentation
in divorce at the bottom labor-service
category (Table 1) may or may not
reflect the actual situation. While it is
relatively simple to classify the upper
and middle occupational groups, it is
more difficult to separate the semiskilled

and the unskilled workers on the basis
of the information contained in the
divorce record. Perhaps the safest generalization would be that the upper
occupational levels are underrepresented, the middle occupational groups
"hold their own," and the lower occupational levels are overrepresented in
divorce actions.

DESERTION

After analyzing the Philadelphia divorce data, it was the writer's belief
that marital patterns of the lowest occupational level—the laborer or unskilled group—might be better understood in terms of the high desertion
rate that is commonly attributed to this
class. For many, many years desertion
has been referred to in family texts as
"the poor man's divorce." The writer
discovered, however, that this latter
phrase is one of the cliches that apparently has no empirical basis. In fact,
the desertion "studies" that are still
being quoted in family texts are, for the
most part, reports that emanated from
social workers or charitable organizations from twenty to fifty years ago;
e.g., reports by Z. Smith in 1901,[21]
Lilian Brandt in 1905,[22] Earle E. Eubank in 1916,[23] Joanna C. Colcord in
1918.[24] Even the statistical studies of

[21] Z. D. Smith, *Deserted Wives and
Deserting Husbands: A Study of 234 Fami-
lies,* Publication No. 75 (Boston: Associated
Charities of Boston, 1901).
[22] Lilian Brandt, *574 Deserters and
Their Families* (New York: The Charity
Organization Society, 1905).
[23] Earle E. Eubank, *A Study of Family
Desertions* (doctoral dissertation, private
edition of the University of Chicago, 1916).
[24] Joanna C. Colcord, "Desertion and
Non-Support in Family Case Work," *The
Annals of the American Academy of Political
and Social Science* (May 1918), 91–102.
Joanna C. Colcord, *Broken Homes, A Study
of Family Desertion and Its Social Treat-*

desertion and nonsupport that were done somewhat later by Patterson[25] and Mowrer[26] contained no clue to the occupations of the husbands, despite the fact that these studies were based on municipal court records.

Failing to unearth any pertinent statistical information, the writer secured the permission of the Philadelphia Municipal Court in 1952 to make an occupational analysis of all the desertion and nonsupport cases for the year 1950. This year was selected so that the desertion cases could be compared occupationally with the decennial census data and also with the aforementioned Philadelphia divorce sample. So far as the writer is aware, the end result was the first series of tabulations in the United States dealing specifically with the occupational distribution of desertion cases.[27] Since the writer was permitted to record the occupational information directly onto the Court's punch-cards, it was possible, in the subsequent analysis, to hold constant such items as the Court routinely collects; e.g., race, nativity, marital status, religion, and type of ceremony. Before

these data are presented, it might be well to comment on the general prevalence of desertion in the United States.

There are various kinds of extralegal or "informal" marital separations, and from time to time United States census figures have given some idea of their prevalence. In addition to the Sample Surveys of the type previously mentioned, the 1940 decennial census revealed that there were 3.1 million married persons who were not living with their spouses as compared to some 1.4 million who stated that they had been divorced.[28]

Many of these separations ultimately become divorces, although apparently large numbers do not. It is quite possible that of the various kinds of extralegal separations, desertion is numerically the most significant. In metro-

ment (New York: Russell Sage Foundation, 1919).

[25] S. H. Patterson, "Family Desertion and Non-Support," *Journal of Delinquency* (September 1922), 249–82, and (November 1922), 299–333.

[26] E. R. Mowrer, *Family Disorganization* (rev. ed.) (Chicago: University of Chicago Press, 1939). See also "The Trend and Ecology of Family Disintegration in Chicago," *American Sociological Review*, 3 (June 1938), 344–53.

[27] The writer is indebted to John Reinemann, Director of Probation for the Philadelphia Municipal Court, who was instrumental in making the Court records available, and to Thomas Monahan, Assistant Statistician for the Court, who made the necessary runs on the I.B.M. cards and who provided a number of invaluable suggestions.

TABLE 2. DIVORCES AND DESERTIONS: PHILADELPHIA, SELECTED YEARS

Year	Number of Divorces	Number of Desertions
1915	878	3,832
1920	1,960	3,924
1925	1,780	4,559
1930	1,825	4,178
1935	1,497	3,617
1940	1,842	3,584
1945	3,476	3,600
1950	3,167	2,191*

* The relatively small number of desertions in 1950 is due primarily to a different system of classifying "friendly service" cases; i.e., those cases involving intrafamily quarreling which resulted in no formal action. In recent years the number of these cases has increased.

[28] See William F. Ogburn, "Marital Separations," *American Journal of Sociology,* 49 (January 1944), 316–23.

politan areas, for example, there is evidence to indicate that, over the years, desertion is much more prevalent than divorce. Comparative figures for Philadelphia reveal that for a period of almost four decades the number of desertions has greatly exceeded that of divorces. (See Table 2.)

The figures in Table 2 do not denote the actual number of desertions in Philadelphia for those years, but represent only the cases reported to the Municipal Court. The term "desertion," incidentally, as it refers to Philadelphia data, signifies desertion or non-support of the wife, the wife and child, or the child only. In typical desertion cases the wife comes to court primarily because the husband has reneged on his financial obligations. The court endeavors to locate the husband and—with the ultimate recourse to a support order—attempts to get him to resume his familial responsibilities. The legal involvements which a deserted wife formerly encountered have been

largely eliminated under a policy by which the court more or less "takes the side of the wife" in her quest for family support. The impetus for handling desertion cases in this manner increased greatly following the establishment of the first family court in Cincinnati, Ohio, in 1914.

It should also be mentioned that the racial factor is much more significant in desertion than in divorce. While the Negro divorce rate in Philadelphia has been increasing, the figure is still somewhat below the rate of divorce among whites. In desertion cases, however, Negroes are overrepresented, as the following figures indicate:

Year	Number of Philadelphia Desertions	Per Cent Nonwhite	Per Cent Nonwhite Married Males in Philadelphia
1940	3,584	24.0	12.5
1950	2,191	40.3	17.1

TABLE 3. PERCENTAGE DISTRIBUTION BY OCCUPATIONAL CATEGORY, RACE, NATIVITY, AND PREVIOUS MARITAL STATUS OF DESERTING HUSBANDS, PHILADELPHIA, 1950

	All Cases (N=2191)	White (N=1305)	Native White (N=1143)	Native White First Marriages (N=922)	Nonwhite (N=886)	Nonwhite First Marriages (N=783)	Foreign Born (N=162)
Professional	2.4	3.4	3.1	2.7	0.9	1.0	5.6
Proprietors	6.3	9.3	8.5	7.5	1.9	1.4	14.8
Clerical and sales	10.1	11.9	12.5	12.7	7.6	7.4	7.4
Skilled	13.7	19.0	18.8	18.6	5.8	5.4	20.3
Semiskilled	30.2	30.6	31.3	31.8	29.6	30.4	25.9
Service	8.2	8.2	6.1	6.0	11.2	11.1	6.2
Unskilled	14.2	6.3	6.1	6.6	26.0	25.9	7.4
Unemployed	9.0	7.6	7.9	8.1	11.0	11.4	5.6
Not reported	5.9	5.8	5.7	6.0	6.0	6.0	6.8
	100.0	100.0	100.0	100.0	100.0	100.0	100.0

For most purposes, also, it is desirable to give separate statistical treatment to the foreign born and to the remarried.[29]

Turning now to the data that were collected from the Municipal Court records, Table 3 shows the occupational distribution of the foregoing groups as they were involved in the 1950 Philadelphia desertion cases.

While the data in Table 2 show the nonwhites to be concentrated in the lower occupational classes, the remarkable finding is that in none of the white groups represented is there any substantial justification for referring to desertion as the "poor man's divorce"! As a matter of fact, *43.6 per cent of the white desertions are derived from the upper half of the occupational ladder.* Moreover, when the occupational distribution of Philadelphia desertion cases is compared to that of the Philadelphia divorce sample, a surprising degree of similarity is evident. These comparative figures are shown in Table 4. In order to make the divorce and desertion cases comparable, both sets of data have been refined to include only native-white first marriages.

The figures in Table 4 are indeed striking. The supposed preponderance of desertion cases in the lower occupational levels fails to emerge. True, in the bottom labor-service category the desertion cases show a slightly higher figure than in the divorce sample—14.8 to 11.8 per cent respectively—but this situation is reversed in the semiskilled class. Combining the two lowest groups —the labor-service and the semiskilled —we find 50.3 per cent of the divorces falling into these categories as com-

---

TABLE 4. PERCENTAGE DISTRIBUTION BY OCCUPATIONAL CATEGORY OF MALE DESERTERS AND DIVORCEES: NATIVE WHITE FIRST MARRIAGES, PHILADELPHIA, 1950

Occupational Category	Divorce Sample (N=939)	Desertion Cases (N=922*)
Professional	4.9	3.1
Proprietors	4.4	8.7
Clerical and sales	20.4	14.8
Skilled	20.0	21.6
Semiskilled	38.6	37.0
Labor-service	11.7	14.8
	100.0	100.0

* Including seventy-five unemployed and fifty-five cases in which the occupation was not reported.

pared to 51.8 per cent of the desertions. Moreover, in both the proprietor and skilled worker groups the desertions show a higher percentage than the divorces!

Perhaps the most meaningful comparison, for our purposes, is that between the occupational distribution of males in the Philadelphia desertion cases and the occupational distribution found in the Philadelphia male population, with race held constant. Unfortunately for sociologists, the 1950 Census volumes were concentrated on metropolitan areas rather than on cities with respect to items such as occupation and income. However, it was possible to procure satisfactory occupational data by race for the City of Philadelphia by utilizing 1950 census tract figures. The resulting comparison between the occupational categories existing in the city and those represented in the Philadelphia desertion cases is shown in Table 5.

Among both whites and Negroes it is

---

[29] For a tabular analysis of the extent to which these groups are involved in Philadelphia divorce and desertion cases, see Kephart and Monahan, *op. cit.*, pp. 724, 726.

evident that the upper occupational classes are underrepresented in desertions (Table 5). When the bottom three occupational categories (service,

TABLE 5. PERCENTAGE DISTRIBUTION BY OCCUPATIONAL CATEGORY AND RACE OF TOTAL MALES AGED 14 AND OVER, AND OF DESERTING HUSBANDS, PHILADELPHIA, 1950

Occupational Category	Whites		Nonwhites	
	Total Males*	Deserting Husbands†	Total Males‡	Deserting Husbands§
Professional	8.2	3.7	2.2	1.0
Proprietors	11.4	9.8	2.8	2.0
Clerical and sales	17.8	12.6	8.0	8.0
Skilled	22.6	20.2	10.1	6.1
Semiskilled	22.3	32.5	21.5	31.5
Service	7.0	6.4	17.0	12.0
Laborer	4.6	6.7	25.0	27.6
Unemployed	6.1	8.1	13.4	11.8
	100.0	100.0	100.0	100.0

Sources: United States Bureau of the Census, *U. S. Census of Population, 1950,* Vol. III, Census Tract Statistics, pp. 57, 205–11. The nonwhite figures, column 3, are based on Census Tracts containing 250 or more nonwhite persons. The white figures, column 1, include total civilian labor force for Census Tracts containing fewer than 250 nonwhites.

* N=502, 481, including 4,905 cases in which occupation was not reported.

† N=1,305, including seventy-six cases in which occupation was not reported.

‡ N=92,956, including 1,595 cases in which occupation was not reported.

§ N=886, including fifty-three cases in which occupation was not reported.

laborer, and unemployed) are combined, the figures indicate that for the whites these classes are slightly overrepresented in desertions, while among Negroes, surprisingly, these classes are slightly underrepresented. Again, the supposed *predominance* of desertions at the lower end of the occupational scale fails to emerge. Among the whites the laborer and semiskilled groups are equally overrepresented in desertion cases, while among the Negroes the greatest overrepresentation is found in the semiskilled category. Also among whites, and to a lesser extent among Negroes, it can be seen that the proprietor group is well in evidence in Philadelphia desertions.

The Philadelphia Municipal Court has not published occupational tables in any of its Annual Reports, the present material being derived and classified by the writer directly from Court records. In the 1952 Annual Report, however, a small statistical study is reported, one section of which shows some similarity to the occupational data reported above.

> The study was based on a random sample of 118 cases of wives coming to court with a complaint of assault and battery. . . . In this small group of cases no professional occupations were found and only one semiprofessional person, a draftsman. . . . The clerical group was only moderately in evidence; but the proprietor and official class were well represented . . . among the whites the indication is that the husbands are primarily found in the skilled and semi-skilled occupations . . . therefore, the cases coming to court are from the middle economic classes. . . .[30]

Prior divorce in desertion cases. It should be kept in mind that a signifi-

---

[30] Philadelphia Municipal Court, *Annual Report* (1952), pp. 155–58.

cant percentage of desertion cases end in the divorce court, although under present reporting procedures it is not possible to determine what this figure is. Our Philadelphia data do show that in 15.9 per cent of the native white and 7.9 per cent of the Negro desertion cases one or both spouses had a prior divorce. The Negro group was too small to permit an occupational analysis, although among the native whites a previous divorce experience was found to vary directly with occupational level. (See Table 6.)

Type of marriage ceremony in desertion cases. Evidence adduced from various marital adjustment studies suggest a positive relationship between religious devoutness and marital happiness. There also seems to be a relation between type of marriage ceremony and later adjustment. Locke, for example, states that "Being married by a justice of the peace is not preferred in our culture and is unquestionably associated with maladjustment in marriage ... more than 1 in 4 divorced men and women were married by a justice of the peace as compared with 1 in 8 happily married men and women."[31] "Gretna Green" marriages have also been found to be characterized by a relatively high divorce rate.[32] It would be expected therefore, that marriages which ultimately end in desertion or divorce would show a relatively high percentage of civil ceremonies—and such seems to be the case. Philadelphia data reveal that for native-white first marriages approximately one-fifth of the divorce and one-fourth of the desertion cases had been married by a civil ceremony. This is probably higher than the city-wide marriage figure, although

TABLE 6. PERCENTAGE DISTRIBUTION BY OCCUPATIONAL CATEGORY OF NATIVE WHITE DESERTIONS INVOLVING A PRIOR DIVORCE BY ONE OR BOTH PARTIES, PHILADELPHIA, 1950

Occupational Category	Number of Cases	Prior Divorce
Professional	36	25.0
Proprietors	97	24.7
Clerical and sales	143	24.7
Skilled	215	15.8
Semiskilled	358	16.5
Service	69	13.0
Laborer	70	11.4
Unemployed	90	10.0
Not reported	65	9.2
Total	1,143	

comparative data are not currently available.

Since there appears to be a rough inverse relationship between frequency of divorce and desertion, and occupational level, it is also logical to expect that the lower occupational classes would be characterized by an undue proportion of civil ceremonies. While comparable occupational-marriage data are not presently available, the Philadelphia desertion data show the expected occupational trend *for native whites.* A discernible pattern for nonwhites fails to emerge. Both sets of data, refined to include first marriages only, are shown in Table 7.

The religious factor in desertion cases. Ever since Mowrer's Chicago studies in the 1920's and 1930's[33] it has been known that the major religious groups are not proportionately represented in white desertions. The Chicago data revealed that Catholics were overrepresented while the Protes-

31 Locke, *op. cit.*, p. 238.
32 Kephart and Strohm, *op. cit.*, pp. 291–96.

33 See footnote 26.

TABLE 7. PERCENTAGE MARRIED IN RELIGIOUS CEREMONY BY OCCUPATION AND COLOR

Per Cent Married in Religious Ceremony:

Occupational Category*	Native Whites	Nonwhites
Professional	88.0	75.0
Proprietors	79.7	100.0
Clerical and sales	75.2	93.1
Skilled	76.6	71.4
Semiskilled	72.7	76.9
Service	71.4	73.0
Laborer	67.2	82.3
Unemployed	69.3	82.0
Not reported	63.6	87.2

* For numerical totals see Table 3.

tants and Jews were underrepresented. This situation also obtains in Baltimore[34] and Philadelphia,[35] at least in those years for which data are available. The disproportionate religious representation in desertions is believed to be of importance in the present analysis since there is also a general occupational distortion among Catholics, Protestants, and Jews. It it theoretically possible, for example, that Catholics are overrepresented in desertions because they are unduly concentrated in the desertion-prone occupational categories. In an effort to shed some light on this question, the Philadelphia desertion data were analyzed in terms of occupational-religious frequencies. Table 8 shows the percentage distribution of occupational categories in native-white desertions as they occur among the various religious and mixed-religious groupings.

Philadelphia data show clearly that Jewish desertions are found primarily in the upper occupational brackets, in

TABLE 8. PERCENTAGE DISTRIBUTION BY OCCUPATIONAL CATEGORY OF NATIVE WHITE MALE DESERTERS, BY RELIGION OF HUSBAND, AND WIFE, PHILADELPHIA, 1950*

Occupational Category	Both Catholic (N=431)	Both Protestant (N=197)	Both Jewish (N=83)	Husband Protestant, Wife Catholic (N=100)	Husband Catholic, Wife Protestant (N=95)
Professional	1.6	4.1	7.2	2.0	1.0
Proprietors	5.6	7.1	22.9	7.0	3.2
Clerical and sales	11.1	13.7	30.1	6.0	8.4
Skilled	17.2	21.8	13.3	19.0	24.2
Semiskilled	35.5	28.4	12.1	38.0	33.7
Service	7.2	6.1	4.8	4.0	3.2
Laborer	7.4	5.6	0.0	10.0	6.3
Unemployed	8.6	7.1	4.8	11.0	9.5
Not reported	5.8	6.1	4.8	3.0	10.5
	100.0	100.0	100.0	100.0	100.0

* Excludes sixteen cases classified " other " religion.

[34] See Probation Department, Supreme Bench of Baltimore City, *Annual Reports, 1935–1938.*

[35] See Thomas P. Monahan and William M. Kephart, "Divorce and Desertion by Religious and Mixed-Religious Groups," *American Journal of Sociology*, 59 (March 1954), 454–65.

contrast to the Catholic, Protestant, and mixed Catholic-Protestant groups (Table 8). It is evident also that the Protestant desertions, on the whole, derive from a higher occupational level than Catholic cases. However, with the exception of the professional category, the differences between the Protestant and the Catholic occupational hierarchies are only moderate, albeit consistent. In the absence of *city-wide* occupational figures classified by major religious groups, no definitive statement can be made regarding the data in Table 8. In view of the moderate differences between the Protestant and Catholic occupational derivations in Philadelphia desertion cases, however, it appears that the overrepresentation of Catholics in these cases is only partially explainable by the occupational factor.

Other possible reasons involved in Catholic desertions are: (a) marital conflicts which stem from differing nationality backgrounds, (b) the fact that the Catholic Church does not recognize divorce, (c) differential reporting rates between Catholics and non-Catholics insofar as those desertion cases coming to court are concerned.

CONCLUDING REMARKS

On the basis of the Philadelphia findings, as well as those of prior studies, there appears to be a rough inverse correlation between frequency of divorce and occupational level. When Philadelphia desertion cases were analyzed by occupational level, the idea of the "poor man's divorce" failed to materialize, at least to the degree that had been expected; in fact, when the bottom three occupational categories (service, laborer, unemployed) are combined, the figures indicate that for the whites these groups are only slightly overrepresented in desertion cases, while among Negroes, surprisingly, these categories are slightly underrepresented.

The above findings raise a perplexing question, namely, what *is* the family stability pattern of the lowest occupational level? Is it possible that this bottom socioeconomic rung maintains stronger family ties than has been supposed? This is questionable in view of the marital-adjustment studies wherein a positive correlation is found between marital happiness and home ownership, steadiness of income, etc.

Another possibility is underreporting; i.e., perhaps the lowest occupational groups experience widespread desertions which are not reported in the same ratio as the middle or upper occupational groups. Deserted wives in this instance may not wish to see their husbands return and may not report their spouses to the Court. This could account for the fact that among Negroes the lowest classes are underrepresented in reported desertion cases, since in these groups the failure of the husband to assume his marital responsibilities is still a lingering tradition. Another reason for possible underreporting among the wives of the bottom class might involve ignorance of the law, or a sense of futility in "trying to get blood out of a stone."

Balanced against such possibilities is the fact that these (lower class) wives *must* have family support, and they cannot get relief from the Department of Public Assistance so long as they have a husband whom they have not reported to the Court. Since the Department of Public Assistance is the only money-giving organization in the city, it can be argued logically that if there is any underreporting of desertion and nonsupport it would be expected to occur in the upper occupational levels, where poverty and the need for family support might not be such pressing problems.

It is the writer's belief that insofar as the family patterns of the lowest occupational level are concerned, nobody knows very much. Most of our premarital and marital research has centered around the college population. Whether or not family research should, or could, be oriented more in the direction of the lowest rather than the highest socioeconomic groups is a matter of opinion, but until more factual material is gathered from the former category, it would seem wise for text writers to restrict their generalizations regarding family stability to the socioeconomic categories for which data have been collected.

MARITAL INSTABILITY AND ITS RELATION TO EDUCATION, INCOME, AND OCCUPATION: AN ANALYSIS BASED ON CENSUS DATA*

Karen G. Hillman

Evanston Township High School, Evanston, Illinois

INTRODUCTION

The relationship between socioeconomic status and marital instability has been the subject of considerable discussion among sociologists. Various writers have found an inverse relationship between income levels, educational background and occupational status on the one hand, and marital instability on the other.[1] Goode "supposes" that in the upper socioeconomic strata there are more "external supports" to marriage than in the lower levels. Among these external supports he lists a greater continuity of social relations, more long term investments, greater difference between the husband's and the wife's earning power, and less anonymity in the event of a marital rupture.[2]

It was not until the publication of the census of 1950 that any substantial body of data on this topic became available. Thereupon it became possible to study the problem on a more com-

---

* From *Selected Studies in Marriage and the Family*, Revised Edition, edited by Robert F. Winch, Robert McGinnis, and Herbert Barringer. Copyright 1953, © 1962 by Holt, Rinehart and Winston, Inc. Reprinted by permission of Holt, Rinehart and Winston, Inc.

[1] Studies in which this inverse relationship is shown most clearly are the following: H. Ashley Weeks, "Differential Divorce Rates by Occupation," *Social Forces*, 21 (1943), 334–37; August B. Hollingshead, "Class Differences in Family Stability," *American Academy of Political and Social Science*, 272 (1950), 39–46; William A. Kephart, "Occupational Level and Marital Disruption," *American Sociological Review*, 20 (1955), 456–65; William J. Goode, *After Divorce* (Glencoe, Ill.: Free Press, 1956).

[2] Goode, *op. cit.*, Chap. 5.

prehensive basis than the quite limited and local evidence used in previous studies. The purpose of this paper is to use the United States population as reported in the 1950 census in order to examine the relationship between socioeconomic status and marital instability.

In terms of the operations employed in this study, a person whose marriage has proved unstable is one who was recorded as either "divorced" or "separated" on the day in 1950 when the census-taker entered that person on the record. For fairly obvious reasons education is an index of socieconomic status of both sexes, irrespective of marital status, but occupation and income are available as indexes only for males. With respect to education and income it is possible to present the data for whites and nonwhites separately. This breakdown is not available for the data on occupations.

RESULTS

Table 1 shows the number of divorced and separated per 1000 persons ever married, by sex and race for several levels of education. The most obvious fact in the table is that the rates of marital instability for nonwhites run between two and three times as high as for whites. Almost equally obvious is the fact that among whites divorces account for well over half of the marital instability whereas among the nonwhites divorces account for only about a third. Table 2 presents divorce and separation rates for white and nonwhite men by income, and Table 3 does so by occupational grouping.

To determine whether or not these data show a negative correlation between socioeconomic status and marital instability rank correlations were computed. With respect to education eight

ranks were used; those reported as "school years not known" were omitted. With respect to occupation nine ranks were used in the order shown in Table 3 from "Professional ... " to "Laborers ... " The farm occupations and "occupations not listed" (last three rows) were omitted. The results appear in Table 4.

It is seen that in general the data support the negative relationship. For white men all the correlations are negative, irrespective of the index of socioeconomic status or of the nature of the instability. For separations all the correlations are negative, irrespective of sex or the index of socioeconomic status. In addition to negative coefficients, however, Table 4 has some in the high positive range and also two fairly close to zero. (The values of the latter two are actually —.17.) One of these, for nonwhite males, represents two contradictory trends—a negative correlation between separation rate and educational level, and a positive correlation between divorce rate and educational level. The other, for nonwhite women, reflects a curvilinear relationship wherein the highest rate of separations occurs near the middle of the range of educational level.

DISCUSSION

Let us notice some of the limitations and implications of the operations used:

1. Since persons with annulled marriages are classified as single, they cannot enter into this analysis of marital instability.
2. Under the census definition, the category "separated" includes not only persons with legal separations but also those who live, permanently or temporarily apart from their

TABLE 1. NUMBER OF PERSONS IN UNITED STATES 25 YEARS OF AGE AND OVER EVER MARRIED, SEPARATED, AND DIVORCED, 1950, BY EDUCATION, SEX, AND RACE*

White Males

Education	Ever Married	Separated	Divorced	Separated per 1000 of Ever Married	Divorced per 1000 of Ever Married	Both Divorced and Separated per 1000 of Ever Married
No school	681,150	18,510	15,510	27.17	22.77	49.94
Elementary 1–4 years	2,516,700	56,550	71,820	22.47	28.54	51.01
5–7 years	5,317,290	102,060	155,610	19.19	29.26	48.45
8 years	7,561,710	106,560	206,610	14.09	27.32	41.41
High school 1–3 years	5,885,820	76,500	166,590	13.00	28.30	41.30
4 years	6,387,240	63,300	156,360	9.91	24.48	34.39
College 1–3 years	2,451,030	22,890	63,450	9.34	25.89	35.23
4 years or more	2,543,760	15,900	44,040	6.25	17.31	23.56
School years not known	922,890	32,760	38,970	35.50	42.22	77.72
Total	34,267,590	495,030	918,960	14.45	26.26	41.47

Nonwhite Males

Education	Ever Married	Separated	Divorced	Separated per 1000 of Ever Married	Divorced per 1000 of Ever Married	Both Divorced and Separated per 1000 of Ever Married
No school	266,520	20,340	4,080	76.32	15.30	91.62
Elementary 1–4 years	1,006,440	84,510	18,750	83.99	18.63	102.62
5–7 years	917,670	78,690	23,040	85.74	25.11	110.85
8 years	379,320	32,040	12,120	84.45	31.95	116.40
High school 1–3 years	393,120	34,020	14,010	86.54	35.64	122.18
4 years	240,390	17,220	9,180	71.63	38.19	109.82
College 1–3 years	89,670	5,310	3,630	59.22	40.48	99.70
4 years or more	67,320	2,640	2,040	39.22	30.30	69.52
School years not known	130,770	14,010	4,200	107.13	32.12	139.25
Total	3,491,220	288,780	91,050	82.71	26.08	108.79

White Females

Nonwhite Females

Education	Ever Married	Separated	Divorced	Separated per 1000 of Ever Married	Divorced per 1000 of Ever Married	Both Divorced and Separated per 1000 of Ever Married	Ever Married	Separated	Divorced	Separated per 1000 of Ever Married	Divorced per 1000 of Ever Married	Both Divorced and Separated per 1000 of Ever Married
No school	776,640	16,860	11,220	21.71	14.45	36.16	214,980	13,920	3,210	64.75	14.93	79.68
Elementary 1–4 years	2,245,590	48,840	45,960	21.75	20.47	42.22	891,420	87,090	17,910	97.70	20.09	117.79
5–7 years	5,401,560	114,780	135,390	21.25	25.06	46.31	1,137,870	123,960	34,980	108.94	30.74	139.68
8 years	7,786,620	129,090	207,570	16.58	26.66	43.24	478,350	55,140	21,240	115.27	44.40	159.67
High school 1–3 years	6,748,380	115,440	239,850	17.11	35.54	52.65	557,430	69,480	28,950	124.64	51.93	176.57
4 years	8,711,670	108,960	289,140	12.51	33.19	45.70	330,150	33,330	19,020	100.95	57.61	158.56
College 1–3 years	2,823,570	28,110	104,700	9.96	37.08	47.04	111,870	8,490	6,480	75.89	57.92	133.81
4 years or more	1,647,060	14,310	58,500	8.69	35.52	44.21	79,020	4,500	5,100	56.95	64.54	121.49
School years not known	778,681	18,330	28,650	23.54	36.79	60.33	101,280	11,760	3,750	116.11	37.02	153.13
Total	36,919,770	594,720	1,120,980	16.11	30.36	46.47	3,902,370	407,670	140,640	104.47	36.04	140.51

* Compiled from U. S. Bureau of the Census, *U. S. Census of Population: 1950, Special Reports, Education*, Table 8 (Washington, D. C.: Government Printing Office, 1953).

TABLE 2. NUMBER OF MEN 14 YEARS OF AGE AND OLDER IN U.S POPULATION EVER MARRIED, DIVORCED, AND SEPARATED, BY INCOME RECEIVED IN 1949 AND RACE*

White Men

Income	Ever Married	Separated	Divorced	Separated per 1000 of Ever Married	Divorced per 1000 of Ever Married	Both Divorced and Separated per 1000 of Ever Married
No income	1,794,750	46,950	64,800	26.16	36.10	62.26
$1–$999	4,242,940	119,940	188,580	28.27	44.44	72.71
$1000–$1999	5,211,410	98,130	167,190	18.82	32.08	50.90
$2000–$2999	8,334,000	131,220	255,150	15.74	30.62	46.36
$3000–$3999	7,320,240	70,740	167,610	9.66	22.90	32.56
$4000 and over	7,261,920	5,100	18,090	0.70	2.49	3.19
Total	34,165,260	472,080	861,420	13.82	25.21	39.03

Nonwhite Men

Income	Ever Married	Separated	Divorced	Separated per 1000 of Ever Married	Divorced per 1000 of Ever Married	Both Divorced and Separated per 1000 of Ever Married
No income	254,660	28,590	7,770	112.27	30.51	142.78
$1–$999	1,096,740	98,130	25,440	89.47	23.20	112.67
$1000–$1999	1,022,010	86,190	23,700	84.33	23.19	107.52
$2000–$2999	802,860	57,120	19,650	71.14	24.48	95.62
$3000–$3999	239,670	12,870	6,840	53.70	28.54	82.24
$4000 and over	63,390	210	210	3.31	3.31	6.62
Total	3,479,330	283,110	83,610	81.37	24.03	105.40

* Compiled from U.S. Bureau of the Census, U.S. Census of Population: 1950, Special Reports, Marital Status, Tables 6 and 7 (Washington, D.C.: Government Printing Office, 1953).

TABLE 3. NUMBER OF MEN 14 YEARS OF AGE AND OVER IN U. S.
POPULATION, 1950, EVER MARRIED AND DIVORCED, BY
OCCUPATIONAL GROUPING*

Occupational Grouping	Ever Married	Divorced	Divorced per 1000 of Ever Married
Professional, technical, and kindred workers	2,493,870	46,110	18.49
Managers, officials, and proprietors, except farm	3,979,230	66,030	16.59
Sales workers	2,074,230	50,250	24.22
Clerical and kindred workers	1,991,190	51,180	25.70
Craftsmen, foremen, and kindred workers	6,945,840	167,610	24.15
Operatives and kindred workers	6,859,560	179,550	26.18
Service workers, except private household	1,933,680	81,900	42.35
Private household workers	57,150	2,700	47.24
Laborers, except farm and mine	2,630,340	86,280	32.80
Farmers and farm managers	3,735,150	29,370	7.86
Farm laborers and foremen	923,070	37,620	40.76
Occupations not reported	516,030	23,850	46.22
Total	34,139,340	822,450	24.09

* Compiled from U. S. Bureau of the Census, *U. S. Census of Population, 1950: Special Reports, Occupational Characteristics*, Table 8, (Washington, D. C.: Government Printing Office, 1953).

TABLE 4. RANK CORRELATIONS BETWEEN INDICES OF MARITAL
INSTABILITY AND INDICES OF SOCIOECONOMIC STATUS,
BY RACE AND SEX

Index of Socioeconomic Status	Sex	Race	Index of Marital Instability		
			Separations	Divorces	Divorces and Separations
Education	Male	White	−1.00	−0.43	−0.95
		Nonwhite	−0.55	+0.76	−0.17
	Female	White	−0.95	+0.88	+0.57
		Nonwhite	−0.17	+1.00	+0.33
Income	Male	White	−0.94	−0.94	−0.94
		Nonwhite	−0.49	−1.00	−1.00
Occupational grouping (except farms)	Male	All		−0.88	

spouses because of marital discord but who have not obtained legal separations.

3. The Bureau of the Census indicates that the number of divorced persons is underestimated.[3] Jacobson esti-

mates that as many as one fifth of the divorced persons are not enumerated as divorced in the census. He suggests that a number of divorced men are probably reported as single, as are women without children. Di-

---

[3] U. S. Bureau of the Census, *U. S. Census of Population: 1950. Special Reports, Education* (Washington, D.C.: Government Printing Office, 1953), p. 5B-9.

vorced women with children probably are frequently recorded as
widowed.[4]

4. The census takes its data as of a
single day in the respondent's life.
That is, the records show the marital
status of the respondent on that one
day rather than any such marital
status as "ever divorced." Accordingly divorced persons who have remarried do not enter into our category of having unstable marriages.

5. There is a correlation between age
and rate of remarriage. Glick suggests that "under current conditions
... about two-thirds of the divorced
women and three-fourth of the divorced men will eventually remarry."[5] He found a high positive
correlation between income and remarriage rates. Before the data were
standardized for age, he discovered
a strong negative correlation between
educational attainment and number
of times married for both sexes.
After such standardization, however,
the relationship becomes positive for
women. As Glick indicates, the age
factor is important because older
persons are the ones most likely to
remarry, and they received their
education at a time when the average

level of education was considerably
lower than it is today. Thus when
figures are not standardized for age,
the remarriages of older persons with
preponderantly lower education influence the trend so as to show an
inverse relationship between education and remarriage. But if age is
controlled, a different trend is discovered—a direct relationship between remarriage rate and education. The data in this paper have
not been standardized for age.

Taking the foregoing considerations
into account and qualifying our findings
accordingly, we conclude that for
American white males there was as of
1950 a negative correlation between
socioeconomic status (whether measured by education, income, or occupation) and marital dissolution (whether
separation or divorce). For nonwhite
males and for females, both white and
nonwhite, no such clear-cut relationship
emerged. Some relationships were curvilinear and some showed positive correlations. According to this evidence,
then, any general statement concerning
the negative relationship between socioeconomic status and marital instability
will have to be confined to white males.

---

[4] Paul H. Jacobson, *American Marriage
and Divorce* (New York: Holt, Rinehart &
Winston, Inc., 1959), pp. 6-7.

[5] Paul C. Glick, *American Families*

(New York: John Wiley & Sons, Inc., 1957),
p. 199.

The excerpt below from *The Family* by Willard Waller and Reuben Hill
describes several aspects of marital conflict in the middle class. Their illustration
of how middle-class couples typically express and attempt to handle marital stress
can be compared with the case studies of lower-class couples by Roach and by
Lee Rainwater presented in Chapter Four.

In the Waller and Hill case study the ideal of marriage is a "complete and
unreserved intimacy." This ideal is shared by many, perhaps the majority of,
middle-class couples. In contrast, the value placed on confiding one's innermost
thoughts to one's mate is incomprehensible and is generally rejected by typical
lower-class couples. From Rainwater's research on white and Negro lower-class
families (Chapters Four and Five) and from the account of the Crawford family
case (Chapter Four), psychic unity or the neurotic quest for it appears to be

uncommon in lower-class families.[1] In large measure, the absence of this characteristic follows from what Rainwater calls the "high degree of role segregation" in the lower class.

Also standing in significant contrast to lower-class behavior are the elaborate and subtle techniques employed by middle-class husbands and wives—their intricate negotiations and compromises—in attempts to control each other, and generally, in their expressions of conflict. These techniques are illustrated in various ways in the case below. The couple, especially the man, sought to avoid active conflict, preferring techniques calculated to evoke resentment without eliciting open rage. The typical lower-class wife, however, who attempts to dominate or stand up to her husband with countercharges and accusations may be risking physical assault or at least episodes of cursing, shouting, and smashing of household possessions.

---

[1] Lower-class couples not only often have "problems in communication" (in the language of family counseling), but also seldom have established lines of communication to begin with.

MARITAL CONFLICT*

Willard Waller,† *Barnard College*

Reuben Hill, *University of Minnesota*

Conflict and accommodation are essential processes in the production of the psychic unity of marriage. In the end they produce a social organization which involves its own value system by which it is justified.

We have said that the accommodations issue from conflict and this is true, but it would be a great mistake to overlook the social pressure which is exerted without active conflict. In the following excerpt from a case study by one of the authors, the role of these pressures seems to be particularly clear:

In the marriage which we have in mind the wife was an extremely sensitive person who had strong feelings of

inferiority and compensated for them by capitalizing upon her attractiveness to men. In order for her to live comfortably with her goading demons of inadequacy, it was necessary for her to have constant reassurance concerning her charms. The husband also knew the meaning of pride and could not live happily without asserting his ego in some way. The ego demands of the husband were ostensibly sacrificed in this living arrangement; he was willing to accept any relationship which permitted him to continue living with his wife. In other words, his ego demands were subordinated to his sex demands. His hold upon his wife was for the most part derived from his ability to flatter her in subtle ways.

Let us understand very clearly some

* From *The Family: A Dynamic Interpretation*, Revised Edition, by Willard Waller. Revised by Reuben Hill. Copyright 1938, 1951 by Holt, Rinehart and Winston, Inc. Reprinted by permission of Holt, Rinehart and Winston, Inc.

† Deceased.

further facts about the relationship. There was between this pair almost no social distance. What either of them knew he had great difficulty in holding back from the other. Their ideal of marriage was that of complete and unreserved intimacy. As an index of their psychic unity, we may mention a number of apparently telepathic manifestations on both sides. The wife was definitely the dominating one. She took for granted her right to give orders and to have them obeyed, and because the husband never dared to contest it, the habit of obedience was strong within him. Whenever an issue arose, she carried her point. Usually she was able to exact from the husband an indemnity of self-abasement and the admission that it was all his fault, together with the promise that it would not happen again; all of this went far beyond a mere yielding of the point in debate. The dominance of the wife apparently resulted from a continuation of control on the principle of least interest in the courtship period. The wife had been much sought after, and the husband had won her only after long and arduous wooing. Of the two, the husband was by far the more stable in his emotional organization and was able, therefore, to exert a considerable control without winning any arguments.

The conflicts of this pair over dances may be taken as typical. They belonged to a social organization in which dances were held periodically, and it was more or less a part of the husband's job to attend them with his wife. The husband greatly resented the wife's interest in dances and dancing. Some weeks before every dance, the wife would begin to think about the occasion and would begin to plan her costume; these thoughts she could never refrain from sharing with her husband. Her costume, always successful, was usually the result of much thought, but it caused much pain to the husband, and he too was under the curse of being able to keep none of his thoughts from the other.

Gradually quarrels arose from this situation. The husband, with a memory of his jealous pains on previous occasions, always reacted very unfavorably to the dress: it was immodest; it cost too much; it was unbecoming for married women to spend so much time in trying to be attractive to other men. Soon the conflict had spread to include the whole subject of dances. The husband objected to his wife's dancing, which he considered a trifle sensual. Although he had rarely given any indications of being excessively moral, he worked up a fine fit of moral indignation regarding dancing as an amusement for married persons. He borrowed the phrases for his Jeremiad from the unlettered evangelists of his rural youth, and became excessively crude. The wife, insulted and aroused, struck back with all her force. She brought in her best weapon, the threat of separation. The husband was always silenced by this big gun. When the evening of the dance arrived, the issue had sometimes been completely settled—in favor of the wife. More often the husband was still grumbling and obstructive. The wife tried to win him at the last moment by cajolery and sexual concessions. If the wife's behavior at the dances did not please the husband, there were bitter quarrels afterwards. The husband always lost, although sometimes he pushed matters so far as to force the wife to go through the motions of packing her trunk and getting ready to leave.

There were, of course, occasional compromises. These compromises usually embodied the wishes of the dominant party, the wife. More important than compromises was the soft pressure of the wishes of each upon the wishes of the other. When an issue was sharp and single, like the dancing, the wife always won. When her temper was aflame, she did not care—perhaps was not aware of—what she did to herself or to anyone else so long as she carried her point. But where there was no clear issue, the husband was able to make his wishes felt. The wife was bound to him by her unvarying need for his admiration and approval. If he withheld his praise on some matter, she strove doubly to attain it. If he praised some aspects of her personality, she developed it to the full. As long as issue was not joined on some particular point of conflict, the husband dominated the relationship. The wife cooked the dishes that he liked, dressed to please him, cultivated mannerisms which he considered charming, and attempted in a thousand ways to gain his approval. The husband cultivated a technique of pushing a struggle up to the point where her anger was evoked and then dropping it; in this way he gained more than he could ever have gained by actual combat. The husband often regained in time of peace the ground that he had lost in time of war. In addition, the wife, because of her instability, was very likely to concede the point which she had gained the day before in combat, illustrating the principle so often met with in cases of divorce, the complete reversal of a position which had previously been too costly and identification with the standard of the other person. The husband, being much more stable and much more clear in his mind as to just what he wanted, and also having less to lose, was much less a prey to repentance and therefore conceded less.

As a result, many of the compromise arrangements which ostensibly represented only the interest of the wife were softened in the periods of relative peace. The impact of the husband, prosaic and steady, upon the wife's personality was extremely heavy, and he was always right on the basis of the mores accepted by the pair. It seems extremely likely that the pressure of his desires, exerted evenly and constantly, was an important factor in producing the flaming rebellion of the wife against the husband and his demands which came to expression in the occasional quarrels.

There were, in addition, a great number of sheer habit adjustments between this pair. The husband, Spartan by training and inclination, was accustomed to arising at the first tinkle of his alarm clock. The wife, more luxuriating, set the clock fifteen minutes early so that she could slowly prepare herself for the ordeal of arising. The husband adopted her habit. At the beginning of the marriage, the husband liked strong coffee and weak tea, the wife weak coffee and strong tea; they ended by becoming accustomed to strong coffee and strong tea. The husband adopted from the wife a greater respect for clothes and other middle class attitudes which emphasize appearances; the wife took from the husband his characteristically rural notion that good food is one of the most important things in life. In all these adjustments the will of the husband, because it was so uniform and clear-cut, was likely to prove superior. The two discussed this with one another—as they discussed everything else—and they had a saying that the wife won all the battles and the husband won all the wars. For the further enlightenment of the reader, it should be recorded that this marriage ended in divorce.

This case makes it clear that the social pressures which do not attain the level of obvious conflict are important determinants of the living arrangements of a pair. In many marriages there is little that could be called by the name of conflict and yet there are compromises and accommodations. Each person exerts pressure upon the other, but it is the pressure of expectations, and if the expectations are not fulfilled there is no expression of hostility, merely the failure to express approval or the lack of the customary warmth in one's praise. These pressures are effective in shaping one personality to the needs of another, but shall we call them conflict?

SUICIDE

Data relating rates of suicide to indices of stratification are relatively scarce.[1] One of the few studies of this subject is Elwin Powell's, presented below. He finds that the rates are higher for occupational prestige categories at the upper and lower ends of the prestige scale. Similar studies conducted in Europe support his results. Following the Durkheimian tradition, Powell relies heavily on the concept of anomie in his explanation of these rates.

---

[1] In addition to the two studies reproduced here, see also Ronald Maris, "Suicide, Status, and Mobility in Chicago," *Social Forces*, 46 (December 1967), 246–55; Andrew F. Henry and James F. Short, Jr., *Suicide and Homicide* (Glencoe, Ill.: The Free Press, 1954); Norman L. Farberow and Edwin S. Schneidman, *The Cry for Help* (New York: McGraw-Hill Book Company, 1961). For a general review of sociological factors in suicide—including stratification variables—see Jack P. Gibbs, "Suicide" in *Contemporary Social Problems*, eds. Robert K. Merton and Robert A. Nisbet (New York: Harcourt, Brace & World, Inc., 1966), pp. 222–61.

OCCUPATION, STATUS, AND SUICIDE: TOWARD A REDEFINITION OF ANOMIE*†

Elwin H. Powell

State University of New York at Buffalo

By definition suicide presupposes the existence of a self. Because the self has its being in the social process, suicide rates will vary with the character of society. While some psychologists doubt the validity of all statistics on the subject,[1] there is fairly convincing evidence that suicide is not randomly distributed throughout the population. Numerous investigations have shown an ecological component in suicide. Rural rates are usually lower than urban rates. Within the city itself the central business district and the zone of transition—the skid-row region—have abnormally high rates.[2] When stable residential areas of

---

*From Elwin H. Powell, "Occupation, Status, and Suicide: Toward A Redefinition of Anomie," *American Sociological Review* (April 1958), pp. 131–38. Reprinted by permission of the American Sociological Association.

† I am indebted to W. L. Kolb of Tulane University for many of the basic ideas and certain criticisms of this study.

[1] Gregory Zilboorg, in "Suicide Among Civilized and Primitive Races," *American Journal of Psychiatry*, 92 (1936), says that present-day statistical data "deserve little

if any credence." F. Achille-Delmos, *Psychologie Pathologique du Suicide* (Paris: Alcan, 1933), would dispense with suicide statistics altogether. However, statistics confined to the limited universe of a single community are not subject to the inaccuracies found on a national or international scale.

[2] Ruth Cavan, *Suicide* (Chicago: University of Chicago Press, 1928); Calvin Schmid, *Suicide in Seattle, 1914–1925: An Ecological and Behavioristic Study* (Seattle: University of Washington Press, 1928).

the city are compared, however, the wealthier sections appear to have more suicide than the low-income neighborhoods.[3] Although in the United States religious affiliation does not seem to be a decisive factor, there is a rate differential by age, sex, ethnicity and socioeconomic level.[4]

The central thesis of the sociological approach to the study of suicide can be stated as follows: The nature and incidence of suicide varies with social status. Status is defined here *not* as rank but as any position in any social system; role is the function or behavior called forth by the rights and obligations of status.[5] The nature of early socialization varies from one culture to another and largely depends on the adult status for which the individual is being prepared.[6] The roles which the person plays, first as a child in the family, later in the peer group, and finally as an adult in the larger community, become incorporated into the structure of the self.

In the simple folk society most people have rather well-defined statuses which are sustained and reinforced by direct participation in communal life. Although conflict and ambiguity mark social position in our contrasting type of society, nevertheless the status of the adult white male in America depends primarily on occupation.[7] It is through work—the performance of a *specific* role—that most men relate themselves to the world.[8] Moreover, vocation determines the individual's *general* social status, i.e., his relationship to the larger society.

Status is the embodiment and concretization of a conceptual system.[9] Roughly the equivalent of a common-value system, the conceptual structure is a framework of categories through which the culture defines reality. It is only through a conceptual system that the individual "sees" his world in its totality and can respond to that world. The institutional order (status system) is founded on a conceptual framework

---

[3] Austin Porterfield, "Suicide and Crime in the Social Structure of an Urban Setting," *American Sociological Review,* 17 (June 1952), 341–49. Apparently the same relationship holds for London; see Peter Sainsbury, *Suicide in London: An Ecological Study* (London: Chapman & Hall, Ltd., 1955), p. 50.

[4] James M. Weiss, "Suicide: An Epidemiological Analysis," *Psychiatric Quarterly,* 28 (1954), 225–52, shows an age, sex, and socioeconomic differential but can detect no differences between religious groups. The city he studied, New Haven, was three-fourths Catholic, though its suicide rate was not below the national average. A few clinical studies indicate that American and Canadian Catholics have higher suicide rates than Protestants or Jews; see B. Pollack, "A Study of the Problem of Suicide," *Psychiatric Quarterly,* 12 (1938), 306–30.

[5] Ralph Linton, "Status and Role," in *Sociological Analysis,* eds. Logan Wilson and William Kolb (New York: Harcourt Brace and Co., 1949), pp. 211–23.

[6] Abram Kardiner *et al., The Psychological Frontiers of Society* (New York: Columbia University Press, 1945).

[7] "In a word . . . occupation is the supreme determinant of human careers." H. D. Anderson and Percy E. Davidson, *Occupational Trends in the United States* (Palo Alto, Calif.: Stanford University Press, 1940), p. 1.

[8] Despite much evidence of job dissatisfaction, work is still a major source of meaning for the great majority of people. Cf. Nancy Morse and Robert S. Weiss, "The Function and Meaning of Work," *American Sociological Review,* 20 (April 1955), pp. 191–98.

[9] Stanley Taylor, *Conceptions of Institutions and the Theory of Knowledge* (New York: Bookman Associates, 1956), pp. 103–17. The term "conceptual system" is more comprehensive than the often-used "common-value system" for it suggests the cognitive as well as the moral elements in human action.

and defines for the individual the ideal ends or goals of action.

When the ends of action become contradictory, unaccessible, or insignificant, a condition of anomie arises.[10] Characterized by a general loss of orientation and accompanied by feelings of "emptiness" and apathy, anomie can be simply conceived as meaninglessness.[11] Meaning, however, is not given in the conceptual scheme as such; it emerges in action. The self creates meaning by its active encounter with the world.[12] When dissociated from a conceptual framework, communication breaks down and self can not validate its existence as a "me."[13] At the other extreme, if totally enveloped by the norms of the culture, the self cannot act as an "I" but, instead, mechanically reacts to a rigidly structured "me."[14] In both cases the self is rendered impotent—unable to act—which engenders the meaninglessness of anomie.

Anomie is a crucial factor in the etiology of suicide. Thus suicide rates can serve as empirical data for testing a general theory of action; conversely, such a theory casts light on the problems of suicide—and by extension—other forms of psychopathology. It would be fallacious to assume that a sociological theory could explain a single, unique case of suicide. But, behind the diverse manifestations of the act of self-destruction, there is a common sociological ground—anomie.

The present inquiry is cast in statistical terms, treating *types*, not individuals. Nevertheless, the claim here is that a person in status X has a greater probability of becoming anomic, other things being equal, than an individual in status Y. This does not mean, of course, that all members of X are anomic or that the individual suicide was in fact anomic. It does mean, however, that psychologistic theories of suicide, which base self-destruction in individual psychopathology,[15] are unsatisfactory.

Based on the postulate that self-destructiveness is rooted in social conditions, the argument of this study is

---

10 Emile Durkheim, *Suicide*, trans. John A. Spaulding and George Simpson (Glencoe, Ill.: The Free Press, 1951), pp. 241–76; Robert K. Merton, "Social Structure and Anomie," in Wilson and Kolb, *op. cit.*, pp. 771-80; Sebastian de Grazia, *The Political Community: A Study of Anomie* (Chicago: University of Chicago Press, 1948), pp. 47–76.

11 Anomie is both a social condition and a psychic state. It is sometimes referred to as a "social and emotional void" or "separation anxiety" (de Grazia). Merton on the other hand stresses the idea of normlessness. The term *meaninglessness* can serve as a common denominator for these different perspectives.

12 The conception of the self employed here is taken from George H. Mead. The self is both an "I"—a subject—and a "me" —an object. The "me" is an incorporated social role or complex of roles; the "I" an actor. The "I" calls into being a "me" appropriate to a given situation and then responds to that "me." Thus the "me" conditions and directs but does not determine the response of the "I." *Mind, Self and Society* (Chicago: University of Chicago Press, 1934), pp. 133–226, especially p. 178.

13 R. E. L. Faris and H. Warren Dunham in *Mental Disorders in Urban Areas* (Chicago: University of Chicago Press, 1939), pp. 158–59, describe the disorganization which results from social isolation.

14 Cf. Erich Fromm, *The Sane Society* (New York: Rinehart and Co., Inc., 1956), p. 16, who speaks of this pattern as the "pathology of normalcy," in which the person is not insane or dissociated from the culture but suffers a defect of spontaneity. The person "experiences himself as the person he thinks he is supposed to be" rather than as the persons he is.

15 Cf. Karl Menninger, *Man Against Himself* (New York: Harcourt, Brace & Co., 1938); A.A. Brill, "The Concept of Psychic Suicide," *International Journal of Psychoanalysis*, 20 (1939), 246–51.

that occupation provides function and determines the individual's social status, which is an index to his conceptual system. The conceptual system is the source of anomie, which is a primary variable in suicide. Therefore, suicide is correlated with occupation.

PROCEDURE

The relationship between occupation and suicide has not been thoroughly examined.[16] Since no national data are available, studies must be based on local samples, which are, of necessity, small. Hence a slight error in recording may produce a great distortion of the results; moreover, occupational data on death certificates are scanty and often inaccurate. To remedy this insufficiency of data, the present study

---

[16] Philip Piker in "Eighteen Hundred and Seventeen Cases of Suicidal Attempts: A Preliminary Statistical Survey," *American Journal of Psychiatry,* 95 (1938), 97–115, surveyed a large number of cases but was able to get occupational information on only half of them; further, his classification did not correspond to the city census statistics, so rates could not be given. A. B. Siavers and E. Davidoff in "Attempted Suicide: Comparative Study of Psychopathic and General Hospital Patients," *Psychiatric Quarterly,* 17 (1943), 520–34, present some fragmentary but inconclusive evidence on occupation. Margaret von Andics in *Suicide and the Meaning of Life* (London: William Hodge, 1947), pp. 49–94, understands the relevance of occupation but unfortunately approaches the subject so unsystematically as to render her work useless from a statistical standpoint. Louis I. Dublin and Bessie Bunzel in *To Be or Not to Be* (New York: Harrison Smith and Robert Hass, 1933), p. 399, present one occupational table based on 1930 British data. Andrew F. Henry and James F. Short, Jr. in *Suicide and Homicide* (Glencoe, Ill.: The Free Press, 1954) correlate suicide with income groups but offer no material on occupations as such.

draws on microfilmed files of the city's two daily newspapers for verification of the occupational status officially given on death certificates. Where discrepancies between the two sources were discovered, the city directory and police files were consulted. In a few instances dubious cases were clarified by the personnel departments of various local firms. A reasonably exact picture of occupational status was thus attained for all but 6 per cent of the male suicides who were residents of the community between 1937 and 1956.

This is a study of suicide in Tulsa, Oklahoma, a city of over 250,000 people. Tulsa County is almost exclusively urban with less than 3 per cent of its population listed as "rural-farm," and virtually all of the county's population is concentrated within the Tulsa Standard Metropolitan Area. While it is impossible to know whether the suicide pattern for Tulsa corresponds to that of American society as a whole, Tulsa is a rather typical, midwestern city. Founded about 1900, it has grown rapidly and is now a managerial center for the oil industry. Its employed male population in 1950 was divided almost equally between white- and blue-collar workers, 31,592 and 30,477, respectively. The population of the metropolitan area remained virtually constant during the 1930s, with 11 per cent of employable males listed as "seeking work." In the early 1940s war industry—mainly aircraft manufacturing—and the general national prosperity revived the economic life, unemployment declined, and the population of the metropolitan area increased by 28 per cent, from 193,363 to 251,686, in the decade of the 1940s. During the 1940s home ownership increased from 56 to 65 per cent, placing the city ninth in the nation in the number of homes which are "owner occupied"; the median annual income for employed males in 1950 was $3,061.[17] Since 1950 the metropolitan area has grown by 50,000 according to Tulsa Chamber of Commerce estimates. Oklahoma City, 100 miles to the west, is of comparable size (325,352) but has a somewhat lower average income, more murders, and fewer suicides than Tulsa. In ranking 105 American cities by 1936–1945 suicide rates, Porterfield and Talbert place Tulsa (rate 14.3 per 100,000) in thirty-ninth place, and Oklahoma City (rate 10.2) in eighty-ninth place.[18]

DATA

During the 20 years between 1937 and 1956 at least 426 residents of Tulsa County over 14 years of age committed suicide. The average annual rate is 13.0 per 100,000; the adult white male rate (27.0) is over four times as high as the

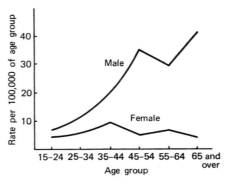

Fig. 1. Suicide by Age and Sex.

female rate (6.6) and ten times as high as the Negro male rate (2.7).

Figure 1 presents a differential pattern of rate increase by age and sex. The female rate attains its zenith in the 35–44 year-old period and then declines; the male rate rises continuously and reaches its peak after 65, suggesting an association between occupational role and suicide.

Table 1 gives the suicide rates for males in the standard (census) occupational categories. Because of the changes which have occurred in Tulsa County over the past two decades, it is revealing to compare the rates by 5-year intervals. During World War II suicide rates throughout the nation dropped to the lowest point since 1917, and Tulsa County followed the national trend.[19] For all males the rate for the half-decade between 1942 and 1946 was 32 per cent below the 1937–1941 rate, whereas the female rate during this time rose by 7 per cent. Moreover, it appears that occupational groups reacted differently to the war and its accompanying prosperity: The combined suicide rates for professional-managerial, service, and unskilled workers dropped 39.6 per cent while the sales-clerical, skilled, and semi-skilled rate declined by 20.1 per cent. Over the entire 20-year period it appears that both extremes of the vocational hierarchy generate a high suicide rate, while the middle groups maintain a fairly constant and low rate.[20]

---

[17] The above demographic data are taken from U. S. Department of Commerce, *Sixteenth Census of the United States: 1940, Population,* Vol. II, Part 5, and *Seventeenth Census of the United States: 1950, Population,* Vol. II, Part 36 (Washington, D.C.: Government Printing Office, 1952), pp. 200 –201, 244.

[18] Austin L. Porterfield and Robert H. Talbert, *Crime, Suicide and Social Well Being* (Fort Worth, Texas: Texas Christian University Press, 1948), p. 99.

[19] "Suicide and War," *Statistical Bulletin of the Metropolitan Life Insurance Company,* 23, No. 9 (1942), 1–2. Unlike the national rate, however, the Tulsa rata did not rise again until the 1950s.

[20] The 6 per cent of our sample which was occupationally unclassified would not alter the picture appreciably. From available

TABLE 1. SUICIDE BY OCCUPATIONAL CATEGORY FOR THE ADULT WHITE MALE POPULATION OF TULSA COUNTY, 1937–1956

Category	1937–1941			1942–1946			1947–1951			1952–1956			Total 1937–1956	
	Number	Population[a]	Rate per 100,000	Number	Population[b]	Rate per 100,000	Number	Population[d]	Rate per 100,000	Number	Population[b]	Rate per 100,000	Number	Average Annual Rate per 100,000
Professional-managerial	36	11,462	63.0	19	13,962	27.3	20	18,851	21.2	30	20,759	29.0	105	35.1
Sales-clerical	9	10,988	16.4	7	11,352	12.4	6	12,111	9.9	5	12,831	7.8	27	11.6
Craftsmen (skilled labor)	7	7,975	17.7	8	9,757	16.3	6	14,537	8.3	12	15,987	15.0	33	14.3
Operatives (semiskilled labor)	10	7,645	26.1	8	8,530	18.7	12	10,339	23.2	8	11,366	14.0	38	20.5
Unskilled labor	5	2,535	39.4	4	2,945	27.2	8	3,020	53.0	6	3,380	35.4	23	38.7
Service	4	2,427	33.0	3	2,677	22.5	1	2,431	8.2	4	2,502	32.1	12	23.9
Retired	9	2,000[c]	90.0	8	2,000	80.0	7	2,215	63.0	13	2,415	100.8	37	83.4
Unemployed and unclassified	8	—	—	6	—	—	1	—	—	5	—	—	20	—
Agriculture	2	5,688	7.1	1	5,688	3.5	2	3,637	11.0	2	3,590	11.1	7	8.1
Student	6	8,064	13.9	0	8,064	—	3	9,562	6.3	5	10,131	9.9	14	7.5
Total	96			64			66			90			316	
Average annual rate			34.0			23.1			22.4			27.2			27.0

a 1940 census.
b Population estimate of the Oklahoma Employment Commission.
c Estimated population over 65 and not in labor force (not given in 1940 census).
d 1950 census.

Schmid and van Arsdol suggest the possibility that blue-collar workers have a higher suicide rate than white-collar.[21] Our findings, however, do not support this contention. For the combined professional-managerial and sales-clerical population the average annual rate was 24.6 as opposed to 19.6 for manual workers. There seems to be a qualitative as well as quantitative difference between the white- and blue-collar suicide. The former is more apt to be a premeditated act, whereas working-class suicide is more impulsive: six times as many murder-suicides occur in the blue-collar world. While the average age of the two groups is roughly comparable—48.2 for the white-collar, 45.2 for the blue-collar suicide—the latter is more apt to be marked by disorganized family life. Table 2 reveals some of these differences.

Eighteen per cent of the blue-collar suicides as opposed to 2.8 per cent of the white-collar workers lived outside the city limits but within the county. This may indicate that a geographic marginality carries with it a psychosocial marginality which is a major factor in working-class suicide. Many of the manual workers were recent rural migrants.[22]

Within the professional-managerial category, professions as a whole have

TABLE 2. SUICIDE IN THE WHITE-COLLAR AND BLUE-COLLAR WORLDS*

	White-Collar (Professional-Managerial and Sales-Clerical)		Blue-Collar (Skilled, Semiskilled and Unskilled)	
	Number	Per Cent	Number	Per Cent
Single, widowed, divorced, estranged	43	30.8	44	42.5
Murder plus suicide	3	2.8	15	16.0
Residence outside city limits	4	3.2	17	18.0

* Data on estrangement and murder plus suicide were taken from the Tulsa *Daily World* and Tulsa *Tribune*.

the lowest rate, followed by salaried managers and officials, and finally the self-employed proprietors, who have the highest rate. Pharmacists and physicians have unusually high rates, while engineers and accountants rank low. Among certain professions—authors, editors, and reporters (population 150), the clergy (population 285), teachers (male population 463), college professors (population 115)—no suicides occurred. Nurses have an incidence of suicide six times that of females in general, while women sales-clerical workers have a rate below the general female population. In blue-collar occupations, cab drivers have a rate four times higher than the general male population, while truck drivers fall below the mean. Though the size of our sample precludes generalization, the data presented in Table 3 may be suggestive.

---

ecological and miscellaneous information these twenty cases could be divided into three groups: (1) a probable middle class (eight cases); (2) probable lower class (eight cases), and (3) unclassified (four cases).

21 Calvin F. Schmid and Maurice D. van Arsdol, Jr., "Completed and Attempted Suicides: A Comparative Analysis," *American Sociological Review*, 20 (June 1955), 273–83.

22 Cf. W. W. Schroeder and J. A. Beegle, "Suicide: An Instance of High Rural Rates," *Rural Sociology*, 17 (1953), 45–52.

TABLE 3. SUICIDE BY SPECIFIC OCCUPATION, 1937–1956*

White-Collar				Blue-Collar			
Occupation	Number	Population	Rate	Occupation	Number	Population	Rate
Pharmacists	6	162	120	Cab drivers	7	402	86.9
Physicians	5	309	83	Welders	5	974	25
Nurses	6	776	38	Machinists	4	1,154	17
Lawyers	4	544	36	Truck drivers	7	2,847	12
Engineers	6	1,953	15	Mechanics	8	3,776	10
Accountants	3	2,054	7	Carpenters	2	1,804	5

* Data from *Seventeenth Census of the United States: 1950, Population*, Vol. II, Part 36 (Washington, D. C.: Government Printing Office, 1952), pp. 206–7. The actual rates would be somewhat higher than those given here as the population has grown 28 per cent since 1940.

Evidently, the greatest strain of all —for the male—derives from lack of occupation. Over the past 20 years the retired have a suicide rate of 89.0, almost five times that of the adult male population and twice that of all males of the same age group. While the female rate declines slightly after 65, the male rate increases sharply, as is shown in Table 4.

INTERPRETATION

Suicide is an ultimate expression of accumulated self-contempt. Psychiatric theories often trace the origin of self-hatred to guilt generated by early childhood experiences.[23] It is our contention that both guilt and self-contempt are rooted in anomie, which results in the inability to act, i.e., impotence. Whether turned inward on the self or outward on the world, destructiveness is the "outcome of an unlived life."[24]

The relationship between self-destruction and anomie is revealed in the suicide rates for the aged. As Fig. 1 shows, the male rate rises continuously throughout life with a sharp increase after 65, while the female rate declines after 40. Theories which trace all suicides to the insecurities of childhood must explain why the effect of early life diminishes with age for the woman but increases for the man. Nor is suicide due to the weariness of long life, for women over 65 have a rate 1.7 per cent below those under 65 (Table 4). Without denying the influence of early socialization and the physiological strains of aging, it appears that the suicide of the elderly male is connected primarily with the loss of occupational status. The suicide rate for men increases by 146 per cent after 65; moreover, the *retired* male over 65 has a rate (83.4 per 100,000) almost twice that for all males of the same age (42.6 per 100,000). Retirement in our society is a virtual excommunication. Men with no history of sickness develop

[23] Elizabeth Kilpatrick, "A Psychoanalytic Understanding of Suicide," *American Journal of Psychoanalysis*, 8 (1948), 13–23; Herbert Hendin, "Psychodynamic Motivational Factors in Suicide," *Psychiatric Quarterly*, 25 (1951), 672–78.

[24] Erich Fromm, *Man for Himself* (New York: Rinehart and Co., 1947), p. 45. Fromm's work has been freely utilized in this discussion.

TABLE 4.   SUICIDE BY AGE AND SEX OF THE ADULT WHITE POPULATION
IN TULSA COUNTY, 1937–1956

	Population 14–64			Population Over 65			
	Number	Population[b]	Rate	Number	Population	Rate	Per Cent Rate Change
Male[a]	257	74,776	17.1	56	6,402	42.6	146.0
Female	96	81,207	5.9	7	7,024	4.9	−1.7

[a] Three of the male suicides were of unknown age and are not included in this table.
[b] Average population of the 1940 and 1950 censuses.

chronic illnesses after retirement; it is certainly plausible to suggest that such unemployment is a primary and not merely precipitating factor in the suicide of the aged male. To be without work is to live without purpose.[25]

Work, however, provides no absolute immunity against suicide, and it appears that the quality and extent of anomie varies by standard occupational categories—used here as ideal types. The type, an abstraction, does not fully describe all (or any) of the particular cases subsumed by it. It does, however, serve as an index to social roles, as follows:

OCCUPATIONAL TYPE[26]	AVERAGE ANNUAL RATE PER 100,000
I. Professional-managerial	35.4
II. Sales-clerical	11.6
III. Skilled workers (craftsmen)	14.3
IV. Semiskilled workers (operatives)	20.5
V. Unskilled labor	38.7

Each of the above types must be viewed in relationship to the others. Factors "causing" suicide in I or V will also be at work with II, III, or IV. But our task is to find specific differences between the types which may account for the observed variation of suicide rates.[27]

"The whole occupational sphere," Parsons writes, "is dominated by a single, fundamental goal, that of 'success'."[28] The idea of success is derived from a larger conceptual framework which defines the nature of man in terms of the active mastery of existence. The determining factor in the distribution of suicide by occupation is the relationship between the self and the success ideology.

Anomie as dissociation: type V. Alienated from the larger society, type V is composed mainly of men in retreat from the world, either downwardly mobile individuals or those unable to assume responsibility for the improve-

---

25 Cf. Bohan Zawadski and Paul Lazarsfeld, "The Psychological Consequences of Unemployment," *Journal of Social Psychology*, 6 (1935), 224–50; Eugene A. Friedman and Robert Havighurst, *The Meaning of Work and Retirement* (Chicago: University of Chicago Press, 1950).

26 Based on Table 1. Service occupations

---

are not included because of their ambiguity.

27 That there is a significant difference in the outlook and attitude of the occupational types is substantiated by Richard Centers, *The Psychology of Social Classes* (Princeton: Princeton University Press, 1949), pp. 57, 229.

28 Talcott Parsons, "The Motivations for Economic Activities," *Essays in Sociological Theory, Pure and Applied* (Glencoe, Ill.: The Free Press, 1949), p. 214.

ment of their status.[29] Lacking "ambition" the unskilled laborer lives a hand-to-mouth existence, both physically and psychically. As a casual worker, employment is sporadic even in prosperous times; routines for the organization of everyday life are either absent or ineffective. Discontinuity in the occupational sphere coupled with the absence of the regulating mores of the wider society creates an atmosphere of pervasive disorder.

Type V individuals have not internalized the success ideology and have no subculture of their own to draw on for orientation. (This is especially true of the locality in question, where there are few ethnic communities.) In an individuated culture the person without dominant, long-range goals becomes increasingly the victim of whim and egoistic impulse. He has little rationale for the delay or regulation of response.[30] Here we have the picture of an "I" without a "me"—a desocialized personality. Devoid of a coherent conceptual structure, the individual cannot sufficiently organize his world so that he can act effectively within it. That which cannot be integrated into the conceptual system—the unknown— is a source of fear, and fear produces two characteristic reactions: flight and aggression. Fear rather than frustration

by external circumstances is the primary source of the aggression of type V. Incapacitated by fear the suicide either sinks into apathy or finally strikes out at the world impulsively—one-third of the type V suicides occurred in conjunction with unpremeditated murder.[31] Having exhausted his resources for coming to terms with a threatening chaos, the individual annihilates the world by killing the self.[32]

Integration: types IV, III, and II. With reference to the conceptual system of the society, these three types represent a middle ground between the dissociation of V and the total involvement of I.

Insofar as V and IV are distinguishable categories the dividing line between them is the concept of success. There is a certain coherence in the life of the semiskilled worker: regularity of employment, some participation in associations (e.g., unions), and at least a nominal membership in the community. For the semiskilled worker success comes to mean immediate gains in income rather than advancement to a managerial position.[33] Nevertheless,

---

29 Type V is roughly the "lower-lower" class. Cf. W. Lloyd Warner and Paul S. Lunt, *The Social Life of a Modern Community* (New Haven: Yale University Press, 1941), pp. 178–95, 200.

30 G. M. Davidson in "The Problem of Suicide," *Medical Record*, 39 (1934), 24–28, sees the dynamic of suicide in the loss of a goal which results in an inattention to life itself, giving rise to an organic depression where the higher centers of the nervous system are unable to comply with and control incoming impulses and unable thus to choose an action.

31 Lower-class suicides are more irrational than middle-class. It appears that flight reactions such as physical drifting, alcoholism, and schizophrenia are associated with low-prestige occupations. Robert E. Clark, "Psychoses, Income and Occupational Prestige," *American Journal of Sociology*, 54 (1949), 433–40; A. B. Hollingshead and F. C. Redlich, "Social Stratification and Schizophrenia," *American Sociological Review*, 19 (June 1954), 302–6.

32 C. W. Wahl in "Suicides as a Magical Act," *Bulletin of the Menninger Clinic*, 21 (1957), 91–99, sets forth the interesting theory that the suicide has regressed to a stage of infantile omnipotence which equates the world with the self and, therefore, kills the self to annihilate the world. We would add that regression itself is a socially structured phenomena.

33 Ely Chinoy, *Automobile Workers and the American Dream* (Garden City, N.Y.:

type IV workers have the goal of raising the personal and family consumption level: Success means a new car, a house in the suburbs, the security of a bank account, freedom from debt.[34]

With type III the drive for an active mastery of existence is more clearly revealed. All of V and many of IV occupations are "jobs" as distinct from "trades." Men drift into jobs but they learn a trade. The trade is a "determinate role" and calls for specialized training.[35] The individual motivated to learn a trade has to some degree internalized the success philosophy. His craft moreover may bring some satisfaction to the urge for creative activity. Both factors combine to reduce anomie: The suicide rate for type III was the lowest of the manual workers during the 20 years covered by this study.

Type II has an unusually low suicide rate. More conservative in political and economic philosophy than the manual worker, type II maintains a middle-class style of life with its emphasis on propriety, restraint, and (a somewhat illusory) individual responsibility. Like the craftsman, the sales-clerical person is disciplined by his occupational role, and the fact that he works directly with people may give him a sense of meaningful participation in society.[36] Mobility drives are frequently transferred to the children but still provide an orientation for striving. The numerous tensions of lower white-collar life may be expressed in psychosomatic and psychoneurotic disorders, but they do not seem to result in a high incidence of suicide.

Anomie as envelopment: type I. With lower-grade manual workers, especially type V, anomie seems to be associated with a fragmentation of the conceptual scheme and "results from man's activity lacking regulation... ultimately [the product of] society's insufficient presence in the individual."[37]

The success concept supplies a general framework of orientation for types IV, III, and II, but a large segment of behavior, especially nonoccupational, is relatively unrestrained and spontaneous. But in type I the self is almost completely enveloped by the success ideology and presents the paradox of what may be called *institutionalized anomie,* i.e., meaninglessness arising from normative regulation itself.[38]

Almost the whole of life for type I people is structured around the concept of success. But, as Tumin writes, "Now the emphasis has shifted from the importance of work and striving to the urgency of appearing to be successful... [and] *being* successful is measured by power and property which one openly consumes."[39] Success comes to be equated with possession of prestige symbols, which signify "belongingness" and serve as protection against the fear of disapproval. Consequently a compulsive adherence to the conceptual framework supports the idea of success; to question

Doubleday & Company, Inc., 1955).

34 Gladys L. Palmer, "Attitudes Toward Work in an Industrial Community," *American Journal of Sociology*, 63 (July 1957), 17–26.

35 R. W. Mack, "Occupational Ideology and the Determinate Role," *Social Forces*, 36 (1957), 37–44; Henri de Man, *Joy in Work,* trans. Eden and Cedar Paul (London: George Allen & Unwin, Ltd., 1929), pp. 59–63.

36 C. Wright Mills, "The Middle Class in Middle-Sized Cities," in Wilson and Kolb, *op. cit.,* pp. 443–53.

37 Durkheim, *op. cit.,* p. 258.

38 This corresponds to Durkheim's altruism in several ways. *Ibid.,* pp. 217, 225.

39 Melvin M. Tumin, "Some Unapplauded Consequences of Social Mobility in a Mass Society," *Social Forces*, 36 (October 1957), pp. 32–37.

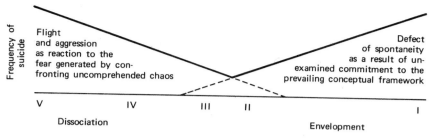

Fig. 2. Conceptual System.

the validity of the culturally sanctioned prestige symbols is a treat to the foundations of the psyche. In Tumin's apt phrase, a "cult of gratitude" [40] emerges with a concomitant paralysis of the critical faculties: The individual cannot sufficiently detach himself from the prevailing institutional order to gain an objective view of it or himself. Psychologically speaking, the person is not "free" to analyze his own motivations. Since he does not know himself, he cannot trust his own judgment and cannot act on his own convictions. Enveloped by the culture, he seems to have no life of his own—no inner coherence.[41]

The source of anomie is not the destruction of ends or the quest for infinitely receding goals but the inability of the self to reconstruct its own ends from the raw material (concepts) presented to it by the culture. Action is not only a matter of fitting means to ends but of selecting ends, and selection presupposes critical analysis. Living by the unexamined directives of the culture, the person has the sense of being totally controlled by forces outside himself. Hence he feels that he is not really living at all. The boredom of "not living" grows into a general loss of

spontaneity that culminates in the inner deadness which precedes the physical death of the suicide.

SUMMARY AND CONCLUSIONS

As opposite poles of a continuum, two forms of anomie can be discerned: The one results from the self's dissociation from, the other from its envelopment by, the conceptual system of the culture. Both render the individual impotent and thus give rise to self-contempt, which in extreme cases eventuates in suicide.

Occupational types can be arranged along the anomie continuum as shown in Fig. 2 above. At V is a disorganized way of life becoming more coherent as we move toward I, with increasing involvement in the success ideology. Moving from I toward V we see a diminishing rigidity, a relaxation of the success norms. Although occupational status is but one component of the total social setting it is an essential key (in our culture) to the relationship between the self and society. The occupation tends to create both by selection and by the nature of the role itself either a dissociated or an enveloped— "self-less"—personality. Thus society

---

[40] *Ibid.*, p. 35.
[41] Max Scheler in *The Nature of Sympathy* (New Haven, Conn.: Yale University Press, 1954), p. 42, describes a type foreshadowing Riesman's "other-directed": "where . . . there is no authentic fellow feeling present but because there is a sort of identifi-

cation with the other person . . . life acquires a tendency to dissipate itself in a vicarious re-enactment of the doings of one or more other people. His very acts and decisions are determined by the implicit demands inherent in the other's conception of him."

generates as well as precipitates suicide.

The self, however, is not a mirror image of the social order. One of the unintended consequences of Durkheim's work has been to encourage an over-simplified social determinism which conceives the self as a mere reflection of the culture. But the self not only reacts to but acts on its environment, creating its own world of concepts and symbols which have their ultimate origin in society.

Warren Breed also explores the relationship between occupational status and suicide. He examines the influence of downward mobility—as manifested by the failure in work roles—in the occurrence of suicide. Using Durkheim's concept of anomie as a point of departure, Breed proposes a structural–interactional explanation of suicide.

OCCUPATIONAL MOBILITY AND SUICIDE AMONG WHITE MALES[*][†]

Warren Breed

Newcomb College, Tulane University

Durkheim maintained that high suicide rates appear with certain broad societal conditions, such as malintegration and lack of "social regulation."[1] His four categories of suicide refer as much to these conditions as to suicide rates. This broad frame of reference, as well as the official data available to him, prevented his dealing with two subjects which are the focus of the present study: the individual process of suicide and social class.

Many *individual* conditions, Durkheim argued, are "not general enough" for sociological analysis.[2] The first four chapters, written partly as an attack on psychological reductionism, were devoted to exorcising individual determinants, as well as other "extrasocial" causes of suicide. Yet in various places Durkheim showed uncertainty about his macrosociological bias. Chapter 6 specified several individual forms of suicide ("Stoic," "Epicurean," etc.), but these turn out to be rather discontinuous versions of his four societal types. He repeatedly spoke of "greed," individual "passions," and "purpose" and "desires," recognizing the relevance of in-

* From "Occupational Mobility and Suicide Among White Males," *American Sociological Review*, 28 (April 1963), 179–88. Reprinted by permission of the American Sociological Association.

† I wish to acknowledge the advice and assistance of Thomas Ktsanes, Robert K. Merton, Henry Orenstein, Robert E. Barnes, and Jane Ledford, and the Tulane University Council on Research for financial support.

1 Emile Durkheim, *Suicide* (Glencoe, Ill.: The Free Press, 1951). The book was originally published in 1897.

2 *Ibid.*, p. 51.

dividual aspirations and their relationship to achievement. In his treatment of anomic suicide, he noted briefly that those individuals "less favored by nature" would require additional amounts of moral discipline in accepting their lesser social rewards. And, in the crucial passage on anomic suicide (". . . when society is disrupted by some painful crisis . . ."), he moved immediately to the notion that some individuals are faced with "declassification"—casting them into a lower social position.[3]

Evidence that such a loss occurs and that particular kinds of individuals show this behavior is not produced. Durkheim provided very little information of any kind relating suicide to class. He did not resolve the question of why the lower classes show high rates whereas they possess attributes which elsewhere Durkheim associates with low rates. He was unclear about who was involved in such categories as "the liberal professions,"[4] "public officials,"[5] and "industrial occupations."[6] The latter, by his own designation, are not occupations at all but individuals engaged in industry—including laborers. (He acknowledges his regret on this point.[7]) His belief that "anomic" rates rise during prosperity as well as depression has been found incorrect by Henry and Short, who also showed more clearly than Durkheim that economic depression is accompanied by higher rates mostly among the higher-income groups.[8] In dealing with this question, Durkheim imputed causation to bankruptcy rates when only correlation with

suicide was warranted.[9] One might ask, if high rates accompany depressions, what accounts for the still-considerable numbers of "anomic" suicides during prosperity? The closest he came to class *mobility* in the lives of individuals was brief mention of declassification or disappointment, as with the bankrupt man or the artist whose work is criticized.[10]

To throw light on these questions, which Durkheim either specifically acknowledged he would not study or was unable to study, research was designed to relate class and class mobility to the lives of individual suicides. Many sociologists woud agree that individual role performance, within a normative system and in interaction with other individuals, is as properly "social" as societal states and rates of behavior. As Inkeles put it, the Durkheimian macrosociological model is an "S-R proposition" (for "State-Rate"), analogous to the psychological S-R model; questions about intervening variables of normatively oriented role performance and deviance are not covered.[11]

Instead of using annual reports, the data to be analyzed are detailed materials on selected portions of the life experiences of 103 white males who committed suicide. The major variable intervening between the societal state and the individual suicide, in this section of the report, is taken to be the quality of work-role performance, with special attention to job instability and downward mobility. Because the theory was developed largely after collection of data

---

3 *Ibid.*, pp. 251–52.
4 *Ibid.*, p. 164.
5 *Ibid.*, p. 166.
6 *Ibid.*, pp. 257–58.
7 *Ibid.*, p. 257.
8 A. F. Henry and J. F. Short, *Suicide and Homicide* (Glencoe, Ill.: The Free Press, 1954).

9 *Op. cit.*, p. 242.
10 *Ibid.*, pp. 288–89.
11 Alex Inkeles, "Personality and Social Structure," in *Sociology Today*, eds. R. K. Merton, Leonard Broom and Leonard S. Cottrell, Jr. (New York: Basic Books, Inc., Publishers, 1959), pp. 249–56. Inkeles recommends the work of Henry and Short, *op. cit.*, as providing an intervening variable in the form of psychodynamics.

began, further discussion of the theory will follow presentation of the findings.

PROCEDURE

The data come from interviews with persons who knew men who had committed suicide. Most of the respondents were relatives, but information was also obtained from friends, employers, and coworkers, and, in some cases, neighbors, landlords, physicians, psychiatrists, and government records. For purposes of reliability, where the first interview was with a female relative, we attempted to gain a second interview with a male nonrelative, and so on. Rapport in most cases was good; respondents seemed to welcome the opportunity to once again go over the "possible causes" of death. The refusal rate was 4.4 per cent. At least one interview was obtained for 103 of the 105 cases in the sample. In twenty-two cases there is one interview, in forty-five cases there are two interviews, and in the remaining thirty-six there are three or more. In every case attempts were made to get at least two interviews; for the twenty-two cases, either there was only one respondent available or the details seemed so clear that further information was not sought. In several of the thirty-six cases, the details were so problematic that five and six interviews were made. The data were coded by two coders, who agreed 93 per cent of the time on all categories used in this report.

The sample consisted of 105 consecutive white male suicides in New Orleans for the years 1954–1959 inclusive, of men between the ages of 20 and 60 and who had lived in the city for at least 6 months. No murder-suicides and no attempted suicides were incuded. Of the 304 deaths called suicides by the authorities during that period, there were also sixty white females; nine murder-suicides—all white; forty white Orleans males aged 61 or more and one under 20; twenty-six Negro males and eight Negro females; and forty-two white males and thirteen white females not residing in the city for 6 months—most of whom had entered the city a day or two before death. The decision to restrict the study to men between the ages of 20 and 60 stems from the interest in the male role of work and performance in that role.

To obtain an estimate for comparing the suicides with their peers, a control group was established. Interviewers were sent to each of the 103 blocks where the suicides had lived, with a modification of the schedule used for the suicides. They followed a plan designed to obtain two interviews at random (but keeping five doors away from the suicide's former residence) on that block, or across the street if necessary. Two respondents were asked to give information about one male each, who became members of the control sample of 206 men. This departure from the usual two-person interviewer-respondent relationship was successful in gathering data by the same method standardized for the suicides but resulted in a much higher refusal rate—18 per cent. People are apparently slow to give information about a still-living third person.

Suicides and controls were matched on the three variables of sex, race, and age. Further, by asking for a relative who lived in that neighborhood, it was hoped to match for a fourth variable, social class. As it turned out, the two groups differed significantly in class—a substantive matter important for the mobility hypothesis (see Table 1). They were quite similar, however, in

TABLE 1. OCCUPATIONAL DISTRIBUTION OF SUICIDES AT TIME OF DEATH AS COMPARED TO CONTROL GROUP AND WHITE MALES IN THE CITY, PER CENT

	Suicides	City, Census	Controls
Professional	7	15	13
Managers	16	17	23
Clerical	7	13	11
Sales	6	11	6
Craftsmen-foremen	14	19	22
Operatives	17	14	14
Service	19	7	7
Farm laborers	0	0	0
Laborers	13	5	3
Totals	103	92,320	206

TABLE 2. FATHERS' OCCUPATIONS OF SUICIDES AND CONTROLS, PER CENT

	Suicides	Controls
Professional	17	12
Managers	24	27
Clerical	3	8
Sales	8	4
Craftsmen	17	23
Operatives	17	13
Service	4	7
Farm laborers	4	3
Laborers	7	4

the class of their fathers; suicides and controls were raised in similar class surroundings (see Table 2). The control group is also interesting in that, although it was not designed as a random sample, its occupational distribution closely parallels that of the city for white males.

THE VALIDITY OF OFFICIAL DATA

Generally the only question sociologists have asked about suicide data taken from coroners' files is that of representativeness in terms of possible underreporting: Are these all the suicides that took place during this period? Two further questions are also relevant, dealing with possible overreporting and with the *quality* of the data. This study deals with all three questions.

All studies of suicide, including this one, conclude that some suicides may not have been registered as such or may have taken place in another jurisdiction. Underreporting is said to occur because officials favor influential persons by stating relatives' cause of death as natural or accidental, rather than as suicide. In this study, such biases may be present. However, during the 6-year period several persons high in influence were declared suicides, including at least ten physicians, lawyers, wealthy businessmen and clubmen, and a relative of one of the two or three most powerful local politicians. A second possible source of underreporting stems from the fact that New Orleans is a Catholic city (some two-thirds of the whites are Catholics). This potential bias is sharply minimized, in fact, by an institutional mechanism: Authorities usually delay stating "cause of death" until final rites are completed. The word "suicide" rarely appears in the local press; cases are said to be "under-investigation." A final source of underreporting is the suicide who leaves town and kills himself in another jurisdiction. During the field work this practice was mentioned by several persons, but closer questioning always ended with the admission that the speaker himself knew of no specific case for the years covered.

Overreporting is also a possibility. In

some eight cases relatives claimed that death was accidental or a consequence of grief. In two or three of these cases, the investigators were left with genuine doubts about mode of death.

Far greater sources of error are inherent, however, in the *quality* of data available from official records. In our investigation and interviewing, we found the following types and frequencies of errors in the 103 cases.

Officially reported occupation higher than actually held	14
Officially reported occupation lower than actually held	8
Officially reported occupation different but of same class level	2
Suicide's occupation given and implied as working, actually not working full-time (unemployed, part-time, retired)	37
Officially reported as married, actually divorced or separated	8
Officially reported as widowed, actually separated	1
Officially reported as divorced, actually in common-law marriage	3

These are sizeable discrepancies, and, while some may partly cancel one another out in gross totals, it seems clear that the careful study of such behavior requires validation checks through data gathered by other than official methods. It is thus not surprising that previous sociological studies of suicide have not embraced the downward mobility hypothesis—their data probably have been overgenerous as to class. In sum, while little can be done about the conventional problem of underreporting, the quality of data can be improved through validation procedures.

OCCUPATION AND WORK STATUS AT DEATH

The question about the social class of suicides has long been open. A recent review of the subject cites the scanty knowledge available and concludes that in general there is a tendency for higher rates at both extremes of the occupational continuum.[12] Much less attention has been paid to mobility and suicide. A study published after this one was under way dealt with mobility but concluded—perhaps partly for the methodological reasons just discussed—that downward mobility (intergenerational) was only somewhat more frequent than upward mobility among male suicides.[13]

The New Orleans data show disproportionately high rates in the lower ranks, as compared to controls and census figures (Table 1). All of the five highest work strata show low rates relative to their portion of the population. Whereas only one-fourth of the city's white male labor force works as operatives, service workers, and laborers, one-half of the suicides were in those categories at time of death. The meaning of this relationship will be sought below.

One of the single most striking findings is that only fifty-two of the suicides —50 per cent—were working full-time just before they committed suicide. The others showed these work situations:

Unemployed	22
Working part-time	11
Sick or disabled	8
Retired before age 60	5
On vacation or leave, killed self within day of return to work	3

---

12 Jack P. Gibbs, "Suicide," in *Contemporary Social Problems*, eds. R. K. Merton and Robert A. Nisbet (New York: Harcourt, Brace, 1961), pp. 222–61. See also the several studies of Norman L. Farberow and Edwin S. Schneidman; their most recent work is *The Cry for Help* (New York: McGraw-Hill Book Company, 1961).

13 Austin L. Porterfield and Jack P. Gibbs, "Occupational Prestige and Social Mobility of Suicides in New Zealand," *American Journal of Sociology*, 66 (September 1960), 147–52.

*Willing and able to work, waiting turn
on roster*   2

More of the suicides between ages 20 and 39 were working full-time (63 per cent) than the 40—49 group (43 per cent) and the 50—60 group (49 per cent). Only 40 per cent of those in the lowest occupational group (service and laboring workers) were working full-time. All but one of the five retired men were white-collar men in their fifties. The three on vacation or leave had given signs of disaffection from work before leaving their job —but all three also had difficulties apart from the work sphere.

Why were they not working full-time? Above and beyond those who were sick, retired, on vacation or a work roster, the remainder show this pattern:

*Fired (includes three who were laid
off with others in a work force)*   13
Quit 1–6 days prior to suicide   3
Quit 7 days or more prior to suicide   12

The nonwork status in most cases was of considerable duration. Of the fifty-one men not working full-time, only nine had been in this condition less than 21 days. The rest had been out of work or working part-time for 3 weeks or more, and the period stretched out to several years for some.

VERTICAL MOBILITY

As important as class is for the definition of life chances, the longitudinal direction of movement over time is equally vital. This is seen, for example, in studies of prejudice, political conservatism, and other apparent correlates of "skidding."[14] The working hypothesis

in this study singled out downward mobility as an independent variable in male suicide. Here we will be examining behavior Durkheim saw as "anomic." His discussion of anomic suicide is not static but implies a temporal sequence of events. In stable times, he noted, "society" (internalized in the conscience) sets limits on individual desires. This regulation collapses when society is disturbed by a painful crisis, and society is momentarily unable to exercise this influence. A new scale of controls cannot be quickly institutionalized.[15] The relationship between ends and means is no longer clear to the individual. It was at this point that Durkheim spoke of "declassification" of the individual, coming as close to downward mobility as he ever came. The materials to be presented here provide some insight into the process of declassification, but they also show that this happens in individual cases and in good times as well as bad.

Intergenerational mobility. When the occupational level of the suicide and his father are compared, considerable mobility—mostly downward—appears. Using North-Hatt categories for the cases for whom comparative data were available, we find:

	SUICIDES	CONTROLS
Subject's father higher	*53 per cent*	*31 per cent*
Subject's father lower	25	38
Same	22	31
Totals	75	169

14 Bruno Bettelheim and Morris Janowitz, *The Dynamics of Prejudice* (New York: Harper, 1950); Melvin M. Tumin, *Desegregation* (Princeton, N.J.: Princeton University Press, 1958), pp. 127–41; Richard Hofstadter, "The Pseudo-Conservative Revolt," in *The New American Right*, ed. Daniel Bell (New York: Criterion Books, 1955); and other works cited in Harold L. Wilensky and Hugh Edwards, "The Skidder," *American Sociological Review*, 24 (April 1959), 216.

15 *Op. cit.*, pp. 248–53.

A similar pattern is found when the census classification of occupations is used. The effect of intergenerational mobility on suicide is clearly related to age, as shown in Table 3. Almost two-thirds of the younger suicides held a position lower than their father's, but this proportion recedes for each age group. Likewise, the proportion of occupational levels shared by father and son is smallest for the young suicides. The "stress and strain" often ascribed to adolescents may continue into the early work life of many men if these trends are representative.

Work-life mobility. Most studies of mobility have used intergenerational data. There is recent evidence, however, that work-life mobility—experienced by the individual during his own career—is likewise relevant.[16] Among the suicides, considerable downward mobility—"skidding"—is found and relatively little upward mobility. This tendency should not come as a surprise in view of the wide prevalence of non-work in the group, already reported. In this section, however, the status "unemployment" is not taken as a work status to be compared with earlier jobs; all work-life mobility comparisons are made between the last (or present) job held and prior jobs.

TABLE 3. INTERGENERATIONAL
MOBILITY OF SUICIDES BY
AGE, PER CENT

	20–39	40–49	50–60
Son higher	22	30	24
Same	13	19	32
Son lower	65	52	44
Totals	23	27	25

16 Wilensky and Edwards, *op. cit.*

One would expect that those suicides not working full-time at death had also experienced more work-life skidding than those who remained at work. This expectation is borne out in the data. Also evident, however, is the finding that more of the terminally employed had experienced downward than upward mobility during the last years of life (see Table 4).

A final index of occupational performance comes from questions about financial income. Incomes were compared for the last year before death and 2 years before that; for the controls, we used present income as against income received 2 years earlier. (Some one-fifth of the income figures were estimated, using wage and salary scales prevailing in the city.) Decreasing incomes characterized more than half the suicides, whereas men of the control group were showing gains. The proportions, excluding cases for which data were incomplete, were:

	SUICIDES	CONTROLS
Income increased	*8 per cent*	*35 per cent*
Income decreased	*51*	*11*
Income same	*41*	*54*
Totals	*101*	*164*

Taking all forms of downward mobility as given individually above, and all 103 cases of suicide, it is found that seventy-seven men—75 per cent—suffered at least one of these forms of drop in status. Intergenerational skidding amounts to 53 per cent of the cases and income loss to 51 per cent, while work-life skidding varies in its contribution from 35 to 43 per cent, depending upon the base and scale employed. One-half of the intergenerational skidders were also work-life skidders. Evidence is at hand that three-fourths of the suicides showed one or more forms of skidding, with its potential consequences of disappointment, frustration, decreased ap-

TABLE 4. WORK-LIFE MOBILITY OF WORKING AND NONWORKING SUICIDES AND CONTROLS, USING TWO OCCUPATIONAL SCALES, PER CENT*

	Suicides		
Work Status	Full-Time	Not Full-Time	Con-trols
Using census categories			
Upward	19	9	12
Same (or only one job)	57	45	83
Downward	24	47	5
Using North-Hatt categories			
Upward	17	9	12
Same (or only one job)	50	41	83
Downward	33	50	5
Totals	52	51	187

* The work-life comparison for the suicides is between last job held and the one preceding. For the controls the comparison was restricted to the past 10-year period; more mobility in both directions would have been shown had a longer work period been studied.

proval granted by peers, and decreased self-respect. In some of the remaining twenty-six cases, it is still possible that similar disappointments with work were present, such as the failure to receive an expected promotion or raise, but such conditions were not coded. It must not be forgotten that, also among the remaining twenty-six cases, adequate work performance was being carried out and in some upward work-life mobility was present. Also, skidding was present among the controls. In short, skidding cannot be hypothesized as anything more than one highly significant

factor in the complex suicide syndrome. Studies of suicide from the individual point of view which neglect skidding, on the other hand, are overlooking a variable which may be crucial in the etiology of suicide.

Skidding in the three classes. Skidding does not occur in random fashion throughout the class hierarchy. Intergenerationally, enormous differences are found between the three occupational strata (see Table 5). The top group (white-collar men) actually contained more upward than downward cases. The ratio is reversed for the middle group, and the lowest stratum shows 88 per cent downward mobility. A similar pattern is found with respect to work-life mobility (see Table 6).

The findings about vertical mobility among the white-collar men pose a

TABLE 5. INTERGENERATIONAL MOBILITY OF SUICIDES, BY OCCUPATIONAL CLASS, PER CENT

	White Collar	Skilled, Operative	Service, Labor
Son higher	37	38	0
Same	41	8	13
Son lower	22	54	88
Totals	27	24	24

TABLE 6. WORK-LIFE MOBILITY OF SUICIDES, BY OCCUPATIONAL CLASS, PER CENT

	White Collar	Skilled, Operative	Service, Labor
Upward	22	13	3
Same (or only one job)	54	50	33
Downward	24	37	64
Totals	33	26	30

direct challenge to a central hypothesis of this paper. Further analysis, using the variable of income trend, supplies at least part of the rebuttal. As shown in Table 7, the white-collar men were experiencing the highest rate of income loss of the three work strata. Almost three-fifths of them showed decreasing income over the last· 2-year period. Thus this stratum too was "downward," although the form it took was more specifically financial than work-level in nature.

Further information on this point about the twenty-four men in the categories "professional, managerial, proprietors, and officials" shows a range of strains. Three, for example, were very ill; two others had accidents that impaired regular work and other activities; five or six had alcohol problems; three at most had something of a mental-nervous-emotional problem, although none of these was serious from the evidence obtained; three were former blue-collar men who had entered business and were doing poorly. And about half showed strains from either the mother or the wife relationship; several appeared to have been dominated by their mother and showed characteristics of dependency.[17] (Some individuals displayed more than one of these symptoms.)

None of these factors present so clear a picture for these top-level men, however, as the "work-performance" factor. Above and beyond the three former working men with failing businesses, three professional and managerial men failed to receive promotions after many years with a concern; and one manager was demoted after a merger (the respondent's description of the reduced physical dimensions and other status symbols of the man's new office

was both vivid and poignant). In only one case, that of an official, was there an outright dismissal. Four had retired; all but one of these had money; one closed his successful business on the death of his wife, with whom he had been inseparable; and one retired to drink a great deal while still talking of business expansion. It is not difficult to form the impression that these men felt acute dissatisfaction with their performance and standing in their respective business and professional circles. They appear to be classic cases of anomic suicide in the world of commerce and industry as depicted by Durkheim.

The work stratum which actually shows the fewest signs of work problems—despite the small amount of technical skidding among the white-collar men—is that of the skilled worker. This is the only working-class stratum which is underrepresented among the suicides. Work-life skidding is almost nonexistent in this stratum. Perhaps having learned a trade in a day of relatively low supply and high demand for these skills, their work status is secure. Furthermore, most of these men were said to be *good* workers. They showed as many domestic and

TABLE 7. INCOME TREND OF
SUICIDES, BY OCCUPATIONAL
CLASS, PER CENT*

	White Collar	Skilled, Operative	Service, Labor
Upward	14	6	3
Same	28	50	42
Downward	58	44	55
Totals	36	32	33

* The comparison is between income gained during the last year of life as against income gained 2 years before that. About one-fifth of the income figures were estimated from rates prevailing in the city.

---

17 Farberow and Schneidman, *op. cit.*

health problems as the others, but in the work sphere it may be that their very security as artisans turned their aspirations up to entrepreneurial and managerial positions, with all the frustrations and complications of this possible shift in work providing considerable strain. This possibility was suggested by several cases.

In his Tulsa study, Powell found several occupations with much higher suicide rates than others.[18] These included pharmacists, cab drivers, physicians, nurses, and lawyers. In New Orleans there were no pharmacist suicides during the 6-year period and no nurses were included in the all-male sample. While only one physician appeared in the city sample, two others were among the larger total of 304 but were living in suburbs and thus were excluded from study. Two lawyers were among the 103, however, and four cab drivers. Occupations ranking low in both cities were carpenter, accountant, mechanic, truck driver, engineer, machinist, and welder.

Several occupations appeared to be disproportionately represented in New Orleans. These were watchman or guard, 7; police and sheriff employees, 6; sales workers, 8, with an added 3 for route man; bar proprietors, 3; and other small proprietors, 3. Differences with Powell's findings may be due in part to the possible bias stemming from the use of official job titles in the Tulsa study. It seems clear that two jobs (cab driver and watchman-guard) may be deadends in the downward path, that sales work is associated with job strains, and that several other men had experienced a chaotic work pattern rather than the smoothly rising gradient typical of successful careers.

While there are differences between the classes in rates of suicide, no such variation appears in the process. Men decide to take their lives in the same way, and for the same kinds of reasons, throughout the class structure.

DOWNWARD MOBILITY AND THE DRIFT HYPOTHESIS

Sociological and ecological data about deviant behavior, when analyzed in terms of class factors, meet the problem of possible "drift": To what extent do data on suicide, mental ill-health, etc., reflect "real" differences in classes and residential areas, or do individuals with morbidity problems "drift" into these classes and neighborhoods? Studies in Chicago and New Haven have shown that the drift by schizophrenics from higher class residential areas to slums is not great.[19] The New Haven study revealed also that schizophrenics did not drift downward (intergenerationally) from higher-class levels but were of the same class level as their parents. No data are available from existing studies of suicide; ecological studies agree, however, that the highest rates are found in slum areas.

Our data show that geographical drift, from higher- to lower-class neighborhoods, was infrequent among the 103 suicides. Only three of them clearly moved to the slums within 2 years before death, and some six or eight others might have—the data are problematic. In any event, well over ninety of the men did not make such a move. When

---

[18] Elwin H. Powell, "Occupation, Status and Suicide," *American Sociological Review*, 23 (April 1958), pp. 131–39.

[19] See August B. Hollingshead and Frederick C. Redlich, *Social Class and Mental Illness* (New York: John Wiley & Sons, Inc., 1958), pp. 244–48.

the address-at-death data of the men are plotted on a map, it is seen that they lived in all of the predominantly white areas of the city.

These data suggest an interpretation of the findings in other cities showing high suicide rates in the zones in transition. It will be recalled that our 103 cases had all resided in the city for at least 6 months, but that during the same 6-year period forty-two white males without this residential history had committed suicide within the city limits. Most of these men took their lives in the central areas, in hotels or rooming house districts—that is, they "drifted" in. Had they been included in this study, the ecological distribution would have more closely resembled that found in Chicago, Seattle, etc., where no restriction was placed upon length of residence. From the point of view of this paper, which takes into account reciprocal role performance over time, these in-migrants do not have roots in the community. Other studies of suicide —and of other morbidities—could control for this factor when official data indicate the length of residence in the city.

If the drift hypothesis is recast in terms of vertical mobility, our suicide data show a clear picture of downward drift. Although few suicides drifted to the slums, it might be that the skidders felt they would soon be forced into cheaper housing. This added barb may have strengthened their tendency to end an intolerable situation.

EGOISTIC AND ALTRUISTIC SUICIDE

This report has focused on the relationship between white male suicide, work, and class mobility. These factors appear to be more characteristic of Durkheim's "anomic" type of suicide than of his egoistic and altruistic forms. Space limitations prohibit extended discussion of findings under the latter headings, but it should be stated that the 103 suicides also showed marked characteristics of egoistic suicide, as seen in family, group, and religious membership and attachment to a set of shared values. Forms of altruistic suicide, quite different from those hypothesized by Powell, were also found. As for related pathologies, mental problems, alcoholism, physical health, and police problems were present, with rates not markedly different from those reported in other studies. Most individual suicides are complex phenomena, involving the individual's role performance in several positions over a period of time; the purpose of this paper was to highlight the relevance of the work role for American males but not to insist that this is the only major factor involved.

TOWARD A STRUCTURAL-INTERACTIONAL THEORY OF SUICIDE

Numerous hypotheses have been advanced to account for deviant behavior. Only those dealing with structured strain and interactional process will be considered here. Merton's theory of social structure and anomie posits social and cultural standards, the individual being said to accept or reject goals or institutionally prescribed means when under strain brought on by the malintegration of goals and means.[20] While Merton asks whether or not the individual accepts or rejects (or strives to change) structural conditions, a further notion is being advanced here. Once the

---

[20] Robert K. Merton, *Social Theory and Social Structure* (Glencoe, Ill.: The Free Press, 1957), pp. 121–94.

individual has decided to accept or reject cultural prescriptions, he acts. Our interest is on the quality of his action, as evaluated by self and others. A focus on the interpersonal consequences of action is contained in the Cooley-Mead tradition and developed by Lemert to apply to deviance.[21]

The process can be reviewed most simply in terms of Cooley's "looking-glass self." The actor acts, alter assesses, and actor reacts to the other's assessment with a self-feeling, such as pride or shame. A favorable evaluation pleases the actor; a negative one hurts, is damaging to the actor's ego. Now when a man—one of our suicides—is fired or not rehired or when a businessman continually fails to show a profit, these actions may result in encounters with others eventuating in a sense of "shame." On telling his wife the news, or facing colleagues and coworkers in the community, the fact of his inadequate work performance may be reflected in their eyes and lodged in the actor's self-awareness. Even before the news is out, he can anticipate these negative evaluations, having internalized the community's work standards. The norm that American men should be working, and working in adequate fashion, can be taken as axiomatic.

The process sketched here is most clearly informed by the theoretical position of Lemert, which embodies much of the Cooley-Mead tradition. Although he criticized "interaction theory" as insufficient in itself to explain deviance, he has proposed a theory of deviation which emphasizes the social self, the differentiation of the deviant from the group, and progressive sanctions from alter following deviation. Ego's deviations increase until he accepts for himself the deviant role imputed to him by a growing number of alters.

Several studies suggest the relationship between low achievement and deviation. A psychiatric study of attempted suicides found that many patients mentioned job and work problems as contributing to their feelings of despondency, although none of them reported work as their biggest single problem.[22] Pearlin found that hospital nurses with low job achievement showed high alienation scores, although such feelings were reduced with higher income.[23] Haskell has reported that delinquents who secured and kept jobs did not recidivate, whereas nonworking boys did.[24] From a more social-psychological approach, Reckless and his associates found that a group of "good" boys (not considered prone to delinquency) showed more favorable self-conceptions than "bad" boys.[25]

The notion of the quality of role performance is seldom used explicitly by sociologists. Actually it is never far from social-psychological concern. When we use concepts like prestige, esteem, self-conception, and the social self, quality of role performance is implied. Parsons, for example, in his treatment of deviance used the notion of "adequacy" in terms of alter's evaluation of ego's performance and ego's

---

[21] Edwin M. Lemert, *Social Pathology* (New York: McGraw-Hill Book Company, 1951), pp. 3–98.

[22] Eli Robins, Edwin H. Schmitt, and Patricia O'Neal, "Some Interrelations of Social Factors and Clinical Diagnosis in Attempted Suicide," *American Journal of Psychiatry*, 114 (1957), 221–31.

[23] Leonard Pearlin, "Alienation from Work," *American Sociological Review*, 27 (June 1962), 314–26.

[24] Martin R. Haskell, "Toward a Reference Group Theory of Juvenile Delinquency," *Social Problems*, 8 (Winter 1960–61), 220–30.

[25] Walter C. Reckless, Simon Dinitz, and Ellen Murray, "Self Concept as an Insulator Against Delinquency," *American Sociological Review*, 21 (December 1956), 744–46.

awareness of that judgment.[26] Many sociologists make the assumption, usually implicit, that men have certain "needs," such as approval and recognition.

Bredeméier and Toby have recently approached this topic in terms of human standards. "Four kinds of standards, which nearly all human beings acquire, can be distinguished."[27] These are standards of adequacy, worthiness, gratification, and security. All of them are relevant to potential deviance, in that they relate the individual to structural forces and requisites, but for present purposes the most crucial is "adequacy." "Measuring up to the standard gives the individual a feeling of achievement and self-satisfaction; falling below it produces a painful sense of failure, or self-devaluation, of shame." Using this criterion, many of our suicides were shown to lack competence on the job. And, because in American society the work role is central for the man, work failure is not inadequancy in just one role among many but spreads through other roles and the self-image to threaten a general collapse of the life organization.

CONCLUSION

New Orleans white male suicides showed substantial problems associated

---

[26] Talcott Parsons, *The Social System* (Glencoe, Ill.: The Free Press, 1951), pp. 259–62.

[27] Harry C. Bredemeier and Jackson Toby, *Social Problems in America* (New York: John Wiley & Sons, Inc., 1960), pp. 3–10.

with work, as seen in downward mobility, reduced income, unemployment, and other job and business difficulties. This finding can be used to refine Durkheim's treatment of anomic suicide. His data did not permit him to specify the differential consequences of anomie on particular strata of the labor force. Further, Durkheim was committed to focusing on the *increase* in suicide during periods of anomie. This left him in a weak position to account for the existence of substantial amounts of anomic suicide in periods of the kinds of integration he dealt with in the *Division of Labor in Society*. Anomic suicide can and does occur under integrated conditions as well as during anomie, and low-achievement performances promote suicide in good times or bad. The questions asked in the two studies differ, but anomie is the focus of both. It was also demonstrated that official data on suicides may be of questionable validity, and that suicides "drift" downward in class but not so much in the ecological sense.

All downwardly mobile men do not, of course, commit suicide (as shown in the control group), just as all entrepreneurs do not kill themselves during economic crisis. The probabilities of both, however, are higher. It is suggested that certain other aspects of evaluated role performance, as in family relationships, may also yield associations with suicide, and that a structural-interactional approach may be profitably employed in studying the etiology of other individual pathologies such as alcoholism and mental illness.

DELINQUENCY

Studies of the relationship between social stratification and delinquency provide examples of the interplay between theory and research. Using an ecological framework early studies of official delinquency confirmed the widely held impression that lower socioeconomic areas were breeders of deviant behavior.[1] Later

TABLE 9.1. NUMBER AND RATE* OF YOUTHFUL CRIMINALS, BY SEX AND RATING OF SOCIOECONOMIC FAVORABILITY** OF RESIDENCE, FOR A 3-YEAR PERIOD (1958–1960), UNDUPLICATED COUNT†

					Rating							
	I		II		III		IV		Unknown		Total	
Sex	Number	Rate	Number	Rate	Number	Rate	Number	Rate	Number	Rate	Number	Rate
Male	182	74.0	271	85.0	621	136.1	1326	224.1	334	—	2734	169.6
Female	8	2.8	27	7.3	52	9.0	215	30.0	48	—	350	18.0
Unknown	0	—	0	—	6	—	5	—	0	—	11	—
Total	190	35.7	298	43.2	679	65.8	1546	118.1	382	—	3095	86.9

* Number of youthful criminals in specified category per 1,000 persons in specified category, 16–20
** I=most favorable
IV=least favorable
† From Orville R. Gursslin, *Youth Crime, 1958–60* (Buffalo, N. Y.: Buffalo Youth Board, 1961), p. 10.

TABLE 9.2. NUMBER AND RATE* OF YOUTHFUL CRIMINALS, BY RACE AND RATING OF SOCIOECONOMIC FAVORABILITY** OF RESIDENCE, FOR A 3-YEAR PERIOD (1958–1960), UNDUPLICATED COUNT†

					Rating							
	I		II		III		IV		Unknown		Total	
Race	Number	Rate	Number	Rate	Number	Rate	Number	Rate	Number	Rate	Number	Rate
White	185	35.1	276	40.8	535	56.8	807	83.5	314	—	2117	68.1
Nonwhite	5	106.4	21	148.9	132	146.5	727	212.1	63	—	948	209.9
Unknown	0	—	1	—	12	—	12	—	5	—	30	—
Total	190	35.7	298	43.2	679	65.8	1546	118.1	382	—	3095	86.9

* Number of youthful criminals in specified category per 1,000 persons in specified category, 16–20
**I=most favorable
IV=least favorable
† From Orville R. Gursslin, *Youth Crime, 1958–60* (Buffalo, N. Y.: Buffalo Youth Board, 1961), p. 10.

[1] One of the first of these ecological investigations was Clifford R. Shaw and Henry D. McKay, "Social Factors in Juvenile Delinquency," *Report on the Causes of Crime*, The National Commission on Law Observance and Enforcement, Vol. 2 (Washington, D.C.: Government Printing Office, 1931).

studies of official delinquency have generally supported these findings.[2] The data in Tables 9.1 and 9.2 are representative of findings on the distribution of delinquency by socioeconomic areas, based upon research in Buffalo, New York.

Some studies of the prevalence of delinquency in the youth population have attempted to determine whether the relationship between delinquency and class obtains for unofficial data. Those who use unofficial data claim that there is a serious bias in official delinquency reports in favor of the middle class.[3]

Studies using self-reports rather than official data have attempted to measure the "real" association between class and delinquency. John Clark and Eugene Wenninger review some of these findings and conclude that minimal association is typical in self-report studies. They give special attention in their research to community types as significant variables. As communities increase in size to the point of becoming large metropolitan areas, the relationship between class and delinquency increases. Since official data are most often drawn from large communities and most previous self-report studies are based upon small communities, Clark and Wenninger conclude that differences in results may reflect differences in method.

---

[2] For a general review of such studies see Orville R. Gursslin, "The Formulation and Partial Test of a Class-Linked Explanation of Delinquency," (unpublished Ph.D. dissertation, State University of New York at Buffalo, 1961), Chap. 1. Also, Robert A. Gordon, "Issues in the Ecological Study of Delinquency," *American Sociological Review*, 32 (December 1967), 927–44.

[3] For example, F. Ivan Nye, James F. Short, and Virgil J. Olson, "Socio-Economic Status and Delinquent Behavior," *American Journal of Sociology*, 63 (January 1958), 381–89.

SOCIOECONOMIC CLASS AND AREA AS CORRELATES OF ILLEGAL BEHAVIOR AMONG JUVENILES*†

John P. Clark, *University of Illinois*

Eugene P. Wenninger, *Kent State University*

Until recently almost all efforts to discover characteristics that differentiate juveniles who violate legal norms from those who do not have compared institutional and noninstitutional populations. Though many researchers still employ a "delinquent" or "criminal" sample from institutions,[1] there is a growing awareness that the process through which boys and girls are selected to populate our "correctional" institutions may cause such comparison studies to distort seriously the true picture of illegal behavior in our society. Therefore, conclusions based upon such studies are subject to considerable criticism[2] if generalized beyond the type of population of the particular institution at the time of the study. Although the study of adjudicated offenders is important, less encumbered studies of the violation of legal norms hold more promise for those interested in the more general concept of deviant behavior.

Though it, too, has methodological limitations, the anonymous-questionnaire procedure has been utilized to obtain results reflecting the rates and patterns of illegal behavior among juveniles from different social classes, ages, sexes, and ethnic groups in the general population.[3] The results of these studies have offered sufficient evidence to indicate that the patterns of illegal behavior among juveniles may be dramatically different than was heretofore thought to be the case.

Some of the most provocative findings have been those that challenge the almost universally accepted conclusion

* From John P. Clark and Eugene P. Wenninger, "Socioeconomic Class and Area as Correlates of Illegal Behavior Among Juveniles," *American Sociological Review*, 27 (December 1962), 826–34. Reprinted by permission of the American Sociological Association.

† The total project of which this paper is a part was sponsored by the Ford Foundation and the University of Illinois Graduate Research Board. Professor Daniel Glaser was very helpful throughout the project and in the preparation of this paper.

[1] An outstanding example of this type of research design is Sheldon and Eleanor Glueck, *Unraveling Juvenile Delinquency* (New York: The Commonwealth Fund, 1950).

[2] See Marshall B. Clinard, *Sociology of Deviant Behavior* (New York: Rinehart, 1958), p. 124, for his assessment of the validity of the study by the Gluecks, *op. cit.*

[3] Most outstanding are those by Austin L. Porterfield, *Youth in Trouble* (Fort Worth, Texas: Leo Potishman Foundation, 1946); F. Ivan Nye and James F. Short, "Scaling Delinquent Behavior," *American Sociological Review*, 22 (June 1957), 326–31; and Robert A. Dentler and Lawrence J. Monroe, "Early Adolescent Theft," *American Sociological Review*, 26 (October 1961), 733–43; Fred J. Murphy, Mary M. Shirley, and Helen L. Witmer, "The Incidence of Hidden Delinquency," *American Journal of Orthopsychiatry*, 16 (October 1946), 686–96.

that the lower socioeconomic classes have higher rates of illegal behavior than do the middle or upper classes. For example, neither the Nye-Short study[4] nor that of Dentler and Monroe[5] revealed any significant difference in the incidence of certain illegal or "deviant'" behaviors among occupational-status levels—a finding quite at odds with most current explanations of delinquent behavior.

Although most of the more comprehensive studies in the social-class tradition have been specifically concerned with a more-or-less well-defined portion of the lower class (i.e., "delinquent gangs,"[6] or "culture of the gang," or "delinquent subculture"[7]), some authors have tended to generalize their findings and theoretical formulations rather specifically to the total lower-class population of juveniles.[8] These latter authors certainly do not profess that *all* lower-class children are equally involved in illegal behavior, but by implication they suggest that the incidence of illegal conduct (whether brought to the attention of law enforcement agencies or not) is more pervasive in this class than others because of some unique but fundamental characteristics of the lower social strata. For example, Miller has compiled a list of "focal concerns" toward which the lower class supposedly is oriented and because of which those in this class violate more legal norms with greater frequency than other classes.[9] Other authors point out that the lower classes are disadvantaged in their striving for legitimate goals and that they resort to deviant means to attain them.[10] Again, the result of this behavior is higher rates of illegal behavior among the lower socioeconomic classes.

Therefore, there *appears* to be a direct conflict between the theoretical formulations of Miller, Cohen, Merton, Cloward and Ohlin, and those findings reported by Nye and Short and Dentler and Monroe. This apparent discrepancy in this literature can be resolved, however, if one hypothesizes that the rates of illegal conduct among the social classes vary with the type of community[11] in which they are found. Were this so, it would be possible for studies which have included certain types of communities to reveal differential illegal

---

4 James F. Short, "Differential Association and Delinquency," *Social Problems*, 4 (January 1957), 233–39; F. Ivan Nye, *Family Relationships and Delinquent Behavior* (New York: John Wiley & Sons, Inc., 1958); James E. Short and F. Ivan Nye, "Reported Behavior as a Criterion of Deviant Behavior," *Social Problems*, 5 (Winter 1957–1958), 207–13; F. Ivan Nye, James F. Short, and Virgil J. Olson, "Socio-Economic Status and Delinquent Behavior," *American Journal of Sociology*, 63 (January 1958), 381–89.

5 Dentler and Monroe, *op. cit.*

6 Richard A. Cloward and Lloyd E. Ohlin, *Delinquency and Opportunity: A Theory of Delinquent Gangs* (New York: The Free Press of Glencoe, Inc., 1961).

7 Albert K. Cohen, *Delinquent Boys: The Culture of the Gang* (Glencoe, Ill.: Free Press, 1955).

8 Walter B. Miller, "Lower Class Culture as a Generating Milieu of Gang Delinquency," *Journal of Social Issues*, 14, No. 3 (1958), 5–19.

9 *Ibid.* The matter of class difference in "focal concerns" or values will be explored in subsequent articles.

10 Cohen, *op. cit.*; Cloward and Ohlin, *op. cit.*; and Robert K. Merton, *Social Theory and Social Structure* (Glencoe, Ill.: Free Press, 1957), pp. 146–49.

11 In this report "type of community" is used to refer in a general way to a geographic and social unit having certain distinctive demographic qualities, such as occupational structure, race, social class, and size. Designations such as "rural farm" or "Negro lower-class urban" or "middle-class suburbia" have long been utilized to describe such persistent physical-social characteristics.

behavior rates among social classes, while studies which have involved other types of communities might fail to detect social-class differences.

Whereas the findings and formulations of Merton, Cohen, Cloward and Ohlin, and Miller are oriented, in a sense, toward the "full range" of social situations, those of Nye-Short and Dentler-Monroe are very specifically limited to the types of populations used in their respective studies. It is important to note that the communities in which these latter studies were conducted ranged only from rural to small city in size. As Nye points out, "They are thus urban but not metropolitan."[12] Yet, most studies of "delinquent gangs" and "delinquent subcultures" have been conducted in metropolitan centers where these phenomena are most apparent. Perhaps, it is only here that there is a sufficient concentration of those in the extreme socioeconomic classes to afford an adequate test of the "social-class hypothesis."

In addition to the matter of social-class concentration and size, there is obviously more than one "kind" of lower class and each does not have rates or types of illegal behavior identical to that of the others. For example, most rural farm areas, in which occupations, incomes, and educational levels are indicative of lower-class status, as measured by most social-class indices, consistently have been found to have low rates of misconduct—in fact lower than most urban middle-class communities.

Therefore, to suggest the elimination of social class as a significant correlate to the quantity and quality of illegal behavior before it has been thoroughly examined in a variety of community situations seems somewhat premature. Reiss and Rhodes concluded as a result of study of class and juvenile court rates by school district that "it is clear that there is no simple relationship between ascribed social status and delinquency."[13] In order to isolate the factor of social class, to eliminate possible effects of class bias in the rate at which juvenile misbehavior is referred to court, as well as to vary the social and physical environs in which it is located, we chose in this study to compare rates of admitted illegal behavior among diverse communities within the northern half of Illinois. Our hypotheses were:

1. Significant differences in the incidence of illegal behavior exist among communities differing in predominant social-class composition, within a given metropolitan area.
2. Significant differences in the incidence of illegal behavior exist among similar social-class strata located in different types of community.
3. Differences in the incidence of illegal behavior among different social-class populations within a given community are not significant.

THE STUDY

The data used to test the above hypotheses were gathered in 1961 as part of a larger exploratory study of illegal behavior (particularly theft) among juveniles, and its relationship to socioeconomic class, type of community, age, race, and various attitudinal variables, such as attitude toward law, feelings of alienation, concept of self, and feelings

---

[12] Nye, Short, and Olson, *op. cit.*, p. 383.

[13] Albert J. Reiss and Albert L. Rhodes, "The Distribution of Juvenile Delinquency in the Social Class Structure," *American Sociological Review*, 26 (October 1961), 720–32.

TABLE 1. DUNCAN SOCIOECONOMIC-INDEX SCORES BASED ON
OCCUPATION OF FATHER

| Score | Type of Community | | | |
	Rural Farm, Per Cent	Lower Urban, Per Cent	Industrial City, Per Cent	Upper Urban, Per Cent
(1) 0–23	75.9	40.4	36.4	5.7
(2) 24–47	9.9	15.5	19.3	4.8
(3) 48–71	4.7	12.5	22.9	43.9
(4) 72–96	1.5	4.2	10.0	34.6
(5) Unclassifiable*	8.0	27.4	11.4	11.0
Total	100	100	100	100
	(N=274)	(N=265)	(N=280)	(N=335)

*This category included those respondents from homes with no father and those respondents who did not furnish adequate information for reliable classification.   The 27.4 per cent figure in the lower urban community reflects a higher proportion of "fatherless" homes rather than greater numbers of responses which were incomplete or vague in other ways.

of being able to achieve desired goals. Subsequent reports will deal with other aspects of the study.

A total of 1154 public school students from the sixth through the twelfth grades in the school systems of four different types of communities were respondents to a self-administered, anonymous questionnaire given in groups of from twenty to forty persons by the senior author. Considerable precaution was taken to insure reliability and validity of the responses. For example, assurances were given that the study was not being monitored by the school administration; questions were pretested to eliminate ambiguity; and the administration of the questionnaire was made as threat-free as possible.

The four communities represented in the study were chosen for the unique social-class structure represented by each. The Duncan "Socio-Economic Index for All Occupations"[14] was used to determine the occupational profile of each community by assigning index scores to the occupation of the respondents' fathers. The results are summarized in Table 1.

The overwhelming majority of the respondents comprising the *rural farm* population live on farms, farming being by far the most common occupation of their fathers. Many of the fathers who were not listed as farmers were, in fact, "part-time" farmers. Therefore, though the Duncan Index would classify most of the residents in the lower class, most of these public school children live on farms in a prosperous section of the Midwest. The sixth, seventh, and eighth graders were drawn from schools located in very small villages. Grades 9–12 were drawn from the high school, which was located in open farm land.

The *lower urban* sample is primarily composed of children of those with occupations of near-equal ranking but

---

14 Albert J. Reiss, Jr., Otis Dudley Duncan, Paul K. Hatt, and Cecil C. North,

Occupations and Social Status (New York: The Free Press of Glencoe, Inc., 1961), especially pp. 109–61 prepared by Duncan.

certainly far different in nature from those of the rural farm community. The lower urban sample was drawn from a school system located in a very crowded and largely Negro area of Chicago. The fathers (or male head of the family) of these youngsters are laborers in construction, waiters, janitors, clean-up men, etc. Even among those who place relatively high on the Duncan Scale are many who, in spite of their occupational title, reside, work, and socialize almost exclusively in the lower-class community.

As Table 1 demonstrates, the occupational structure of the *industrial city* is somewhat more diffuse than the other communities, though consisting primarily of lower-class occupations. This city of about 35,000 is largely autonomous, although a small portion of the population commutes daily to Chicago. However, about two-thirds of these students have fathers who work as blue-collar laborers in local industries and services. The median years of formal education of all males age 25 or over is 10.3.[15] The median annual family income is $7,255.[16] The population of this small city contains substantial numbers of Polish and Italian Americans and about 15 per cent Negroes.

Those in the *upper urban* sample live in a very wealthy suburb of Chicago. Nearly three-fourths of the fathers in these families are high-level executives or professionals. The median level of education for all males age 25 or over is 16 plus.[17] The median annual family income is slightly over $20,000—80 per cent of the families make $10,000 or more annually.[18]

With two exceptions, representative sampling of the public school children was followed within each of these communities: (1) those who could not read at a fourth grade level were removed in all cases, which resulted in the loss of less than one-half per cent of the total sample, and (2) the sixth grade sample in the industrial city community was drawn from a predominantly Negro, working-class area and was, therefore, nonrepresentative of the total community for that grade level only. All the students from grades 6 through 12 were used in the rural farm community "sample."

MEASURE OF ILLEGAL BEHAVIOR

An inventory of thirty-six offenses was initially assembled from delinquency scales, legal statutes, and the FBI Uniform Crime Reports. In addition to this, a detailed list of theft items, ranging from candy to automobiles, was constructed. The latter list was later combined into two composite items (minor theft and major theft) and added to the first list, enlarging the number of items in this inventory to thirty-eight items as shown in Table 2. No questions on sex offenses were included in this study, a restriction found necessary in order to gain entrance into one of the school systems.

All respondents were asked to indicate if they had committed each of these offenses (including the detailed list of theft items) *within the past year*, thus furnishing data amenable to age-level analysis.[19] If the respondents admitted commission of an offense, they so indicated by disclosing the number

---

15 *U.S. Census of Population: 1960,* Final Report PC (1)–15C, p. 15–296.

16 *Ibid.,* p. 15–335.

17 *Ibid.,* p. 15–305.

18 *Ibid.,* p. 15–344.

---

19 Rates of illegal behavior were found to increase until age 14–15 and then to decrease.

of times (either 1, 2, 3, or 4 or more) they had done so. The first four columns of Table 2 reveal the percentage of students who admitted having indulged in each specific behavior one or more times *during the past year*.

Specific offense items were arranged in an array from those admitted by the highest percentage of respondents to those admitted by the lowest percentage of respondents. Obviously the "nuisance" offenses appear near the top while the most serious and the more situationally specific fall nearer the end of the listing.[20] Several offenses are apparently committed very infrequently by school children from the sixth to twelfth grades regardless of their social environs.

FINDINGS

In order to determine whether significant differences exist in the incidence of illegal behavior among the various types of communities, a two-step procedure was followed. First, each of the four communities was assigned a rank for each offense on the basis of the percentage of respondents admitting commission of that offense. These ranks were totaled across all offenses for each community. The resultant numerical total provided a very crude overall measure of the relative degree to which

the sample population from each community had been involved in illegal behavior during the past year. The results were (from most to least illegal behavior) : industrial city, lower urban, upper urban, and rural farm. However, there was little overall difference in the sum of ranks between upper urban and rural farm and even less difference between the industrial city and lower urban areas.

In the second step the communities were arranged in the order given above and then the significance of the difference between adjacent pairs was determined by applying the Wilcoxon matched-pairs signed-ranks test. Only those comparisons which involve either industrial city or lower urban versus upper urban or rural farm result in any significant differences.[21] This finding is compatible with the above crude ranking procedure.

On the basis of these findings the first hypothesis is supported, while the second hypothesis received only partial support. Lower urban juveniles reported significantly more illegal behavior than did the juveniles of the upper urban community, and the two lower-class communities of industrial city and lower urban appear to be quite similar in their high rates, but another lower-class area composed largely of farmers has a much lower rate, similar to that of the upper urban area.

---

20 Ordinarily, not receiving 100 per cent admission to the first few offenses listed would have raised doubt as to the validity of those questionnaires on which these extremely common offenses were not admitted. In the Nye-Short study such questionnaires were discarded. However, since the respondents were asked in this study to admit their offenses during the past year only, it was thought that less than 100 per cent admission would be highly possible when one considers the entire age range. Undoubtedly some of the respondents who did not admit these minor offenses were falsifying their questionnaires.

21 Significance of differences was calculated between pairs of communities across *all* thirty-eight offenses by using the Wilcoxon matched-pairs signed-ranks test (described in Sidney Siegel, *Non-Parametric Statistics* [New York: McGraw-Hill Book Company, 1956], pp. 75–83). The results of this procedure were:

1–2—*P* 0.35	1–3—*P* 0.00006
2–3—*P* 0.0034	1–4—*P* 0.0006
3–4—*P* 0.90	2–4—*P* 0.016

TABLE 2. PERCENTAGE OF RESPONDENTS ADMITTING INDIVIDUAL OFFENSES AND SIGNIFICANCE OF DIFFERENCES BETWEEN SELECTED COMMUNITY COMPARISONS

Offense	(1) Industrial City N=280	(2) Lower Urban N=265	(3) Upper Urban N=335	(4) Rural Farm N=274	Significance of Differences* (1–2)	(2–3)	(3–4)
1. Did things my parents told me not to do.	90	87	85	82	X	X	X
2. Minor theft (compilation of such items as the stealing of fruit, pencils, lipstick, candy, cigarettes, comic books, money less than $1, etc.).	79	78	80	73	X	X	X
3. Told a lie to my family, principal, or friends.	80	74	77	74	X	X	X
4. Used swear words or dirty words out loud in school, church, or on the street so other people could hear me.	63	58	54	51	X	X	X
5. Showed or gave someone a dirty picture, a dirty story, or something like that.	53	39	58	54	1	3	X
6. Been out at night just fooling around after I was supposed to be home.	49	50	51	35	X	X	3
7. Hung around other people who I knew had broken the law lots of times or who were known as " bad " people.	49	47	27	40	X	2	4
8. Threw rocks, cans, sticks, or other things at passing car, bicycle, or person.	41	37	33	36	X	X	X
9. Slipped into a theater or other place without paying.	35	40	39	22	X	X	3
10. Major theft (compilation of such items as the stealing of auto parts, autos, money over $1, bicycles, radios and parts, clothing, wallets, liquor, guns, etc.).	37	40	29	20	X	2	3
11. Gone into another person's house, a shed, or other building without their permission.	31	16	31	42	1	3	4

(continued on next page)

TABLE 2 (CONT'D)

Offense	(1) Indus-trial City N=280	(2) Lower Urban N=265	(3) Upper Urban N=335	(4) Rural Farm N=274	Significance of Differences* (1–2)	(2–3)	(3–4)
12. Gambled for money or something else with people other than my family.	30	22	35	26	X	3	3
13. Got some money or something from others by saying that I would pay them back even though I was pretty sure I wouldn't.	35	48	26	14	2	2	3
14. Told someone I was going to beat up on them unless they did what I wanted them to do.	33	28	24	32	X	X	4
15. Drank beer, wine, or liquor without my parents' permission.	38	37	26	12	X	2	3
16. Have been kicked out of class or school for acting up.	27	28	31	22	X	X	3
17. Thrown nails or glass or cans in the street.	31	29	21	17	X	X	X
18. Used a slug or other things like this in candy, coke, or coin machines.	24	35	18	12	2	2	3
19. Skipped school without permission.	24	36	18	11	2	2	3
20. Helped make a lot of noise outside a church or school or any other place in order to bother the people inside.	17	37	18	15	X	2	X
21. Threw rocks or sticks or any other thing in order to break a window or street light or thing like that.	24	26	22	16	X	X	3
22. Said I was going to tell something on someone unless they gave me money, candy, or something else I wanted.	23	28	17	19	X	2	X
23. Kept or used something that I knew had been stolen by someone else.	29	36	15	16	X	2	X

Community

486

TABLE 2 (CONT'D)

| Offense | Community | | | | Significance of Differences* | | |
	(1) Indus- trial City $N=280$	(2) Lower Urban $N=265$	(3) Upper Urban $N=335$	(4) Rural Farm $N=274$	(1–2)	(2–3)	(3–4)
24. Tampered or fooled with another person's car, tractor, or bicycle while they weren't around.	26	13	19	24	1	3	X
25. Started a fist fight.	26	22	15	18	X	2	X
26. Messed up a restroom by writing on the wall or leaving the water running to run onto the floor or upsetting the waste can.	18	33	14	17	X	2	X
27. Hung around a pool hall, bar, or tavern.	21	18	10	23	X	2	4
28. Hung around the railroad tracks and trains.	16	13	23	16	X	3	3
29. Broken down or helped to break down a fence, or door on another person's place.	15	14	8	8	X	2	X
30. Taken part in a "gang fight."	12	18	7	7	X	2	X
31. Ran away from home.	12	12	8	7	X	X	X
32. Asked for money, candy, a cigarette, or other things from strangers.	12	12	6	7	X	2	X
33. Carried a razor, switchblade, or gun to be used against other people.	8	16	3	4	2	2	X
34. "Beat up" on kids who hadn't done anything to me.	8	5	5	6	X	X	X
35. Broke or helped break up the furniture in a school, church, or other public building.	8	4	2	8	X	X	4
36. Attacked someone with the idea of killing them.	3	6	1	3	2	n	n
37. Smoked a reefer or used some sort of dope (narcotics).	3	4	1	3	X	n	n
38. Started a fire or helped set a fire in a building without the permission of the owner.	3	2	1	3	X	n	n

* Code: X=no significant difference
1, 2, 3, or 4=significant differences at 0.05 level or higher. The numbers indicate which of the communities in the comparison is higher in incidence of the offense.
n=too few offender cases to determine significant level

Much more contrast among the rates of juvenile misconduct in the four different communities than is indicated by the above results becomes apparent when one focuses on individual offenses. As the last column in Table 2 reveals, and as could be predicted from the above, there are few significant differences in the rates on each offense between the industrial city and lower urban communities. The few differences that do occur hardly fall into a pattern except that the lower urban youth seem to be oriented more toward violence (carrying weapons and attacking persons) than those in the industrial city.

However, sixteen of a possible thirty-five relationships are significantly different in the upper urban-rural farm comparison, a fact that could not have been predicted from the above results. Apparently, variation in one direction on certain offenses tends to be neutralized by variation in the opposite direction on other offenses when the Wilcoxon test is used. There are greater actual differences in the nature of illegal behavior between these two communities than is noticeable when considered in more summary terms. (It might be pointed out here, parenthetically, that this type of finding lends support to the suggestion by Dentler and Monroe that the comparison of criterion groups on the basis of "omnibus scales" may have serious shortcomings.[22])

Rural farm youngsters are more prone than those in the upper urban area to commit such offenses as trespassing, threatening to "beat up" on persons, hanging around taverns, and being with "bad" associates—all relatively unsophisticated acts. Although some of the offenses committed more often by those who live in the upper urban community are also unsophisticated (throwing rocks at street lights, getting kicked out of school classes, and hanging around trains), others probably require some skill to perform successfully and probably depend on supportive peer-group relationships. For example, these data reveal that upper urban juveniles are more likely than their rural farm counterparts to be out at night after they are supposed to be at home, drink beer and liquors without parents' permission, engage in major theft, gamble, skip school, and slip into theaters without paying. In addition to their likely dependence upon peer groups, perhaps these offenses are more easily kept from the attention of parents in the urban setting than in open farm areas.

The greatest differences between rates of illegal conduct occur between the lower urban and upper urban communities, where twenty-one of a possible thirty-five comparisons reach statistical significance, the lower urban rates being higher in all except five of these. Although the upper urban youngsters are more likely to pass "dirty pictures," gamble, trespass, hang around trains, and tamper with other people's cars, their cousins in the lower-class area are more likely to steal major items, drink, skip school, destroy property, fight, and carry weapons. The latter offenses are those normally thought to be "real delinquent acts," while the upper urban offenses (with the exception of vehicle tampering) are not generally considered to be such.

To summarize briefly, when the rates of juvenile misconduct are compared on individual offenses among communities, it appears that as one moves from rural farm to upper urban to industrial city and lower urban, the incidence of most offenses becomes greater, especially in the more serious

---

22 Dentler and Monroe, *op. cit.*, p. 734.

offenses and in those offenses usually associated with social structures with considerable tolerance for illegal behavior.

While most emphasis is placed here on the differences, one obvious finding, evident in Table 2, is that in most of the nuisance offenses (minor theft, lying to parents, disobeying parents, swearing in public, throwing objects to break things or into the streets) there are no differences among the various communities. Differences appear to lie in the more serious offenses and those requiring a higher degree of sophistication and social organization.

The Reiss-Rhodes findings tend to refute theories of delinquent behavior which imply a high delinquency proneness of the lower class regardless of the "status area" in which it is found.[23] In view of this report and since Nye-Short and Dentler-Monroe were unable to detect interclass differences, interclass comparisons were made within the four community types of this study. Following the technique employed by Nye and Short, only those students age 15 and younger were used in these comparisons in order to neutralize the possible effects of differential school drop-out rates by social classes in the older categories.

With the exception of the industrial city, no significant interclass differences in illegal behavior rates were found within community types when either the Wilcoxon test was used for all offenses or when individual-offense comparisons were made.[24] This finding supports hypothesis 3. It could account for the inability of Nye-Short and Dentler-

Monroe to find differences among the socioeconomic classes from several relatively similar communities in which their studies were conducted. It is also somewhat compatible with the Reiss and Rhodes findings. However, we did not find indications of higher rates of illegal conduct in the predominant socioeconomic class within most areas, as the Reiss and Rhodes data suggested.[25] This may have been a function of the unique manner in which the socioeconomic categories had to be combined for comparison purposes in this study. These findings, however, are logical in that boys and girls of the minority social classes within a "status area" would likely strive to adhere to the norms of the predominant social class as closely as possible whether these norms were legal or illegal.

Within the industrial city the second socioeconomic category (index scores 24–47) was slightly significantly lower than either extreme category when the Wilcoxon test was used. Since the largest percentage of the sample of the industrial city falls in the lowest socioeconomic category (0–23) and since this category evidences one of the highest rates of misconduct, the finding for this community is somewhat similar to the Reiss-Rhodes findings.

---

23 Reiss and Rhodes, *op. cit.*, p. 729. The concept of "status areas" is used here as it was used by Reiss and Rhodes to designate residential areas of a definite social-class composition.

24 Because of small numbers in social classes within certain communities, categories were collapsed or ignored for comparison

purposes as shown below. Refer to Table 1 for designation of categories. The Wilcoxon matched-pairs signed-ranks test was used.

Rural farm
    category 1 versus 2,3,4   insignificant
Lower urban
    category 1 versus 2,3,4   insignificant
    category versus 5   insignificant
    categories 2,3,4 versus 5   insignificant
Industrial city
    category 1 versus 2   significant
    category 2 versus 3,4   significant
    category 1 versus 3,4   insignificant
Upper urban
    category 3 versus 4   insignificant
    25 Reiss and Rhodes, *op. cit.*, p. 729.

CONCLUSIONS

The findings of this study tend to resolve some of the apparent conflicts in the literature that have arisen from previous research concerning the relationship between the nature of illegal behavior and socioeconomic class. However, some of the results contradict earlier reports.

Our findings are similar to those of Nye-Short and Dentler-Monroe in that we failed to detect any significant differences in illegal-behavior rates among the social classes of rural and small urban areas. However, in keeping with the class-oriented theories, we did find significant differences, both in quantity and quality of illegal acts, among communities or "status areas," each consisting of one predominant socioeconomic class. The lower-class areas have higher illegal-behavior rates, particularly in the more serious types of offenses. Differences among the socioeconomic classes within these "status areas" were generally insignificant (which does not agree with the findings of Reiss and Rhodes), although when social-class categories were compared across communities, significant differences were found. All this suggests some extremely interesting relationships.

1. The pattern of illegal behavior within small communities or within "status areas" of a large metropolitan center is determined by the predominant class of that area. Social-class differentiation within these areas is apparently not related to the incidence of illegal behavior. This suggests that there are community-wide norms which are related to illegal behavior and to which juveniles adhere regardless of their social-class origins. The answer to the obvious question of how large an urban area must be before socioeconomic class becomes a significant variable in the incidence of illegal behavior is not provided by this study. It is quite likely that, in addition to size, other considerations such as the ratio of social-class representation, ethnic composition, and the prestige of the predominant social class relative to other "status areas" would influence the misconduct rates. The population of 20,000 of the particular upper urban community used in this study is apparently not of sufficient size or composition to provide for behavior autonomy among the social classes in the illegal-behavior sense. There is some evidence, however, that an industrial city of roughly 40,000, such as the one included here, is on the brink of social-class differentiation in misconduct rates.

2. Though the juveniles in all communities admitted indulgence in several nuisance offenses at almost equal rates, serious offenses are much more likely to have been committed by lower-class urban youngsters. Perhaps the failure of some researchers to find differences among the social classes in their misconduct rates can be attributed to the relatively less serious offenses included in their questionnaires or scales. It would seem to follow that any "subculture" characterized by the more serious delinquencies would be found only in large, urban, lower-class areas. However, the data of this study, at best, can only suggest this relationship.

3. Lastly, these data suggest that the present explanations that rely heavily on socioeconomic class as an all-determining factor in the etiology of illegal behavior should be further specified to include data such as this study provides. For example, Cohen's thesis that a delinquent subculture emerges when lower-class boys discover that they must satisfy their need for status by means other than those advocated in the middle-class public schools should be

amended to indicate that this phenomenon apparently occurs only in large metropolitan centers where the socioeconomic classes are found in large relatively homogeneous areas. In the same manner, Miller's theory of the relationship between the focal concerns of the lower-class culture and delinquency may require closer scrutiny. If the relationship between focal concerns and illegal behavior that Miller has suggested exists, then those in the lower social class (as determined by father's occupation) who live in communities or "status areas" that are predominantly of some other social class are apparently not participants in the "lower class culture"; or, because of their small numbers, they are being successfully culturally intimidated by the predominant class. Likewise, those who are thought to occupy middle-class positions apparently take on lower-class illegal-behavior patterns when residing in areas that are predominantly lower class. This suggests either the great power of prevailing norms within a "status area" or a limitation of social class, as it is presently measured, as a significant variable in the determination of illegal behavior.

RESEARCH QUESTIONS

At least three general questions that demand further research emerge from this study:

1. What dimension (in size and other demographic characteristics) must an urban area attain before socioeconomic class becomes a significant variable in the determination of illegal-behavior patterns?

2. What are the specific differences between lower-class populations and social structures located in rural or relatively small urban areas and those located in large, concentrated areas in metropolitan centers that would account for their differential illegal-behavior rates, especially in the more serious offenses?

3. The findings of this study suggest that the criteria presently used to determine social-class levels may not be the most conducive to the understanding of variation in the behavior of those who fall within these classes, at least for those within the juvenile ages. A substitute concept is that of "status area" as operationalized by Reiss and Rhodes. For example, the differentiating characteristics of a large, Negro, lower-class, urban "status area" could be established and would seem to have greater predictive and descriptive power than would the social-class category as determined by present methods. Admittedly, this suggestion raises again the whole messy affair of "cultural-area typologies" but area patterns of behaviors obviously exist and must be handled in some manner. Research effort toward systematically combining the traditional socioeconomic-class concept with that of cultural area might prove extremely fruitful by providing us with important language and concepts not presently available.

Sociologists have used various theoretical explanations to account for the high incidence of official delinquency in lower-class areas. The ecological view holds that lower socioeconomic areas are inhabited by a heterogeneous, economically depressed, and highly mobile population. Differences in value orientation give rise to confusion and uncertainty on the part of the young. Insufficient internalization of normative patterns results and in turn produces delinquency.[1] An alternative explanation is offered by Edwin H. Sutherland's differential-association theory, which emphasizes exposure of the young person to criminal values in high-delinquency areas. He sees delinquent behavior as the result of an excess of definitions favorable to violation of the law over definitions favoring legal conformity.[2]

Still other explanations of lower-class delinquency have been developed in recent years. Walter Miller,[3] for one, contends (in contrast to those who favor the status-frustration thesis[4]) that lower-class delinquency is directly a product of a distinct lower-class culture rather than of exposure and reaction to the middle-class value system.[5] Miller refers to lower-class focal concerns—trouble, toughness, smartness, excitement, fate, and autonomy—which can lead to or come to be labeled as delinquent acts. Whatever the process, Miller's position is that the origins of this delinquency are in the lower-class cultural milieu.

The works of Robert Merton,[6] Albert K. Cohen,[7] Richard A. Cloward and Lloyd E. Ohlin[8] collectively represent a separate body of theory linking social class with delinquency. The paper by Gursslin and Roach discusses their theoretical contributions, with particular attention to the work of Cohen. It emphasizes the need to specify the way in which class, as an independent variable, is associated with delinquency as a dependent variable. Such specifications should make clear the social-psychological assumptions and intervening variables on which the framework is based.

---

1 Shaw and McKay, *op. cit.* A view derived from this ecological approach but departing from the thesis of disorganization as set forth by Shaw and McKay is the culture-conflict school. In general, this framework is based on the following assumptions: (1) Groups arise because they serve important needs of their members (i.e., members share common values and frames of reference). (2) Groups come in conflict when the interests or the purposes they serve are competitive with one another. (3) If one group is successful in having its values, interests, and purposes protected by the legal code, then the members of the opposing group may be defined as criminals. This theory is often tied to ethnic or class differences. See Thorsten Sellin, *Culture Conflict and Crime,* Bulletin No. 44 (New York: Social Science Research Council, 1938).

For a brief discussion of the similarities and differences between the social-disorganization and the culture-conflict approaches, see Albert K. Cohen and James F. Short, Jr., "Juvenile Delinquency," in Merton and Nisbet, *op. cit.*, pp. 104–6.

2 *Principles of Criminology* (Philadelphia: J. B. Lippincott Co., 1939).

3 "Lower Class Culture as a Generating Milieu of Gang Delinquency," *Journal of Social Issues,* 14 (April 1958), 5–19.

4 We discuss advocates of this school of thought, notably Robert Merton, Albert K. Cohen, and Richard Cloward and Lloyd Ohlin, subsequently.

5 As Miller notes, "In the case of 'gang delinquency', the cultural system which exerts the most direct influence on behavior is that of the lower-class community itself—a long-established, distinctively patterned tradition with an integrity of its own—rather than a so-called 'delinquent subculture' which has arisen through conflict with middle-class culture and is oriented to the deliberate violation of middle-class norms." *Op. cit.*, p. 5.

6 *Op. cit.*, pp. 131–60.

7 *Delinquent Boys* (Glencoe, Ill.: The Free Press, 1955).

8 *Delinquency and Opportunity* (Glencoe, Ill.: The Free Press, 1960).

SOCIAL CLASS AND DELINQUENCY:
A THEORETICAL RESTATEMENT*

Orville R. Gursslin, *Ohio University*

Jack L. Roach, *University of Connecticut*

This paper concerns the relationship between social class and delinquency as set forth in anomie theory.[1] The writings of Merton, Cohen, and Cloward and Ohlin[2] represent the clearest statement of this relationship. Our focus is mainly on Cohen's work as an example of this body of theory.

Essentially, Cohen employed a framework derived from Merton's earlier paper, "Social Structure and Anomie". Merton directed attention to the disjunction in American society between culturally prescribed goals and socially organized access to them. This disjunction is particularly acute for those in lower-class positions, who have little opportunity to achieve success. Cohen elaborated this thesis by pointing out that lower-class persons lack certain personal qualifications for success as a result of class-linked socialization patterns. The combination of blocked opportunity (a theme developed more

---

* This paper is based in part on Orville R. Gursslin's unpublished Ph.D. dissertation, "The Formulation and Partial Test of a Class-Linked Theory of Delinquency," State University of New York at Buffalo, February 1961.

[1] It is not our purpose to consider the present status of anomie theory, delinquency theory in general, or alternative theories linking social class and delinquency. For accounts bearing upon one or several of these areas see, among others, Marshall Clinard, ed., *Anomie and Deviant Behavior* (New York: The Free Press of Glencoe, Inc., 1964); John M. Martin and Joseph P. Fitzpatrick, *Delinquent Behavior: A Redefinition of the Problem* (New York: Random House, Inc., 1965); Muzafer Sherif and Carolyn Sherif, eds., *Problems of Youth* (Chicago: Aldine, 1965); Herbert C. Quay, ed., *Juvenile Delinquency: Research and Therapy* (Princeton, N.J.: D. Van Nostrand Company, Inc., 1965); Scott Briar and Irving Pilliavin, "Delinquency, Situational Inducements and Commitment to Conformity," *Social Problems*, 13 (Summer 1965), 35–45; William C. Kvaraceus and Walter B. Miller, *Delinquent Behavior: Culture and Individual* (Washington, D.C.:

National Education Association, 1959); David Matza, *Delinquency and Drift* (New York: John Wiley & Sons, Inc., 1964); Ralph W. England, Jr., "A Theory of Middle Class Juvenile Delinquency," *Journal of Criminal Law, Criminology and Police Science*, 50 (March–April 1960), 535–40; Robert E. Stanfield, "The Interaction of Family Variables and Gang Variables in the Aetiology of Delinquency," *Social Problems*, 13 (Spring 1966), 411–17; T. R. Fyvel, *Trouble Makers: Rebellious Youth in an Affluent Society* (New York: Schocken, 1962); Muzafer Sherif and Carolyn Sherif, *Reference Groups: Exploration into Conformity and Deviation of Adolescents* (New York: Harper & Row, Publishers, 1964); Gerald Marwell, "Adolescent Powerlessness and Delinquent Behavior," *Social Problems*, 14 (Summer 1966), 35–47.

[2] Robert K. Merton, "'Social Structure and Anomie," *American Sociological Review*, 3 (October 1938), 672–82; Albert K. Cohen, *Delinquent Boys: The Culture of the Gang* (Glencoe, Ill.: The Free Press, 1955); Richard A. Cloward and Lloyd E. Ohlin, *Delinquency and Opportunity* (New York: The Free Press of Glencoe, Inc., 1960).

extensively by Cloward and Ohlin) and class-linked personal inadequacy creates status frustration,[3] seen by Cohen as a key precipitating factor in lower-class delinquency.

Cohen moved much beyond Merton's original formulation by postulating that the delinquent subculture offers a "solution" to the status problem of the lower-class boy. Since he cannot succeed in culturally defined terms, the lower-class boy seeks an alternative avenue to the attainment of status. Cohen suggests that for the child who completely breaks with middle-class norms, there are "no moral inhibitions on the free expression of aggression against the sources of his frustration."[4] This aggression consists of flagrant violation of the norms of "respectable" middle-class society and is characterized by "irrational, malicious, and unaccountable hostility." Such behavior, according to Cohen, is an overreaction which "becomes intelligible when we see that it has the function of reassuring the actor against an inner threat to his defenses as well as the function of meeting an external situation on its own

terms."[5] It should be emphasized that this interpretation assumes that the lower-class boy internalizes middle-class values to a degree sufficient to produce a problem and consequent overreaction.

Cohen devotes only a few pages of *Delinquent Boys* to a discussion of middle-class delinquency. He holds that middle-class delinquency is apt to be an expression of revolt against identification with the mother and an assertion of masculinity. The boy in the typical middle-class family has few emotional relationships with adults other than parents. Often the mother is the principal exemplar of morality, source of discipline, and object of identification. In some cases his revolt against this identification takes the form of delinquency.[6]

Cohen's explanation of middle-class delinquency refers, then, to a different set of conditions than those to which his explanation of lower-class delinquency refers. In brief, he assumes his status-frustration hypothesis is relevant to lower-class delinquency but not to middle-class delinquency. The tenability of these assumptions will now be examined, but, before doing so, let us briefly consider the use of class labels. In *Delinquent Boys*, Cohen applies the terms *lower class* and *working class* interchangeably. This is not unusual in the sociological literature. It can, however, result in misleading interpretations. There are important differences between the upper-lower and the lower-lower classes. Basic among these differences is the fact that the lower-lower class lives at or below the subsistence level, while the upper-lower class lives somewhat above the subsistence level. Henceforth, we shall refer to the lower-

---

3 Status frustration as used in this paper refers to severe or intensely felt feelings of status deprivation.

4 Cohen, *op. cit.*, p. 133. Short and Strodtbeck do not find evidence that gang boys completely break with middle-class norms. They suggest, "An explanation for the disparity between the theories and these particular data might be found in the distinction between moral validity and legitimacy." James F. Short and Fred Strodtbeck, *Group Process and Gang Delinquency* (Chicago: University of Chicago Press, 1965), p. 59. It is possible, also, that the lower-class boy with a status-frustration problem may seek a nondelinquent retreatist solution. Such a conclusion is supported by Elliott's study of school dropouts. Cf. Delbert S. Elliott, "Delinquency, School Attendance and Dropout," *Social Problems*, 13 (Winter 1966), 307–14.

5 Cohen, *op. cit.*, p. 133.

6 This view, originally stated by Parsons in more general terms, is thought by Cohen to be particularly relevant to the middle class. *Ibid.*, p. 162.

lower class as the *lower* class and the upper-lower class as the *working* class. Both classes collectively shall be referred to as the *lower classes*.

DELINQUENCY IN THE LOWER CLASSES

Cohen's theory of delinquency in the lower classes is based, in part, on the following propositions: Persons in the lower classes (1) have internalized the success goals of American culture and are motivated to achieve; (2) perceive the causes of their lack of opportunity as originating in the social structure; (3) experience a high level of status frustration, and (4) have evolved a delinquent subculture as a "solution" to the status-frustration problem.

LOWER CLASS

An implied assumption in Cohen's formulation is that the foregoing propositions are equally valid for both the working class and the lower class. However, available evidence does not support the application of these propositions to the lower class. The following generalizations are based upon empirical studies of the characteristics of lower-class persons.[7] After each generalization, we comment on its implication for the relevant proposition in Cohen's theory.

(a) Lower-class persons have low aspiration levels. They have limited interest in educational or occupational achievement. *The empirical evidence*

does not support proposition 1, which *assumes that lower-class persons have high aspiration levels.*

(b) Lower-class persons have little knowledge of the outside world. They make plans with inadequate comprehension of their implications or understanding of the alternatives. *Empirical findings do not support proposition 2, which assumes that lower-class persons have the cognitive sophistication to perceive that the social structure causes lack of opportunity.*

(c) Lower-class people are primarily concerned with subsistence maintenance rather than status. In general, they experience a low level of status frustration. *The evidence does not support proposition 3, which postulates the existence of intense status frustration in the lower class.*

(d) The self-system of lower-class persons is poorly integrated and characterized by weak ego controls. Lower-class persons have limited role skills; they lack subtleties in role-playing and have difficulties in shifting perspectives. *It is implausible that persons with such deficiencies could develop delinquent subcultures,[8] as stated in proposition 4.*

WORKING CLASS

In contrast to the lower class, in

---

[7] For specific references supporting these empirical generalizations, see Jack L. Roach and Orville R. Gursslin, "The Lower-Class, Status Frustration and Social Disorganization," *Social Forces*, 43 (May 1965), 501–10.

[8] This is not to deny that some group patterns exist in the lower class, approximating what Yablonsky refers to as "near groups." Lewis Yablonsky, *The Violent Gang* (New York: The Macmillan Company, Publishers, 1962). However, Cohen's thesis implies the existence of a strong delinquent subculture which persists from one generation to the next as a solution to the lower-class boy's problem. For a discussion of requisites for the emergence and persistence of this kind of subculture, see Jack L. Roach and Orville R. Gursslin, "An Evaluation of the Concept 'Culture of Poverty'," *Social Forces*, 45 (March 1967), 383–92. [Reproduced in Chapter Four.]

which the requisites for an experience of intense status frustration and for the development of a viable subculture are missing, evidence with respect to the working class suggests that its members (1) at least partially internalize success goals, (2) are aware of their position in the class structure and their lack of opportunity, (3) experience status frustration, and (4) are capable of evolving a subculture.[9] Adequate grounds are present, therefore, to conclude that Cohen's status-frustration theory is applicable to the working class.

DELINQUENCY IN THE MIDDLE CLASS

Following the lines of Merton's argument, Cohen assumes that because middle-class boys have opportunities to achieve success goals they do not experience status frustration. Since Cohen does not see the status-frustration framework as applicable to the mid-

dle-class, he turns to an alternative explanation in which different structural origins are hypothesized for middle-class delinquency. We contend that Cohen does not have to move away from the status-frustration hypothesis in his explanation of middle-class delinquency. The basic question is not whether opportunities are available to middle-class boys but whether all middle-class boys have the capacity to utilize available opportunities.

Two relatively distinct factors derived from the middle-class social structure may lead to the status frustration of some middle-class adolescents. First, despite learning advantages and much better job opportunities, not all middle-class adolescents can attain an equally high degree of "success." The structure of the middle-class school system and of the middle-class world in general is such that some middle-class children and adolescents are relegated to inferior positions among their contemporaries. This separation is particularly the case in homogeneous middle-class communities, where young people must compete with each other for top positions in school and in extracurricular activities. That middle-class persons attach significance to even minor status distinctions suggests that some middle-class children suffer from problems of relative status frustration. Evidence also indicates that a minority of these children do not attain positions which the middle class views as being of adequate status.[10]

---

9 Among a large number of studies supporting statements 1 through 4, are Robert H. Guest, "Work Careers and Aspirations of Automobile Workers," *American Sociological Review*, 19 (April 1954), 153–63; Ely Chinoy, *Automobile Workers and the American Dream* (Garden City, N.Y.: Doubleday & Company, Inc., 1955); August B. Hollingshead, *Social Class and Mental Illness* (New York: John Wiley & Sons, Inc., 1958), p. 104; Herbert Hyman, "The Value Systems of Different Classes: A Social-Psychological Contribution to the Analysis of Stratification," in *Class, Status and Power*, eds. Reinhard Bendix and Seymour Lipset (Glencoe, Ill.: The Free Press, 1953), pp. 426–42; Bernard C. Rosen, "Race, Ethnicity and the Achievement Syndrome," *American Sociological Review*, 24 (February 1959), 47–60; Herbert Gans, *The Urban Villagers* (Glencoe, Ill.: The Free Press, 1962); August B. Hollingshead, *Elmtown's Youth* (New York: John Wiley & Sons, Inc., 1949), pp. 102–3; William F. Whyte, *Street Corner Society* (Chicago: University of Chicago Press, 1943).

---

10 Seymour Lipset and Reinhard Bendix, *Social Mobility in Industrial Society* (Berkeley, Calif.: University of California Press, 1959), p. 190. A study by Martin Gold reaches a similar conclusion: "Perhaps the most important implication of this study is that delinquency among higher-status boys seems to follow upon the same set of pro-

When middle-class parents perceive that their child is not "succeeding," they may bring pressure upon him to do better, thus creating serious problems for the child. Seeley, Sim, and Loosley provide a description of those pressures and resulting problems in their study of "Crestwood Heights," a middle-class suburban community.

> One final and particularly devastating strain upon the family occurs when the child is required by parents to meet certain culturally approved standards of behavior which are beyond his innate abilities.... It is all too common to find in Crestwood Heights that many children are driven toward unrealistic goals. ... Such demands produce disturbance in the child, frustrate family hopes, and endanger status.[11]

Such accounts suggest the problems that may develop when the adolescent lacks the capacity for the achievement intensely demanded of him. The lack of capacity may be present and the demands are present in the middle class.

The second factor which may lead to status frustration in some middle-class adolescents is the learning of achievement prowess. In addition to

the innate ability to achieve, the capacity for showing achievement prowess is dependent upon a learning process which prepares the young person for effective status-striving. Despite their general training for achievement, particularly in the area of academic preparation and the learning of interpersonal skills, some middle-class boys are handicapped by a learned incapacity. Unlike working-class boys, who are caught in the disjunction between middle-class goals and working-class means, the middle-class boy is trapped by a contradiction in the middle-class child-rearing pattern. This contradiction has been most clearly expressed by Arnold Green,[12] who contends that (1) middle-class parents emphasize the importance of love, (2) the child's need for love is experienced precisely because he has been conditioned to need it, (3) the threat of withdrawal of love is the most characteristic means of punishment used by middle-class parents, and (4) to avoid this threat the child develops a submissive and compliant mode of adaptation. However, according to Green, the middle-class child who relieves anxiety and guilt by blind obedience and "love" for his parents cannot easily form relationships with others. He soon discovers that he is involved in competition with others, as an individual with his contemporaries and as a representative of his family. For some middle-class boys this transition is sufficiently difficult to create achievement problems.

To summarize, because of lack of innate ability or learned incapacity or both, some middle-class boys have serious achievement problems. As they grow older, increasing pressure is ex-

vocative circumstances [conditions leading to status deprivation]; but delinquency occurs less often among higher-status boys because fewer of them are subject to such status problems." Martin Gold, *Status Forces in Delinquent Boys* (Ann Arbor, Mich.: Institute for Social Research, University of Michigan, 1963), pp. 182–83. For an account suggesting a somewhat different basis for status frustration among middle-class youth, see Robert H. Bohlke, "Social Mobility, Stratification Inconsistency and Middle-Class Delinquency," *Social Problems*, 8 (Spring 1961), 351–63.

[11] John R. Seeley, R. Alexander Sim, and Elizabeth W. Loosley, *Crestwood Heights* (New York: Basic Books, Inc., Publishers, 1956), pp. 220–21.

[12] "The Middle-Class Male Child and Neurosis," *American Sociological Review*, 11 (February 1945), 31–41.

erted upon them to develop the characteristics of competitiveness, initiative, and intellectual productivity, which are essential for success in the middle-class world. This pressure reaches a high point during the adolescent period for it is then that the middle-class boy must demonstrate that he has these characteristics. The inability to achieve, derived from the sources we have suggested, together with strong pressures to achieve, causes some middle-class adolescents to strongly experience status frustration.

We have discussed the applicability of Cohen's status-frustration hypothesis to the lower, working, and middle classes. It is our contention that this hypothesis is not applicable to the lower class, where Cohen does apply it, but that it is applicable to the middle class, where Cohen does not apply it. We agree with Cohen that it is applicable to the working class. We shall now use this critique as the basis for a theoretical restatement of the relationship between social class and delinquency.

THEORETICAL REFORMULATION[13]

Below we briefly sketch an alternative theoretical scheme linking social-class factors and delinquency. We outline the relationships between antecedents and consequences in quasi-logical form. After each set of statements, we comment on the nature of the linkages and suggest the salient types of delinquency for each class. We believe that lower-class delinquency is largely a consequence of undersocialization, and that

---

13 For a detailed statement of this reformulation, as well as partial empirical support, see Gursslin, *op. cit.*

working- and middle-class delinquency are products of socialization. We hypothesize that the delinquent acts of both working- and middle-class male adolescents are forms of aggression directed against the major source of status frustration—the middle-class value system, and the middle-class people or institutions or both embodying these values. Applying Cohen's framework, we postulate that delinquency in the middle class, as well as in the working class, is an overreaction and that the delinquent group provides an alternative avenue to social recognition.

Lower-Class Delinquency

1.1. Persons minimally affected by cultural patterning are incompletely socialized.

1.2. Lower-class male adolescents are minimally affected by cultural patterning.

1.3. Therefore, lower-class male adolescents are incompletely socialized.

1.4. Persons who are incompletely socialized are prone to impulsive behavior.

1.5. Lower-class male adolescents are incompletely socialized (see 1.3).

1.6. Therefore, lower-class male adolescents are prone to impulsive behavior.

2.1. Persons who are prone to impulsive behavior are apt to be delinquents.

2.2. Lower-class male adolescents are prone to impulsive behavior (see 2.6).

2.3. Therefore, lower-class male adolescents are apt to be delinquents.

Lower-class persons are governed primarily by basic-need deprivation rather than by status deprivation. They have not internalized the central cultural value of success or other values functionally related to it and can be considered, accordingly, as inadequately socialized.[14] Yablonsky discusses the connections among inadequate socialization, sociopathic personality, and delinquency in the lower class. He describes sociopathic personalities as "essentially characterized by (a) a lack of social conscience; (b) a limited ability to relate, identify, or empathize with others except for egocentric objectives; (c) manifestations of impulsive, aggressive, and socially destructive violent behavior when impulsive immediate needs are not satisfied."[15] Lower-class adolescents are therefore more likely to commit delinquent acts of a violent nature. As Yablonsky[16] points out, the near-group violent gang is found in the slum environment.[17]

WORKING-CLASS DELINQUENCY

1.1. Persons who have partially internalized success-goal values but do not have legitimate or illegitimate success channels or who lack the ability to take advantage of them experience status frustration.

1.2. Many working-class male adolescents have partially internalized success-goal values but do not have legitimate or illegitimate channels of success or lack ability to take advantage of them.

1.3. Therefore, many working-class male adolescents experience status frustration.

2.1. Status frustration among working-class male adolescents leads to out-group aggression directed against the middle class.

2.2. Working-class male adolescents' out-group aggression directed against the middle class involves rejection of culturally prescribed, essentially middle-class means and goal values.

2.3. Rejection of culturally prescribed means and goal values produces delinquent behavior.

Working-class delinquency is a result of status frustration. It leads to out-group aggression consisting of rejection of culturally prescribed, essentially middle-class means and goal values. Such rejection is possible in the working class because of the relatively weak means values in American society and the fact that working-class youth only partially internalize the goal values. Vandalism and acts of public disorder[18] are examples of the kind of delinquent behavior directed against middle-class values and institutions representing these values.[19]

---

[14] For a discussion of the relationship between conditions of poverty and sociocultural deprivation, see Jack L. Roach, "Economic Deprivation and Lower-Class Behavior" (unpublished Ph.D. dissertation, State University of New York at Buffalo, 1964).

[15] Yablonsky, *op. cit.*, p. 161.

[16] *Ibid.*

[17] In addition to evidence of more serious crimes of violence in the lower class, findings show that a larger proportion of all lower-class crimes are in this category. See Gursslin, *op. cit.*, p. 134. Moreover, evidence indicates that a larger proportion of lower-class than middle-class delinquents is engaged in crimes of violence. Cf. Leon F. Fannin and Marshall B. Clinard, "Differences in the Conception of Self as a Male Among Lower and Middle Class Delinquents," *Social Problems*, 13 (Fall 1965), 205–14.

[18] For evidence that destruction of property constitutes the higher proportion of all working-class crimes, see Gursslin, *op. cit.*, p. 136.

[19] Implied here is not only the rejection of means and goal values but also, in line with Cohen's conception, the substitution of anithetical values. This state of mind contains some of the elements of *ressentiment* and some of the elements of Merton's conception of rebellion. Cf. Robert K. Merton, *Social Theory and Social Structure* (rev. ed.) (Glencoe, Ill.: The Free Press,

MIDDLE-CLASS DELINQUENCY

1.1. Persons who strongly internalize success-goal values but do not have the ability to make use of legitimate success channels experience status frustration.

1.2. Some middle-class male adolescents have strongly internalized success-goal values but do not have the ability to make use of legitimate success channels.

1.3. Therefore, some middle-class male adolescents experience status frustration.

2.1. Status frustration among middle-class male adolescents leads to in-group aggression directed against middle-class parents and the middle-class community.

2.2. Middle-class male adolescents' in-group aggression consists of rejection of culturally prescribed means but not goal values.

2.3. Rejection of culturally prescribed means but not goal values produces delinquent behavior.

Middle-class delinquency is also the result of status frustration. It leads to in-group aggression involving the rejection of middle-class means but not goal values. This in-group aggression is directed against middle-class parents and the middle-class community in general, both of which stress the development of legitimate means abilities. The middle-class boy can reject the relatively weak means values but, unlike the working-class boy, he cannot reject the strongly internalized middle-class goal values. Crimes of property acquisition are examples of the kind of delinquency which represents the nonnormative attainment of strongly internalized culturally prescribed goals.[20]

SUMMARY AND CONCLUSION

The work of Merton, Cohen, and Cloward and Ohlin,[21] *in toto*, represents the most developed theoretical statement, to date, of the relationship between social class and delinquency. We have used Cohen's thesis as a basis for examining the nature of this relationship. He emphasizes the existence of differential opportunities in the social structure and assumes a relatively uniform degree of socialization throughout society. As a consequence, the lower classes experience status frustration and seek a deviant solution. We have suggested that (1) the conditions for status frustration exist in the middle class as well as in the working class and (2) lower-class delinquency results from a relative lack of personal control not from status frus-

---

1957), pp. 155–56. In the formulation for the working class, reference is made to the failure to develop abilities to take advantage of illegitimate means. Some evidence shows that, although an illegitimate opportunity structure exists in the working class, only a few working-class male adolescents are able to avail themselves of it. We omit reference to illegitimate-means abilities in the formulation for the middle class because, for middle-class male adolescents, the illegitimate opportunity structure is negligible. Such a structure is available only to middle-class adults who have obtained an occupational status making possible white-collar crime.

---

[20] A study by Wattenberg and Balistrieri indicates that middle-class delinquents are more apt to be automobile thieves than are lower-class delinquents. William W. Wattenberg and James J. Balistrieri, "Automobile Theft: A Favored-Group Delinquency," *American Journal of Sociology*, 62 (May 1952), 575–79. For evidence that crimes of property acquisition in general constitute the higher proportion of all middle-class crimes, see Gursslin, *op. cit.*, p. 134.

[21] Merton, *op. cit.*; Cohen, *op. cit.*; Cloward and Ohlin, *op. cit.*

tration. Sociopathic behavior in the lower class is a product of undersocialization, which is, in turn, a consequence of the rudimentary lower-class social structure. This rudimentary social structure results from the conditions of economic deprivation, which make it impossible for lower-class persons to become full-fledged social actors.

Merton's essay "Social Structure and Anomie" was a reaction against the explanation of deviance in terms of an undersocialized conception of man. More recently, and in more general terms, Dennis Wrong and others[22]

have reacted against the oversocialized conception of man in sociology. Both a socialized and an undersocialized conception of man are required for an adequate understanding of delinquency. In addition to the social-structural factors which propel relatively socialized man to deviant behavior, sociologists must identify and take account of the societal conditions which lead either directly or indirectly to undersocialization and consequent deviance.

---

[22] Dennis H. Wrong, "The Oversocialized Conception of Man in Modern Sociology," *American Sociological Review*, 26 (April 1961), 183–193; Richard Quinney, "A Conception of Man and Society for Criminology," *Sociological Quarterly*, 6 (Spring 1965), 119–27. In addition to discussing the critics of the oversocialized conception of man, Quinney refers to the critics of a complementary conception, the over-integrated society.

SELECTED BIBLIOGRAPHY

AUBERT, VILHELM, "White-Collar Crime and the Social Structure," *American Journal of Sociology*, 58 (November 1952), 263–71.

BATES, WILLIAM, "Caste, Class and Vandalism," *Social Problems*, 9 (Spring 1962), 306–10.

BAUM, O. EUGENE, *et al.*, "Psychotherapy, Dropouts, and Lower Socioeconomic Class Patients," *American Journal of Orthopsychiatry*, 36 (July 1966), 620–35.

BELL, WENDELL, "Anomie, Social Isolation, and the Class Structure," *Sociometry*, 20 (June 1957), 105–16.

CHAMBLISS, WILLIAM J., and MARION F. STEELE, "Status Integration and Suicide: An Assessment," *American Sociological Review*, 31 (August 1966), 524–41.

CLARK, ROBERT E., "Psychoses, Income, and Occupational Prestige," *American Journal of Sociology*, 54 (March 1949), 433–40.

CLOWARD, RICHARD A., and LLOYD E. OHLIN, *Delinquency and Opportunity.* Glencoe, Ill.: The Free Press, 1960.

COHEN, ALBERT K., *Delinquent Boys.* Glencoe, Ill.: The Free Press, 1955.

CONGER, JOHN J., and WILBER C. MILLER, *Personality, Social Class and Delinquency.* New York: John Wiley & Sons, Inc., 1966.

CURTIS, JAMES E., and JOHN W. PETRAS, "The Current Literature on Social Class and Mental Disease in America: Critique and Bibliography," *Behavioral Science*, 13 (September 1968), 382–98.

DOHRENWEND, BRUCE P., "Social Status and Psychological Disorder: An Issue of Substance and an Issue of Method," *American Sociological Review*, 31 (February 1966), 14–34.

DUBLIN, LOUIS I., *Suicide: A Sociological and Statistical Study.* New York: The Ronald Press Co., 1963.

DUNHAM, H. WARREN, *Community and Schizophrenia.* Detroit: Wayne State University Press, 1965.

ENGLAND, RALPH W., JR., "A Theory of Middle Class Juvenile Delinquency," *Journal of Criminal Law, Criminology, and Police Science*, 50 (March–April 1960), 535–40.

FARIS, ROBERT E. L., and H. WARREN

DUNHAM, *Mental Disorders in Urban Areas.* Chicago: University of Chicago Press, 1939.

FLEISHER, BELTON M., *The Economics of Delinquency.* Chicago: Quadrangle Books, 1966.

GOODE, WILLIAM J., "Economic Factors and Marital Stability," *American Sociological Review*, 16 (December 1951), 808–12.

GORDON, ROBERT A., "Issues in the Ecological Study of Delinquency," *American Sociological Review*, 32 (December 1967), 927–44.

GURSSLIN, ORVILLE R., *et al.*, "Social Class and the Mental Health Movement," *Social Problems*, 7 (Winter 1959–60), 210–18.

HENRY, ANDREW F., and JAMES F. SHORT, JR., *Suicide and Homicide.* Glencoe, Ill.: The Free Press, 1954.

HOLLINGSHEAD, AUGUST B., and FREDERICK REDLICH, *Social Class and Mental Disorders.* New York: John Wiley & Sons, Inc., 1958.

HUNT, RAYMOND G., "Social Class and Mental Illness: Some Implications for Clinical Theory and Practice," *American Journal of Psychiatry*, 116 (June 1960), 1065–69.

———, "Socio-Cultural Factors in Mental Disorder," *Behavioral Science*, 4 (April 1959), 96–106.

KANTOR, MILDRED B., ed., *Mobility and Mental Health.* Springfield, Ill.: Charles C Thomas, Publisher, 1965.

KLEINER, ROBERT J., and SEYMOUR PARKER, "Goal-Striving, Social Status, and Mental Disorder: A Research Review," *American Sociological Review*, 28 (April 1963), 189–203.

KOOS, EARL L., *The Middle Class Family and Its Problems.* New York: Columbia University Press, 1948.

KOTLAR, SALLY L., "Middle-Class Marital Role Perceptions and Marital Adjustment," *Sociology and Social Research*, 49 (April 1965), 283–93.

KRIESBERG, LOUIS, "Socio-Economic Rank and Behavior," *Social Problems*, 10 (Spring 1963), 334–52.

LEAVEY, STANLEY A., and L. Z. FREEDMAN, "Psychoneurosis and Economic Life," *Social Problems*, 4 (July 1956), 55–67.

McDERMOTT, JOHN F., *et al.*, "Social Class and Mental Illness in Children: The Question of Childhood Psychosis," *American Journal of Orthopsychiatry*, 37 (April 1967), 548–57.

MARIS, RONALD, "Suicide, Status, and Mobility in Chicago," *Social Forces*, 46 (December 1967), 246–56.

MAYER, JOHN C., *The Disclosure of Marital Problems: An Exploratory Study of Lower and Middle Class Wives.* New York: Community Service Society of New York, 1966.

MERTON, ROBERT K., "Social Structure and Anomie," in *Social Theory and Social Structure.* Glencoe, Ill.: The Free Press, 1957.

MILLER, KENT S., and CHARLES M. GRIGG, *Mental Health and the Lower Social Classes.* Tallahassee: Florida State University, 1966.

MILLER, S. M., and ELLIOT G. MISHLER, "Social Class, Mental Illness and American Psychiatry: An Expository Review," *Milbank Memorial Fund Quarterly*, 37 (April 1959), 1–26.

MILLER, WALTER B., "Violent Crimes in City Gangs," *The Annals of the American Academy of Political and Social Science*, 364 (March 1966), 96–112.

MIZRUCHI, EPHRAIM H., *Success and Opportunity.* Glencoe, Ill.: The Free Press, 1964.

MYERS, JEROME K., and BERTRAM H. ROBERTS, *Family and Class Dynamics in Mental Illness.* New York: John Wiley & Sons, Inc., 1959.

MYERS, JEROME K., *et al.*, "Social Class and Psychiatric Disorders: A Ten Year Follow-up," *Journal of Health and Human Behavior*, 6 (Summer 1965), 74–79.

NYE, F. IVAN, *et al.*, "Socio-Economic Status and Delinquent Behavior," *American Journal of Sociology*, 63 (January 1958), 381–89.

PARKER, SEYMOUR, and ROBERT J. KLEINER, *Mental Illness in the Negro Community.* New York: The Free Press of Glencoe, Inc., 1966.

REISS, ALBERT J., JR., and ALBERT LEWIS

RHODES, "The Distribution of Juvenile Delinquency in the Social Class Structure," *American Sociological Review,* 26 (October 1961), 720–32.

——, "Status Deprivation and Delinquent Behavior," *Sociological Quarterly,* 4 (Spring 1963), 135–49.

RIESSMAN, FRANK, *et al.,* eds., *Mental Health of the Poor.* New York: The Free Press of Glencoe, Inc., 1964.

ROACH, JACK L., and ORVILLE R. GURSSLIN, "The Lower Class, Status Frustration and Social Disorganization," *Social Forces,* 43 (May 1965), 501–10.

ROBERTS, ROBERT W., *The Unwed Mother.* New York: Harper & Row, Publishers, 1966.

ROBINS, LEE N., *et al.,* "Interaction of Social Class and Deviant Behavior," *American Sociological Review,* 27 (August 1962), 480–92.

ROMAN, PAUL M., and HARRISON M. TRICE, *Schizophrenia and the Poor.* Ithaca, N.Y.: New York State School of Industrial and Labor Relations, Cornell University, 1967.

ROTH, JULIUS, and ROBERT F. PECK, "Social Class and Social Mobility Factors Related to Marital Adjustment," *American Sociological Review,* 16 (August 1951), 478–87.

SHANLEY, FRED J., "Middle-Class Delinquency as a Social Problem," *Sociology and Social Research,* 51 (January 1967), 185–98.

SIEGEL, NATHANIEL H., *et al.,* "Social Class, Diagnosis, and Treatment in Three Psychiatric Hospitals," *Social Problems,* 10 (Fall 1962), 191–96.

STANFIELD, ROBERT E., "The Interaction of Family Variables and Gang Variables in the Etiology of Delinquency," *Social Problems,* 13 (Spring 1966), 411–17.

STOCKWELL, EDWARD G., "Infant Mortality and Socioeconomic Status: A Changing Relationship," *Milbank Memorial Fund Quarterly,* 40 (January 1962), 101–11.

SUTHERLAND, EDWIN H., *White-Collar Crime.* New York: Dryden, 1949.

TUCKMAN, JACOB, *et al.,* "Occupational Level and Mortality," *Social Forces,* 43 (May 1965), 575–78.

UDRY, J. RICHARD, "Marital Instability by Race and Income Based on 1960 Census Data," *American Journal of Sociology,* 72 (May 1967), 673–75.

VAZ, EDMUND G., ed., *Middle-Class Delinquency.* New York: Harper & Row, Publishers, 1966.

VOSS, HARWIN L., "Differential Association and Reported Delinquent Behavior: A Replication," *Social Problems,* 12 (Summer 1964), 78–85.

WHITE, MARY ALICE, and JUNE CHARRY, eds., *School Disorder, Intelligence, and Social Class.* New York: Teachers College Press, Columbia University, 1966.

WILLIAMSON, ROBERT C., "Socio-Economic Factors and Marital Adjustment in an Urban Setting," *American Sociological Review,* 19 (April 1954), 213–16.

WILLIE, CHARLES V., "The Relative Contribution of Family Status and Economic Status to Juvenile Delinquency," *Social Problems,* 14 (Winter 1967), 326–35.

YABLONSKY, LEWIS, *The Violent Gang.* New York: The Macmillan Company, Publishers, 1962.

YAMAMOTO, JOE, and MARCIA K. GOIN, "On the Treatment of the Poor," *American Journal of Psychiatry,* 122 (September 1965), 267–71.

CHAPTER TEN

Social Mobility

An analysis of the American stratification system is incomplete without some treatment of the phenomenon of social mobility[1]—a fundamental characteristic of class behavior. Mobility is often referred to as the dynamic aspect of stratification.[2] Thus it can be said that mobility is related to stratification in the same way that social change is related to social systems (social structure). Just as stratification appears to be an essential aspect or component of social systems, so mobility appears to be an essential aspect or component of social change. Although these analogies are crude and incomplete, they suggest some of the complexities inherent in defining the conceptual and empirical properties of social mobility.[3]

---

[1] Actually, much of the discussion and many of the papers in previous chapters have either dealt directly with or anticipated this treatment of mobility. See, for example, the references to mobility in Chapters One and Three, the descriptions of life styles in Chapters Four and Five (particularly the accounts of aspirations and status values) and the bearing of mobility on the topics of Chapters Eight and Nine.

[2] As Reissman suggests, with reference to a class society, "An individual's behavior and his attitudes may be less a function of the class he is in at the moment and much more a function of the class to which he aspires." Leonard Reissman, *Class in American Society* (Glencoe, Ill.: The Free Press, 1959), p. 295.

[3] While there is some consensus on the general meaning of social mobility as movement up or down the class ladder, Westoff *et al.* point out that it is a "complex multidimensional concept consisting presently of an indeterminate but substantial number of components." Charles F. Westoff, Marvin Bressler, and Philip C. Sagi, "The Concept of Social Mobility: An Empirical Inquiry," *American Sociological Review*, 25 (June 1960), 375. For a similar

Sociologists have viewed mobility as a source, a consequence, and an index of social change. If mobility is a consequence of social change, which of the latter's numerous dimensions are most significant for explaining the former? Some writers suggest that those changes which contribute to mobility depend largely on general processes in social systems.[4] Is this merely another way of stating that mobility is a consequence of social change, or are social organization and social stratification assumed as intervening conditions? Is mobility a crucial condition of social organization? Or, if not, what assumptions should be made about the relationship between the two? A variety of viewpoints on the role of these several concepts as independent, dependent, and intervening variables are implicit, if not manifest, in the studies of mobility presented in this chapter.[5]

Those who are higher on the scale of stratification possess and have greater opportunities to acquire highly valued goods and services. They have more opportunities to pursue chosen educational aims and more freedom to follow occupational and recreational interests. They can avoid the harmful effects of inadequate diet and shelter, neighborhood lawlessness, and mental and physical illness, as well as other pathologies frequently associated with life in the lower classes. In general, the resources of the higher classes allow them to engage in a wide variety of activities not available to those in lower socioeconomic levels.

A significant aspect of this situation is the visibility of upper-class privileges to nearly all members of a society. Mainly for this reason, most people seek higher status than that which they have; families attempt to raise their position in each new generation, and, in some cases, larger collectivities attempt to elevate their standing in society. This kind of movement or mobility within a system of stratification has fostered studies of the attributes of different strata together with their expansion and contraction.

TYPES OF MOBILITY

There are two types of mobility—horizontal and vertical. Horizontal mobility refers primarily to changes in status or role, especially occupation, which are not accompanied by corresponding changes in class or strata position. Such mobility is also known as *situs* mobility, meaning, in Richard T. Morris and Raymond J. Murphy's terms, the movement from one functional category (situs) to another equally valued one.[6] Examples are the machinist who leaves a job in one factory

---

view, see S. M. Miller, "The Concept of Mobility," *Social Problems*, 3 (October 1955), 65–72.

4 For a significant attempt to clarify relationships among several general sets of variables, see Judah Matras, "Social Mobility and Social Structure: Some Insights from the Linear Model," *American Sociological Review*, 32 (August 1967), 608–14.

5 Compare the discussion in Chapter Two of alternative views of the relationships among social differentiation, social stratification, and social organization.

6 "The Situs Dimension in Occupational Structure," *American Sociological Review*, 24 (April 1959), 231–39.

to accept a similar job in another or the cashier who becomes a waitress in the same or another restaurant.

Vertical mobility[7] refers to changes in status or occupation accompanied by changes in class or strata position in either an upward or downward direction. American society places great emphasis on the value of success through upward mobility. This ethic is nourished by the parallel belief that opportunities exist for those who want to exploit them. It is supported by widely publicized examples of those who have risen from rags to riches in the tradition of Horatio Alger. These examples are thought to establish the importance of rational, purposeful, and industrious behavior[8] for achieving mobility.

Within the context of this success ethic, studies of social mobility in American sociology take on special meaning. Most of the research concerns either the extent of upward mobility or the factors associated with it. Empirical studies of the extent of downward mobility in the American stratification system have been infrequent. As one writer suggests, "This scarcity seriously hampers the evaluation of 'familistic' and 'hereditary' forces aimed at maintaining the existing structure."[9]

Although the study of upward mobility reflects in part the predominant cultural concern, there are other reasons for its importance in the area of stratification. We shall consider several of these reasons in the subsequent discussion of the consequences of mobility.

DEGREE OF MOBILITY

Most descriptive accounts of the degree of social mobility deal with mobility at one or more periods of time or compare American society with other societies for a given period of time. Some accounts concern movement into or out of a particular group. In almost all cases, the choice of population reflects an interest in either the circulation or continuity of middle- and upper-level groups in Ameri-

---

[7] Our emphasis in this chapter is on vertical mobility, henceforth referred to as either *mobility* or *social mobility*. However, in American society, there is an intricate relationship between horizontal (situs) and vertical mobility, heightened by extensive geographical mobility in this country.

[8] The reference here, of course, is to the behavioral attributes idealized in the Protestant ethic.

[9] Egon E. Bergel, *Social Stratification* (New York: McGraw-Hill Book Company, 1962), p. 351.

Again, our reference is to the relative absence of attention to downward mobility. Substantial data do exist but typically they are provided in studies where the primary concern is with measuring upward mobility or with issues pertaining to rigidity or changing opportunities in the class structure. See, for example, Otis Dudley Duncan, "The Trend of Occupational Mobility in the United States," *American Sociological Review*, 30 (August 1965), 491–98. Page 491 of this study cites similar investigations which include findings on downward mobility.

can society.[10] Since such studies require time-comparative data, researchers must use indices based on past as well as on present data. Occupation is viewed as best satisfying this pragmatic requirement.[11] In addition, it is relatively precise and correlates highly with other indicators of class, such as income, education, and residence. Nevertheless, occupation as a criterion has the shortcomings previously discussed in Chapter Three.[12]

Studies of occupational mobility are of two types: (1) comparison of the son's occupation with that of his father (intergenerational mobility); or (2) comparison of the individual's occupational position at two or more periods in his work history (intragenerational mobility).[13] Studies of intergenerational mobility commonly find that about two-thirds of the sons have occupations which are not in the same categories as those of their fathers.[14] This result points to considerable upward and downward mobility. However, evidence indicates that the extent of this shift is slight, the son's occupation often being only one level removed from

[10] For example, Stuart N. Adams, "Trends in Occupational Origins of Business Leaders," *American Sociological Review*, 19 (October 1954), 541–48; Charles H. Coates and Roland J. Pellegrin, "Executives and Supervisors: A Situational Theory of Differential Occupational Mobility," *Social Forces*, 35 (December 1956), 121–26; Robert Perrucci, "The Significance of Intra-Occupational Mobility: Some Methodological and Theoretical Notes, Together with a Case Study of Engineers," *American Sociological Review*, 26 (December 1961), 875–83; Albert J. Reiss, Jr., "Occupational Mobility of Professional Workers," *American Sociological Review*, 20 (December 1955), 693–700; W. Lloyd Warner and James Abegglen, *Big Business Leaders in America* (New York: Harper, Inc., 1955); Vincent H. Whitney and Charles M. Grigg, "Patterns of Mobility Among a Group of Families of College Students," *American Sociological Review*, 23 (December 1958), 643–52.

[11] But, as Mayer points out, "Occupation indicates changes in class position more directly than it reflects mobility up or down in either the prestige or the power hierarchy, about which very little quantitative information exists." Kurt B. Mayer, *Class and Society* (New York: Random House, Inc., 1962), p. 69.

See also, Morris' comment on the few studies of mobility using subjective or reputational approaches. Richard T. Morris, "Social Stratification" in *Sociology*, eds. Leonard Broom and Philip Selznick (New York: Harper & Row, Publishers, 1963), pp. 204–5.

For one of the relatively few studies using income as an index of mobility with variant conclusions about the changing shape of the class structure, see Gabriel Kolko, "Economic Mobility and Social Stratification," *American Journal of Sociology*, 63 (July 1957), 30–38.

[12] In brief, just as questions must be raised about the tendency to equate occupational stratification with social stratification, so reservations must be expressed "regarding social mobility and occupational mobility as even approximately synonymous." Westoff *et al., op. cit.,* p. 379.

[13] As several writers have pointed out, much of the divergence in conclusions about mobility trends originates in the failure either to differentiate intergenerational from intragenerational mobility or to control one type while studying the other. Gerhard E. Lenski, "Social Stratification," in *Contemporary Sociology*, ed. Joseph S. Roucek (New York: Philosophical Library, 1958), pp. 521–38; Saburo Yasuda, "A Methodological Inquiry into Social Mobility," *American Sociological Review*, 29 (February 1964), p. 16.

Blau discusses several aspects of the interdependence of these two types of mobility and measures their interaction in a sophisticated research design. Peter M. Blau, "The Flow of Occupational Supply and Recruitment," *American Sociological Review*, 30 (August 1965), 475–90.

[14] Joseph A. Kahl, *The American Class Structure* (New York: Holt, Rinehart & Winston, Inc., 1957), p. 259; Walter Slocum, *Occupational Careers* (Chicago: Aldine Publishing Co., 1966), p. 172.

that of his father.[15] The more likely shift is upward rather than downward.[16] Studies of intragenerational mobility show much horizontal movement, with upward mobility typically consisting of a rise of one or two steps on the occupational ladder.[17] These studies generally indicate that the greatest cleavage in the occupational system exists between manual and nonmanual categories.[18]

Perhaps the most significant research on occupational mobility in America in the past several decades is Natalie Rogoff's study[19] which attempted to control for the influence of structural factors[20] while measuring intergenerational mobility. A major conclusion of her work is that most mobility in American society is a function of the expanding job market. Seymour Lipset and Reinhard Bendix reach a similar conclusion. In their study of mobility patterns in Western industrial countries, they found high rates of upward mobility, which they attributed to economic expansion and industrialization. These factors "are more significant in determining the extent of social mobility in a given society than variations in political, economic, or cultural value systems."[21] The evidence suggests, therefore, that the high degree of mobility in American society is a general characteristic of all advanced industrial nations and not a peculiar feature of American open-class society.[22]

The article by Elton Jackson and Harry Crockett assesses the rate of intergenerational occupational movement in America since the end of World War II. This research is of special importance because it attempts to differentiate mobility due to structural change from mobility due to occupational circulation, which in Jackson and Crockett's usage is the mutual exchange among occupational cate-

---

15 Kahl, *op. cit.*, p. 261; A. J. Jaffe and R. O. Carleton, *Occupational Mobility in the United States, 1930–1960* (New York: Kings Crown Press, 1954).

16 Kahl, *op. cit.*, p. 262; Seymour M. Lipset and Reinhard Bendix, *Social Mobility in Industrial Society* (Berkeley, Calif.: University of California Press, 1963), p. 88; Duncan, *op. cit.*, p. 498.

17 Jaffe and Carleton, *op. cit.*; Lipset and Bendix, *op. cit.*, Chap. 6.

18 *Ibid.* Later research suggests that the boundary between manual and nonmanual categories is based increasingly upon lessening downward mobility from the nonmanual into the manual ranks rather than upon restrictions on upward mobility. Blau, *op. cit.*

Moreover, as indicated in our discussion of the lower class (Chapter Four), a more significant cleavage within the manual category is that between working class and lower class. In the recent past, 10 years or less of education did not prevent large numbers of the unskilled from moving up the ladder into the semiskilled and even skilled ranks. Today this level of education poses an almost insuperable barrier for the vast majority at the bottom of the class hierarchy. For more detailed discussion, see Orville R. Gursslin and Jack L. Roach, "Some Issues in Training the Unemployed," *Social Problems*, 12 (Summer 1964), 86–98.

19 *Recent Trends in Occupational Mobility* (Glencoe, Ill.: The Free Press, 1953).

20 Structural factors encompass a number of variables usually classified under the rubrics of technological and social-organizational changes. We discuss these factors more fully in the ensuing account of the sources of mobility.

21 Most students of mobility support this assessment. To mention only a few, Kahl, *op. cit.*; Mayer, *op. cit.*; Blau, *op. cit.*

22 Lipset and Bendix, *op. cit.*, p. 13. Recent research by Lopreato shows that this generalization also holds for Italy, previously thought to be an exception. Joseph Lopreato, "Social Mobility in Italy," *American Journal of Sociology*, 71 (November 1965), 311–14.

gories. For example, upward mobility is balanced by downward mobility, and movement from rural to urban employment is balanced by the reverse sequence.

OCCUPATIONAL MOBILITY IN THE UNITED STATES: A POINT ESTIMATE AND TREND COMPARISON*†

Elton F. Jackson, *Indiana University*

Harry J. Crockett, Jr., *University of Nebraska*

Vertical mobility has come to be recognized as a crucial attribute of systems of structured inequality. Stimulated and to some extent foreshadowed by Sorokin's classic *Social Mobility*,[1] studies of social origins and mobility are an outstanding example of cumulative research in modern sociology. Most of this research has concentrated either on the individual effects of mobility or on comparing rates of mobility between societies or within the same society at different times.[2]

This paper reports research in the latter area, the study of mobility trends. We shall first present a reading as of 1957 on intergenerational occupational mobility in the United States and then compare the 1957 findings with several earlier national studies of mobility, paying particular attention to the hypothesis of growing rigidity in the system of occupational inheritance.

OCCUPATIONAL MOBILITY IN 1957

The data for our 1957 estimate of mobility come from a national sample survey conducted in the spring of that year by Gurin, Veroff, and Feld at the University of Michigan Survey Research Center.[3] The area probability (cluster) sample consisted of American adults living in private households.

* From Elton F. Jackson and Harry J. Crockett, Jr., "Occupational Mobility in the United States: A Point Estimate and Trend Comparison," *American Sociological Review*, 29 (February 1964), 5–15. Reprinted by permission of the American Sociological Association.

† The authors wish to thank Richard F. Curtis, Gerhard E. Lenski, and Richard L. Simpson for their valuable criticism and advice, Gerald Gurin for permission to use the data; and Harry P. Sharp for facilitating the analysis. This paper is a revision and expansion of a paper read at the annual meetings of the American Sociological Association, August 1962.

[1] Pitirim A. Sorokin, *Social Mobility* (New York: Harper, 1927).

[2] For a recent survey and discussion of findings on rates, consequences, and conditions of social mobility, see Seymour Martin Lipset and Reinhard Bendix, *Social Mobility in Industrial Society* (Berkeley, Calif.: University of California Press, 1959).

[3] The major findings of this survey are reported in Gerald Gurin, Joseph Veroff, and Sheila Feld, *Americans View Their Mental Health* (New York: Basic Books, Inc., Publishers, 1960). The complete interview schedule is given in Appendix I and details of the sampling procedure in Appendix II.

We shall confine our analysis to the 1023 males in the sample for whom occupational data were available for themselves and their fathers.[4]

Occupational mobility is measured from responses to the following questions: "What kind of work do you do?" and "What kind of work did your father do for a living while you were growing up?" In order to match our occupational categories, for a trend comparison, with those used by Centers in 1945, we employed his criteria[5] to recode both fathers' and sons' occupations into a seven-category scale: (1) professional, (2) business, (3) white collar, (4) skilled manual, (5) semi-skilled, (6) unskilled, and (7) farmer.[6]

For other comparisons, these are collapsed into the familiar nonmanual-manual-farm scale by combining categories 1, 2, and 3 and categories 4, 5, and 6.[7]

Table 1 presents occupational origins and destinations for the 1957 sample, using the seven-point occupational scale. These data show that in every origin category (except unskilled worker) the most common destination is the occupational category of the father—30 per cent of the men in the sample had, in this sense, "inherited" their fathers' occupational level. When movement does occur, it is usually to an adjacent or near-adjacent category. Sons of farmers who do not remain in farming tend to go into manual occupations. Although farmers' sons do

---

4 Fifty-four males had to be dropped for lack of such occupational data. The remaining 1023 males include 885 employed full-time, 103 retired, twenty-four unemployed, and eleven employed part-time. Since our object was to estimate the mobility experience of all adult U.S. males, we did not restrict the analysis to full-time employees (except when necessary for comparative purposes). The white, full-time employed sample yields very similar findings, however.

5 Centers' analysis of male mobility is presented in Richard Centers, "Occupational Mobility of Urban Occupational Strata," *American Sociological Review*, 13 (April 1948), 197–203. Somewhat more detailed statements of his occupational coding criteria can be found in his "Marital Selection and Occupational Strata," *American Journal of Sociology*, 54 (May 1949), 530–35, especially footnote 6, and *The Psychology of Social Classes* (Princeton, N.J.: Princeton University Press, 1949), pp. 48–50.

6 The following occupational codes from the 1957 survey were included in the seven categories: (1) professional: professional, technical and kindred workers, and officers in the Armed Forces; (2) business: managers, proprietors, and officials; (3) white collar: minor technicians, clerical and kindred workers, and sales workers; (4) skilled manual: craftsmen, foremen and kindred workers, skilled and semiskilled service workers, and government service workers;

(5) semiskilled: operatives and kindred workers, Armed Forces enlisted men, and unskilled service workers dealing primarily with people (barbers, beauticians, etc.); (6) unskilled: unskilled nonfarm laborers and private household workers; and (7) farmer: farm owners, managers, tenants, and laborers. The content of these categories follows Centers as closely as possible so as to permit an accurate comparison between the 1945 and 1957 data (Table 3).

7 It would have been fruitful to assess mobility using a regression analysis based on Duncan's socioeconomic index of occupations. Many of the interviews, however, did not provide sufficient detail for coding in the Duncan scheme, and, in any case, comparison with earlier studies required that we match their methods as closely· as possible. For details of this index see Otis Dudley Duncan, "A Socioeconomic Index for All Occupations" and "Properties and Characteristics of the Socioeconomic Index," Chaps. 6 and 7 in *Occupations and Social Status,* Albert J. Reiss, Jr., *et al.* (New York: Free Press of Glencoe, Inc., 1961), pp. 109–61. For an example of regression analysis of social mobility employing these scores, see Otis Dudley Duncan and Robert W. Hodge, "Education and Occupational Mobility: A Regression Analysis," *American Journal of Sociology*, 68 (May 1963), 629–44.

TABLE 1. OCCUPATION OF MALES, BY FATHER'S OCCUPATION, 1957

Occupation of Respondent's Father	Occupation of Male Respondents (in Percentages and Mobility Ratios)[a]							
	Professional, per cent	Business, per cent	White Collar, per cent	Skilled Manual, per cent	Semiskilled, per cent	Unskilled, per cent	Farmer, per cent	N (100.0 per cent)
Professional	40.4 (4.81)	19.1 (1.45)	12.8 (0.91)	19.1 (0.72)	2.1 (0.12)	4.3 (0.47)	2.1 (0.18)	47
Business	18.3 (2.18)	25.8 (1.96)	22.5 (1.61)	15.0 (0.57)	12.5 (0.72)	1.7 (0.18)	4.2 (0.36)	120
White collar	20.3 (2.41)	17.4 (1.32)	24.6 (1.76)	20.3 (0.77)	10.1 (0.59)	5.8 (0.64)	1.4 (0.13)	69
Skilled manual	8.5 (1.02)	13.6 (1.03)	15.6 (1.11)	42.2 (1.59)	14.6 (0.84)	4.5 (0.50)	1.0 (0.09)	199
Semiskilled	2.3 (0.28)	6.3 (0.47)	17.2 (1.23)	28.9 (1.09)	32.8 (1.90)	10.2 (1.12)	2.3 (0.20)	128
Unskilled	1.5 (0.18)	6.1 (0.46)	10.6 (0.76)	36.4 (1.37)	27.3 (1.58)	15.2 (1.66)	3.0 (0.26)	66
Farmer	2.5 (0.30)	11.2 (0.85)	8.4 (0.60)	21.6 (0.81)	16.5 (0.95)	13.5 (1.48)	26.4 (2.29)	394
All respondents (N's)	86	135	143	271	177	93	118	1023

Summary mobility measures : Per cent mobile :
Observed   70.0 per cent
Structural movement   27.0
Circulation   43.0
Full-equality model   84.8
Cramér's V 0.246

a Cell entries in parentheses are mobility ratios, defined as the ratio of the observed cell frequency to the cell frequency expected under conditions of full equality of opportunity.
b Some rows do not total to exactly 100.0 per cent because of rounding.

not move into nonmanual jobs as often as sons of skilled manual workers, they are more likely than sons of semiskilled and unskilled workers to go into business positions.

If we assume that our six urban occupational categories are ranked roughly in order of prestige, despite considerable intracategory variation, we can categorize urban movers as upwardly or downwardly mobile. Under this assumption, nearly a quarter of the men in the sample have moved up from an urban origin to a higher urban occupation and about a sixth have moved down.

Information beyond these simple descriptive statements may be garnered from Table 1 by comparing the observed data with two analytic models—one of maximum stability, the other of equal opportunity.

Comparison with a maximum stability model allows us to divide occupational circulation from structural movement.[8] We see in Table 1 that the number of sons in each urban occupational category is larger than the corresponding number for fathers, and that the reverse is true for the farmer category. This, of course, is partly due to the national expansion of urban occupations and contraction of rural occupations. Another source of the discrepancy is the differential fertility of fathers in various occupational groups, producing a surplus of sons in some categories and an insufficient number for full replacement in others. These differences between the fathers' and sons' marginal distributions reflect structural conditions which, in a sense, *force* occupational mobility.

Our figures indicate that if inheritance, or stability, had been at a maximum, all sons of urban fathers could have inherited their fathers' occupational level, about a quarter of the farmers' sons could have inherited, and the remaining farmers' sons would have been forced by lack of farm positions to go into the vacant urban occupations. In other words, under conditions of maximum inheritance or stability, 73 per cent of the sample would have inherited and 27 per cent (all farmers' sons) would necessarily have moved due to structural change.

The observed data, on the other hand, show much more movement than this necessary minimum generated by structural conditions. Even in urban occupations, where complete inheritance was possible, in no case did a majority of sons of a given origin inherit their fathers' occupational level. Comparison with the maximum stability model, then, indicates that of the 70 per cent who did in fact move, the movement of 27 per cent can be attributed to structural conditions; the remaining 43 per cent may be counted as circulators. "Circulation" represents mutual exchange among the occupational categories, for example, upward mobility balanced by downward, and (less frequently) movement from the farm balanced by movement from urban to rural employment. The amount of circulation suggests how open the system would be in times of structural stability.

In our second comparison, we calculate how the mobility table would look if all sons had equal occupational opportunity. This full-equality model assumes that the occupation of the father has no effect on that of the son and therefore depicts, in a sense, a situation of maximum mobility. The expected figures are computed using

---

[8] A similar analysis, employing Swedish data, can be found in Gösta Carlsson, *Social Mobility and Class Structure* (Lund: Gleerup, 1958), pp. 103–4.

the marginals in exactly the manner employed in a chi-square test. Since the full-equality model thus reflects the structural conditions expressed in the marginal distributions, deviations from the model cannot be simply attributed to structural conditions.

Several sorts of deviation from the full-equality model will be of interest to us here. In parentheses below the percentages in Table 1 are shown ratios of the observed frequency in that cell to the frequency predicted by the full-equality model. These mobility ratios indicate whether each form of movement or inheritance occurs more often than expected (ratios greater than one) or less often than expected (ratios less than one).[9] The ratios show a pattern similar to that of the percentages—a tendency for sons disproportionately to enter their father's occupational category or one nearby. Inheritance beyond random expectation is especially marked for sons of professionals and farmers. Among sons of urban workers, deviations in the direction of upward mobility are larger and more common than those indicating disproportionate downward mobility. The model figures can also be summed to yield the expected proportion experiencing all types of movement. About 85 per cent of the sample would have moved (i.e., would not have inherited) under conditions of full equality; this compares to an observed movement of 70 per cent of the men.

An overall comparison between the observed and the full-equality figures can be obtained by computing Cramér's V, a measure of association that is based on chi-square and thus reflects

the divergence of the observed from the model figures.[10] In other words, the value of V indicates the strength of the relation betwen fathers' and sons' occupations, reflecting all forms of contingency and not only direct occupational inheritance. The value of V, 0.246, is consistent with the above analysis, showing that movement in our sample departs only moderately from a system of full occupational equality.[11]

Gross Occupational Mobility. When we collapse the relatively fine occupational scale of Table 1 into a simple nonmanual-manual-farm scale, the data show that almost one-third of the sons of nonmanual workers fall into the manual stratum and the same proportion of manual sons rise into nonmanual jobs; about two-thirds of the sons from both origins are stable (detailed figures are given in Table 4 on p. 520). Farmers are recruited almost entirely from the sons of farmers, but almost three-quarters of the sons of farmers move into urban occupations, over half into the manual stratum. Farmers' sons do not attain nonmanual positions quite as often as do sons of urban manual workers.

The gross mobility table, of course, counts part of the movement appearing in Table 1 as stability, and thus gives the impression of less mobility than Table 1. When the gross mobility figures are compared with the maxi-

---

[9] For a discussion of these ratios and an extended example of their use and interpretation, see Natalie Rogoff, *Recent Trends in Occupational Mobility* (Glencoe, Ill.: Free Press, 1953), especially pp. 29–33.

[10] For a description of this measure, see Hubert M. Blalock, Jr., *Social Statistics* (New York: McGraw-Hill Book Company, 1960), p. 230.

[11] Duncan and Hodge, *op. cit.*, pp. 634–35, obtained a similarly modest zero-order correlation between fathers' and sons' occupations, using 1950 data from Chicago (r = approximately 0.30). Of course, the values of the two coefficients are not directly comparable since ours is a chi-square measure and theirs a product-moment correlation.

TABLE 2. OCCUPATION OF MALES, BY FATHER'S
OCCUPATION AND AGE, 1957

	Respondent's Father Nonmanual Worker			
	Respondent's Occupation			
Respondent's Age in 1957	Nonmanual	Manual	Farm	$N(100.0$ per cent)[a]
21–29	63.8 per cent	36.2 per cent	0.0 per cent	47
30–39	72.7	25.0	2.3	44
40–49	73.8	26.2	0.0	65
50–59	67.6	24.3	8.1	37
60 and over	52.4	40.5	7.1	42

	Respondent's Father Manual Worker			
	Respondent's Occupation			
	Nonmanual	Manual	Farm	$N(100.0$ per cent)[a]
21–29	33.3 per cent	65.4 per cent	1.3 per cent	78
30–39	33.6	65.5	0.9	110
40–49	29.9	68.8	1.3	77
50–59	27.0	68.3	4.8	63
60 and over	25.0	73.4	1.6	64

	Respondent's Father Farmer			
	Respondent's Occupation			
	Nonmanual	Manual	Farm	$N(100.0$ per cent)[a]
21–29	17.1 per cent	53.7 per cent	29.3 per cent	41
30–39	23.0	60.9	16.1	87
40–49	30.9	49.4	19.8	81
50–59	29.2	48.6	22.2	72
60 and over	12.5	46.4	41.1	112

[a] Some rows do not total to exactly 100.0 per cent because of rounding. These N's total to only 1020 because the ages of three respondents were not ascertained.

mum stability model (Table 4), the percentage of mobility attributable to structural change is still 27 per cent, because the only structural movement is from farm to urban occupations and the farm category was not collapsed when the occupational scale was reduced to three categories. The percentage of men who can be regarded as circulators thus drops to about 21 per cent. In our second comparison, the full-equality model predicts movement of about two-thirds of the sample, compared to an observed figure of about 48 per cent. The value of Cramér's V for the gross table is 0.348, still a moderate relation between the occupations of father and son.

Occupational mobility and age. In Table 2 we present the gross occupational mobility of our sample within 10-year age groups (the small sample size prevented finer age or occupational breaks). Age should have two opposed effects on occupational mobility in modern urban industrialized societies. In the first place, as a man grows older he has more opportunity to gain education, accumulate capital and experience and in other ways improve his chances for attaining or maintaining a high occupational position. Also, young men who are training for high-status occupations often must delay their entry into the labor force until a later age than persons entering low-status positions. For these reasons, age should be *positively* correlated with upward mobility and with inheritance of high occupational status. This is a cyclic effect, recurring as each generation passes through the occupational structure. On the other hand, a long-term trend effect stems from expanding educational opportunities and an increasing number of high-status positions. Age here indicates the period during which the man trained for and began his occupational career. Younger men entered the system at a later period and thereby received more advantages, thus producing a *negative* relation between age and upward mobility.

To separate these two effects, we need comparative data by age for different time periods.[12] Lacking such

data, we present our age analysis in relatively simple form, expecting the two opposing effects to produce a curvilinear relationship—men of middle age should enjoy some of the benefits and avoid most of the hardships of both effects, and thus should hold better occupational positions than younger or older men. The data in Table 2 do indeed show such a curvilinear relationship for sons of nonmanual workers and for sons of farmers. Middle-aged sons of nonmanual workers are more likely than either older or younger sons to have remained in or returned to a nonmanual job, and less likely to have moved down to a manual job. Among sons of farmers, the middle-aged cohorts are the most likely to have attained nonmanual urban employment. Among the sons of manual workers, however, the relationship is roughly monotonic—the older a man, the more likely he is to have remained in the manual category, the less likely to have moved up to a nonmanual job. Apparently the educational and occupational trends discussed above affect sons of manual workers, but the career- mobility cyclic effect is weaker than in other origin groups, perhaps because manual sons in the early years of their working careers are less likely to accumulate the financial or educational

---

12 For an attempt to separate these factors through an age-cohort analysis, see Gerhard E. Lenski, "Trends in Inter-Generational Occupational Mobility in the United States," *American Sociological Review*, 23 (October 1958), 514–23. Our age categories mask some of the effects of the economic depression which Lenski identified since the 1903–1912 cohort is split and combined with adjacent 5-year groups. When the same cohorts as used by Lenski are examined, sons of nonmanual workers in the depression cohort were less likely to remain nonmanual and more likely to move down to a manual job than in adjacent older or younger cohorts.

capital necessary for upward career mobility.

In summary, our 1957 estimate of mobility rates in the U.S. suggests that despite a clear tendency for sons to follow occupations within or near the occupational categories of their fathers, the influence of father''s occupation on son's is only moderate. In other words, the behavior of the system of occupational transmission is closer to that of a full-equality model than to a model of maximum inheritance. We now turn to comparisons of our findings with those of earlier national studies of mobility.

TREND COMPARISONS OF OCCUPATIONAL MOBILITY

In 1955 Ely Chinoy[13] assessed the empirical and theoretical studies on mobility trends in the U.S. and concluded that they had failed to establish with any convincing degree of accuracy whether national mobility rates were rising, falling, or remaining stationary. Few empirical studies on the question have appeared in the ensuing years. Lenski, employing age cohort estimates,[14] concluded that upward mobility increased in the last half-century (largely for structural reasons), that downward mobility rose and then fell to the original rate, and that upward mobility opportunities for sons of farmers declined relative to those of urban sons. Perrucci's study of engineers[15] concluded that the structure of opportunities for this group became more rigid from 1911 to 1950, since the father's position increasingly influenced the (engineering) position of the son.

In this section we shall attempt to estimate mobility trends by comparing our 1957 findings to the three available national reports on U.S. occupational mobility: Centers' 1945 study,[16] the 1947 "Jobs and Occupations" survey of the National Opinion Research Center,[17] and the Survey Research Center's 1952 election study, as reported by Lenski.[18] Our comparisons do not span nearly as long a time period as some earlier studies; but they do make a start at the *direct* measurement of national mobility trends.

It is important to examine the comparability of these surveys, both with regard to the sampling procedure and to the questions on occupation. None of these studies was primarily directed toward the assessment of occupational mobility; hence, neither the sampling designs nor the questions on occupation are especially adapted to mobility research.

The 1952 and 1957 Survey Research Center studies use area cluster samples, which are usually closely representative of the national population of noninstitutionalized adults.[19] The 1945 and

---

13 Ely Chinoy, "Social Mobility Trends in the United States," *American Sociological Review*, 20 (April 1955), 180–86.

14 Lenski, *op. cit.* This is the only previous attempt known to the authors to estimate mobility trends empirically using national sample data.

15 Robert Perrucci, "The Significance of Intra-Occupational Mobility: Some Methodological and Theoretical Notes, Together

with a Case Study of Engineers," *American Sociological Review*, 26 (December 1961), 875–83.

16 Centers, "Occupational Mobility of Urban Occupational Strata," *op. cit.*

17 National Opinion Research Center, "Jobs and Occupations," *Opinion News* (September 1, 1947), pp. 3–13. The data used in the present paper are those derived from the NORC report by Natalie Rogoff and published in Lipset and Bendix, *op. cit.*, p. 21.

18 Lenski, *op. cit.*

19 For a detailed statement of the sampling design of the 1952 study, see Angus

1947 studies, however, employ quota sampling procedures, which typically over-represent persons from higher social strata.[20] (Centers reports such a bias in a comparison of the occupational distribution of his sample with the 1940 U.S. Census distribution.[21]) We assume that the effect of this bias is not so great nor so focused as to distort any overall mobility trend.

The occupational questions in the three comparison studies were as follows:

1945:[22] "What do you do for a living"?
"What was or is your father's occupation?"

1947:[23] "What kind of work do you do?"
"What is (was) your father's main occupation?"

1952:[24] "What is your occupation? I mean, what kind of work do you do?"
"What kind of work did your father do for a living while you were growing up?"

The minor variations in the questions concerning respondent's occupation do not seem likely to make for serious difficulties in comparing the four studies. Variations in questions regarding occupation of respondent's father seem more troublesome: the questions used in the 1952 and 1957 studies focus on father's occupation while the respondent was "growing up," but the 1945 and 1947 questions do not specify the period for which father's occupation should be given. Respondents in these earlier studies might have tended to take advantage of the less restrictive question by reporting as father's occupation the most prestigeful job he ever held; this might produce lower rates of upward mobility and higher rates of downward mobility in the two earlier studies as compared with the 1952 and 1957 studies. The size of this bias, if any, unfortunately cannot be estimated.

1945–1957 comparison. Centers' is the earliest national sample study on male occupational mobility of which we are aware. We compare his findings with ours separately from the other two studies since he uses a relatively fine occupational break and also because he presents no data on sons of farmers, as the other studies do. To make this comparison two sorts of alteration were necessary: (1) in order to match occupational categories, we merged Centers' two Business categories into one and his two Farmer categories into one, since our 1957 occupational data were not sufficiently precise to permit such fine distinctions; (2) we reduced our sample of adult males to whites, employed full- or part-time, whose fathers were not farmers, since Centers presented data for this group only. The comparison, then, is in terms of six occupational origins and seven destinations and applies only to white employed men of urban occupational origin.

The general pattern of occupational movement and stability is similar in the 1945 and 1957 samples. Inheritance or movement to an adjacent occupational group is the most common destination for sons of all origins in both studies. The summary mobility measures in Table 3, however, reveal several differences between the two samples.

Campbell, Gerald Gurin, and Warren E. Miller, *The Voter Decides* (Evanston, Ill.: Row, Peterson, 1954).

[20] For a description of these samples, see: 1945 study—Centers, *The Psychology of Social Classes*, pp. 34–38; 1947 study—Reiss *et al., op. cit.*, p. 6.

[21] Centers, *The Psychology of Social Classes*, p. 38.

[22] *Ibid.*, pp. 232, 234.

[23] Reiss, *op. cit.*, pp. 259–60.

[24] Campbell *et al., op. cit.*, p. 226.

First, somewhat more mobility was observed in the later sample: 67.7 per cent had moved from their father's occupation in 1957, compared to 61.5 per cent in 1945.[25] The bottom line of Table 3 indicates that more urban sons experienced upward mobility in 1957 than in 1945 (urban upward and downward mobility are defined as in the first section). When the observed mobility figures are compared to the model of maximum stability, the percentage who were "forced" to move by structural conditions is similar in the two samples; the difference between the two studies is essentially in the amount of circulation.

Mobility differences are also indicated by comparing the deviations of the two samples from their respective models of equal opportunity. Mobility ratios are presented in Table 3 for men from each origin and for the whole sample; these are the ratios of the observed numbers inheriting, moving up, or moving down to the numbers expected under a situation of full equality. For each occupational origin, the 1945 inheritance ratio is higher than that for 1957, indicating that the tendency to depart from full equality was greater in the earlier sample. The tendency toward upward mobility was uniformly higher in 1957. Lastly, the values of Cramér's V indicate that in the 1945 sample the son's occupation was more closely related to his father's than in the 1957 sample.

Although these differences are not strikingly large, the figures consistently indicate, then, that white, employed, urban-born men in the 1957 sample experienced somewhat more mobility

than did those in the 1945 sample. Our task is now to account for this result. Our analysis rules out structural change as an explanation. Unfortunately, we cannot definitely dismiss the possibility that the mobility "trend" is due at least partly to differences in the age distributions of the two samples. Centers' study was completed just before World War II ended. Therefore, despite a quota sample control for persons above and below 40 years of age, his interviewers were unable to sample the millions of men who were at that time serving in the Armed Forces. The proportion below age 30 in his sample is therefore smaller than in ours, and the proportion in the age 30–40 category larger.[26] Our data on age and mobility presented in the previous section indicate that if this complement of young men had been added to the 1945 sample, that sample would probably have shown more mobility, thus reducing the differences between the two compared studies.

A second interpretation, which could either supplement or replace the first, is that the effect of military service on many men was to broaden their occupational aspirations and, in the form of post-war assistance in technical and academic training, provide for implementation of some of these aspirations. In many cases, too, by interrupting careers, military service might also have produced downward mobility. In other

---

25 Unfortunately, this comparison and those to follow all involve quota samples; tests of statistical significance were not applied because the assumption of random sampling is not met.

26 These remarks are based on an age distribution presented in Centers' *The Psychology of Social Classes*, p. 167. This distribution includes 825 of his 1100 respondents. Since the degree of correspondence between this 825-person sample and the 637-person mobility sample is unknown, these figures cannot be used for an indirect age standardization of the two mobility samples, which might otherwise have indicated the extent to which age differences produced the mobility differences.

words, the war might have loosened the ties between fathers' occupation and sons' occupation for the cohort beginning their careers at that time. Therefore, even if the 1945 sample had included more young men, the 1957 sample might still have had a higher mobility rate, since it includes those veterans after the effects of military service have had time to emerge.

A third explanation is that the findings represent at least in part a long-term relaxation in the system of occupational transmission, due to such factors as increased educational opportunities and the decreasing importance of inherited financial capital in occupational success. The postwar comparisons, to which we now turn, tend to support this conclusion.

1947–1952–1957 comparison. Our second comparison differs from the previous one in that all three samples consist of all adult U.S. males, including nonwhite and sons of farmers, thus yielding a more comprehensive picture of occupational mobility in the U.S. at three points in time. The nature of the reported data for the two earlier studies, however, restricts our occupational measurement to simple Nonmanual, Manual, and Farm categories. Centers' 1945 study is not included here because his sample included no nonwhites and because he did not report data for sons of farmers.

Table 4 indicates that the general pattern of occupational movement is similar for all three samples. The only consistent difference of any size is the rise from 1947 to 1957 in the percentage of farmers' sons going into manual occupations, and the corresponding fall in the percentage remaining on the farm. The mobility ratios for this row, however, show only a small variation over time, indicating that this trend is mainly attributable to structural shifts

in the availability of farm and manual occupations.

As for the amount of mobility, Table 4 shows a slight increase in the percentage of movers in the samples from 1947 to 1957. When the observed figures are broken down into the movement due to structural conditions (from the maximum stability model) and the remaining circulation, we see that the percentage of structural movement increased between 1947 and 1952, producing a small drop in the movement attributable to circulation, despite the increased total amount of movement. Neither of these changes continued from 1952 to 1957. The context of this change, however, is such that it may be spurious. In all three samples, structural movement is entirely due to the excess of sons with farmer fathers over sons currently employed in farming, meaning that considerable numbers of farm sons could not inherit their fathers' occupation and were "forced" to move to urban jobs. The true percentage of men with farmer fathers in the U.S. is probably decreasing consistently over time.[27] The percentage is indeed smaller in the 1957 sample than in the 1952 sample, but the percentage of men with farmer fathers in the 1947 sample is lower than in either of the two later studies. This suggests that the 1947 quota interviewers failed to contact a representative number of respondents with farm fathers. If the percentage of farmer fathers in the 1947 sample had been even one percentage point higher

---

[27] Our age data and those of Lenski, *op. cit.*, support this assumption. In both samples the percentage of men who are sons of farmers falls consistently from the older to the younger age cohorts. Also, with one exception, each of the age cohorts in the 1957 sample had a smaller percentage of farmers' sons than did the same age cohort in the 1952 sample.

TABLE 4. OCCUPATIONAL MOBILITY OF MALES IN THREE NATIONAL SAMPLES

Occupation of Respondent's Father	Occupation of Male Respondents (in Percentages and Mobility Ratios)[a]									N's (100.0 per cent)[b]		
	Nonmanual			Manual			Farm					
	1947	1952	1957	1947	1952	1957	1947	1952	1957	1947	1952	1957
	per cent	per cent	per cent	per cent	per cent	per cent	per cent	per cent	per cent			
Nonmanual	70.8 (1.74)	64.7 (1.90)	66.5 (1.87)	25.1 (0.58)	34.0 (0.67)	30.5 (0.58)	4.1 (0.26)	1.3 (0.09)	3.0 (0.26)	319	153	236
Manual	35.1 (0.86)	31.1 (0.91)	30.5 (0.86)	60.9 (1.41)	67.1 (1.32)	67.7 (1.28)	4.0 (0.25)	1.8 (0.12)	1.8 (0.15)	430	280	393
Farm	23.0 (0.56)	22.0 (0.64)	22.1 (0.62)	39.1 (0.90)	44.3 (0.87)	51.5 (0.97)	37.9 (2.37)	33.8 (2.23)	26.4 (2.29)	404	314	394
All respondents (N's)	470	255	364	499	379	541	184	113	118	1153	747	1023

Summary mobility measures	1947	1952	1957
Per cent mobile	per cent	per cent	per cent
Observed	44.4	47.4	48.5
Structual movement	19.1	26.9	27.0
Circulation	25.3	20.5	21.5
Full-equality model	67.0	67.6	67.0
Cramér's V	0.390	0.372	0.348

a Cell entries in parentheses are mobility ratios.
b Some rows do not total to exactly 100.0 per cent due to rounding.

than in 1952, the structural movement percentage would have been practically constant for all three samples. We may plausibly infer, then, that the increase in structural mobility and the resultant decrease in circulation from 1947 to 1952 are probably due to undersampling of farmers' sons in the earlier study.

At any rate, the difference stems solely from the movement of farm sons. If the three samples are compared in terms of the mobility of urban workers' sons alone, no such trend is apparent. If anything, the amount of movement attributable to structural conditions decreased slightly, as our 1945–1957 comparison, confined to sons of urban workers, indicated.

The final comparison involves the deviations of each of the three samples from the distributions expected under a random, or full-equality model. The value of Cramér's V decreases somewhat over the period, suggesting a decrease in the degree to which the samples depart from the model. If the pattern of occupational transmission has changed at all in the U.S. in these years, it has moved toward a situation of full equality of opportunity.

SUMMARY AND CONCLUSIONS

The following conclusions are suggested by our data:

1. In 1957 differential replacement rates and changes in occupational structure had produced movement of about a quarter of U.S. men from farm origins into urban, especially manual, occupations. Considerable circula-

tion, however, occurred beyond this minimal structural mobility: Using a relatively fine measure of occupation, the amount of movement was much closer to that expected in a situation of full equality of opportunity than to the minimum imposed by the differences between fathers' and sons' occupational distributions. The relation between fathers' and sons' occupations was only moderate.

2. Comparisons with earlier national mobility studies yield an impression that no striking changes have occurred in mobility patterns and rates since World War II. The conservative interpretation might be that of essentially no change. What movement has occurred, however, is in the direction of increasing rates of movement and decreasing influence of father's occupation on that of his son.

The scope of these findings should be carefully qualified. They pertain only to intergenerational occupational mobility, they are based on total national samples, and they cover only the years since World War II. Entirely different forms of change may have occured in educational, financial, or other forms of mobility; the national data may mask important variations among communities, occupations, and other sub-groups; and mobility changes in earlier (or later) periods might be of quite a different order. The data suggest, however, that the rate of occupational mobility in the United States has increased somewhat since the end of World War II. At the least, we found scant evidence that the system of occupational inheritance is growing more rigid.

In a concluding remark Jackson and Crockett note certain limitations on the scope of their research. These limitations stem mainly from the fact that their findings are based on total national samples. They suggest that their national data "may mask important variations among communities, occupations, and other sub-groups." These and other qualifications were subjected to intensive study by Peter M. Blau and Otis Dudley Duncan in their large-scale analysis of occupational mobility, *The American Occupational Structure*.[1] The excerpt below is from a preliminary report based on their research. It presents conclusions on the "significance for occupational attainment of education, ethnic background, community size, migration, and parental family." Their documentation of the variation in the patterns of mobility of different subcategories in the population emphasizes the need to study differential motivation and opportunity structures in separate populations.

---

[1] *The American Occupational Structure* (New York: John Wiley & Sons, Inc., 1967).

SOME PRELIMINARY FINDINGS ON SOCIAL STRATIFICATION IN THE UNITED STATES*

Peter M. Blau, *University of Chicago*

Otis D. Duncan, *University of Michigan*

We have illustrated our procedures as well as some preliminary findings from our research in this paper. The complexity of the analysis required when several factors influence occupational success has undoubtedly become evident. Since the condensed discussion may well have been difficult to follow at various points, it might be useful to summarize in conclusion the main substantive findings.

There is much intergenerational occupational mobility in the United Sweden and Britain. The correlation than in other Western countries such as Sweden and Britain. The correlation between father's and son's SES is +0.38. The influence of father's on son's status is largely mediated through education, in apparent contrast to the situation in some other countries, but socioeconomic origins also influence career chances independent of education.

It hardly comes as a surprise that racial discrimination in the United States is reflected in the Negro's inferior chances of occupational success, although the extent to which Negroes with the same amount of education as whites remain behind in the struggle for desirable occupations is striking. Negroes receive much less occupational return for their educational investments than whites do, and their consequent lesser incentive to acquire an education further disadvantages them in the labor market. What may be surprising, however, is that white ethnic minorities, on the average, appear to have as good occupational chances as

---

* From Peter M. Blau and Otis D. Duncan, "Some Preliminary Findings on Social Stratification in the United States," *Acta Sociologica*, 9 (1965), 21–22.

the majority group. At least, the occupational achievements of foreign-born and second-generation Americans are no worse than those of native whites of native parentage with the same amount of education.

Urban migrants are more likely to occupy desirable occupational positions and to have moved up from the socioeconomic status of their fathers than nonmigrants. Migration to urban areas brings occupational success more often than migration to rural areas (for the nonfarm population here under consideration), and migration from urban areas to small cities is particularly advantageous. The larger the place where a migrant grew up, the greater are the chances of his occupational success, regardless of the type of place where he ends up working. Indeed, for non-migrants as well as migrants, there is a direct correlation between the size of the place where a man was reared and his occupational achievement.

Size of parental family and sibling position affect careers. The occupational attainments of men with many siblings, with whom they had to share parental resources, are inferior to those of men with few siblings, but only children do not achieve higher socioeconomic positions than men from small families. Oldest and youngest children tend to have more successful careers than middle ones. In small families, though not in large ones, finally, having no older brothers appears to give a middle child a slight advantage in the struggle for occupational success, which suggests that older sisters improve future life chances.

Robert Perrucci's research represents a different methodological approach to the study of intragenerational mobility. He is concerned with the origins, as determined by fathers' occupations, of persons in only one occupation—engineer. More specifically, he is interested in the influence of socioeconomic background upon prestige positions. His findings bear upon the question of trends in the openness of class structure.[1]

---

[1] Debate on the degree of openness of the American class structure has been a continuing theme in the stratification literature since its beginnings. A number of writers hold with Perrucci that the opportunity structure is becoming more rigid. Others oppose this view and claim either that no significant changes are discernible or that, if anything, opportunities may have increased in recent decades. Still others suggest that our knowledge of this problem is so incomplete or inconsistent that judgment must be reserved. Duncan, *op. cit.*, a supporter of the position of increasing opportunities, reviews a number of the major studies representing both positions.

Of special note is the important historical research conducted by Thernstrom; it raises serious questions about mobility studies conducted within a short-term, ahistorical framework. Thernstrom's conclusions do not support the belief that it is now more difficult to move up the social ladder than it was in the "idyllic" past. Stephen Thernstrom, *Poverty and Progress: Social Mobility in a Nineteenth Century City* (Cambridge, Mass.: Harvard University Press, 1964); See, especially, the appendix.

SIGNIFICANCE OF INTRAOCCUPATIONAL MOBILITY*†

Robert Perrucci

Purdue University

Researchers concerned with stratification and social mobility have usually attempted to make some statement regarding whether the American social structure is becoming more open or closed. By and large there has been little agreement among sociologists. One group has seen the door of opportunity slowly closing, leaving the Horatio Alger myth as part of a bygone era.[1] Another group looks with optimism toward expanding horizons with increased opportunities for all.[2] These differing conclusions have, for the most part, resulted from the use of different populations as the unit of analysis and from the employment of different methodological procedures for determining social-economic positions. Some studies have utilized a sample representing a wide range of occupations, while others have focused on more "elite" occupational roles. Similarly, most studies have differed in the use of a classificatory scheme for father's and son's occupation. Because of the varied approaches, there seems to be little conclusive evidence concerning changes in the American opportunity structure.

One of the more recent efforts to attack the question of change in the American social structure has been Natalie Rogoff's study of occupational mobility.[3] Being most sensitive to the shortcomings of previous work, Rogoff considered the factor of changes in the composition of the occupational structure as crucial in any attempt to evaluate the amount of movement taking place between occupational categories over time. As such, Rogoff's study has received considerable attention by sociologists, primarily in terms of accepting her conclusion that no significant change has occurred in overall mobility rates in the time periods included in her study.[4]

* From Robert Perrucci, "The Significance of Intraoccupational Mobility: Some Methodological and Theoretical Notes, Together with a Case Study of Engineers," *American Sociological Review*, 26 (December 1961), 874–83. Reprinted by permission of the American Sociological Association.

† The author is indebted to James M. Beshers, Department of Sociology, Purdue University, for his valuable suggestions and advice in the preparation of this paper. He is also indebted to Robert L. Eichhorn, Philip M. Marcus, and Ephraim H. Mizruchi for a critical reading of an earlier draft.

1 See, e.g., F. W. Taussig and C. S. Joslyn, *American Business Leaders* (New York: The Macmillan Company, Publishers, 1932); J. O. Hertzler, "Some Tendencies Toward a Closed Class System in the United States," *Social Forces*, 30 (March 1952), 313–23.

2 See, e.g., W. Lloyd Warner and James C. Abegglen, *Occupational Mobility in American Business and Industry, 1928–1952* (Minneapolis: University of Minnesota Press, 1955); Stuart Adams, "Trends in Occupational Origins of Business Leaders," *American Sociological Review*, 19 (October 1954), 541–48.

3 *Recent Trends in Occupational Mobility* (Glencoe, Ill.: Free Press, 1953).

4 See, e.g., Bernard Barber, *Social Stratification* (New York: Harcourt, Brace and

This paper will be concerned with several related problems. First, an examination will be made of some of the major difficulties involved in attempts to measure the relative openness of a social structure; this refers to the variation that can exist *within* a gross occupational category and the implications this variation has for estimating variation *among* occupational categories. Secondly, we will re-examine the meaning of an "opening" or "closing" social structure and suggest the kinds of data needed to test such a proposition. Thirdly, a time-comparative sample of college graduates whose job positions fall within *one* occupational category will be examined to estimate the effect of their social class origins upon the relative prestige of their present job position within the engineering profession.

VARIATION WITHIN OCCUPATIONAL CATEGORIES

Efforts to study change over time must involve the establishment of a set of social categories whose change is measured. Hence, studies seeking to examine movement in social space have taken occupations as their basic unit since one's position in economic life is a major factor affecting position in the social-class structure. The result is that most mobility research utilizes some means of occupational classification whereby those occupations assumed to be so similar as to form a social-economic grouping are combined into broad categories. The most widely used set of categories in the United States is that developed by Alba Edwards and

used by the United States Census Bureau.[5] While all mobility studies do not use Edward's categories specifically, their variations on the Edwards scale still make the same assumption of categorizing occupations assumed to be similar along some dimension.

The use of these broad occupational categories in mobility studies involves the assumption that those people who fall into a particular category (e.g., professional) are similar as to social and economic characteristics. This assumption, however, does not seem quite valid in light of the very large variations within a single occupational category. For example, to treat all persons in the category "professional" as similar with respect to social-economic position is to lose sight of the variations which may range from a $70,000 per year surgeon to a $10,000 per year general practitioner. In fact, these variations within a single category may provide a better picture of the openness of a social structure since they involve the very factors that remain more or less hidden when broad groupings are used. If one were to find, for example, that a person's relative position within the category "professional"[6] is related to his class origins (i.e., father's occupation), then we have a hidden effect that raises further questions concerning the openness of our opportunity structure. An example of these wide variations within the category "professional" may be seen in Table 1. Table 1 contains a sample

Company, 1957); Joseph A. Kahl, *The American Class Structure* (New York: Rinehart and Company, 1953).

[5] Alba M. Edwards, "A Social-Economic Grouping of the Gainful Workers of the United States," *Journal of the American Statistical Association*, 28 (December 1933), 377–87.

[6] We assume that all those occupations that fall into the general category of "professional" (or any other category) are not equally valued occupations; hence, we may speak of a person's relative position within any occupational category.

TABLE 1. PER CENT DISTRIBUTION OF PRESENT JOB POSITION BY
FATHER'S OCCUPATION OF ENGINEERING GRADUATES (1911–1950)

Job Position	Father's Occupation			
	Professional, Semi-professional	Clerical and Sales	Skilled and Semi-skilled	Unskilled
President and vice-president	20.9	13.8	11.8	12.1
Assistant chief engineer and chief engineer	24.0	25.4	25.6	20.8
Assistant superintendent and district engineer	21.4	22.3	21.9	20.3
Design engineer and project engineer	33.7	38.4	40.7	46.7
Total per cent	100.0	99.9	100.0	99.9
Number of cases	705	614	577	571

$\chi^2=41.5 \ p \leq 0.001$
Chi squares for controlled analysis are:
  1911–1930 graduates: $\chi^2=21.18 \ p \leq 0.02$
  1931–1940 graduates: $\chi^2=26.63 \ p \leq 0.01$
  1941–1950 graduates: $\chi^2=27.93 \ p \leq 0.001$

of engineering graduates[7] arranged according to the occupational category of their father's occupation at the time the graduates were in college and the relative prestige of their present job position[8] within the engineering profession. The distribution with respect to father's occupation and present job position of sons indicates that the sons of fathers of high-status occupations are more likely to occupy high-status job positions in the engineering profession than are sons of fathers of low-status occupations. This would indicate a substantial loss of precision which results from combining all respondents under the general category of "professional" and giving each an

equal weight in the amount of mobility achieved. The mere fact that sons of fathers of low-status occupations become engineers cannot be used as full evidence of an opening social structure. It is generally assumed that both economic and demographic changes have made it necessary to recruit sons of lower-class origins into high-status occupations.[9] The important fact, however, is the relative position of the lower-class sons as compared to the upper-class sons. From one viewpoint, a stratification system at any particular point in time may be considered as a rank order of statuses. Hence, if the economy changes so that everyone moves up we have the impression of increased mobility, while everyone still

7 See footnote 20 for an explanation of the sampling procedures.

8 See the section on procedure for an explanation of the means used to determine the relative prestige of the engineers' present job positions.

9 Elbridge Sibley, "Some Demographic Clues to Stratification," *American Sociological Review*, 7 (May 1941), 322–33.

remains in the same rank order.[10] This very impression of increased mobility is a further source of error in the use of gross occupational categories.

With this variation within an occupational category in mind, let us turn our attention to the statistical problems involved in attempting to make statements concerning changes in movement in and out of categories over time.

The usual procedure has been to present a matrix arrangement of father's occupation against son's occupation for two separate time periods for the purpose of determining whether any occupational shifts have taken place. Thus for Time 1 we have a matrix of X_{ij} entries, and for Time 2 a matrix of Y_{ij} entries. The hypothesis tested by previous researchers is that the means of all the individual cell frequencies in each time period do not differ significantly from each other. Symbolically it is:

$$\Sigma\Sigma(X_{ij} - Y_{ij}) = 0$$

or

$$\frac{\Sigma\Sigma X_{ij}}{N} - \frac{Y_{ij}}{N} = 0$$

Stated in terms of the data, the hypothesis is that the movement of sons out of their father's occupational category and into another category has not changed significantly between Time 1 and Time 2. The statistical procedures used to test this hypothesis warrant some consideration and comment.

Using Rogoff's technique as more or less typical of most recent mobility research (conceptually if not statistically), our first concern is with the procedure

of computing "mean mobility rates."[11] A "mean mobility rate" is obtained by summing across all individual cell rates for a particular time period (e.g., Time 1); it is repeated again for a second time period (e.g., Time 2), with the two means being compared to ascertain whether there has been an increase or decrease in total mobility. This procedure, however, pays no attention to the particular cell in which overrepresentation or underrepresentation has occurred. For example, an examination of Rogoff's tables[12] from which "mean mobility rates" were computed indicates that the individual cell ratios could be completely rearranged without affecting the overall mobility rate. Since the marginal frequencies in Rogoff's tables do not determine the internal cell frequencies, there are a large number of possible combinations of internal cell frequencies (hence cell ratios) that would yield the same "mean mobility rate." However valid this procedure may be statistically, a rearrangement of cell ratios would present an entirely different picture regarding where the sons of professionals are moving or how many sons of skilled workers remain skilled workers. The two time periods might also contain a complete reversal in the direction of mobility which would not or could not be revealed by the mean rate.

In short, then, the lumping together of all individual cell mobility rates in order to compute a mean or average rate fails to identify between which occupational categories the most or least movement is taking place. When we try to answer the crucial question of how open a social structure is, the rate of movement of sons of professionals into unskilled occupations is more important

---

[10] For an expanded discussion of this general point, see James M. Beshers, *Urban Social Structure* (Glencoe, Ill.: Free Press, 1962).

[11] For a discussion of this procedure, see Rogoff, *op. cit.*, Chap. IV.

[12] Rogoff, *op. cit.*, pp. 47–48.

than their rate of movement into semi-professional occupations.[13] Similarly the rate of movement for sons of unskilled workers into professional occupations is more significant, again from the point of view of the flexibility of the social structure, than their rate of movement would be into skilled occupations.

Secondly, the amount of hidden variation that takes place *within* gross occupational categories (as seen in Table 1) must be accounted for in any attempt to assess the amount of variation between two groups (on gories for two separate time periods. In statistical terminology, the presence of variation between two groups (on some criterion) is established when the variation within groups is minimized. Hence, in the problem at hand, a considerable variation within groups makes it most difficult to establish variation between groups. This may account for the inability of the Rogoff data to account for any significant change in occupational movement between the two time periods.

THE RELATIVE OPENNESS OF SOCIAL STRUCTURES

The second objective of this paper is to re-examine the meaning of an "open" or "closed" structure and to suggest an alternative approach for assessing changes in the social structure over time.

The studies cited above have been primarily concerned with the question of how much movement has taken place between father's and son's occupations over time. The focus has been on occupations in each stratum, from top to bottom, in order to see where the sons of professionals move or where the sons of unskilled workers move, i.e., what occupational position they hold. Any change over time in the amount of movement that takes place between occupations is then used as an index of the relative openness or rigidity of the social structure. In this way a view of the total structure is obtained by establishing the rates of movement *in* and *out* of occupations in each stratum.[14]

This particular approach, however, has certain limitations. Aside from the increased error which may result from the research design and the statistical techniques used to compute mobility rates, as indicated above, there is the further question of the precise meaning attached to an increase or decrease in occupational shifts over time. An increase in movement out of the occupational category of the fathers, by the sons, may indicate that the structure is opening, or it may only indicate a shift

---

can Sociological Review, 22 (August 1957), 392–99; and Charles F. Westoff, Marvin Bressler, and Philip C. Sagi, "The Concept of Social Mobility," *American Sociological Review,* 25 (June 1960), 375–85.·

14 By way of comparison, "elite" studies of mobility have assumed that, if you look at people who have arrived at the top and see where they came from, you can make statements concerning the openness of the social structure. One of the shortcomings of this approach is, presumably, that if all the members of an elite occupation came from the very bottom of the structure, it would still be possible to have a very closed social structure, in terms of the *proportions* of people in each of the strata below the top who stay where they are, move up only slightly, or drop.

---

13 For a specific discussion of the lesser importance of movement in and out of contiguous occupational categories, see Melvin M. Tumin and Arthur S. Feldman, "Theory and Measurement of Occupational Mobility," *American Sociological Review,* 22 (June 1957), 281–88. For a general discussion of the problems involved in the measurement of mobility, see Peter M. Blau, "Occupational Bias and Mobility," *Ameri-*

in the occupational structure related to the changing nature of the economy. For example, a reduction in the number of skilled occupations needed, along with an attendant increase in the need for clerical workers, would necessarily cause such occupational shifts.

Being unable to partial out and control the various sources of error in the "total-structure" approach, we can perhaps find other indicators of the openness of a structure by looking at those aspects of stratification systems that are used to classify a structure as "open" or "closed." These classificatory aspects may be found in the nature of the institutionalized norms concerning social mobility. Thus, in examining the ideology associated with the traditional Indian social structure, an archetype of the "closed" structure, we find a disapproval of social mobility, a legitimization of inequality, and a relative absence of specific means or channels for legitimate mobility. The open class ideology in the United States, an archetype of the "open" structure, emphasizes equality of opportunity, approves of upward mobility, and specifies the means by which legitimate mobility is to be achieved.[15]

Still another aspect of an open social structure is the existence of legitimate means for movement in and out of *any* position in society. For example, the son of a laborer can become a doctor *provided* he uses the appropriate means. Given the existence of certain means for mobility, there are two tests which may be utilized to assess change in the relative openness of a social structure. The first test relates to the question of differential access to the institutionalized means for mobility, e.g., who can or does go to college. The second test involves the question of differential distribution of rewards after the utilization of appropriate institutionalized means.[16] When the son of a laborer who has not finished high school becomes a stock clerk, and the son of a lawyer who goes to medical school becomes a physician, we have a situation of differential access to institutionalized avenues of mobility. We cannot apply the differential rewards test because in the case of the laborer's son the appropriate institutionalized means for mobility have not been utilized, while in the case of the lawyer's son they have been utilized. If, however, the son of a laborer and the son of a lawyer both go to medical school with the former becoming a neighborhood general practitioner and the latter a "Park Avenue specialist," we then have a situation of differential rewards related to social-economic origins despite the utilization of the appropriate institutionalized means. This reward distribution is not legitimized because both sons "played the game" and were not similarly rewarded.

---

15 It should be noted that occupational shifts in India have been associated with efforts to obtain more favored caste status and, as such, operate as a channel of mobility. However, there is a relative absence of specific normative directives and accompanying institutionalized means for social mobility comparable to those found in the educational system in the United States. See, Barber, *op. cit.*, Chap. 13, for a discussion of institutional norms and social mobility.

16 Our formulation here, has some further implications that are related to Merton's discussion of the structural sources of deviant behavior; unlike Merton, however, our concern would be focused upon the latent consequences of a "conformity" mode of adaptation when the cultural rewards are not realized even after the utilization of the appropriate institutionalized means. See Robert K. Merton, "Social Structure and Anomie," in *Social Theory and Social Structure* (Glencoe, Ill.: Free Press, 1957).

It is suggested, therefore, that an examination of the institutionalized norms which define legitimate means of achieving mobility will result in a better understanding of the openness of our social structure. Since education is the predominant institutionalized avenue of mobility in our society,[17] we will compare the relative prestige of the present job positions of a sample of college graduates who completed their engineering training between the years 1911 through 1950; we will examine the extent to which graduates of varying social-class backgrounds do or do not hold job positions of equal prestige in the engineering profession.

In this way, we shall be able to control many of the sources of error not accounted for in previous mobility research. For example, all respondents in the sample can be assumed to be equally prepared for their present occupation since each person has been trained and graduated in the same area of specialized knowledge. This also holds constant, to some extent, such factors as level of aspiration and mobility orientation of the respondent. Secondly, all the respondents in the sample are in the same profession and thus would presumably be equally affected by any changes in the economy or occupational structure.

What we have outlined, then, is a preliminary model for estimating whether our social structure is becoming more open or closed. The model is not concerned with the movement of sons into any occupational category but the relative prestige of their present job position in one occupational category, namely "professional."[18] To test the

utility of such a model we would need the following kinds of data:

(a) A sample of college graduates whose training has been in the same professional area, e.g. medicine, law, engineering. The sample should cover at least two separate time periods in order to be able to make some "trend" statement.

(b) Some measure of the social-class origins of the graduates at the time they entered college.

(c) A relative prestige ranking of the various job positions within the particular professional occupation being used, e.g. corporation lawyer, criminal lawyer, divorce lawyer; or, surgeon, general practitioner, pediatrician.

(d) The job positions of the graduates at various stages in their professional careers. For example, the job position after graduation, after 10 years, after 20 years, etc., up to the present job position. In this fashion we can control the effect of time upon career mobility patterns.[19]

Unfortunately, since the data to be presented in this paper were not collected for the specific purpose of testing the above model, we lack information of the type required for step (d).

---

17 Kahl, *op. cit.*, p. 200.

18 We have focused upon the "professional" category primarily because the professions have been viewed as examples of

"careers open to talent," where advancement is judged by such general criteria as "ability." See, e.g., Morris Rosenberg, *Occupations and Values* (Glencoe, Ill.: Free Press, 1957), p. 54; Patricia Salter West, "Social Mobility Among College Graduates," in *Class, Status and Power*, eds. Reinhard Bendix and Seymour Lipset (Glencoe, Ill.: Free Press, 1953), p. 473.

19 The effect of "time" upon career mobility patterns has not always been considered in past mobility research. Rogoff's sample, for example, consisted primarily of persons in the very early stages of their career, which would eliminate the possibility of getting at those changes which would occur with time.

PROCEDURE

A sample of engineering graduates from 1911 through 1950 responded to a mailed questionnaire concerning their career patterns since graduation and their opinions on the academic preparation of the engineering student.[20] The graduates were grouped into three eras of graduation in order to compare early graduates with more recent ones. The time periods used were 1911 through 1930 graduates, 1931 through 1940 graduates, and 1941 through 1950 graduates. These particular groupings were selected in order to include those years in each era that were somewhat stable with respect to economic conditions of the country. It was assumed that all the graduates in each era would have been subjected to the same general types of problems in job-seeking, job selection, and job maintenance.

The social-class origin of the engineers was established through the use of the *Sims Social Class Identification Occupational Rating Scale.*[21] Each respondent checked those occupations listed in the questionnaire which he considered less desirable than his father's occupation at the time the engineer entered college.[22] Fathers' oc-

cupations were then grouped into four main categories: (1) professional and semiprofessional; (2) clerical and sales; (3) skilled and semiskilled; and (4) unskilled.

Each respondent was asked to indicate his present work in engineering by selecting a job position, out of a predetermined list, which was most similar to his own job in duties and responsibility. The relative prestige of these job positions within the engineering profession was established by having a sample of engineering faculty members rate each occupation along a prestige dimension. The resulting ranking of positions, in order of increasing prestige, are as follows: design engineer, project engineer, assistant superintendent, district engineer, assistant chief engineer, chief engineer, vice-president, president. Table 2 contains the raw data on our sample as to father's occupation, present job position of sons, and era of graduation. Following Rogoff's procedure for controlling any possible changes in the job structure within the engineering profession,[23] the raw data were converted to ratios of the actual cell value to the expected cell value. In this fashion, all cell ratios may be compared regarding whether the sons of fathers who were "professionals" or "unskilled" are underrepresented or overrepresented in any particular job position. A ratio of "one" indicates that

---

[20] The total population of engineering graduates between 1911 and 1950 was stratified by year of graduation, from which every nth graduate was selected; the sampling interval used was varied according to the size of the graduating class in order to insure adequate returns. Of the 5,429 graduates receiving a questionnaire, 3,799 (70.0 per cent) were returned in completed form.

[21] Verner M. Sims, "A Technique for Measuring Social Class Identification," *Educational and Psychological Measurement,* 11 (Winter 1951), 541–48.

[22] The particular method of establishing social-class origins used in this study has several shortcomings: (1) a subjective identification and placement of father's occupation provides no information as to what

dimension of the occupation the respondent is rating; (2) the respondents were ranking their father's occupation at the time the graduates entered college, thereby introducing a rather large time discrepancy which may affect the actual status dimension of the occupation; and (3) the impact of time and the socialization process of a college education may affect certain changes in attitudes toward a particular occupation. At any rate, the actual occupations of the fathers would have been more desirable.

[23] Rogoff, *op. cit.,* Chap. II.

TABLE 2. PRESENT JOB POSITION OF ENGINEERS BY FATHER'S OCCUPATION AND ERA OF GRADUATION (RAW DATA)

	Era of Graduation											
	1911–1930 (Time 1)				1931–1940 (Time 2)				1941–1950 (Time 3)			
	Father's Occupation											
Son's Job Position	Professional and Semi-professional	Clerical and Sales	Skilled and Semi-skilled	Un-skilled	Professional and Semi-professional	Clerical and Sales	Skilled and Semi-skilled	Un-skilled	Professional and Semi-professional	Clerical and Sales	Skilled and Semi-skilled	Unskilled
President and vice president	43	34	36	38	54	29	17	23	50	22	24	17
Assistant chief engineer and chief engineer	32	39	50	36	58	56	49	32	80	61	46	49
Assistant superintendent district engineer	16	13	40	31	49	38	34	19	86	86	50	64
Design engineer and project engineer	14	28	24	24	44	38	49	51	179	170	158	187
Number of Cases	105	114	150	129	205	161	149	125	395	339	278	317

TABLE 3. RATIO OF ACTUAL ENGINEERS TO EXPECTED ENGINEERS BY FATHER'S OCCUPATION AND ERA OF GRADUATION

	Era of Graduation											
	1911–1930 (Time 1)				1931–1940 (Time 2)				1941–1950 (Time 3)			
	Father's Occupation											
Son's Job Position	Professional and Semiprofessional (a)	Clerical and Sales (b)	Skilled and Semiskilled (c)	Unskilled (d)	Professional and Semiprofessional (a)	Clerical and Sales (b)	Skilled and Semiskilled (c)	Unskilled (d)	Professional and Semiprofessional (a)	Clerical and Sales (b)	Skilled and Semiskilled (c)	Unskilled (d)
President and vice president (1)	1.32	0.99	0.79	0.97	1.32	0.94	0.59	0.96	1.43	0.76	1.02	0.62
Assistant chief engineer and chief engineer (2)	0.97	1.09	1.06	0.88	0.93	1.14	1.08	0.84	1.13	1.01	0.93	0.87
Assistant superintendent and district engineer (3)	0.76	0.57	1.33	1.20	1.09	1.08	1.04	0.69	0.98	1.18	0.84	0.94
Design engineer and project engineer (4)	0.68	1.36	0.88	1.03	0.75	0.83	1.16	1.44	0.86	0.96	1.13	1.13

Significant Differences:
* = 0.05
** = 0.01

Time 1:
a_1-c_1**
a_3-c_3*
b_3-c_3*
b_3-d_3*
a_4-b_4*

Time 2:
a_1-c_1**
a_4-d_4**
b_4-d_4**
c_4-d_4**

Time 3:
a_1-b_1**
a_1-d_1**
b_3-c_3*
a_4-c_4**
a_4-d_4**
b_4-d_4*

there are as many sons in a particular job position as would be expected if there were no relation between son's job position and father's occupational class position. Similarly, a ratio of "two" would indicate that twice as many sons are found in a particular job position than would be expected if there were no relationship between son's job position and father's occupational class position. Tests of significance were run in order to determine if the number of sons found in any particular job position differed according to the social-class origins of the engineers.

FINDINGS AND DISCUSSION

An examination of the ratios in Table 3 indicates, first of all, that the sons of fathers of high-status occupation are overrepresented in high-prestige job positions, while sons of fathers of low-status occupations are underrepresented in high-prestige job positions. Similarly, sons of fathers of low-status occupations are overrepresented in low-prestige job positions, while sons of fathers of high-status occupations are underrepresented in low-prestige job positions. This is true for all three time eras. To determine, however, which time era was more open or closed with respect to a more random distribution of sons in all job positions, we must turn to the internal differences in each time era.

Looking at the highest prestige job position in Time 1 (vice-president and president), we see that sons of fathers who were "professionals" are found in significantly greater numbers than sons of fathers who were "skilled" (a_1—c_1). The lowest prestige job position (design engineer and project engineer) finds sons of fathers who were "clerical and sales" in significantly greater numbers

than sons of fathers who were "professionals" (a_4—b_4). The most revealing finding in Time 1 is that there are no significant differences among the four extreme cells (i.e., a_1—d_1; a_4—d_4). The extreme cells, however, are the most important cells theoretically. If class origin is, in fact, significantly related to the job position held by an engineer, we would expect to find its influence in the lowest occupational class. We find in Time 1, however, that the sons of "professionals" are not differently represented in any job position than the sons of "unskilled" fathers (a_1—d_1; a_2—d_2; a_3—d_3; a_4—d_4).

Another factor influencing our focus on the four extreme cells is that, if, in fact, the occupational-class categories do form a rank order of statuses and if class origins do influence the job position an engineer holds, we would expect to find some internal consistency among the differences observed. For example, if more presidents are sons of "professionals" than they are sons of "clerical and sales," we would also expect more presidents to be sons of "professionals" than sons of "skilled" workers and sons of "unskilled" workers since "clerical and sales" is a higher rank order occupational class than "skilled" and "unskilled." Since the differences found in Time 1 do not reveal any internal consistency with respect to occupational class origins, we might conclude that those differences found (a_1—c_1 and a_4—b_4) are due to chance variations. Hence the data for Time 1 graduates closely approximates an "open" structure, i.e., the reward distribution of various job positions are randomly distributed rather than related to class origins.

Time 2 differences show a tendency toward our criterion of internal consistency in *one* of the extreme cell combinations. The distribution of sons in the lowest prestige job position (design engineer and project engineer) reveals that the sons of "professionals" are found in significantly fewer numbers than sons of "unskilled," $(a_4—d_4)$; sons of "clerical and sales" are found in significantly fewer numbers than sons of "unskilled" $(b_4—d_4)$; and sons of "skilled" are found in significantly fewer numbers than sons of "unskilled" $(c_4—d_4)$. In the highest prestige job position (vice-president and president) the only difference found $(a_1—c_1)$ is neither an extreme cell difference nor does it meet the internal-consistency criterion. We might conclude, then, that the Time 2 data reveals a slightly more "closed" opportunity structure than we found in Time 1.

In Time 3, we find extreme cell differences in both the highest and lowest prestige job positions, as well as the closest approximation of our ideal internal-consistency criterion. The data in this time period indicate a much more "closed" opportunity structure than we found in either of the two previous time periods. That is, the relative prestige of the job position held by our Time 3 graduates is much more likely to be a function of social-economic origins (occupation class of the father) of the engineer than was found in either Time 1 or Time 2.

The first and most obvious possible objection to our conclusion that the social structure is more closed in the most recent sample is the fact that the Time 3 engineers have been in the engineering profession only from 10 to 19 years, while the Time 1 graduates have been engineers from 30 to 49 years. In other words, given sufficient time in the engineering profession our Time 3 graduates would appear quite similar to our Time 1 graduates with respect to holding job positions that are not related to social-economic origins. This particular difficulty was pointed out above when we outlined the kinds of data needed to test the proposition embodied in our conception of what an "open" or "closed" structure meant. Since we have no data for our Time 1 engineers that would indicate their job positions at earlier stages in their career, we have been unable to control the effect of time in the profession upon the job position an engineer holds.

However, we hold to our conclusion concerning a trend toward a more closed structure in view of the following assumption concerning the effect of time upon job position. We assume that the job positions held by engineers at graduation and in the early stages of their career are most likely to be the result of such general criteria as the needs of the industry and the particular specialized qualifications of the engineer, while particular factors, such as the selection for promotion of those engineers who are from upper- and middle-class backgrounds, are most likely to be operative at later stages in their careers. We predict that the social-economic differences found among our Time 3 engineers will become greater when they reach the stage in their career that our Time 1 engineers are in (30 to 49 years in the profession).

Despite the lack of data to test the validity of this assumption, we tentatively conclude that the evidence presented in this paper indicates a possible trend toward rigidity in the American opportunity structure.

SOURCES AND CONSEQUENCES OF MOBILITY

Research on social mobility falls roughly into three general areas. The first
deals with the structural characteristics which promote or impede mobility. It
attempts to uncover those factors which determine the degree of circulation within
the class system and to assess the extent to which structural changes increase or
decrease the possibility of mobility. While there may be disagreement over the
structural factors included as independent variables in Leo F. Schnore's[1] ecologi-
cal-demographic framework, his taxonomy is useful for comprehending the range
of determinants attended to by students of mobility. Schnore lists four general
sets of factors: demographic, organizational, technological, and environmental.
Under demographic he lists differential fertility,[2] mortality, and immigration;[3]
under technological, innovations in production, distribution, transportation, and
communication;[4] under organizational, changes in and introduction of new industries, increases in sizes of firms, and redistribution of wealth resulting from
increased productivity or political action or both; under environmental, growth of
control over the physical environment, including the discovery of natural resources
and the exhaustion of nonreplaceable resources. Studies of structural determinants
essentially concern the extent of role vacancies in the society. Role vacancies
increase the likelihood of upward and downward movement, providing they are
filled on the basis of achieved rather than ascribed criteria.

The second general area of research on mobility deals with the social-psychological factors influencing the mobility of individuals.[5] The third focuses on
the consequences of mobility for the individual and society. In the remainder of
this chapter, we consider these last two areas of study.

---

[1] "Social Mobility in Demographic Perspective," *American Sociological Review*, 26
(June 1961), 441–42. The major variables in Schnore's scheme—especially their relative
contribution to mobility—are discussed more fully and analyzed in Kahl, *op. cit.*, Chap. 9.

[2] A few examples of the numerous studies on the role of fertility in mobility are H.
Yuan Tien, "The Social Mobility/Fertility Hypothesis Reconsidered," *American Sociological
Review*, 26 (April 1961), 247–57; Carolyn Cummings Perrucci, "Social Origins, Mobility
Patterns and Fertility," *American Sociological Review*, 32 (August 1967), 615–25.

[3] Few studies of the part played by immigration in mobility are comparable to Kahl's
excellent analysis, *op. cit.*

[4] The advent of automation epitomizes much of what is meant by technological innovations and their consequences for social organization and social change. For examples
of the relationships among automation, mobility, and stratification, see William A. Faunce
and Donald A. Clelland, "Professionalization and Stratification Patterns in an Industrial
Society," *American Journal of Sociology*, 72 (January 1967), 341–50; Gursslin and Roach,
op. cit. The latter study reviews much of the literature on automation, especially as it
relates to stratification.

[5] While we are treating social-psychological studies separately from those focusing on
structural variables, we do not mean to minimize their mutual effect on mobility. We agree
with Lipset and Bendix "that by merging the sociological and psychological approaches to

Research on the social-psychological antecedents of vertical mobility investigates the extent to which various population groups embrace the success ethic. In short, emphasis is on the social-psychological correlates of upward, rather than downward, mobility. To some degree, the substantive accounts of the classes in Part II dealt with these correlates in the context of class structure. For this reason, only research which deals with attitudes toward mobility will be treated here. The study by Bernard Rosen reveals a complex relationship among demographic factors and achievement motivation. The extensive interest in this area reflects societal concern for the development of talent. We do not intend to review this vast literature.[6] However, we offer a sample of this research because it represents an appreciable segment of empirical investigations on the social-psychological factors predictive of mobility.

the study of mobility we may be able to advance the study of the mechanisms by which individuals and groups reach their positions in the stratification structure." *Op. cit.*, p. 259.

Needless to say, agreement with this statement presents fewer difficulties than does its implementation in practice. For one of the relatively few attempts to study personality variables in conjunction with sociological or structural variables in mobility research, see Harry J. Crockett, Jr., "The Achievement Motive and Differential Occupational Mobility in the United States," *American Sociological Review*, 27 (April 1962), 191–204.

[6] For an extensive survey and compilation of relevant research, see Bernard C. Rosen *et al.*, eds., *Achievement in American Society* (Cambridge, Mass.: Schenkman Publishing Co., 1967).

FAMILY STRUCTURE AND ACHIEVEMENT MOTIVATION*†

Bernard C. Rosen

Cornell University

This paper is a study of the relationship of certain demographic factors to family structure and personality development. Specifically, it examines the ways in which family size, ordinal position, mother's age, and social class influence the quality and quantity of patterned parent-child interaction and their impact upon the development of achievement motivation.

Achievement motivation has been defined as the redintegration of affect

* From Bernard C. Rosen, "Family Structure and Achievement Motivation," *American Sociological Review*, 26 (August 1961), 574–85. Reprinted by permission of the American Sociological Association.

† Part of an address before the annual meeting of the Brazilian Society for the Advancement of Science (Sociedade Brasileira Para O Progresso Da Ciencia), Piracicaba, Brazil, July 6, 1960. This research was supported by a research grant (M2283) from the National Institute of Mental Health, United States Public Health Service. The paper was written while the author held a

aroused by cues in situations involving standards of excellence.[1] Such standards are typically learned from parents who urge the child to compete against these standards, rewarding him when he performs well and punishing him when he fails. In time parental expectations become internalized, so that when later exposed to situations involving standards of excellence the individual re-experiences the affect associated with his earlier efforts to meet them. In our culture, the behavior of people with strong achievement motivation is characterized by persistent striving and general competitiveness.

Recent empirical data show that strong achievement motivation tends to develop when parents set high goals for their child to attain, when they indicate a high evaluation of his competence to do a task well, and impose standards of excellence upon problem-solving tasks, even in situations where such standards are not explicit. This complex of socialization practices has been called *achievement training*. Also related to achievement motivation is another set of socialization practices called *independence training*. This type of training involves expectations that the child be *self-reliant* in situations where he competes with standards of excellence. At

Special Research Fellowship (MF-10,795) awarded by the Research Fellowships Branch of the National Institute of Mental Health and sponsored by the Universidade de São Paulo, Brazil. The contributions of Marian Winterbottom for her work in scoring the TAT protocols, and June Schmelzer, Miriam Witkin, and William Erlbaum for their assistance in reviewing the literature are greatly appreciated. My thanks also to Dr. Carolina Martuscelli Bori of the Faculdade Filosofia, Ciencias e Letras, Universidade de São Paulo for her helpful comments.

[1] D. C. McClelland, J. Atkinson, R. Clark, and E. Lowell, *The Achievement Motive* (New York: Appleton-Century-Crofts, 1953).

the same time the parent grants him relative *autonomy* in problem-solving and decision-making situations where he is given both freedom of action and responsibility for success or failure. The role of independence training in generating achievement motivation is exceedingly complex and can only be understood in the context of what appears to be a division of labor between the fathers and mothers of boys with high achievement motivation. Observation of parent-child interaction in an experimental problem-solving situation has shown that both of the parents of boys with high achievement motivation stress achievement training. When compared with the parents of boys with low achievement motivation, it was found that the fathers and mothers of boys with high achievement motivation tend to be more competitive and interested in their sons' performance; they set higher goals for him to attain and have a greater regard for his competence at problem-solving. They also react to good performance with more warmth and approval or with disapproval if he performs poorly. The pattern changes with respect to independence training. Much of this type of training comes from the father, who (in an experimental situation at least) expected his son to be self-reliant in problem-solving and gave him a relatively high degree of autonomy in making his own decisions. The mothers of boys with high achievement motivation, on the other hand, were likely to be more dominant and to expect less self-reliance than the mothers of boys with low motivation. ·

It appears that the boy can take, and perhaps needs, achievement training from both parents, but the effects of independence training and sanctions (a crucial factor determining the child's affective reaction to standards of excellence) are different depending on whether they come from the father or mother. In order for strong achievement motivation to develop, the boy seems to need more autonomy from his father than from his mother. The authoritarian father may crush his son —and in so doing destroy the boy's achievement motive—perhaps because he views the boy as a competitor and is viewed as such by his son. On the other hand, the mother who dominates the decision-making process does not seem to have the same effect, possibly because she is perceived as imposing her standards on the boy, while a dominating father is perceived as imposing himself on his son. It may be that mother-son relations are typically more secure than those between father and son, so that the boy is able to accept higher levels of dominance and hostility from mother than father without adverse effect upon his achievement motivation. It should be remembered, however, that while the mother of a boy with high achievement motivation is willing to express hostility at poor performance she is also more likely to show approval and warmth when he does well than is the mother of a boy with low motivation.[2]

A number of investigators have remarked upon the differences in parent-child relationships associated with certain demographic characteristics of the family. It has been said that life in a small family is more competitive than in a large family and that the parents of the former are more likely to have higher aspirations for their children and to place a greater stress upon personal achievement. Furthermore, fathers of small families, particularly in the middle class, are described as less authoritarian than those of large, lower-class families. With respect to the variable of ordinal position, early born children are said to be reared more anxiously, to be more "adult-oriented," and to command more of their parents' attention than later born. And as regards parental age, it has been noted that parents as they grow older have less energy to enforce their socialization demands. They are also said to be more indulgent and solicitous, placing less emphasis upon self-reliance and achievement in child-rearing. For these and other reasons which will be spelled out in more detail, this study hypothesized that (a) children from small families will tend to have stronger achievement motivation than children from larger families, (b) early born (first or only) would tend to have higher achievement motivation scores than later born, and (c) children of young mothers would tend to have higher motivation than the children of old mothers.

RESEARCH PROCEDURE

The data for this study were collected from two independent samples. The first was a purposive sample of 427 pairs of mothers and their sons who resided in four northeastern states. This sample (which we will call Sample *A*) was deliberately designed to include subjects from a very heterogenous population.[3] The interviewers, all of whom were upper-classmen enrolled in two sociology courses, were instructed to draw respondents from six racial

---

[2] The above two paragraphs are paraphrased from B. C. Rosen and R. D'Andrade, "The Psychosocial Origins of Achievement Motivation," *Sociometry*, 22 (September 1959), 185–218.

[3] Cf. B. C. Rosen, "Race, Ethnicity, and the Achievement Syndrome," *American Sociological Review*, 24 (February 1959), 47–60.

and ethnic groups: French-Canadians, Greeks, Italians, Jews, Negroes, and white Protestants, as well as from various social classes. Most of the mothers and all of the sons were native-born. The boys ranged in age from 8 to 14, with a mean age of about 11. At a later date, a second group of respondents (Sample *B*) was obtained in connection with another and larger research program by interviewing systemically virtually the entire universe of boys, 9 to 11 years of age, in the elementary schools of three small northeastern Connecticut towns. This sample of 367 subjects had a mean age of about 10 years and was much more homogeneous with respect to race and ethnicity. All the respondents were white, and predominantly Protestant or Roman Catholic. Also, the interviewers were two carefully trained graduate assistants employed specifically for this purpose. For both samples, the respondent's social position was determined by a modified version of Hollingshead's Index of Social Position, which uses the occupation and education of the main wage-earner, usually the father, as the principal criteria of status. Respondents were classified according to this index into one of five social classes, from the highest status group (Class 1) to the lowest (Class V).

A measure of the boy's achievement motivation was obtained by using a Thematic Apperception-type test.[4] This projective test involves showing the subject four ambiguous pictures and asking him to tell a story, under time pressure, about each one. The stories are then scored by counting the frequency of imagery about evaluated per-

formance in competition with a standard of excellence. This test assumes that the more the individual shows indications of connections between affect and evaluated performance in his fantasy, the greater will be the degree to which achievement motivation is a part of his personality. The boys in both samples were given this test privately and individually. In the case of the first sample the testing was done in the home; in the second at school in a private office. The subject's imaginative responses were scored by two judges, and a product-moment correlation between the two scorings of 0.86 for the first sample and 0.92 for the second was obtained.

For Sample *A*, information about the size of the family, ordinal position of the boy, mother's age, and occupation-education characteristics of the father was obtained from the mother in personal interviews in the home. In the case of Sample *B*, these data were secured from the boy through questionnaires administered in the classroom. Data on the age of mother are lacking for subjects in Sample *B*, as the boys were frequently uncertain of their mother's age.

RESEARCH FINDINGS

Family size and achievement motivation. Considering the sociologist's traditional and continuing concern with group size as an independent variable (from Simmel and Durkheim to the recent experimental studies of small groups), there have been surprisingly few studies of the influence of size upon the nature of interaction in the family. However, such studies as do exist (Bossard's work especially) strongly point to the importance of family size as a variable affecting the socialization process in ways that are relevant to the

---

[4] The test was administered under neutral conditions, using pictures 33, 26, 9, 24 in that order. For more information about this test, see D. C. McClelland *et al.*, *op. cit.*

development of achievement motivation. In fact, when comparing small and large families, investigators tend to regard what we have called achievement and independence training as among the more important criteria differentiating one type of family from the other.[5]

The small family has been described as a planned unit driven by ambition. Middle-class small families are regarded as particularly oriented toward status-striving and upward mobility. To achieve this end, the parents stress planning and achievement not only for themselves but for their children as well. Considerable attention can be given to the child's progress in the small family since its limited size affords the parents a relatively greater opportunity to devote more of their time and effort to each child than would be possible in the large family. In fact, life in many small families seems to be organized around plans for the child's development and future achievement. There may be, for example, an intense concern with his performance in school. In such families, parental reaction to the child's success or failure in competition with his peers is frequently immediate and strong. Evidences of achievement are likely to be lavishly applauded and rewarded, while failure will elicit numerous signs of parental disappointment or displea-

sure. Of course, the parent's motives are not always altruistic. In some cases the child's achievements serve to improve the family's status or may represent the working out through the child of the parent's unfulfilled personal aspirations. McArthur suggests that children in small families are sometimes "exploited to fulfill the expectations, even the frustrated desires of the parents."[6] Whatever the motives may be, and surely they are many and complex, it seems safe to say that in cases where parents are ambitious for themselves and their children, we may expect to find much emphasis upon standards of excellence, coupled with expectations for high achievement and intense parental involvement in the child's performance. Competition with standards of excellence, and rivalry with peers and siblings are, in fact, oft noted characteristics of the behavior of children from small, particularly middle-class, homes.[7]

---

[5] See, for example, J. H. Bossard, *Parent and Child* (Philadelphia: University of Pennsylvania Press, 1953); J. H. Bossard and E. S. Boll, "Personality Roles in the Large Family," *Child Development*, 26 (March 1955); D. E. Damrin, "Family Size and Sibling Age, Sex, and Position as Related to Certain Aspects of Adjustment," *The Journal of Social Psychology*, 26 (February 1949), 93–102; R. Stagner and E. T. Katyoff, "Personality as Related to Birth Order and Family Size," *Journal of Applied Psychology*, 20 (May–June 1936) 340–46.

[6] C. McArthur, "Personalities of First and Second Children," *Psychiatry*, 19 (February 1956), 47–54.

[7] Cf. M. Mead, *And Keep Your Powder Dry* (New York: William Morrow & Company, Inc., 1943), especially Chaps. VI–VII. The variables examined in this paper do not of course, exhaust the list of possible causal factors. It is quite possible that other demographic factors, such as the number and ordinal position of male and female siblings and the number of years separating each child, may also be important. Furthermore, nondemographic factors, such as parental values, could also play a significant role in the development of achievement motivation. Thus family size and achievement motivation may *both* reflect the achievement-oriented values of the parents. We know, also, that other persons besides parents, for example, peers, play an important part in the socialization process. Cf. B. C. Rosen, "Multiple Group Membership: A Study of Parent-Peer Group Cross-Pressures," *American Sociological Review*, 20 (April 1955), 155–61.

The pattern of independence training known to be related to the development of achievement motivation is also believed to be more characteristic of life in the small family. The achievement-oriented values of parents of small families and their recognition of the importance of self-reliant mastery for advancement in our competitive society will cause them to urge the child to be self-reliant *in situations where he competes with standards of excellence.* Also, the small family is said to be more democratic and relatively free from the authoritarian, patriarchal leadership that is more common to the large family. In the small family, particularly in the middle-class, the parent typically seeks to obtain the cooperation of the child through the employment of conditional love and the manipulation of guilt feelings rather than by the use of coercion. Of course, the very intensity of parent-child relations in this type of family, especially between mother and son, sets definite limits to the child's freedom of action. But an intensely involved, "pushing" mother appears to promote the development of achievement motivation in boys. It is the authoritarian father, not the mother, who represents a greater threat to the boy and inhibits the development of achievement motivation.

The large family is a different social system, both qualitatively as well as quantitatively. The larger number of persons in the group creates a greater degree of interdependence between members and an increased need for cooperative effort and consensus. The precarious equilibrium of the large family would be threatened by excessive emphasis upon competition and achievement. Rivalry exists, of course, but it must be muted. Hence, in contrast to the small family, the large family is more likely to value responsibility

above individual achievement, conformity above self-expression, cooperation and obedience above individualism. Children are more likely to be disciplined for the sake of family harmony than to assure their meeting achievement goals. Bossard maintains that there is a greater degree of specialization of roles in the large family. Each child tends to become functionally specialized, his behavior being more influenced by the family division of labor than by parental aspirations for achievement. He notes that his material on the large family contains "little mention of a child who excels at large, as is so common with small-family children; there is little comparison with neighbor's children; there is emphasis on duty, not spectacular achievement."[8]

As the size of the family increases, better internal organization and a higher degree of discipline are required. It is perhaps for this reason that the authoritarian father is often associated with the large-family system. But in families where the father is overly dominant the amount of autonomy permitted the son will be severely curtailed. The child will have little opportunity to experience the pleasures of autonomous mastery that appear important to the development of strong achievement motivation. On the other hand, although the child may not be granted very much autonomy in the large family, he typically receives considerable training in self-reliance. In the large family the child normally receives a smaller amount of attention and surveillance from his parents than would be the case in the small family. Hence, he is expected to be self-reliant but

---

8 J. H. Bossard, *The Large Family System* (Philadelphia: University of Pennsylvania Press, 1956).

usually in areas involving self-caretaking (e.g., feeding, dressing, amusing and defending oneself) rather than in situations where he competes with standards of excellence. Research has shown that self-reliance training in caretaking areas is not related to high achievement motivation.

In view of these differences between the socialization practices of parents with families of different sizes, we predicted that the children from small families would tend to have higher achievement motivation than those from large families. To test this hypothesis, we divided the families into three groups. Families with one or two children were called "small," those with three or four children "medium," and those with five or more children "large." This procedure was performed for both samples. In Table 1 are shown the boy's mean achievement motivation scores, cross-tabulated by family size and social class[9] for samples *A* and *B*. The data tend to support our hypothesis, especially for subjects in sample *A*. Considering for the moment only the means for family groups without regard to social class, we find a clear

inverse relationship between family size and achievement motivation: The mean score for boys from small families in sample *A* is 5.43, medium families 4.64, and large families 2.48. Thus, the mean score of boys from small families is more than twice as great as that of boys from large families, and the mean score of boys from medium-size families almost twice as great. The difference between the scores of boys from large families and those from medium and small families is statistically significant at the 0.001 level. However, the difference between small and medium families is not statistically significant. Social class is also related to achievement motivation, as has been reported elsewhere[10] and, in fact, accounts for more of the variance ($F=5.67$, $P<0.01$) than family size ($F=3.70$, $P<0.05$). However, for sample *A*, the relationship between family size and achievement motivation tends to persist even when social class is controlled. An internal examination of the table reveals that for each social class, in eleven out of twelve cells, the boys from small families have the highest mean scores, with somewhat lower motivation scores for boys from medium-size families, while the scores of boys from large families are the lowest in every social class.

For sample *B*, the relationship of family size to achievement motivation is also an inverse one (small family 6.61, medium 6.57, large 6.22), but the differences between groups are small and statistically insignificant. Social class continues to be related significantly to achievement motivation—this time at the 0.05 level—and displays a pattern

---

[9] An analysis was made to determine the relationship of religion and race to family size since achievement motivation is known to be related to these factors. (See footnote 3.) It was found that Roman Catholics and Negroes have larger families than white Protestants, Greeks, and Jews. But these differences virtually disappear when social class is controlled. For example, in the middle class the average number of children in Negro families is 3.0, Catholic families 2.7 as compared with 2.5 for Greeks, 2.6 for Jews, and 2.8 for white Protestants. In the lower class the differences are somewhat larger but not statistically significant: Jews 2.1, Greeks 2.4, white Protestants 3.0, Catholics 3.3, and Negroes 3.6. This finding is one reason why social class was introduced as a controlling variable throughout this study.

[10] See B. C. Rosen, "The Achievement Syndrome: A Psychocultural Dimension of Social Stratification," *American Sociological Review*, 21 (April 1956), 203–11.

TABLE 1.   MEAN ACHIEVEMENT SCORES BY
FAMILY SIZE AND SOCIAL CLASS

| | Sample A* | | | | Sample B** | | | |
| | Family Size | | | | Family Size | | | |
Social Class	Small	Medium	Large	$\bar{x}$	Small	Medium	Large	$\bar{x}$
I–II	5.20	6.41	2.33	5.46	7.28	7.93	2.25	7.11
III	6.49	6.14	5.83	6.28	7.67	7.36	6.13	7.32
IV	5.06	3.40	2.82	4.00	6.33	6.15	7.29	6.29
V	4.57	3.67	1.48	3.31	4.15	5.00	2.00	4.69
$\bar{x}$	5.43	4.64	2.48		6.61	6.57	6.22	
N	178	193	54		155	166	45	

* Information lacking for two cases.
** Information lacking for one case.

identical to that found in Sample A: The highest score is in class III, a somewhat lower score in class I–II, with progressively declining scores in classes IV and V.

There are other similarities between samples A and B. For example, the rank of mean scores for class Ǐ—II and III are similar for both samples. That is, in class I-II the relationship between family size and motivation is curvilinear: highest score in medium-size families, a somewhat lower score in the small family, and a considerably lower score in large families. In class III there is an inverse relationship between motivation and family size: The smaller the family the larger the motivation score. Furthermore, in both samples the large-size families in classes I–II and V have the lowest scores of all groups. Why should this be so? Perhaps because at both extremes of the status continuum the pressure to excel is not so intense; there may be less stress on striving, less emphasis on standards of excellence and fewer pressures on the child to compete with them, possibly because in one class the need to succeed is not so great, and in the other because the objective possibility is so limited.

Generally, then, boys from large families tend to have lower achievement motivation than those from small and medium families (with one exception: class IV in sample B), but it must be added that any statement about the relationship of family size to achievement motivation would be on firmer ground if the F ratio for sample B had been statistically significant.

Birth order and achievement motivation. Influenced, perhaps, by Freud's observation that "a child's position in the sequence of brothers and sisters is of very great significance for the course of his later life,"[11] a considerable number of researchers have studied the relationship between ordinal position, socialization, and a variety of personality characteristics. Though sometimes conflicting, many of their findings have relevance for a study of the develop-

---

[11] S. Freud, *A General Introduction to Psycho-Analysis* (Garden City, N.Y.: Doubleday & Company, Inc., 1938), p. 182.

ment of achievement motivation.[12]

A disproportionate degree of attention has been concentrated on the first born, so that an impressive amount of data has been collected on this position. While the term "achievement training" is not used explicitly, several studies indicate that the first-born child (i.e., eldest child in a family containing two or more children) typically receives more achievement training than the later born. To begin with, the amount and degree of interaction between parent and first born is likely to be large and intense. Also, as the only child (at least for a time), he is the sole object of parental expectations. These tend to be high, and sometimes involve an overestimate of the child's abilities, in part because there are no other children to provide a realistic standard against which his performance may be evaluated. This may lead the parent to accelerate his training, a process which receives further impetus with arrival of younger siblings. Thus, it has been noted that the first-born child tends to talk earlier than the later born. Koch has found that first-born children are more competitive than the later born.[13]

[12] A. Adler, "Characteristics of First, Second, and Third Child," *Children, the Magazine For Parents*, 3 (May 1928), 14–52; H. E. Jones, "Order of Birth," in *Handbook of Child Psychology*, ed. C. Murchison (Worcester, Mass.: Clark University Press, 1933); M. H. Krout, "Typical Behavior Patterns in Twenty-Six Ordinal Positions," *Journal of Genetic Psychology*, 55 (September 1939), 3–30; J. P. Lees, "The Social Mobility of a Group of Eldest-Born and Intermediate Adult Males," *British Journal of Psychology*, 43 (August 1952), 210–21; R. R. Sears, "Ordinal Position in the Family as a Psychological Variable," *American Sociological Review*, 15 (June 1950), 397–401.

[13] H. L. Koch, "Some Personality Correlates of Sex, Sibling Position and Sex of Siblings Among Five and Six Year Old Children," *Genetic Psychology Monographs*, 52 (August 1955), 3–50.

Furthermore, in part because of his greater access to his parents, the first born tends to become intensely involved with them and very sensitive to their expectation and sanctions. The first-born child has been described as "adult-oriented," serious, conscientious, and fond of doing things for his parents, while the second born is said to be more "peer oriented."[14] Of course, this close association may make him more dependent upon his parents, although with the advent of younger siblings he is likely to receive considerable and even abrupt independence training. Frequently, where the family is large, the oldest child will act as a parent-surrogate, and is given very early self-reliance training, so that at times he may behave more like a responsible little man than a child. However, in the absence of achievement training this type of self-reliance training is likely to generate a personality oriented more toward accepting responsibility than striving for achievement.

In the beginning, the positions of the oldest and the only child are identical—neither have siblings, and one would expect that their socialization experiences would be similar. This is likely to be the case with respect to achievement training, although the only child will miss the extra push that the oldest child receives with the advent of the next-born. The major difference seems to be with respect to independence training. Only children are said to be anxiously trained: Some are reared overstrictly, others are excessively indulged. They run the risk of being "smothered" by their parents and of becoming excessively dependent. An overdominated child may be only externally driven and "run out of gas" as soon as parental pressures are removed. The excessively

[14] McArthur, *op. cit.* p. 54.

indulged child may simply not internalize the expectations of his parents. Thus, Sears reports that "high conscience" is found more frequently in children whose parents employed both rewards and punishments than among children who experienced only rewards.[15] In either event, the only child is not likely to receive the training in self-reliance and autonomy that is more frequently the experience of the oldest child with several siblings.

The socialization experiences of the youngest child may involve considerable achievement training for with approaching freedom from child care the mother tends to accelerate the youngest child to the level of mastery attained by his elder siblings. Thus, Lasko found, in comparing second children who are youngest with second children who have younger siblings, that parents tend to accelerate the younger in a two-child family to the level imposed upon the oldest child.[16] Where there were younger sibs no such attempt was made since the parents were able to estimate more realistically the child's capabilities. The youngest child, however, does run considerable risk with regard to independence training. Research in this connection indicates that parents are more warm and solicitous toward the youngest child than toward other children in the birth order. The youngest child is likely to be pampered, over-protected, and overindulged, not only by his parents but also by elder siblings. Such indulgence and overprotectiveness is antithetical to the development of achievement motivation, which requires that parents set and enforce high expectations for achievement, self-reliance, and autonomy.

Very little has been written about the socialization of the intermediate child in the birth sequence. Perhaps this is because the intermediate child is not so much a fixed position in the birth order as a residual category. The intermediate child could be anyone of several children in the ordinal sequence; e.g., the second child in the ordinal sequence; e.g., the second child in a three-child family, the third or fourth child in a five-child family, and so on. Despite this ambiguity, there has been some speculation that the position of the intermediate child is the most comfortable in the birth order.[17] There is less pressure on the intermediate child to conform to the levels of mastery attained by his siblings and less anxiety about his development. Furthermore, the intermediate child is more likely to come from a large family than a small family; he must, of course, come from a family with at least three children. It is probable, then, if our observations about socialization in the large family are correct, that his training will involve a greater emphasis upon cooperation and responsibility than on achievement.

Given these descriptions of the socialization experiences associated with different positions in the birth order, we predicted that achievement motivation would be highest among boys who are oldest in the birth sequence, somewhat lower among only and youngest children, and lowest among the intermediate boys. As can be seen in Table 2,

15 R. R. Sears, E. E. Maccoby, and H. Levin, in collaboration with E. L. Lowell, P. S. Sears, and J. W. M. Whiting, *Patterns of Child Rearing* (Evanston, Ill.: Row, Peterson, 1957).

16 J. K. Lasko, "Parent Behavior Towards First and Second Children," *Genetic Psychology Monographs*, 49 (February 1954), 97–137.

17 W. Toman, "Family Constellation as a Basic Personality Determinant," *Journal of Individual Psychology*, 15 (November 1959), 199–211.

TABLE 2. MEAN ACHIEVEMENT SCORES BY
BIRTH ORDER AND SOCIAL CLASS

| Social Class | Sample A* | | | | | Sample B** | | | | |
| | | Birth Order | | | | | Birth Order | | | |
	Only	Oldest	Inter-mediate	Youn-gest	$\bar{x}$	Only	Oldest	Inter-mediate	Youn-gest	$\bar{x}$
I–II	3.50	6.03	4.28	5.34	5.46	5.33	7.76	5.76	8.29	7.11
III	8.50	6.38	5.61	5.62	6.28	9.83	6.63	7.16	7.88	7.32
IV	2.92	3.73	4.02	4.70	4.00	3.91	7.36	7.27	4.29	6.29
V	4.14	3.36	2.89	4.95	3.31	4.28	5.84	4.21	2.66	4.69
$\bar{x}$	5.08	4.97	3.45	5.12		5.41	7.02	6.59	5.97	
N	36	162	103	124		31	139	106	90	

* Information missing for two cases.
** Information missing for one case.

the data do not confirm our hypothesis. It is true that the mean score for oldest boys in sample *B* is higher than those for other ordinal positions, as predicted. But, unfortunately for our hypothesis, the oldest boys in sample *A* have a lower mean score than only or youngest, although the differences between the positions are very small and statistically insignificant. The intermediate boys in sample *A* have the lowest mean score, again as predicted, but in sample *B* their mean score is higher than that for only or youngest boys. Most significant is the fact that an analysis of the variance for each sample revealed that the effects of ordinal position are not statistically significant. The effects of social class, however, are statistically significant; at the 0.01 level for sample *A*, and the 0.05 level for sample *B*.

Since family size has been shown to be related to achievement motivation, it occurred to us that the difference between these two samples might be a function of the effects of this variable. That is, perhaps the oldest boys in sample *A* come from large families, while

those from sample *B* tend to be from small families. Similarly, youngest and intermediate boys in the two samples might also come from families of markedly different size. We decided to introduce family size as a test variable. Table 3 shows the relationship between birth order and achievement motivation with family size and social class controlled. Class III has been grouped with classes I—II, and class IV with class V in order to reduce the number of cells without cases. We will call the former group middle class, the latter group lower class. Only the data derived from sample *A* are presented. Unfortunately, the smaller number of cases in sample *B* made a multivariate analysis of this complexity impossible—there proved to be too many empty cells or cells with very few cases—so we were not able to test our hypothesis about the different composition of the two samples. Only children, for whom of course family size is not a variable, are also not included.

Table 3 shows how perilous it is to speak about the relationship of birth

TABLE 3. MEAN ACHIEVEMENT MOTIVATION SCORES BY BIRTH ORDER, FAMILY SIZE, AND SOCIAL CLASS

	Social Class I–II–III			Social Class IV–V		
	Family Size			Family Size		
Birth Order	Small	Medium	Large	Small	Medium	Large
Oldest	5.82	7.52	5.75	4.31	2.86	1.00
Intermediate	*	5.44	10.00	*	3.43	1.96
Youngest	5.94	5.21	2.00	5.93	3.90	2.84

* There are, of course, no intermediate children in a two-child family.

order to achievement motivation without taking into account the influence of family size and social class. For each ordinal position, with the exception of only two out of seventeen cells, achievement motivation declines as the size of the family increases. The decline is greatest and most consistent in the lower class. For example, the mean score for oldest children from small families is 4.31, medium families 2.86, and large families 1.00. Similar consistent declines also apply to lower-class intermediate and youngest children. The motivation score of the youngest child is most consistently affected by family size: The mean scores for both middle- and lower-class boys who are youngest in the birth sequence decline as the size of the family increases. In the middle class, the mean score for youngest boys from small families is 5.94, from large families 2.00. In the lower class the score for youngest boys from small families is 5.93, from large families 2.84. On the other hand, only in the lower class does family size affect the scores of the oldest child. In the middle class, the mean motivation scores for oldest boys increase from 5.82 in small families to 7.52 in medium families and drop negligibly to 5.75 in large families. But in the lower class

the scores for oldest boys drop rapidly as family size increases: small family 4.31, medium 2.86, large 1.00.

Why should family size have this differential effect? Probably because the socialization practices associated with ordinal position vary with the size of the family and its social class. We have noted that oldest children in large, lower-class families are often expected to be parent-surrogates, performing some of the child-rearing duties for which the overburdened parents have neither the time nor energy. This condition is especially likely to occur when both parents are working (as is increasingly the case for both middle- and lower-class families), and are unable or unwilling to hire help. In situations where the mother is absent from the home or where one parent is missing for some reason, the oldest child must frequently assume her functions. Often he must defer his own ambitions and gratifications in order to help raise the family and to insure the education of younger siblings. Under these conditions a concern with training him for achievement may go by the board. In the middle class, however, financial pressures are not so likely to force parents to place so much of the burden of child-rearing on the oldest child. If the mother is working, it is usually possible for the family to hire someone to perform some of her functions.

The situation is quite different for the youngest child. In large families the youngest child is frequently indulged, overprotected, and may in general be exposed to few of the socialization experiences associated with the development of high achievement motivation. *In this connection it is particularly interesting that the impact of family size on achievement-motivation scores of boys who are youngest in the birth order appears to be more important than social class.* The pervasive achievement orientation of the middle class, which may have been responsible for the maintenance of relatively high scores among oldest boys of large middle-class families, seems *not* to have had the same effect on the youngest child; i.e., the youngest child from a large family has a lower mean achievement-motivation score than any other middle-class group.

Social class seems clearly to influence the impact of family size on ordinal position and achievement motivation. As we have noted, *in the lower class* the scores for oldest, intermediate, and youngest children all decline as family size increase. This decline is more precipitate among oldest than intermediate or youngest children. Also the mean motivation scores of the youngest and intermediate boys are higher than those for oldest children. Thus in the lower class the mean scores for youngest boys are as follows: small family 5.93, medium 3.90, large 2.84. The scores for oldest boys are consistently lower: small family 4.31, medium 2.86, large 1.00. But *in the middle class* the scores for oldest children are higher than those for intermediate and youngest, except in small families where

the score for youngest children is slightly and negligibly higher.

It is difficult to assess the relative effects of these three variables—ordinal position, family size, and social class—since unfortunately the empty cells in this table make an analysis of variance impracticable. But it appears probable that social class is the greatest and most consistent factor, followed by family size and ordinal position.

Mother's age and achievement motivation. When considering the relationship of mother's age to the achievement motivation of the child, the question arises as to the nature of the changes that occur in the socialization process with increments in the parent's age. Systematic data on this factor are exceedingly skimpy, although the frequent use of such terms as "young mother" or "old mother" suggest that the parent's age is commonly considered important.[18]

Perhaps the most obvious difference between young and older women is that of sheer physical stamina. Older mothers on the average have less energy to cope with very young children, who normally seethe with activity, and may have difficulty enforcing their socialization demands. It is said, also, that older mothers tend to be more solicitous and indulgent toward children than their younger counterparts. The older mother, particularly where the child represents a long-delayed fulfillment, may be unwilling to make strong demands upon her child for self-reliance and achievement. Or, if the demands are made, she may not enforce them with the negative sanctions that appear important to the development of achievement mo-

---

[18] See J. H. Bossard, *Parent and Child* (Philadelphia: University of Pennsylvania Press, 1953).

tivation. The tendency for the young mother, on the other hand, especially in the middle class, to be intensely competive about the speed with which her child learns to master his environment —as compared with his peers—has excited frequent and disapproving comment. She may, for example, constantly compare her child's skill in walking or talking with that of his playmates. Later in school, his performance relative to that of his peers is closely watched and strong pressure may be exerted if he falls behind. Where the competitive spirit is not a factor, the young mother may accelerate her child's training simply through inexperience and an inability to correctly gauge his abilities. It was for these reasons that we hypothesized that children of younger mothers would tend to have higher achievement motivation than those of older mothers.

In order to test this hypothesis the mothers were divided into three age groups: mothers 34 years of age or less are called "young," those between 35 and 44 "middle age," and those 45 years or more "old." These data were obtained only from subjects in sample *A*, where it was possible to interview the mother personally.

Table 4 shows the relationship between mother's age and the boy's achievement motivation with social class controlled. An analysis of variance of the data revealed that mother's age is significantly related to achievement motivation ($F=5.56$, $P<0.01$). The effects of social class are also significant ($F=5.79$, $P<0.01$): *within all mother's age groups* the boy's mean achievement-motivation scores decline as the mother's status decreases, except for a slight increase from class I–II to class III. However, our hypothesis that the children of young mothers would have higher achievement-motivation scores

TABLE 4. MEAN ACHIEVEMENT-MOTIVATION SCORES BY MOTHER'S AGE AND SOCIAL CLASS

Social Class	Mother's Age			
	Young	Middle	Old	$\bar{x}$
I–II	5.00	5.57	6.50	5.65
III	9.14	5.78	6.18	6.32
IV	2.37	4.78	3.58	4.01
V	0.57	4.33	2.87	3.43
$\bar{x}$	3.61	5.09	4.75	
N	75	266	69	

Information missing on seven cases

than those of older mothers was not confirmed. Disregarding social class, the relationship between mother's age and the boy's motivation is curvilinear: Children of young mothers have the lowest mean scores (3.61), those of middle-age mothers the highest (5.09), and the sons of old mothers the intermediate score (4.75). However, when social class is controlled the picture becomes quite confused. In class I—II, the achievement-motivation scores of the boys increase as mother's age increases—just the opposite of what we had predicted. However, in class III, the reverse is true: The boys of younger mothers have higher scores than those of old mothers.

Some of this confusion is reduced when family size is introduced as a specifying variable. The data in Table 5 show the relationship of mother's age to son's achievement motivation when the variables of social class and family size are controlled. In small-size families the sons of young mothers have higher mean scores than the sons of old mothers, but this relationship is reversed as the size of the family increases. In medium- and large-size families of both the middle and lower classes, the sons of old mothers have higher scores than the sons of young mothers. The effect of increased family size, however, is much greater in the lower than in the middle class and greatest of all upon the sons of young, lower-class mothers. Thus, the mean scores of the sons of young, lower-class mothers drop precipitately as the size of the family increases: from 4.23 in small families, to 0.02 in medium size, and 0.33 in large families. The mean scores of the sons of older mothers also decline as family size increases, but the drop is more modest; i.e., small family 3.81, medium family 3.53, large family 2.36. Why should the motivation scores of sons of young mothers be so much more adversely affected by increased family size than are the scores of sons of older mothers? Perhaps because the children of a young mother with a large family are all young, so that the older children are not able to provide much help in taking care of younger siblings. In this case the young mother, particularly if she is lower class and unable to obtain help, may simply be overwhelmed. She will have little time or energy for the supervision and complex training in achievement that the development of achievement motivation requires.

The introduction of family size as a specifying variable requires a rephrasing of our original hypothesis about the relationship of mother's age to achievement motivation. Our prediction that the sons of young mothers would have higher motivation than the sons of old mothers is correct *but only when the family is small and primarily when the parents are middle class*. As the family increases in size, the motivation scores of children of older mothers are higher than the scores of children of younger mothers, and indeed in the lower class the sons of middle-age mothers have the highest scores of all.

CONCLUSION

Perhaps the most important generalization to be drawn from this study is that it is exceedingly unwise to single out any one demographic factor as an explanation of achievement motivation. It is true that social class is consistently related to achievement motivation: The data show that the motivation scores of class I–II–III boys are significantly higher than are the scores of boys from classes IV–V. Also, we have noted time and again that boys from small families tend to have higher achievement motivation than their peers from large families. But the effects of social class and family size, as well as the impact of birth order and mother's age,

TABLE 5.   MEAN ACHIEVEMENT-MOTIVATION SCORES BY MOTHER'S AGE, FAMILY SIZE, AND SOCIAL CLASS

	Social Class I–II–III			Social Class IV–V		
	Family Size			Family Size		
Mother's Age	Small	Medium	Large	Small	Medium	Large
Young	7.64	7.33	*	4.32	0.02	0.33
Middle	5.79	5.70	4.50	5.58	4.29	2.70
Old	5.86	7.60	5.33	3.81	3.53	2.36

* No cases.

can only be properly understood in a large context in which all of these variables (and others, undoubtedly) interact.

For example, the impact of family size on the boy's achievement motivation varies with his social class. It was shown that while, in general, motivation scores decline as family size increases, the effect of family size on motivation scores is much greater at the upper-middle (class I–II) and lower-class (class V) levels than at the lower-middle (class III) and upper-lower class (class IV) levels. Furthermore the effect of birth order is intimately related to family size and social class. Hence it is not very helpful in predicting an individual's achievement motivation to know his position in the birth order—indeed this information may be misleading rather than useful—unless the social class and size of his family of orientation are also known. In small middle-class families, for example, the effect of ordinal position seems to be relatively unimportant: The oldest and youngest child in a two-child, middle-class family have almost identical motivation scores, but *as the size of the*

family increases the scores for the oldest child *in the middle* class become higher than those for the youngest child. However, *in the lower class* the reverse is true: The youngest child has a higher achievement-motivation score on the average than the oldest child—a position that is maintained even when the size of the family increases. Similarly, the effect of mother's age upon the child's achievement motivation varies with the size of her family and social class. Thus the hypothesis that the sons of young mothers would have higher achievement motivation than the sons of old mothers proved to be correct, *but only when the family is small.* As the size of the family increases, *particularly in the lower class,* the scores of sons of young mothers drop rapidly and are surpassed by the scores of sons of middle age and old mothers.

These data, then, indicate that the demographic factors examined in this study have relevance for the development of achievement motivation, but their effects are complicated, interconnected, and interdependent upon one another and difficult to assess individually.

The preceding articles focus on mobility resulting from individual and societal antecedents. Other studies focus on mobility as an independent variable which produces significant social consequences. Insofar as classes are somewhat discrete cultures and social systems, movement from one class position to another requires an adjustment in attitudes, values, and group identification. A change in class status also means a change in the conditions of life of the mobile person. The study by Robert Ellis and W. Clayton Lane[1] shows that attitudinal and environmental changes may be highly disruptive for the socially mobile person.

---

1 This research considers some of the important linkages among mobility, stress, and behavior. Several of the studies presented in Chapter Nine suggest that some of these linkages can be operative in the manifestation of social pathology.

SOCIAL MOBILITY AND SOCIAL ISOLATION: A TEST OF SOROKIN'S DISSOCIATIVE HYPOTHESIS*†

Robert A. Ellis, *University of Oregon*

W. Clayton Lane, *San Jose State College*

The stratification system generally operates in our society to bind persons to the class circumstances to which they are born. Nevertheless, in any given generation a number of individuals do free themselves of the restraints of their class of origin and change their position in the social structure. Just what consequences these shifts in status have for the individual, especially where major mobility is involved, has been a matter of recurring concern but little consensus.

One line of thought portrays the upwardly mobile as isolated, lonely individuals who, because of their ascent, find themselves unable to form satisfactory personal relationships in their new environment. This point of view—what we term the *dissociative hypothesis*—was introduced by Sorokin over a quarter of a century ago. Although in discussing the effects of mobility Sorokin mentions such benefits to society as increased creativity and adaptability, he points out that they come at a psychological cost to the individual. Part of this cost is an experience of rootlessness, for upward mobility is a disruptive social experience that, to use Sorokin's terms, "diminishes intimacy and increases psychosocial isolation and loneliness." The mobile man in contemporary society he thus depicts as one who is unattached to anything or anybody.[1]

* From Robert A. Ellis and W. Clayton Lane, "Social Mobility and Social Isolation: A Test of Sorokin's Dissociative Hypothesis," *American Sociological Review*, 32 (April 1967), 237–53. Reprinted by permission of the American Sociological Association.

† Expanded version of a paper read at the annual meeting of the Western Psychological Association, April 1964. The research has been supported by Public Health Grant MH-04968 from the National Institute of Mental Health and by grants from the Society for the Investigation of Human Ecology, the Social Science Research Council, and Stanford University Facility Research Funds. Data analysis was supported in part by a contract with the United States Department of Health, Education, and Welfare, Office of Education.

In a project of this duration, it is impossible to acknowledge the services of all the persons who have contributed time, energy, and ideas. Special appreciation, however, is due to the following individuals: Richard H. Anderson, Milton Bloombaum, John Koval, Virginia Olesen, Robert Von der Lippe, and William Zwerman.

[1] Pitirim A. Sorokin, *Social Mobility* (New York: Harper & Bros., 1927), pp. 522–25. More recent statements of this view are found in Robert H. Bohlke, "Social Mobility, Stratification Inconsistency and Middle Class Delinquency," *Social Problems*, 8 (Spring 1961), 351–63; Peter M. Blau, "Oc-

An alternative view, the *compensatory hypothesis*, has been advanced by psychoanalytically oriented social scientists. They treat social isolation as more the cause than the effect of upward mobility. Status strivings, from this standpoint, are evoked to compensate for social deprivation arising from childhood and early adolescent experiences.[2] While those who rise in the social structure may, as adults, encounter inordinate difficulties in establishing close ties with others, this isolation is construed as only "a continuation of [the same] superficial, impermanent primary group relations" that originally motivated them to alter their class circumstances.[3]

Still another approach is to be found in the *ameliorative hypothesis* set forth in reference-group theory. An upward shift of one's class position is acknowledged to have a potentially disruptive effect but one that is not inevitable. The disruptive tendencies can be substantially ameliorated, if not alleviated entirely, by prior social experiences. Conceiving anticipatory socialization to be the usual mechanism for achieving upward mobility, proponents of this hypothesis contend that lower-class persons who have had opportunity to absorb the values, norms, and judgmental standards of the middle class to which they aspire should easily gain acceptance by that segment of society.[4]

In essence, then, these represent three competing interpretations of the

---

cupational Bias and Mobility," *American Sociological Review*, 22 (August 1957), 392–99; Richard Hoggart, *The Uses of Literacy: Changing Patterns in English Mass Culture* (Boston: Beacon Press, Inc., 1961), pp. 246–49; Jerome K. Myers and Bertram H. Roberts, *Family and Class Dynamics in Mental Illness* (New York: John Wiley & Sons, Inc., 1959), pp. 147–49, 152–53; Jurgen Ruesch, "Social Technique, Social Status, and Social Change in Illness" in *Personality in Nation, Society, and Culture*, eds. Clyde Kluckhohn and Henry A. Murray (New York: Alfred A. Knopf, Inc., 1949), pp. 117–30 (especially p. 125); Robert P. Stuckert, "Occupational Mobility and Family Relations," *Social Forces*, 41 (March 1963), 301–7; W. Lloyd Warner and James C. Abegglen, *Big Business Leaders in America* (New York: Harper & Bros., 1955), pp. 70–105; and Harold L. Wilensky and Hugh Edwards, "The Skidder: Ideological Adjustments of Downward Mobile Workers," *American Sociological Review*, 24 (April 1959), 215–31 (especially pp. 216 and 230).

[2] Russell R. Dynes, Alfred C. Clarke, and Simon Dinitz, "Levels of Occupational Aspiration: Some Aspects of Family Experience as a Variable," *American Sociological Review*, 21 (April 1956), 212–15; Evelyn Ellis, "Social Psychological Correlates of Upward Social Mobility Among Unmarried Career Women," *American Sociological Review*, 17 (October 1952), 558–63; Karen Horney, *The Neurotic Personality of Our Time* (New York: W. W. Norton & Company, Inc., Publishers, 1937), pp. 80–82, 162–87.

[3] Ellis, *op. cit.*, p. 563.
[4] Robert K. Merton, *Social Theory and Social Structure* (rev. ed.) (Glencoe, Ill.: The Free Press, 1957), pp. 254–55, 265–66, 384–85; Ralph H. Turner, *The Social Context of Ambition: A Study of High-School Seniors in Los Angeles* (San Francisco: Chandler Publishing Company, 1964), pp. 207–8, 219–22. For findings consistent with the ameliorative hypothesis see Julius Roth and Robert F. Peck, "Social Class and Social Mobility Factors Related to Marital Adjustment," *American Sociological Review*, 16 (August 1951), 478–87 (especially pp. 485–86).

The ameliorative hypothesis, as Merton formulates it, has relevance only for the individual's relation to his class of destination. With respect to one's class of origin, Merton clearly views upward mobility as a disruptive experience, the individual becoming progressively alienated from the old group in attitude, in value, and in interaction, even as this response is being reciprocated by the old group. See Merton, *op. cit.*, pp. 269–71, 294–95.

personal consequences of upward mobility. The dissociative hypothesis stipulates that a prolonged period of estrangement is the normal, direct consequence of upward mobility. Conversely, social isolation is treated in the compensatory hypothesis as a concomitant of mobility but not a direct consequence, and in the ameliorative hypothesis as a potential consequence of mobility but not a normal one. The validity of these hypotheses remains, however, to be demonstrated.

Methodologically, a test of Sorokin's hypothesis against its two theoretical alternatives requires capturing upwardly mobile individuals at a time of major status transition. This would permit determining whether a significant step in upward mobility is, in fact, accompanied by a period of social dislocation. If social isolation is a result, independent evidence needs to be gathered as to whether this isolation can be attributed either to (1) earlier inability to form effective social relationships or (2) the absence of effective anticipatory socialization.

RESEARCH PROBLEM

This paper endeavors to provide such a test by examining a situation of extreme mobility. We draw upon findings from a panel research undertaken at Stanford University over a complete undergraduate sequence to ascertain the intellectual and social adjustment students make to college life. As the discussion makes clear, the elaborate institutionalization of behavior at Stanford, plus the wide discrepancy between the past and present status circumstances of the upwardly mobile, make it an excellent natural experimental setting for testing the effects of social mobility.

Of primary interest in this inquiry are the highly selected students who come to Stanford from lower-class backgrounds. Clearly in the minority at this university, constituting only 3 per cent of the total undergraduate student body, they are upon matriculation confronted with the task of assuming full-time residence in what, from their perspective, may seem an alien and stressful social environment. Stanford is, in terms of its personnel, policies, and values, a predominantly upper-middle-class institution. Moreover, it is a highly competitive setting. This partially results from the characteristically upper-middle-class emphasis put on striving for achievement. In part, it is the direct consequence of admissions procedures that recruit youths who have been eminently successful in high school, having in the majority of cases been outstanding leaders in both scholastic and non-scholastic endeavors.

Yet this is not a world for which such lower-class youth as these are unprepared. The joint circumstances of self- and institutional selection have operated to bring to Stanford students from lower social backgrounds who have already adopted a middle class reference group and many of its attendant norms and values.[5] It is nevertheless problematical (1) whether their anticipatory socialization into middle-class practices and beliefs enables them to be readily assimilated into the Stanford undergraduate society; and (2) if not, whether the social estrangement that results is attributable to a chronic inability on their part to establish effective primary group ties.

---

[5] See Robert A. Ellis and W. Clayton Lane, "Social Mobility and Career Orientation," *Sociology and Social Research,* 50 (April 1966), 280–96.

METHOD

The subjects for this report consist of 126 male undergraduates who entered Stanford as first-year freshmen in the fall of 1958. Of these, ninety-nine were selected by means of a standard probability sample. Designated the Regular Sample, it furnishes a reliable and accurate estimate of the characteristics of the Stanford undergraduate population. The remaining twenty-seven students represent an oversample taken of all lower- and lower-middle-class freshmen not originally contained in the Regular Sample so as to compensate for the underrepresentation of persons from these social levels in the student body. The oversample is used to augment the Regular Sample whenever the factor of social class is analyzed.

Social-class background was determined by the Index of Class Position (ICP), a two-factor intercommunity measure of stratification developed and validated specifically for research on college populations.[6] ICP is based on the two components of father's occupation and the student's subjective identification of the class position of the family. This index yields a six-class scale ranging as follows:

SOCIAL CLASS	NOMINAL DESIGNATION
I	*Upper*
II	*Upper-Middle*
III	*Middle-Middle*
IV	*Lower-Middle*
V	*Upper-Lower*
VI	*Lower-Lower*

For a student to be categorized in the lower stratum by ICP, his father would have to be employed in a blue-collar occupation, and the student would have to perceive the family as being in the working or lower class.

Since background factors other than social class might be presumed to alienate individuals from their peers, appropriate controls were imposed. Race, ethnicity, and age were controlled by sample exclusion, so that nonwhites, foreign-born, and persons over 20 and under 17 were eliminated from the sample frame, a step that resulted in only a negligible reduction of the parent universe. Non-Protestants among the Stanford student body were too few to permit systematic partialling of the effects of Catholic, Jewish, and Protestant backgrounds. Nevertheless, all class differences obtained for the Regular Sample were recomputed for only the Protestants in the sample so as to insure that the effect of religion did not spuriously contribute to the results. All class differences reported below have been found to stand up independently of the effect of religion. Finally, the incidence of broken homes among Stanford students was found to be evenly distributed among the social classes and thus required no special treatment.

Data on social background, as well as all other information gained through students' self-reports, were obtained from hour-long interviews held early in the freshman year and, so long as the students remained in college, at the end of the freshman, sophomore, and senior years—which for some involved a time span of up to 7 years. Two additional sources of data were provided by administrative records and by judgments made of the students by other persons with the opportunity to observe and evaluate them in a social context. Included among the latter were high school teachers, dormitory counselors, and college administrators.

---

6 Robert A. Ellis, W. Clayton Lane, and Virginia Olesen, "The Index of Class Position: An Improved Intercommunity Measure of Stratification," *American Sociological Review*, 28 (April 1963), 271–77.

These outside judgments furnish an especially vital datum. Their use permits us to avoid exclusive reliance on individual self-reports, which may very well mask the more sensitive social and personal side effects of upward mobility. Moreover, since these evaluations span the time from high school to the senior year at Stanford, they help make it possible to pinpoint the premobility characteristics of the students and then to discern over an extended period the social impact that results from their movement in the social structure.

Finally, we should emphasize the strategic nature of the Stanford setting, which allows us to concentrate on persons taking a major step in upward mobility. This circumstance lends special weight to whatever negative findings may be uncovered regarding the compensatory hypothesis; for, as Lipset and Bendix and Evelyn Ellis note, it is extreme mobility that may be expected to attract "personality configurations which are a result of childhood deprivation."[7]

PRECOLLEGE POTENTIAL FOR SOCIAL SUCCESS

Our first concern is with the social potential exhibited by lower-class students prior to the time they come to Stanford. Is there early indication that they lack the skills neccessary for making an effective social and personal adjustment to college life?

By their record of extracurricular accomplishments in high school, it is readily evident that social maladjustment is the exception, characterizing no more

than 5 to 10 per cent of all class V and VI students. It is much more the rule for the upwardly mobile to be the prototype of the much-fabled "all-American boy." They have been able to combine a record of scholastic excellence with a prominent leadership role in the nonscholastic activities of high school life and even in the community at large. Not infrequently, these youngsters have achieved scholastic distinction as class valedictorian or National Merit Scholarship holder, while at the same time accumulating a series of nonscholastic honors, such as leadership in extracurricular organizations, class or student body officership, and major athletic awards. Many, in addition, have held offices that would bring them to the attention of the community at large, as, for example, in the City Youth Council or Junior Red Cross. In addition, almost half of the lower class were recipients of such "general honors" as American Legion Award for Outstanding Citizen of the Year or Senior Voted Most Likely to Succeed. Of equal significance is the fact that their record of leadership in nonscholastic endeavors falls only slightly below that of Stanford undergraduates in general: 64 per cent of class V and VI students, as compared to 76 per cent of the Regular Sample, have had the kind of awards and offices that would stamp them as outstanding leaders in the student culture.[8] (See Table 1.) Conse-

---

[7] Evelyn Ellis, *op cit.*, p. 563; Seymour Martin Lipset and Reinhard Bendix, *Social Mobility in Industrial Society* (Berkeley and Los Angeles, Calif.: University of California Press, 1960), pp. 252–53.

[8] Information on students' accomplishments in high school was obtained in the interviews held early in the fall of the freshman year when the students' high school experiences still were fresh in their minds. This information was subsequently checked for completeness and accuracy against the students' high school records on file in the Stanford Admissions Office.

The activities, accomplishments, and awards in each of the four role spheres of scholarship, athletics, student government,

TABLE 1. HIGH SCHOOL ACCOMPLISH-
MENTS OF LOWER-CLASS AND
OTHER STANFORD FRESHMEN,
PER CENT

Per cent Who Achieved High Success in :	Classes V and VI (N=22)	Regular Sample (N=99)
Area of success		
Scholastic	86	63
Nonscholastic*	64	76
Voluntary associations	18	30
Student government	32	51
Athletics	32	36
General honors	45	25
Pattern of success		
Both scholastic and nonscholastic areas	50	54
Scholastic area alone	36	10
Nonscholastic area alone	14	22
Neither area	0	14

* Success has been achieved in athletic activities and/or voluntary associations and/or student government.

quently, their high school accomplishments not only mark these class V and VI students as atypical of other persons coming from their background, but also indicate that they have essentially the same potential for social success as stu-

and school-sponsored voluntary associations were classified by use of a high school achievement scale specifically developed for this purpose. The scale makes it possible to classify students' accomplishment in each role sphere according to whether they yield *very high, high, medium, low,* or *no* social recognition in the high school setting. For the present paper, students with a record of high or very high achievement in a role sphere are treated as "successful" in that area.

A manual describing the use of the high school achievement scale is in preparation.

dents coming to Stanford from higher status levels.

Conclusions of a similar nature can be drawn from the recommendations that the high schools furnish the Stanford Admissions Office on each prospective student. Included in the recommendation form is a check list of academic and personal qualifications that is filled out by the high school principal or counselor assigned this responsibility. Tabulation of these items (see Table 2) shows that class V and VI students are viewed by high school administrators as slightly more motivated and able than other Stanford freshmen to do academic work—a finding that is not too surprising since almost all lower-class freshmen come to Stanford on scholarships.

It is also clear from the high school reports that these lower-class youth are thought to possess the social potential to fit into the Stanford undergraduate culture. Slightly more than half are regarded as having been good leaders in the high school student body, a result comparable to that obtained for the Regular Sample. Furthermore, they are even more likely than other Stanford freshmen to be judged free from those "personal or social problems . . . that would interfere with academic and personal success at Stanford," and not a single lower-class student is reported as being "more likely than the typical student" to be experiencing such problems. Moreover, in spite of their families' socioeconomic status—which almost inevitably was the subject for comment in the high school's report— the students from classes V and VI are described as possessing those personal and social characteristics which stamp an individual as "middle class." Almost without exception they are described as: (1) generally neat and clean in appearance, (2) responsible and trust-worthy in social and academic affairs, (3) likely to accept suggestions and corrections gracefully, (4) respectful and cooperative toward teachers and school officials, and (5) able to get along well with students and be respected by them.

Thus, from both their high school records and the judgments of high school personnel, it is clear that before they enter Stanford these upwardly mobile youth are not the socially inept, constrained individuals that the compensatory hypothesis of upward mobility would imply. Nor do they give evidence of having missed the significant anticipatory socialization into middle-class practices and beliefs that the ameliorative hypothesis suggests would pave the way for their making an easy and effective adjustment to the new social world they are entering.

Let us now turn our attention to the social reaction made to these students at the time they enter Stanford and over the course of the undergraduate years. Does the reaction by the other Stanford students indicate that the upwardly mobile encounter special difficulty in gaining social acceptance in this new milieu?

SOCIAL REACTION TO THE UPWARDLY MOBILE

Initial reaction. The task of selecting undergraduate judges is simplified by Stanford's practice of having twenty-four undergraduate counselors assigned as residents to the freshman dormitory, one to approximately every thirty freshmen. After the initial list of applicants is screened by the administration, these counselors, known at Stanford as "freshman sponsors," are elected to their post each year by the preceding group. Their role in the dormitory consists

TABLE 2. HIGH SCHOOL RECOMMENDATIONS OF LOWER-CLASS AND OTHER STANFORD FRESHMEN, PER CENT

Items Checked	Classes V and VI (N=22)	Regular Sample (N=99)
1. Great desire to achieve academic success at college	59	52
2. Possibility of achieving academic distinction in college	59	40
3. Very unlikely to have personal or social problems leading to emotional instability that would interfere with academic and personal success at Stanford	68	50
4. A good leader [in high school student body]	55	52
5. Generally neat and clean in appearance	95	93
6. Responsible and trustworthy in social and academic affairs	95	94
7. Accepts suggestions and corrections gracefully	91	89
8. Respectful and cooperative toward teachers and school officials	95	92
9. Gets along well with students and is respected by them	91	87

TABLE 3. SOCIAL CHARACTERISTICS
OF STANFORD FRESHMEN AND
SPONSORS, PER CENT

Social Characteristic	Regular Sample (N=99)	Sponsors (N=24)
Resident of California	61	54
Social class of family (ICP)[a]		
Class I (upper class)	12	21
Class II (upper-middle class)	49	50
Occupation of father		
High-level executive or major proprietor	22	38
Major professional	27	33
Educational background of one or both parents		
College graduate	68	75
Undergraduate attendance at a prestige university or college[b]	38	42
Stanford alumnus	21	21
Religious affiliation of student		
High-status Protestant[c]	44	42
Graduate of private secondary school	14	04
Recipient of freshman scholarship	38	42

[a] Social class was measured by the Index of Class Position. See Robert A. Ellis, W. Clayton Lane, and Virginia Olesen, "The Index of Class Position: An Improved Intercommunity Measure of Stratification," *American Sociological Review*, 28 (April 1963), 271–77.

[b] An institution was coded as a prestige college or university if it was included either in the *Chicago Tribune*'s 1957 survey of the forty best schools or in the Knapp and Greenbaum list of fifty undergraduate colleges and universities that have been most productive of future Ph. D's. See Robert H. Knapp and Joseph J. Greenbaum, *The Young American Scholar: His Collegiate Origins* (Chicago: University of Chicago Press, 1953); Chester Manly, "Greatest Schools in Nation: A Survey by the

partially of acting as institutionally approved socializing agents. They are expected to interpret the undergraduate culture for the new students and to serve as a prototype of the model Stanford undergraduate. Their job also requires acting as agents of social control in maintaining house discipline and reporting signs of trouble to the administration.

Apart from convenience, two basic advantages accrue from using sponsors as judges. First, they typify the core upper-middle-class undergraduate society faced by students coming from lower social strata. (See Table 3.) Second, they are by virtue of the functions of their role put in a position to know the incoming students intimately —a premise well borne out by the data. High agreement is found between sponsors and students on their expectations of how the student will fare in college (e.g., getting very good grades, joining a fraternity, being an important person in school affairs, being a good athlete, etc.). The percentage of agreement ranges from 61 to 94, with the median level of agreement being 70 per cent. Moreover, it is found that the sponsors' judgments accurately predict the actual performance of the students in those areas where data are available. For example, a 0.58 correlation (Pearson r) is obtained between the sponsors' grade estimates and the students' first-year grade-point averages, while 71 per cent of the students they expect to make fraternities during spring rushing actually do so (a figure that increases to 80 per cent if the academically disqualified are omitted from consideration).

Chicago Tribune (April 21–June 9, 1957).

[c] Protestant denominations classified as high status are Episcopalian, Presbyterian, and Congregational.

The sponsors' evaluations of the students in their charge were obtained through individual interviews held 2 months after the start of the school year. The number of students judged by each sponsor ranged from three to eleven, the median being five.

One measure of the extent to which lower-class students are integrated into the undergraduate culture was provided by gauging the sponsors' own personal reaction to the students in their charge. Sponsors were asked whether they, themselves, had found any of these students "difficult to know or to understand as a person" and, if so, why? From their replies, two different categories of "difficult" students can be identified:

1. Those who are socially withdrawn (e.g., "he keeps to himself")
2. Those whose attitudes are in some way interpreted as peculiar (e.g., 'he has a don't-give-a-damn attitude")

The distribution of the sponsors' answers for the several social classes is presented in Table 4. As the findings show, the phenomenon of social withdrawal is concentrated disproportionately in the lower class where one-third of the students are perceived as socially isolated, withdrawn individuals. In con-

TABLE 4. SOCIAL-CLASS DIFFERENCES IN STUDENTS REPORTED "DIFFICULT TO KNOW" BY SPONSORS IN FRESHMAN YEAR, PER CENT

				Social Class			
Difficult to Know		I	II	III	IV	V and VI	Regular Sample
Category	(N)	(12)	(49)	(27)	(16)	(22)	(99)
Social isolates		8	10	4	25	32[a]	11
Unusual attitudes		17	10	11	0	0	10

[a] One-tailed exact probability test of difference between classes V and VI and Regular Sample yields a *P* of 0.02.

TABLE 5. SOCIAL-CLASS DIFFERENCES IN SPONSORS' PERCENTILE ESTIMATES OF STUDENTS' FUTURE POPULARITY AT STANFORD

				Social Class			
Percentile Estimates		I	II	III	IV	V and VI	Regular Sample
	(N)	(12)	(49)	(27)	(16)	(22)	(99)
Mean		54	59	55	51	40[a]	55
Standard deviation		16.4	16.5	18.9	21.9	16.2	18.0
Per cent in unpopular category[b]		25	14	15	38	55[c]	20

[a] One-tailed *t* test (35d.f.) between classes V and VI and Regular Sample = 3.85; $P < 0.001$.
[b] The fortieth percentile and below are treated as negative estimates.
[c] One-tailed $\chi^2 c$ (1d.f.) = 9.22; $P < 0.01$, when classes V and VI are compared with the Regular Sample.

trast, only 11 per cent of the Regular Sample are reacted to in this fashion.

A second measure of social estrangement was obtained by having the sponsors make percentile estimates of the popularity the students in their charge would eventually enjoy by the time they are seniors. The results, summarized in Table 5, present the mean and standard deviation of the percentile estimates for each social class and the percentage by class that is judged unpopular (defined by the percentile estimates' falling at or below the fortieth percentile).[9]

The data offer some confirmation for the social dominance earlier premised for the upper-middle class for it is to these individuals that the greatest popularity accrues in the eyes of the sponsor. The data furnish additional proof, too, of the social disadvantage at which lower-class freshmen initially find themselves in the Stanford environment. Their average popularity rating falls at the fortieth percentile. This is 19 percentile points below the average rating sponsors give class II students and, indeed, is at the level we have taken as the cut-

ting point for designating unpopularity. Only one other group at Stanford is perceived to be as unpopular as the lower class on campus. These are the Jews in the sample, who, on the average, receive a popularity rating that falls at the thirty-sixth percentile.

When the results on unpopularity and withdrawal are combined, as has been done in Table 6, we are in the best position to appraise the initial social impact of upward mobility. Despite the earlier data indicating that the lower class had in high school made a dramatic shift to a middle-class reference group and, at that time, given evidence of fully the same potential for social success as students from the Regular Sample, once the lower class enter Stanford they are quickly reacted to as marginal individuals on campus. Fully two-thirds of the lower class are perceived as failing to become integrated into the undergraduate society.

Subsequent reaction. That this experience of estrangement is not a transitory phenomenon is shown by the data in Table 7, where we present the social reaction to the students at the end of

TABLE 6. SOCIAL-CLASS DIFFERENCES AMONG STUDENTS REPORTED BY SPONSORS AS SOCIAL ISOLATES AND/OR UNPOPULAR EARLY IN FRESHMAN YEAR, PER CENT

		Social Class					Regular Sample
	(N)	I (12)	II (49)	III (27)	IV (16)	V and VI (22)	(99)
Social isolates and/or unpopular		33	16	15	44	64[a]	23

[a] One-tailed χ^2c (1d.f.) = 12.00; $P < 0.001$ when class V and VI are compared with Regular Sample.

[9] For a description of the linear rating procedure, see Robert A. Ellis and Thomas C. Keedy, Jr., "Three Dimensions of Status: A Study of Academic Prestige," *The Pacific Sociological Review*, 3 (Spring 1960), 23–28.

TABLE 7. SOCIAL-CLASS DIFFERENCES IN NEGATIVE SOCIAL REACTION
MADE TO STUDENTS LATER IN THEIR UNDERGRADUATE
CAREER, PER CENT

	Social Class					Regular Sample
	I	II	III	IV	V and VI	
End of freshman year						
Social isolates	0	21	9	25	38	17
Unpopular	11	12	5	0	12	8
Social isolates and/or unpopular	11	27	14	25	50[a]	23
(N)	(9)	(33)	(22)	(12)	(16)	(71)
Later undergraduate years						
Social isolates	12	18	25	38	64	24
Unpopular	12	6	7	0	29	6
Social isolates and/or unpopular	25	24	25	38	79[b]	29
(N)	(8)	(34)	(16)	(13)	(14)	(66)

[a] One-tailed $\chi^2 c$ (1d.f.) $= 3.65$; $P < 0.05$ when classes V and VI are compared with Regular Sample.

[b] One-tailed $\chi^2 c$ (1d.f.) $= 10.18$; $P < 0.001$ when classes V and VI are compared with Regular Sample.

freshman year and during the later undergraduate years. For these data it was necessary to turn to administrative records. Throughout the time a student is an undergraduate, Stanford compiles a series of confidential reports that carefully chronicle his academic and social progress. At the end of freshman year, these reports are prepared by the sponsors and by the faculty residents assigned to the freshman dormitory. In subsequent years, they are prepared by resident assistants (usually graduate students) assigned to the dormitory or the fraternity in which the student lives. While the reports vary in quality and completeness, they do furnish a rich body of information on the student's behavior through the undergraduate years and the reactions it evokes. Of particular importance are the detailed comments provided on the student's ability for getting along with others, his personal traits, and the extent and

kind of involvement he manifests in social life and extracurricular activities.

Use of these confidential reports as a data source yields essentially the same definition of social isolation as relied upon in the preceding section. The fact that a student may be depicted as quiet and shy is not, by itself, sufficient to classify him as socially isolated. He is categorized as socially isolated only when there are explicit statements that he has withdrawn from his peers.[10]

---

[10] The following three examples illustrate the kind of statement relied on for categorizing students as socially isolated.

John had trouble adjusting to college life. It took him nearly the entire year to become accustomed to being away from home. He tended to live quite unaware of activity around him. In fact, he did not converse with anyone at length. It is only in the past few weeks he has begun to come out of his shell.

He is not well integrated into house activities. Only recently has he begun

The shift to a new data source does, however result in a more restricted definition of unpopularity. From the confidential reports it was relatively easy to discern when a student was being depicted as socially rejected by his peers. However, it was not possible on the basis of these reports to identify the more passive form of "unpopularity" where the student, though not socially rejected, is perceived as not being popular among his classmates. Thus, we were unable to incorporate into our analysis many of the more passive cases of unpopularity which occur in conjunction with social isolation. Exclusion of these cases undoubtedly contributes to the lower frequency of unpopularity found in Table 7 as compared to Table 5. It does not, however, appear to affect the combined category of "social isolates and/or unpopular," which is the main datum for assessing the impact of upward mobility.

Inspection of Table 7 reveals that as a group the upwardly mobile do not succeed in overcoming the social barriers initially encountered. At the end of freshman year, still one-half of class V and VI students are depicted as social isolates or as unpopular in the eyes of their classmates. Moreover, in later undergraduate years, when they have moved out of the freshman dormitory to which they were assigned on

a random basis and taken up residence in new quarters and with friends more of their own choosing, an even greater proportion of them encounter social difficulties. Seventy-nine per cent are reported during this later period to be socially isolated or rejected by their peers.

The exact extent of their estrangement in their new surroundings is best seen by examining Table 8, which summarizes the findings obtained over the undergraduate years. As the results show, the vast majority (77 per cent) of class V and VI students have at some point in their undergraduate career encountered difficulty in establishing effective peer-group relations. For a few, the social disruption that occurs is of relatively short duration, lasting less than a year. For 60 per cent of the upwardly mobile, however, the period

---

to be seen often with his roommate. He is the only fellow in the dorm who did not come to our cottage [the faculty resident's] for our evening get-togethers. [The sponsor notes: "He seems to let the group go its own way as long as he can go his."]

I cannot say I know him well, although he has been one of my charges (certainly, one of my brighter ones) all year long. He is extremely independent, quiet in a forceful rather than a meek way, his relations with his neighbors are polite but minimal, and he keeps his own counsel.

TABLE 8. SUMMARY OF NEGATIVE REACTIONS TO LOWER-CLASS STUDENTS THROUGHOUT THE UNDERGRADUATE YEARS, PER CENT

Reacted to as Social Isolates and/or Unpopular	Classes V and VI	Regular Sample
At least once while at Stanford		
Per cent	77[a]	35
(N)	(22)	(99)
For 1 year or more		
Per cent	60[b]	19
(N)	(20)	(91)
For the entire period at Stanford		
Per cent	40[c]	10
(N)	(20)	(91)

[a] One-tailed $\chi^2 c$ (1d.f.) = 11.25; $P < 0.001$.
[b] One-tailed $\chi^2 c$ (1d.f.) = 12.44; $P < 0.001$.
[c] One-tailed test of exact probability yields a P of 0.003.

TABLE 9. SOCIAL-CLASS DIFFERENCES IN SPONSORS' EXPECTATIONS OF
ACHIEVEMENT IN FOUR SELECTED SPHERES OF THE STUDENT
ROLE, PER CENT

Achievement Expectations	(N)	Social Class					Regular Sample
		I (12)	II (49)	III (27)	IV (16)	V and VI (22)	(99)
Join a fraternity		75	67	63	56	36[a]	64
Get very good grades		25	55	52	69	50	53
Be a good athlete		33	24	41	19	32	28
Be an important person in school affairs		8	24	19	6	5	18
Success in one or more role spheres		92	88	93	88	82	88
Success in both scholastic and nonscholastic roles[b]		8	39	37	38	14[c]	33

[a] One-tailed $\chi^2 c$ (1d.f.) = 4.46; $P < 0.05$, when classes V and VI are compared with the Regular Sample.

[b] Nonscholastic success is defined as a person who is expected to join a fraternity, be a good athlete, and/or be a very important person in schools affairs.

[c] One-tailed $\chi^2 c$ (1d.f.) = 2.46; $P \approx 0.05$:

of social dislocation lasts at least a year or longer; and for 40 per cent, it continues unabated throughout the time they are at Stanford. Thus, for many, although not for all, the price of social mobility is social isolation.[11]

Perceived success in college. A fuller comprehension of the social disadvantage at which the upwardly mobile find themselves in their new surroundings is gained by examining Table 9, which presents the sponsors' expectations early in the freshman year of the success students in the sample would later attain in four areas of undergraduate achievement: scholastic, extracurricular, athletic, and social (i.e., fraternity membership). It can be seen that some measure of successful accomplishment is expected of most freshmen, regardless of their class of origin. Moreover, students from classes V and VI are viewed as not handicapped in the scholastic and athletic spheres of undergraduate life where success depends more upon technical proficiency than upon social

[11] That this isolation is the consequence of mobility, not its precursor, is clearly revealed by the sharp and abrupt contrast between the lower-class students' precollege potential for social success and their actual college experiences. This conclusion is further underscored by findings obtained on twelve lower-class boys who had been specifically singled out in their high school recommendations as "good leaders." Consistent with these recommendations, the majority had either been major officers in the student body or had held important positions in student government. Those who had not done so had distinguished themselves by major accomplishments in extracurricular activities or in athletics. By all indications, none should have experienced inordinate difficulty in adjusting socially to college life. Yet, once they enter Stanford there is a sharp reversal in their social fortunes. Eight out of the twelve are reported at some juncture in their undergraduate career as socially isolated or rejected by their peers, and for six, this period of estrangement lasts for a year or more.

TABLE 10. SOCIAL-CLASS DIFFERENCES IN SPONSORS' PERCENTILE
ESTIMATES OF STUDENTS' FUTURE SUCCESS IN
EXTRACURRICULAR AFFAIRS

	Social Class					Regular Sample
Percentile Estimates (N)	I (12)	II (49)	III (27)	IV (16)	V and VI (22)	(99)
Mean	42	51	49	47	29[a]	48
Standard deviation	17.7	22.2	20.2	21.5	18.7	21.4
Per cent judged inactive[b]	75	39	37	38	82[c]	43

[a] One-tailed t test (36d.f.) between classes V and VI and the Regular Sample = 4.19; $P < 0.001$.

[b] The fortieth percentile and below are treated as negative estimates.

[c] One-tailed $\chi^2 c$ (1d.f.) = 9.13; $P < 0.001$, when classes V and VI are compared with the Regular Sample.

skills. It is only when successful accomplishment requires some degree of social facility that social class considerations loom as important. One such instance is fraternity membership,[12] which is seen to decline consistently with class position—and abruptly so for class V and VI students. The latter are deemed half as likely as other undergraduates to make a fraternity, a prediction which, if true, would importantly shape their social experiences on campus. Similarly, only a negligible minority of lower-class students are expected to attain a position of prominence in school affairs, this being viewed as mainly the domain of classes II and III.

The extent to which the lower class is perceived as uninvolved in extracurricular activities is obscured by our

12 Unlike many schools, where fraternity rushing is held at the start of the freshman year, at Stanford rushing takes place in mid-spring of the freshman year. Thus, sponsors' expectations about fraternity membership are as much predictions about future social behavior as are their expectations about athletic success, prominence in extracurricular activities, and scholastic performance.

dichotomizing such participation at the extreme end of the continuum. Many students who are not "very important persons in school affairs" may nevertheless take an active part in extracurricular activities. For this reason, data are also included on the sponsors' percentile estimates of the future success students would achieve in the area of extracurricular activities. The findings, as presented in Table 10, indicate how completely the lower class are seen to be removed from this arena of undergraduate behavior. Their average percentile rating of 29 falls 13 points below the rating given any other class and 19 points below that given the Regular Sample. Equally significant is the fact that 82 per cent of class V and VI students, as compared to 43 per cent of the Regular Sample, receive ratings at or below the fortieth percentile, the cutting point relied upon for categorizing a student as judged to be inactive in extracurricular endeavors. A similarly high percentage of low participation is also reported for class I students but for entirely different reasons. Rather than indicating a lack of social acceptance, it reflects the presumed preoccupation of the upper class with the social life available to them in fraternities and in nearby San Francisco society. A final point regarding Table 10 is that students from the lower-middle class (class IV) are judged to be as deeply involved in extracurricular activities as are students from classes II and III. While the lower-middle class may not be viewed as attaining prominence in this area, they are not regarded as socially excluded from it—a fact that underscores the special plight of the lower class in this setting.

The findings on perceived success in college, thus, temper what might otherwise be an overly bleak picture of the upwardly mobile. While the data continue to emphasize the failure of the lower class to find ready social acceptance among their peers, they reveal that the opportunity for success is not closed to them in college. Rather, their success is perceived to lie in those spheres where achievement is largely a matter of technical proficiency.

BEHAVIORAL EVIDENCE OF SOCIAL ISOLATION

The evidence so far has been based on observations by others officially in a position to be in close contact with the students and familiar with their progress in college. Their judgments, reflecting as they do the prevailing norms of the Stanford culture, give us considerable insight into the social dislocation that accompanies upward mobility. Nevertheless, it is germane to inquire whether or not the portrait that is gained of the lower class has its counterpart in the actual social and academic experiences of the students. Is there independent behavioral evidence that students from the lower class do not gain social acceptance from their peers? Do their actual accomplishments in college

take on the segmental pattern predicted by the freshman sponsors?

Social acceptance. One indicator of peer acceptance on campus is living-group affiliation. In spring of the freshman year, the student is faced with the choice of joining a fraternity, joining an eating club, or remaining independent.[13] An eating club, an institution distinctive to Stanford (at least in its function), gives the student an intermediate option between the highly organized group life characterizing fraternity living and the socially autonomous existence of being an independent. Like the fraternity, the eating club is a socially exclusive organization electing its own members. Members of each eating club eat together in their own dining hall, but, unlike fraternity members, do not live together in a separately established house. Instead, members of all eating clubs are quartered in a common dormitory. The eating club thus provides companionship and a sense of belonging to a chosen group without the total strictures of organized fraternity life. In this way, eating-club life also contrasts sharply with the dormitory existence facing independents who are more prone to look upon their living quarters as a "boarding house" than as a place for social companionship.

As may be seen from Table 11, a student's affiliation with a living group provides a rough index of his popularity among his peers. Regardless of whether student popularity is measured by spon-

---

[13] The choice of living group made at the end of freshman year is not irrevocable. Eleven per cent of the Regular Sample, but none of the lower class, switch their affiliation at some later date. In the majority of cases, this entails a move away from the status of being an independent. For purposes of analysis, a student's living-group affiliation is classified according to the highest status he attains on a scale running from fraternity to eating club to independent.

TABLE 11. DIFFERENCES BY LIVING GROUP IN STUDENT POPULARITY

	Fraternity (49)	Eating Club (18)	Independents (26)
(N)[a]			
Popularity rating by sponsors			
Mean percentile	65	47	44
Standard deviation	14.8	14.3	18.3
Rating of "Personal Potential" by admissions office			
Per cent rated high	73	56	38

[a] Analysis is restricted to the ninety-three males in the Regular Sample attending Stanford long enough to participate in rush activities.

sors' estimates early in the freshman year or by admissions office ratings of students' "personal potential" for Stanford, fraternities are found to recruit the most popular students on campus, and eating clubs, those intermediate in popularity. In turn, those who remain independents receive the lowest ratings of popularity.[14]

Social-class differences in living-group affiliation, summarized in Table 12, offer striking evidence of the extent to which the upwardly mobile are out of the mainstream of undergraduate society. Three-fourths of students in all social classes except V and VI manage to join either a fraternity or an eating club, with one-half affiliating with a fraternity. In contrast, only 45 per cent of the lower class join a fraternity or an eating club, and only 20 per cent a fraternity. Even their acceptance into a fraternity or an eating club does not necessarily signify that the upwardly mobile have made a successful adjustment to the social demands of undergraduate life. Some have, but the majority fail to become integrated into the living group. Instead, they later appear

TABLE 12. SOCIAL-CLASS DIFFERENCES IN FRATERNITY–EATING-CLUB AFFILIATION, PER CENT

		Social Class					Regular Sample
		I	II	III	IV	V and VI	
Affiliation	(N)	(11)	(46)	(26)	(15)	(20)	(93)
Fraternity		55	57	54	47	20[b]	53
Fraternity or eating club		73	74	73	74	45[c]	72

[a] Analysis is limited to students still attending Stanford long enough to participate in rush activities.
[b] One-tailed $\chi^2 c$ (1 d.f.) = 5.81; $P < 0.01$ when classes V and VI are compared with the Regular Sample.
[c] One-tailed $\chi^2 c$ (1 d.f.) = 4.34; $P < 0.05$ when classes V and VI are compared with the Regular Sample.

14 Further evidence that living-group affiliation serves as a rough index of a student's popularity among his peers is found in the association between fraternity membership and "sociability" reported by Levine and Sussman and by Goldsen et al. See Gene Norman Levine and Leila A. Sussman, "Social Class and Sociability in Fraternity Pledging," *American Journal of Sociology*, 65 (January 1960), 391–99; and Rose K. Goldsen, Morris Rosenberg, Robin Williams, Jr., and Edward A. Suchman, *What College Students Think* (Princeton, N.J.: D. Van Nostrand Company, Inc., 1960), especially pp. 60–80.

in administrative records as "loners"—persons who do not mix with the other members of the house or club. Yet those who remain independent are not exempted from the necessity of having to cope with living in an upper-middle-class environment, for class II students still constitute the model group in the dormitories reserved for independents.[15]

A second indicator of social acceptance on campus is popularity with the opposite sex. Dating is such an elaborately institutionalized facet of campus life that, as Willard Waller long ago noted, it serves as a sensitive barometer of an undergraduate's informal standing in the college peer group.[16] Moreover, the gradient of dating desirability is so clearly recognized and adjusted to on the college campus that it can be an especially traumatic event for the student to perceive himself—and have others perceive him—as one who is unable to get a date. Yet the same barriers that set the lower class apart from other college males also appear to restrict their relationships with college coeds. Information to this effect was obtained by asking students in each of the four interviews how often each month they have coffee and study dates and how often each month they have other kinds of dates. No effort was made to restrict answers to dates with Stanford coeds, though in the majority of cases the dates were with girls attending Stanford. The results are presented in Table 13. They reveal that

64 per cent of the boys in classes V and VI, but only 29 per cent of the Regular Sample, have gone through at least one period in college of not having dated. While for some this experience of not dating is relatively short-lived, for 45 per cent of class V and VI students it lasts a year or longer. Equally important is its distinctive pattern of persistence among class V and VI students. In all four interviews, a substantial minority of the upwardly mobile report being in

TABLE 13. PER CENT OF LOWER-CLASS AND OTHER STANFORD STUDENTS WHO REPORT THEY DO NOT DATE AT COLLEGE

Time of Report	Classes V and VI	Regular Sample
Beginning of freshman year		
Per cent	41[a]	17
(N)	(22)	(99)
End of freshman year		
Per cent	30[b]	17
(N)	(20)	(90)
End of sophomore year		
Per cent	29[c]	14
(N)	(17)	(81)
End of senior year		
Per cent	33[d]	10
(N)	(15)	(71)
At least once while at Stanford		
Per cent	64[e]	29
(N)	(22)	(99)
For 1 year or more		
Per cent	45[f]	26
(N)	(20)	(93)

[a] One-tailed $\chi^2 c = 4.69$; $P < 0.05$.
[b] One-tailed exact probability test yields $P = 0.15$.
[c] One-tailed exact probability test yields $P = 0.11$.
[d] One-tailed exact probability test yields $P = 0.03$.
[e] One-tailed $\chi^2 c = 7.83$; $P < 0.01$.
[f] One-tailed $\chi^2 c \approx 2.08$; $P < 0.05$.

[15] Examination of interview data on persons cited as close friends also reveals that the lower class do not seek each other out at any point in their undergraduate years, a fact that would appear to reflect their disinclination to associate with class equals at this juncture in their mobility experience as well as their being part of a numerically small minority on campus.

[16] "The Rating and Dating Complex," *American Sociological Review*, 2 (October 1937), 727–34.

a situation of not dating.[17] That this situation is clearly in evidence during freshman year, before students have a chance to affiliate with fraternities or eating clubs, rules out considering the low frequency of dating to be a side effect of living-group affiliation.

Success achieved in college. A more balanced picture of the impact of upward mobility is gained by examining the students' record of accomplishment in college. In each interview from the end of freshman year to the time they left college (in some cases, 7 years later) a continuing inventory was taken of students' activities, achievements, and awards in all areas of undergraduate endeavor. This information was subsequently checked against class yearbooks and a variety of administrative records. Besides insuring completeness and accuracy, this check made it possible to include in the final inventory those achievements realized after the

TABLE. 14.   SOCIAL-CLASS DIFFERENCES IN COLLEGE
ACCOMPLISHMENTS, PER CENT

		Social Class					Regular Sample
	(N)	I (12)	II (49)	III (27)	IV (16)	V and VI (22)	(99)
1. Area of success							
Scholastic		0	18	15	12	32[a]	16
Athletic		8	4	7	19	9	5
Social		33	22	30	25	5[b]	25
Extracurricular		33	39	15	6	18	28
2. Pattern of success							
Scholastic or athletic		8	22	22	31	41[c]	21
Social or extracurricular		50	43	33	31	18[d]	39
Success in any area		58	57	52	38	50	53

[a] One-tailed test of exact probability yields $P = 0.09$ when classes V and VI are compared with the Regular Sample.
[b] One-tailed test of exact probability yields $P = 0.02$ when classes V and VI are compared with the Regular Sample.
[c] One-tailed χ^2_c (1 d.f.) $= 2.76$; $P < 0.05$ when classes V and VI are compared with the Regular Sample.
[d] One-tailed χ^2_c (1 d.f.) $= 2.16$; $P < 0.05$ when classes V and VI are compared with the Regular Sample.

[17] Undoubtedly, financial factors contribute to the social plight of the lower class, but a simple economic interpretation is not feasibly. Seventy-one per cent of class V and VI students report owning or having access to a car while they are at college—a figure that is somewhat, but not materially, less than that obtained for the Regular Sample, 86 per cent of whom own or have access to a car. Students from the lower class, on the other hand, are handicapped by having considerably less money per month than class I and II students to spend for recreational purposes. (The median amount of spending money available to class V and VI students is $18; for students in classes I and II, $51 and $40.) Nevertheless, they are no more handicapped than students from classes III and IV, who have a similarly restricted budget for recreational purposes but do not encounter the same barriers to fraternity membership and dating behavior. Thus the sharp and abrupt decline in social participation observed for the lower class would appear to be more a function of social than financial factors.

TABLE 15. ATTAINMENTS, SOCIAL EXPERIENCES, AND ROLE STRESSES OF UPWARDLY MOBILE WHO ACHIEVE SUCCESS IN COLLEGE

Student	Inventory of Attainment[a]	Social Experiences[b]		Evidence of Alienation[c]
		First Year	Later Years	
A	Scholastic: 1. Phi Beta Kappa, 2. graduation with great distinction, 3. departmental honors.	—	—	Continuous pattern
B	Scholastic: 1. graduation with distinction.	—	—to+	None
C	Scholastic and extracurricular: 1. graduation with distinction, 2. election to student legislature.	—	+	Intermittent pattern
D	Scholastic: 1. departmental honors.	—	—to+	Intermittent pattern
E	Athletic: 1. three varsity letters in major sport.	+	—	None
F	Athletic: 1. three varsity letters in minor sport.	—	—	None
G	Scholastic and extracurricular: 1. Phi Beta Kappa, 2. Tau Beta Kappa, 3. graduation with distinction, 4. scholastic award from national professional society, 5. vice-president and treasurer of undergraduate professional society, 6. secretary of campus voluntary association.	0	0	None
H	Scholastic: 1. Phi Beta Kappa, 2. graduation with great distinction.	—to+	—	Initial response
I	Extracurricular: 1. editor of major campus publication.	—	No data	Continuous pattern
J	Social and extracurricular: 1. rush chairman and social chairman of eating club, 2. one of five elected to major legislative post.	+	+	Continuous pattern for first 2 years
K	Scholastic: 1. graduation with distinction.	—	—	Initial response

[a] Graduation with distinction at Stanford is an honor comparable to graduating *magna cum laude* at other universities; graduation with great distinction is comparable, in turn, to graduating *summa cum laude*.

[b] Data on social reaction to students are coded for freshman year and later undergraduate years as follows: — =student perceived as socially isolated and/or unpopular, 0=student perceived as having average acceptance among peers, + =student perceived as popular among peers.

[c] Alienation is defined by the student's reporting in one or more interviews that he has experienced difficulty at Stanford in "feeling you are a nobody." The patterns of answers are coded as follows: (1) none, (2) initial response [in first interview only], (3) intermittent response [in four interviews], (4) continuous pattern for first 2 years [but not in senior-year interview], and (5) continuous pattern [reported in all four interviews].

terminal spring interviews (e.g., honors and awards conferred at graduation and awards received for spring sports). Using a procedure closely patterned after the high school achievement scale referred to above,[18] we classified students as to whether they had been highly or very highly successful in four main spheres of undergraduate life: scholastic, athletic, extracurricular, and social (i.e., achievements centering around the living group). Students classified as successful were ones who had clearly gained general recognition on campus for being top scholars or athletes, being very important persons in school affairs, or being elected leaders of their living group.

The findings reveal what may be best described as a qualified success story for the upwardly mobile. (See Tables 14 and 15.) They are as likely as students from more favored backgrounds to compile a record of outstanding accomplishment over the undergraduate years. Their achievements, however, take on the segmental pattern predicted originally by the freshman sponsors, being concentrated disproportionately in scholastic and athletic endeavors rather than in the realm of social and extracurricular pursuits. The latter is, instead, the domain of class I and II students who together hold 69 per cent of the major positions of social and extracurricular leadership on campus.

RESPONSE TO ESTRANGEMENT

Evidence of alienation. As Table 15 makes clear, the successful attainments of the upwardly mobile have been realized at a social cost. Nine of the eleven who are successful have undergone the estranging experience of mov-

ing abruptly from a situation of peer acceptance to one where they are socially isolated or rejected for an extended period. That they are not impervious to this reversal of their social fortunes is shown by the feeling of self-alienation that emerges. As is true of the upwardly mobile in general, two-thirds of those in classes V and VI who have been outstandingly successful report experiencing difficulty at college in "feeling you are a nobody"—a response given only by a minority of the Regular Sample.[19]

Interrupted pattern of academic achievement. Not surprisingly, the social shock of their mobility experience appears to have had a temporarily adverse effect on their performance in the classroom. As may be seen from Table 16 their grades in freshman year suffer but in a subtle fashion.[20] Compared to

---

[19] Sixty-four per cent of class V and VI students, compared to 38 per cent of students in the Regular Sample, report experiencing difficulty at college in feeling they are a nobody $[\chi^2_c \ (1 \text{d.f.}) = 3.71; P < 0.05]$. The incidence of self-alienation by the four interview phases is as follows:

	Early in first year	End of first year	End of second year	End of fourth year
Lower Class	55 per cent	35 per cent	47 per cent	33 per cent
Regular Sample	24 per cent	20 per cent	22 per cent	13 per cent

[20] The skewed distribution of grades has dictated using the median rather than the mean as the measure of central tendency.

For upper-middle- as well as lower-class students at Stanford, freshman grading practices pose a situation of anomic stress in the sense that there is a sharp disparity between socially reinforced academic aspirations and socially structured avenues for realizing these aspirations. The administration's practice of grading on the curve necessitates that only a minority of the 80 per cent of students planning to attain a *B* average or better at Stanford and attaching major importance to this attainment can actually realize that goal in freshman year—despite their record of

---

[18] See footnote 8.

TABLE 16. PATTERN OF SCHOLASTIC ACHIEVEMENT BY LOWER-CLASS
AND OTHER STANFORD UNDERGRADUATES

	Median GPA				
	High School	First Year	Second Year	Third Year	Fourth Year
Varied N^a					
Classes V and VI	3.89	2.34	2.81	3.12	3.13
Regular Sample	3.64	2.37	2.66	2.62	2.93
difference	+0.25	−0.03	+0.15	+0.50	+0.20
Constant N^b					
Classes V and VI	3.88	2.56	2.81	3.12	3.13
Regular Sample	3.64	2.47	2.67	2.62	2.93
difference	+0.24	+0.09	+0.14	+0.50	+0.20

[a] N varies by interview phase. For classes V and VI, $N = 22$, 22, 18, 16, and 15; for Regular Sample, $N = 98$; 98, 90, 77, and 77.

[b] Analysis is limited to students who complete the undergraduate sequence at Stanford. N for classes V and VI = 15; for Regular Sample, $N = 77$.

other undergraduates, they do not perform poorly on the average. Nevertheless, it is only in the freshman year that they fail to maintain the relatively superior academic record realized both in high school and in the later undergraduate years. Thus their interrupted pattern of academic achievement appears to serve as apt testimony both to the disruptive consequences of upward mobility and to the resilience of those who succeed in achieving upward mobility.

CONCLUSIONS

The findings detailed above offer convincing confirmation for Sorokin's dissociative hypothesis of upward mobility against its two competing alternatives. The high potential for social suc-

outstanding success in high school. Moreover, these aspirations are reinforced, and perhaps made inflexible for many, by the fact that 75 per cent of entering male freshmen clearly expect to go on to graduate school, for which a B-level record of performance is usually required.

cess manifested by the lower class before coming to college, plus the evidence we have of their having already made a behaviorally significant shift to a middle-class reference group, rule out the possibility of attributing their social difficulties in their new upper-middle-class surroundings either to a chronic inability on their part to form socially effective relationships with their peers or to the absence of anticipatory socialization. The extended period of estrangement the lower class has undergone, their interrupted pattern of scholastic performance, as well as their own response of self-alienation, clearly attest to the disruptive effects of social mobility. Whether such disruptive efects also accompany mobility achieved through different institutional channels or through educational settings having different institutional arrangements poses significant questions for future empirical research, but ones that lie outside the realm of the present inquiry.[21]

[21] This does not imply that the present findings have no application beyond the

Stanford setting. Though considerable caution needs to be exercised in generalizing beyond these parameters, it is our expectation that similar social difficulties will be encountered by lower-class youth at other prestige colleges and universities in which students must assume residence in a predominantly upper-middle-class environment if they are to avail themselves of the intellectual, economic, and social advantages such schools have to offer.

Some support for this inference is found in Harvard's experiences with its "risk-gamble fund" scholarship program. For the past decade Harvard has actively sought out a small number of disadvantaged youth that could each year be admitted to Harvard College with substantial scholarship support. During the very early stages of the program Harvard discovered the need to break with its traditional laissez-faire policy of permitting each undergraduate to determine his own educational and personal affairs. Although this policy was effective with students coming to Harvard through normal channels, it was found that for those entering under the "risk-gamble fund," 'the price paid for failure . . . was too high, and the early failures too frequent." Corrective measures, therefore, had to be taken so that these bright but disadvantaged youth would not find "Harvard incomprehensible academically and another planet personally."

One series of measures involved the admissions procedures. In addition to the tangible evidence of scholastic potential required of all admitted to the program, two nonscholastic criteria have been introduced. One requires evidence of some extracurricular skill that would give the candidate a chance at Harvard "to find diversion and to maintain self-esteem." The other is an assessment (among other qualities) of the candidate's "toughness and resilience" for this undergraduate experience.

Even with these precautions, corrective measures have had to be enacted *after* matriculation. One is a deliberate but discreet effort to maximize the social contacts these "risk-gamble" undergraduates have with adults variously connected with the university (study counselors, psychiatric workers, personnel service people, Financial Aid Office staff, directors of activities, coaches, etc.). The purpose is quite explicitly to "find for every student [in the program] some adult in this community who can get close to the student and inspire his confidence, trust, and friendship." A second corrective step, taken during the critical first year in college, entails the careful selection of roommates for this group and the provision of living quarters in the freshman dormitory such that they are "physically as well as spiritually" close to the quarters of their graduate-student proctors. The proctors, much like the Stanford sponsors, are thus in a position to note which students are "participating and chatting and dating least." The Harvard authorities have found such elaborate arrangements to be a practical necessity if they are to break down the communication barriers that *almost inevitably* separate the boys in the "risk-gamble" program from the undergraduate world they enter. This experience, in turn, bears testimony that the disruptive consequences of mobility which we have demonstrated are not unique to Stanford.

The information is drawn from memoranda kindly made available by Henry P. Briggs, Jr., Director of Freshman Scholarships at Harvard College.

The research by Ellis and Lane is not congruent with the common belief in American society that upward social mobility is always a positive gain for the individual and society. Melvin Tumin's essay discusses additional negative consequences stemming from the emphasis on moving up the ladder. It places in wider perspective the range of the effects of mobility and heightened expectations.[1]

---

1 Empirical investigations showing the effects of mobility upon various forms of personal and social organization support Tumin's speculative essay. In addition to several of the studies reproduced in Chapter Nine, see Peter M. Blau, "Social Mobility and Interpersonal Relations," *American Sociological Review*, 21 (June 1956), 290–95; Mildred B. Kantor, ed., *Mobility and Mental Health* (Springfield, Ill.: Charles C Thomas, Publisher, 1965); Robert J. Kleiner and Seymour Parker, "Goal-Striving, Social Status and Mental

SOME UNAPPLAUDED CONSEQUENCES OF SOCIAL MOBILITY IN A MASS SOCIETY*

Melvin M. Tumin

Princeton University

The process of getting to be better-off than one used to be does not ordinarily make one sit and reflectively balance what he may have lost against the advantages gained. For, if being reasonably well-off is a novel experience —as is implied when we talk of mobility—it may take a long time for the novelty to wear off. One begins to spend time and energy in cultivating the new habits of consumption and the new modes of living appropriate to his new position. And, perhaps one's most ardent wish is that no one should rock the boat, or raise questions about other dimensions of life on which this experience of mobility may be having an impact.

But this is what I propose to do here, briefly, and, in large part, impressionistically, since while much attention has been given to measuring mobility and to comparing the mobility rates of various groups in various societies,[1] relatively little attention has been paid to the range of consequences generated.

I

In the broadest sense, any economic improvement of heretofore disadvan-

---

* From Melvin M. Tumin, "Some Unapplauded Consequences of Social Mobility in a Mass Society," *Social Forces*, 36 (October 1957), 32–37.

[1] See, for instance, three book length studies: N. Rogoff, *Recent Trends in Occupational Mobility* (Glencoe, Ill.: The Free Press, 1954); W. L. Warner and J. G. Abeg-glen, *Occupational Mobility in American Business and Industry, 1928–1952* (Minneapolis: University of Minnesota Press, 1955); D. V. Glass, ed., *Social Mobility in Britain* (Glencoe, Ill.: The Free Press, 1954); also, an earlier review of the literature in P. Sorokin, *Social Mobility* (New York: Harper & Bros., 1927).

Disorder: A Research Review," *American Sociological Review*, 28 (April 1963), 189–203; E. E. LeMasters, "Social Class Mobility and Family Integration," *Marriage and Family Living*, 16 (August 1954), 226–32; Fred B. Silberstein and Melvin Seeman, "Social Mobility and Prejudice," *American Journal of Sociology*, 65 (November 1959), 258–64; Robert P. Stuckert, "Occupational Mobility and Family Relationships," *Social Forces*, 41 (March 1963), 301–7; Harold L. Wilensky and Hugh Edwards, "The Skidder: Ideological Adjustments of Downward Mobile Workers," *American Sociological Review*, 24 (April 1959), 215–31.

Much of the literature on anomie and deviance, focusing as it does on blocked opportunity structures (inability to achieve success goals), also bears on the relationship between mobility and pathology. See Marshall B. Clinard, ed., *Anomie and Deviant Behavior* (New York: The Free Press of Glencoe, Inc., 1964).

The growing body of research on status inconsistency suggests similar consequences for behavior. See, for example, Elton F. Jackson, "Status Consistency and Symptoms of Stress," *American Sociological Review*, 27 (August 1962), 469–80. Much of this literature is summarized in H. M. Blalock, Jr., "Status Inconsistency, Social Mobility, Status Integration and Structural Effects," *American Sociological Review*, 32 (October 1967), 790–801.

taged persons strikes us as valuable.[2] This is true whether we start with a Marxist orientation toward the factors which determine man's fate, or a twentieth century liberal's version of what constitutes the good life; or the most conservative of political orientations, which, ultimately joins with a version of Marxism in insisting that the economic welfare of the society is the basis of the total welfare of that society.

Even a smattering of sociological sophistication, however, informs us that economic changes do not occur in a vacuum;[3] that other conditions precede, accompany and follow; that a range of values is affected; and that general social change, and not simply economic change, is necessarily implied. Surely, then, the consequences of any phenomenon as broadsweeping as socioeconomic mobility are likely to be diverse and mixed—diverse in their institutional ramifications and mixed in their implications for other values.

The same bit of sociological sophistication will also inform us that mobility is too broad a term to allow for more than vague generalization, unless we further specify the kinds of mobility, the rates of occurrence, the conditions under which it transpires, and the segments of the population affected.[4]

With these requirements in mind I wish now to specify more closely the mobility about which I am here talking. I refer first to the current American scene, and, within that, to the improvement in the standard of living, both relative and absolute, of large numbers of members of various ethnic minority groups. This improvement is preceded and accompanied by a reallocation of persons to higher-rated occupational groups, in which these higher incomes are earned.[5] I refer secondly to the fact that much of this has occurred within the last fifty years, or less than two demographic generations; and that a very substantial portion of the change is attributable to the opportunities presented by the second World War and the Korean incident. I cite these specific events only as convenient indicators of the time periods involved.

These transformations have occurred in a context of what we are now wont to call a "mass society." The referents of that term are numerous and mixed.[6] For our purposes here, as a minimum, when we speak of a "mass society" we shall have reference to the following things:

1. There are media for rapid interchange and transfer of ideas, persons, incentives and styles.
2. Economic motives include specific intents to produce for and distribute to all available segments of the population.
3. Inexpensive duplication of elite items of consumption is a dominant theme in production and consumption.
4. Traditional criteria of prestige, such as membership in exclusive kinship groups, are rapidly vanishing. First appraisals and apprisals of status-rank are made increasingly on the

---

2 Robin Williams, Jr., *American Society: A Sociological Interpretation* (New York: Alfred A. Knopf, Inc., 1951) on the dominant values of American society.

3 See Wilbert Moore, *Economy and Society* (Garden City, N.Y.: Doubleday & Company, Inc., 1955), especially Chap. 2.

4 Melvin Tumin and Arnold Feldman, "Theory and Measurement of Occupational Mobility in Puerto Rico," *American Sociological Review*, XXII, No. 3 (June 1957).

5 See H. P. Miller, *Income of the American People* (New York: Wiley & Sons, Inc., 1955).

6 Daniel Bell, "The Theory of the Mass Society," *Commentary*, 22, No. 1 (July 1956), 75–83, presents a historical survey of the meanings ascribed to the term "mass society."

basis of apparent income, as manifested in items openly consumed.

5. The "ideal" values insist that existing lines of social differentiation, including class and caste barriers, are temporary, and in the long run, insignificant; that all men are ultimately equal, some temporarily more equal than others; but that in some way we take turns at being more equal, since this is a condition which is theoretically available to everyone under the right happenstances.

6. It is theoretically permissible and even well-mannered to compete with everyone, no matter what his rank.

Running through this type of social order is a major theme of status striving which, for our present purposes, we need not try to explain, but rather will take as given. Sometimes and some places this motif is at bottom a search for some token by which to assure oneself of the rightness of self-esteem. Other times and other places it is egregiously insistent upon formal and overt recognition by others of one's right to an elevated place and a differentiated set of powers. Whatever the motive to which status-rivalry can be reduced, and whatever the forms it may assume, it is an intense focus of social activity and interpersonal relations, especially among mobile-minded Americans.[7]

These features then roughly and approximately describe the types, conditions, rates, and participants in social mobility to which we have reference.

A further word of caution needs to be inserted before we proceed to the main analysis in hand. Some of the consequences to be cited will refer only

[7] In Melvin Tumin, "Some Disfunctions of Institutional Imbalance," *Behavioral Science*, I, No. 2 (July 1956), the consequences of heavy emphasis upon status as measured by economic achievement are argued in some detail.

to some of the most mobile segments of the population; some of them and those with whom they come in contact during their movement or at their temporary resting places; some to the relations between them and their kin; some have to do with phenomena which emerge in the interplay between strains toward mobility and those toward stability; some are only dimly visible while others are already well-developed. In short, the sweep, coverage, intensity, and importance of the consequences we are about to specify are as mixed as the conditions which give rise to them.

II

1. THE FRAGMENTATION OF THE SOCIAL ORDER

I have reference here in general to the numerous ways in which rapid social mobility, in a mass society in which status rivalry is a dominant theme, leads to the proliferation of interest groups, associations and temporary social congeries, all oriented toward the accumulation and symbolization of prestige.

This proliferation is set in motion when status-mobiles, with full credentials in hand, knock upon the doors of elite membership groups, demanding acceptance and recognition, and are then denied the final bestowals of grace on grounds quite irrelevant to those which presumably determine one's right to such recognition. Even though sufficient income, education, occupational rank, commodiousness of residence, and auxiliary criteria have been met, the occupants of the top statuses invoke other criteria, such as kinship, ethnic origin, table and bar manners, and coldness of emotional toning, in order to justify the denial to the status-mobiles of access to intimacy with them in their own highly-ranked associations.

These criteria—precious and refined —are not only irrelevant to the major themes in the culture, but essentially hostile to democratic values. Their invocation, in denying admission to aspirants, leads to actions on the part of the mobiles which intensify certain antidemocratic and antiopen-society tendencies.

Thus, for instance, one finds the rejected aspirants creating dual and triple sets of elite facilities such as social clubs, country clubs, recreational facilities, residential sites, and even colleges and universities. These tend to be justified on the grounds that where opportunity has been illegitimately cut off, it is proper to create such facilities. Whatever pleasures and proprieties these dual facilities may insure for the participants and whatever pleasure of restricted intimacy this may residually grant to the older elite, the creation of such facilities, along lines of ethnic, racial, and religious distinctions, gives further strength to these antidemocratic distinctions. Moreover, because the *elites* of various ethnic and religious persuasions engage in such distinctions, these styles of social intercourse are likely to be emulated at other class levels.

Within these separate hierarchies status-rivalry becomes heightened and intensified, and there is sharper insistence on class-oriented behavior. This intensification of class distinctions within ethnicoreligious status-hierarchies is not unmixed in its implications for a democratic, open society.

Under these circumstances, one may expect some loss of faith in the fairness of the social process and in the democratic quality of the culture. For if the major criteria of equal status have been satisfied, but personal recognition is nevertheless withheld, there is good ground to disbelieve the value-themes which emphasize the equality of all men and the worthwhileness of supporting the society in general, without reference to ethnic or religious origin.

Still another consequence may be cited. Highly mobile members of ethnic and religious groups tend to impose upon their less mobile co-ethnics the same criteria of disability with which they were earlier afflicted. Thus, Negroes use color as bases of distinction within their groups; Jews use Jewish folk characteristics of language, gesture, and food. In short, denigrated minority groups absorb, accept, and apply to themselves the very antidemocratic criteria which their status-superiors earlier imposed upon them. In the extreme cases, the ethnics tend to blame their own rejection upon the persistence of these identifying traits of origin among their less mobile co-ethnics. The phenomenon of Negro and Jewish self-hatred has often been partially and correctly explained on these grounds.

The implications for self-esteem and mental health of such self-depreciation are obvious. What may not be quite so obvious is the way in which this shift of focus misplaces the responsibility for the existing barriers to social mobility, redirecting it mistakenly from the institutional restraints and antidemocratic tendencies in the older elites where it properly belongs.

2. The Denial of Work

A good deal of the social energy and drive which have made mobility possible for many of the heretofore underprivileged groups in America derived from the belief that hard work pays off. This belief was tied in and compatible with prior value commitments to the inherent virtue of work.

But now the emphasis has shifted from the importance of work and striving to the urgency of appearing to be successful. In at least some important elite circles, the social productivity of one's occupation, the social value of products which one distributes, and the skill required to produce these items are systematically ignored. Instead, almost exclusive preference is given to the open portrayal of *being* successful, as measured by the power and property which one openly consumes.

No one in any society has more quickly oriented himself to what is the right way to succeed in our status-conscious society than the new-mobile. Being a mobile and seeking further mobility makes it imperative that one adopt the standards which rule the market. In adopting those standards, and playing the game by them, he helps institutionalize them and make them the themes into which the next generations are socialized and indoctrinated. In this manner, the fact of rapid social mobility contributes importantly to the loss of a theme of the instrumental importance and the inherent dignity of work. In their place has been substituted the cult of the quick buck, with its theme that nothing succeeds like success.

Most of the major consequences of the triumph of the cult of the quick buck are well known. Some of the less obvious but equally important consequences bear scrutiny for a moment.

We may note, in the first place, the development of a Cult of Opportunity, Unlimited. That is, there has spread through the younger members of the more mobile groups in our population a sense that only success is in store for them; that the paths to this success are pretty clearly indicated; that no downward turns of the economy are possible; and that the insistence upon a horizon of despair is simply a neurotic hankering for the past on the part of those who have not quite made the grade.

This set of attitudes leads to an uncritical acceptance of the strength and durability of those economic and social arrangements which have recently yielded such high standards of living. In turn, this makes any ideas regarding the need for checks, controls, and contingency mechanisms, designed to cushion cyclical downturns, seem like morbid, gloomy, and radical prophecies of doom. Such policies and legislation as may be required to provide just these contingency cushions and provisions for possible economic disaster, fail to receive at least the kind of attention which our past history has indicated they merit. It would be one thing to reject them after scrutiny, on the grounds that the fears for the possible future are pointless. It is quite another to dismiss them out of hand as undeserving of consideration. Nothing is likely to contribute so much to the possibility of a bust as the denial, during the boom, of that possibility.

The denial of work also has consequences for social integration. For the only system of social recognition which makes it possible for all men in a society to achieve a sense of their worthiness to that social order, and thus to be integrated within it, must contain important reference to the dignity of work, *at any level,* and to the worthiness of conscientiousness regardless of the level of skill or income associated with the work. Any tendency which denies the dignity of work and which, in turn, insists upon consumption of high income as a criterion of social worth, undermines the possibility of widespread social integration. For, thereby, large numbers of men are deprived of the only basis on which they can achieve a sense of their equality. It is extremely difficult for a democratic ideology to have vital meaning at all levels of skill and income when we denigrate work and applaud income.

3. THE LOSS OF SOCIAL CRITICISM

I have reference here at the outset to the numerous ways in which the ranks of social critics and the ideas of social criticism are being depleted under the impact of the illusions and fantasies which social mobility for large numbers has generated.

There are evident signs of the emergence of "a cult of gratitude" among significant sections of the mobile population. Members of this cult tend to lose sight of the history of effort and struggle which have been required for past mobility. They engage in a type of euphoric wallowing in present comforts. They organize their perspectives around a sense of gratitude to the social order for making the present pleasures possible.

A prime case in point concerns some intellectuals. Perhaps never before has there been so much room in the well-paying portions of the occupational ladder for the skills and talents of intellectuals. Again it may be inconsequential that ideas now become commodities, or gain much of their value from their marketability. It is consequential, however, for the total society, that many of the ablest critics of the social order, whose criticism and ideas were important in making past mobility and present comfort possible, have been in a sense, bought off by the social order. This reference is not alone to political critics operating directly in the field of political ideology, but also to men of creative imagination and ideas operating in the fields of literature, mass entertainment and the media of mass-know-how-enlightenment.

Any social order stands in danger when it becomes smug regarding its past and even smugger about its future. The presence of an alert, critical-minded and creatively-oriented group of men of ideas is an indispensable antidote to such smugness. The mobility of the society in general has made creative criticism highly undesired and unpopular. And the mobility of prior critics has made significant numbers of them deny their histories and the value of their prior criticism. Those denials have helped them move quickly and surely into the ranks of those who feel it important to applaud. The active pursuit of open and sharp debate—an indispensable condition for the maintenance of an open society—is thus seriously endangered.

4. THE DIFFUSION OF INSECURITY

Anomie spreads through any social order when its personnel moves rapidly through a series of statuses and roles, whose definitions of rights and responsibilities are constantly shifting. This is generally what occurs in any society when much of the population experiences rapid social mobility, and when styles of behavior are oriented primarily toward status-acceptance and prestige-ranking, rather than some persistent and assured sense of what the social welfare requires.

In its simplest terms one sees this process occurring when the primary orientation is upon moving out of given levels into others as rapidly as possible; and when each of the major roles at any of these levels—whether parental, occupational, or community-member role—is defined in accordance with the class level. There is neither time nor inclination to become absorbed in a set of traditional responsibilities and to cultivate the expectations of traditional rights. The stability of bearing and the security deriving from adequate role-playing are thereby surrendered in preference for the constant readaptation of oneself and his role performances to the requirements of the next income level.[8]

Insecurity is also spread under conditions, when, in addition, one takes his bearings on his worth to himself and his social order by his position on the prestige-ladder, and when that position is primarily defined by income and its correlates. For in a society with differentiated income-classes, almost everyone is outranked by someone else who, by his own criteria, is more worthy.

Moreover, no source or criterion of prestige is quite so shaky and unstable as wealth, especially when that wealth flows from commerce rather than from proprietary estates based on land. Many of the very same persons who today are wealthy and therefore prestigeful have known in their own lifetimes what it has meant to be poor, therefore low-ranking, to become wealthy and improve their ranking, to become impoverished once again and lose their ranking, and finally, now once again, to be wealthy and be back in the high ranks. It is difficult to see how there could be any deeply built-in sense of security under such circumstances. It is easy to see how a gnawing, though perforce, concealed, sense of the ephemerality and impermanence of their present conditions might permeate such a population.

Rapid social mobility of the type we have experienced, and under the circumstances which have prevailed, has led to an extreme emphasis upon income-accumulation and consumption as the basis of ranking. Thus, there has tended to diffuse throughout significant portions of the population at all levels an insecurity regarding place and position. An illustration in point is the intense demand for reassurance that we are loved. This is exemplified in its most unself-conscious form in the cult of "palship" among cafe society habitués. To insist that a true friend is one who sticks by one through all varying economic fortunes, and, in turn, to place the value of that kind of friend above all other values except money, is to testify to the instability of money as a measure of worth in general, and the uncertainty regarding one's personal worth, so measured, in particular.

III

Time forbids the detailed analysis of any other set of consequences of social mobility. Yet a number of these may be mentioned in passing, to indicate how truly mixed are those consequences, in contrast to the general bland assumption that social mobility is eminently and predominantly a benign process.

5. We must recognize, therefore, that rapid social mobility, under the conditions stated, leads to a severe imbalance of institutions, insofar as it encourages the invasion of such institutions as family, religion, and education by criteria derived from the market place. The success of role-performances in these institutions tends to be measured by some income yardstick, thus endangering seriously the major functions they have traditionally performed.[9]

6. Comparably, the possibilities of genuine cultural pluralism in our society are seriously diminished by some results

---

[8] See Melvin Tumin, "Rewards and Task Orientations," *American Sociological Review*, XX (August 1955).

[9] Melvin Tumin, "Some Disfunctions of Institutional Imbalance," *op. cit.*

of the process of rapid social mobility. For in leading to the creation of dual and triple hierarchies on new class levels, ethnic groups become converted into status-competing hierarchies rather than the culture-contributing peer groups which a theory of the pluralist society envisions.

7. Along with the loss of social critics and criticism, goes the depreciation of taste and culture which occurs in a highly mobile society when marketability becomes the criterion of aesthetic worth, and when one consumes such products as the taste-merchants assure us that the elite are presently enjoying.

8. Finally, it may be observed that rapid social mobility generates in the older portions of the population a cranky and bitter conservatism and worship of the past; and in the new-mobile segments a vituperative contempt for traditions. If it is true that the age of a custom is no guarantee of its contemporary fitness, it is equally true that the age of a custom is no guarantee of its inadequacy. Any society will be the loser which either wallows in its past indiscriminately, or, equally indiscriminately, rejects it.

IV

Marx somewhere says that the philosopher with his eyes upon the stars is betrayed by his lower parts into a ditch. Without being silly enough to try to improve upon that formulation, I would try to adapt it to the present situation, by noting that the mobiles, with their eyes upon the higher reaches of the social ladder, are betrayed into their ditches by their overly careful devotion to how and where they might next move.

As can be seen from the foregoing discussion and papers, the study of mobility is a highly specialized area of research, posing many complex issues for theoretical and empirical analysis. The integration of findings pertinent to these issues is essential to the understanding of problems of mobility, change, and social stratification.

By emphasizing long-range perspectives on change in the American class system, Kurt Mayer's paper may aid in visualizing some of the broad implications of research on mobility. His essay also reminds us how little we know about social mobility when other than occupational dimensions are considered.

THE CHANGING SHAPE OF THE AMERICAN CLASS STRUCTURE*

Kurt B. Mayer

University of Bern

.... When one looks at the history of Western societies one is impressed with the fact that preindustrial social structures were all characterized by clearcut, highly visible and relatively unambiguous divisions not only of social positions but also of social strata. Despite many concrete differences in time and place, the various classes of people were then clearly demarcated and sharply set off from each other because they occupied congruent positions in each of the separate rank orders and because their positions were also hereditary. In feudal society, for example, a man's estate was not only hereditary and legally fixed but also generally implied well-matched positions in the economic, prestige, and power hierarchies. Differing sharply in wealth, honor, prestige, and political power, each class was characterized by distinctive patterns of conduct, by a sharp sense of social distance, and by outward symbols of a distinct way of life which placed narrow limits on intermarriage and social intercourse. At the same time, the prevailing ideologies and religious creeds explained and justified the existing hierarchical arrangements.

The situation is quite different, however, in modern industrial societies where social classes are no longer set apart by tangible, legal boundaries. Of course, the three rank orders of posi-

tions exist here, too, and if anything they have become considerably more differentiated and more complex. But in the absence of legal restrictions, dynamic economic, technological and demographic forces have greatly increased the social mobility of individuals and families and of entire groups. This has been accompanied by a democratization of behavior patterns and a change in ideology toward equalitarianism. The result of these massive changes has been two-fold: many individuals now move up or down the separate rank orders at different rates of speed, thereby creating sizeable proportions of the total population who find themselves at noticeably different levels of the three hierarchies of social position at any given time, a fact which bedevils all unidimensional, conceptual schemes of social stratification. At the same time, the increased mobility has also greatly weakened the inheritance of positions, particularly in the middle ranges of the economic, prestige, and power orders. In modern, industrial societies, therefore, social classes still clearly inhabit both the top and the bottom of the rank hierarchies, but they are now beginning to dissolve in the middle. Moreover, since the middle ranges have been greatly expanding, this portends major changes in the shape of the social structure.

If we now focus specifically on American society, we note that impressive changes have taken place during the last quarter century in the position-

* From Kurt B. Mayer, "The Changing Shape of the American Class Structure," *Social Research*, 30 (Winter 1963), 462–68.

al hierarchies. The most obvious transformation has occurred in the economic hierarchy which no longer represents a pyramid with a broad base, a smaller middle and a narrow top. The pyramid diagram was indeed applicable before World War II, but during the past two decades major shifts have occurred in the occupational structure and in the distribution of incomes. The unskilled occupations and the farm jobs have contracted sharply while the proportion of the labor force working in white collar jobs and in the skilled manual categories has expanded. Well over half of the labor force today is employed in white collar and skilled manual jobs.

The shifts in the distribution of income which have accompanied these changes in the occupational structure have been even more dramatic. In terms of constant (1959) dollars, median family incomes rose 50 per cent during the 1950's alone.[1] Underlying this increase in median family incomes has been a major shift of families upward along the entire income scale. The proportion of families with incomes of less than $5,000 declined from 80 per cent in 1949 to 42 per cent in 1959, while the proportion receiving incomes between $5,000 and $10,000 increased from 17 per cent to 43 per cent during the decade, and families with income of $10,000 and over rose from 3 per cent to 15 per cent. Note, however, that despite the remarkable overall rise in income, somewhat more than one-fifth of all American families still had incomes of less than $3,000 in 1959. Despite this very significant lag, to which we shall return later, it is no ex-

aggeration to conclude that the economic rank order of American society has changed its shape from the traditional pyramid to a diamond bulging at the middle and somewhat flat at the bottom.

The transformation of the economic structure has also significantly affected the shape of the prestige hierarchy. The time-honored invidious distinctions between the style of life of white collar employees and of manual workers have become blurred to a considerable extent. The rising standard of living has made many elements of a middle class style of life, such as home ownership, suburban living, paid vacations, and highly valued consumer goods, available not only to white collar employees but also to large numbers of manual wage earners. Nor has this trend been confined to material status symbols. The economic leveling has been accompanied by a visible "democratization" of behavior patterns. The gap in formal education which has traditionally set the wage worker sharply apart from the white collar employee has been reduced considerably as the median number of school years completed by the American population twenty-five years of age and over rose from 8.6 in 1940 to 10.6 in 1960.[2] The rise in educational achievements, combined with the increasing exposure to the mass media of communication, has induced large numbers of people at the lower social levels to adopt behavior patterns which differ little from those of the higher status circles who, quite significantly, seem to have relaxed stiff etiquette and elaborate social rituals in favor of greater informality, partly because domestic servants have become a vanishing breed.

Most visible, perhaps, has been the

---

[1] U. S. Bureau of the Census, *U. S. Census of Population: 1960, General and Economic Characteristics, United States Summary.* Final Report PC (1)–1C (Washington, D.C.: Government Printing Office, 1962), p. xxix.

[2] *Ibid.*, p. xxi.

diminishing difference in wearing apparel: as the factories have installed lockers and cafeterias, the traditional blue shirts and lunch boxes of the workers have largely disappeared. The sports shirts and slacks they now wear to and from work resemble the increasingly informal attire of the supervisory personnel. Indeed, in growing numbers workers now wear the sports shirts on the job, as automation reduces the number of "dirty" jobs. Similarly, "correct speech" patterns are being diffused more widely by schools and mass media at the same time that standards of English usage are constantly becoming more lax among the well-educated.

To be sure, this assimilation of life styles has not obliterated all status differentials. There remain important differences in food habits, reading tastes, leisure time pursuits, participation in formal and informal associations, church attendance, and so forth, which all serve as badges of belonging to separate status groups. In fact, there is reason to believe that emphasis on subtle prestige differences is increasing precisely because crude and highly visible status differences have become blurred. But the heightening emphasis on symbolic minutiae counts little as compared to the growing proportion of Americans whose style of life is becoming steadily more similar.

Unfortunately, we have much less information about what is happening in the power dimension. This an area where empirical research has barely begun to penetrate the surface, especially at the national level. Until we get the urgently needed information, it would appear that this hierarchy still retains its pyramid shape. The great mass of the population is apathetic and participates little in the decision-making process. This leaves the field to the relatively small minorities of policy makers and the somewhat larger groups who execute the policies. At the present time it is far from clear whether the national structure of power is monolithic or pluralistic, but there is no doubt that both access to and exercise of power remain more concentrated than the distribution of positions in the economic and prestige rank orders.

Finally, the crucial question of the effects which structural changes in the various hierarchies of roles and positions have had on the collectivities of people who occupy these roles must be raised. How have these changes affected the intergenerational transmission of positions, or the opportunities to attain them? It would appear that we still find rather clearly delimited classes both at the top and the bottom of the positional hierarchies. Here there are segments of the population whose position in all three rank orders is congruent and continues to be transmitted by ascription.

At the top is a numerically small but influential upper class of big businessmen, top corporation officials, independently wealthy men and women, and some professionals who originate from this class or are associated with it. It is difficult to estimate their numbers but one may hazard a guess that they comprise about one half of one per cent of the total population. These people are our economic elite, and most though not all of them move in top prestige circles. Many of them also belong to the power elite, although not all of them avail themselves of the opportunities to exercise power, nor are all men in top power positions necessarily members of the upper class. It is true that this class is not really homogeneous; there are status differences between old upper-class families who have been wealthy for generations and whose hallmark is inconspicuousness, and the newer, flashy café society circles and Texas billionaires. Still, their way of life, their attitudes, values and tastes differ from those of the rest in many respects and they successfully endeavor to pass on their positions on a hereditary basis.

At the other end of the scale there is a lower class of impoverished people. It comes as something of a shock that in our affluent society there is still a great mass of people who are literally poor and underprivileged in every respect. Who are they? They are the unskilled workers, migrant farm workers, unemployed workers who have been displaced by automation, and many of the nonwhites. How many of them are there? This depends upon the statistical standards used, but even the most conservative yardstick indicates well over thirty million people. This is "the other America" as Michael Harrington has so poignantly described it in a recent book,[3] a submerged fifth of our total population, literally forgotten and invisible to the rest of society. For them poverty is a permanent way of life. Here, too, the three dimensions coincide and the positions at the bottom are also transmitted from father to son. Particularly dismaying is the fact that the prospects for improving their lot and reducing their numbers are not at all bright.

Who is in between these two classes? There are first of all the skilled and semiskilled urban manual workers, the core of what has been traditionally the working class. They account for about a third of the population, but the traditional dividing line between manual workers and white collar employees no

---

[3] Michael Harrington, *The Other America: Poverty in the United States* (New York: The Macmillan Company, Publishers, 1962).

longer holds, because large segments of the working class now share a "white collar" style of life and many also accept middle class values and beliefs. To be sure, we still have a sizeable segment of workers who are not socially mobile, who live in a separate working class culture, emphasizing a philosophy of "getting by" rather than "getting ahead." They, too, form a stable class with congruent, hereditary positions. But one of the great gaps in our current knowledge in the field of social stratification is that we have no reliable information about the size of this group as compared to those manual workers who are mobile or are at least encouraging and urging, successfully for the most part, their children to move out of the working class. These latter form an important segment of the population, of indeterminate size, which is quite literally in transition, with positions no longer congruent and no longer hereditary.

Immediately beyond them is the white collar world, a truly heterogeneous aggregate of salaried employees, independent enterprisers, and professionals. They comprise well over two-fifths of the population. It has been customary to call them middle class and to distinguish between an upper and a lower middle class. It seems to this writer, however, that these designations are losing their validity. Here we have so much mobility that many people hold different positions in the various rank orders and the situation is becoming so fluid that one can no longer truly speak of classes in the middle ranges of positional hierarchies. We therefore boldly conclude that what we have been accustomed to calling the middle class or middle classes is well on the way to losing its class character altogether. What is emerging here is social differentiation without stratification.

More and more the bulk of white collar positions are opened up to competition through achievement and ability. They are less and less passed on from generation to generation on the basis of monopolistic pre-emption. Increasingly, there is free upward and downward mobility all the way up and down the widening middle ranges of the economic and prestige hierarchies.

To sum it up, America's social structure today and in the proximate future can be perceived as a diamond where the top and bottom are still pretty rigidly fixed, inhabited by upper and lower classes. A working class of the traditional sort also persists but comprises nowadays only a part of the manual workers. Between the extremes, however, classes are disappearing. To

be sure, prestige, power and economic differentials persist here too, of course, and prestige differentials tend even to become accentuated as crude economic differences diminish and lose their visibility. But these differentials are no longer the hallmarks of social classes. In the middle ranges of the various rank orders we are witnessing the beginnings of a classless society in a modern industrial economy. It already involves roughly one-half of our population and may well involve more than that in the future although there are no signs that the top and bottom classes are likely to disappear altogether. This is a somewhat different classless society from that envisaged by Marx a century ago, but it is at least a partially classless society nevertheless.

SELECTED BIBLIOGRAPHY

ADAMS, STUART A., "Origins of American Occupational Elites, 1900–1955," *American Journal of Sociology*, 62 (January 1957), 360–68.

AIKEN, MICHAEL, and LOUIS A. FERMAN, "Job Mobility and Social Integration of Displaced Workers," *Social Problems*, 14 (Summer 1966), 48–56.

ANDERSON, C. ARNOLD, "A Skeptical Note on the Relation of Vertical Mobility to Education," *American Journal of Sociology*, 66 (May 1961), 560–70.

BALTZELL, E. DIGBY, "Social Mobility and Fertility Within an Elite Group," *Milbank Memorial Foundation Quarterly*, 31 (October 1953), 411–20.

BLAU, PETER M., "Social Mobility and Interpersonal Relations," *American Sociological Review*, 21 (June 1956), 290–95.

————, and OTIS DUDLEY DUNCAN, *The American Occupational Structure*. New York: John Wiley & Sons, Inc., 1967.

BONJEAN, CHARLES M., *et al.*, "Social Mobility and Job Satisfaction: A Replication and Extension," *Social Forces*, 45 (June 1967), 492–501.

CROCKETT, HARRY J., JR., "Achievement Motive and Differential Occupational Mobility in the United States," *American Sociological Review*, 27 (April 1962), 191–204.

CURTIS, RICHARD F., "Conceptual Problems in Social Mobility Research," *Sociology and Social Research*, 45 (July 1961), 387–95.

————, "Income and Occupational Mobility," *American Sociological Review*, 25 (October 1960), 727–30.

CUTRIGHT, PHILLIPS, "Occupational Inheritance: A Cross-National Analysis," *American Journal of Sociology*, 73 (January 1968), 400–16.

DUNCAN, OTIS DUDLEY, and ROBERT W. HODGE, "Education and Occupational Mobility: A Regression Analysis," *American Journal of Sociology*, 68 (May 1963), 629–44.

ELLIS, ROBERT A., and CLAYTON W. LANE, "Structural Supports for Upward Mobility," *American Sociological Review*, 28 (October 1963), 743–56.

EMPEY, LAMAR T., "Social Class and Occupational Aspiration: A Comparison of Absolute and Relative Measurement," *American Sociological Review*, 21 (December 1956), 703–9.

FAUNCE, WILLIAM A., "Automation and the Division of Labor," *Social Problems*, 13 (Fall 1965), 149–60.

FOOTE, NELSON N., and PAUL K. HATT, "Social Mobility and Economic Advancement," Supplement, *American Economic Review*, 43 (May 1953), 364–78.

GESCHWENDER, JAMES A., "Continuities in Theories of Status Consistency and Cognitive Dissonance," *Social Forces*, 46 (December 1967), 160–71.

GOLDNER, FRED H., and R. R. RITTI, "Professionalization as Career Mobility," *American Journal of Sociology*, 72 (March 1967), 489–502.

GOLDSTEIN, SIDNEY, "Migration and Occupational Mobility in Norristown, Pa.," *American Sociological Review*, 20 (August 1955), 402–8.

GOODE, WILLIAM J., "Family and Mobility," in *Class, Status and Power* (2nd ed.), eds. Reinhard Bendix and Seymour M. Lipset. New York: The Free Press of Glencoe, Inc., 1966.

GURSSLIN, ORVILLE R., and JACK L. ROACH, "Some Issues in Training the Unemployed," *Social Problems*, 12 (Summer 1964), 86–98.

HANDLIN, OSCAR, and MARY F. HANDLIN, "Ethnic Factors in Social Mobility," *Explorations in Entrepreneurial History*, 9 (October 1956), 1–7.

HILTON, ALICE M., *The Evolving Society*. New York: Institute for Cybercultural Research, 1966.

HODGE, ROBERT W., and PATRICIA HODGE, "Occupational Assimilation as a Competitive Process," *American Journal of Sociology*, 71 (November 1965), 249–64.

HOSELITZ, BERT F., "Population Pressure, Industrialization and Social Mobility," *Population Studies*, 11 (November 1957), 123–35.

JACKSON, ELTON F., "Status Consistency and Symptoms of Stress," *American Sociological Review*, 27 (August 1962), 469–80.

JAFFE, A. J., and R. O. CARLETON, *Occupational Mobility in the United States*. New York: Kings Crown Press, 1954.

JANOWITZ, MORRIS, "Some Consequences of Social Mobility in the United States," *Transactions of the Third World Congress of Sociology*, 3 (1956), 191–201.

KAHL, JOSEPH A., *The American Class Structure*. New York: Holt, Rinehart & Winston, Inc., 1957. Chaps. 9 and 10.

———, "Education and Occupational Aspirations of 'Common Man' Boys," *Harvard Educational Review*, 23 (Summer 1953), 186–203.

KOLKO, GABRIEL, "Economic Mobility and Social Stratification," *American Journal of Sociology*, 63 (July 1957), 30–38.

LADINSKY, JACK, "Occupational Determinants of Geographic Mobility Among Professional Workers," *American Sociological Review*, 32 (April 1967), 253–64.

LENSKI, GERHARD E., "Trends in Inter-Generational Mobility in the United States," *American Sociological Review*, 23 (October 1958), 514–23.

LIPSET, SEYMOUR M., and REINHARD BENDIX, *Social Mobility in Industrial Society*. Berkeley, Calif.: University of California Press, 1959.

———, and HANS L. ZETTERBERG, "A Theory of Social Mobility," in *Class, Status and Power* (2nd ed.), eds. Reinhard Bendix and Seymour M. Lipset. New York: The Free Press of Glencoe, Inc., 1966.

LITTIG, LAWRENCE W., and CONSTANTINE A. YERACARIS, "Achievement Motivation and Inter-Generational Occupational Mobility," *Journal of Personality and Social Psychology*, 1 (April 1965), 386–89.

MCCLELLAND, DAVID C., et al., *The Achieving Society*. Princeton, N.J.: D. Van Nostrand Company, Inc., 1961.

———, *Talent and Society*. Princeton, N.J.: D. Van Nostrand Company, Inc., 1958.

MACK, RAYMOND W., et al., *Social Mobility: Thirty Years of Research and Theory, and Annotated Bibliography*. Syracuse: Syracuse University Press, 1957.

———, *Transforming America: Patterns of Social Change*. New York: Random House, Inc., 1967.

MARSH, ROBERT M., "Values, Demand and Social Mobility," *American Sociological Review*, 28 (August 1963), 565–75.

MILLER, S. M., "Comparative Social Mobility," *Current Sociology*, 9 (1960), 1–89.

———, "The Concept of Mobility," *Social Problems*, 3 (October 1955), 65–73.

MUSTIAN, R. DAVID, and C. HORACE HAMILTON, "Measuring the Extent, Character, and Direction of Occupational Changes," *Social Forces*, 45 (March 1967), 440–44.

NATIONAL COMMISSION ON TECHNOLOGY, AUTOMATION AND ECONOMIC PROGRESS, "The Outlook for Technological Change and Employment," Vol. 1, and "Educational Implications of Technological Change," Vol. 4, *Technology and the American Economy*. Washington, D.C., Government Printing Office, 1966.

PERRUCCI, CAROLYN CUMMINGS, "Social Origins, Mobility Patterns and Fertility," *American Sociological Review*, 32 (August 1967), 615–25.

PERRUCCI, ROBERT, "Education, Stratification, and Mobility," in *On Education—Sociological Perspectives*, eds. Donald A. Hansen and Joel E. Gerstl. New York: John Wiley & Sons, Inc., 1967.

REISS, ALBERT J., JR., "Occupational Mobility of Professional Workers," *American Sociological Review*, 20 (December 1955), 693–700.

REISSMAN, LEONARD, "Levels of Aspiration and Social Class," *American Sociological Review*, 18 (June 1953), 233–42.

ROGOFF, NATALIE, *Recent Trends in Occupational Mobility*. Glencoe, Ill.: The Free Press, 1953.

ROSEN, BERNARD C., *et al.*, eds., *Achievement in American Society*. Cambridge, Mass.: Schenkman Publishing Co., 1967.

SCANZONI, JOHN, "Socialization, n Achievement, and Achievement Values," *American Sociological Review*, 32 (June 1967), 449–56.

SCHNORE, LEO F., "Social Mobility in Demographic Perspective," *American Sociological Review*, 26 (June 1961), 407–23.

SEWELL, WILLIAM H., *et al.*, "Social Status and Educational and Occupational Aspiration," *American Sociological Review*, 22 (February 1957), 67–73.

SHEPPARD, HAROLD L., and HARVEY BELITSKY, *The Job Hunt*. Baltimore: The Johns Hopkins Press, 1966.

SIMPSON, RICHARD L., "Parental Influence, Anticipatory Socialization, and Social Mobility," *American Sociological Review*, 27 (August 1962), 517–22.

SLOCUM, WALTER, *Occupational Careers*. Chicago: Aldine Publishing Co., 1966.

SMELSER, NEIL J., and SEYMOUR M. LIPSET, eds., *Social Structure and Mobility in Economic Development*. Chicago: Aldine Publishing Co., 1966.

SOROKIN, PITIRIM A., *Social and Cultural Mobility*. New York: Harper and Bros., 1927.

SPADY, WILLIAM G., "Educational Mobility and Access: Growth and Paradoxes," *American Journal of Sociology*, 73 (November 1967), 273–86.

STEPHENSON, RICHARD M., "Mobility Orientation and Stratification of 1,000 Ninth Graders," *American Sociological Review*, 22 (April 1957), 204–12.

STRAUS, MURRAY A., "Deferred Gratification, Social Class, and the Achievement Syndrome," *American Sociological Review*, 27 (June 1962), 326–35.

THERNSTROM, STEPHAN, *Poverty and Progress: Social Mobility in a Nineteenth Century City*. Cambridge, Mass.: Harvard University Press, 1964.

TIEN, HUAN Y., *Social Mobility and Controlled Fertility*. New Haven, Conn.: College and University Press, 1965.

TUMIN, MELVIN M., and ARNOLD S. FELDMAN, "Theory and Measurement of Occupational Mobility," *American Sociological Review*, 22 (June 1957), 281–88.

TURNER, RALPH, *The Social Context of Ambition*. San Francisco: The Chandler Press, 1964.

———, "Upward Mobility and Class Values," *Social Problems*, 11 (Spring 1964), 359–71.

WARNER, W. LLOYD, and JAMES ABEGGLEN, *Occupational Mobility in American Business and Industry, 1928–1952*. St.

Paul: University of Minnesota Press, 1955.

WESTOFF, CHARLES F., *et al.*, "The Concept of Social Mobility: An Empirical Inquiry," *American Sociological Review*, 25 (June 1960), 375–85.

WHITE, HARRISON C., "Cause and Effect in Social Mobility Tables," *Behavioral Science*, 8 (January 1963), 14–27.

WILEY, NORBERT, "The Ethnic Mobility Trap and Stratification Theory," *Social Problems*, 15 (Fall 1967), 147–59.

YASUDA, SABURO, "A Methodological Inquiry into Social Mobility," *American Sociological Review*, 29 (February 1964), 16–23.

CHAPTER ELEVEN

Postscript: The Language and Logic of Stratification

The best way to study social stratification, of course, is to look at the phenomena to which it refers and to report the results in a language acceptable to the academic reader. This is the usual process and one that easily recommends itself. Nevertheless it overlooks a consideration of more than passing significance. Put simply, most of the phenomena of social stratification and all reports about it consist of verbal data. Anyone who "sees" group hierarchies and class relations sees or hears primarily words and responds by using words. To give an understanding of the implications of this fact is the purpose of this chapter. But first, we present a summary of the chapter's assumptions.

The sociologist has built his discipline from everyday vocabulary.[1] His conceptual schemes are attempts to improve on that vocabulary—to reconstruct it by clarifying and systematizing the human experience to which it refers. In some cases, he uses words in their common-sense meanings; in other cases he defines common-sense meanings beyond the recognition of laymen. Whenever sociologists use words foreign to laymen, they are influenced by traditions that stand in opposition to common-sense viewpoints. Consider, for example, the influence of natural science models and metaphors on sociological language. Probably all

---

1 "Indeed, almost all of the established technical vocabulary of sociology has been taken over from the common stock of words in ordinary language, and there is hardly a widely received sociological term that was not long ago assigned a nonprofessional and yet clearly sociological meaning." Edward Rose, "The English Record of a Natural Sociology," *American Sociological Review*, 25 (April 1960), 196.

attempts to separate sociological from everyday language must contend with the following conditions.

(1) Everyday language is a loose and shifting network of verbal connections, a tangled skein in which the meaning of a word is dependent upon the meaning of numerous others. The relation of two or more words cannot be understood without knowing their intermediaries and without knowing how they may act as synonyms or antonyms of one another.

(2) All words can be taken as contributing to some essential condition of experience, to some form of thought or description of things. Certain words, the so-called *categories of understanding*, serve as centers of meaning around which others converge and cluster. The importance of such categories, identified by names like "substance," "quality," "quantity," "relation," "time," and "place," rests upon the analysis of word hierarchies—words prior to and generative of all others.

(3) Insofar as sociological and ordinary language share a common heritage the former participates in the alleged "liabilities" of the latter. Among these liabilities are ambiguity, nonempirical reference (in the positivistic science sense), and valuational representation. Ordinary language is inherently valuational because it is used to conduct the affairs of society or, more specifically, to detail the proper conduct of social affairs. As long as human affairs affect human beings, they will affect their language. Thus, both the language of human affairs and that part of it borrowed by sociologists are normative in character. People speak of and classify one another in ways which are of the greatest concern to them. The words they frequently use are clues to what they usually perceive and attend to—the things of greatest value in their lives.

Because of these conditions, language is open to change and clarification and thus we can use it to describe any new kind of social order. From the infirmities of language, scholars have built images of social life in infinite variety. We give below a few hints on how they have done this.

COMMON CATEGORIES OF UNDERSTANDING

We have suggested that the vocabulary of social stratification is drawn primarily from the vocabulary of everyday usage. Although certain words are repeated many times, the ideas they transmit are continually rearranged into new patterns. Each combination is a variant statement of a fundamental core of ideas that appears in new guises whenever it is given verbal shape. The individuality of an author's phrasing is his private way of publicly expressing what is at root a universal grammar of the intellect.

Collective experience is affirmed when widely understood word categories are successful guides to social action. The things felt and seen by each individual are largely, though not entirely, the things felt and seen by previous others—contemporaries as well as predecessors. Seeing without public verbalization or thought without categories for ordering experience is devoid of significance. For anything to be significant it must be assimilated into the vocabulary of a people, into the shared language of human discourse. To give a clear understanding of these points we present a short resumé of categories common to sociology and ordinary language. We then examine the applicability of these categories to stratification.

Perhaps the most fundamental category is that of existence—"the inclusive *term* which designates the state or *condition* of anything regarded as occurring in space or time, as distinct or apart from all other *things*, and as having a *nature* or substance of its own; as 'customs which have recently come into existence' "[2] (*Webster's Dictionary of Synonyms*, italics added). Notice how the word or idea of existence relates to other words or ideas. It supports the word "category," interpreted as a form of thought that embraces some class or condition of predictable or existent things. And, condition and thing are included in the definition of both existence and category.

Returning to the italicized words in the definition of existence, we note that *term* stands for word, expression, limit, or boundary line designating a definite thing. *Condition* is the state or mode in which a person or thing exists; a modifying circumstance including, by definition, situation, posture, status, or estate (cf. *Webster's Dictionary of Synonyms*), and "a grade or rank, especially high social position" (cf. *Britannica World Language Dictionary*). *Thing* is a comprehensive term applicable to whatever is apprehended as having actual, distinct, and demonstrable existence. *Nature* is the character or essential traits of a person, thing, or class, especially if original rather than acquired.

Apparently, *thing* is contained in the definitions of existence, category, term, condition, and nature. *Term* appears explicitly in the definitions of existence and thing and implicitly in those of category, condition, and nature. *Condition* suggests things, situations, and positions. *Nature* refers to things and existence; it is a category and must, therefore, describe a condition. Other words linked to existence, such as "designate," "state," "occur," "distinct," and "substance," perform similar functions. Shared meanings—the intended significance of objects or things—is the basis for this cross-referencing of terms.

Consider now two other widely used categories in sociological and in ordinary language—relation and quantity. *Relation* is the condition of being connected either objectively or in the mind (*Britannica World Language Dictionary*). Anything that is associated, corresponding, correlative, complementary, identical, like, analogous, uniform, or different stands in relation to some other thing. Agreement and consensus are relations. Difference, as a relation, calls forth such words as "variance," "diversity," "divergence," "disparity," "dissimilarity," "disagreement," "distinction," "contrast," and "inconsistency."

Quantity refers to the condition of an object or thing regarded as having a

---

[2] Anything that exists is said to be real or actual or matter of fact; to rank and endure; to have character, type, quality, and presence at some time and place.

determinable mass, volume, or number. Analogous terms include "unit," "factor," "amount," "sum," "aggregate," "total," "whole." The idea of "sameness of quantity or degree" includes equality, equivalence, equilibrium, coordination, and adjustment. The idea of "difference of quantity or degree" includes inequality, disparity, imbalance, disequilibrium, and maladjustment. Many of these terms suggest the word "surplus"—that which remains over and above what is required. When quantity is used (comparatively) with reference to standards, ideas of magnitude, size dimension, and scale arise. When it is used (comparatively) with reference to similar objects, ideas of supremacy, superiority, primacy, majority, minority, inferiority, and subordination arise. Roget's *Thesaurus* includes the category "concrete quantity," which involves such ideas as element, part-whole, integrity, universality, component, and composition. When the meaning of the category "order" is joined to those of relation and quantity, it includes the concepts of system, uniformity, continuity, and subordination.

The student of general sociology immediately recognizes the importance of the terms "relation" and "quantity," and of their numerous synonyms and antonyms in scholarly writings. The literature contains countless references to class "relations," to "correlated" variables, to ethnic "differences," to group "consensus," to cultural "diversity," to personality "factors," to system "equilibrium," to "surplus" goods, to status "dimensions," to "elements" of social interaction, to social "order," etc.

Before discussing the relevance of these categories for social stratification, let us look at other category words frequently found in sociology. The term "position" refers to (1) the manner in which a thing is placed—its location, posture, relative social standing, rank, or circumstance; (2) the ground for, argument over, attitude about or point of view toward a subject; and (3) a person's employment or job. We sometimes use function and position synonomously with office and situation. Position and location suggest the category "space," which, in turn, gives rise to ideas of existence, situation, habitation, content, size, distance, interval, layer, height, depth, form, and motion. All these terms have entered the vocabulary of social stratification.

The term "structure" refers to the arrangement and organic union of parts in a body or object. We often use it interchangeably with framework, organization, system, and scheme. More specifically, it designates any part of the makeup of a particular body, organism, edifice, building, or machine or the subdivisions, connections, and interrelations that reveal its underlying design.

The term "function" may appear in any one of several ordinary-language contexts. It may refer to (1) agency, operation, action, performance, and effect, or to (2) utility, service, instrumentality, and applicability. Such references are probably more common in the sociological literature than are those of (3) ceremony, ritual, rite, observance, or (4) duty, responsibility, and obligation. Also, in sociological usage, number and formula are less frequently suggested, while product, result, or consequence are more frequently found meanings for the term.

Three general categories inherited from the past and thus of historical significance for sociology are those of intellect, affections, and volition; or knowledge, emotion, and action. By common usage, intellect includes perception, thought, mind, rationality, understanding, belief, judgment, expectation, evidence, inquiry, comparison, prediction, and, in general, all communication of ideas in respect to both their nature and means. It is an expression of human power, ability, and education. Affections include feeling, sensibility, emotion, disposition, friendship, love, sociability, sentiment, obligation, right and duty, and many of the aspirational characteristics of legal and religious institutions. Volitions include motive, will, choice, decision, habit, action, activity, behavior, skill, opposition, authority, subjection, acquisition, cooperation, method, means, and importance (as in subservience to ends). Force and coercion are distinguishing antonyms.

The preceding paragraphs provide a suitable context for introducing two commonly used sociological terms, norms and values. In everyday usage a *norm* is "a rule or authoritative standard; a model, type, pattern, or value considered as representative of a specified group" (*Britannica World Language Dictionary*). Performance of a noun belongs in the category "volitions." But it can also be viewed as an abstract relation, a condition of existence, or a quantity. Or it can be seen as a regularity and thus as a member of the category "order" (consider, for instance, its closeness to the word "rule").

Value is the desirability or worth of a thing—the equivalence in money, goods, and services that may be asked or given in its exchange. Among its synonyms are merit, esteem, importance, significance, usefulness, and rank in a system of classification. In some contexts it refers to quantity (magnitude) as well as to quality. As a magnitude it belongs to the category "intellect." As something having utility, importance, or goodness, it belongs to the category "volitions." And, when signifying esteem, appreciation, approval, or honor, it belongs to the category "affections."

THEORETICAL INTERPRETATIONS OF STRATIFICATION

Having discussed some widely adopted word categories and their pervasiveness in both sociological and everyday language, we turn to an exploration of their significance in studies of social stratification.

We have seen how words from everyday usage frequently appear in sociological writing. In many instances ordinary and sociological meanings are the same or are similar; in other instances, transference of meanings produces ambiguity. However, there is little support for the view that the differences of usage among sociological authors are fewer than the differences of usage between sociologists and laymen. Moreover, common usage can be a standard of comparison for ferreting out the atypical meanings of the professional writer—in respect to both conceptualization and detailed description. If sociological usage can be comprehended only by understanding its relationship to ordinary words, then a conscious retention of the latter is helpful in understanding the former. A few examples of what can be done by holding familiar words in mind make these points clear.

In Chapter Two we quoted Bernard Barber's definition of social stratification as "a *structure* of *regularized inequality* in which men are *ranked higher and lower* according to the *value* accorded their *various social roles* and *activities*."[3] As we noted in the previous section, in ordinary usage *structure* is a combination or arrangement of related parts in a body or object. Sometimes it includes the makeup or substance of such an arrangement. Its synonyms include organization, system, and integration, all of which belong to the category *order*. *Regularized* suggests form, system, and uniformity, all of which belong to the categories *order* and *space*. *Inequality,* as we have seen, is a difference of quantity. When Barber says that "men are *ranked as higher and lower*," he uses quantity comparatively, as in superiority and inferiority. *Value*, we found, suggests the desirability or worth of things, hence the categories intellect (and quantity), volition, and affections. *Various* and its synonyms difference, dissimilarity, etc. are, again, aspects of relation and quantity. The word *social* can be placed in the category affections, and *roles and activities* in the category volition.

Note how Barber's definition of stratification can be restated by successively substituting for each word some other belonging to the same category. Drawing from related words in ordinary language we can say that *social stratification is a system of ordered ranks in which men are placed as superior or inferior according to the worth of their different duties (affections) and skills (volitions).* This sentence may be restated in other ways by further substitutions—by rotating terms within the categories shared by both the original sentence and ours. In some instances, sentence structure may be awkward or distorted but not necessarily less intelligible or comprehensive.

As a second example, take Talcott Parsons' statement on stratification in which he holds that it is "a condition of the stability of social systems that there should be an integration of the value standards of the component units to constitute a common value system."[4] We may express this statement in different words without essentially changing the meaning. Consider, for instance, one possible substitution: *It is a requisite of regularity in institutional organizations that there should be an equilibrium of the norms of the component elements to constitute a common normative organization.* For norms one could substitute sentiments; for equilibrium, balance, etc. Some sociologists may claim that these substitutions are not strictly equivalent since expert linguists can find margins of meaning in one term

---

3 *Social Stratification: A Comparative Analysis of Structure and Process* (New York: Harcourt, Brace & World, Inc., 1957), p. 7, italics added.

4 "A Revised Analytical Approach to the Theory of Social Stratification," in *Class, Status, and Power,* eds. Reinhard Bendix and Seymour Lipset (Glencoe, Ill.: The Free Press, 1953), p. 93.

that are absent in the other. The important consideration, however, is not whether the author's intentions are violated in small ways but whether the reality described is any less factual, accurate, or correct from a sociological viewpoint.

For a third interpretation of social stratification, consider Walter Buckley's: "Stratification involves the existence of strata, generally agreed to refer to specifiable collectivities or subgroups that continue through several generations to occupy the same relative positions and to receive the same relative amounts of material ends, prestige, and power."[5] No matter how this definition is converted into other words, it differs more from those of Barber and Parsons than do the latter from each other. Obviously, considerable latitude of expression is available to the writer who would follow one or another precedent in phrasing his personal views.

The number of statements that can be linked to considerations of social stratification is probably infinite. This diversity will be clear to any student who experiments with the word categories and related synonyms discussed in the opening pages of this chapter. A cursory inspection of Roget's *Thesaurus* supports the likelihood that nearly every word in the English language can be put to use in stratification studies. Roget's category "inorganic matter" appears to be furthest removed from the subject. Yet such terms as materiality, friction, density (cf. permeability), hardness (cf. rigidity), tenacity and toughness (cf. cohesion), texture (cf. structure and organization), fluidity (cf. mobility), conduct (cf. channel), and their synonyms appear in discussions of social stratification. Least likely to appear are such words as gravity, levity, pulverulence, liquifaction, moisture, and pulpiness. But with the widespread use of metaphor (an imaginative identification of one object or word with another, ascribing to the first the qualities of the second, e.g., "Life's but a walking shadow"), it is a mistake to predict the unacceptability of these words in future work on stratification. Some author may, for instance, decide to label the movement of a population toward the center of the class structure "social gravity" or may label the accelerating tendency of classes to develop class interests "stratum gravity." He may then regard countertendencies as "liquifaction." If these labels sound unnatural, common repetition would erase this impression as it has erased the unnatural sound of many other words.

Saying that the whole English language may be used to support studies of social stratification is not the same as giving authenticity to any kind of relationship among words. Associations between terms are not entirely random. There are, it seems, a limited number of logical alternatives. These alternatives can be thought of as patterns of word options, restricted in scope but not excluding mixed categories. The reader knows that the word "stratification" has been applied to positions, people, groups, roles, statuses, powers, wealth, income, occupation, education, religion, land ownership, marriage patterns, eating habits, dress, speech, etc.

---

5 "Social Stratification and the Functional Theory of Social Differentiation," *American Sociological Review*, 23 (August 1958), 370.

We easily view some of these terms as variables. Minutely divisible, they fluctuate in value under changing conditions (like the amount of money people have). We view other terms (like "dogs" and "cats") as existing in all-or-none amounts—as referring to clearly distinguishable characteristics of categories. One group of critics claims that social classes are best represented as subdivisions on a continuum. Another claims that they are more like separate and distinct categories. A third believes they may be a combination of both possibilities. Here, then, is a simple example of how interpretations of a subject are limited by its logical alternatives. Things differ by gradual degrees or they differ in kind or they, in certain respects, do both. There are no other possibilities, although there may be many refinements in the basic distinctions, each refinement capable of being represented by some unique combination of words. For instance, if we accept the idea of separate classes, or strata, then we may question their number, their rigidity and distinctiveness, their identifiable characteristics, the variations within and between them, the changes in them over time, their sources and consequences, etc. The list could be extended; but, when problems of content (i.e., what is stratified?) are not considered, the number of abstract relations is limited to a few logical categories.

If he grants the preceding assumption, the student can make an enlightening discovery: Analysts of social stratification seldom utilize even the few logical alternatives available to them. For Karl Marx, classes are based on material conditions, on the conflict of economic interests. For W. Lloyd Warner, classes are based on status factors, primarily family lineage, and not on conflicting economic interests. Thorstein Veblen combines both economic and prestige factors; the object of economic competition is, for him, prestige. To prestige and the economic factor, Max Weber adds power. He speaks of the economic order, the social order (prestige and esteem), and the legal order (power). Consideration of these factors as sources of stratification did not follow a neat line of historical development. Nevertheless, we may conjecture that with the accumulation of research every logical form of ranking will have its time of ascendency, perhaps under the press of social circumstances or scholarly imagination. Today, education, as a symbol of technological advance, is becoming the salient criterion of class standing. Tomorrow a dual system of community life may appear: one for the public sector (educational capacities?), the other for the private sector (recreational capacities?). Logically speaking, all scales for ranking people are expressions of differences in material resources or in human capacities. One stratum has more goods or more ability than another, and most members of society recognize this distinction. Later analysis may determine whether status, power, prestige, etc. are separately or in some combination the product of resources or capacities. Researchers will make this analysis once they realize that all criteria of stratification are but logical alternatives of these two categories—however they are labeled or whatever their names.

We find in studies of power another illustration of the restrictions placed by logical categories on empirical interpretations of stratification. We know, prior to any observation, that a characteristic of a population may be primarily in one part of it, in two parts of it, in more than two parts of it, or in all of it. Any such characteristic must be distributed in equal amounts throughout, or be distributed at random, or be concentrated in some one of or fewer than all the parts. (Of course, such distributions may vary over time.) There are no other possibilities except the total·absence of the characteristic. Thus, we find John Walton classifying studies of community power structures as pyramidal (single concentrated leadership group), factional (at least two durable factions), coalitional (fluid coalitions), and amorphous (absence of persistent patterns of leadership).

Logical limitations apply, in like manner, to the process of locating people in a class structure. They may be ranked on some scale of presumably objective reference, such as income, occupation, or education. Or they may be ranked by a variety of subjective criteria, less clearly understood. People may rate themselves, they may rate others, or they may be rated by professionals. Within the range of these logical possibilities, sociologists have developed several methods of class placement. So-called objective ratings rest on professional rankings of people in respect to manifest differences in some characteristic such as socioeconomic standing. Self-placement ratings are usually rankings that community members give themselves. Reputational ratings are based on the identification of people in terms of their community statuses. These people may be identified by laymen or from a list prepared in advance by professionals. Only two logical alternatives have been overlooked. (1) Laymen have not rated one another on the so-called objective rankings. (2) Although professionals have engaged in self-ratings and they have been ranked by laymen with other professionals overseeing their efforts, laymen have not conducted independent studies. If our scheme of logical alternatives is complete, new methods of class placement will develop as variations within it. From this assumption, the student can make intelligent guesses about the categories likely to emerge in later research and, in some cases, about the new language that may be used to describe them.

Once he understands the logical structure of old theories, the student may apply imagination and ingenuity to constructing new theories. Consider, for instance, the Davis-Moore theory of stratification, which may be summarized[6] in this way:

(1) Higher positions have greater degrees of functional importance (i.e., make greater contributions to societal preservation or survival).

(2) Adequate performance in higher positions requires greater amounts of talent and training.

(3) Personnel with greater amounts of talent and training are scarce.

(4) Greater awards are attached to those positions which require greater amounts of

---

[6] In most respects this summarization closely follows our discussion of Davis and Moore in Chapter Two. However, the original statement of the theory favors the word "different" rather than "higher" or "greater" in statements (1) and (2). The latter must be assumed if (4) and (5) are to make sense.

talent and training, thus assuring the mobility of the more talented and trained into the more highly rewarded positions.

(5) The attachment of unequal rewards to higher positions (i.e., stratification) makes for societal preservation or survival.

Roughly translated this theory affirms a correlation among the importance of a position, the amounts of talent and training required to fill it, and the awards attached to it. We can develop a structurally similar theory with different conceptual content by replacing (1) higher positions with higher levels of coordination, (2) talent and training with power and privilege, and (3) preservation and survival with coordination and control. The following statements outline such a theory:

(1) Higher levels of coordination involve greater degrees of social control.
(2) Adequate performance at higher levels requires greater amounts of power and privilege.
(3) Personnel with greater amounts of power and privilege are scarce.
(4) Greater awards are attached to those positions which require greater amounts of power and privilege, thus assuring the mobility of the more powerful and privileged into the higher levels of coordination.
(5) The attachment of unequal rewards to higher positions (i.e., stratification) makes for societal coordination and control.

The parallels between this theory and that of Davis and Moore are not so close as one could make them.[7] Nevertheless, the resemblance is sufficient to establish the point that alternative sociological interpretations are not difficult to find.[8] Although power and privilege are central categories, as in Gerhard

---

[7] The following simpler series of statements is more directly comparable to the Davis-Moore theory but less interesting: (1) Higher positions have greater degrees of functional importance. (2) Adequate performance in higher positions requires greater amounts of power and privilege. (3) Personnel with greater amounts of power and privilege are scarce. (4) Greater awards are attached to those positions which require greater amounts of power and privilege, thus assuring the mobility of the more powerful and privileged into the more highly rewarded positions. (5) The attachment of unequal rewards to higher positions makes for societal preservation or survival.

We can produce still another variation on the Davis-Moore theory by substituting coordination and integration for functional importance or societal preservation or survival in statements (1) and (5). Should the student wish to construct his own theory he may turn to the following quotation, which lends support to some portion of each version of stratification discussed in these pages. "As division of labor increases and the social units become more numerous and diverse, the need for coordination and integration also increases and, when satisfied, enables the larger groups to survive and develop. Those who occupy coordinating positions acquire power and prestige. They do so because their actions partly control the behavior of the individuals who look to them for direction. Within this simple control there is power. Those who exercise such power either acquire prestige directly from it or have gained prestige from other sources sufficiently to be raised to a coordinating position." See W. Lloyd Warner, Marchia Meeker, K. W. Eells, *Social Class in America* (Chicago: Science Research Associates, Inc., 1949), p. 8.

[8] The placing of empirical restrictions on theory formation is, in most instances, quite arbitrary. Consider for example the reasonableness of adding a sixth statement to our theory: The maintenance of the more powerful and privileged at higher levels is supported by legally established patterns of status ascription.

Lenski's theory,[9] our reconstruction more nearly resembles that of Davis and Moore. We have every reason to believe, then, that the proposed "theory" could have at least the same degree of empirical support that underlies the other two.

EMPIRICAL INTERPRETATIONS OF STRATIFICATION

To now we have discussed some possible contributions of language and logic to an understanding of social stratification. To some extent, the importance of these contributions depends on their empirical substantiation. If knowledge of social stratification is based on direct observation, on tangible data, we need give slight attention to the niceties of symbolic expression. When observable signs are clear and unambiguous, we discourage arbitrary verbalizations. But, when observable signs and the experiences they generate are unreliable or when they fail to provide clearly understood symbols, ordinary language and its logical reconstruction become the primary sources of emperical support. What then can be said about the reliability of the so-called empirical data upon which stratification studies rest?

Turning to such studies we find that most of their data consist of literal transcriptions of spontaneous (off-the-cuff) expressions, usually restated in language familiar to the educated layman. The terms of reference are open to multiple interpretations because they rest largely on private judgment. As a result, the conceptual gap between data and language is wide, allowing for extremely different, even contradictory, viewpoints. Here are a few examples.

A working-class woman is asked if she is a member of any clubs or other organizations. She replies by saying, "I haven't been asked to any club, I'm not very social myself. I'm too shy and reserved; I'd like to join, but I will wait until I'm asked. I'd like to have some place to go. They don't interest me at all; you have to have an interest and I'm no pusher."[10] Thus, the woman's responses range from "I'd like to join" to "they don't interest me at all." What is she communicating or trying to communicate? Ambivalence of attitude or lack of knowledge? Is she saying something closer to "well, it depends upon what happens"? Can we say that the only clear answer she is giving to the question of club membership is a not-so-positive "no"?

From the preceding replies and others resembling them, the author draws a number of conclusions.[11]

---

9 See our discussion of Lenski's theory in Chapter Two.

10 Lee Rainwater *et al.*, *Workingman's Wife* (New York: MacFadden-Bartell Corp., 1962), p. 51.

11 We wish to state in the strongest terms that the comments which follow are not meant to reflect on the value of the contributions included. Indeed, we believe the writings of Rainwater and Gans and of the other authors used illustratively here to be among the best in sociology. If they did not provide new understanding we would gain little from a

(1) A central characteristic of the working-class wife is her underlying conviction that most significant action originates from the world external to herself rather than from within herself; (2) she expresses a certain internal immobility and a reliance upon the outer world coming to her in terms that are specific, clearly defined, and readily understood; (3) she sees the world beyond her doorstep and neighborhood as fairly chaotic and potentially catastrophic; and (4) in comparison with the middle-class wife, reality is, in its ordinary presentation to her, flat, unvarnished, and not highly differentiated.[12]

These conclusions appear to be far removed from the data upon which they are based, the working-class wife's verbal responses. In what ways do her replies show an "underlying conviction" as a central characteristic. In what ways are they indicative of her concern for "significant action"? By what inference do her words express "internal immobility"? From the author's statements it appears that her outer world is (1) specific, clearly defined, and readily understood; (2) fairly chaotic and potentially catastrophic; and (3) flat, unvarnished, and not highly differentiated. Can it be said therefore that the world of the working-class wife is highly differentiated, confused, or undifferentiated? If these alternatives include every logical possibility, the empirical characteristics of working-class wives cannot be definitely identified from this study.

The following statement is Gans's description of the peer-group society of the Urban Villagers:

> In view of the severity of social control, it would be easy to caricature peer-group life as a prison for its members. To the outsider the concern for social control and self-control might indeed seem oppressive. But he must also take into account that there is little desire for voluntary nonconformity and, consequently, little need to require involuntary conformity. . . . Tensions and problems exist in the peer group, as in every other group, but they are overshadowed by the gratification that it provides for the individual. Perhaps the best illustration of this was given by a young man who was suffering from an ulcer and was faced with a choice between his health and his group. As he explained it: "I can't stop drinking when I'm with my friends; I eat and drink like they do, and when I'm alone I take care of my ulcer. But I don't care if it kills me; if it does, that's it."
>
> In summary, social relationships within the peer group follow a narrow path between individualistic display and strictly enforced social control. The group is set up to provide its members with an opportunity for displaying, expressing, and acting out their individuality, as long as this does not become too extreme.[13]

Assuming, as the author does, that "there is little desire for voluntary non-

---

close examination of the empirical bases of their work. Their deficiencies are among the lesser deficiencies of sociology—to which your editors claim no immunity. For instance, our account of the Crawfords (Chapter Four) justifies the same line of criticism.

12 Rainwater, *op. cit.*, p. 52.

13 Herbert J. Gans, *The Urban Villagers* (Glencoe, Ill.: Free Press, 1962), p. 88.

conformity and, consequently, little need to require involuntary conformity," should we draw the conclusion that there is much desire for voluntary conformity and, consequently, much need to require involuntary nonconformity? The latter statement seems to represent the remaining logical alternative—unless some mixed state of desire and need is intended. If these alternatives are neither clarifying nor intellectually satisfying, it is less the fault of the author than it is of the un-developed state of sociology. In providing the reader with significant insights, the author must, in the face of limited knowledge, consider both social conformity and individuality as explanatory hypotheses. Thus, the peer group follows "a narrow path," but its members have the opportunity for "acting out their individuality." And the Urban Villager continues to drink even though it kills him!

Interpretation and informal response intertwine in the following account of the Negro way of life:

> The whole atmosphere of middle-class life is one of tension, particularly at upper-middle-class levels, or among people on the way up but not yet secure in their position. The drive to get ahead, to "lay a little something by," to prepare for the education of children, and at the same time to keep up "front" by wearing the right kind of clothes, having a "nice home," and belonging to the proper organizations—pursuit of these goals brings into being definite social types which Bronzeville calls "strivers" and "strainers." . . . Sometimes the family units break under the strain, particularly if one of the partners is oriented toward excessive conspicuous consumption. The testimony of the husband quoted below may be a rationalization in his individual case, but it does indicate a type of domestic tragedy that occurred often enough in upper-middle-class circles to excite widespread comment: "One reason my wife and I couldn't make it was that she wanted to spend everything on good times and clothes. I wanted to have something some day. My wife makes good money as a schoolteacher, but she spends more than she makes all the time. Just about the time she gets out of debt, she's back in again in a big way. Our paths are just two different ones. We'll never be able to make it. We've agreed to disagree, and my mother's here taking care of the child.[14]

The preceding passages are informative because they exhibit a linguistic device widely prevalent in sociology, indeed in all of science—the use of metaphors. The author speaks of "atmosphere" (a meteorological term), "tension" and "break" (originally physical terms), "the way up" (a spatial term), the "drive to get ahead" (a mechanical term), to "lay a little something by" (an agrarian term), "keeping up front" (another spatial term), "right," "nice," and "proper" (evaluational terms), "tragedy" (a dramatic term), etc. Some of these words as well as others quoted from respondents ("good money," "making it," etc.) are slang or akin to slang. Again, sociological and everyday usage are closely joined. Both are deficient as the type of empirical support required in the physical sciences.

---

14 St. Clair Drake and Horace R. Cayton, *Black Metropolis* (New York: Harcourt, Brace & Co., 1945), p. 668.

Turning now to studies of upper-class life, Negro and white, we shall consider the similarities and differences in method, content, and conceptualization. The following statement applies to the Negro upper class:

> The general tone of upper-class life is conveyed by phrases used when people are explaining what they mean by "dicties," "hincties," "mucktimucks"—i.e., "upper-class people." Among such phrases are: "... have money, culture, influence, and surplus money in the bank to go on ...," "... dress according to the latest styles and with quality ...," "... try to give their children the very best in life—education, luxuries, and things like that—according to their money ...," "... have reached their aim in life and become leaders of The Race ...," "... believe in taking life easy and taking trips wherever they want to without thought of work...."[15]

We can draw at least two conclusions from this extract. First, the coined words (neologisms) used to describe the upper class convey no empirical content until learned, but after that they have the power to conjure "experience" in the same way that popular fiction does. Their ambiguities are not unlike those found in everyday language[16] Second, both coined words and everyday discourse may be as clear as the professional language for describing stratification. All these modes of expression fall short of meeting the requirements for precise and unambiguous communication.

What kind of knowledge can we obtain of the white upper class? Here is the authors' report:

> I learned that Mr. Dobson was not the only one of his social class who seemed to have an inner freedom and an easy way of dealing with his "impulse life." True, they are conventional in manner, their business roles are exemplary, and their moral behavior without reproach, but some of them find joy in life and are capable of having fun.
>
> While we were having a drink before I left, the conversation turned to his civic and social life and the kinds of clubs and organizations to which he and his wife belonged. I told him I'd like to know what they were and how he felt about them.
>
> "I must belong to hundreds of associations. I'm constantly trying to weed them out. I've taken a pretty active part in some; sometimes I spread myself too thin. I belong to the National and State Chambers of Commerce, the NAM, American Banking Institute, and to the Harvard and Racquet Clubs.... I am on the board of the Art Museum; I'm on the boards of two prep schools.... I'm not society minded at all, only my wife is. I'm usually involved in extracurricular activities so much that I don't gad about...."
>
> The birth elite are active in a greater variety of philanthropic and civic organizations and social clubs.[17]

---

15 *Ibid.*, p. 526.

16 These two observations are not supported by Drake and Cayton's data. Like other sociologists we find it useful to go beyond the empirical materials at hand. Is this not another testimonial to the thesis of the present chapter?

17 W. Lloyd Warner and James C. Abegglen, *Big Business Leaders in America* (New York: Harpers, 1955), pp. 147–48.

Some of the authors' conclusions although clearly substantiated, are of questionable significance, while others, although significant, are not substantiated. That Mr. Dobson is active in a variety of organizations and social clubs is evident from his statements. However, the significance of these statements for stratification needs to be shown. The authors' reference to Dobson's inner freedom and easy way of dealing with his impulses is significant but not substantiated by Dobson's replies. We can readily believe that some of those in Dobson's social class "find joy in life and are capable of having fun" because our common stereotypes accord with this belief. But little in the authors' account lends credence to it. Could not one as readily draw a contrary interpretation? Mr. Dobson is "conventional in manner"; his "moral behavior" is "without reproach"; he does not "gad about"; he spreads himself too thin; he is active in too many clubs. As one who has inherited the obligations of a social role and must meet its expectations, he hardly has the freedom of the socially (institutionally) uncommitted. On very similar grounds the claim of special freedoms could be made for all classes of people.[18]

LIMITS OF UNDERSTANDING

The difficulties in establishing adequate empirical foundations for theories of social stratification stem from restrictions inherent in the character of man and in his social world. Application of the criteria for identifying phenomena is limited by the number of observations and conceptual distinctions which can be held in mind. Since humans have a limited capacity for acquiring and storing information, they direct most of their attention to events of immediate concern which for reasons of adjustment or personal expression make a difference in their freedom to act. "We can stretch our limited span of attention by carefully organizing information hierarchically and then dealing with our problems at a rather abstract level, relatively secure in the belief that, when necessary, the more detailed information can be reconstructed from the hierarchy stored in memory.[19] Confronted in immediate experience with countless elements of concrete reality, the individual has no choice but to organize them under a few abstract categories or principles.

[18] We should see the above remarks in wider perspective. The limitations placed by language on the literature of stratification apply to the entire field of sociology. These authors, not to mention others, should not be held responsible for difficulties deeply rooted in the human condition—biological, historical, cultural, and scientific. Although we question the widespread assumptions that sociological knowledge is clearly superior to subjectively informed judgment and that sociology is close to achieving scientific goals, the student should not conclude that popular beliefs are adequate substitutes for sociological understanding. Undeveloped though sociology is, few other fields of study offer a more intelligible account of human behavior.

[19] George A. Miller, "Some Psychological Perspectives on the Year 2000," *Daedalus* (Summer 1967), p. 886.

A related limitation stems from what might be called the *ontology of social structure*. Suppose society were ordered in every detail, with each person holding a fixed position within it or with each limited to holding only a few social positions. Individual initiative would be absent or severely curtailed, and environmental alterations inconsequential. Under these circumstances human beings would not have the characteristics with which they are presently identified. Consider, now, the opposite situation, that of a social structure without any order. No person would have a social position or role; his anonymity would be complete. Communication and human planning, indeed the attempt to organize one's life, would be senseless. The first assumption requires total stability for all time; the second requires total and continuous change—the absence of repetition or reproductivity. Neither kind of social structure is plausible, given human beings as they are now known. Some mixture of the two processes of order and randomness remains, and this mixture is what social scientists have found.[20] Replication of data always produces varying degrees of association. Some events appear to be more closely related or more directly connected than do others. We assume that some explanations of social stratification are more probable or plausible than others. We believe more easily some descriptions of stratum or class differences than others. However, no interpretation is fully adequate or satisfactory. We can support not even the most abstractly stated proposition without criticism or modification. Hence, the ubiquity of intellectual variety. It matters little whether this variety is inherent in social phenomena or in the human mind. The consequences are the same—an endemic infirmity which eludes the exactness of a physical science.

Does the mixture of order and chance manifested in intellectual variety arise largely from the difficulties of fixing upon some stable content for observation and conceptualization? Perhaps, but we must consider other reasons. People seek to increase their freedom, to escape the constraints of life, by engaging in contrivance, invention, and creative effort. They do not always want clarity and certainty, especially when these aims are accompanied by physical and emotional deprivation. The possibility of knowing how another person is put together in-

---

[20] Aubert's analysis of conceptual possibilities is a variation of that described above. He speaks of (1) random distribution, (2) equal distribution, and (3) systematic and unequal distribution of contributions and sanctions. He regards (1) and (2) as equalitarian systems and (3) as conducive to a social system based on such complementary inequalities as age and sex. Defining stratification as a distribution of contributions and sanctions among individuals and roles, he writes, "By 'contribution' is meant those qualities or performances of actors which qualify for sanctions. 'Sanctions' refer to both rewards and penalties. The distribution may conform to one of three principles or to a combination of these. Contributions and sanctions may be *equally* distributed. Everybody gives and receives the same, regardless of who he is and of the amount of access that he has to other values. Contributions and sanctions may be *randomly* distributed: There are differences among actors, for example, in intelligence or income but [they are] not systematically related to other social criteria. Finally, contributions and sanctions may be systematically and *unequally* distributed, that is, related to the distribution of other values." Vilhelm Aubert, *Elements of Sociology* (New York: Charles Scribner's Sons, 1967), p. 101.

cludes, at the same time, the possibility of being known in these terms. When one's capacities and deficiencies are publicly known, one can be more easily victimized by social circumstance, including the wills of those close at hand. Severe criticism, real or imagined, thwarts the search for novelty, suspense, and personal adventure. Few people, if any, can withstand a full exposure of their motivations. What would become of aspirations and ambitions if one knew precisely what he could and could not hope for, if he knew with certainty which situations were beyond his capacities, if the superiority of others could not be doubted? Would he be able to meet the difficulties of living, including the stress of boredom? What would happen to his curiosity and enthusiasm?[21]

Freedom and creative effort thrive not only on uncertainty but also on surprise, perplexity, verbal elaboration, and dramatic exaggeration. In Thurman Arnold's view, the following situation holds:

> Every individual, for reasons lying deep in the mystery of personality, constructs for himself a succession of little dreams in which he is the principal character. No one escapes the constant necessity of dressing himself in a series of different uniforms or silk hats and watching himself go by. In primitive conditions, man may get along with only a few principal roles. As life becomes more complex, the number of plays which he must write for himself increases. Those who are unable to construct a worthwhile character for themselves in any particular situation lose morale; they, become discouraged, ineffective, confused.[22]

Why are men confirmed role-players and word-makers? Are they seeking relief from environmental restrictions? Are they escaping from unwanted employment by flight into imaginary worlds? Do they have strong dramaturgical needs for spontaneous entertainment and mastery over hostile forces? Do they derive esthetic

---

21 "Secrecy, reserve, discretion, concealment, deception all serve to create what might be called a sphere of nebula around the individual, a kind of buffer. . . . The nebular content is an essential element in social life for it is what keeps human intercourse wound up and ticking. . . . Throughout human history and in different societies the nebular content has been promoted by different structural elements—magic, religion, theology, drug, literature, philosophy." Peter Park, "The Cretan Dictum: A Functional Analysis of Sociology," *The American Sociologist* (August 1967), pp. 156–77.

22 *The Symbols of Government* (New Haven, Conn.: Yale University Press, 1935), p. 9. A similar theme, directly relevant to stratification, has been propounded by Hugh Duncan. He writes, "Fixed positions of superiority, inferiority, or equality are impossible when social relations are intimate and personal because in such relationships we play many roles, and we must shift quickly from one to another. . . . Dislike and hatred of authority rise within us even as we express devout loyalty. Enemies evoke deep compassion—as we are about to destroy them. We struggle to suppress bursts of merriment in the midst of solemn ceremony. A chaotic whirl of images and ideas swarms through us; moods shift and change swiftly and intensely. The order and precision of military drill suddenly become a grotesque pantomime whose rigidity oppresses us as we long for the freedom of walking and talking together. Only in the abrupt shifts of imagery and mood in dance and music, where rage and serenity follow in swift yet harmonic progression, do we find anything similar to the fleeting intensity of the conscious and unconscious states we experience in our relations as superiors, inferiors, and equals." Hugh Dalziel Duncan, *Communication and Social Order* (New York: The Bedminister Press, 1962), p. 271.

satisfaction from playing games with language, gestures, and ceremonies? Whatever the reasons for man's role-playing, it is clear that most men wish to shape
their futures, to adapt the world to their own values. Without values, the multi-
tude of acts and verbal expressions that constitute the drama of human existence
would be unintelligible. For this reason, one finds valuational interpretations
in every linguistic product, including books on social stratification.[23] Consider the
value implications of such words as supreme, dominant, paramount, superlative,
pre-eminent, incomparable, exultant, heightened, enhanced, ascendant, and sur-
passing as possible vocabularies of social stratification. Even snob, almost totally
neglected by sociologists, is rich in implications. A snob is "one who makes both
wealth or education the sole criterion of worth, especially one who is cringing to
superiors and overbearing with inferiors in position; also, anyone pretending to
gentility" (*Britannica World Language Dictionary*). Indeed, sociologists seem to
have missed an opportunity by not only failing to adopt the term but also not
using it as the basis for a typology of social stratification. Russell Lynes's humorous
analysis suggests this possibility.

> Snobbery has assumed so many guises, in fact, that it is, I believe, time that someone
> attempt to impose order on what is at best a confused situation. There are a few
> basic categories of snobs that seem to include most of the more common species that
> one is likely to encounter, or, indeed, to be. . . . The Intellectual Snob is of such dis-
> tinguished lineage and comes from such established precedent that he is dignified by
> a mention in Webster's ("one who repels the advances of those whom he regards as
> his inferiors; as, an intellectual snob"). The other categories are less well known and
> less well documented. For convenience, let us call them the Regional Snobs, the
> Moral Snobs, the Sensual Snobs, the Emotional Snobs, the Physical Snobs, the Occupa-
> tional Snobs, and finally, the Reverse Snobs, or Antisnob Snobs.[24]

Historians make less effort to keep value judgments from entering analysis.
Their interpretations of social stratification are apt to be richer in detail, more
metaphorical, and more idiomatic than those of sociologists. The following quotation mixes literary and sociological categories. Skill in historical research does
not prevent the writer from introducing values which are unacceptable to many
sociologists. For example, after the British industrial revolution the concept of
class became, in his words, a bludgeon rather than a scalpel. The passage as a

---

23 Note, for instance, how sociological words are dramatized as values in popular
literature: "*Act* upon it if you can" "The *act* lies in his true nature." "*Adjust,* amend
and heal." "When bad men combine, the good must *associate.*" "In *authority* settled and
calm." "Every man must have an *authority.*" "All doth in *change* delight." "*Change* for
the worse." "Neither to *change* nor falter." "More than a game, an *institution.*" "Deep
stake in such a glorious *institution.*" "Your laws, *institutions,* and false gods." "*Systems:*
away with '*System*'!" "Our little *systems.*" "I must create a *system.*" "Oppose every *system.*" "All things began in *order.*" "Decently and in *order.*" "In a wonderful *order.*"
"*Order* is heaven's first law." "Good *order* is the foundation." "Set thine house in *order.*"

24 "The New Snobbism," in *An Encyclopedia of Modern American Humor,* ed. Bennett
Cerf (Garden City, N.Y.: Doubleday & Company, Inc., 1954), p. 36.

whole reveals how the boundaries between history, sociology, and literature can be ignored, fused, or erased. Since readership cannot be controlled for homogeneity of interest (or field), class conceptions become a composite (melange?) of whatever each or all projects onto the printed page.

> Class is not the only or inevitable division of a hierarchical society. The very concept of class, in the modern sense of broad, mutually hostile, horizontal bands based on conflicting economic interest, is a product of the British industrial revolution. Until then the word was used in its neutral, "classifying" sense and its place supplied by the "ranks," "orders," and "degrees" of a more finely graded hierarchy of great subtlety and discrimination. In that older society the horizontal solidarities and vertical antagonisms of class were usually latent, overlain by the vertical bonds of patronage and dependency and horizontal antagonisms between different interests, such as the landed, East and West Indian, cloth-manufacturing, and wool-exporting interests. In the small communities—village or tiny town—which made up most of the old society, a man was highly conscious of his exact position in the social hierarchy, not by comparison with his anonymous fellows on his own level elsewhere but by his face-to-face relationship with his immediate neighbors above and below him. In regard to such a society the concept of class is a bludgeon rather than a scalpel and crushes what it tries to dissect.[25]

The paragraph below further illustrates the influence of values on class concepts. After giving a seemingly objective account of how the meaning of bourgeois has changed in his lifetime, the author discusses its normal linguistic usage. His interpretation is an example of the ambiguities found in most of the vocabulary of social stratification.

> All my life the epithet *bourgeois* has been, in many contexts, a term of contempt, but not for the same reason. When I was a boy—a *bourgeois* boy—it was applied to my social class by the class above it; *bourgeois* meant "not aristocratic, therefore vulgar." When I was in my twenties this changed. My class was now vilified by the class below it; *bourgeois* began to mean "not proletarian, therefore parasitic, reactionary." Thus it has always been a reproach to assign a man to that class which has provided the world with nearly all its divines, poets, philosophers, scientists, musicians, painters, doctors, architects, and administrators. When the bourgeoisie is despised for not being proletarian, we get an exception to the general principle stated above. The name of the higher status implies the worse character and behavior. This I take to be the peculiar, and transitory, result of a revolutionary situation. The earlier usage—*bourgeois* is "not aristocratic"—is the normal linguistic phenomenon.[26]

---

25 H. J. Perkins, "Social History" in *Approaches to History*, ed. H. P. R. Finberg (Toronto: University of Toronto Press, 1962), pp. 64–65.

26 C. S. Lewis, *Studies in Words* (London: Cambridge: University Press, 1960), p. 21. Particularly dramatic are sudden shifts toward acceptance of the language of "poverty." Consider the following passage, published as recently as 1964: "It is, of course, a well-known fact that there are no longer any poor in America, only the *underprivileged* who happen to fall into a *low-income group*. Nor are there poor children in the public schools,

What can we conclude from the materials of this chapter? Are not all studies of social stratification handicapped by the infirmities of language and the illusions of the external world? Attempts to describe stratification as a social phenomenon are never complete and almost never representative, because words are not closely joined to particular things; they symbolize both the dispositions of their users and the changing appearances of distant realities. Social phenomena are filtered and unwittingly distorted to serve the special needs and purposes of human respondents, whether citizens or scientists. Without incorrigible criteria for gauging collective judgments, definitive standards of truth are beyond our reach.

Despite these limitations we can support some statements descriptive of social stratification with confidence. The existence of wide differences in human capacities and resources is not disputed. Certain overt signs of power and poverty are understood by most people, even when they disagree on implications. Nearly everyone recognizes the search for status and acceptance, although agreement on specific manifestations may never be achieved. Some social arrangements, found everywhere by social scientists, appear to be certain because we cannot easily imagine how they could be otherwise. Other arrangements appear to be certain they apply to a narrow range of phenomena—to events which occurred in a brief period of time in a small sector of society. And who then can dispute their authenticity?

Such a state of affairs need not produce pessimism. As we suggested earlier, it permits more ingenuity and creativeness than might otherwise be possible. New discoveries may be responsive to but not dependent on the claims of classical sociology and its founding fathers. Indeed, if sociologists were to regard any statement about stratification indisputably true by virtue of indisputable canons of science, further research would be unnecessary. And where is the sociologist who is prepared to take such a stand? If and when sociology discovers some "absolutely true" propositions, other such propositions will follow in rapid succession. The millenium of social science will be at hand and will put an end to books of this kind.

---

only *children unable to secure much beyond the necessities of today's world because of the modest finances of the family.* ... Those who cling to the bottom of their class in school are not necessarily poor students or even lazy; they are simply *children with untapped potential* or perhaps children *with latent ability or underachievers.* If they fail to receive passing grades they may still qualify for social promotion. None of them lives in a slum, for there no slums, although every big city has its older, more overcrowded areas." L. Barnett, *The Treasure of Our Tongue* (New York: Alfred A. Knopf, Inc., 1964), pp. 191–92.

Index